When should I travel to get the best airfare?
Where do I go for answers to my travel questions?
What's the best and easiest way to plan and book my trip?

frommers.travelocity.com

Frommer's, the travel guide leader, has teamed up with **Travelocity.com**, the leader in online travel, to bring you an in-depth, easy-to-use resource designed to help you plan and book your trip online.

At **frommers.travelocity.com**, you'll find free online updates about your destination from the experts at Frommer's plus the outstanding travel planning and purchasing features of Travelocity.com. Travelocity.com provides reservations capabilities for 95 percent of all airline seats sold, more than 47,000 hotels, and over 50 car rental companies. In addition, Travelocity.com offers more than 2,000 exciting vacation and cruise packages. Travelocity.com puts you in complete control of your travel planning with these and other great features:

Expert travel guidance from Frommer's - over 150 writers reporting from around the world!

Best Fare Finder - an interactive calendar tells you when to travel to get the best airfare

Fare Watcher - we'll track airfare changes to your favorite destinations

Dream Maps - a mapping feature that suggests travel opportunities based on your budget

Shop Safe Guarantee - 24 hours a day / 7 days a week live customer service, and more!

Whether traveling on a tight budget, looking for a quick weekend getaway, or planning the trip of a lifetime, Frommer's guides and Travelocity.com will make your travel dreams a reality. You've bought the book, now book the trip!

A New Star-Rating System & Other Exciting News from Frommer's!

In our continuing effort to publish the savviest, most up-to-date, and most appealing travel guides available, we've added some great new features.

Frommer's guides now include a new **star-rating system.** Every hotel, restaurant, and attraction is rated from 0 to 3 stars to help you set priorities and organize your time.

We've also added **seven brand-new features** that point you to the great deals, in-the-know advice, and unique experiences that separate travelers from tourists. Throughout the guide, look for:

Finds	Special finds—those places only insiders know about
Fun Fact	Fun facts—details that make travelers more informed and their trips more fun
Kids	Best bets for kids—advice for the whole family
Moments	Special moments—those experiences that memories are made of
Overrated	Places or experiences not worth your time or money
Tips	Insider tips—some great ways to save time and money
Value	Great values—where to get the best deals

We've also added a **"What's New"** section in every guide—a timely crash course in what's hot and what's not in every destination we cover.

Other Great Guides for Your Trip:

Frommer's Seattle & Portland

Frommer's Vancouver & Victoria

Frommer's Washington State

Frommer's Great Outdoor Guide to Washington & Oregon

Frommer's USA

Oregon
3rd Edition

by Karl Samson & Jane Aukshunas

Here's what the critics say about Frommer's:

"Amazingly easy to use. Very portable, very complete."

—*Booklist*

"The only mainstream guide to list specific prices. The Walter Cronkite of guidebooks—with all that implies."

—*Travel & Leisure*

"Complete, concise, and filled with useful information."

—*New York Daily News*

"Hotel information is close to encyclopedic."

—*Des Moines Sunday Register*

"Detailed, accurate, and easy-to-read information for all price ranges."

—*Glamour Magazine*

Hungry Minds™

Best-Selling Books • Digital Downloads • e-Books • Answer Networks
e-Newsletters • Branded Web Sites • e-Learning

New York, NY • Cleveland, OH • Indianapolis, IN

About the Authors

Husband-and-wife travel-writing team **Karl Samson** and **Jane Aukshunas** make their home in Oregon, where they spend their time juggling their obsessions with traveling, outdoor sports, and gardening. Each winter, to dry out their webbed feet, they flee the soggy Northwest to update the *Frommer's Arizona* guide, but they always look forward to their return to the land of good coffee. Karl is also the author of *Frommer's Great Outdoor Guide to Washington & Oregon* and *Frommer's Nepal.*

Published by:

Hungry Minds, Inc.

909 Third Ave.
New York, NY 10022

ISBN 0-7645-6555-9
ISSN 1093-7455

Editor: Margot Weiss
Production Editor: Suzanna R. Thompson
Photo Editor: Richard Fox
Cartographer: John Decamillis
Production by Hungry Minds Indianapolis Production Services

Front cover photo: Seastacks on the Southern Oregon Coast
Back cover photo: Spring at the Japanese Gardens in Portland

Special Sales

For general information on Hungry Minds' products and services, please contact our Customer Care department; within the U.S. at 800-762-2974, outside the U.S. at 317-572-3993, or fax 317-572-4002. For sales inquiries and reseller information, including discounts, bulk sales, customized editions, and premium sales, please contact our Customer Care department at 800-434-3422.

Manufactured in the United States of America

5 4 3 2 1

Contents

List of Maps

An Invitation to the Reader

In researching this book, we discovered many wonderful places—hotels, restaurants, shops, and more. We're sure you'll find others. Please tell us about them so that we can share the information with your fellow travelers in upcoming editions. If you were disappointed with a recommendation, we'd love to know that, too. Please write to:

Frommer's Oregon, 3rd Edition
Hungry Minds, Inc. • 909 Third Avenue • New York, NY 10022

An Additional Note

Please be advised that travel information is subject to change at any time—and this is especially true of prices. We therefore suggest that you write or call ahead for confirmation when making your travel plans. The authors, editors, and publisher cannot be held responsible for the experiences of readers while traveling. Your safety is important to us, however, so we encourage you to stay alert and be aware of your surroundings. Keep a close eye on cameras, purses, and wallets, all favorite targets of thieves and pickpockets.

New! Frommer's Star Ratings & Icons

Every hotel, restaurant, and attraction listing in this guide has been ranked for quality, value, service, amenities, and special features using a star-rating scale. In country, state, and regional guides, we also rate towns and regions to help you narrow down your choices and budget your time accordingly. Hotels and restaurants in the Very Expensive and Expensive categories are rated on a scale of one (highly recommended) to three stars (exceptional). Those in the Moderate and Inexpensive categories rate from zero (recommended) to two stars (very highly recommended). Attractions, towns, and regions are rated according to the following scale: zero stars (recommended), one star (highly recommended), two stars (very highly recommended), and three stars (must-see).

In addition to the rating system, we also use seven icons to highlight insider information, useful tips, special bargains, hidden gems, memorable experiences, kid-friendly venues, places to avoid, and other useful information:

(Finds   (Fun Fact   (Kids   (Moments   (Overrated   (Tips   (Value

The following abbreviations are used for credit cards:

AE	American Express	DISC	Discover	V	Visa
DC	Diners Club	MC	MasterCard		

FROMMERS.COM

Now that you have the guidebook to a great trip, visit our website at **www.frommers.com** for travel information on nearly 2,000 destinations. With features updated regularly, we give you instant access to the most current trip-planning information available. At Frommers.com, you'll also find the best prices on airfares, accommodations, and car rentals—and you can even book travel online through our travel booking partners. At Frommers.com, you'll also find the following:

- Daily Newsletter highlighting the best travel deals
- Hot Spot of the Month/Vacation Sweepstakes & Travel Photo Contest
- More than 200 Travel Message Boards
- Outspoken Newsletters and Feature Articles on travel bargains, vacation ideas, tips & resources, and more!

What's New in Oregon

The world of travel is always changing. New hotels and museums open. Restaurants and nightclubs close. Establishments move. Oregon is no exception, so, in this book, we've tried to keep tabs on what's new and noteworthy throughout the state. The following are some of the highlights.

PORTLAND Orientation The **Portland Oregon Visitors Association (POVA)**, 1000 SW Broadway, Suite 2300, Portland, OR 97205 (© **877/678-5263** or 503/275-9750; www.travelportland.com), moved its visitor center into a new and very conveniently located facility right on (actually under) Pioneer Courthouse Square, downtown Portland's central plaza. This plaza is the site of various events throughout the year and is within a few blocks of most of Portland's top downtown hotels.

At the new visitor center, you'll find **Ticket Central** (© **503/275-8358**), which sells both full-price advance-purchase tickets to a wide range of Portland area concerts and events, but also sells half-price day-of-show tickets.

On the public transportation front, Portland continues to break new ground. Summer 2001 saw the opening of the **Portland Streetcar** (© **503/238-RIDE;** www.portlandstreetcar.org), which now connects downtown Portland with the Pearl District and the Nob Hill neighborhood, Portland's two trendiest neighborhoods. This streetcar line is the first new streetcar in the U.S. in 50 years. By the time you read this the new **Airport Max** (© **503/238-7433;** www.tri-met.org),

should be up an running, making Portland the only city on the West Coast with a light-rail system with tracks right up to an airport terminal.

To make Portland even easier to get around by public transit, Tri-Met also expanded downtown's Fareless Square (an area in which all buses, trolleys, and streetcars are free) to include the Rose Quarter neighborhood on the east side of the Willamette River. The Rose Quarter is the site of the Rose Garden arena, the Oregon Convention Center, and the Lloyd Center Mall.

Where to Dine With the closing of the restaurant Atwater's, which was located high atop a downtown skyscraper, Portland lost its best restaurant with a view. However, for view-seeking visitors to Portland, there is a great alternative that we've added to this edition of the book. The **Chart House,** 5700 SW Terwilliger Blvd. (© **503/246-6963**), offers not only great views across Portland to Mount Hood and Mount St. Helens but also the best clam chowder in Portland (and plenty of good seafood and steaks as well). Another restaurant worth searching out is the **Veritable Quandary,** 1220 SW First Ave. (© **503/227-7342**), which, though it has been around for many years, recently went through a renovation and an upgrading of its menu.

Seeing the Sights After many years of moving from one temporary space to another, Portland's **American Advertising Museum,** 211 NW Fifth Ave. (© **503/226-0000;** www.ad museum.org) finally settled into a permanent space this year. The new museum facility, located between Chinatown and the trendy Pearl District, is small but packs a lot of fun exhibits into its small space.

If you'll be visiting Portland with your kids, be sure to check out the new home of Portland's children's museum. **CM2—Children's Museum 2nd Generation,** 4015 SW Canyon Rd. (© **503/223-6500;** www.portlandcm2.org), as the museum is now known, is conveniently located across the parking lot from the Oregon Zoom, which makes for a great double whammy of a kids' outing. Both the zoo and the children's museum are located in Washington Park, a sprawling green space in the forested hills to the west of downtown Portland.

THE WILLAMETTE VALLEY Don't be surprised if you run into a phone number with the new 971 area code in Yamhill, Polk, or Marion counties, which include the wine country and the state capital of Salem.

The North Willamette Valley Wine Country After its long, slow migration north from Long Beach, California, the Spruce Goose, Howard Hughes's famous wooden flying boat, has finally come to roost in the huge new **Evergreen Aviation Museum,** 3685 NE Three Mile Lane (© **503/434-4180;** www.sprucegoose.org), outside McMinnville. Since this is wine country, the museum is surrounded by vineyards.

The **Oregon Garden,** 879 W. Main St. (© **877/674-2733** or 503/874-8100; www.oregongarden.org), a large display garden outside Silverton, is finally up and blooming after many years of preparations. Although Butchart Gardens in Victoria, British Columbia, doesn't have to worry too much about the new kid on the block yet, these gardens are certainly impressive. If you know a peony from a pachysandra, you'll want to schedule a visit.

Salem If you happen to be traveling through the Willamette Valley with kids, don't miss an opportunity to check out the Salem waterfront where you'll find not only **Salem's Riverfront Carousel,** 101 Front St. NE (© **503/540-0374**), but also lots of lawns where the kids can burn off excess energy, and the **A.C. Gilbert Discovery Village,** 116 Marion St. NE. (© **503/371-3631;** www.acgilbert.org), and the dock for the *Willamette Queen* (© **503/371-1103;** www.willamettequeen.com), a paddlewheeler that cruises the Willamette River.

THE COAST Astoria In 2001, the **Columbia River Maritime Museum,** 1792 Marine Dr. (© **503/325-2323;** www.crmm.org), underwent an extensive renovation that was scheduled to be completed sometime in the spring of 2002. The museum focuses on the maritime history of the Oregon coast and the Columbia River, and the museum's many exhibits are even fascinating for landlubbers.

Tillamook County The quaint beach community of Manzanita is now home to some of the most comfortable cottages on the Oregon coast. **Coast Cabins,** 635 Laneda Ave., Manzanita (© **503/368-7113;** www.coastcabins.com), with their cedar siding and terraced perennial gardens, capture the very essence of an Oregon coast getaway.

Lincoln City For excellent Northwest cuisine and creative seafood dishes, be sure to have a meal or two at the **Blackfish Café,** 2733 NW Hwy. 101 (© **541/996-1007;** www.blackfishcafe.com), located at the north end of town. **Eden Hall,** 6675 Gleneden Beach Loop Rd. (© **541/764-3826**), at the south end of Lincoln City, is a new jazz club that has given this beach town a new lease on nightlife.

Newport Although Keiko the killer whale (star of the *Free Willy* movies) has long since departed for the waters of the north Atlantic, the **Oregon Coast Aquarium,** 2820 SE Ferry Slip Rd. (℗ **541/867-3474;** www. aquarium.org), is still the coast's top attraction. In the huge tank once inhabited by Keiko, large open-ocean sharks now patrol the waters. An underwater see-through tunnel provides visitors with a very unusual way to explore the ocean depths without ever getting wet.

Yachats   Although it doesn't look like much from the outside, **The Drift Inn,** 124 U.S. 101 (℗ **541/547-4477**), in Yachats, is a deceptive place. Sure it's not much more than a local tavern, but at night, the menu is surprisingly creative. Definitely not to be missed if you are staying in the Yachats area.

THE GORGE The Columbia Gorge National Scenic Area   High atop the basalt cliffs of the Columbia Gorge at Crown Point stands the historic 1916 **Vista House visitor center** (℗ **503/695-2230;** www.vistahouse. com), which boasts a commanding view of the gorge and the Columbia River. In 2001, the Vista House underwent an extensive renovation and is now, once again, one of the crowning achievements along the Historic Columbia River Highway.

At exit 40 of I-84, at the **Bonneville Fish Hatchery** (℗ **541/ 374-8393**), be sure not to miss the **Sturgeon Viewing Center,** which has an underwater viewing window that lets you get up close and personal with several huge sturgeon. Across I-84 from the fish hatchery, you'll find a trail head for a section of the **Historic Columbia River Highway State Trail,** a paved multi-use trail that connects the town of Cascade Locks with Bonneville Dam. This trail incorporates abandoned sections of the Historic Columbia River Highway and is open to hikers and bikers.

Hood River   Fans of carousels won't want to miss the **International Museum of Carousel Art,** 304 Oak St. (℗ **541/387-4622;** www.carousel museum.com). Although this museum doesn't actually have a functioning carousel, it does have the nation's largest collection of carousel animals.

East of Hood River, you'll find a second section of the **Historic Columbia River Highway State Trail.** This is actually the more interesting section of trail because it passes through the Mosier Twin Tunnels, which were blasted into the basalt cliffs almost a century ago. The tunnels are a sort of gateway between the wetter west end of the gorge and the dry east end.

The Dalles   If you are planning on crossing the Columbia River into Washington to visit the Maryhill Museum, be sure to leave some time in your schedule to visit two new area wineries as well. **Maryhill Winery,** 9774 Hwy. 14, Maryhill (℗ **877/ 627-9445;** www.maryhillwinery.com) has the best view of any winery in the Northwest and also produces some very good wines. **Marshal's Winery,** 150 Oak Creek Rd., Dallesport (℗ **509/767-4633**), is a tiny family-run winery that produces some of Washington's smoothest Cabernet Sauvignons and Merlots.

SOUTHERN OREGON Ashland By the time you read this, the **Oregon Shakespeare Festival,** 15 S. Pioneer St. (℗ **541/482-4331;** www. osfashland.org), should have its new theater up and running. The new theater will replace the Black Swan, which for years was the festival's main venue for new works and experimental theater productions.

The historic **Ashland Springs Hotel,** 212 E. Main St. (℗ **800/ 325-4000** or 541/488-1700; www. westcoasthotels.com), the finest hotel in the southern half of the state, opened after an extensive and time-consuming renovation. The high-rise hotel originally opened in 1925 and was built to cash in on what was at that time Ashland's burgeoning reputation as a health spa.

At the other end of the spectrum, **The Palm,** 1065 Siskiyou Blvd. (© 877/482-2635 or 541/482-2636; www.palmcottages.com), a former motor court, has also been renovated and now has the look and feel of Cape Cod cottages. Room rates are considerably more economical than at the Ashland Springs Hotel.

CENTRAL OREGON North Central Oregon & the Lower Deschutes River At The Cove Palisades State Park (© **541/546-3412**) near the town of Madras, you can now paddle a sea kayak through the sort of flooded canyon country most people associate with the Southwest, not the Northwest. The naturalist-guided sea-kayak tours are offered throughout the year on the waters of Lake Billy Chinook.

Bend The **High Desert Museum,** 59800 S. Hwy. 97. (© **541/382-4754**), south of Bend is one of Oregon's top attractions and continues to expand its facilities. The most recent additions are an extensive exhibit on the Plateau Indians, who have long inhabited the inland Northwest, and a birds of prey center, which houses a wide variety of live raptors.

1

The Best of Oregon

Perhaps you've heard that Oregonians have webbed feet or that they don't tan—they rust. Even if you are otherwise unfamiliar with Oregon, you probably have heard that it rains a lot here. There's simply no getting around the fact that few states receive as much rain or cloudy weather as Oregon (except Washington, Oregon's northern neighbor). However, Oregon's rainfall no longer seems to have the effect it once did. Sure, it still keeps the landscape green, but it's no longer keeping people from moving here.

Once Oregon was the promised land of 19th-century pioneers, and today it is an amalgam of American life and landscapes. Within its boundaries, the state reflects a part of almost every region of the country. Take a bit of New England's rural beauty, its covered bridges, and its steepled churches. Temper the climate with that of the upper South to avoid harsh winters. Now bring in some low, rolling mountains such as the Appalachians; rugged, glaciated mountains such as the Rockies; and Hawaiian-style volcanoes and lava fields. Add a river as large and important as the Mississippi—complete with paddle-wheel steamers—and a coastline as rugged as California's. Of course, there would have to be sagebrush and cowboys and Indians. You could even throw in the deserts of the Southwest and the wheat fields of the Midwest. A little wine country would be a nice touch, and so would some long, sandy beaches. Finally, you'll need a beautiful city, one whose downtown skyscrapers are framed by high, forested hills and whose gardens are full of roses.

To explore such a diverse state takes quite a bit of advance planning, and knowing ahead of time the best that the state has to offer can make a visit much more enjoyable. After traveling the length and breadth of the state, we've chosen what we feel are the very best attractions, activities, lodgings, and restaurants. These are the places and experiences you won't want to miss. Most are described in more detail elsewhere in this book, but this chapter will give you an overview and get you started.

1 The Best Natural Attractions

- **The Oregon Coast:** Rocky headlands, offshore islands and haystack rocks, natural arches, caves full of sea lions, giant sand dunes, and dozens of state parks make this one of the most spectacular coastlines in the country. See chapter 6.
- **Columbia Gorge National Scenic Area:** Carved by Ice Age floods that were as much as 1,200 feet deep, the Columbia Gorge is a unique feature of the Northwest landscape. Waterfalls by the dozen cascade from the basalt cliffs of the gorge. Highways on both the Washington and the Oregon sides of the Columbia River provide countless memorable views. See "The Columbia Gorge National Scenic Area" in chapter 7.

- **Mount Hood:** As Oregon's tallest mountain and the closest Cascade peak to Portland, Mount Hood is a recreational mecca par excellence. Hiking trails, lakes and rivers, and year-round skiing make this the most appealing natural attraction in the state. See "Mount Hood: Skiing, Hiking & Scenic Drives" in chapter 8.

- **Crater Lake National Park:** At 1,932 feet deep, Crater Lake is the deepest lake in the United States, and its sapphire-blue waters are a bewitchingly beautiful sight when seen from the rim of the volcanic crater that contains them. See "Crater Lake National Park" in chapter 8.

- **Central Oregon Lava Lands:** Throughout central Oregon and the central Cascades region, from the lava fields of McKenzie Pass to the obsidian flows of Newberry National Volcanic Monument, you'll find dramatic examples of the volcanic activity that gave rise to the Cascade Range. See chapters 8 and 10.

- **Hells Canyon:** Deeper than the Grand Canyon, this massive gorge along the Oregon-Idaho border is remote and inaccessible, and that is just what makes it fascinating. You can gaze down into it from on high, float its waters, or hike its trails. See "Hells Canyon & the Southern Wallowas" in chapter 11.

2 The Best Outdoor Activities

- **Biking the Oregon Coast:** With U.S. 101 clinging to the edge of the continent for much of its route through Oregon, this road has become one of the most popular cycling routes in the Northwest. The entire coast can be done in about a week, but there are also plenty of short sections that make good day trips. See "Biking the Oregon Coast" in chapter 6.

- **Windsurfing at Hood River:** Winds that rage through the Columbia Gorge whip up white-capped standing waves and have turned this area into the windsurfing capital of the United States, attracting windsurfers from around the world. See "Hood River: The Windsurfing Capital of the Northwest" in chapter 7.

- **Fly-Fishing for Steelhead on the North Umpqua River:** Made famous by Zane Grey, the North Umpqua is the quintessential steelhead river (and for part of its length it's open to fly-fishing only). The river and the elusive steelhead offer a legendary fishing experience. See "The North

Umpqua–Upper Rogue River Scenic Byway" in chapter 8.

- **Rafting the Rogue River:** Of all the white-water-rafting rivers, none is more famous than the Rogue. Meandering through remote wilderness in the southern part of the state, this river has been popular with anglers since early in the 20th century and attracted Zane Grey with its beauty and great fishing. Today, you can splash through roaring white water by day and spend your nights in remote lodges that are inaccessible by car. See "Ashland & the Oregon Shakespeare Festival" in chapter 9.

- **Mountain Biking in Bend:** Outside the town of Bend, in central Oregon, dry ponderosa pine forests are laced with trails that are open to mountain bikes. Routes pass by several lakes, and along the way you'll get great views of the Three Sisters, Broken Top, and Mount Bachelor. See "Bend & Sunriver: Skiing, Hiking, Fishing, Mountain Scenery & More" in chapter 10.

Oregon

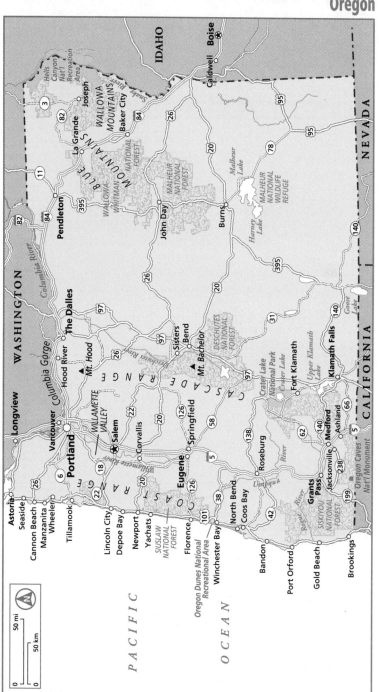

- **Skiing Mount Bachelor:** With ski slopes dropping off the very summit of this extinct volcano, Mount Bachelor ski area, in central Oregon, is the state's premier ski area. Seemingly endless runs of all levels of ability make this a magnet for skiers and snowboarders from around the state, and lots of high-speed quad chairs keep people on the snow instead of standing in line. See "Bend & Sunriver: Skiing, Hiking, Fishing, Mountain Scenery & More" in chapter 10.

3 The Best Beaches

See chapter 6 for details on the beaches listed below.

- **Cannon Beach/Ecola State Park:** With the massive monolith of Haystack Rock rising up from the low-tide line and the secluded beaches of Ecola State Park just north of town, Cannon Beach offers all the best of the Oregon coast. See "Cannon Beach" in chapter 6.
- **Oswald West State Park:** At this state park south of Cannon Beach, it's a 15-minute walk through the woods to the beach, which keeps the sand from ever getting too crowded. The crescent-shaped beach is on a secluded cove backed by dense forest. This also happens to be a popular surfing spot. See "Cannon Beach" in chapter 6.
- **Sunset Bay State Park:** Almost completely surrounded by sandstone cliffs, this little beach near Coos Bay is on a shallow cove. The clear waters here get a little bit warmer than unprotected waters elsewhere on the coast, so it's sometimes possible to actually go swimming. See "The Coos Bay Area" in chapter 6.
- **Bandon:** It's difficult to imagine a more picturesque stretch of coastline than the beach in Bandon. Haystack rocks rise up from sand and sea as if strewn there by some giant hand. Motels and houses front this scenic beach, which ensures its popularity no matter what the weather. See "Bandon" in chapter 6.
- **The Beaches of Samuel H. Boardman State Scenic Corridor:** Within this remote south coast state park are to be found some of the prettiest, most secluded, and least visited beaches on the Oregon coast. Ringed by rocky headlands, the many little crescents of sand in this park provide an opportunity to find *the* perfect beach. See "The Southern Oregon Coast" in chapter 6.

4 The Best Hikes

- **Cape Lookout Trail:** Leading 2½ miles through dense forests to the tip of this rugged cape on the north Oregon coast, this trail ends high on a cliff above the waters of the Pacific. Far below, gray whales can often be seen lolling in the waves, and the view to the south takes in miles of coastline. See "Tillamook County" in chapter 6.
- **Umpqua Dunes Trail:** If you've ever dreamed of joining the French Foreign Legion or simply want to play at being Lawrence of Arabia, then the Oregon Dunes National Recreation Area is the place for you. Within this vast expanse of sand dunes, you'll find the highest dunes on the Oregon coast—some 500 feet tall. See "Florence & the Oregon Dunes National Recreation Area" in chapter 6.
- **Eagle Creek Trail:** This trail in the Columbia Gorge follows the

tumbling waters of Eagle Creek and passes two spectacular waterfalls in the first 2 miles. Along the way, the trail climbs up the steep gorge walls, and in places it is cut right into the basalt cliffs. See "The Columbia Gorge National Scenic Area" in chapter 7.

- **Timberline Trail:** As the name implies, this trail starts at the Timberline, high on the slopes of Mount Hood. Because the route circles Mount Hood, you can start in either direction and make a day, overnight, or multiday hike of it. Paradise Park, its meadows ablaze with wildflowers in July and August, is a favorite for both day hikes and overnight trips. See "Mount Hood: Skiing, Hiking & Scenic Drives" in chapter 8.
- **McKenzie River Trail to Tamolitch Pool:** The McKenzie River Trail stretches for 26 miles along the banks of this aquamarine river, but by far the most rewarding stretch of trail is the 2-mile hike to Tamolitch Pool, an astounding pool of turquoise waters formed as the McKenzie River wells up out of the ground after flowing underground for several miles. The trail leads through rugged, overgrown lava fields. See "The Santiam Pass, McKenzie Pass & McKenzie River" in chapter 8.
- **Deschutes River Trail:** The Deschutes River, which flows down from the east side of the Cascades, passes through open ponderosa pine forest to the west of Bend. Paralleling the river and passing tumultuous waterfalls along the way, it is an easy trail that's popular with hikers, mountain bikers, and joggers. See "Bend & Sunriver: Skiing, Hiking, Fishing, Mountain Scenery & More" in chapter 10.

5 The Best Scenic Drives

- **Gold Beach to Brookings:** No other stretch of U.S. 101 along the Oregon coast is more breathtaking than the segment between Gold Beach and Brookings. This remote coastline is dotted with offshore islands, natural rock arches, sea caves, bluffs, and beaches. Take your time, stop at the many pull-offs, and make this a leisurely all-day drive. See "The Southern Oregon Coast" in chapter 6.
- **Historic Columbia River Highway:** Built between 1914 and 1926 to allow automobiles access to the wonders of the Columbia Gorge, this narrow, winding highway east of Portland climbs up to the top of the gorge for a scenic vista before diving into forests where waterfalls, including the tallest one in the state, pour off of basalt cliffs. See "The Columbia Gorge National Scenic Area" in chapter 7.
- **The Santiam and McKenzie Passes:** This loop drive, which crosses the Cascade crest twice, takes in views of half a dozen major Cascade peaks, negotiates a bizarre landscape of lava fields, passes several waterfalls, and skirts aptly named Clear Lake, the source of the McKenzie River. This is one of the best drives in the state for fall color. See "The Santiam Pass, McKenzie Pass & McKenzie River" in chapter 8.
- **Crater Lake Rim Drive:** This scenic drive circles the rim of the massive caldera that holds Crater Lake. Along the way are numerous pull-offs where you can admire the sapphire-blue waters and the ever-changing scenery. See "Crater Lake National Park" in chapter 8.

• **Cascade Lakes Highway:** This road, formerly known as Century Drive, covers roughly 100 miles as it loops out from Bend along the eastern slope of the Cascades. Views of Broken Top and the Three Sisters are frequent, and along the way are numerous lakes, both large and small. See "Bend & Sunriver: Skiing, Hiking, Fishing, Mountain Scenery & More" in chapter 10.

6 The Best Museums

• **Portland Art Museum:** Although the main focus is on bringing blockbuster, touring shows to town, the Portland Art Museum also has respectable permanent collections of Northwest contemporary art, as well as a superb collection of Native American artifacts. See p. 91.
• **Evergreen Aviation Museum** (McMinnville): Looking like a cross between a gigantic airplane hangar and a huge barn, this new museum is home to Howard Hughes' "Spruce Goose," the largest wooden plane ever built. There are also plenty of smaller planes on display to provide a little perspective for this behemoth of the air. See p. 129.
• **Jensen Arctic Museum** (Monmouth): This museum is not very big, but it contains an amazingly diverse collection of artifacts from the Arctic. Even more surprising than the thoroughness of the collection is the fact that the museum is here in Oregon and not in Alaska. See p. 140.
• **Favell Museum of Western Art and Indian Artifacts** (Klamath Falls): This museum houses an overwhelming assortment of Native American artifacts, including thousands of arrowheads, spear points, and other stone tools. See p. 285.
• **The Museum at Warm Springs** (Warm Springs Reservation): Set in a remote valley in Central Oregon, this modern museum houses an outstanding collection of artifacts from the area's Native American tribes. See p. 300.
• **The High Desert Museum** (Bend): With its popular live-animal exhibits, this is more a zoo than a museum, but exhibits also offer glimpses into the history of the vast and little-known high desert that stretches from the Cascades eastward to the Rocky Mountains. See p. 309.
• **National Historic Oregon Trail Interpretive Center at Flagstaff Hill** (Baker City): The lives of 19th-century pioneers, who gave up everything to venture overland to the Pacific Northwest, are documented at this evocative museum. Set atop a hill in sagebrush country, the museum overlooks wagon ruts left by pioneers. See p. 324.

7 The Best Family Attractions

• **Oregon Museum of Science and Industry** (Portland): With an OMNIMAX theater, a planetarium, a submarine, and loads of hands-on exhibits, this Portland museum is fun for kids and adults alike. See p. 92.
• **Oregon Coast Aquarium** (Newport): This modern aquarium is the biggest attraction on the coast. Tufted puffins and sea otters are always entertaining, while tide pools, jellyfish tanks, and a giant octopus also contribute to the appeal of this very realistically designed public aquarium. See p. 193.

- **Sea Lion Caves** (north of Florence): This massive cave, the largest sea cave in the country, is home to hundreds of Steller's sea lions that lounge on the rocks beneath busy U.S. 101. See p. 202.
- **West Coast Game Park** (Bandon): The opportunity to pet wild baby animals, including leopards and bears, doesn't come often, so it's hard to pass up this roadside

attraction on the southern Oregon coast. See p. 216.
- **Wildlife Safari** (Winston): Giraffes peer in your window and rhinoceroses thunder past your car doors as you drive the family through this expansive wildlife park. The savanna-like setting is reminiscent of the African plains. See p. 294.

8 The Best Historical Sites

- **Fort Clatsop National Memorial** (Astoria): This small log fort is a replica of the fort that explorers Lewis and Clark built during the winter of 1805–06. During the summer, costumed interpreters bring the history of the fort to life. See p. 160.
- **Jacksonville:** With more than 80 buildings listed on the National Register of Historic Places, this 19th-century gold-mining town is the best-preserved historic community in Oregon. Here you'll also find two inns housed in buildings constructed in 1861, which makes these Oregon's oldest buildings being used as inns. See "Jacksonville & Medford: After the Gold Rush" in chapter 9.
- **Oregon Trail Wagon Ruts** (Baker City): It's hard to believe that

something as seemingly ephemeral as a wagon rut can last more than 150 years, but the path made by the thousands of pioneers who followed the Oregon Trail cut deep into the land. One place you can see ruts is near Baker city's National Historic Oregon Trail Interpretive Center. See p. 323.
- **Kam Wah Chung & Co. Museum** (John Day): This unusual little museum is way off the beaten track but is well worth a visit if you're anywhere in the vicinity. The museum preserves the home, office, and apothecary of a Chinese doctor who ministered to the local Chinese community in the early part of the 20th century. See p. 329.

9 The Best B&Bs

- **Heron Haus** (Portland; © **503/ 274-1846**): Located in one of Portland's prettiest neighborhoods, this elegant old mansion is surrounded by lush grounds and has a view over the city. If you want to sample the epitome of bathroom luxury circa 1920, ask for the room with the multiple-head shower. See p. 68.
- **Springbrook Hazelnut Farm** (Newberg; © **800/793-8528** or 503/538-4606): Set in the midst

of the Yamhill County wine country, this working hazelnut farm captures the essence of rural Oregon and distills it into a tranquil and restorative retreat. You can opt to stay in the main house, a carriage house, or a cottage. See p. 130.
- **Willamette Gables Riverside Estate** (Newberg; © **503/678-2195**): Designed as a replica of a Natchez, Mississippi, plantation home, this modern B&B is set on

the banks of the Willamette River and is among the finest reproductions of a historic home in which you are likely to ever stay. See p. 130.

- **The Secret Garden** (Eugene; ② **888/484-6755** or 541/484-6755): Housed in what was once a sorority house and before that the home of one of Eugene's founding families, this very elegant inn is utterly tasteful. The garden has some very interesting secrets. See p. 155.

- **St. Bernards** (Cannon Beach; ② **800/436-2848** or 503/436-2800): Patterned after a French château, this mansion-sized B&B may seem oddly out of place on the Oregon coast, but no one staying here seems to mind. It could be the huge guest rooms and castle-like ambience, or it could be the abundance of European antiques and original art. See p. 171.

- **Channel House** (Depoe Bay; ② **800/447-2140** or 541/765-2140): Situated on the cliff above the channel into tiny Depoe Bay, this B&B offers one of the most striking settings on the Oregon coast. The contemporary design includes guest rooms made for romance—a hot tub on the balcony, a fireplace, and an unsurpassed view out the windows. See p. 191.

- **Newport Belle Bed & Breakfast** (Newport; ② **800/348-1922** or 541/867-6290): The rooms at this B&B may not be the most luxurious nor are they the largest, but the fact that they are on a replica paddlewheeler moored in Yaquina Bay near the Oregon Coast Aquarium certainly makes them some of the most unusual. See p. 196.

- **Heceta Head Lightstation** (Yachats; ② **541/547-3696**): Ever dreamed of staying at a lighthouse? Well, on the Oregon coast, your dream can come true at this former lighthouse keeper's home. The Victorian B&B, which claims one of the most spectacular locations on the entire coast, is set high on a hill above the crashing waves. See p. 203.

- **Ziggurat Bed & Breakfast** (Yachats; ② **541/547-3925**): A boldly styled, contemporary, pyramid-shaped home built right on the beach, this is the Oregon coast's most visually stunning B&B. Its setting, near one of the most breathtaking stretches of coast, makes the inn even more worth recommending. See p. 203.

- **Chetco River Inn** (Brookings; ② **541/670-1645** or 800/327-2688): Want to get away from it all without sacrificing luxury and great food? Book a room at this remote B&B on the crystal-clear Chetco River. The setting in the middle of a national forest is as tranquil as you could wish. See p. 225.

10 The Best Small Inns

- **Stephanie Inn** (Cannon Beach; ② **800/633-3466** or 503/436-2221): Combining the look of a mountain lodge with a beachfront setting in Oregon's most artistic town, the Stephanie Inn is a romantic retreat that surrounds its guests with unpretentious luxury. See p. 172.

- **Coast Cabins** (Manzanita; ② **503/368-368-7113**): Although not actually an inn or a lodge, this collection of four modern cottages is so thoroughly enchanting that we had to include it here. Beautiful perennial gardens surround the cottages, two of which have two stories (with the bedroom on the upper floor). See p. 175.

- **Sylvia Beach Hotel** (Newport; ✆ **888/SYLVIAB** or 541/265-5428): Taking literature as its theme and decorating its rooms to evoke authors from Edgar Allan Poe to Dr. Seuss, the Sylvia Beach Hotel is the most original small inn in the Northwest. The fact that it's only a block from the beach is just icing on the cake. See p. 197.

- **Tu Tu Tun Lodge** (Gold Beach; ✆ **800/864-6357** or 541/247-6664): Though some might think of this as a fishing lodge, it's far too luxurious for anglers to keep to themselves. A secluded setting on the lower Rogue River guarantees tranquillity, and choice guest rooms provide the perfect setting for forgetting about your everyday stress. The dining room serves excellent meals. See p. 223.

- **Steamboat Inn** (Steamboat; ✆ **800/840-8825** or 541/498-2230): Oregon's North Umpqua River is legendary for its steelhead fishing, and this is where you stay if you want to return to elegance and comfort after a day on the water. The word is out on this inn, and many guests now show up with no intention of casting a fly into the river's waters. They'd rather just sit back and watch the river flow. See p. 262.

- **The Winchester Country Inn** (Ashland; ✆ **800/972-4991** or 541/488-1113): Located only 2 blocks from the theaters of the Oregon Shakespeare Festival, this inn has the feel of a country inn though it's located right in town. Rooms are in three different buildings, including a modern Victorian cottage that has four spacious suites. See p. 273.

- **Pine Ridge Inn** (Bend; ✆ **800/600-4095** or 541/389-6137): This luxurious inn is located on the outskirts of Bend on a bluff overlooking the Deschutes River. With its spacious rooms and suites, antiques, and regional art, it provides both elegance and a Northwest flavor. See p. 313.

- **Pine Valley Lodge** (Halfway; ✆ **541/742-2027**): Set in the tiny hamlet of Halfway just outside Hells Canyon National Recreation Area, this lodge is everything that contemporary rustic Western lodges wish they could be. Owned and operated by two artists, the lodge conjures up the image of an old stage stop with its unusual architecture, while unique details add a very personal feel. See p. 337.

11 The Best Historic Hotels & Lodges

- **The Benson** (Portland; ✆ **800/426-0670** or 503/228-2000): With its crystal chandeliers and Circassian walnut paneling in the lobby, this 1912 vintage hotel is the lodging of choice for presidents, dignitaries, and celebrities visiting Portland. See p. 63.

- **Columbia Gorge Hotel** (Hood River; ✆ **800/345-1921** or 541/386-5566): Built in 1915 to handle the first automobile traffic up the Columbia Gorge, this Mission-style hotel commands a stunning view across the gorge and is surrounded by colorful gardens. The breakfasts are legendary. See p. 238.

- **Timberline Lodge** (Mount Hood; ✆ **800/547-1406** or 503/622-7979): Built by the WPA during the Great Depression, this stately mountain lodge with grand stone fireplace, exposed beams, and wide plank floors, showcases the skills of the craftspeople who created it.

The views of Mount Hood's peak and the Oregon Cascades to the south are superb. See p. 251.

- **Crater Lake Lodge** (Crater Lake National Park; ℂ **541/830-8700**): Perched on the rim of the caldera (not crater) that holds the blue waters of Crater Lake, this modern mountain lodge incorporates a few details from the original lodge that used to stand on this same site. The setting is breathtaking. See p. 264.
- **Ashland Springs Hotel** (Ashland; ℂ **800/325-4000** or 541/488-1700): This recently renovated historic high-rise hotel was originally built to cash in on Ashland's mineral springs, but today it is, instead, a superb choice for anyone attending the Oregon Shakespeare Festival. See p. 271.
- **Geiser Grand Hotel** (Baker City; ℂ **888/GEISERG** or 541/523-1889): Originally opened in 1889 at the height of the Blue Mountains gold rush, this Baker City grande dame has been completely renovated, and, with its corner turret, stained-glass ceiling, and abundance of crystal chandeliers, succeeds in capturing the feel of a Wild West luxury hotel without sacrificing any modern conveniences. See p. 327.

12 The Best Dining with a View

- **Chart House** (Portland; **503/246-6963**): Perched high on a hillside, this restaurant boasts the best view of any restaurant in Portland. The Willamette River is directly below and off in the distance stand Mount Hood and Mount St. Helens. See p. 81.
- **Roseanna's Oceanside Café** (Oceanside; ℂ **503/842-7351**): You can expect a long wait to get a table here on a summer weekend, but the view of the haystack rocks just offshore makes this an absolute legend on the Three Capes Scenic Loop. See p. 181.
- **Pelican Pub & Brewery** (Pacific City; ℂ **503/965-7007**): Cheap pub food and good microbrews are usually enough to keep an Oregon brewpub packed, but this one also has a head-on view of Haystack Rock and is right on the beach. Popular with surfers. See p. 181.
- **Tidal Raves** (Depoe Bay; ℂ **541/765-2995**): When the surf's up, you can practically forget about getting a table at this oceanfront restaurant. The windows overlook a rugged shoreline known for putting on some of the coast's best displays of crashing waves. See p. 192.
- **Lord Bennett's Restaurant and Lounge** (Bandon; ℂ **541/347-3663**): The beach in Bandon is strewn with dozens of huge monoliths that make this one of the most impressive stretches of shoreline in the state, and this restaurant has the perfect view for enjoying sunset over the sand, surf, and giant rocks. See p. 218.
- **Multnomah Falls Lodge** (Columbia Gorge; ℂ **503/695-2376**): This historic lodge is at the base of Oregon's tallest waterfall, and although not every table has a view of the waterfall, there are plenty that do, especially in the summer when there is outside seating. See p. 234.
- **Broken Top Club Restaurant and Lounge** (Bend; ℂ **541/383-8210**): Golf course views are always nice, but the golf-course view at this Bend restaurant also takes in the restaurant's namesake mountain, which, as the name implies, is one of the more jagged peaks in the Cascades. See p. 316.

13 The Best Off-the-Beaten-Path Restaurants

- **The Joel Palmer House** (Dayton; ℂ **503/864-2995**): Mushrooms are an obsession of the chef at this wine-country restaurant, and you'll find them in almost every dish on the menu (with the exception of the desserts). The restaurant is quite formal and is housed in an immaculately restored old home. See p. 133.

- **Cascade Dining Room** (Mount Hood; ℂ **503/622-0700**): Located inside the historic Timberline Lodge, the Cascade Dining Room is Oregon's premier mountain-lodge restaurant and has long kept skiers and other hotel guests happy. Since the windows here are small, it isn't the view that keeps diners content, but rather the creative cuisine. See p. 253.

- **Steamboat Inn** (North Umpqua Valley; ℂ **800/840-8825** or 541/498-2230): Set on the bank of the North Umpqua River, this is ostensibly a fishing-lodge dining room, but the multicourse gourmet meals served here have become the stuff of legends. See p. 262.

- **Kokanee Café** (Camp Sherman; ℂ **541/595-6420**): Located amid the ponderosa pines on the bank of the Metolius River near the Western theme town of Sisters, this rustic restaurant has the look of an upscale fishing lodge, but its clientele is much broader than just the foolish fly anglers who come to test the waters of the Metolius. The trout is, of course, always a good bet. See p. 308.

- **The Halfway Supper Club** (Halfway; ℂ **541/742-2027**): Halfway is an unlikely town for a restaurant that can rank among the top in the state, but the imaginative, rustic Western decor combined with the chef/co-owner's love of cooking always make a meal here a highlight of a trip to the Wallowa Mountains region. See p. 337.

2

Planning Your Trip to Oregon

This chapter covers everything you need to plan a trip to Oregon.

1 The Regions in Brief

Geography and climate play important roles in dividing Oregon into its various regions.

The Willamette Valley This is Oregon's most densely populated region and site of the state's largest cities, including Portland, Eugene, and the state capital of Salem. The valley's fabled farmland grows the greatest variety of crops of any region of the United States. These include hops, mint, grass seed, berries, hazelnuts, irises, tulips, Christmas trees, and an immense variety of landscape plants. The Willamette Valley is also one of the nation's finest wine regions, with vineyards cropping up along its entire length.

Summer, when farm stands pop up alongside rural highways, is by far the best time of year to visit the Willamette Valley. However, if you are interested in wine, you might also want to consider October, when vineyards pick and crush their grapes.

The Oregon Coast Stretching for nearly 300 miles, the Oregon coast is one of the most spectacular coastlines in the country. Backed by the Coast Range mountains and alternating sandy beaches with rocky capes and headlands, this mountainous shoreline provides breathtaking vistas at almost every turn of the road. Haystack rocks—large monoliths just offshore—lend the coast an unforgettable drama and beauty. Along the central coast,

huge dunes, some as much as 500 feet high, have been preserved as the Oregon Dunes National Recreation Area. Small towns, some known as fishing ports and some as artists' communities, dot the coast. Unfortunately, waters are generally too cold for swimming, and a cool breeze often blows even in summer.

Of course, summer is the most popular time of year on the coast, and crowds can be daunting. In Seaside, Cannon Beach, Lincoln City, and Newport, traffic backups try the patience of many vacationers. The north coast, because of its proximity to Portland, is the most visited section of the coast, and it is also one of the most dramatic. The south coast is even more spectacular than the north, and because of its distance from major metropolitan areas is not nearly as crowded as other stretches of the coast. The central coast, though it boasts the Oregon Dunes National Recreation Area, is less spectacular than the north and south coasts.

The Columbia Gorge Beginning just east of Portland, the Columbia Gorge is one of the region's most breathtaking attractions. Declared a national scenic area, the Gorge is the site of numerous waterfalls, including Multnomah Falls, the fourth highest in the United States. The winds that regularly blast through the Gorge attract windsurfing enthusiasts. The town of Hood River is now one of the

Oregon's Regions

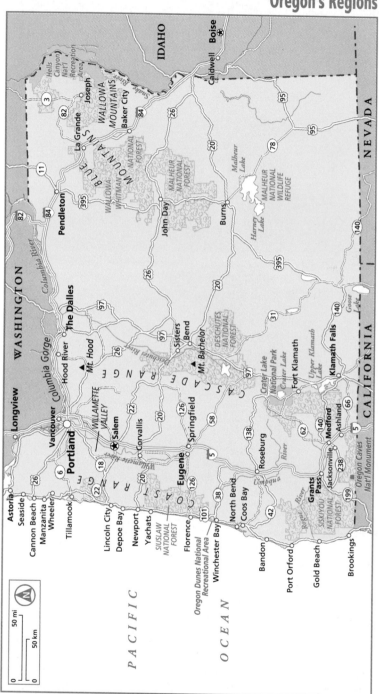

world's top windsurfing spots. Rising above the Gorge on the south side is Mount Hood, the tallest peak in Oregon.

Although the Gorge can be explored in a day or two, if you are an avid hiker or windsurfer, you might want to plan a longer visit. Springtime is the best time of year to visit. March through May, countless wildflowers, some of which grow nowhere else but in the Columbia Gorge, burst into bloom, and Gorge wildflower hikes are annual rites of spring for many Oregonians.

The Cascade Range Stretching from the Columbia River in the north to the California state line in the south, this mountain range is a natural dividing line between eastern and western Oregon. Dominated by conical peaks of volcanic origin (all currently inactive), the Cascades are almost entirely encompassed by national forests that serve as both sources of timber and year-round recreational playgrounds. Throughout these mountains are several designated wilderness areas in which all mechanized travel is prohibited. Among these, the Mount Hood Wilderness, the Mount Jefferson Wilderness, and the Three Sisters Wilderness are the most scenic and heavily visited. In the southern Cascades, an entire mountain once blew its top, leaving behind a huge caldera that is now filled by the sapphire-blue waters of Crater Lake, Oregon's only national park.

With little private property and few lodges other than rustic (and often run-down) cabin "resorts," the Cascades are primarily a camping destination during the warmer months. The one exception is the area stretching from Sisters to Sunriver, which abounds in upscale family and golf resorts. In winter several ski areas and many miles of cross-country ski trails attract skiers and snowboarders.

Southern Oregon Lying roughly midway between San Francisco and Portland, southern Oregon is a jumbled landscape of mountains and valleys through which flow two of the state's most famous rivers. The North Umpqua and the Rogue rivers have been fabled among anglers ever since Zane Grey popularized these waters in his writings. A climate much drier than that of the Willamette Valley to the north gives this region the look of parts of northern California, and, in fact, several towns in the region are very popular with retired Californians. Among these are Ashland, site of the Oregon Shakespeare Festival, and Jacksonville, a historic gold-mining town that is now the site of the Britt Festivals, an annual summer festival of music and modern dance. Also in the region are quite a few wineries that take advantage of the warm climate to produce Oregon's best Cabernet Sauvignon and Merlot.

Although summer is the most popular time of year to visit this region, with the Oregon Shakespeare Festival running through much of the spring and fall, Ashland stays busy almost year-round.

Central Oregon When the rain on the west side of the Cascades becomes too much to bear, many of the state's residents flee to Central Oregon, the drier and sunnier part of the state. Consisting of the east side of the Cascade Range from the Columbia River to just south of Bend, the region spans the eastern foothills of the Cascades and the western edge of the Great Basin's high desert. Known primarily for its lack of rain and proximity to the cities of the Willamette Valley, central Oregon is the state's second-most-popular summer vacation destination (after the coast), with resorts clustered around Sisters and Bend. The biggest and most popular resort is Sunriver, an entire community (complete with three golf courses, a shopping center, and thousands of vacation homes and condos) south of Bend. A volcanic legacy has left the region with some of the most fascinating geology in the state, much of which is preserved in Newberry National Volcanic Monument. Also in this region is the High Desert Museum, a combination museum and zoo that is among the state's most popular attractions.

Although summer is the peak season here, with Mount Bachelor ski area providing the best skiing in the Northwest, central Oregon is also quite popular in winter.

Eastern Oregon   Large and sparsely populated, eastern Oregon is primarily high desert interspersed with small mountain ranges. Despite the desert climate, the region is also the site of several large shallow lakes that serve as magnets for a wide variety of migratory birds. In the northeast corner of the region rise the Blue and Wallowa Mountains, which are remote, though popular, recreation areas. Carving North America's deepest gorge, and partially forming the border with Idaho, are the Snake River and Hells Canyon. Throughout this region, signs of the Oregon Trail can still be seen.

Because this region is so remote from Portland and the Willamette Valley, it is little visited. However, the breathtaking Wallowa Mountains offer some of the finest backpacking in the state. The town of Joseph, on the north side of these mountains, is one of the nation's foremost centers for casting bronze sculptures.

2 Visitor Information

Contact the **Oregon Tourism Commission,** 775 Summer St. NE, Salem, OR 97310 (© **800/547-7842** or 986-0000; www.traveloregon.com), or the **Portland Oregon Visitors Association (POVA),** 1000 SW Broadway, Suite 2300, Portland, OR 97205 (© **877/678-5263** or 503/ 275-9750; www.travelportland.com).

Most cities and towns in Oregon have either a tourist office or a chamber of commerce that provides information. When approaching cities and towns, watch for signs along the highway directing you to these information centers. See the individual chapters for addresses.

For Oregon regional websites, try the Oregon Tourism Commission's website at **www.traveloregon.com**. Learn about local Oregon news, sports, and entertainment at *The Oregonian* newspaper's site, www. oregonlive.com. And if you're planning an active vacation, check Gorp at **www.gorp.com/gorp/location/ or/or.htm**.

You can also get travel information covering Oregon from the American Automobile Association (AAA) if you're a member.

To get information on outdoor recreation in the national forests of Oregon, contact the **Nature of the Northwest Information Center,** 800 NE Oregon St., Room 177, Portland, OR 97232 (© **503/872-2750;** www. naturenw.org). For information on Crater Lake, the only national park in Oregon, contact **Crater Lake National Park** (© **541/594-2211;** www.nps.gov/crla).

For information on camping in Oregon state parks, contact the **Oregon State Park Information Center** (© **800/551-6949;** www. oregonstateparks.org).

3 Money

ATMs are linked to a national network that most likely includes your bank at home. **Cirrus** (© **800/424-7787**; www.mastercard.com) and **PLUS** (© **800/843-7587**; www.visa.com) are the two most popular networks; check the back of your ATM card to see which network your bank uses. Use the 800 numbers to locate ATMs in your destination. Other ATM networks found in the Portland area are Accel, The Exchange, and Interlink.

At most banks, you can get a cash advance with your credit card at the ATM if you know your PIN number.

Almost every credit-card company has an emergency toll-free number that you can call if your wallet or purse is stolen. The toll-free information directory will provide the number if you dial © **800/555-1212. Citicorp Visa's** U.S. emergency number is © **800/336-8472. American Express** cardholders and traveler's check holders should call © **800/221-7282** for all money emergencies. **MasterCard** holders should call © **800/307-7309.**

For more information, see chapter 3.

4 When to Go

Summer is the peak season in Oregon. In summer, hotel and car reservations are almost essential; the rest of the year, they're highly recommended, but not imperative. If you visit in one of the rainier months between October and May, hotel rates are lower. It will also be easier to get reservations, especially on the coast. However, you will have to bring good rain gear. Whenever you go, keep in mind that you usually get better rates by reserving at least 1 or 2 weeks in advance, whether you're booking a plane, hotel, or rental car. Summer holiday weekends are the hardest times of year to get room reservations, especially on the coast. Book months in advance for Memorial Day, Fourth of July, and Labor Day.

Though Oregon is famous for its gray skies and mild temperatures, the state is actually characterized by a diversity of climates almost unequaled in the United States. For the most part, moist winds off the Pacific Ocean keep temperatures west of the Cascade Range mild year-round. Summers in the Willamette Valley and southern Oregon can see temperatures over 100°F, but on the coast you're likely to need a sweater or light jacket at night, even in August. The Oregon rains that are so legendary fall primarily as a light, but almost constant, drizzle between October and early July. Sure, there are windows of sunshine during this period, but they usually last no more than a week or so. There are also, unfortunately, occasional wet summers, so be prepared for wet weather whenever you visit. Winters usually include one or two blasts of Arctic air, usually right around Christmas or New Year's, that bring snow and freezing weather to the Portland area. Expect snow in the Cascades any time during the winter, and even some Coast Range passes can get icy.

If you visit the coast, expect grayer, wetter weather than in the Portland area. It can be quite cool here in the summer and is often foggy or rainy throughout the year. In fact, when the Willamette Valley is at its hottest in July and August, you can be sure that the coast will be fogged in. The best month for the coast is usually September, with good weather often holding on into October.

In the Cascades and eastern Oregon's Blue and Wallowa Mountains, snowfall is heavy in the winter and skiing is a popular sport. Summer doesn't come until late in the year here, with snow lingering into July at higher elevations (for instance, the Timberline Lodge area at Mount Hood and the Eagle Cap Wilderness in the Wallowas). At such elevations, late July and on through August are the best times to see the wildflowers in alpine meadows.

The region east of the Cascades is characterized by lack of rain and temperature extremes. This high desert area can be very cold in the winter, and at higher elevations it receives considerable amounts of snow. In summer, the weather can be blazingly hot at lower elevations, though nights are often cool enough to require a sweater or light jacket.

If you're planning to go wine touring, avoid January and February, when most wineries are closed. Also keep in mind that many wineries are open daily during the summer months, but on weekends only in spring and fall.

Portland's Average Monthly Temperatures & Rainfall

	Jan	Feb	Mar	Apr	May	June	July	Aug	Sept	Oct	Nov	Dec
Temp. (°F)	40	43	46	50	57	63	68	67	63	54	46	41
Temp. (°C)	4	6	8	10	14	17	20	20	17	12	8	5
Days of Rain	18	16	17	14	12	10	4	5	8	13	18	19

OREGON CALENDAR OF EVENTS

February

The Portland International Film Festival, Portland. Although not one of the country's top such festivals, plenty of interesting films are shown. Screenings are held at various theaters around the city. Tickets go on sale 2 weeks before the festival starts, and weekend shows usually sell out. ✆ **503/ 221-1156;** www.nwfilm.org. Last 3 weeks of February.

Oregon Shakespeare Festival, Ashland. The repertory company features about a dozen plays—some by Shakespeare and others by classical and contemporary playwrights—in three unique theaters. Backstage tours, a museum, and lectures round out the festival. Call ✆ **541/ 482-4331** or check **www.osf ashland.org** for details and ticket information. February through October.

Newport Seafood and Wine Festival, Newport. Taste local seafood dishes and wines while shopping for art. ✆ **800/262-7844** or 541/265-8801; www.newport chamber.org/swf. Last full weekend in February.

March

Oregon Dune Mushers' Mail Run, Florence. An endurance dog run over the varied terrain of the Florence coastline commemorates routes used before roads were constructed. ✆ **541/269-1269.** Second weekend in March.

Woodburn Tulip Festival, Woodburn. Here's a chance to do some hot-air ballooning and wine tasting, but the main attraction is the blazing red and yellow of the tulip fields. ✆ **503/981-3441;** www. woodenshoe.com. Late March to early April.

April

Hood River Blossom Festival, Hood River. Celebrates the blossoming of the orchards outside the town of Hood River. ✆ **800/366- 3530;** www.hoodriver.org. Third weekend in April.

May

Mother's Day Rhododendron Show, Crystal Springs Rhododendron Gardens. Blooming rhododendrons and azaleas transform this tranquil garden into a mass of blazing color. ℂ **503/771-8386** or 503/777-1734; www.arsportland. org. Mother's Day.

Memorial Day Wine Tastings, throughout the wine country surrounding Portland. This is one of 2 weekends celebrated by Yamhill County and other area wineries with special tastings and events. Many wineries not usually open to the public open on this weekend. ℂ **503/ 646-2985;** www.yamhillwine.com. Memorial Day weekend.

Azalea Festival, Brookings. Attractions include food booths, a craft fair, and of course the colorful native azaleas. ℂ **800/535-9469.** Memorial Day weekend.

Boatnik, Grants Pass. Jet boats and hydroplanes race on the Rogue River, and there's also a parade and carnival. ℂ **800/547-5927.** Memorial Day weekend.

June

Cannon Beach Sand Castle Festival, Cannon Beach. Artistic sand-sculpted creations appear along the beach. ℂ **503/436-2623;** www. cannonbeach.org. Early June.

Sisters Rodeo and Parade, Sisters. A celebration of the West in this duded-up Western town near Bend. ℂ **800/827-7522.** Second weekend of June.

Portland Rose Festival. From its beginnings back in 1888 the Rose Festival has blossomed into Portland's biggest celebration. The festivities now span nearly a month and include a rose show, parade, rose queen contest, music festival, art show, car races, footrace, boat races, and even an air show. Contact the Portland Rose Festival Association, 5603 SW Hood Ave., Portland, OR 97201 (ℂ **503/ 227-2681;** www.rosefestival.org), or Ticketmaster (ℂ **503/224-4400**) for tickets to specific events. Tickets are also available through the Rose Festival website. Most of the events (some of which are free) take place during the middle 2 weeks of June, and hotel rooms can be hard to come by, so plan ahead.

Britt Festivals, Jacksonville. Performing arts festival with world-class jazz, classical, folk, country, dance, musical theater, and pop performances in a beautiful natural setting. Bring a picnic. ℂ **800/88-BRITT,** 541/773-6077, or www.brittfest.org for details and ticket information. June through September.

Oregon Bach Festival, Eugene. One of the biggest Bach festivals around serves up Bach's big oratorio works such as the *B Minor Mass,* but also various other concerts including chamber music and a program for kids. ℂ **800/457-1486** or www.bachfest.uoregon. edu. Late June to early July.

July

Fourth of July Fireworks, Vancouver, Washington. Vancouver, which is part of the Portland metropolitan area, hosts the biggest fireworks display west of the Mississippi. ℂ **360/693-5481.** July 4.

World Championship Timber Carnival, Albany. Logging events, parade, food, and fireworks. ℂ **800/ 526-2256.** Fourth of July weekend.

Oregon Country Fair, Eugene. Counterculture craft fair and festival for Deadheads young and old. ℂ **800/992-8499** or 541/343-4298; www.oregoncountryfair.org. Second weekend in July.

Sisters Quilt Show, Sisters. The entire town gets decked out in colorful handmade quilts. ℂ **541/ 549-0251.** Second Saturday of July.

Da Vinci Days, Corvallis. Three-day celebration of science and technology with performances, art, interactive exhibits, children's activities, food, and wine. ✆ **800/334-8118** or 541/757-6363; www.davinci-days. org. Mid-July.

Salem Arts Festival, Salem. The largest juried art fair in Oregon, under the trees in Bush Park, with musical entertainment and food booths. ✆ **503/581-2228;** www. salemart.org. Third weekend in July.

Oregon Brewers Festival, Tom McCall Waterfront Park. America's largest festival of independent craft brewers features lots of local and international microbrews and music. ✆ **503/778-5917;** www.oregon brewfest.com. Last weekend in July.

August

Mount Hood Jazz Festival, Mount Hood Community College, Gresham (less than 30 min. from Portland). For the serious jazz fan, this is *the* festival of the summer, featuring the greatest names in jazz. Tickets are $28.50 to $50 per day or $70 to $175 for a 3-day pass. ✆ **503/219-9833;** www.mthood jazz.com. Tickets are available through the Web address or Fastixx (✆ **800/992-8499** or 503/224-8499). First weekend in August.

Oregon State Fair, Salem. A typical agricultural state fair. ✆ **800/ 833-0011** in Oregon, or 503/947-3247. The 12 days before and including Labor Day.

Cascade Festival of Music, Bend. Classical and world music in a park setting. ✆ **541/382-8381;** www. cascademusic.org. Last weekend in August.

September

Mt. Angel Oktoberfest, Mount Angel. Biergarten, Bavarian-style oompah bands, food booths. ✆ **503/ 845-9440;** www.oktoberfest.org. Second weekend after Labor Day.

Shrewsbury Renaissance Faire, Corvallis. Go back 500 years to celebrate the age of Elizabeth I and Shakespeare with jousting and period costumes in an Elizabethan village. ✆ **541/929-4897;** www. shrewfaire.com. Second weekend of September.

Pendleton Round-Up and Happy Canyon Pageant, Pendleton. Rodeo, Native American pageant, country-music concert. ✆ **800/ 457-6336** or 541/276-2553; www.pendletonroundup.com. Mid-September.

Bandon Cranberry Festival, Bandon. Cranberry bog tours, arts and crafts. ✆ **541/347-9616.** Early to mid-September.

Eugene Celebration, Eugene. Street party celebrating the diversity of the community. Festivities include the crowning of a Slug Queen. ✆ **541/ 681-4108;** www.eugenecelebration. com. Mid-September.

Kite Festival, Lincoln City. Kite carnival including the world's largest spinning windsock and lighted night kite flights. ✆ **800/ 452-2151;** www.oregoncoast.org. Late September.

October

Hood River Valley Harvest Fest, Hood River. At the Hood River Expo Center, enjoy fruit products of the region, crafts, and entertainment; drive the Fruit Loop to visit farm stands and wineries. ✆ **800/ 366-3530;** www.hoodriver.org. Mid- to late October.

November

Wine Country Thanksgiving, Yamhill County. About 30 miles outside of Portland, more than two dozen wineries open their doors for tastings of new releases, usually with food and live music. ✆ **503/ 646-2985;** www.yamhillwine.com. Thanksgiving weekend.

Holiday Lights and Open House at Shore Acres State Park, Charleston. Extravagantly decorated gardens near dramatic cliffs at the Oregon coast. ⓒ **541/756-5401.** Thanksgiving to early January.

December

Holiday Festival of Lights, Ashland. Thousands of lights decorate the town. ⓒ **541/482-3486;** www. ashlandchamber.com. Month of December.

Holiday Parade of Ships, Willamette and Columbia Rivers. Boats decked out in fanciful holiday lights parade and circle on the rivers after nightfall. www. christmasships.org. Mid-December.

5 Tips for Travelers with Special Needs

FOR TRAVELERS WITH DISABILITIES

When making airline reservations, always mention your disability. Airline policies differ regarding wheelchairs and Seeing Eye dogs. Almost all hotels and motels in Oregon, aside from bed-and-breakfast inns and older or historic lodges, offer accommodations accessible for travelers with disabilities. However, when making reservations, be sure to ask. Oregon lodgings that are accessible are listed in the *Oregon Traveler's Guide to Accommodations.* To get a copy of this magazine, contact the **Oregon Tourism Commission,** 775 Summer St. NE, Salem, OR 97310 (ⓒ **800/547-7842**).

The public transit systems found in most Oregon cities either have regular vehicles that are accessible for riders with disabilities or offer special transportation services for people with disabilities.

Oregon State Parks has a TDD (Telephone Device for the Deaf) information line (ⓒ **800/858-9659**) that provides recreation and camping information.

If you plan to visit any national parks or monuments, you can avail yourself of the **Golden Access Passport.** This lifetime pass is issued free to any U.S. citizen or permanent resident who has been medically certified as disabled or blind. The pass permits free entry into national parks and monuments.

A World of Options, a book of resources for travelers with disabilities, costs $35 ($31.50 for members) and is available from **Mobility International USA,** P.O. Box 10767, Eugene, OR, 97440 (ⓒ **541/343-1284,** voice and TDD; www.miusa.org).

Many of the major car-rental companies now offer hand-controlled cars with advance reservations. **Wheelchair Getaways** (ⓒ **800/642-2042;** www.wheelchair-getaways.com) rents specialized vans with wheelchair lifts and other features for travelers with disabilities in about 40 cities across the United States. In the Pacific Northwest Wheelchair Getaways is located near Seattle in the suburb of Woodinville (ⓒ **888/376-1500** or 425/788-3718).

Both **Amtrak** (ⓒ **800/USA-RAIL;** www.amtrak.com) and **Greyhound** (ⓒ **800/752-4841;** www.greyhound. com) offer special services for the disabled. Amtrak also offers special fares. Call at least a week in advance of your trip for details.

FOR GAY & LESBIAN TRAVELERS

Gay and lesbian travelers visiting Portland should be sure to pick up a free copy of *Just Out* (ⓒ **503/236-1252;** www.justout.com), a bimonthly newspaper for the gay community. You can usually find copies at **Powell's Books,** 1005 W. Burnside St. *Just Out* also publishes the *Just Out Pocketbook,* a statewide gay and lesbian business directory. Another publication to look for is *Portland's Gay & Lesbian Community Yellow Pages* (© **503/230-7701;** www.pdxgayyellowpages.com), which is also usually available at Powell's.

FOR SENIORS

Don't be shy about asking for discounts, but always carry some kind of identification, such as a driver's license, that shows your date of birth.

Mention the fact that you're a senior when you first make your travel reservations, since many airlines and hotels offer discounts. Both **Amtrak** (© **800/USA-RAIL;** www.amtrak.com) and **Greyhound** (© **800/752-4841;** www.greyhound.com) offer discounts to persons over 62. Many attractions, some theaters and concert halls, and tour companies also offer senior discounts.

Save on National Park and Monument admissions by getting a **Golden Age Passport,** which is available for $10 to U.S. citizens and permanent residents 62 and older. This federal government pass allows lifetime entrance privileges. You can apply in person for this passport at a national park, a national forest, or any other location where it's honored, as long as you can show reasonable proof of age.

If you aren't a member of the **American Association of Retired Persons (AARP),** 601 E St. NW, Washington, DC 20049 (© **800/424-3410;** www.aarp.org), you should consider joining. This association provides discounts for many lodgings, car rentals, airfares, and attractions throughout Oregon.

Older travelers (either you or your spouse must be 55 years old or older) interested in educational trips should look into programs by **Elderhostel,** 11 Avenue de Lafayette, Boston, MA 02110-1746 (© **877/426-8056;** www.elderhostel.org).

6 Planning Your Trip Online

With a mouse and a modem, Internet users can tap into the same travel-planning databases that were once accessible only to travel agents. Sites such as **Travelocity, Expedia,** and **Orbitz** allow consumers to comparison shop for airfares, book flights, learn of last-minute bargains, and reserve hotel rooms and rental cars.

But don't fire your travel agent just yet. Although online booking sites offer tips and hard data to help you bargain shop, they cannot endow you with the hard-earned experience that makes a seasoned, reliable travel agent an invaluable resource, even in the Internet age. And for consumers with a complex itinerary, a trusty travel agent is still the best way to arrange the most direct flights.

Still, there's no denying the Internet's emergence as a powerful tool in researching and plotting travel time.

The benefits of researching your trip online can be well worth the effort:

- **Last-minute specials,** known as "E-savers," such as weekend deals or Internet-only fares, are offered by airlines to fill empty seats. Most of these are announced on Tuesday or Wednesday and must be purchased online. They are only valid for travel that weekend, but some can be booked weeks or months in advance. Sign up for weekly e-mail alerts at airline websites or check megasites that compile comprehensive lists of E-savers, such as Smarter Living (smarterliving.com) or WebFlyer (www.webflyer.com).
- All major airlines offer **incentives**—bonus frequent-flier miles, Internet-only discounts, sometimes even free cellphone rentals—when you purchase online or buy an e-ticket.

Frommers.com: The Complete Travel Resource

For an excellent travel planning resource, we recommend **Arthur Frommer's Budget Travel Online** (www.frommers.com). Among the special features are: **"Ask the Expert"** bulletin boards, where Frommer's authors answer your questions via online postings; **Arthur Frommer's Daily Newsletter,** for the latest travel bargains and inside travel secrets; and Frommer's **Destinations Archive,** where you'll get expert travel tips, hotel and dining recommendations, and advice on the sights to see for more than 200 destinations around the globe. Once your research is done, the **Online Reservation System** (www.frommers.com/booktravelnow) takes you to Frommer's favorite sites for booking your vacation at affordable prices.

- Advances in mobile technology provide business travelers and other frequent travelers with **the ability to check flight status, change plans, or get specific directions** from handheld computing devices, mobile phones, and pagers. Some sites will e-mail or page a passenger if a flight is delayed.

TRAVEL PLANNING & BOOKING SITES

The best travel planning and booking sites cast a wide net, offering domestic and international flights, hotel and rental-car bookings, plus news, destination information, and deals on cruises and vacation packages. Keep in mind that free (one-time) registration is often required for booking. Because several airlines are no longer willing to pay commissions on tickets sold by online travel agencies, be aware that these online agencies will either charge a $10 surcharge if you book a ticket on that carrier—or neglect to offer those air carriers' offerings.

The sites in this section are not intended to be a comprehensive list, but rather a discriminating selection to get you started. Recognition is given to sites based on their content value and ease of use and is not paid for—unlike some website rankings, which are based on payment. Remember: This is a press-time snapshot of leading websites—some undoubtedly will have evolved or moved by the time you read this.

- **Travelocity** (www.travelocity.com or www.frommers.travelocity.com) and **Expedia** (www.expedia.com) are the most longstanding and reputable sites, each offering excellent selections and searches for complete vacation packages. Travelers search by destination and dates coupled with how much they are willing to spend.

- The latest buzz in the online travel world is about **Orbitz** (www.orbitz.com), a site launched by United, Delta, Northwest, American, and Continental airlines. It shows all possible fares for your desired trip, offering fares lower than those available through travel agents.

- **Qixo** (www.qixo.com) is another powerful search engine that allows you to search for flights and hotel rooms on 20 other travel-planning sites (such as Travelocity) at once. Qixo sorts results by price, after which you can book your travel directly through the site.

SMART E-SHOPPING

Here are a few tips to help you navigate the Internet successfully and safely.

- **Shop around.** Compare results from different sites and airlines—and against a travel agent's best fare, if you can. If possible, try a range of times and alternate airports before you make a purchase.
- **Stay secure.** Book only through secure sites (some airline sites are not secure). Look for a key icon (Netscape) or a padlock (Internet Explorer) at the bottom of your Web browser before you enter credit-card information or other personal data.
- **Avoid online auctions.** Sites that auction airline tickets and frequent-flier miles are the number-one perpetrators of Internet fraud, according to the National Consumers League.
- **Maintain a paper trail.** If you book an e-ticket, print out a confirmation, or write down your confirmation number, and keep it safe and accessible—or your trip could be a virtual one!

ONLINE TRAVELER'S TOOLBOX

Following is a selection of online tools to bookmark.

- **Visa ATM Locator** (www.visa.com/pd/atm) or **MasterCard ATM Locator** (www.mastercard.com/atm). Find ATMs in hundreds of cities in the U.S. and around the world.
- **Intellicast** (www.intellicast.com). Weather forecasts for all 50 states and cities around the world. *Note:* Temperatures are in Celsius for many international destinations.
- **Mapquest** (www.mapquest.com). This best of the mapping sites lets you choose a specific address or destination, and in seconds, it will return a map and detailed directions.
- **Cybercafes.com** (www.cybercafes.com) or **Net Café Guide** (www.netcafeguide.com/mapindex.htm). Locate Internet cafes at hundreds of locations around the globe. Catch up on your e-mail and log onto the Web for a few dollars per hour.

7 Getting There

BY PLANE

The major carriers to **Portland Airport** (www.portlandairportpdx.com) include: **Alaska Airlines** ✆ 800/426-0333, www.alaskaair.com; **America West** ✆ 800/235-9292, www.americawest.com; **American** ✆ 800/433-7300, www.aa.com; **Continental** ✆ 800/525-0280, www.continental.com; **Delta** ✆ 800/221-1212; delta.com; **Frontier** ✆ 800/432-1359, www.frontierairlines.com; **Horizon Air** ✆ 800/547-9308, www.horizonair.com; **Northwest/KLM** ✆ 800/225-2525, www.nwa.com; **Skywest** ✆ 800/241-6522, www.skywest.com; **Southwest** ✆ 800/435-9792, www.southwest.com.

For information on flights to the U.S. from other countries, see chapter 3.

FLY FOR LESS: TIPS FOR GETTING THE BEST AIRFARES

If you're flying to Portland from another city in the Western U.S., check with Frontier Airlines, Shuttle by United, Alaska Airlines, Horizon Airlines, or Southwest. These airlines often have the best fares between western cities.

Check your newspaper for advertised discounts or call the airlines directly and ask if any **promotional rates** or special fares are available. You'll almost never see a sale during

Site Seeing: The Best of Oregon on the Web

- **Oregon Tourism Commission (www.traveloregon.com):** With a slide show illustrating the state's geographical diversity, an online hotel reservations system, and loads of links to other helpful websites, this should be your online starting point for planning a trip to Oregon.
- **CitySearch (portland.citysearch.com):** Another in CitySearch's excellent line of city sites, CitySearch Portland offers, in a familiar format, much of what a visitor needs to know about the culinary, artistic, theatrical, and musical scenes in town. The site is searchable by time, venue, date, or neighborhood. Also check out the dozens of restaurant reviews.
- **Portland Oregon Visitors Association (www.pova.com):** The Portland Oregon Visitors Association (POVA) is eager to have you see and do all you can in its city. Click on "Visitor Info" for advice on sightseeing, performing arts, shopping, outdoor activities, and an online hotel reservation service. The site also offers a calendar of events and tools to help business travelers plan meetings and conventions.
- **The Oregonian (www.oregonlive.com):** A service of the state's largest newspaper, the *Oregonian,* Oregon Live offers news updates, events calendars, local entertainment listings, online classifieds, and chat rooms.
- **Nature of the Northwest (www.naturenw.org):** This is sort of a clearinghouse for information on reservations and rentals on public lands in the Northwest. The website also has information on passes that you'll need in order to park at trail heads and in snow-parks. Plenty of links, too.
- **Oregon State Parks (www.oregonstateparks.org):** With detailed information on every park in the system and lots of photos, this website is enough to get anyone planning a state parks of Oregon road trip.
- **Forest Service (www.fs.fed.us/r6/):** This website will give you links to all the national forests in Oregon (and Washington), and although the individual national forest websites vary in their usefulness and ease of use, all have lots of information on campgrounds and current trail conditions.
- **Great Outdoors Recreation Pages (www.gorp.com/gorp/location/or/or.htm):** With an overwhelming amount of information, this website is a weekend warrior's dream come true. Although much of the information is copied straight from handouts available at ranger stations and other public information sources, here you can find it all in one place.

peak summer vacation months or during the Thanksgiving or Christmas seasons; but in periods of low-volume travel, you should pay no more than $400 for a cross-country flight. If your schedule is flexible, ask if you can secure a cheaper fare by staying an extra day or by flying midweek. If you already hold a ticket when a sale breaks, it may even pay to exchange your ticket, which usually incurs a $50 to $75 charge. Note, however, that the lowest-priced fares are often nonrefundable, require advance purchase of 1 to 3 weeks and a certain length of stay, and carry penalties for changing travel dates.

Consolidators, also known as bucket shops, are a good place to find low fares. Consolidators buy seats in bulk from the airlines and then sell them back to the public at prices below even the airlines' discounted rates. Their small, boxed ads usually run in the Sunday travel section of newspapers at the bottom of the page. Before you pay, however, ask for a confirmation number from the consolidator and then call the airline itself to confirm your seat. Be prepared to book your ticket with a different consolidator—there are many to choose from—if the airline can't confirm your reservation. Also be aware that bucket shop tickets are usually nonrefundable or rigged with stiff cancellation penalties, often as high as 50% to 75% of the ticket price. And when an airline runs a special deal, you won't always do better with a consolidator.

Council Travel (© 800/226-8624; www.counciltravel.com) and **STA Travel** (© 800/781-4040; www.statravel.com) cater especially to young travelers, but their bargain basement prices are available to people of all ages. **Travel Bargains** (© 800/AIR-FARE;** www.1800airfare.com) offers deep discounts on many airlines, with last-minute purchases available. For discount and last-minute bookings, contact **McCord Consumer Direct** (Air for Less) (© **800/FLY-FACTS** or 800/FLY-ASAP; www.better1.com), which can often get you tickets at significantly less than full fare. Other reliable consolidators include **1/800-FLY-CHEAP** (www.flycheap.com); and

TFI Tours International (© 800/745-8000 or 212/736-1140), which serves as a clearinghouse for unused seats. There are also "rebators," such as **Travel Avenue** (© 800/333-3335 or 312/876-1116; www.travelavenue.com), which rebate part of their commissions to you.

BY CAR

The distance to Portland from Seattle is 175 miles; from Spokane, 350 miles; from Vancouver, B.C., 285 miles; from San Francisco, 640 miles; and from Los Angeles, 1,015 miles.

If you're driving up from California, I-5 runs up through the length of the state and continues up toward the Canadian border; it will take you through both Portland and Seattle. If you're coming from the east, I-84 runs from Idaho and points east into Oregon, eventually ending in Portland.

One of the most important benefits of belonging to the **American Automobile Association** (© 800/222-4357) is that they supply members with emergency road service. In Portland, AAA is located at 600 SW Market St. (© **503/222-6734;** www.aaa.com).

BY TRAIN

Amtrak's (© 800/872-7245; www.amtrak.com) *Coast Starlight* train connects Portland with Seattle, San Francisco, Los Angeles, and San Diego and stops at historic **Union Station,** 800 NW Sixth Ave. (© **503/273-4866),** about 10 blocks from the heart of downtown Portland. Between Portland and Seattle there are both regular trains and modern European-style Talgo trains, which make the trip in 3½ to 4 hours versus 4½ hours for the regular train. One-way fares on either type of train run $23 to $36. Talgo trains run between Eugene, Oregon, and Vancouver, British Columbia.

8 Getting Around

BY CAR

A car is by far the best way to see Oregon. There just isn't any other way to get to the more remote natural spectacles or to fully appreciate such regions as the Oregon coast or eastern Oregon.

The major car-rental companies are all represented in Portland and have desks at Portland International Airport, which is the most convenient place to pick up a car. There are also many independent and smaller car-rental agencies listed in the Portland Yellow Pages. Currently, weekly rates for an economy car in July (high-season rates) are about $188 with no discounts. Expect lower rates in the rainy months.

At Portland International Airport on the ground floor of the airport parking deck, across the street from the baggage-claim area, you'll find the following companies: **Avis** (© 800/ 831-2847 or 503/249-4950; www.avis. com), **Budget** (© 800/527-0700 or 503/249-6500; www.budget.com), **Dollar** (© 800/800-4000 or 503/ 249-4792; www.dollar.com), **Hertz** (© 800/654-3131 or 503/249-8216; www.hertz.com), and **National** (© 800/227-7368 or 503/249-4900; www.nationalcar.com). Outside the airport, but with desks adjacent to the other car-rental desks, are **Alamo** (© 800/327-9633 or 503/252-7039; www.alamo.com), **Enterprise** (© 800/ 736-8222 or 503/252-1500; www. enterprise.com), and **Thrifty,** at 10800 NE Holman St. (© 800/367-2277 or 503/254-6563; www.thrifty.com).

For the best deal on a rental car, make your reservation at least a week in advance. It also pays to shop around and call the same companies a few times over the course of a couple of weeks. If you decide on the spur of the moment to rent a car, check to see whether any weekend or special rates are available. If you're a member of a frequent-flyer program, be sure to mention it; you might get mileage credit for renting a car. Always ask about special promotions and try different combinations of where to pick up and drop off your car.

RENTER'S INSURANCE Before you drive off in a rental car, be sure you're insured. If you already hold a **private auto insurance** policy, you are most likely covered in the United States for loss of or damage to a rental car, and liability in case of injury to any other party involved in an accident. Be sure to find out the details of your policy for the type of vehicle you are renting and the area you are visiting.

Most **major credit cards** provide some degree of coverage as well— provided they were used to pay for the rental. Terms vary widely, however, so be sure to ask your credit-card company directly. Credit cards *will not cover liability,* or the cost of injury to an outside party and/or damage to an outside party's vehicle. If you do not hold an insurance policy, you may want to consider purchasing additional liability insurance from your rental company.

The basic insurance coverage offered by most car-rental companies, known as the **Loss/Damage Waiver (LDW)** or **Collision Damage Waiver (CDW),** can cost as much as $20 a day. It usually covers the full value of the vehicle with no deductible if an outside party causes an accident or other damage to the rental car.

GASOLINE Oregon is a big state, so keep your gas tank as full as possible when traveling in the mountains or on the sparsely populated east side of the Cascades. There are no self-service gas stations.

Value Driving a Bargain in Oregon

If there's any way you can arrange to pick up your car somewhere other than the airport, you can save the 11% airport concession fee. If you can pick up your car in Beaverton or Hillsboro (western suburbs of Portland), you can also avoid the 12.5% Multnomah county tax that applies at the airport and at downtown Portland car-rental offices.

MAPS Maps are available at most highway tourist information centers, at the tourist information offices listed earlier in this chapter and throughout this book, and at gas stations throughout the region. For a map of Oregon, contact the **Oregon Tourism Commission** (✆ **800/547-7842**). Members of AAA can get detailed road maps of Oregon by calling their local AAA office.

SPECIAL DRIVING RULES You may turn right on a red light after a full stop, and if you are in the far-left lane of a one-way street, you may turn left into the adjacent left lane of a one-way street at a red light after a full stop. Everyone in a moving vehicle is required to wear a seat belt.

BREAKDOWNS/ASSISTANCE In the event of a breakdown, stay with your car, lift the hood, turn on your emergency flashers, and wait for a police patrol car. *Do not leave your vehicle.*

DRIVING TIMES It takes about 1½ hours to drive from Portland to Canon Beach on the Oregon coast; from Portland to Mount Hood, about 1 hour; and from Portland to Bend, about 3 hours. Portland to Seattle is about a 3½-hour trip, depending on traffic conditions.

BY PLANE

Although there are airports with regular commercial service in Redmond, Eugene, and Medford, flying isn't usually a very appropriate way to get around Oregon. However, if you are heading to the central or southern Oregon coast, you might want to consider flying into either the Eugene or the Medford Airport. If you are headed to Bend or Sunriver, flying into Redmond might work for you. If you are headed to Ashland for some Shakespeare, you could consider the Medford airport.

BY RECREATIONAL VEHICLE (RV)

An economical way to tour Oregon is with a recreational vehicle. If you're considering renting an RV, look under "Recreational Vehicles—Rent and Lease" in the Yellow Pages of your local phone book. They can be rented for a weekend, a week, or longer. In Portland, you might try **Cruise America,** 8400 SE 82nd Ave. (✆ **800/327-7799** or 503/777-9833). If you're going to be traveling in the peak season of summer, it's important to make reservations for your RV at least 2 months ahead of time. The rest of the year, a couple of weeks' lead time is usually sufficient.

9 The Active Vacation Planner

The abundance of outdoor recreational activities is one of the main reasons people choose to live in and visit Oregon. With both mountains and beaches within an hour's drive of the major metropolitan areas, there are numerous choices for the active vacation.

OUTDOOR CLASSES & ORGANIZED TRIPS
ACTIVITIES A TO Z
BIKING/MOUNTAIN BIKING

The Oregon coast is one of the most popular bicycling locales in the nation, and each summer attracts thousands of dedicated pedalers. Expect to spend about a week to pedal the entire coast if you're in good shape and are traveling at a leisurely pace. During the summer months, it's best to travel from north to south along the coast because of the prevailing winds. Also keep in mind that many state parks have designated hiker/biker campsites. You can get a free Oregon coast bicycle map, as well as other bicycle maps for the state of Oregon, by calling the Oregon Department of Transportation's **Oregon Bicycle Map Hot Line** (© 503/986-3556).

Other regions growing in popularity with cyclists include the wine country of Yamhill County and other parts of the Willamette Valley. Portland, Salem, Corvallis, Eugene, Cottage Grove, and Central Point all have easy bicycle trails that either are in parks or connect parks. In addition, the region's national forests provide miles of logging roads and single-track trails for mountain biking. Among the most popular mountain-biking areas are the east side of Mount Hood, the Oakridge area southeast of Eugene, the Ashland area, and the Bend and Sisters areas of central Oregon.

If you're interested in a guided bike tour in the state, try **Bicycle Adventures,** P.O. Box 11219, Olympia, WA 98508 (© **800/443-6060** or 360/786-0989; www.bicycleadventures.com). Tour prices range from $836 to $2,262 per person.

For less expensive bike tours through less traveled regions of the state, contact **Pathfinders,** P.O. Box 210, Oakridge, OR 97463 (© **800/778-4838;** www.path-finders.com), which charges around $700 for a 7-day camping bike tour. Five-day tours are around $600.

Although it isn't actually an organized tour, the annual **Cycle Oregon** bike ride is a weeklong sponsored ride along some of Oregon's most scenic roads. The ride, which takes place in September, follows a different route each year. The fee has been about $600, which includes meals, baggage transportation, and camping or homestays. For information, contact Cycle Oregon, P.O. Box 15339, Portland,

---

Finds Cruising the Columbia River

Paddle-wheel steamboats played a crucial role in the settling of Oregon, shuttling people and goods down the Columbia River before railroads came to the region. Today, the *Queen of the West,* a paddle-wheel cruise ship operated by the **American West Steamboat Company,** 2101 Fourth Ave., Suite 1150, Seattle, WA 98121 (© **800/434-1232;** www.columbiariver cruise.com), is cruising the Columbia offering a luxury never before known in Columbia River paddlewheelers. Fares for the 7-night cruise range from $1,155 to $4,636 per person. Shorter cruises are also available.

If you'd rather cruise aboard a smaller vessel, consider a trip with **Cruise West,** Fourth and Battery Building, Suite 700, Seattle (© **800/426-7702** or 206/441-8687; www.cruisewest.com), which offers an 8-day cruise from Portland on the Columbia and Snake Rivers. Fares range from $795 to $3,895 per person. Similar trips, though with naturalists and historians on board, are offered by **Lindblad Expeditions** (© **800/762-0003** or 212/765-7740; www.expeditions.com) at similar rates.

Tips **Serious Reservations**

The days of spontaneous summer weekends are a thing of the past in Oregon. If you want to be assured of getting a room or a campsite at some of the busier destinations, you'll need to make your reservations months in advance, especially if you're going on a weekend.

To be sure that you get the state park campsite, yurt (circular domed tents with electricity, plywood floors, and beds), cabin, teepee, house-boat, or covered wagon you want, you'll need to make your reserva-tions as much as 9 months in advance (that's the earliest you can reserve) through **Reservations Northwest** (© **800/452-5687** or 503/731-3411), which handles reservations at both Oregon and Washington State Parks. Reservations are accepted for dates between April 1 and September 30, with Memorial Day, the Fourth of July, and Labor Day weekends, of course, requiring the most advance planning. A $6 reser-vation fee is charged.

While National Forest Service campgrounds are generally less devel-oped and less in demand than state park campgrounds, many do stay full throughout the summer months, especially those at the beach. For reservations at forest service campgrounds, call the **National Recreation Reservation Service** (© **800/280-CAMP** or www.reserveusa.com), which charges an $8.65 reservation fee. These sites can be reserved up to 8 months in advance.

The same sort of advance planning also applies to such accommo-dations as Crater Lake Lodge (Crater Lake National Park does not, however, accept camping reservations), Timberline Lodge, and just about any lodging on the coast on a summer weekend. Making rooms even more difficult to come by are the many festivals scheduled around the state throughout the summer months. Be sure to check whether your schedule might coincide with some popular event.

OR 97293-5339 (© **800/292-5367;** www.cycleoregon.com).

BIRD-WATCHING   Oregon offers many excellent bird-watching spots. Malheur National Wildlife Refuge, in central Oregon, is the state's premier bird-watching area and attracts more than 300 species yearly. Nearby Summer Lake also offers good bird-watching, with migratory waterfowl and shorebirds most prevalent. There's also good bird-watching on Sauvie Island, outside Portland, where water-fowl and eagles can be seen, and along the coast, where you can see tufted puffins, pigeon guillemots, and per-haps even a marbled murrelet. The Klamath Lakes region of south-central Oregon is well known for its large population of bald eagles, which are best seen in the winter months.

Throughout the year, the National Audubon Society sponsors expeditions and field seminars. For more informa-tion, contact the **Audubon Society of Portland** (© **503/292-6855**). You can also call this number to listen to the Rare Bird Alert hot line.

CAMPING   Public and private campgrounds abound across Oregon; those along the coast are among the most popular. Campgrounds on lakes also stay busy. During the summer, campground reservations are almost a necessity at most state parks, especially those along the coast. For information on making campsite reservations, see the "Serious Reservations" box on p. 33.

Various state parks also offer a variety of camping alternatives. Tops among these are yurts (circular domed tents with electricity, plywood floors, and beds), which make camping in the rain a bit easier. Yurts, which rent for $27 a night, can be found at 14 coastal parks, as well as at five inland state parks (Champoeg, Valley of the Rogue, Tumalo, LaPine, and Wallowa Lake).

Log cabins are available at Loeb, Cape Blanco, Emigrant Springs, Farewell Bend, LaPine, Prineville Reservoir, Silver Falls, The Cove Palisades, and Umpqua Lighthouse State Parks. Nightly rates range from $35 to $65. At Farewell Bend and Deschutes River State Parks, there are covered wagons for rent ($27 per night). Unity Lake, Farewell Bend, Lake Owyhee, Tumalo, and Clyde Holliday State Parks, have teepees for $27 per night. On Lake Billy Chinook at The Cove Palisades State Park, you can rent a houseboat for $1,995 to $2,195 per week. Call Cove Palisades Marina (© 541/546-3521; www.covepalisades marina.com).

FISHING The fish of Oregon enjoy near-legendary status, and although there may be few streams in the region of national importance among anglers, there are still plenty of great rivers. Salmon of half a dozen species, steelhead, sturgeon, wild cutthroat, and rainbow trout are all available, as are mackinaw trout, kokanee salmon, Atlantic salmon, and bass. Offshore fishing for salmon, tuna, and bottom fish is also popular.

The most important thing to know about fishing in Oregon is that the rules are complicated and always in flux. It is essential you know all the regulations for the body of water you are fishing in. To find out what the current regulations are, you'll need to pick up a copy of *Oregon Sport Fishing Regulations.* This publication is free and is available at sporting goods stores and bait-and-tackle shops. Alternatively, order copies by contacting the **Oregon Department of Fish and Wildlife,** P.O. Box 59, Portland, OR 97207-0059 (© **503/872-5268;** www.dfw.state.or.us).

GOLF Oregon has around 200 private and public golf courses, including numerous resort courses, most of which are in the Portland and Bend-Redmond areas. There are also quite a few excellent courses along the coast.

HIKING & BACKPACKING Oregon has an abundance of hiking trails, including the Pacific Crest Trail, which runs along the spine of the Cascades from Canada to the California line (and onward all the way to Mexico). The state's thousands of miles of hiking trails are concentrated primarily in national forests, especially in wilderness areas, in the Cascade Range. Along the length of the Pacific Crest Trail are such scenic hiking areas as the Mount Hood Wilderness, the Mount Jefferson Wilderness, the Three Sisters Wilderness, the Diamond Peak Wilderness, the Mount Thielsen Wilderness, and the Sky Lakes Wilderness. However, many state parks also have extensive hiking-trail systems.

The Oregon Coast Trail is a designated route that runs the length of the Oregon coast. In most places it travels along the beach, but in other places it climbs up and over capes and headlands through dense forests and windswept meadows. The longest stretches of the trail are along the southern coast in Samuel H. Boardman State Park. There's also a long beach stretch in the Oregon Dunes National Recreation Area.

Other coastal parks with popular hiking trails include Saddle Mountain State Park, Ecola State Park, Oswald

West State Park, and Cape Lookout State Park. Silver Falls State Park, east of Salem, is also a popular hiking spot. The many trails of the Columbia Gorge National Scenic Area are also well trodden, with Eagle Creek Trail being a longtime favorite. For a quick hiking fix, Portlanders often head for the city's Forest Park. The trails leading out from Timberline Lodge on Mount Hood lead through forests and meadows at the tree line and are particularly busy on summer weekends.

If you'd like to do your hiking with a guide, contact Joe Whittington at **Oregon Peak Adventures,** P.O. Box 25576, Portland, OR 97298 (© **503/ 297-5100** or 877-965-5100; www. oregonpeakadventures.com). Whittington leads hikes in the Columbia Gorge, on the Oregon coast, and on Mount St. Helens, as well as climbs to the summits of Mount St. Helens and Mount Adams. Prices start at around $70 per person with a four-person minimum. Nonhiking tours are also available.

KAYAKING & CANOEING   While Puget Sound, up in Washington, is the **sea kayaking** capital of the Northwest, Oregonians are also taking to this sport. However, sea kayaks in Oregon very rarely make it to the sea, where waters are usually far too rough for kayaks. There are, however, numerous protected bays along the Oregon coast that are popular paddling spots. Also, the Lewis & Clark National Wildlife Refuge on the Columbia River not far from Astoria offers miles of quiet waterways to explore.

White-water kayaking is popular on many of the rivers that flow down out of the Cascade Range in Oregon, including the Deschutes, the Clackamas, the Molalla, and the Sandy. Down in southern Oregon, the North Umpqua and the Rogue provide plenty of white-water action.

Sundance Expeditions (© **888/ 777-7557** or 541/479-8508; www. sundanceriver.com), which is located near Grants Pass, is one of the premier kayaking schools in the country. They offer a 9-day beginner's program that does a multiday trip down the wild-and-scenic section of the Rogue River after several days of initial instruction. Also in southern Oregon, you'll find the **Siskiyou Kayak School,** 4541 W. Griffin Creek Rd., Medford, OR 97501 (© **888/59KAYAK** or 541/ 772-9743; www.siskiyou-kayak.com), which offers various classes lasting from 1 to 4 days. Prices for classes range from $85 to $325, and trips are also offered.

Canoeing is popular on many of Oregon's lakes. Some of the best are Hosmer and Sparks Lakes west of

---

Tips Travel Tip

Before heading out to a national forest anywhere in Oregon, be sure to get a Northwest Forest Pass. Most trail head parking areas in the state now require such a permit, and though they can sometimes be purchased from machines at the most popular trail heads, it's better to have one before heading out. To find out if you need a pass for your particular destination, contact the **Nature of the Northwest Information Center,** 800 NE Oregon St., Room 177, Portland, OR 97232 (© **503/872-2750;** www. naturenw.org). Passes are available at national forest ranger stations throughout the state and also at many outdoors supply stores, such as REI. Day passes cost $5 and annual passes are $30. In some cases such passes are required not just for trail heads but for other national forest recreational areas as well.

Bend, Clear Lake south of Santiam Pass, Waldo Lake near Willamette Pass southeast of Eugene, and Upper Klamath Lake (where there's a canoe trail).

MOUNTAINEERING   Mount Hood and several other Cascades peaks offer challenging mountain climbing and rock climbing for both the novice and the expert. If you're interested in learning some mountain-climbing skills or want to hone your existing skills, contact **Timberline Mountain Guides,** P.O. Box 1167, Bend, OR 97709 (© **541/312-9242;** www.timberlinemtguides.com), a company that offers snow-, ice-, and rock-climbing courses. They also lead summit climbs on Mount Hood. A 2-day Mount Hood mountaineering course with summit climb costs $375.

ROCK CLIMBING   Smith Rock State Park, near Redmond in central Oregon, is a rock-climbing mecca of international renown, and many climbers claim that sport climbing got its American start here. Smith Rock abounds in climbing routes, some of which are among the toughest in the world. If you're a serious climber, pick up a copy of Alan Watts's *Climber's Guide to Smith Rock* (Chockstone Press, 1992), an exhaustive guide to the many climbing routes here.

SKIING   Because the winter weather in Oregon is so unpredictable, the state is not known as a ski destination. Most of the state's ski areas are relatively small and cater primarily to local skiers. Mount Bachelor, in central Oregon outside of Bend, is the one exception. Because of its high elevation and location on the drier east side of the Cascades, it gets a more reliable snowpack and isn't as susceptible to midwinter warming spells, which tend to bring rain to west-side ski slopes with irritating regularity.

Ski areas in Oregon include Mount Hood Meadows, Mount Hood Ski Bowl, Timberline Ski Area, Cooper Spur Ski Area, and Summit Ski Area, all of which are on Mount Hood outside Portland. Farther south, there are Hoodoo Ski Bowl (east of Salem), Willamette Pass (east of Eugene), and Mount Bachelor (outside Bend). In the eastern part of the state, Anthony Lakes and Spout Springs provide a bit of powder skiing. Down in the south, Ski Ashland is the only option. There's also snow-cat skiing north of Crater Lake on Mount Bailey.

Many downhill ski areas also offer groomed **cross-country ski trails.** Cross-country skiers will find an abundance of trails up and down the Cascades. Teacup Lake, Trillium Basin, and Mount Hood Meadows, all on Mount Hood, offer good groomed trails. Near Mount Bachelor, there are also plenty of groomed trails. Crater Lake is another popular spot for cross-country skiing. Backcountry skiing is also popular in the Wallowa Mountains in eastern Oregon.

WHALE-WATCHING   Gray whales, which can reach 45 feet in length and weigh up to 35 tons, migrate annually between Alaska and Baja California, and pass close by the Oregon coast between December and May. However, with more and more whales stopping to spend the summer off the Oregon coast, it is now possible to see them just about any month of the year.

Depoe Bay, north of Newport, is not only the smallest harbor in the world, but also a home port for several whale-watching boats that head out throughout the year to look for gray whales. It's also possible to whale watch from shore, with Cape Meares, Cape Lookout, Cape Kiwanda, Devil's Punchbowl, Cape Perpetua, Sea Lion Caves, Shore Acres State Park, Face Rock Wayside (in Bandon), Cape Blanco, Cape Sebastian, and Harris Beach State Park being some of the better places from which to watch.

Educational & Volunteer Vacations

The **Nature Conservancy** is a nonprofit organization dedicated to the global preservation of natural diversity. For information about field trips in Oregon, contact the Nature Conservancy, 821 SE 14th Ave., Portland, OR 97214 (© **503/230-1221;** www.tnc.org).

Sierra Club Service Trips helps build, restore, and maintain hiking trails in wilderness areas. For more information, contact the **Sierra Club Outing Department,** 85 Second St., Second Floor, San Francisco, CA 94105 (© **415/977-5500;** www.sierraclub.org), or call the local chapters of the Sierra Club. In Oregon, the Portland Chapter is at © **503/238-0442.**

Earth Watch Institute, 3 Clock Tower Place, Suite 100 (Box 75), Maynard, MA 01754 (© **800/776-0188** or 978/461-0081; www. earthwatch.org), sends volunteers on scientific research projects. Contact them for a catalog listing trips and costs.

The **Northwest School of Survival,** 2870 NE Hogan Rd., Suite E, #461, Gresham, OR 97030 (© 503/667-9455 or 503/702-3514; www.nwsos.com), can teach you everything from how to start a fire with a stick to how to evaluate an avalanche hazard.

WHITE-WATER RAFTING Plenty of rain and snowmelt and lots of mountains combine to produce dozens of good white-water-rafting rivers in Oregon, depending on the time of year and water levels. Central Oregon's Deschutes River and southern Oregon's Rogue River are the two most popular rafting rivers. Other popular rafting rivers include the Clackamas outside Portland, the McKenzie outside Eugene, and the North Umpqua outside Roseburg. Out in the southeastern corner, the remote Owyhee River provides adventurers with still more white water. See the respective chapters for information on rafting companies operating on these rivers.

WINDSURFING The Columbia River Gorge is one of the most renowned windsurfing spots in the world. As the winds whip up the waves, skilled sailors rocket across the water and launch themselves skyward to perform aerial acrobatics. On calmer days and in spots where the wind isn't blowing so hard, there are also opportunities for novices to learn the basics. Summer is the best sailing season, and the town of Hood River is the center of the boarding scene, with plenty of windsurfing schools and rental companies. The southern Oregon coast also has some popular spots, including Floras Lake just north of Port Orford and Meyers Creek in Pistol River State Park, south of Gold Beach.

10 Tips on Accommodations

It's always a good idea to make hotel reservations as soon as you know your trip dates. Reservations usually require a deposit of 1 night's payment. Portland and the Oregon coast are particularly busy during summer months, and hotels book up in advance—especially on holiday and festival weekends. If you do not have reservations, it is best to look for a room in the midafternoon because hotels may be filled by evening. Major downtown hotels, which cater primarily to business travelers, commonly offer weekend discounts of as much as 50% to entice vacationers to fill up the empty rooms. However, resorts and hotels near tourist attractions tend to have higher rates on weekends.

For information on B&Bs in Oregon, contact the **Oregon Bed and Breakfast Guild**, P.O. Box 3187, Ashland, OR 97520 (© **800/944-6196;** www.obbg.org). For B&B reservations, call **Northwest Bed and Breakfast Reservation Service,** 3559 SW Valley View Dr., Redmond, OR 97756 (© **503/243-7616** or 877/243-7782; nwbedandbreakfast.com). This service represents more than 350 homes throughout Oregon, Washington, and British Columbia. All homes have been inspected.

 FAST FACTS: Oregon

AAA If you're a member of the American Automobile Association and your car breaks down, call © **800/AAA-HELP** for 24-hour emergency road service.

American Express **The American Express Travel Service Office,** 1100 SW Sixth Ave. (© **503/226-2961**), at the corner of Sixth and Main, is open Monday through Friday from 8:30am to 5:30pm. You can cash American Express traveler's checks and exchange the major foreign currencies here. Call the Portland office for information on American Express services in other outlying towns. To report lost or stolen traveler's checks, call © **800/221-7282.**

ATM Networks Automatic teller machines (ATMs) (with Star, Cirrus, Plus, Accel, and the Exchange networks widely available) are nearly ubiquitous throughout Oregon, so you can get cash as you travel; however, some small-town banks still do not have ATMs.

Car Rentals See "Getting Around," earlier in this chapter.

Climate See "When to Go," earlier in this chapter.

Driving Rules See "Getting Around," earlier in this chapter.

Drugstores Rite Aid Pharmacies and Walgreens (© **800/WALGREENS** for locations) are two large pharmacy chains found in the Northwest.

Embassies & Consulates See chapter 3.

Emergencies Call © **911** for fire, police, and ambulance.

Information See "Visitor Information," earlier in this chapter.

Liquor Laws The legal minimum drinking age in Oregon is 21. Bars can legally stay open until 2am. Beer and wine can often be purchased in supermarkets, but liquor can be purchased only in state-licensed liquor stores, of which there are very few.

Maps See "Getting Around," earlier in this chapter.

Pets Some hotels and motels in Oregon accept small well-behaved pets. However, a small fee often is charged to allow them into guest rooms. Many places, in particular bed-and-breakfast inns, don't allow pets at all. (Policies can change frequently, so always be sure to confirm.) On the other hand, many bed-and-breakfasts have their own pets, so if you have a dog or cat allergy, be sure to mention it when making a B&B reservation. Pets are usually restricted in national parks for their own safety, so call each park's ranger station to check before setting out.

Police To reach the police, dial © **911.**

Smoking Many restaurants in Oregon are no-smoking establishments.

Taxes Oregon is a shopper's paradise—there's no sales tax.

Time Zone With the exception of far-eastern Oregon near Ontario, the state is on Pacific Standard Time (PST) and observes daylight saving time from the first Sunday in April to the last Sunday in October, making it consistently 3 hours behind the East Coast.

3

For International Visitors

Although American trends have spread across Europe and other parts of the world to the extent that America may seem like familiar territory before your arrival, there are still many peculiarities and uniquely American situations that any international visitor will encounter.

1 Preparing for Your Trip

ENTRY REQUIREMENTS

Immigration laws are a hot political issue in the United States these days, and the following requirements may have changed somewhat by the time you plan your trip. Check at any U.S. embassy or consulate for current information and requirements. You can also access the U.S. State Department's Internet site at www.state.gov.

VISAS The U.S. State Department has a Visa Waiver Pilot Program allowing citizens of certain countries to enter the United States without a visa for stays of up to 90 days. At press time these included Andorra, Argentina, Australia, Austria, Belgium, Brunei, Denmark, Finland, France, Germany, Iceland, Ireland, Italy, Japan, Liechtenstein, Luxembourg, Monaco, the Netherlands, New Zealand, Norway, San Marino, Slovenia, Spain, Sweden, Switzerland, and the United Kingdom. Citizens of these countries need only a valid passport and a round-trip air or cruise ticket in their possession upon arrival. If they first enter the United States, they may also visit Mexico, Canada, Bermuda, and/or the Caribbean islands and return to the United States without a visa. Further information is available from any U.S. embassy or consulate. Canadian citizens may

enter the United States without visas; they need only proof of residence.

Citizens of all other countries must have (1) a valid passport that expires at least 6 months later than the scheduled end of their visit to the United States, and (2) a tourist visa, which may be obtained without charge from any U.S. consulate.

OBTAINING A VISA To obtain a visa, the traveler must submit a completed application form (either in person or by mail) with a 1½-inch-square photo, and must demonstrate binding ties to a residence abroad. Usually you can obtain a visa at once or within 24 hours, but it may take longer during the summer rush June through August. If you cannot go in person, contact the nearest U.S. embassy or consulate for directions on applying by mail. Your travel agent or airline office may also be able to provide you with visa applications and instructions. The U.S. consulate or embassy that issues your visa will determine whether you will be issued a multiple- or single-entry visa and any restrictions regarding the length of your stay.

To pick up an application for a regular 10-year passport (the Visitor's Passport has been abolished), visit your nearest passport office, major post office, or travel agency. You can also contact the **London Passport Office** at © **020/271-3000** or search its website at www.open.gov.uk/ukpass/ukpass.htm. Passports are £21 for adults and £11 for children under 16.

MEDICAL REQUIREMENTS

Unless you're arriving from an area known to be suffering from an epidemic (particularly cholera or yellow fever), inoculations or vaccinations are not required for entry into the United States. If you have a disease that requires treatment with narcotics or syringe-administered medications, carry a valid signed prescription from your physician to allay any suspicions that you may be smuggling narcotics (a serious offense that carries severe penalties in the U.S.).

For HIV-positive visitors, requirements for entering the United States are somewhat vague and change frequently. For up-to-the-minute information concerning HIV-positive travelers, contact the Centers for Disease Control's National Center for HIV (© **800/HIV-0440;** www.hivatis.org) or the Gay Men's Health Crisis (© **800/243-7692** or 212/807-6655; www.gmhc.org).

DRIVER'S LICENSES Foreign driver's licenses are mostly recognized in the U.S., although you may want to get an international driver's license if your home license is not written in English.

CUSTOMS REQUIREMENTS

Every visitor over 21 may bring in, free of duty, the following: (1) 1 liter of wine or hard liquor; (2) 200 cigarettes, 100 cigars (but not from Cuba), or 3 pounds of smoking tobacco; and (3) $100 worth of gifts. These exemptions are offered to travelers who spend at least 72 hours in the United States and who have not claimed them within the preceding 6 months. It is altogether forbidden to bring into the country foodstuffs (particularly fruit, cooked meats, and canned goods) and plants (vegetables, seeds, tropical plants, and the like). Foreign tourists may bring in or take out up to $10,000 in U.S. or foreign currency with no formalities; larger sums must be declared to U.S. Customs on entering or leaving, which includes filing form CM 4790. For more specific information regarding U.S. Customs, call your nearest U.S. embassy or consulate, or the U.S. Customs office at © **202/927-1770** or www.customs.gov/travel/travel.htm.

INSURANCE

Although it's not required of travelers, health insurance is highly recommended. Unlike many European countries, the United States does not usually offer free or low-cost medical care to its citizens or visitors. Doctors and hospitals are expensive, and in most cases will require advance payment or proof of coverage before they render their services. Other policies can cover everything from the loss or theft of your baggage and trip cancellation to the guarantee of bail in case you're arrested. Good policies will also cover the costs of an accident, repatriation, or death. Packages such as Europ Assistance in Europe are sold by automobile clubs and travel agencies at attractive rates. Worldwide Assistance Services (© **800/821-2828**) is the agent for Europ Assistance in the United States.

Though lack of health insurance may prevent you from being admitted to a hospital in nonemergencies, don't worry about being left on a street corner to die: The American way is to fix you now and bill the living daylights out of you later.

MONEY

CURRENCY The U.S. monetary system has a decimal base: one American dollar ($1) = 100 cents (100¢).

Dollar bills commonly come in $1 (a "buck"), $5, $10, $20, $50, and $100 denominations. (The last two are not welcome when paying for small purchases and are generally not accepted in taxis.) There are also $2 bills (seldom encountered). Note that newly redesigned $100 and $50 bills were introduced in 1996, a redesigned $20 bill in 1998, and redesigned $10 and $5 notes in the year 2000. Despite rumors to the contrary, the old-style bills are still legal tender.

There are six denominations of coins: 1¢ (1 cent, or a "penny"), 5¢ (5 cents, or a "nickel"), 10¢ (10 cents, or a "dime"), 25¢ (25 cents, or a "quarter"), 50¢ (50 cents, or a "half dollar"), and, prized by collectors, the rare $1 piece (the older, large silver dollar and the newer, small Susan B. Anthony coin). A new gold $1 piece, the Sacagawea dollar, was introduced in 2000. Note that U.S. coins are not stamped with their numeric value.

The foreign-exchange bureaus so common in Europe are rare even at airports in the United States, and non-existent outside major cities. Try to avoid having to change foreign money or traveler's checks not denominated in U.S. dollars at a small-town bank, or even a branch bank in a big city. In fact, leave any currency other than U.S. dollars at home—it may prove more nuisance to you than it's worth.

TRAVELER'S CHECKS   Traveler's checks denominated in U.S. dollars are readily accepted at most hotels, motels, restaurants, and large stores, but may not be accepted at small stores or for small purchases. The best place to change traveler's checks is at a bank. Do not bring traveler's checks denominated in other currencies. The three traveler's checks that are most widely recognized are Visa, American Express, and Thomas Cook.

CREDIT CARDS & ATMs   Credit cards are the most widely used form of payment in the United States: Visa (BarclayCard in Britain), MasterCard (EuroCard in Europe, Access in Britain, Chargex in Canada), American Express, Diners Club, Discover, and Carte Blanche. You must have a credit or charge card to rent a car. There are, however, a handful of stores and restaurants that do not take credit cards, so be sure to ask in advance. Most businesses display a sticker near their entrance to let you know which cards they accept. (*Note:* Often, businesses require a minimum purchase price, usually around $10, to use a credit card.)

It is strongly recommended that you bring at least one major credit card. Hotels, car-rental companies, and airlines usually require a credit-card imprint as a deposit against expenses, and in an emergency a credit card can be priceless.

You'll find automatic teller machines (ATMs) on just about every block—at least in almost every town—across the country. Some ATMs will allow you to draw U.S. currency against your bank and credit cards. Check with your bank before leaving home, and remember that you will need your personal identification number (PIN) to do so. Most accept Visa, MasterCard, and American Express, as well as ATM cards from other U.S. banks. Expect to be charged up to $1.50 per transaction, however. One way around these fees is to ask for cash back at grocery stores that accept ATM cards and don't charge usage fees. Of course, you'll have to purchase something first.

SAFETY
GENERAL SAFETY SUGGESTIONS   Although tourist areas are generally safe, U.S. urban areas tend to be less safe than those in Europe or Japan. You should always stay alert. This is particularly true of large U.S. cities. It is wise to ask your hotel front-desk staff or the city's or area's tourist office if you're in doubt about which neighborhoods are safe.

> **Tips** **Travel Tip**
>
> Be sure to keep a copy of all your travel papers separate from your wallet or purse, and leave a copy with someone at home should you need it faxed in an emergency.

Avoid deserted areas, especially at night, and don't go into public parks at night unless there's a concert or similar occasion that will attract a crowd.

Avoid carrying valuables with you on the street, and don't display expensive cameras or electronic equipment. If you are using a map, consult it inconspicuously—or better yet, try to study it before you leave your room. Hold onto your pocketbook, and place your billfold in an inside pocket. In theaters, restaurants, and other public places, keep your possessions in sight.

Remember also that hotels are open to the public, and in a large hotel, security may not be able to screen everyone entering. Always lock your room door—don't assume that once inside your hotel you are automatically safe and no longer need to be aware of your surroundings.

DRIVING   Safety while driving is particularly important. Ask your rental agency about personal safety or request a brochure of traveler safety tips when you pick up your car. Get written directions or a map with the route marked in red from the agency to show you how to get to your destination. If possible, arrive and depart during daylight hours.

Recently more and more crime has involved cars and drivers. If you drive off a highway into a doubtful-looking neighborhood, leave the area as quickly as possible. If you have an accident, even on the highway, stay in your car with the doors locked until you assess the situation or until the police arrive. If you are bumped from behind on the street or are involved in a minor accident with no injuries, and the situation appears to be suspicious, motion to the other driver to follow you to the nearest police precinct, gas station, or open store. Never get out of your car in such situations.

Park in well-lit, well-traveled areas if possible. Always keep your car doors locked, whether the vehicle is attended or unattended. Look around you before you get out of your car and never leave any packages or valuables in sight. If someone attempts to rob you or steal your car, do not try to resist the thief/carjacker—report the incident to the police department immediately by calling ⓒ 911.

Also, make sure that you have enough gasoline in your tank to reach your intended destination, so that you're not forced to look for a service station in an unfamiliar and possibly unsafe neighborhood, especially at night.

2 Getting to the United States

For an extensive listing of airlines that fly into Portland, see "Getting There," in chapter 2.

A number of U.S. airlines offer service from Europe to the United States. If they do not have direct flights from Europe to Seattle or Portland, they can book you straight through on a connecting flight. You can make reservations by calling the following numbers in Great Britain: **American** (ⓒ 0345/789 789; www.aa.com), **Continental** (ⓒ 0800/776-464; www.continental.com), **Delta** (ⓒ 0800/414-767;

www.delta.com), **Northwest/KLM** (© 08705/074-074; www.nwa.com, and **United** (© 0800/888-555; www. united.com).

International carriers that fly from Europe to Los Angeles and San Francisco include **Aer Lingus** (© 01/886-8888 in Ireland; www.aerlingus. com) and **British Airways** (© 0845/773-3377; www.britishairways.com), which also flies direct to Seattle from London.

From New Zealand and Australia, there are flights to Los Angeles on **Qantas** (© 13-13-13; www.qantas. com.au) and **Air New Zealand** (© 0800/737-000 in Auckland; www. airnewzealand.co.nz). Continue on to Portland on a regional airline such as **Alaska Airlines** (© 800/426-0333; www.alaskaair.com) or Southwest (© 800/435-9792; www.iflyswa.com).

From Toronto, there are flights to Seattle and Portland on: **Air Canada** (© 888/247-2262; www.aircanada.ca), **American** (© 800/433-7300; www. aa.com), **Northwest** (© 800/225-2525; www.nwa.com), and **United** (© 800/241-6522; www.united.com).

From Vancouver, B.C., there are flights to Seattle and Portland on **Air Canada, United,** and **Alaska Airlines** (© 800/426-0333; www.alaskaair. com).

AIRLINE DISCOUNTS Travelers from overseas can take advantage of the advance-purchase excursion (APEX) fares offered by the major U.S. and European carriers. For more money-saving airline advice, see "Getting There," in chapter 2.

IMMIGRATION & CUSTOMS CLEARANCE The visitor arriving by air, no matter what the port of entry, should cultivate patience before setting foot on U.S. soil. Getting through Immigration Control may take as long as 2 hours on some days, especially summer weekends. Add the time it takes to clear Customs, and you'll see that you should make a very generous allowance for delay in planning connections between international and domestic flights—an average of 2 to 3 hours at least.

Travelers arriving by car or by rail from Canada will find increasing delays at border-crossing points.

3 Getting Around the United States

For specific information on traveling to and around Portland and Oregon, see "Getting There" and "Getting Around," in chapter 2.

BY PLANE Some large airlines (for example, Northwest and Delta) offer travelers on their transatlantic or transpacific flights special discount tickets under the name Visit USA, allowing mostly one-way travel from one U.S. destination to another at very low prices. These discount tickets are not on sale in the United States and must be purchased abroad in conjunction with your international ticket. This system is the best, easiest, and fastest way to see the United States at low cost. You should get information well in advance from

your travel agent or the office of the airline concerned, since the conditions attached to these discount tickets can be changed without advance notice.

BY CAR The United States is a car culture through and through. Driving is the most cost-effective, convenient, and comfortable way to travel through the West. The interstate highway system connects cities and towns all over the country, and in addition to these high-speed, limited-access roadways, there's an extensive network of federal, state, and local highways and roads. Driving will give you a lot of flexibility in making, and altering, your itinerary and in allowing you to see some off-the-beaten-path destinations that cannot be reached easily by public transportation. You'll also have easy access to inexpensive motels at interstate highway off-ramps.

BY TRAIN   International visitors can also buy a **USA Railpass,** good for 15 or 30 days of unlimited travel on **Amtrak** (© **800/USA-RAIL;** www. amtrak.com). The pass is available through many foreign travel agents. Prices in 2001 for a 15-day pass are $295 off-peak, $440 peak; a 30-day pass costs $385 off-peak, $550 peak. (With a foreign passport, you can also buy passes at staffed Amtrak offices in the United States, including locations in San Francisco, Los Angeles, Chicago, New York, Miami, Boston, and Washington, D.C.) Reservations are generally required and should be made for each part of your trip as early as possible. Amtrak also offers an **Air/Rail Travel Plan** that allows you to travel by both train and plane; for information call © **800/440-8202.**

BY BUS   Although bus travel is often the most economical form of public transit for short hops between U.S. cities, it can also be slow and uncomfortable—certainly not for everyone (particularly when Amtrak, which is far more luxurious, offers similar rates). **Greyhound/Trailways** (© **800/231-2222;** www.greyhound. com), the sole nationwide bus line, offers an Ameripass for unlimited travel for 7 days at $185, 15 days at $285, 30 days at $385, and 60 days at $509. Special rates are available for seniors and students. Passes can be purchased at a Greyhound terminal or on the Greyhound website. (If you plan to purchase your ticket on the website, please do so well in advance.)

 ***FAST FACTS:* For the International Traveler**

Automobile Organizations Auto clubs will supply maps, suggested routes, guidebooks, accident and bail-bond insurance, and emergency road service. The American Automobile Association (AAA) is the major auto club in the United States. If you belong to an auto club in your home country, inquire about AAA reciprocity before you leave. You may be able to join AAA even if you're not a member of a reciprocal club; to inquire, call AAA (© **800/222-4357**). AAA is actually an organization of regional auto clubs, so look under "AAA Automobile Club" in the White Pages of the telephone directory. AAA has a nationwide emergency road service telephone number (© **800/AAA-HELP**).

Business Hours The following are general open hours; specific establishments may vary. Banks: Monday through Friday from 9am to 5pm (some are also open Sat mornings); there's usually 24-hour access to ATMs at most banks and other outlets. Offices: generally open weekdays from 9am to 5pm. Stores: typically open Monday through Saturday between 9 and 10am and close between 5 and 6pm. Some department stores have later hours and are open on Sunday from 11am to 5 or 6pm, and stores in malls are usually open until 9pm. Bars: stay open until 1 or 2am; dance clubs often stay open much later.

Climate See "When to Go" in chapter 2.

Currency See "Money" under "Preparing for Your Trip," earlier in this chapter.

Currency Exchange You will find currency-exchange services in major airports with international service. At Portland International Airport there is **Travelex America** (© 503/281-3045), on the main floor across from the Southwest Airlines desk. Elsewhere, they may be quite difficult to come by.

To exchange money in Portland, go to **American Express,** 1100 SW Sixth Ave. in the Standard Plaza Building (© 503/226-2961), or **Thomas Cook** at Powell's Travel Store at Pioneer Courthouse Square, 701 SW Sixth Ave. (© 503/222-2665).

Drinking Laws The legal age for purchase and consumption of alcoholic beverages is 21; proof of age is required and often requested at bars, nightclubs, and restaurants, so it's always a good idea to bring ID when you go out. Beer and wine can often be purchased in supermarkets, but liquor laws vary from state to state.

Do not carry open containers of alcohol in your car or any public area that isn't zoned for alcohol consumption. The police can, and probably will, fine you on the spot. And nothing will ruin your trip faster than getting a citation for DUI ("driving under the influence"), so don't even think about driving while intoxicated.

Electricity Like Canada, the United States uses 110 to 120 volts AC (60 cycles), compared to 220 to 240 volts AC (50 cycles) in most of Europe, Australia, and New Zealand. If your small appliances use 220 to 240 volts, you'll need a 110-volt transformer and a plug adapter with two flat parallel pins to operate them here. Downward converters that change 220 to 240 volts to 110 to 120 volts are difficult to find in the United States, so bring one with you.

Embassies & Consulates All embassies are located in the nation's capital, Washington, D.C. Some consulates are located in major U.S. cities, and most nations have a mission to the United Nations in New York City. If your country isn't listed below, call for directory information in Washington, D.C. (© 202/555-1212), for the number of your national embassy.

The embassy of Australia is at 1601 Massachusetts Ave. NW, Washington, DC 20036 (© 202/797-3000; www.austemb.org). The nearest consulate is in San Francisco at 625 Market St., Suite 200, San Francisco, CA 94105-3304 (© 415/536-1970). There are also consulates in Atlanta, New York, Honolulu, and Los Angeles.

The embassy of Canada is at 501 Pennsylvania Ave. NW, Washington, DC 20001 (© 202/682-1740; www.canadianembassy.org). The regional consulate is at Plaza 600 Building, Sixth Ave. and Stewart St., Seattle, WA 98101-1286 (© 206/443-1777). Other Canadian consulates are in Buffalo (N.Y.), Detroit, New York, and Los Angeles.

The embassy of Ireland is at 2234 Massachusetts Ave. NW, Washington, DC 20008 (© 202/462-3939; www.irelandemb.org). The nearest consulate is at 44 Montgomery St., Suite 3830, San Francisco, CA 94104 (© 415/392-4214). Other Irish consulates are in Boston, Chicago, and New York.

The embassy of New Zealand is at 37 Observatory Circle NW, Washington, DC 20008 (© 202/328-4800; www.nzemb.org). There is a consulate in Los Angeles at 12400 Wilshire Blvd., Suite 1150, Los Angeles, CA 90025 (© 310/207-1605). Other New Zealand consulates are in Atlanta, Boston, Chicago, Hawaii, Houston, New York, Salt Lake City, San Diego, and San Francisco. There is also an honorary consulate in Seattle.

The embassy of the United Kingdom is at 3100 Massachusetts Ave. NW, Washington, DC 20008 (© 202/462-1340; www.britain-info.org). There is a consulate in Seattle at 900 Fourth Ave., Suite 3001, Seattle, WA 98164 (© 206/622-9255). Other British consulates are in Atlanta, Boston, Chicago, Dallas, Denver, Houston, Los Angeles, Miami, New York, and San Francisco.

Emergencies Call © **911** to report a fire, call the police, or get an ambulance. This is a toll-free call. (No coins are required at a public telephone.)

If you encounter problems, check the local telephone directory to find an office of the **Traveler's Aid Society,** a nationwide nonprofit social-service organization geared to helping travelers in difficult straits. The society's services might include reuniting families separated while traveling, providing food and/or shelter to people stranded without cash, or even emotional counseling. If you're in trouble, seek it out.

Gasoline (Petrol) Petrol is known as gasoline (or simply "gas") in the United States, and petrol stations are known as both gas stations and service stations. Gasoline costs less here than it does in Europe, and taxes are already included in the printed price. One U.S. gallon equals 3.8 liters or 0.85 Imperial gallons.

Holidays Banks, government offices, post offices, and many stores, restaurants, and museums are closed on the following legal national holidays: January 1 (New Year's Day), the third Monday in January (Martin Luther King, Jr. Day), the third Monday in February (Presidents' Day, Washington's Birthday), the last Monday in May (Memorial Day), July 4 (Independence Day), the first Monday in September (Labor Day), the second Monday in October (Columbus Day), November 11 (Veterans' Day/Armistice Day), the fourth Thursday in November (Thanksgiving Day), and December 25 (Christmas). Also, the Tuesday following the first Monday in November is Election Day and is a federal government holiday in presidential-election years (held every 4 years, and next in 2004).

Internet Access Checking the Yellow Pages under Internet Access may turn up a few cybercafes. Alternatively, many copy shops (**Kinko's** is one large national chain) provide Internet access. See "Planning Your Trip Online" in chapter 2 for more information. Also, if you are traveling with your laptop computer, note that many hotels, especially those frequented by business travelers, have telephones with dataports and dual phone lines in guest rooms.

Legal Aid The foreign tourist will probably never become involved with the American legal system. If you are "pulled over" for a minor infraction (for example, of the highway code, such as speeding), never attempt to pay the fine directly to a police officer; this could be construed as attempted bribery, a much more serious crime. Pay fines by mail, or directly into the hands of the clerk of the court. If accused of a more serious offense, say and do nothing before consulting a lawyer. Here the burden is on the state to prove a person's guilt beyond a reasonable doubt, and everyone has the right to remain silent, whether he or she is suspected of a crime or actually arrested. Once arrested, a person can make one telephone call to a party of his or her choice. Call your embassy or consulate.

Mail If you aren't sure what your address will be in the United States, mail can be sent to you, in your name, c/o General Delivery at the main post office of the city or region where you expect to be (call © **800/ 275-8777** for information on the nearest post office). The addressee must pick mail up in person and must produce proof of identity (driver's license or passport). Most post offices will hold your mail for up to 1 month, and many post offices are open Monday through Friday from 8am to 5pm, and Saturday from 9am to 3pm.

Generally found at intersections, mailboxes are blue with a red-and-white stripe and carry the inscription U.S. MAIL. If your mail is addressed to a U.S. destination, don't forget to add the five-digit postal code (or ZIP code), after the two-letter abbreviation of the state to which the mail is addressed.

At press time, domestic postage rates were 22¢ for a postcard and 34¢ for a letter. International mail rates vary. For example, a 1-ounce first-class letter to England costs 80¢, or 60¢ to Canada and Mexico; a first-class postcard to England costs 70¢ or 50¢ to Canada and Mexico; and a preprinted postal aerogramme to England costs 70¢.

Medical Emergencies To call an ambulance, dial © **911** from any phone. No coins are needed.

Newspapers/Magazines National newspapers include the *New York Times, USA Today,* and the *Wall Street Journal.* National newsweeklies include *Newsweek, Time,* and *U.S. News & World Report.* In large cities most newsstands offer a small selection of the most popular foreign periodicals and newspapers, such as *The Economist, Le Monde,* and *Der Spiegel.*

Safety See "Safety" in "Preparing for Your Trip," earlier in this chapter.

Taxes The United States does not have a value-added tax (VAT) or other indirect tax at a national level. Every state, and each county and city in it, is allowed to levy its own local tax on purchases and services (including hotel and restaurant bills, airline tickets, and so on). Taxes are already included in the price of certain services, such as public transportation, cab fares, telephone calls, and gasoline. The amount of sales tax varies from about 4% to 12%, depending on the state and city; so when you're making major purchases, such as photographic equipment, clothing, or stereo components, it can be a significant part of the cost.

In Portland and the rest of Oregon, there is no sales tax. At Portland International Airport, you'll pay 23% when you rent a car. You'll save 11% to 23% by renting somewhere other than the airport. Hotel room taxes range from around 9% to 15.6%. Travelers on a budget should keep both car-rental and hotel-room taxes in mind when planning a trip.

Telephone, Telegraph, Telex & Fax The telephone system in the United States is run by private corporations, so rates, especially for long-distance service and operator-assisted calls, can vary widely. Generally, hotel surcharges on long-distance and local calls are astronomical, so you're usually better off using a public pay telephone, which you'll find clearly marked in most public buildings and private establishments as well as on the street. Convenience grocery stores and gas stations always have them. Many convenience groceries and packaging services sell prepaid calling cards in denominations up to $50; these can be the least expensive way to call home. Many public phones at airports now accept American Express, MasterCard, and Visa credit cards. Local calls made from public pay phones in most locales cost 25¢, 35¢, or 50¢. Pay phones do not accept pennies, and few will take anything larger than a quarter.

Most long-distance and international calls can be dialed directly from any phone. For calls within the United States and to Canada, dial 1 followed by the area code and the seven-digit number. For other international calls, dial 011 followed by the country code, city code, and the telephone number of the person you are calling.

Calls to area codes 800, 888, and 877 are toll-free. However, calls to numbers in area codes 700 and 900 (chat lines, bulletin boards, "dating" services, and so on) can be very expensive—usually 95¢ to $3 or more per minute, and they sometimes have minimum charges that can run as high as $15 or more.

For reversed-charge or collect calls, and for person-to-person calls, dial 0 (zero, not the letter O) followed by the area code and number you want; an operator will then come on the line, and you should specify that you are calling collect, or person-to-person, or both. If your operator-assisted call is international, ask for the overseas operator.

For local directory assistance (information), dial ℂ **411;** for long-distance information, dial 1, then the appropriate area code and ℂ **555-1212.**

Most hotels have fax machines available for guest use (be sure to ask about the charge to use them). A less expensive way to send and receive faxes may be at stores such as Kinko's (see "Internet Access," above) or Mail Boxes Etc., a national chain of packing service shops (look in the Yellow Pages directory under "Packing Services").

There are two kinds of telephone directories in the United States. The so-called **White Pages** list private households and business subscribers in alphabetical order. The inside front cover lists emergency numbers for police, fire, ambulance, the U.S. Coast Guard, poison-control center, crime-victims hot line, and so on. The first few pages will tell you how to make long-distance and international calls, complete with country codes and area codes. Government numbers are usually printed on blue paper within the White Pages. Printed on yellow paper, the so-called **Yellow Pages** list all local services, businesses, industries, and houses of worship according to activity with an index at the front or back. (Drugstores/pharmacies and restaurants are also listed by geographic location.) The Yellow Pages also include city plans or detailed area maps, postal ZIP codes, and public transportation routes.

Time The United States is divided into six time zones. From east to west, they are Eastern Standard Time (EST), Central Standard Time (CST), Mountain Standard Time (MST), Pacific Standard Time (PST), Alaska Standard Time (AST), and Hawaii Standard Time (HST). Seattle and Portland run on Pacific Standard Time. Always keep the changing time zones in mind if you are traveling (or even telephoning) long distances in the United States. For example, noon in New York City (EST) is 11am in Chicago (CST), 10am in Phoenix (MST), 9am in Los Angeles (PST), 8am in Anchorage (AST), and 7am in Honolulu (HST).

Tipping Tipping is so ingrained in the American way of life that the annual income tax of tip-earning service personnel is based on how much they should have received in light of their employers' gross revenues. Accordingly, they may have to pay tax on a tip you didn't actually give them.

Here are some rules of thumb:

In hotels, tip bellhops at least $1 per bag ($2–$3 if you have a lot of luggage) and tip the chamber staff $1 to $2 per day (more if you've left a disaster area to clean up, or if you're traveling with kids and/or pets). Tip the doorman or concierge only if he or she has provided you with some specific service (for example, calling a cab for you or obtaining difficult-to-get theater tickets). Tip the valet parking attendant $1 every time you get your car.

In restaurants, bars, and nightclubs, tip service staff 15% to 20% of the check, tip bartenders 10% to 15%, tip checkroom attendants $1 per garment, and tip valet-parking attendants $1 per vehicle. Tipping is not expected in cafeterias and fast-food restaurants.

Tip cab drivers 15% of the fare.

As for other service personnel, tip skycaps at airports at least $1 per bag ($2–$3 if you have a lot of luggage) and tip hairdressers and barbers 15% to 20%.

Tipping gas-station attendants and ushers at movies and theaters is not expected.

Toilets You won't find public toilets or "restrooms" on the streets in most U.S. cities, but they can be found in hotel lobbies, bars, restaurants, museums, department stores, railway and bus stations, or service stations. Note, however, that restaurants and bars in resorts or heavily visited areas may reserve their restrooms for the use of their patrons. Some establishments display a notice that toilets are for the use of patrons only. You can ignore this sign or, better yet, avoid arguments by paying for a cup of coffee or a soft drink, which will qualify you as a patron. Large hotels and fast-food restaurants are probably the best bet for good, clean facilities.

Portland

Situated at the confluence of the Willamette and Columbia rivers, Portland, Oregon, with a population of roughly 1.8 million in the metropolitan area, is a city of discreet charms. That the city claims a rose garden as one of its biggest attractions should give you an idea of just how laid-back it is. Sure, Portlanders are just as attached to their cellphones and pagers as residents of other major metropolitan areas, but this is the City of Roses, and people still take time to stop and smell the flowers. Spend much time here, and you, too, will likely feel the city's leisurely pace seeping into your bones.

While nearby Seattle, Washington, has zoomed into the national consciousness, Portland has, until recently, managed to dodge the limelight and the problems that come with skyrocketing popularity. For many years now Portland has looked upon itself as a small, accessible city, vaguely European in character. *Clean* and *friendly* are the two terms that crop up most often in descriptions of the city. However, as word has spread about overcrowding in Seattle, people looking for the good life and affordable housing have turned to Portland, which is now experiencing the same sort of rapid growth that Seattle began going through more than a decade ago.

Portland does not have any major tourist sights. Instead, it is a city of quiet charms that must be searched for and savored—the shade of the stately elms in the South Park Blocks, the tranquillity of the Japanese Garden, the view from the grounds of Pittock Mansion, the miles of hiking trails in Forest Park. Sure, there's a good art museum and a world-class science museum, but these are not nearly as important to the city's citizenry as its many parks and public gardens. Not only does Portland claim beautiful rose gardens, the most authentic Japanese Garden in North America, and the largest classical Chinese garden in the country, but it also can lay claim to both the world's smallest city park and the largest forested urban park in the country.

The city's other claim to fame is as the nation's microbrew capital. Espresso may be the beverage that gets this town going in the morning (this *is* the Northwest), but it is microbrewed beer that helps the city maintain its mellow character. There are so many brewpubs here in Portland that the city has been nicknamed Munich on the Willamette. Wine is also popular, which shouldn't come as a surprise, considering how close the city is to wine country.

Portland itself may be short on things for visitors to do, but the city's surroundings certainly are not. Within a 1½- to 2-hour drive from Portland, you can be strolling a Pacific Ocean beach, strolling beside a waterfall in the Columbia Gorge, hiking on Mount Hood (a dormant volcano as picture perfect as Mt. Fuji), driving through the Mount St. Helens blast zone, or sampling world-class Pinot Noirs in the Oregon wine country. It is this proximity to the outdoors that makes Portland a great city to use as a base for exploring some of the best of the Northwest.

1 Orientation

ARRIVING

BY PLANE

Portland International Airport (PDX) (© 877/739-4636; www.portlandairport pdx.com) is located 10 miles northeast of downtown Portland, adjacent to the Columbia River. There's an information booth by the baggage-claim area where you can pick up maps and brochures and find out about transportation into the city. Many hotels near the airport provide courtesy shuttle service to and from the airport; be sure to ask when you make a reservation.

GETTING INTO THE CITY BY CAR   If you've rented a car at the airport and want to reach central Portland, follow signs for downtown. These signs will take you first to I-205 and then I-84 west, which brings you to the Willamette River. Take the Morrison Bridge exit to cross the river. The trip takes about 20 minutes and is entirely on interstates. For more information on renting a car, see section 2 of this chapter, "Getting Around," below.

GETTING INTO THE CITY BY TAXI, SHUTTLE, BUS, OR LIGHT RAIL   If you haven't rented a car at the airport, the best way to get into town is to take the new **Airport MAX (Red Line)** light-rail system, which at press time, was scheduled to go into service in September 2001. This light-rail line will operate daily every 15 minutes between 5am and 11:30pm and the trip from the airport to Pioneer Courthouse Square in downtown Portland will take approximately 40 minutes. (All but one or two of the downtown hotels lie within 4 or 5 blocks of the square; plan on walking since there are not usually any taxis waiting here. Folks arriving with a lot of luggage will be better off taking a cab or shuttle van from the airport.) The fare is $1.55. For information on this new service, contact **Tri-Met** (© 503/238-7433; www.tri-met.org).

Alternatively, you can take the **Gray Line Airport Shuttle** (© 800/422-7042 or 503/285-9845), which picks you up outside the baggage-claim area and can drop you at any of 16 downtown hotels. One-way fares are $15 for adults, $12 seniors, $8 for children 4 to 12, and free for children under 4. It operates every 45 minutes from 5:15am to midnight.

Tri-Met public bus no. 12 leaves the airport approximately every 15 minutes from 5:30am to 11:45pm for the trip to downtown Portland. The trip takes about 40 minutes and costs $1.25. The bus between downtown and the airport operates between 5:15am and 12:30am and leaves from SW Sixth Avenue and Main Street.

A taxi downtown generally costs between $20 and $25 and is cheaper and faster than the Gray Line Airport Shuttle if there are two or more of you traveling together.

BY TRAIN/BUS

Amtrak trains stop at the historic **Union Station,** 800 NW Sixth Ave. (© 503/ 273-4866), about 10 blocks from the heart of downtown Portland. Taxis are usually waiting to meet trains and can take you to your hotel. Alternatively, you might be able to get your hotel to send a van to pick you up, or, if you are renting a car from a downtown car-rental office, the agency will usually pick you up at the station. Public buses stop within a block of the station and are free within the downtown area if you catch the bus south of Hoyt Street (2 blocks away).

The **Greyhound Bus Lines** station is at 550 NW Sixth Ave. (© 800/ 231-2222 or 503/243-2357) on the north side of downtown near Union Station. As with getting into downtown from the train station, if you walk south 2 blocks

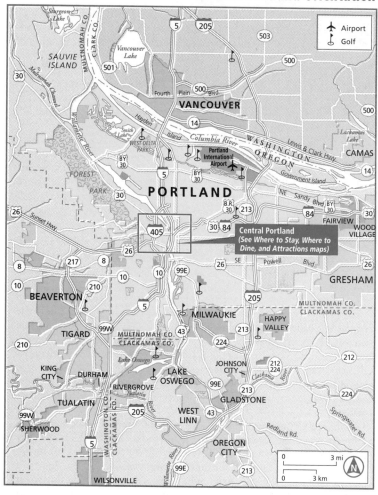

to Hoyt Street, you reach the edge of downtown Portland's Fareless Square area, within which all buses and light-rail trolleys are free.

Although you could easily walk from the station into the heart of downtown, you have to pass through a somewhat rough neighborhood for a few blocks. This area is currently undergoing a renaissance and is not nearly as bad as it once was.

VISITOR INFORMATION

The **Portland Oregon Visitors Association (POVA) Information Center,** 701 SW Sixth Ave., Suite 1 (✆ **877/678-5263** or 503/275-9750; www.travelportland. com), is in Pioneer Courthouse Square in downtown Portland. There's also an information booth by the baggage-claim area at the Portland Airport.

If you happen to see a person walking down a Portland street wearing a very bright green jacket, he or she is probably a member of the **Portland Guides** service run by the Association for Portland Progress (✆ **503/224-7383**). The guides will be happy to answer any question you have about the city.

CITY LAYOUT

Portland is in northwestern Oregon at the confluence of the Columbia and Willamette Rivers. To the west are the West Hills, which rise to more than 1,000 feet. Some 90 miles west of the West Hills are the spectacular Oregon coast and the Pacific Ocean. To the east are rolling hills that extend to the Cascade Range, about 50 miles away. The most prominent peak in this section of the Cascades is Mount Hood (11,235 ft.), a dormant volcanic peak that looms over the city on clear days. From many parts of Portland it's also possible to see Mount St. Helens, the volcano that famously erupted in 1980.

With about 1.8 million people in the entire metropolitan area, Portland remains a relatively small city. This is especially evident when you begin to explore the compact downtown area. Nearly everything is accessible on foot, and the city authorities do everything they can to encourage walking.

MAIN ARTERIES & STREETS   I-84 (**Banfield Fwy. or Expressway**) enters Portland from the east. East of the city is **I-205**, which bypasses downtown Portland and runs past the airport. I-5 (**East Bank Fwy.**) runs through on a north-south axis, passing along the east bank of the Willamette River directly across from downtown. I-405 (**Stadium Fwy. and Foothills Fwy.**) circles around the west and south sides of downtown. U.S. 26 (**Sunset Hwy.**) leaves downtown heading west toward Beaverton and the coast. **Oregon Highway 217 (Beaverton-Tigard Hwy.)** runs south from U.S. 26 in Beaverton.

The most important artery within Portland is **Burnside Street.** This is the dividing line between north and south Portland. Dividing the city from east to west is the **Willamette River,** which is crossed by eight bridges in the downtown area. From north to south these bridges are the Fremont, Broadway, Steel, Burnside, Morrison, Hawthorne, Marquam, and Ross Island. Additional bridges beyond the downtown area include the Sellwood Bridge between downtown and Lake Oswego and the St. John's Bridge from northwest Portland to north Portland.

For the sake of convenience, we have defined downtown Portland as the 300-block area within the **Fareless Square.** This is the area (shaded in on the maps on p. 64, p. 74, and p. 88) in which you can ride for free on the city's public buses and the MAX light-rail system. In downtown, the Fareless Square is bounded by I-405 on the west and south, by Hoyt Street on the north, and by the Willamette River on the east. A Fareless Square extension now allows transit riders to travel between downtown Portland and both the Oregon Convention Center and Lloyd Center Mall for free. There is no charge to ride either the MAX light-rail trolleys or any of the 10 buses that connect downtown with the Rose Quarter and Lloyd District across the Willamette River in northeast Portland.

FINDING AN ADDRESS   Finding an address in Portland can be easy. Almost all addresses in Portland, and for miles beyond, include a map quadrant—NE (Northeast), SW (Southwest), and so forth. The dividing line between east and west is the Willamette River; between north and south it's Burnside Street. Any downtown address will be labeled either SW (Southwest) or NW (northwest). An exception to this rule is the area known as North Portland, which is the area across the Willamette River from downtown going toward Jantzen Beach. Streets here have a plain "North" designation. Also, Burnside Street is designated either "East" or "West."

Avenues run north–south and streets run east–west. Street names are the same on both sides of the Willamette River. Consequently, there is a Southwest

> **Fun Fact** **Did You Know?**
>
> • The flasher in the famous "Expose Yourself to Art" poster is none other than Bud Clark, the former mayor of Portland.
> • Portland is the only city in the United States with an extinct volcano—Mount Tabor—within the city limits.
> • Matt Groening, creator of *The Simpsons,* got his start in Portland.
> • More Asian elephants have been born in Portland (at the Metro Washington Park Zoo) than in any other city in North America.
> • Twenty downtown water fountains were a gift to the city from teetotaling early-20th-century timber baron Simon Benson, who wanted his mill workers to have something other than alcohol to drink during the day.

Yamhill Street and a Southeast Yamhill Street. In northwest Portland, street names are alphabetical going north from Burnside to Wilson. Naito Parkway is the street nearest the Willamette River on the west side, and Water Avenue is the nearest on the east side. Beyond these are numbered avenues. On the west side you'll also find Broadway and Park Avenue between Sixth Avenue and Ninth Avenue. With each block, the addresses increase by 100, beginning at the Willamette River for avenues and at Burnside Street for streets. Odd numbers are generally on the west and north sides of the street, and even numbers on the east and south sides.

Here's an example: You want to go to 1327 SW Ninth Ave. Because it's in the 1300 block, you'll find it 13 blocks south of Burnside and, because it's an odd number, on the west side of the street.

STREET MAPS Stop by the **Portland Oregon Visitors Association Information Center,** 701 SW Sixth Ave., Suite 1 (© **877/678-5263** or 503/275-9750; www.travelportland.com), in Pioneer Courthouse Square in downtown Portland for a free map of the city; they also have a more detailed one for sale.

Powell's City of Books, 1005 W. Burnside St. (© **800/878-7323** or 503/228-4651), has an excellent free map of downtown that includes a walking-tour route and information on many of the sights you'll pass along the way.

Members of the **American Automobile Association (AAA)** can get a free map of the city at the AAA offices at 600 SW Market St. (© **503/222-6734;** www.aaa.com).

PORTLAND NEIGHBORHOODS IN BRIEF

Portland's neighborhoods are mostly dictated by geography. The Willamette River forms a natural dividing line between the eastern and western portions of the city, while the Columbia River forms a boundary with the state of Washington on the north. The West Hills, comprising Portland's prime residential neighborhoods, are a beautiful backdrop for this attractive city. Covered in evergreens, the hills rise to a height of 1,000 feet at the edge of downtown. Within these hills are the Oregon Zoo, the International Rose Test Garden, the Japanese Garden, and several other attractions.

For a map of Portland neighborhoods, turn to the "Portland Attractions" map on p. 88.

DOWNTOWN This term usually refers to the business and shopping district south of Burnside and north of Jackson Street between the Willamette River and 13th Avenue. Here you'll find a dozen or more high-end hotels, dozens of restaurants of all types, and loads of shopping (including the major department stores). Within downtown's **Cultural District** (along Broadway and the South Park Blocks), are most of the city's performing arts venues and a couple of museums.

SKIDMORE HISTORIC DISTRICT Also known as Old Town, this is Portland's original commercial core and centers around Southwest Ankeny Street and Southwest First Avenue. Many of the restored buildings have become retail stores, but despite the presence of the **Saturday Market,** the neighborhood has never become a popular shopping district, mostly because of its welfare hotels, missions, street people, and drug dealing. However, with its many clubs and bars, it has become the city's main nightlife district. The neighborhood is safe during the day, but solo women should exercise caution at night.

CHINATOWN Portland has had a Chinatown almost since its earliest days. This small area, with its numerous Chinese groceries and restaurants, is wedged between the Pearl District and the Skidmore Historic District and is entered through the colorful Chinatown Gate at West Burnside Street and Fourth Avenue. The neighborhood's main attraction is the impressive **Portland Classical Chinese Garden.** Because of its proximity to bars on West Burnside Street and the homeless missions and welfare hotels in Old Town, this is not a good neighborhood to explore late at night.

THE PEARL DISTRICT This neighborhood of galleries, residential and business lofts, cafes, breweries, and shops is bounded by the North Park Blocks, Lovejoy Street, I-405, and Burnside Street. Crowds of people come here on **First Thursday** (the first Thurs of every month) when the galleries and other businesses are open late. This is currently Portland's bid for a hip urban loft scene and is one of the city's main upscale restaurant neighborhoods.

NORTHWEST/NOB   HILL Located along Northwest 23rd and Northwest 21st avenues, this is Portland's most fashionable neighborhood. Here you'll find many of the city's most talked-about restaurants (mostly along NW 21st Ave.), as well as lots of cafes, boutiques, and increasingly, national chain stores. Surrounding the two main business streets of the neighborhood are blocks of restored Victorian homes on shady tree-lined streets. This is where you'll find the city's liveliest street scene.

IRVINGTON Though neither as attractive nor as large as the Northwest/Nob Hill neighborhood, Irvington, centered around Broadway in northeast Portland, is almost as hip. For several blocks along Broadway (around NE 15th Ave.) you'll find interesting boutiques and numerous excellent but inexpensive restaurants.

HAWTHORNE/BELMONT DISTRICT This enclave of southeast Portland is full of eclectic boutiques, moderately priced restaurants, and hip college students from nearby **Reed College.** Just south of Hawthorne Boulevard, beginning at SE 12th Avenue, you'll find the interesting **Ladd's Addition** neighborhood, which has five rose gardens, a great pastry shop, and a brewpub that features live music several nights a week. Along Belmont Street, just north of Hawthorne Boulevard, is one of the city's up-and-coming hip neighborhoods.

SELLWOOD/WESTMORE-LAND Situated in Southeast Portland, this is the city's antiques district and contains many restored Victorian houses. Just north of the Sellwood antiques district, surrounding the intersection of SE Milwaukie Avenue and SE Bybee Boulevard, you'll find the heart of the Eastmoreland neighborhood, home to numerous good restaurants.

2 Getting Around

BY PUBLIC TRANSPORTATION

FREE RIDES Portland is committed to keeping its downtown uncongested, and to this end has invested heavily in its public transportation system. The single greatest innovation and best reason to ride the Tri-Met public buses and the MAX light-rail system is that they're free within an area known as the **Fareless Square.** That's right, free!

There are 300 blocks of downtown included in the Fareless Square, and as long as you stay within the boundaries, you don't pay a cent. The Fareless Square covers the area between I-405 on the south and west, Hoyt Street on the north, and the Willamette River on the east. A Fareless Square extension now also makes it possible to take public transit (either the bus or the MAX light-rail trolley) between downtown Portland and both the Rose Quarter (site of the Oregon Convention Center) and the Lloyd District (site of the Lloyd Center Mall), which are both across the Willamette River in northeast Portland.

BY BUS Tri-Met buses operate daily over an extensive network. You can pick up the *Tri-Met Guide,* which lists all the bus routes with times, or individual route maps and time schedules, at the **Tri-Met Customer Assistance Office,** behind and beneath the waterfall fountain at Pioneer Courthouse Square (© **503/238-7433;** www.tri-met.org). The office is open Monday through Friday from 7:30am to 5:30pm. Bus and MAX passes and transit information are also available at area Fred Meyer, Safeway, and most Albertson grocery stores. Nearly all Tri-Met buses pass through the Transit Mall on SW Fifth Avenue and SW Sixth Avenue.

Outside the Fareless Square, adult fares on both Tri-Met buses and MAX are $1.25 or $1.55, depending on how far you travel. Seniors 65 years and older pay 60¢ with valid proof of age; children 7 through 18 pay 95¢. You can also make free transfers between the bus and the MAX light-rail system. A day ticket costing $4 is good for travel to all zones and is valid on both buses and MAX. Day tickets can be purchased from any bus driver. The **Adventure Pass,** good for 3 days of unlimited rides on both buses and MAX, costs $10 and is available at the Tri-Met Customer Assistance Office and at any of the other outlets mentioned above.

BY LIGHT RAIL The **Metropolitan Area Express (MAX)** is Portland's aboveground light-rail system that connects downtown Portland with the airport (as of Sept 2001), the eastern suburb of Gresham, and the western suburbs of Beaverton and Hillsboro. MAX is basically a modern trolley, but there are also reproductions of vintage trolley cars (© **503/323-7363**) operating between downtown Portland and the Lloyd Center on Sundays between noon and 6pm. One of the most convenient places to catch the MAX is at Pioneer Courthouse

Square. The MAX light-rail system crosses the Transit Mall on SW Morrison Street and SW Yamhill Street. Transfers to the bus are free.

As with the bus, MAX is free within the Fareless Square, which includes all the downtown area. A Fareless Square extension now also makes it possible to ride the MAX between downtown Portland and both the Rose Quarter (site of the Oregon Convention Center) and the Lloyd District (site of the Lloyd Center Mall). Both are across the Willamette River in northeast Portland. If you are traveling outside of the Fareless Square, be sure to buy your ticket and stamp it in the time-punch machine on the platform before you board MAX. There are ticket-vending machines at all MAX stops that tell you how much to pay for your destination; these machines also give change. The MAX driver cannot sell tickets. Fares are the same as on buses. There are ticket inspectors who randomly check to make sure passengers have stamped tickets.

In July 2001, the new **Portland Streetcar** (℃ **503/238-RIDE;** www. portlandstreetcar.org) began operating between the Portland State University neighborhood of downtown through the Pearl District to the Nob Hill neighborhood. The route takes in not only the attractions of the Cultural District, but also all the restaurants and great shopping in the Pearl District and along Northwest 21st and 23rd avenues, which makes this streetcar a great way for visitors to get from the downtown (where most of the hotels are located) to the neighborhoods with the greatest concentrations of restaurants. On Saturdays and Sundays, vintage streetcars operate free of charge (donations are encouraged). Streetcar fares for trips outside the Fareless Square are $1.25 for adults, 95¢ for youths, and 60¢ for seniors.

BY CAR

CAR RENTALS   Portland is a compact city, and public transit will get you to most attractions within its limits. However, if you are planning to explore outside the city—and Portland's greatest attractions, such as Mount Hood and the Columbia River Gorge, lie not in the city itself but in the countryside within an hour of the city—you'll definitely need a car.

The major car-rental companies are all represented in Portland and have desks at Portland International Airport, which is the most convenient place to pick up a car. There are also many independent and smaller car-rental agencies listed in the Portland Yellow Pages. Currently, weekly rates for an economy car in July (high-season rates) are about $188 with no discounts. Expect lower rates in the rainy months.

On the ground floor of the airport parking deck, across the street from the baggage-claim area, you'll find the following companies: **Avis** (℃ 800/831-2847 or 503/249-4950; www.avis.com), **Budget** (℃ 800/527-0700 or 503/249-6500; www.budget.com), **Dollar** (℃ 800/800-4000 or 503/249-4792; www.dollar.com), **Hertz** (℃ 800/654-3131 or 503/249-8216; www.hertz.com), and **National** (℃ 800/227-7368 or 503/249-4900; www.nationalcar.com). Outside the airport, but with desks adjacent to the other car-rental desks, are **Alamo** (℃ 800/327-9633 or 503/252-7039; www.alamo.com), **Enterprise** (℃ 800/736-8222 or 503/252-1500; www.enterprise.com), and **Thrifty,** at 10800 NE Holman St. (℃ 800/367-2277 or 503/254-6563; www.thrifty.com).

PARKING   Parking downtown can be a problem, especially if you show up after workers have gotten to their offices on weekdays. There are a couple of very important things to remember when parking downtown. When parking on the street, be sure to notice the meter's time limit. These vary from as little as 15 minutes (these are always located right in front of the restaurant or museum where you plan to spend 2 hr.) to long term (read: long walk). Most common are 30- and 60-minute meters. You don't have to feed the meters after 6pm or on Sunday.

The best parking deal in town is at the **Smart Park** garages, where the cost is 95¢ per hour for the first 4 hours (but after that the hourly rate jumps considerably and you'd be well advised to move your car), $2 for the entire evening after 6pm, or $5 all day on the weekends. Look for the red, white, and black signs featuring Les Park, the friendly parking attendant. You'll find Smart Park garages at First Avenue and Jefferson Street, Fourth Avenue and Yamhill Street, Tenth Avenue and Yamhill Street, Third Avenue and Alder Street, O'Bryant Square, and Naito Parkway and Davis Street. More than 200 downtown merchants also validate Smart Park tickets if you spend at least $25, so don't forget to take your ticket along with you.

Rates in other public lots range from about $1.50 up to about $4 per hour.

SPECIAL DRIVING RULES   You may turn right on a red light after a full stop, and if you are in the far left lane of a one-way street, you may turn left into the adjacent left lane of a one-way street at a red light after a full stop. Everyone in a moving vehicle is required to wear a seat belt.

BY TAXI

Because most everything in Portland is fairly close, getting around by taxi can be economical. Although there are almost always taxis waiting in line at major hotels, you won't find them cruising the streets—you'll have to phone for one. **Broadway Cab** (© **503/227-1234**) and **Radio Cab** (© **503/227-1212**) both offer 24-hour radio-dispatched service and accept American Express, Discover, MasterCard, and Visa. Fares are $2.50 for the first mile, $1.50 for each additional mile, and $1 for additional passengers. Up to four passengers can share a taxi.

ON FOOT

City blocks in Portland are about half the size of most city blocks elsewhere, and the entire downtown area covers only about 13 blocks by 26 blocks. This makes Portland a very easy place to explore on foot. The city has been very active in encouraging people to get out of their cars and onto the sidewalks downtown. The sidewalks are wide and there are many fountains, works of art, and small parks with benches.

As mentioned above, if you happen to spot a person walking around downtown wearing a bright green jacket, he or she is probably a **Portland Guide.** These informative souls are there to answer any questions you might have about Portland.

 FAST FACTS: Portland

AAA The **American Automobile Association** (© **800/222-4357**; www.aaa.com) has a Portland office at 600 SW Market St. (© **503/222-6734**), which offers free city maps to members.

Airport See "Getting There" in chapter 2 and "Arriving," in section 1 of this chapter.

American Express The **American Express Travel Service Office**, 1100 SW Sixth Ave. (© **503/226-2961**), at the corner of Sixth and Main, is open

Monday through Friday from 8:30am to 5:30pm. You can cash American Express traveler's checks and exchange the major foreign currencies here. For card member services, phone ✆ **800/528-4800**. Call ✆ **800/AXP-TRIP** or go online to www.americanexpress.com for other city locations or general information.

Area Codes The Portland metro area has two area codes—503 and 971—and it is necessary to dial all 10 digits of a telephone number, even when making local calls.

Babysitters If your hotel doesn't offer babysitting services, call **Northwest Nannies** (✆ **503/245-5288**).

Car Rentals See section 2, "Getting Around," earlier in this chapter.

Climate See section 4, "When to Go," in chapter 2.

Dentist Contact **Oregon Dental Referral** (✆ **800/800-1705**) or the **Multnomah Dental Society** (✆ **503/223-4731**) for a referral.

Doctor If you need a physician referral while in Portland, contact the **Medical Society of Metropolitan Portland** (✆ **503/222-0156**). The **Oregon Health Sciences University Hospital**, 3181 SW Sam Jackson Park Rd. (✆ **503/494-8311**) has a drop-in clinic.

Emergencies For police, fire, or medical emergencies, phone ✆ **911**.

Eyeglass Repair Check out **Binyon's Eyeworld Downtown**, 803 SW Morrison St. (✆ **503/226-6688**).

Hospitals Three conveniently located area hospitals are **Legacy Good Samaritan**, 1015 NW 22nd Ave. (✆ **503/413-7711**); **Providence Portland Medical Center**, 4805 NE Glisan St. (✆ **503/215-1111**); and the **Oregon Health Sciences University Hospital**, 3181 SW Sam Jackson Park Rd. (✆ **503/494-8311**), which is just southwest of the city center and has a drop-in clinic.

Hot Lines The **Portland Center for the Performing Arts Event Information Line** is ✆ **503/796-9293**. The **Oregonian's Inside Line** (✆ **503/225-5555**), operated by Portland's daily newspaper, provides information on everything from concerts and festivals to sports and the weather.

Information See "Visitor Information" in section 1 of this chapter.

Internet Access If you need to check e-mail while you're in Portland, first check with your hotel. Otherwise, visit a **Kinko's**. There's one downtown at 221 SW Alder St. (✆ **503/224-6550**) and in Northwest at 950 NW 23rd Ave. ✆ **503/222-4133**). You can also try the **Multnomah County Library**, 801 SW 10th Ave. (✆ **503/988-5123**), which is Portland's main library and offers online services.

Liquor Laws The legal minimum drinking age in Oregon is 21. Aside from on-premise sales of cocktails in bars and restaurants, hard liquor can only be purchased in liquor stores. Beer and wine are available in convenience stores and grocery stores. Brewpubs tend to sell only beer and wine, but some also have licenses to sell hard liquor.

Maps See "City Layout," in section 1 of this chapter.

Newspapers/Magazines Portland's morning daily newspaper is *The Oregonian.* For arts and entertainment information and listings, consult the "A&E" section of the Friday *Oregonian* or pick up a free copy of *Willamette Week* at Powell's Books and other bookstores, convenience stores, or cafes.

Pharmacies Convenient to most downtown hotels, **Central Drug,** 538 SW Fourth Ave. (© **503/226-2222**), is open Monday through Friday from 9am to 6pm, Saturday from 10am to 4pm.

Photographic Needs **Wolfcamera,** 900 SW Fourth Ave. (© **503/224-6776**) and 733 SW Alder (© **503/224-6775**), offers 1-hour film processing. **Camera World,** 400 SW Sixth Ave. (© **503/205-5900**), is the largest camera and video store in the city.

Police To reach the police, call © **911.**

Post Offices The **main post office,** 715 NW Hoyt St., is open Monday through Friday from 7am to 6:30pm, Saturday from 8:30am to 5pm. There is also another convenient post office at 1505 SW Sixth Ave., open Monday through Friday from 7am to 6pm, Saturday from 10am to 3pm. For more information, call © **800/275-8777.**

Restrooms There are public restrooms underneath Starbucks coffee shop in Pioneer Courthouse Square, in downtown shopping malls, and in hotel lobbies.

Safety Because of its small size and progressive emphasis on keeping the downtown alive and growing, Portland is still a relatively safe city; in fact, strolling the downtown streets at night is a popular pastime. Take extra precautions, however, if you venture into the entertainment district along West Burnside Street or Chinatown at night. Certain neighborhoods in north and northeast Portland are the centers for much of the city's gang activity, so before visiting any place in this area, be sure to get very detailed directions so you don't get lost. If you plan to go hiking in Forest Park, don't leave anything valuable in your car. This holds true in the Skidmore Historic District (Old Town) as well.

Smoking Although many of the restaurants listed in this book are smoke-free, there are also many Portland restaurants that allow smoking. At most high-end restaurants, the smoking area is usually in the bar/lounge, and although many restaurants have separate bar menus, most will serve you off the regular menu even if you are eating in the bar. There are very few no-smoking bars in Portland.

Taxes Portland is a shopper's paradise—there's no sales tax. However, there is an 11.5% tax on hotel rooms within the city and a 12.5% tax on car rentals (plus an additional airport-use fee if you pick up your rental car at the airport; this fee is usually an additional 11%). Outside the city, the room tax varies.

Taxis See section 2, "Getting Around," earlier in this chapter.

Time Zone Portland is on Pacific time, 3 hours behind the East Coast. In the summer, daylight saving time is observed and clocks are set forward 1 hour.

Transit Info For bus and MAX information, call the **Tri-Met Customer Assistance Office** (© **503/238-7433**).

Weather If it's summer, it's sunny; otherwise, there's a chance of rain. This almost always suffices, but for specifics, call **Weatherline Forecast Service** (© **503/243-7575**) or the Portland Oregon Visitor Association's **weather information hot line** (© **503/275-9792**). If you want to know how to pack before you arrive, check **www.cnn.com/weather** or **www.weather.com**.

3 Where to Stay

Portland has been undergoing a downtown hotel renaissance for the past decade. Several historic hotels have been renovated, and other historic buildings have been retrofitted to serve as hotels. The Benson, the Governor Hotel, The Heathman Hotel, the Hotel Vintage Plaza, the 5th Avenue Suites, and the Embassy Suites (formerly the Multnomah Hotel) are all part of this trend. These hotels offer some of Portland's most comfortable and memorable accommodations. Several other new hotels have also opened in the past 2 years.

The city's largest concentrations of hotels are in downtown and near the airport. If you don't mind the high prices, downtown hotels are the most convenient for visitors.

However, if your budget won't allow for a first-class business hotel, try near the airport or elsewhere on the outskirts of the city (Troutdale and Gresham on the east side; Beaverton and Hillsboro on the west; Wilsonville and Lake Oswego in the south; and Vancouver, Washington in the north), where you're more likely to find inexpensive to moderately priced motels.

You'll find the greatest concentration of bed-and-breakfasts in the Irvington neighborhood of northeast Portland. This area is close to downtown and is generally quite convenient even if you are here on business.

In the following listings, price categories are based on the rate for a double room in high season. (Most hotels charge the same for a single or double room.) Keep in mind that the rates listed do not include local room taxes, which vary between 7% and 11.5%.

For comparison purposes, we list what hotels call "rack rates," or walk-in rates—but you should never have to pay these highly inflated prices. Various discounts (AAA, senior, corporate, and Entertainment Book) often reduce these rates, so be sure to ask (and check each hotel's website for Internet specials). In fact, you can often get a discounted corporate rate simply by flashing a business card (your own, that is). At inexpensive chain motels, there are almost always discounted rates for AAA members and seniors.

You'll also find that room rates are almost always considerably lower October through April (the rainy season), and large downtown hotels often offer weekend discounts of up to 50% throughout the year. Some of the large, upscale hotel chains have now gone to an airline-type rate system based on occupancy, so if you call early enough before a hotel books up you might get a really good rate. On the other hand, call at the last minute and you might catch a cancellation and still be offered a low rate. Also be sure to ask about special packages (romance, golf, or theater), which most of the more expensive hotels usually offer.

A few hotels include breakfast in their rates; others offer complimentary breakfast only on certain deluxe floors. Parking rates are per day.

Although Portland is not nearly as popular with tourists as Seattle, it's still advisable to make reservations as far in advance as possible if you're planning to visit during the busy summer months.

Most hotels offer no-smoking rooms, and most bed-and-breakfasts are exclusively no-smoking. Most hotels also offer wheelchair-accessible rooms.

HELPING HANDS

If you're having trouble booking a room, try the **Portland Oregon Visitors Association (POVA),** 1000 SW Broadway, Suite 2300, Portland, OR 97205 (© **877/678-5263** or 503/275-9750; www.pova.com), which offers a reservation service for the Portland metro area.

For information on **bed-and-breakfasts** in the Portland area, call the **Portland Oregon Visitors Association** (© 877/678-5263 or 503/275-9750; www.pova.com). Also try contacting the **Oregon Bed and Breakfast Guild,** P.O. Box 3187, Ashland, OR 97520 (© **800/944-6196;** www.obbg.org). You can also try the **Northwest Bed and Breakfast Reservation Service** (© 877/ **243-7782** or 503/243-7616; www.nwbedandbreakfast.com).

DOWNTOWN
VERY EXPENSIVE

RiverPlace Hotel ✦✦✦   With the Willamette River at its back doorstep and the sloping lawns of Waterfront Park to one side, the RiverPlace is Portland's only downtown waterfront hotel. This alone would be enough to recommend the hotel, but its quiet boutique-hotel atmosphere would make it an excellent choice even if it weren't on the water.

The river-view standard king rooms here are the hotel's best deal, but the junior suites are only slightly more expensive and provide a bit more space. In general, furnishings are neither as elegant nor as luxurious as at The Heathman or The Benson; what you're paying for is the waterfront locale. More than half the rooms are suites; some come with wood-burning fireplaces and whirlpool baths. There are also condominiums for long stays.

The hotel's restaurant overlooks the river, and there's also a comfortable bar with live piano music and a casual menu. The bar also has a patio dining area overlooking the river.

1510 SW Harbor Way, Portland, OR 97201. © **800/227-1333** or 503/228-3233. Fax 503/295-6161. www. riverplacehotel.com. 84 units. $219–$379 double; $249–$389 junior suite; $279–$979 suite. Rates include continental breakfast. AE, DC, DISC, MC, V. Valet parking $18. Pets accepted with $45 nonrefundable cleaning fee. **Amenities:** Restaurant (Northwest/Continental), lounge; indoor pool; access to nearby health club; day spa; Jacuzzi; sauna; concierge; 24-hr. room service; massage; babysitting; laundry/dry cleaning. *In room:* A/C, TV, fax, dataport, minibar, hair dryer, iron.

EXPENSIVE

The Benson ✦✦✦   Built in 1912, The Benson exudes old-world sophistication and elegance. In the French baroque lobby, walnut paneling frames a marble fireplace, Austrian crystal chandeliers hang from the ornate plasterwork ceiling, and a marble staircase allows for grand entrances. Presidents stay here whenever they're in town—a good clue that these are the poshest digs in Portland. The guest rooms vary considerably in size, but all are luxuriously furnished in a plush Euro-luxe styling. The deluxe kings are particularly roomy, but the corner junior suites are the hotel's best deal. Not only are these quite large, but the abundance of windows also makes them much cheerier than other rooms. Bathrooms, unfortunately, have little shelf space.

In the vaults below the lobby you'll find the **London Grill,** well known for its Sunday brunch. Just off the lobby, there's El Gaucho steakhouse, and in the Lobby Bar, there's live jazz in the evenings.

309 SW Broadway, Portland, OR 97205. © **800/426-0670** or 503/228-2000. Fax 503/226-4603. www. bensonhotel.com. 287 units. $150–$170 double; $285 junior suite; $500–$900 suite. AE, DC, DISC, MC, V. Valet parking $21. Pets accepted ($100 fee). **Amenities:** Restaurant (Northwest/Continental), lounge; exercise room, access to nearby health club; concierge; business center; 24-hr. room service; massage; dry cleaning. *In room:* A/C, TV, dataport, minibar, coffeemaker, hair dryer, iron.

Embassy Suites ✦✦ *Kids* *Value*   Located in the restored former Multnomah Hotel, which originally opened in 1912, the Embassy Suites has a beautiful large lobby that is a masterpiece of gilded plasterwork. The accommodations here are

Where to Stay in Portland

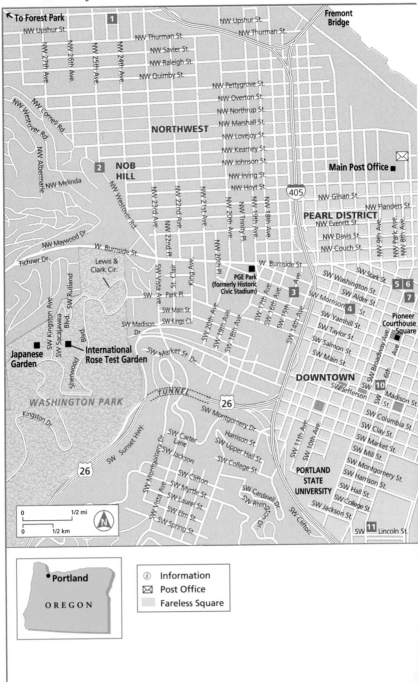

To Forest Park

Fremont Bridge

NW Upshur St.
NW Thurman St.
NW Savier St.
NW Raleigh St.
NW Quimby St.

NW Pettygrove St.
NW Overton St.
NW Northrup St.
NW Marshall St.
NW Lovejoy St.
NW Kearney St.
NW Johnson St.
NW Irving St.
NW Hoyt St.

NW 27th Ave.
NW 26th Ave.
NW 25th Ave.
NW 24th Ave.

NW Westover Rd.
NW Cornell Rd.
NW Albermarle
NW Melinda
NW Westover Rd.
NW Maywood Dr.
Tichner Dr.

NORTHWEST

NOB HILL

NW 23rd Ave.
NW 22nd Ave.
NW 22nd Pl.
NW 21st Ave.
NW 20th Ave.
NW 20th Pl.
NW 19th Ave.
NW 18th Ave.
NW Trinity Pl.

Main Post Office ■

405

NW Glisan St.
NW Flanders St.

PEARL DISTRICT
NW Everett St.
NW Davis St.
NW Couch St.

NW 9th Ave.
NW Park Ave.
NW 8th Ave.

W. Burnside St.
Lewis & Clark Cir.

W. Burnside St.

PGE Park (formerly Historic Civic Stadium)

SW Stark St.
SW Washington St.
SW Alder St.
SW Morrison St.
SW Yamhill St.
SW Taylor St.
SW Salmon St.
SW Main St.

SW 17th Ave.
SW 16th Ave.
SW 15th
SW 14th Ave.

SW Vista Ave.
St. Clair
King Ave.
SW Park Pl.
SW Main St.
SW Madison Dr.
SW Kings Ct.
SW Kings Cl.

SW 20th Ave.
SW 19th Ave.
SW 18th Ave.

3
4

5 6
7

Pioneer Courthouse Square

SW Kingston Ave.
SW Sacajawea Blvd.
SW Rutland

Japanese Garden ■

■ **International Rose Test Garden**

Sherwood Blvd.

SW Market St. Dr.

TUNNEL

26

SW Montgomery Dr.

DOWNTOWN

SW Jefferson

SW Broadway Ave.
6th Ave.

10

SW Madison St.
SW Columbia St.
SW Clay St.
SW Market St.
SW Mill St.
SW Montgomery St.
SW Harrison St.
SW Hall St.
SW College St.
SW Jackson St.

WASHINGTON PARK

Kingston Dr.

SW Sunset Hwy.

26

SW Montgomery Dr.
SW Carter Lane
SW Jackson
SW Clifton
SW Myrtle St.
SW Laurel St.
SW Elm St.
SW Spring St.

Harrison St.
SW Upper Hall St.
SW College St.

SW Cardinell Dr.
SW Riving

SW Vista Ave.

SW 11th Ave.
SW 10th Ave.

PORTLAND STATE UNIVERSITY

11 Lincoln St.

0   1/2 mi
0   1/2 km

N

● Portland

OREGON

ⓘ   Information
✉   Post Office
    Fareless Square

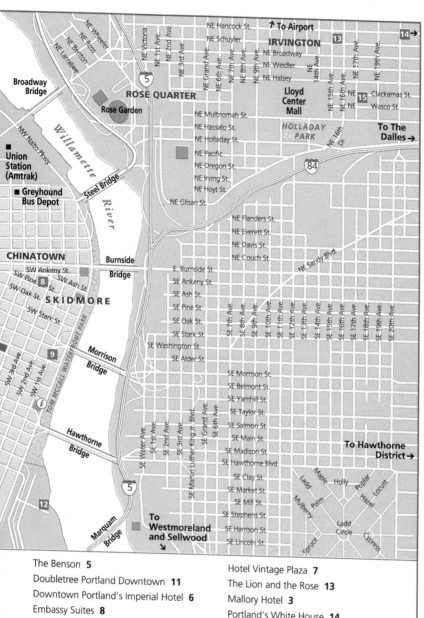

The Benson **5**
Doubletree Portland Downtown **11**
Downtown Portland's Imperial Hotel **6**
Embassy Suites **8**
Four Points Hotel Sheraton **9**
Governor Hotel **4**
The Heathman Hotel **10**
Heron Haus **2**

Hotel Vintage Plaza **7**
The Lion and the Rose **13**
Mallory Hotel **3**
Portland's White House **14**
RiverPlace Hotel **12**
Silver Cloud Inn Portland Downtown **1**
Sullivan's Gulch B&B **15**

primarily two-room suites, with the exception of a handful of studio suites. In keeping with the historic nature of the hotel, the suites have classically styled furnishings. However, what's much more important is that they give you lots of room to spread out, a rarity in downtown hotels. The hotel's Portland Steak and Chophouse has a classic dark and woody steakhouse decor and a large bar. There's a nightly complimentary evening manager's reception.

319 SW Pine St., Portland, OR 97204-2726. © 800/EMBASSY or 503/279-9000. Fax 503/497-9051. www. embassyportland.com. 276 units. $129–$209 double. Rates include full breakfast. AE, DC, DISC, MC, V. Valet parking $15; self-parking $15. Amenities: Restaurant (steak), lounge; indoor pool; exercise room, access to nearby health club; day spa; Jacuzzi; sauna; concierge; car-rental desk; business center; room service; massage; laundry/dry cleaning. In room: A/C, TV, dataport, fridge, coffeemaker, hair dryer, iron.

Governor Hotel ★★★
This historic hotel pays homage to the Lewis and Clark Expedition, and you'll spot references to the famous explorers throughout. However, the historical references are just the icing on the cake at this plush hotel.

Guest rooms vary considerably in size but are all attractively decorated, with perks such as two-line phones and voice mail. The least expensive rooms are rather small but are nevertheless very comfortable. Still, we'd opt for one of the deluxe guest rooms. Unfortunately, bathrooms are, in general, quite cramped by today's standards and lack counter space, although their tile work does give them a classic feel. Suites, on the other hand, are spacious, and some even have huge patios overlooking the city.

Be sure to take a peek at the Dome Room, which is just off the lobby and has a stunning stained-glass skylight. Jake's Grill, a large, old-fashioned restaurant located just off the lobby, serves grilled steak and seafood. There's also a complimentary evening wine tasting Monday through Thursday.

611 SW 10th Ave., Portland, OR 97205. © 800/554-3456 or 503/224-3400. Fax 503/241-2122. www. govhotel.com. 100 units. $165–$195 double; $200 junior suite; $210–$500 suite. AE, DC, DISC, MC, V. Valet parking $16. Amenities: Restaurant (American), lounge; pool; access to adjacent health club with indoor pool, Jacuzzi, saunas, indoor running track; concierge; business center; 24-hr. room service; laundry service; dry cleaning. In room: A/C, TV, dataport, minibar, coffeemaker, hair dryer, iron.

The Heathman Hotel ★★★
With its understated luxury and superb service, The Heathman is one of the finest hotels in the city. Although primarily a top-end business hotel, it's also the address of choice for visiting culture hounds, with its proximity to the theater and an outstanding collection of art ranging from 18th-century oil paintings to Andy Warhol prints. Don't look for a bowl-you-over lobby here; although there is plenty of marble and teak, the lobby itself is tiny. However, just off the lobby is the Tea Court, where the original eucalyptus paneling creates a warm, old-world atmosphere.

The basic rooms here tend to be quite small, but are nonetheless attractively furnished and set up for business travelers. There are no real views to speak of, but rooms on the west side of the hotel look out to a mural done just for the hotel. Basically what you get here is luxury in a small space. The corner rooms are lighter and more spacious.

The **Heathman Restaurant** is one of Portland's finest (see the review on p. 73). Afternoon tea is served in the Lobby Lounge, and there's usually live jazz nightly. There are also complimentary wine tastings several nights a week.

1001 SW Broadway at Salmon St., Portland, OR 97205. © 800/551-0011 or 503/241-4100. Fax 503/790-7110. www.heathmanhotel.com. 150 units. $169–$209 double; $305–$775 suite. AE, DC, DISC, MC, V. Parking $19. Pets accepted for $25. Amenities: Restaurant (Northwest), lounge; exercise room and access to nearby health club; concierge; room service; laundry service; dry cleaning. In room: A/C, TV, dataport, minibar, coffeemaker, hair dryer, iron, high-speed Internet access.

Hotel Vintage Plaza ★★ This hotel, which was built in 1894 and is on the National Register of Historic Places, is *the* place to stay in Portland if you are a wine lover. A wine theme predominates in the hotel's decor, and there are complimentary evening tastings of Northwest wines. There are a wide variety of room types here, and though the standard rooms are worth recommending, the starlight rooms and bi-level suites are the real scene-stealers. The starlight rooms in particular are truly extraordinary. Though small, they have greenhouse-style wall-to-ceiling windows that provide very romantic views at night and let in floods of light during the day. The bi-level suites, some with Japanese soaking tubs and one with a spiral staircase, are equally attractive spaces.

  Pazzo Ristorante, one of Portland's best Italian restaurants, is a dark, intimate trattoria.

422 SW Broadway, Portland, OR 97205. ⓒ **800/243-0555** or 503/228-1212. Fax 503/228-3598. www.vintageplaza.com. 107 units. $150–$225 double; $325–$400 suite. AE, DC, DISC, MC, V. Valet parking $21. Pets accepted. **Amenities:** Restaurant (Italian); lounge; exercise room, access to nearby health club; concierge; business center; 24-hr. room service; massage; laundry service; same-day dry cleaning. *In room:* A/C, TV, fax, dataport, minibar, hair dryer, iron.

MODERATE

Downtown Portland's Imperial Hotel ★ *Value* Although it doesn't quite live up to its regal name, this remodeled older hotel across the street from the Benson is a good bet for moderately priced accommodations at a great downtown location. Although the staff may be young and not as polished as those at more expensive hotels, they usually are good about seeing to guests' needs. Rooms are quite up-to-date. The corner king rooms, with large windows, should be your first choice; barring this, ask for an exterior room. These might get a little street noise, but they're bigger than the interior rooms and get more sunlight. Free local calls are a nice perk.

400 SW Broadway, Portland, OR 97205. ⓒ **800/452-2323** or 503/228-7221. Fax 503/223-4551. www.hotel-imperial.com. 128 units. $90–$130 double. Rates include continental breakfast. AE, DC, DISC, MC, V. Valet parking $15. Pets accepted ($10 fee). **Amenities:** Highly regarded restaurant (Thai); lounge with live jazz; access to nearby health club; dry cleaning. *In room:* A/C, TV, dataport, fridge, hair dryer, iron, safe.

Four Points Hotel Sheraton ★★ *Value* Overlooking Waterfront Park and located on the MAX light-rail line, this 1960s vintage hotel is nondescript from the outside, but the inside has been renovated with a contemporary look that makes it one of the most stylish hotels in town. You are only steps from the Willamette River (although not actually on the water), and are also close to businesses, fine restaurants, and shopping. Guest rooms are as boldly contemporary in design as the lobby and restaurant, which are sort of downscale *Architectural Digest.*

50 SW Morrison St., Portland, OR 97204-3390. ⓒ **800/899-0247** or 503/221-0711. Fax 503/274-0312. www.fourpointsportland.com. 140 units. $99–$140 double. AE, DC, DISC, MC, V. Parking $10. Pets accepted. **Amenities:** Restaurant (American/international), lounge; access to nearby health club; room service; massage; dry cleaning. *In room:* A/C, TV, dataport, coffeemaker, hair dryer, iron.

Mallory Hotel ★ *Finds* The Mallory, which is right on the west-side Max line, has long been a favorite of Portland visitors who want the convenience of staying downtown but aren't on a bottomless expense account. This is an older hotel, and the lobby, with its ornate gilt plasterwork trim and crystal chandeliers, has a certain classic (and faded) grandeur. Time seems to have stood still here. (There's a lounge straight out of the 1950s.)

  The standard rooms are not as luxurious as the lobby might suggest and are smaller than comparable rooms at the Imperial or Days Inn, but are comfortable and clean. With rates this low, you might even want to go for one of the king-size suites, which are as big as they come, with walk-in closets, refrigerators, and sofa beds. Free local calls are a nice perk.

The dining room continues the lobby's grand design, with heavy drapes and faux-marble pillars.

729 SW 15th Ave., Portland, OR 97205-1994. © **800/228-8657** or 503/223-6311. Fax 503/223-0522. www. malloryhotel.com. 130 units. $95–$160 double; $160 suite. AE, DC, DISC, MC, V. Free parking. Pets accepted ($10 fee). **Amenities:** Restaurant (American), lounge; access to nearby health club; concierge; room service. *In room:* A/C, TV, dataport, fridge, iron, safe.

NOB HILL & NORTHWEST PORTLAND
EXPENSIVE
Heron Haus 🌟🌟   A short walk from the bustling Nob Hill shopping and dining district of northwest Portland, the Heron Haus B&B offers outstanding accommodations, spectacular views, and tranquil surroundings. Surprisingly, the house still features some of the original plumbing. In most places this would be a liability, but not here, since the same man who plumbed Portland's famous Pittock Mansion (see p. 95) did the plumbing here. Many of that building's unusual bathroom features are also found at the Heron Haus—one shower has *seven* showerheads. In another room there's a modern whirlpool spa with excellent views of the city. All the rooms have fireplaces.

2545 NW Westover Rd., Portland, OR 97210. © **503/274-1846.** Fax 503/248-4055. www.heronhaus.com. 6 units. $135–$350 double. Rates include continental breakfast. MC, V. Free parking. *In room:* A/C, TV, dataport, hair dryer, iron.

MODERATE
Silver Cloud Inn Portland Downtown 🌟   This hotel is on the edge of Portland's trendy Nob Hill neighborhood, and though it faces the beginning of the city's industrial area, it is still a very attractive and comfortable place (ask for a room away from Vaughn St.). Reasonable rates are the main draw here, but the rooms are also well-designed and filled with plenty of conveniences, such as free local calls. Although the minisuites have wet bars, microwave ovens, and separate seating areas, the king rooms with whirlpool tubs, which happen to be the most expensive rooms, are our favorites. However, the best thing about the hotel is its location within a 5-minute drive (or 15-min. walk) of a half dozen of the city's best restaurants. To find the hotel, take I-405 to Ore. 30 west and get off at the Vaughn Street exit.

2426 NW Vaughn St., Portland, OR 97210. © **800/205-6939** or 503/242-2400. Fax 503/242-1770. www. silvercloud.com. 83 units. $89–$139 double. Rates include continental breakfast. AE, DC, DISC, MC, V. Free parking. **Amenities:** Exercise room; Jacuzzi; business center; coin-op laundry; laundry service; dry cleaning. *In room:* A/C, TV, dataport, coffeemaker, hair dryer, iron.

THE ROSE QUARTER & IRVINGTON
EXPENSIVE
The Lion and the Rose 🌟🌟   This imposing Queen Anne–style Victorian inn is located in the Irvington District, a fairly quiet residential neighborhood 1 block off Northeast Broadway. It's a good choice if you want to keep your driving to a minimum. Restaurants, cafes, eclectic boutiques, and a huge shopping mall are all within 4 blocks. Even without the splendid location, the inn would be a gem. Guest rooms each have a distinctively different decor. In the Lavonna room, there are bright colors and a turret sitting area, while in the deep green Starina room you'll find an imposing Edwardian bed and armoire. Both the Garden room and the Lavonna Room's shared bathroom have claw-foot tubs,

---

Kids Family-Friendly Hotels

Embassy Suites *(see p. 63)*   Located in the center of the city, this renovated historic hotel offers spacious rooms (mostly two-room suites). You and the kids will have room to spread out and can hang out by the indoor pool when you tire of exploring Portland.

Homewood Suites by Hilton Vancouver/Portland *(see p. 71)* Although this hotel is across the Columbia River in Vancouver, Washington, its location right across the street from the river, a paved riverside trail, a fun family restaurant, and a brewpub all add up to convenience for families. That you'll get a one- or two-bedroom apartment with a full kitchen just makes life on vacation that much easier.

The Lakeshore Inn *(see p. 72)*   This reasonably priced inn is right on the shore of the lake and it also has a pool. The big rooms with kitchenettes are great for families; for more space, opt for a one- or two-bedroom suite.

---

while some rooms have rather cramped, though attractive, bathrooms. If you have problems climbing stairs, ask for the ground floor's Rose room, which has a whirlpool tub. Breakfasts are sumptuous affairs, great for lingering.

1810 NE 15th Ave., Portland, OR 97212. © 800/955-1647 or 503/287-9245. Fax 503/287-9247. www. lionrose.com. 6 units (1 with shared bathroom). $95–$140 double. AE, DISC, MC, V. **Amenities:** Concierge. *In room:* A/C, TV, hair dryer, iron.

MODERATE

McMenamins Kennedy School ★★ *Finds*   The Kennedy School is from the same folks who turned Portland's old poor farm into the most entertaining and unusual B&B in the state (see the listing for McMenamins Edgefield on p. 233 in chapter 7). This inn, located well north of stylish Irvington in an up-and-coming neighborhood that dates from the early years of the 20th century, was an elementary school from 1915 to 1975. In the guest rooms you'll still find the original blackboards and great big school clocks (you know, like the one you used to watch so expectantly). However, the classroom/guest rooms here now have their own bathrooms, so you won't have to raise your hand or walk down the hall. On the premises you'll also find a restaurant, a beer garden, a movie theater pub, a cigar bar, and a big hot soaking pool.

5736 NE 33rd Ave., Portland, OR 97211. © 888/249-3983 or 503/249-3983. www.mcmenamins.com. 35 units. $99–$109 double. Rates include full breakfast. AE, DISC, MC, V. **Amenities:** Restaurant (American), 5 lounges; soaking pool; massage. *In room:* Dataports.

Portland's White House ★★   With massive columns framing the entrance, semicircular driveway, and in the front garden, a bubbling fountain, this imposing Greek-revival mansion bears a more than passing resemblance to its namesake in Washington, D.C. Behind the mahogany front doors, a huge entrance hall with original hand-painted wall murals is flanked by a parlor, with French windows and a piano, and the formal dining room, where the large breakfast is served beneath sparkling crystal chandeliers. A double staircase leads past a large stained-glass window to the second-floor accommodations. Canopy and brass queen beds, antique furnishings, and bathrooms with claw-foot tubs further the feeling of classic luxury here. Request the balcony room, and you can gaze out past the Greek columns and imagine you're in the Oval Office. There are also three rooms in the restored carriage house.

1914 NE 22nd Ave., Portland, OR 97212. © **800/272-7131** or 503/287-7131. Fax 503/249-1641. www. portlandswhitehouse.com. 9 units. $98–$169 double. Rates include full breakfast. AE, DISC, MC, V. *In room:* A/C, dataport, fridge, hair dryer, iron.

INEXPENSIVE

Sullivan's Gulch B&B ⚐   Set on a quiet, tree-shaded street just a couple blocks from busy Northeast Broadway, this inn is a 1907 home filled with an eclectic mix of Mission-style furniture, Asian artifacts, and contemporary art. Our favorite room here is the Northwest Room, which is decorated with Northwest Coast Native American masks and has an old Hudson's Bay Company blanket on the bed. There's also a room that draws on Montana and Western art for its decor. A pretty little deck out back is a pleasant place to hang out in summer. The inn is popular with gay and lesbian travelers, and with the MAX stop just a few blocks away it's convenient to downtown.

1744 NE Clackamas St., Portland, OR 97232. © **503/331-1104.** Fax 503/331-1575. www.sullivansgulch. com. 4 units (2 with shared bathroom). $70–$85 double. AE, MC, V. Pets accepted. *In room:* TV, fridge, no phone.

JANTZEN BEACH (NORTH PORTLAND) & VANCOUVER, WASHINGTON

Located on Hayden Island in the middle of the Columbia River, Jantzen Beach, named for the famous swimwear company that got its start here, is a beach in name only. Today this area is a huge shopping mall complex aimed primarily at Washingtonians, who come to Oregon to avoid Washington's sales tax. Jantzen Beach is also home to a pair of large convention hotels that are among the city's only waterfront hotels. Both hotels are, however, in the flight path for the airport, and although the rooms themselves are adequately insulated against noise, the swimming pools and sun decks can be pretty noisy.

MODERATE

Doubletree Hotel Portland Columbia River ⚐⚐   Attractive landscaping and an interesting low-rise design that's somewhat reminiscent of a Northwest Coast Indian longhouse give this convention hotel a resort-like feel and have kept it popular for many years. Although rush-hour traffic problems can make this a bad choice if you're here to explore Portland, it's a good location if you plan to visit Mount St. Helens. Guest rooms are large, though rather nondescript. Be sure to ask for one of the rooms with a view of the Columbia River.

1401 N. Hayden Island Dr., Portland, OR 97217. © **800/222-TREE** or 503/283-2111. Fax 503/283-4718. www.doubletreehotels.com. 351 units. $100–$125 double; $200–$250 suite. AE, DC, DISC, MC, V. Free parking. Pets accepted with $30 nonrefundable deposit. **Amenities:** 2 restaurants (Northwest, American), 2 lounges; outdoor pool; access to exercise room at adjacent hotel; Jacuzzi; concierge; courtesy airport shuttle; room service; laundry/dry cleaning. *In room:* A/C, TV, dataport, coffeemaker, hair dryer, iron.

The Heathman Lodge ⚐⚐ *Value*   Mountain lodge meets urban chic at this suburban Vancouver hotel adjacent to the Vancouver Mall, and though it's a 20-minute drive to downtown Portland, the hotel is well placed for exploring both the Columbia Gorge and Mount St. Helens. With its log, stone, and cedar-shingle construction, this hotel conjures up the Northwest's historic mountain lodges and is filled with artwork and embellished with rugged Northwest-inspired craftwork, including totem poles, Eskimo kayak frames, and Pendleton blankets. Guest rooms feature a mix of rustic pine and peeled-hickory furniture.

7801 NE Greenwood Dr., Vancouver, WA 98662. ℂ **888/475-3100** or 360/254-3100. Fax 360/254-6100. www. heathmanlodge.com. 143 units. $89–$139 double; $159–$550 suite. AE, DC, DISC, MC, V. Free parking. **Amenities:** Restaurant (Northwest), lounge; indoor pool; exercise room; Jacuzzi; sauna; concierge; business center; room service; guest laundry; laundry service; dry cleaning. *In room:* A/C, TV, dataport, fridge, microwave, coffeemaker, hair dryer, iron.

Homewood Suites by Hilton Vancouver/Portland *⋆⋆* *Kids*   Located across the street from the Columbia River, this modern suburban all-suite hotel is a great choice for families. The hotel charges surprisingly reasonable rates for large apartment-like accommodations that include full kitchens. Rates include not only a large breakfast, but afternoon snacks as well (Mon–Thurs). These snacks are substantial enough to pass for dinner if you aren't too hungry. The hotel is right across the street from both a beach-theme restaurant and a brewpub. Across the street, you'll also find a paved riverside path that's great for walking or jogging. The only drawback is that it's a 15- to 20-minute drive to downtown Portland.

701 SE Columbia Shores Blvd., Vancouver, WA 98661. ℂ **800/CALL-HOME** or 360/750-1100. Fax 360/ 750-4899. www.homewood-suites.com. 104 units. $99–$119 double. Rates include full breakfast. AE, DC, DISC, MC, V. Free parking. Pets accepted with $25 nonrefundable deposit plus $10 per night. **Amenities:** Outdoor pool; exercise room; Jacuzzi; sports court; business center; coin-op laundry. *In room:* A/C, TV, dataport, kitchen, fridge, coffeemaker, hair dryer, iron.

THE AIRPORT AREA & TROUTDALE

Moderately priced hotels have been proliferating in the airport area in the past few years, which makes this a good place to look for a room if you arrive with no reservation.

EXPENSIVE

Shilo Inn Suites Hotel Portland Airport *⋆⋆*   If you need to stay near the airport and want a spacious room and the facilities of a deluxe hotel, this is one of your best bets. The rooms are spacious and have many amenities such as large closets with mirrored doors, lots of bathroom counter space, double sinks, and three TVs (including one in the bathroom). The main drawback here is that this is a convention hotel and is often very crowded. To find the Shilo, head straight out of the airport, drive under the I-205 overpass, and watch for the hotel ahead on the left.

11707 NE Airport Way, Portland, OR 97220-1075. ℂ **800/222-2244** or 503/252-7500. Fax 503/254-0794. www.shiloinns.com. 200 units. $79–$169 double. Rates include full breakfast. AE, DC, DISC, MC, V. Free parking. **Amenities:** Restaurant (American), lounge; indoor pool; exercise room; Jacuzzi; sauna; tour desk; courtesy airport shuttle; business center; room service; coin-op laundry; dry cleaning. *In room:* A/C, TV, dataport, fridge, coffeemaker, hair dryer, iron, safe.

MODERATE

Silver Cloud Inn Portland Airport *⋆* *Value*   Conveniently located right outside the airport, this hotel has one of the best backyards of any hotel in the Portland area. A lake, lawns, and trees create a tranquil setting despite the proximity of both the airport and a busy nearby road. Rooms are designed primarily for business travelers, but even if you aren't here on an expense account, they are a good value, especially those with whirlpool tubs (and you even get free local calls). Some suites have gas fireplaces. Best of all, with the exception of two suites, every room has a view of the lake. An indoor pool is another big plus. To find this hotel, take the complimentary airport shuttle or head straight out of the airport, drive under the I-205 overpass, and watch for the hotel sign ahead on the left.

11518 NE Glenn Widing Dr., Portland, OR 97220. © **800/205-7892** or 503/252-2222. Fax 503/257-7008. www.silvercloud.com. 102 units. $89–$105 double; $129–$139 suite. Rates include continental breakfast. AE, DC, DISC, MC, V. Free parking. **Amenities:** Indoor pool; exercise room; Jacuzzi; courtesy airport shuttle; business center; coin-op laundry; dry cleaning. *In room:* A/C, TV, dataport, fridge, coffeemaker, microwave, hair dryer, iron, free local calls.

INEXPENSIVE
The **Super 8 Motel,** 11011 NE Holman St. (© **503/257-8988**), just off Airport Way after you go under the I-205 overpass, is convenient but charges a surprisingly high $66 to $81 a night for a double in summer. Also not far away, in Troutdale, at the mouth of the Columbia Gorge, you'll find a **Motel 6,** 1610 NW Frontage Rd., Troutdale (© **503/665-2254**), charging $43 to $52 per night for a double.

LAKE OSWEGO
INEXPENSIVE
The Lakeshore Inn ★ *Finds* *Kids*   Considering that the town of Lake Oswego is Portland's most affluent bedroom community, this motel is quite reasonably priced. It's right on the shore of the lake, and there's a pool on a deck built on the water's edge, making it a great place to stay in summer. Rooms have standard motel furnishings but are large and have kitchenettes. There are also one- and two-bedroom suites. The 7-mile drive into downtown Portland follows the Willamette River and is quite pleasant. There are several restaurants and cafes within walking distance.

210 N. State St., Lake Oswego, OR 97034. © **800/215-6431** or 503/636-9679. Fax 503/636-6959. www.thelakeshoreinn.com. 33 units. $69–$99 double; $89–$129 suite. AE, DC, DISC, MC, V. **Amenities:** Outdoor pool; access to nearby health club; coin-op laundry. *In room:* A/C, TV, dataport, kitchenette, coffeemaker, hair dryer, iron.

4 Where to Dine

In the past few years the Portland restaurant scene has gotten so hot that the city is beginning to develop a Seattle-style reputation. Excellent new restaurants keep popping up around the city. Several distinct dining districts are full of upscale spots, and though you aren't likely to choose to eat at one of these places on the spur of the moment (reservations are usually imperative), their proximity allows you to check out a few places before making a decision for later.

The Pearl District's renovated warehouses currently house the trendiest restaurants, while Nob Hill's Northwest 21st Avenue boasts half a dozen terrific establishments within a few blocks. The Sellwood and Westmoreland neighborhoods of Southeast Portland make up another of the city's hot restaurant districts, and for good inexpensive food, it's hard to beat the many offerings along NE Broadway in the Irvington neighborhood.

Dinner in Portland isn't complete without an Oregon wine. Pinot Noir and Pinot Gris in particular receive widespread acclaim. However, they can be more expensive than other domestic wines.

DOWNTOWN (INCLUDING THE SKIDMORE HISTORIC DISTRICT & CHINATOWN)
VERY EXPENSIVE
Couvron ★★★ CONTEMPORARY FRENCH   If you're in Portland for a very special occasion and are looking for the most memorable restaurant in town, this is it. Located in the Goose Hollow neighborhood at the foot of the

West Hills and only a few blocks from the PGE Park baseball stadium, this diminutive restaurant has an utterly unremarkable facade yet a thoroughly French and unpretentiously sophisticated interior. The menu is one of the most extraordinary in the city, featuring fine ingredients in unusual flavor combinations that almost always hit the mark. Dinners here are multicourse affairs that change with the seasons. Expect such interesting creations as an ahi salad with avocado, fresh wasabi, and citrus vinaigrette; chilled tomato soup; smoked quail with organic fingerling potatoes, truffles, truffle oil, and wine sauce; saddle of rabbit with lentils and sautéed foie gras; and lobster with polenta, corn, chanterelles and port-wine sauce.

1126 SW 18th Ave. (℮) **503/225-1844.** www.couvron.com. Reservations required. Prix fixe menus only: $65 (vegetarian), $75, or $95. AE, MC, V. Tues–Sat 5:30–9pm.

EXPENSIVE

In addition to the restaurants listed below, two high-end steakhouse chains—**Ruth's Chris Steak House,** 309 SW Third Ave. (℮ **503/221-4518**) and **Morton's,** 213 SW Clay St. (℮ **503/248-2005**)—both have restaurants in downtown Portland.

The Heathman Restaurant and Bar ✸✸✸ NORTHWEST/FRENCH

This grande dame of Northwest-style restaurants serves Northwest cuisine with a French accent, and in 2001, executive chef Philippe Boulot received the James Beard Foundation's "Best Chef in the Northwest" award. Boulot's menu changes seasonally, but one thing remains constant: The ingredients used are the very freshest of Oregon and Northwest seafood, meat, wild game, and produce. The interior is Art Deco inspired, the atmosphere bistro-like. The menu changes daily and is quite extensive. We advise picking appetizers and entrees from the "Northwest Specialties" lists, but the dishes from the grill are also good choices. The bar offers Northwest microbrewery beers on tap, while an extensive wine list spotlights Oregon wines.

The Heathman Hotel has an extensive collection of classic and contemporary art, and on the restaurant walls you'll find Andy Warhol's *Endangered Species* series.

In the Heathman Hotel, 1001 SW Broadway. (℮) **503/790-7758.** Reservations highly recommended. Main courses $7.25–$15 at lunch, $16–$30 at dinner. AE, DC, MC, V. Mon–Fri 6:30–11am and 11:30am–2pm; Sat–Sun 7am–2pm; Mon–Thurs 5–10pm; Fri–Sat 5–11pm.

Higgins ✸✸✸ NORTHWEST/MEDITERRANEAN

Higgins, located just up Broadway from the Heathman Hotel, where chef Greg Higgins first made a name for himself in Portland, strikes a balance between contemporary and classic in both decor and cuisine. The menu, which changes frequently, explores contemporary culinary horizons, while the decor in the tri-level dining room opts for wood paneling and elegant place settings. Yet despite all this, the restaurant remains unpretentious. Portions here can be surprisingly generous for a high-end restaurant. Flavors change with the season, but are often both subtle and earthy. A recent entree of roast pork loin with grilled sweet Walla Walla onions, cherry glace, and Swiss roesti-style potatoes highlighted the restaurant's ability to balance creativity with familiarity. Be sure to leave room for dessert, and if you happen to be a beer lover, you'll be glad to know that Higgins has one of the most interesting beer selections in town (plenty of good wine, too).

1239 SW Broadway. (℮) **503/222-9070.** Reservations recommended. Main courses $7.75–$13.75 at lunch, $16.50–$26.50 at dinner. AE, DC, MC, V. Mon–Fri 11:30am–2pm and 5–10:30pm; Sat–Sun 5–10:30pm; bistro menu served in the bar daily until midnight.

Where to Dine in Portland

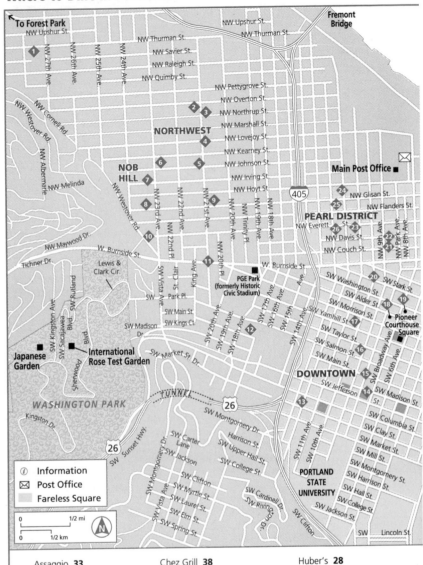

Assaggio **33**
Aztec Willie's,
  Joey Rose Taqueria **48**
Bijou Café **27**
bluehour **26**
Café Azul **22**
Caffe Mingo **5**
Caprial's Bistro & Wine **34**
Castagna **37**
Chart House **30**

Chez Grill **38**
Chez José East **49**
Couvron **12**
Esparza's Tex-Mex Café **45**
Fratelli **24**
Garbonzo's **4**
Genoa **41**
Good Dog/Bad Dog **18**
The Heathman Restaurant **15**
Higgins **14**

Huber's **28**
In Good Taste **23**
Jake's Famous Crawfish **20**
Ken's Home Plate **25**
Kitchen Table Café **43**
McCormick & Schmick's
  Harborside Restaurant **31**
Newport Bay Restaurant **32**
Nicholas's **44**
Old Wives' Tales **46**

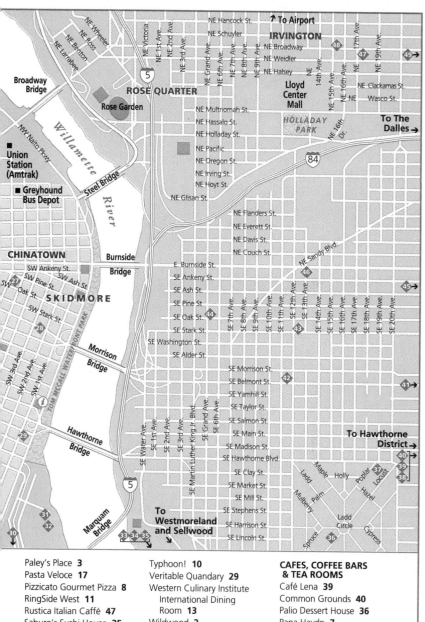

Paley's Place **3**
Pasta Veloce **17**
Pizzicato Gourmet Pizza **8**
RingSide West **11**
Rustica Italian Caffé **47**
Saburo's Sushi House **35**
Southpark Seafood Grill
  & Wine Bar **16**
Swagat **4**
Tapeo **1**

Typhoon! **10**
Veritable Quandary **29**
Western Culinary Institute
  International Dining
  Room **13**
Wildwood **2**

**CAFES, COFFEE BARS
& TEA ROOMS**
Café Lena **39**
Common Grounds **40**
Palio Dessert House **36**
Papa Haydn **7**
Pearl Bakery **21**
Peet's Coffee **19**
Rimsky-Korsakoffee House **42**
Torrefazione Italia **6**

Veritable Quandary ★★ NEW AMERICAN   Located in an old brick building just a block off Tom McCall Waterfront Park, this restaurant is a must for summer meals. The restaurant's garden patio, the prettiest in town, faces a small park. The menu changes daily, but keep an eye out for the grilled prawns, sometimes served with strawberries and green peppercorn sauce, and don't pass up the *osso buco*. The chef here pulls in all kinds of influences, so don't be surprised if you find grilled beef skewers with a Peruvian marinade or prosciutto with fig molasses, fresh figs, and warm bruschetta, or springs rolls filled with duck confit, shiitakes, and Chinese cabbage (served with a side of wasabi-ginger sauce).

1220 SW First Ave. © 503/227-7342. Reservations recommended. Main courses $16–$25. AE, DC, DISC, MC, V. Mon–Fri 11:30am–3pm; Sat–Sun 9:30am–3:30pm; Sun–Thurs 5–10pm; Fri–Sat 5–11pm.

MODERATE

There's an outpost of **Typhoon!** at 400 SW Broadway (© **503/224-8285**), in the Imperial Hotel. See the complete review on p. 80.

Huber's ★ *Finds* AMERICAN   Huber's, Portland's oldest restaurant, first opened its doors to the public in 1879 and is tucked inside the Oregon Pioneer Building down a quiet hallway. The main room has a vaulted stained-glass ceiling, Philippine mahogany paneling, and the original brass cash register.

Turkey dinner with all the trimmings is the house specialty, but you can also gobble turkey enchiladas, turkey Parmesan, and even Moroccan turkey. Another specialty is Spanish coffee made with rum, Kahlua, Triple Sec, coffee, and cream. The preparation, which involves flaming the rum in a wine glass, is a very impressive tableside production. Because Huber's bar is quite popular, you'll probably enjoy your meal more if you come for lunch instead of dinner. Be sure to ask for a table in the old vaulted room.

411 SW Third Ave. © 503/228-5686. www.hubers.com. Reservations recommended. Main courses $6–$20 at lunch, $8–$20 at dinner. AE, DC, DISC, MC, V. Mon–Thurs 11:30am–midnight; Fri 11:30am–1am; Sat noon–1am.

Jake's Famous Crawfish ★★ SEAFOOD   Great seafood at reasonable prices make this place a winner. Jake's has been a Portland institution since 1909, and the back bar came all the way around Cape Horn in 1880. Much of the rest of the decor looks just as old and well worn as the bar and therein lies this restaurant's charm.

There's a daily menu listing a dozen or more specials, but there's really no question about what to eat at Jake's: crawfish, which are always on the menu and are served several different ways. Monday through Friday from 3 to 6pm, bar appetizers are only $1.95. The noise level after work, when local businesspeople pack the bar, can be high, and the wait for a table can be long if you don't make a reservation. However, don't let these obstacles put you off.

401 SW 12th Ave. © 503/226-1419. Reservations recommended. Main courses $5–$13 at lunch, $10–$43 at dinner. AE, DC, DISC, MC, V. Mon–Fri 11:30am–11pm; Sat 4–11pm; Sun 4–10pm.

McCormick and Schmick's Harborside Restaurant ★★ SEAFOOD   Anchoring the opposite end of RiverPlace Esplanade from the RiverPlace Hotel, this large glitzy seafood restaurant serves up a view of the Willamette and excellent seafood. Four dining levels assure everyone a view of the river and marina below, and in summer, customers head out to tables on the Esplanade. Because it's so popular, the place tends to be noisy and the help can sometimes be a bit harried; however, this doesn't detract from the fine food. Although seafood (such as blackened cod with cilantro-lime butter or macadamia-encrusted mahimahi with tropical fruit salsa) is the main attraction here, the menu is quite extensive. The clientele is mostly upscale, especially at lunch and during the after-work hours.

0309 SW Montgomery St. ℭ **503/220-1865.** Reservations recommended. Main courses $9.75–$24. AE, DC, DISC, MC, V. Mon–Thurs 11am–10pm; Fri–Sat 11am–11pm; Sun 10am–3pm and 4–10pm.

Newport Bay Restaurant 🌟 *(Kids)* SEAFOOD   Though there are Newport Bay restaurants all over the Portland area, this one has by far the best location—floating on the Willamette River. Located in the marina at Portland's beautiful RiverPlace shopping-and-dining complex, the Newport Bay provides excellent views of the river and the city skyline, especially from the deck. Popular with young couples, families, and boaters, this place exudes a cheery atmosphere, and service is efficient. Nearly everything on the menu has some sort of seafood in it, even the quiche, salads, and pastas. Entrees are straightforward and well prepared—nothing too fancy. Sunday brunch is a very good deal.

0425 SW Montgomery St. ℭ **503/227-3474.** www.newportbay.com. Reservations recommended. Main courses $10–$23; lunches and light main courses $6–$12. AE, DC, DISC, MC, V. Summer hours Mon–Thurs 11am–11pm; Fri–Sat 11am–midnight; Sun 10am–3pm (brunch) and 3–10pm. Closes 1 hr. earlier in winter.

Southpark Seafood Grill & Wine Bar 🌟🌟 *(Value)* MEDITERRANEAN/ SEAFOOD   Can it be true? An upscale restaurant/wine bar with downscale prices? Yes, that's exactly what you'll find here at Southpark (no relation to the TV show). So what's the catch? Wine prices are not as reasonable as the food prices, so what you save on your food bill, you'll probably spend on your wine. With its high ceiling, long heavy drapes, halogen lights, and interesting wall mural, the wine bar is a contemporary interpretation of a late-19th-century Parisian, and the main dining room is both comfortable and classy. For a starter, don't pass up the fried calamari served with salt-preserved lemons bursting with flavor. Equally delicious is the butternut squash and ricotta-filled ravioli with toasted hazelnuts, which comes in a rich marsala wine sauce that begs to be sopped up with the crusty bread. An extensive wine list presents some compelling choices, and the desserts are consistently fine.

901 SW Salmon St. ℭ **503/326-1300.** www.southpark.citysearch.com. Reservations recommended. Main courses $8–$20. AE, DC, DISC, MC, V. Mon–Thurs 11:30am–midnight; Fri 11:30am–1am; Sat 11am–1am; Sun 10am–midnight.

INEXPENSIVE

Bijou Café 🌟 NATURAL FOODS   The folks who run the Bijou take both food and health seriously. They'll serve you a bowl of steamed brown rice and raisins for breakfast, but you can also get delicious fresh oyster hash or brioche French toast. However, the real hits here are the sautéed potatoes and the muffins, which come with full breakfasts. Don't leave without trying them. Local and organic products are used as often as possible at this comfortably old-fashioned cafe.

132 SW Third Ave. ℭ **503/222-3187.** Breakfast and lunch $4–$9. MC, V. Mon–Fri 7am–2pm; Sat–Sun 8am–2pm.

Pasta Veloce 🌟 ITALIAN   Pasta Veloce, which translates roughly as "noodles in a hurry," really lives up to its name—it's a quick, cheap place to get a tasty Italian meal downtown. Portions are not huge, but they are satisfying and come with rustic grilled bread. We really like the gnocchi with chicken, broccoli, and walnuts in a Gorgonzola sauce. Wine and beer are available at prices that match those of the pastas. There are two convenient locations.

933 SW Third Ave. (① **503/223-8200**) and 1022 SW Morrison St. (① **503/916-4388**). Main courses $5.25–$7.50. AE, DISC, MC, V. Third Ave. location Mon–Thurs 11am–8pm; Fri 11am–8:30pm; Sat noon–8:30pm. Morrison location Mon–Thurs 11:30am–9pm; Fri 11:30am–9:30pm; Sat noon–9:30pm.

Western Culinary Institute International Dining Room ☆ (*Value*
CONTINENTAL/AMERICAN   If you happen to be a frugal gourmet whose palate is more sophisticated than your wallet can afford, you'll want to schedule a meal here. The dining room serves five- to six-course gourmet meals prepared by advanced students at prices even a budget traveler can afford. The dining room decor is modern and unassuming, and the students who wait on you are eager to please. For each course you can choose from among two to half a dozen offerings. A sample dinner menu might begin with velouté Andalouse followed by sautéed vegetables in a puff pastry, a pear sorbet, grilled ahi tuna with black bean salsa, Chinese salad with smoked salmon, and mocha cheesecake. Remember, that's all for under $20! The five-course lunch for only $9.95 is an even better deal.

1316 SW 13th Ave. ① **503/294-9770** or 800/666-0312. Reservations required. 5-course lunch **$9.95**; 6-course dinner $19.95; Thurs buffet $19.95. AE, MC, V. Tues–Fri 11:30am–1pm and 6–8pm.

NORTHWEST PORTLAND (INCLUDING THE PEARL DISTRICT & NOB HILL)
EXPENSIVE

bluehour ☆ FRENCH/ITALIAN   Restaurateur Bruce Carey has long dominated the Portland restaurant scene, and here at his latest high-style restaurant, he continues to woo and wow the local trendsetters. Despite the location in a recently converted warehouse that serves as headquarters for Portland advertising giant Wieden+Kennedy, bluehour has a very theatrical atmosphere. With sophisticated menu items such as pan-seared foie gras and smoked goose prosciutto, it's obvious that bluehour is issuing a challenge to Portland's other high-end restaurants. Unfortunately, the cacophonous noise level and tightly packed tables severely detract from the cultured cuisine. If you value conversation with your meal, steer clear of bluehour. This is definitely the sort of place where being seen by the right people is more important than the food.

250 NW 13th Ave. ① **503/226-3394.** www.bluehour.com. Reservations highly recommended. Main dishes $17.50–$30. AE, MC, V. Mon–Thurs 11:30am–2:30pm and 6–10pm; Fri 11:30am–2:30pm and 6–10:30pm; Sat 5:30–10:30pm.

Café Azul ☆☆ GOURMET MEXICAN   Located in the Pearl District in what was clearly once an old warehouse, Café Azul is a long, narrow space softened by expanses of warm yellow and terra-cotta walls. The food here includes some of the best regional Mexican dishes you're likely to find this side of the border. Tasty margaritas are generous and can be made with a number of different tequilas; sangrita, a spicy nonalcoholic ancho chili and orange drink, also gets two thumbs up. Start by spreading some dangerously tasty chili butter on a crusty roll, then follow this with a taco sampler platter that includes handmade corn tortillas served with Yucatecan-style pork roasted in banana leaves. From Oaxaca, Mexico, comes the inspiration for Café Azul's *mole,* a rich, spicy sauce made with more than two-dozen ingredients, including toasted nuts, chocolate, and chilies, which might be served over chicken or duck. The housemade ice creams and sorbets, often made with unusual tropical fruits, are always a fitting finale. This may be expensive for Mexican food, but it's well worth it.

112 NW Ninth Ave. ① **503/525-4422.** Reservations recommended. Main courses $16.50–$25. DISC, MC, V. Tues–Thurs 5–9pm; Fri–Sat 5–9:30pm.

Paley's Place ★★ NORTHWEST/FRENCH   Located in a Victorian-era house, Paley's is a favorite of Portland foodies. The menu ranges from traditional bistro fare to dishes with a hint of Northwest inspiration and relies extensively on the freshest local organic ingredients. Chef Vitaly Paley and his wife Kimberly run the show here and continue to receive accolades year after year. Whether you're in the mood for steamed mussels or something more unusual (pasta with chickpeas, preserved tuna, dried tuna roe, and mint), you'll certainly find something that appeals. If you've never tried sweetbreads, this is the place to do so, and the signature *frites,* with a mustard aioli, are not to be missed. Big on wines, Paley's offers wine tasting on Wednesdays and an occasional wine-maker dinner. For dessert, we can't pass up the warm chocolate soufflé with ice cream. In good weather, the front porch is the better place to dine. Inside, the restaurant is small and stylishly comfortable but can be quite noisy.

1204 NW 21st Ave. ② **503/243-2403.** www.paleysplace.citysearch.com. Reservations highly recommended. Main courses $15–$26. AE, MC, V. Mon–Thurs 5:30–10pm; Fri–Sat 5:30–11pm; Sun 5–10pm.

RingSide West ★ STEAK   Despite the location on a rather unattractive stretch of West Burnside Street, RingSide has long been a favorite Portland steak house. Boxing may be the main theme of the restaurant, but the name is a two-fisted pun that also refers to the incomparable onion rings that should be an integral part of any meal here. Have your rings with a side order of one of their perfectly cooked steaks for a real knockout meal.

There's also a RingSide East at 14021 NE Glisan St. (② **503/255-0750**), on Portland's east side, with basically the same menu but not as much atmosphere; this one is open for lunch during the week.

2165 W. Burnside St. ② **503/223-1513.** www.ringsidesteakhouse.com. Reservations highly recommended. Steaks $14–$27; other main courses $15–$38. AE, DC, DISC, MC, V. Mon–Sat 5pm–midnight; Sun 4–11:30pm.

Wildwood ★★ NEW AMERICAN   With a menu that changes daily and a spare, elegant interior decor straight out of *Architectural Digest,* Wildwood has for many years been considered one of Portland's best restaurants. Lately, however, dishes have been a bit hit-or-miss, with the appetizers, salads, and desserts often outshining the entrees. But if you love creative cuisine you may still want to give this place a try. Fresh seasonal ingredients combined into simple-yet-imaginative dishes are the hallmark of chef Cory Schreiber's cooking, and often there are no more than four ingredients in a dish so as to let each of the flavors shine through. On a recent evening, there were skillet-roasted Wash-ington mussels with garlic, tomato, and saffron and an excellent oyster-topped salad with pancetta and aioli. This is the only non-Indian restaurant we know of that has a tandoor oven, and you can usually count on the meat dishes that are roasted in this oven. Salads and sorbets are exceptionally good. If you can't get a reservation, you can still usually get served at the bar.

1221 NW 21st Ave. ② **503/248-WOOD.** www.wildwoodrestaurant.citysearch.com. Reservations highly recommended. Main courses $9–$13 at lunch, $16–$25 at dinner. AE, MC, V. Mon–Sat 11:30am–2:30pm and 5:30–10pm; Sun 10am–2pm (brunch).

MODERATE

Caffe Mingo ★★ *Finds* ITALIAN   This intimate little neighborhood restaurant has terrific food, an interior as attractive as that of any other upscale restaurant here on Restaurant Row, and lower prices. If there's any problem with this immensely popular place it's that you almost always have to wait for a table and they only take reservations for larger parties. The solution? Get here as early as pos-sible. The menu is short, and focuses on painstakingly prepared Italian comfort food. Just about all of the items on the menu are winners, from the antipasto platter, which might include roasted fennel, fresh mozzarella, and roasted red pepper, to an unusual penne pasta dish with tender beef braised in Chianti and espresso. The *panna cotta* dessert ("cooked cream" with fruit) is reason enough to come back here again and again, even if you have to wait in the rain to get a seat.

807 NW 21st Ave. ⓒ **503/226-4646.** Reservations accepted only for parties of 6 or more. Main courses $8.50–$18. AE, DISC, MC, V. Sun–Thurs 5–10pm; Fri–Sat 5–11pm.

Fratelli ✿✿ REGIONAL ITALIAN   In this rustic-yet-chic restaurant, cement walls provide a striking contrast to dramatic draperies and candles that drip casually onto the tabletops. Dishes are consistently good, with surprisingly moderate prices for the Pearl District. There's excellent olive oil to go with your bread and an *antipasto* plate that's far more creative than your usual platter of meat, cheese, and pickled vegetables. On a recent visit, everything we tasted, from spring beans with arugula and octopus to chicken wrapped in prosciutto to rabbit *crepinette* (a sort of sausage) to a luscious panna cotta, was thoroughly satisfying. This restaurant's aesthetic and menu are similar to Caffe Mingo's (see above), but at Fratelli you can make reservations.

1230 NW Hoyt St. ⓒ **503/241-8800.** Reservations recommended. Main courses $11–$16.50. AE, DC, MC, V. Sun–Thurs 5:30–9pm; Fri–Sat 5:30–10pm.

Tapeo ✿✿ *(Finds)* SPANISH   This a great place for a light meal or a romantic evening out. With the feeling of an old European restaurant, this small yet plush neighborhood spot nestled deep in Northwest Portland seems intimate, but the noise level rises considerably when the place is full—which is often. People wait around for the tables, which are placed so close together that you might as well be sitting with your neighbor. But it's worth the wait for authentic Spanish tapas such as excellent grilled eggplant thinly sliced and stuffed with goat cheese and deliciously crisp fried calamari served with aioli. The flan is the richest you'll ever taste. Prices on wines, both by the glass and bottle, are decent.

2764 NW Thurman St. ⓒ **503/226-0409.** Reservations not accepted. Tapas $1.75–$9. DISC, MC, V. Tues–Thurs 5:30–10pm; Fri–Sat 5–10:30pm.

Typhoon! ✿ THAI   Located just off NW 23rd Avenue, this trendy spot is a bit pricey for a Thai restaurant, but the unusual menu offerings generally aren't available at other Portland Thai restaurants. Be sure to start a meal with the *miang kum,* which consists of dried shrimp, tiny chilies, ginger, lime, peanuts, shallots, and toasted coconut drizzled with a sweet-and-sour sauce and wrapped up in a spinach leaf. The burst of flavors on your taste buds is absolutely astounding. (We first had this in Thailand and waited years to get it in the United States.) The whole front wall of the restaurant slides away for Thai-style open-air dining in the summer. There is an extensive tea list.

There's another **Typhoon!** at 400 SW Broadway (ⓒ **503/224-8285**), in the Imperial Hotel.

2310 NW Everett St. ⓒ **503/243-7557.** Reservations recommended. Main courses $7–$20. AE, DC, DISC, MC, V. Mon–Fri 11:30am–2:30pm; Sat noon–3pm; Mon–Thurs 5–9:30pm; Fri–Sat 5–10:30pm; Sun 4:30–9:30pm.

INEXPENSIVE

Garbonzo's MIDDLE EASTERN/LATE-NIGHT DINING   This casual little place calls itself a falafel bar and is a popular spot for a late-night meal (but it's also good for lunch or dinner). The menu includes all the usual Middle Eastern offerings, most of which also happen to be American Heart Association approved. You can eat at one of the tiny cafe tables or get your order to go. They even serve beer and wine.

Other Garbonzo's are at 3433 SE Hawthorne Blvd. (© **503/239-6087**) and 6341 SW Capitol Hwy. (© **503/293-7335**).

922 NW 21st Ave. © **503/227-4196**. Sandwiches $4–$5; dinners $7–$9. AE, DISC, MC, V. Sun–Thurs 11:30am–12:30am; Fri–Sat 11:30am–2am (closed 1 hr. earlier Oct–June).

Ken's Home Plate ⟨ℛ⟩ *(Finds)* INTERNATIONAL   You could easily overlook this little hole-in-the-wall, but once you step inside and see the beautifully prepared foods in the display cases, you'll probably be as hooked as we are. Eating here once is enough to have you dreaming about living in the neighborhood, so you could get all your meals here. Chef/owner Ken Gordon turns out dishes that would do justice to the best restaurants in town, and on any given day 15 to 20 different entrees such as salmon strudel, Tuscan meatloaf, chicken marsala, and Louisiana gumbo are available. However, you might have trouble getting past the delicious sandwiches, which come with a side of any of more than half a dozen salads. Desserts are prominently displayed on the countertop, making them very difficult to ignore. Although this is primarily a take-out place, there are a few tables in case you can't wait to dig in.

1208 NW Glisan St. © **503/517-8935**. Plates and sandwiches $5–$8.50. MC, V. Tues–Sat 11am–8pm; until 9pm on 1st Thurs of each month.

Swagat ⟨ℛ⟩ *(Value)* INDIAN   Located on the same corner as Garbonzo's (see above) is an exceptionally good Indian restaurant specializing in south Indian dishes. The *dosas,* crepes made of lentil flour stuffed with vegetable curry and served with a variety of sauces, are deliciously savory, and the tandoori chicken is intriguingly smoky. Be sure to start your meal with the sambar, a thin but flavorful soup. We also like the vegetable samosas, crisp turnovers stuffed with potatoes and peas, and the *keema mattar* (ground lamb with peas). Don't forget to order some of the puffy nan bread. At lunch, there is an extensive buffet that at $6.95 is a very good deal.

Another Swagat is located in the west-side suburb of Beaverton at 4325 SW 109th Ave. (© **503/626-3000**).

2074 NW Lovejoy St. © **503/227-4300**. Reservations not accepted. Main courses $7–$14. AE, DISC, MC, V. Daily 11:30am–2:30pm and 5–10pm.

SOUTHWEST PORTLAND
EXPENSIVE

Chart House ⟨ℛℛ⟩ SEAFOOD   Although this place is a part of a national restaurant chain with lots of outposts all over California and the rest of the West, it also happens to boast the best view of any restaurant in Portland. On top of that, it serves the best New England clam chowder in the state. (The recipe repeatedly won awards in a Boston chowder competition.) While you savor your chowder, you can marvel at the views of the Willamette River, Mount Hood, Mount St. Helens, and nearly all of Portland's east side. Fresh fish, either grilled, baked, or blackened is the house specialty. You'll also find a selection of excellent steaks for the problem child in your group who just won't eat seafood. No dinner here is complete without the hot chocolate lava cake, which has to be ordered at the start of your meal if you want it to be ready when you are.

The Chart House is in an out-of-the-way spot about a 10-minute drive from downtown Portland; be sure to call ahead and get driving directions.

5700 SW Terwilliger Blvd. © **503/246-6963**. Reservations recommended. Main courses $10–$16 at lunch, $15–$40 at dinner. AE, DC, DISC, MC, V. Mon–Fri 11:30am–2pm; Mon–Sat 5–10pm; Sun 5–9pm.

Kids Family-Friendly Restaurants

Aztec Willie & Joey Rose Tacqueria *(see below)* Cheap Mexican and a glassed-in children's play area make this a good choice for families on a budget.

Chez José East *(see below)* Kids under 6 eat free at this friendly Mexican restaurant between 5 and 7pm.

Newport Bay Restaurant *(see p. 77)* A cheery atmosphere, straightforward meals, and a great location on the Willamette River make this a good family pick.

Old Wives' Tales *(see p. 84)* This is just about the best place in Portland to eat if you've got small children. There are children's menus at all meals, and in the back of the restaurant there's a playroom that will keep your kids entertained while you enjoy your meal.

Rustica Italian Caffe *(see below)* A long menu of kiddie-friendly food and an unpretentious atmosphere.

INEXPENSIVE

For Middle Eastern fare, there's a branch of **Garbonzo's** at 6341 SW Capitol Hwy. (© **503/293-7335**). See the complete review on p. 80.

There's also a **Chez José West** at 8502 SW Terwilliger Blvd. (© **503/244-0007**); see the review of Chez José East below.

NORTHEAST PORTLAND (INCLUDING IRVINGTON)
MODERATE

Rustica Italian Caffe ⍟ *Kids* ITALIAN If you're looking for good, moderately priced Italian food in Northeast Portland, look no further than Rustica. The menu is long, portions are large, and they have a nice selection of Chiantis and great bread. What more could you ask for? In addition, the atmosphere is unpretentious, the space light and airy, and it's a popular spot for families. There is also a small pizzeria adjacent to the main restaurant. Among our favorite dishes here are the smoked-salmon cannelloni and the prawns sautéed in olive oil with grapefruit, rosemary, chili flakes, and cream.

1700 NE Broadway. © 503/288-0990. Reservations recommended. Main courses $11–$17. AE, DISC, MC, V. Mon–Fri 11:30am–2:30pm; Mon–Thurs 5–9:30pm; Fri–Sat 5–10:30pm; Sun 5–9pm.

INEXPENSIVE

Aztec Willie & Joey Rose Tacqueria *Kids* MEXICAN It's hard to miss this hip-yet-casual Mexican place with its copper pyramid over the front door and Mayan glyphs decorating the facade. Associated with perennial favorite Mayas Tacqueria in downtown Portland, Aztec Willie is a big place where you order cafeteria-style. For adults, there's a bar, and for kids, there's a glassed-in play area.

1501 NE Broadway. © 503/280-8900. Reservations not accepted. Main courses $3–$9. AE, DISC, MC, V. Daily 11am–11pm.

Chez José East ⍟ *Kids* MEXICAN It's obvious both from the hip decor and the menu that this isn't Taco Bell. Although a squash enchilada with peanut sauce (spicy and sweet with mushrooms, apples, jicama, and sunflower seeds) sounds weird, it actually tastes great. Don't worry, though, there's also plenty of traditional—and traditionally cheap—fare on the menu. Because the restaurant doesn't take reservations, it's a good idea to get here early, before the line starts snaking out the door. This is a family-friendly place, so don't hesitate to bring the kids, and if the kids are under 6, they'll eat for free between 5 and 7pm.

2200 NE Broadway. ✆ **503/280-9888.** Reservations accepted for 7 or more. Main courses $5.75–$11.50. AE, MC, V. Mon–Thurs 11:30am–11pm; Fri–Sat 11:30am–midnight; Sun 5–10pm.

HAWTHORNE, BELMONT & INNER SOUTHEAST PORTLAND
VERY EXPENSIVE

Genoa ✿✿✿ REGIONAL ITALIAN   This has long been the best Italian restaurant in Portland, and with fewer than a dozen tables, it's also one of the smallest. Everything, from the breads to the luscious desserts, is made fresh in the kitchen with the best local seasonal ingredients. This is an ideal setting for a romantic dinner, and service is attentive—the waiter explains dishes in detail as they are served, and dishes are magically whisked away as they're finished. The fixed-price menu changes every couple of weeks, but a typical dinner might start with *bagna cauda*, a creamy garlic and anchovy fondue, followed by spicy mussel soup. The pasta course could be a lasagna, with braised fresh artichokes layered with a béchamel sauce and Parmigiano-Reggiano cheese. There's always a choice of main courses, such as trout stuffed with chanterelle mushrooms, prosciutto, and tomatoes or pan-roasted rabbit with fennel and white wine. It takes Herculean restraint to choose from a selection that includes chocolate and nut tortes, fresh berry tarts, or liqueur-infused desserts.

2832 SE Belmont St. ✆ **503/238-1464.** www.genoarestaurant.com. Reservations required. Fixed-price 4-course dinner $56, 7-course dinner $68. AE, DC, DISC, MC, V. Mon–Sat 5:30–9:30pm (4-course dinner limited to 5:30 and 6pm seatings only).

EXPENSIVE

Castagna ✿✿ FRENCH/ITALIAN   Located on a rather nondescript stretch of Hawthorne Boulevard and much removed from the bustle of this boulevard's central commercial area, Castagna is a magnet for Portland foodies. Considering the less than stylish setting and minimalist (though thoroughly designed) interior, it's obvious that the food's the thing here. Dishes tend toward simple preparations that allow the freshness of the ingredients to express themselves. A friend swears the New York steak, served with a heaping mound of shoestring potatoes, is the best he's ever had; no wonder it's a house favorite here. However, less familiar entrees, such as salmon with fingerling potatoes and preserved Meyer lemon salsa or grilled rack of lamb with mint salsa verde and fava bean salad, flesh out the menu. In addition to the main dining room, there is a more casual and inexpensive cafe dining room serving much simpler fare.

1752 SE Hawthorne Blvd. ✆ **503/231-7373.** Reservations highly recommended. Main dishes $20–$28; cafe main courses $9–$18. AE, DC, DISC, MC, V. Tues–Thurs 6–10pm; Fri 6–10:30pm; Sat 5:30–10:30pm.

MODERATE

Assaggio ✿✿ RUSTIC ITALIAN   This trattoria in the Sellwood neighborhood focuses on pastas and wines; the menu lists 15 pastas, and the wine list includes more than 100 wines, almost all Italian. The atmosphere in this tiny place is theatrical, with indirect lighting, dark walls, and the likes of Mario Lanza playing in the background. The pastas, with surprisingly robust flavors, are the main attraction. Don't be surprised if after taking your first bite, you suddenly hear a Verdi aria. *Assaggio* means a sampling or a taste, and that is exactly what you get if you order salad, bruschetta, or pasta Assaggio-style—a sampling of several dishes, all served family-style. This is especially fun if you're here with a group.

7742 SE 13th Ave. ℭ 503/232-6151. www.assaggiorestaurant.com. Reservations accepted (and recommended) only Tues–Thurs or for parties of 6 or more. Main courses $10–$16. MC, V. Tues–Thurs 5–9:30pm; Fri–Sat 5–10pm.

INEXPENSIVE

For Middle Eastern fare, there's a branch of Garbonzo's at 3433 SE Hawthorne Blvd. (ℭ **503/239-6087**). See the complete review on p. 80.

Chez Grill ⋆ SOUTHWEST   Brought to you by the owners of Portland's popular Chez José restaurants, Chez Grill leans more toward nuevo Mexican or Southwestern flavors. Although the restaurant is at the western end of the Hawthorne district, it looks as if it could have been transported straight from Tucson or Santa Fe. Whatever you do, don't miss the grilled fish tacos; they're the best in town! The grilled prawn enchilada is also exquisite, although you only get one (with rice and beans). Be sure to start a meal with the rough-cut guacamole; for a strangely sweet appetizer, try the unusual stuffed avocado.

2229 SE Hawthorne Blvd. ℭ **503/239-4002**. www.chezgrill.citysearch.com. Main courses $6.25–$14. DISC, MC, V. Mon–Thurs 4–10pm; Fri–Sat 4–11pm; Sun 5–10pm (bar open later nightly).

Esparza's Tex-Mex Café ⋆ *Finds* TEX-MEX   With red-eyed cow skulls on the walls and marionettes, model planes, and stuffed iguanas and armadillos hanging from the ceiling, the decor here can only be described as Tex-eclectic, a description that is just as appropriately applied to the menu. Sure there are enchiladas and tamales and tacos, but they might be filled with ostrich, buffalo meat, or smoked salmon. Rest assured Esparza's also serves standard ingredients such as chicken and beef. Main courses come with some pretty good rice and beans, and if you want your meal hotter, they'll toss you a couple of jalapeño peppers. The *nopalitos* (fried cactus) are worth a try, and the margaritas just might be the best in Portland. While you're waiting for a seat (there's almost always a wait), check out the vintage tunes on the jukebox.

2725 SE Ankeny St. ℭ **503/234-7909**. Reservations not accepted. Main courses $7.25–$14.50. AE, DC, DISC, MC, V. Tues–Sat 11:30am–10pm (in summer Fri–Sat until 10:30pm).

Nicholas's *Finds* MIDDLE EASTERN   This little hole-in-the-wall on an unattractive stretch of Grand Avenue is usually packed at mealtimes, and it's not the decor or ambience that pulls people in. The big draw is the great food and cheap prices. In spite of the heat from the pizza oven and the crowded conditions, the customers and wait staff still manage to be friendly. Our favorite dish is the *Manakish,* Mediterranean pizza with thyme, oregano, sesame seeds, olive oil, and lemony-flavored sumac. Also available are a creamy hummus, baba ghanoush, kabobs, falafel, and gyros.

318 SE Grand Ave. (between Pine and Oak sts.). ℭ **503/235-5123**. Reservations not accepted. Main courses $4.25–$10.75. No credit cards. Mon–Sat 11am–9pm; Sun noon–9pm.

Old Wives' Tales ⋆ *Kids* INTERNATIONAL/VEGETARIAN   Old Wives' Tales is a Portland countercultural institution. The menu is mostly vegetarian, with multi-ethnic dishes such as spanakopita and burritos and a smattering of chicken and seafood dishes. Breakfasts here are excellent and are served until 2pm daily. Old Wives' Tales's other claim to fame these days is as the city's best place to eat out with kids. The restaurant has plenty of meal choices for children, and there's a big playroom where the kids can stay busy while you enjoy your meal.

1300 E Burnside St. ⓒ **503/238-0470.** Reservations recommended for parties of 5 or more. Breakfasts $5–$7; lunch and dinner main courses $6–$13. AE, DC, DISC, MC, V. Sun–Thurs 8am–9pm; Fri–Sat 8am–10pm.

WESTMORELAND & SELLWOOD
EXPENSIVE

Caprial's Bistro and Wine ★★ NORTHWEST   If you're a foodie, you're probably already familiar with celebrity chef Caprial Pence, who helped put the Northwest on the national restaurant map and has since gone on to write several cookbooks and host TV and radio food shows. That her eponymously named restaurant is a fairly casual place tucked away in a quiet residential neighborhood in Southeast Portland may come as a surprise. The menu changes monthly and is limited to four or five main dishes and about twice as many appetizers. Entrees combine perfectly cooked meat and seafood with vibrant sauces such as cherry barbecue sauce. Pork loin is always a good bet here, as are the seasonal seafood dishes. Desserts are usually rich without being overly sweet. There is also a wine bar offering a superb selection of wines at reasonable prices.

7015 SE Milwaukie Ave. ⓒ **503/236-6457.** Dinner reservations highly recommended. Main courses $7–$12 at lunch, $20–$26 at dinner. MC, V. Tues–Fri 11am–3pm; Sat 11:30am–3pm; Tues–Thurs 5–9pm; Fri–Sat 5–9:30pm.

MODERATE

Saburo's Sushi House ★★ JAPANESE   This tiny sushi restaurant is so enormously popular that there is almost always a line out the door, and as people linger over their sushi, frequently ordering "just one more," the line doesn't always move very fast. But when you finally do get a seat and your sushi arrives, you'll know it was worth the wait. The big slabs of fresh fish drape over the sides of the little cubes of rice, leaving no question about whether you get your money's worth here. Our favorites are the *sabu* roll and the maguro tuna sushi, with generous slabs of tuna.

1667 SE Bybee Blvd. ⓒ **503/236-4237.** Reservations not accepted. Main courses $8–$16; sushi $2.50–$7. DISC, MC, V. Mon–Thurs 5–9:30pm; Fri 5–10:30pm; Sat 4:30–10pm; Sun 4:30–9pm.

COFFEE, TEA, BAKERIES & PASTRY SHOPS
CAFES

If you'd like to sample some cafes around Portland that serve not only the full range of coffee drinks, but are also atmospheric, we recommend the following:

Café Lena, 2239 SE Hawthorne Blvd. (ⓒ **503/238-7087**), located in the funky Hawthorne District, has occasional live music and tasty food but is best known for its poetry nights.

Located out beyond Hawthorne Boulevard's main shopping district, **Common Grounds,** 4321 SE Hawthorne Blvd. (ⓒ **503/236-4835**), is a countercultural hangout where the magazine rack is filled with literary reviews, small press journals, and other lefty literature. The crowd of coffee drinkers tends to be tattooed and pierced.

Peet's Coffee ★, 508 SW Broadway (ⓒ **503/973-5540**), a relative newcomer in Portland, is notable not only for its great (and strong) coffee, but also for the fact that the space here is much larger than at any Peet's you'd find in Berkeley, California, where the chain originated.

Torrefazione Italia ★★, 838 NW 23rd Ave. (ⓒ **503/228-1255**), serves its classic brew in hand-painted Italian crockery and has a good selection of pastries to go with your drink. Order a latte just to see what a wonderful job they do with the foam. Other locations are at 1403 NE Weidler (© **503/288-1608**) and 1140 NW Everett (© **503/224-9896**).

BAKERIES & PASTRY SHOPS

Pearl Bakery ⚔⚔, 102 NW Ninth Ave. (© **503/827-0910**), in the heart of the SoHo-like Pearl district, is famous for its breads and European-style pastries. The gleaming bakery cafe is also good for sandwiches, such as the roasted eggplant and tomato pesto on crusty bread.

The **Rimsky-Korsakoffee House** ⚔, 707 SE 12th Ave. (© **503/232-2640**), a classic old-style coffeehouse (complete with mismatched chairs), has been Portland's favorite dessert hangout for more than a decade. Live classical music and great desserts keep patrons loyal. (The mocha fudge cake is small but deadly.) There's no sign on the old house, but you'll know this is the place as soon as you open the door. Open after 7pm and until midnight on weekdays, 1am on weekends.

Say the words *Papa Haydn* to a Portlander, and you'll see a blissful smile appear. What is it about this little bistro that sends locals into accolades of superlatives? The desserts. The lemon chiffon torte, raspberry gâteau, black velvet, and tiramisu at **Papa Haydn West** ⚔⚔, 701 NW 23rd Ave. (© **503/ 228-7317**), are legendary. There's another location at 5829 SE Milwaukie Ave. (© **503/232-9440**) in Sellwood.

Located in Ladd's Addition, an old neighborhood full of big trees and craftsman-style bungalows, **Palio Dessert House** ⚔, 1996 SE Ladd Ave. (© **503/232-9412**), is a very relaxed place with a timeless European quality. Hang out, play chess, or listen to music while you enjoy a slice of Key lime pie or banana bread. To get there, take Hawthorne Boulevard east to the corner of 12th and Hawthorne, then go diagonally down Ladd Avenue.

QUICK BITES & CHEAP EATS

If you're just looking for something quick, cheap, and good to eat, there are lots of great options around the city. Downtown, at **Good Dog/Bad Dog,** 708 SW Alder St. (© **503/222-3410**), you'll find handmade sausages. The bratwurst with kraut and onions is a good deal.

Designer pizzas topped with anything from roasted eggplant to wild mushrooms to Thai peanut sauce can be had at **Pizzicato Gourmet Pizza** ⚔. Find them downtown at 705 SW Alder St. (© **503/226-1007**); in Northwest at 505 NW 23rd Ave. (© **503/242-0023**); and in Southeast at 2811 E. Burnside (© **503/236-6045**).

In the Pearl District, there's **In Good Taste** ⚔ at 231 NW 11th Ave. (© **503/ 241-7960**), a cooking school and store that also serves a bistro lunch. Order such items as caramelized tomato tart and maple-spice pork loin sandwich at the counter and grab a seat.

Over in Southeast Portland, you can't miss the **Kitchen Table Café,** 400 SE 12th Ave. (© **503/230-6977**), in the yellow and purple building on the corner of SE Oak and SE 12th streets. This is a great place for homemade soups, salads, and sandwiches.

5 Seeing the Sights

Most American cities boast about their museums and historic buildings, shopping, and restaurants; Portland, as always, is different. Ask a Portlander about the city's must-see attractions, and you'll probably be directed to the

Japanese Garden, the International Rose Test Garden, and the Portland Saturday Market.

This isn't to say that the Portland Art Museum, which specializes in blockbuster exhibits, isn't worth visiting or that there are no historic buildings around. It's just that Portland's gardens, thanks to the weather here, are some of the finest in the country. What's more, all the rainy weather seems to keep artists indoors creating beautiful art and crafts for much of the year, work that many artists sell at the Portland Saturday Market.

Gardening is a Portland obsession, and there are numerous world-class public gardens and parks within the city. Visiting all the city's gardens alone can take up 2 or 3 days of touring, so leave plenty of time in your schedule if you have a green thumb.

Once you've seen the big attractions, it's time to start learning why everyone loves living here so much. Portlanders for the most part are active types, who enjoy snowskiing on Mount Hood and hiking in the Columbia Gorge just as much as going to art museums. So no visit to Portland would be complete without venturing out into the Oregon countryside. Within 1½ hours you can be skiing on Mount Hood, walking beside the chilly waters of the Pacific, sampling Pinot Noir in wine country, or hiking beside a waterfall in the Columbia Gorge. However, for those who prefer urban activities, the museums and parks listed below should satisfy.

DOWNTOWN PORTLAND'S CULTURAL DISTRICT

Any visit to Portland should start at the corner of Southwest Broadway and Yamhill Street on **Pioneer Courthouse Square.** The brick-paved square is an outdoor stage for everything from flower displays to concerts to protest rallies, but not too many years ago this beautiful area was nothing but a parking lot. The parking lot was created in 1951 when the Portland Hotel, an architectural gem of a Queen Anne–style château, was controversially razed to the ground.

Today the square, with its tumbling waterfall fountain and freestanding columns, is Portland's favorite gathering spot, especially at noon, when the *Weather Machine* ⊛, a mechanical sculpture, forecasts the weather for the next 24 hours. Amid a fanfare of music and flashing lights, the Weather Machine sends up clouds of mist and then either a sun (clear weather), a dragon (stormy weather), or a blue heron (clouds and drizzle) appears.

Keep your eyes on the square's brick pavement, too. Every brick contains a name (or names) or statement, and some are rather curious. Also on the square, you'll find the **Portland Oregon Visitor Association Information Center,** a Starbucks espresso bar, and Powell's Travel Store. Unfortunately, you'll also find plenty of street kids hanging out here all hours of the day and night, so don't be surprised if they ask you for spare change.

Also not to be missed in this neighborhood are *Portlandia* ⊛⊛ and the **Portland Building,** 1120 SW Fifth Ave. Symbol of the city, *Portlandia* is the second-largest hammered bronze statue in the country, second only to the Statue of Liberty. The massive kneeling figure holds a trident in one hand and reaches toward the street with the other. This classically designed figure perches incongruously above the entrance to the controversial Portland Building, considered to be the first postmodern structure in the country. Today anyone familiar with the bizarre constructions of Los Angeles architect Frank Gehry would find it difficult to understand how such an innocuous and attractive building could have ever raised such a fuss, but it did just that in the early '80s.

Portland Attractions

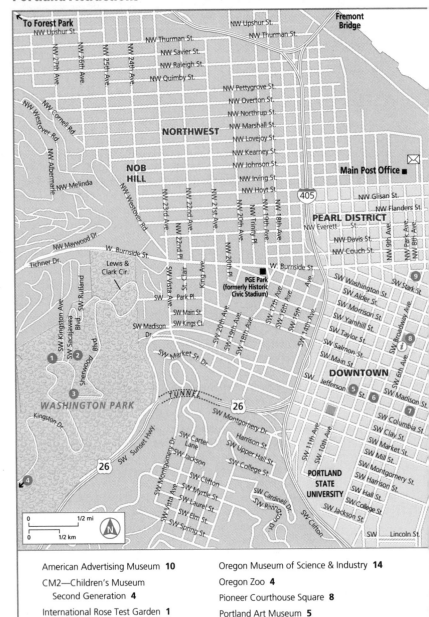

To Forest Park

NW Upshur St.
NW Upshur St.
NW Upshur St.
NW Thurman St.
NW Thurman St.
NW Thurman St.
NW Savier St.
NW Raleigh St.
NW Quimby St.

Fremont Bridge

NW 27th Ave.
NW 26th Ave.
NW 25th Ave.
NW 24th Ave.

NW Westover Rd.
NW Cornell Rd.
NW Pettygrove St.
NW Overton St.
NW Northrup St.
NORTHWEST NW Marshall St.
NW Lovejoy St.
NW Kearney St.
NW Johnson St.
NOB HILL NW Irving St.
NW Melinda NW Hoyt St.

NW Maywood Dr.
NW Albermarle
NW Westover Rd.

Main Post Office ■

405
NW Glisan St.
NW Flanders St.
PEARL DISTRICT
NW Everett St.
NW Davis St.
NW Couch St.

Tichner Dr.
Lewis & Clark Cir.
W. Burnside St.

NW 23rd Ave.
NW 22nd Ave.
NW 21st Ave.
NW 20th Ave.
NW 19th Ave.
NW 18th Ave.
NW Trinity Pl.

NW Park Ave.
NW 9th Ave.
NW 8th Ave.

W. Burnside St.
PGE Park (formerly Historic Civic Stadium)
W. Burnside St.

9

SW Kingston Ave.
SW Rutland
SW Sacajawea Blvd.
Sherwood Blvd.
SW Vista Ave.
Clay Ave.
King Ave.
NW 20th Pl.

SW Park Pl.
SW Main St.
SW Madison Dr.
SW Kings Ct.

SW 20th Ave.
SW 19th Ave.
SW 18th Ave.
SW 17th Ave.
SW 16th Ave.
SW 15th Ave.
SW 14th Ave.

SW Washington St.
SW Alder St.
SW Morrison St.
SW Yamhill St.
SW Taylor St.
SW Salmon St.
SW Main St.

SW Stark St.
SW Broadway Ave.

8

1
2
SW Market St. Dr.

SW
Jefferson
St.
DOWNTOWN
5
6
SW Madison St.

SW 6th Ave.

i

7

3
TUNNEL
26
SW Montgomery Dr.

SW Columbia St.
SW Clay St.
SW Market St.
SW Mill St.
SW Montgomery St.
SW Harrison St.
SW Hall St.
SW College St.

WASHINGTON PARK
Kingston Dr.

26
SW Sunset Hwy.
SW Jackson

SW Carter Lane
SW Upper Hall St.
Harrison St.
SW College St.

SW 11th Ave.
SW 10th Ave.

PORTLAND STATE UNIVERSITY

4

SW Montgomery Dr.
SW Vista Ave.
SW Clifton
SW Myrtle St.
SW Laurel St.
SW Elm St.
SW Spring St.

SW Cardinell Dr.
SW Rivington

SW Jackson St.

SW Lincoln St.

0   1/2 mi
0   1/2 km
N

American Advertising Museum **10**

CM2—Children's Museum
  Second Generation **4**

International Rose Test Garden **1**

Japanese Garden **2**

Mill Ends Park **13**

Oregon History Center **6**

Oregon Museum of Science & Industry **14**

Oregon Zoo **4**

Pioneer Courthouse Square **8**

Portland Art Museum **5**

Portland Classical Chinese Garden **11**

Portlandia & the Portland Building **7**

Portland Saturday Market **12**

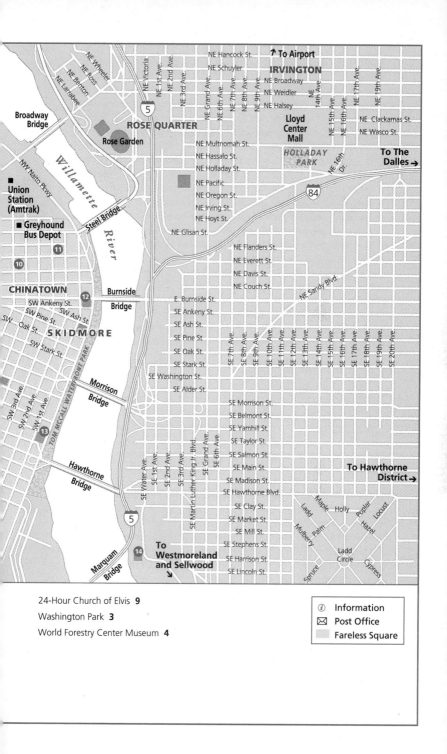

24-Hour Church of Elvis **9**

Washington Park **3**

World Forestry Center Museum **4**

ⓘ	Information
⊠	Post Office
▨	Fareless Square

Frommer's Favorite Portland Experiences

- **Strolling the Grounds at the Japanese Garden.** This is the best Japanese garden in the United States, perhaps the best anywhere outside of Japan. Our favorite time to visit is in June when the Japanese irises are in bloom. There's no better stress-reducer in the city.
- **Beer Sampling at Brewpubs.** They may not have invented beer here in Portland, but they've certainly turned it into an art form. Whether you're looking for a cozy corner pub or an upscale taproom, you'll find a brewpub where you can feel comfortable sampling what local brewmeisters are concocting.
- **Kayaking Around Ross Island.** Seattle may be the sea-kayaking capital of the Northwest, but Portland's not a bad spot for pursuing this sport either. You can paddle on the Columbia or Willamette River, but our favorite easy outing is around Ross Island in the Willamette River. You can even paddle past the submarine at the Oregon Museum of Science and Industry and pull out at Tom McCall Waterfront Park.
- **Mountain Biking the Leif Erickson Road.** Forest Park is the largest forested city park in the country, and running its length is unpaved Leif Erickson Road. The road is closed to cars and extends for 12 miles. Along the way, there are occasional views of the Columbia River. This is a pretty easy ride, without any strenuous climbs.
- **Hanging Out at Powell's.** They don't call Powell's the City of Books for nothing. This bookstore, which sells both new and used books, is so big you have to get a map at the front door. No matter how much time we spend here, it's never enough. A large cafe makes it all that much easier to while away the hours.

Oregon History Center 🌟 In the middle of the 19th century, the Oregon Territory was a land of promise and plenty. Thousands of hardy individuals set out along the Oregon Trail, crossing a vast and rugged country to reach the fertile valleys of this region. Others came by ship around the Horn. Those who wish to learn about the people who came to Oregon before them will enjoy this well-designed museum.

Fascinating educational exhibits chronicle Oregon's history from before the arrival of the first Europeans to well into the 20th century. The displays incorporate Native American artifacts, a covered wagon, nautical and surveying instruments, and contemporary objects. Museum docents, with roots stretching back to the days of the Oregon Trail, are often on hand to answer questions. There's also a research library that includes many journals written by early pioneers. You can't miss this complex—look for the eight-story-high trompe l'oeil mural stretching across the front.

1200 SW Park Ave. ✆ **503/222-1741.** www.ohs.org. Admission $6 adults and seniors, $3 students, $1.50 children 6–12, free for children under 6, free for seniors on Thurs. Tues–Sat 10am–5pm (Thurs until 8pm); Sun noon–5pm. Bus: 6. MAX: Library Station. Portland Streetcar: Art Museum (northbound); 11th Ave. and Jefferson St. (southbound).

- **Free Rides on the Vintage Trolleys.** Tri-Met buses, MAX light-rail trolleys, and Portland Streetcars are all free within a large downtown area known as the Fareless Square. That alone should be enough to get you on some form of public transit while you're in town, but if you're really lucky, you might catch one of the vintage trolley cars. There aren't any San Francisco–style hills, but they're still fun to ride.
- **An Afternoon at the Portland Saturday Market.** This large arts and crafts market is an outdoor showcase for hundreds of the Northwest's creative artisans. You'll find fascinating one-of-a-kind clothes, jewelry, kitchenwares, musical instruments, and much, much more. The food stalls serve up some great fast food, too.
- **Summertime Concerts at the Washington Park Zoo.** Summertime in Portland means partying with the pachyderms. Two to three evenings a week throughout the summer you can catch live music at the zoo's amphitheater. Musical styles include blues, rock, bluegrass, folk, Celtic, and jazz. For the price of zoo admission, you can catch the concert and tour the zoo (if you arrive early enough). Picnics are encouraged, but no alcohol is allowed into the zoo. (However, beer and wine are on sale during concerts.)
- **First Thursday Art Walk.** On the first Thursday of every month, Portland goes on an art binge. People get dressed up and go gallery hopping from art opening to art opening. There are usually hors d'oeuvres and wine available, and sometimes there's even live music. The galleries stay open until 9pm.

Portland Art Museum ★★   Although this relatively small art museum has a respectable collection of European, Asian, and American art, the museum has in recent years been positioning itself as the Northwest stop for touring blockbuster exhibits. Scheduled from June 1 to September 22, 2002, is "Splendors of Imperial Japan (Arts of the Meiji Period from the Khalili Collection)"; and from August 17 to December 1, 2002, the museum will be showing "Grandma Moses in the 21st Century." An expansion a couple of years ago added several new galleries and a small sculpture court to the museum. The galleries of Native American art and Northwest art are now the museum's most impressive displays. October through May, on Wednesday nights, the Museum After Hours program presents live music. The adjacent **Northwest Film Center** is affiliated with the Art Museum and shows an eclectic mix of films.

1219 SW Park Ave. ✆ **503/226-2811.** www.portlandartmuseum.org. Admission $7.50 adults, $6 seniors and students, $4 children 5–18, free for children under 5. Tues–Sat 10am–5pm (Oct–May Wed 10am–8pm); Sun noon–5pm; first Thurs of each month until 8pm. Bus: 6. MAX: Library Station. Portland Streetcar: Art Museum (northbound); 11th Ave. and Jefferson St. (southbound).

SKIDMORE HISTORIC DISTRICT, CHINATOWN & THE WILLAMETTE RIVER WATERFRONT

If Pioneer Courthouse Square is the city's living room, **Tom McCall Waterfront Park** ⭑, along the Willamette River, is the city's party room and backyard play area. There are acres of lawns, shade trees, sculptures, and fountains, and the paved path through the park is popular with in-line skaters and joggers. This park also serves as the site of numerous festivals each summer. Also in the park are the Waterfront Story Garden, dedicated to storytellers, and the Japanese-American Historical Plaza, dedicated to Japanese Americans who were sent to internment camps during World War II.

Just north of this plaza, a pedestrian walkway crosses the Steel Bridge to the east side of the Willamette River and the new **Eastside Promenade,** which stretches for about 1½ miles along the east bank of the river. Although this paved multi-use path gets a lot of traffic noise from the adjacent freeway, it offers great views of the Portland skyline. Along the route there are small parks and gardens, interesting sculptures, and benches for sitting and soaking up the view. The highlight of this path is a section that floats right on the river and is attached to pilings in much the same way that a floating dock is constructed. You can access the Eastside Promenade by way of the pedestrian pathway on the Steel Bridge. This bridge is at the north end of Waterfront Park.

Oregon Museum of Science and Industry (OMSI) ⭑ (Kids)   Located on the east bank of the Willamette River across from the south end of Waterfront Park, this modern science museum has six huge halls, and both kids and adults find the exhibits fun and fascinating. This is a hands-on museum, and everyone is urged to get involved with displays, from a discovery space for toddlers to physics and chemistry labs for older children. Simulated earthquakes and tornadoes are perennial favorites. There's plenty of pure entertainment at an **OMNIMAX theater** and the **Murdock Sky Theater,** which features laser-light shows and astronomy presentations. The USS *Blueback* submarine (used in the film *The Hunt for Red October*) is docked here, and tours are given daily.

Between mid-June and late September, **Samtrak** (© **503/653-2380**), a small open-air train, runs between OMSI and Oaks Park Amusement Center. OMSI is also the departure point for several different boat cruises up and down the Willamette River.

1945 SE Water Ave. © **800/955-6674** or 503/797-4000. www.omsi.edu. Museum or OMNIMAX $7 adults, $5 seniors and children 4–13; $4 submarine tours, $4 planetarium shows, laser-light shows $4 matinee, $7 evening; discounted combination tickets available. Thurs 2pm until closing all tickets are 2-for-1. Mid-June to Labor Day daily 9:30am–7pm; Labor Day to mid-June Tues–Sun 9:30am–5:30pm. Closed Christmas. Bus: 63.

Portland Saturday Market ⭑⭑   The Portland Saturday Market (actually held on both Sat and Sun) is arguably the city's single most important and best-loved event. Don't miss it. For years the Northwest has attracted artists and craftspeople, and every Saturday and Sunday nearly 300 of them can be found selling their creations here. In addition to the dozens of crafts stalls, you'll find ethnic and unusual foods and lots of free entertainment. This is one of the best places in Portland to shop for one-of-a-kind gifts. The atmosphere is always cheerful and the crowds colorful. Located at the heart of the Skidmore District, Portland Saturday Market makes an excellent starting or finishing point for a walk around Portland's downtown historic neighborhood. On Sunday, on-street parking is free.

Underneath the west end of the Burnside Bridge between SW First Ave. and SW Naito Pkwy. © **503/222-6072.** www.portlandsaturdaymarket.com. Free admission. First weekend in Mar–Christmas Eve Sat 10am–5pm and Sun 11am–4:30pm. Bus: 12, 19, or 20. MAX: Skidmore Fountain Station.

WASHINGTON PARK & PORTLAND'S WEST HILLS

Portland is justly proud of its green spaces, and foremost among them are **Washington Park** and **Forest Park.**

Within Washington Park, you'll find the Japanese Garden and International Rose Test Garden, which are adjacent to one another on the more developed east side of the park (see the listings below). On the west side of the park (farther from the city center), you'll find not only the Hoyt Arboretum but also the Oregon Zoo, World Forestry Center, and CM2—Children's Museum 2nd Generation.

The 175-acre **Hoyt Arboretum** ⚘ (⟁ **503/228-8733**) is planted with 800 species of trees and shrubs from temperate regions around the world. The arboretum has 10 miles of hiking trails and is a great place for a quick hike. Between April and October, there are free 1-hour guided tours of the arboretum on Saturdays and Sundays at 2pm. At the south end of the arboretum, adjacent to the World Forestry Center and the Oregon Zoo, is the **Vietnam Veterans Living Memorial.** At the Visitor Center, 4000 SW Fairview Blvd. (open daily 9am–3pm), you can pick up maps and guides to the arboretum. The arboretum can be reached either from the Oregon Zoo/World Forestry Center/CM2—Children's Museum 2nd Generation area or by following the arboretum signs from West Burnside Street.

To the north of Hoyt Arboretum is **Forest Park** ⚘⚘ (⟁ **503/823-PLAY**), which, with nearly 5,000 acres of forest, is the largest forested city park in the United States. Within the park, there are more than 65 miles of trails and old fire roads for hiking, jogging, and mountain biking. More than 100 species of birds call this forest home, making it a great spot for urban bird-watching. Along the forest trails, you can see huge old trees and find quiet picnic spots tucked away in the woods. One of the most convenient park access points is at the top of NW Thurman Street (just keep heading uphill until the road dead-ends). However, if you park at the Hoyt Arboretum Visitor Center (see above) or the Audubon Society (see below), you can pick up a map of Forest Park and head out from either of these locations.

Adjacent to Forest Park, you'll also find the **Portland Audubon Society,** 5151 NW Cornell Rd. (⟁ **503/292-9453**), which has a couple of miles of hiking trails on its forested property. In keeping with its mission to promote enjoyment, understanding, and protection of the natural world, these nature trails are open to the public. You can also visit the Nature Center or Wildlife Care Center here. To find this facility from downtown Portland, first drive to NW 23rd Avenue, and then head uphill on NW Lovejoy Street, which becomes NW Cornell Road. (*Warning:* Car break-ins are commonplace at the parking area just down the road from the Audubon Society, so don't leave anything of value in your car.)

By car, the easiest route to the Washington Park attractions from downtown Portland is to take SW Jefferson Street west, turn right onto SW 18th Avenue, left on SW Salmon Street, right on SW King Street, and then left onto SW Park Place. Although this sounds confusing, you'll find most of the route well marked with "Scenic Drive" signs. Alternatively, you can drive west on West Burnside Street and watch for signs to the arboretum, or take the zoo exit off U.S. 26. All of these attractions can also be reached via Bus 63. You can also take the MAX line to the Washington Park Station, which is adjacent to the Oregon Zoo, World Forestry Center, CM2—Children's Museum 2nd Generation, and Hoyt Arboretum. From here, it is possible (in the summer months) to take a bus shuttle to the Japanese Garden and International Rose Test Garden. There's also a

Great Photo Ops

If you've seen a photo of Portland with conical snow-covered Mount Hood looming in the background and you want to snap a similar photo while you're in town, there are several places to try. Most popular are probably the terraces of the International Rose Test Garden and from behind the pavilion at the Japanese Garden. Another great view can be had from the grounds of the Pittock Mansion. All three of these places are described in detail elsewhere in this chapter.

One other view is located atop Council Crest, a hilltop park in Portland's West Hills. To reach this park, take the Sylvan exit off U.S. 26 west of downtown Portland, turn south and then east (left) on Humphrey Boulevard, and then follow the signs. Alternatively, you can follow SW Broadway south out of downtown Portland and follow the signs. This road winds through attractive hillside neighborhoods for a ways before reaching Council Crest.

miniature train that runs from the zoo to a station near the two public gardens. However, to ride this train, you must first pay zoo admission.

International Rose Test Garden ★★   Covering 4½ acres of hillside in the West Hills above downtown Portland, these are among the largest and oldest rose test gardens in the United States and are the only city-maintained test gardens to bestow awards on each year's best roses. The gardens were established in 1917 by the American Rose Society and are used as a testing ground for new varieties of roses. Though you will probably see some familiar roses in the Gold Medal Garden, most of the 400 varieties on display are new hybrids being tested before marketing. Among the roses in bloom from late spring to early winter, you'll find a separate garden of miniature roses. There's also a Shakespeare Garden that includes flowers mentioned in the Bard's works. After seeing these acres of roses, you'll understand why Portland is known as the City of Roses and why the Rose Festival in June is the city's biggest annual celebration. The small Rose Garden Store (© **503/227-7033**), is packed with rose-inspired products.

400 SW Kingston Ave., Washington Park. © **503/823-3636.** Free admission (donations accepted). Daily dawn–dusk. Bus: 63.

Japanese Garden ★★★   Considered the finest example of a Japanese garden in North America, Portland's Japanese Garden is one of the city's most popular attractions. Don't miss it. Not only are there five different styles of Japanese gardens scattered over 5½ acres, but there's also a view of volcanic Mount Hood, which has a strong resemblance to Mount Fuji.

Although Japanese gardens are traditionally not designed with colorful floral displays in mind, this garden definitely has its seasonal highlights. In early spring there are the cherry trees, in mid-spring there are the azaleas, in late spring a huge wisteria bursts into bloom, and in early summer, huge Japanese irises color the banks of a pond. Among the gardens, there's a beautiful and very realistic waterfall.

This is a very tranquil spot and is even more peaceful on rainy days when the crowds stay away, so don't pass up a visit just because it's raining. Also, on the third Saturday of each of the summer months, there's a demonstration of the Japanese tea ceremony in the garden's teahouse. There are also many special events held here throughout the year (ikebana, bonsai, Japanese-inspired art, and so on).

611 Kingston Ave. (in Washington Park). ☎ 503/223-1321. www.japanesegarden.com. Admission $6 adults, $4 seniors, $3.50 students, free for children under 6. Apr 1–Sept 30 Tues–Sun 10am–7pm; Mon noon–7pm; Oct 1–Mar 31 Tues–Sun 10am–4pm, Mon noon–4pm. Closed Thanksgiving, Christmas, and New Year's Day. Bus: 63. MAX: Washington Park Station (then, in summer months, take the shuttle bus or the Zoo Train).

Oregon Zoo ☆ ⓚⁱᵈˢ   The Oregon Zoo has the largest breeding herd of elephants in captivity and is perhaps best known for its elephants. However, in recent years, the zoo has been adding new exhibits and branching out beyond the world of pachyderms. The Africa exhibit, which includes a very life-like rain forest and a savanna populated by zebras, rhinos, giraffes, hippos, and other animals, is one of the most realistic habitats you'll ever see at a zoo. Equally impressive is the Alaskan tundra exhibit, with grizzly bears, wolves, and musk oxen. The Cascade Crest exhibit includes mountain goat habitat, and in the Steller Cove exhibit, you can watch the antics of Steller's sea lions and sea otters. Don't miss the bat house. At press time, there were plans to open a new Amazon Flooded Forest exhibit in late 2001.

> ### All Aboard!
> The **Washington Park and Zoo Railway** travels between the zoo and the International Rose Test and Japanese gardens. Tickets for the miniature railway are $2.75 for adults, $2 for seniors and children 3 to 11.

In the summer, there are **outdoor concerts** in the zoo's amphitheater; admission prices vary.

4001 SW Canyon Rd., Washington Park. ☎ 503/226-1561. www.oregonzoo.org. Admission $7.50 adults, $6 seniors, $4.50 children 3–11, free for under 2; free 2nd Tues of each month from 1pm to closing. Apr 1–Sept 30 daily 9am–6pm; Oct 1–Mar 31 daily 9am–4pm. Bus: 63. MAX: Washington Park Station.

Pittock Mansion ☆   At nearly the highest point in the West Hills, 1,000 feet above sea level, stands the most impressive mansion in Portland. Once slated to be torn down to make way for new housing, this grand château, built by the founder of Portland's *Oregonian* newspaper, is fully restored and open to the public. Built in 1914 in a French Renaissance style, the mansion featured many innovations, including a built-in vacuum system and amazing multiple shower-heads in the baths. Today it's furnished with 18th- and 19th-century antiques, much as it might have been at the time the Pittocks lived here. With an expansive view over the city to the Cascade Range, the lawns surrounding the mansion are great for picnics. You can also access Forest Park's Wildwood Trail from here.

3229 NW Pittock Dr. ☎ 503/823-3624. Admission $5.50 adults, $5 seniors, $3 children 6–18. Daily noon–4pm. Closed 3 days in late Nov, most major holidays, and the month of Jan.

World Forestry Center Museum ☆   Although Oregon depends less and less on the timber industry with each passing year, the World Forestry Center Museum is still busy educating visitors about the importance of our forest resources. Step inside the huge wooden main hall, and you come face to bark with a very large and very life-like tree. Press a button at its base and it tells you the story of how trees live and grow. In other rooms you can see exhibits on forests of the world, old-growth trees, a petrified wood exhibit, and a rain-forest exhibit developed by the Smithsonian Institution. There are also interesting temporary exhibits staged here throughout the year, from photographic exhibits to displays of the woodworker's art.

4033 SW Canyon Rd. © **503/228-1367**. www.worldforestry.org. Admission $4.50 adults, $3.50 seniors and children under 6. Daily 10am–5pm (9am–5pm Memorial Day–Labor Day). Closed Christmas. Bus: 63. MAX: Washington Park Station.

PORTLAND'S OTHER PUBLIC GARDENS

For Portland's two best-loved public gardens, the **International Rose Test Garden** and the **Japanese Garden,** see "Washington Park & Portland's West Hills," earlier in this chapter.

If roses are your passion, you'll also want to check out the **Peninsula Park Rose Garden** at the corner of N. Portland Boulevard and N. Albina Avenue (take the Portland Blvd. exit off I-5 and go 2 blocks east), which has even more rose bushes than the International Rose Test Garden.

The Berry Botanic Garden 🎇   Originally founded as a private garden, the Berry Botanic Garden is now one of Portland's favorite public gardens. Among the highlights is a large, forestlike collection of mature rhododendron shrubs. There are also a native plant trail, a fern garden, and rock gardens with unusual plants. The garden is open by reservation only.

11505 SW Summerville Ave. © **503/636-4112**. www.berrybot.org. Adults $5. Open daylight hours by appointment. Bus: 35 or 36.

Crystal Springs Rhododendron Garden 🎇   Nowhere do rhododendrons do better than in the cool, rainy Northwest, and nowhere in Portland is there a more impressive planting of rhodies than at Crystal Springs. Eight months out of the year, this is a tranquil garden, with a waterfall, a lake, and ducks to feed. But when the rhododendrons and azaleas bloom from March to June, it becomes a spectacular mass of blazing color. The Rhododendron Show and Plant Sale is held here on Mother's Day weekend.

SE 28th Ave. (1 block north of SE Woodstock Blvd.). © **503/771-8386** or 503/777-1734. Admission $3 Mar 1–Labor Day Thurs–Mon 10am–6pm; free at other times. Open year-round daily dawn to dusk. Bus: 19.

Elk Rock Garden of the Bishop's Close 🎇   Set on a steep hillside above the Willamette River between Portland and Lake Oswego, this was once a private garden but was donated to the local Episcopal bishop of Oregon on the condition that it be opened to the public. The mature gardens are at their best through the spring and early summer. There's also an excellent view of Mount Hood from the grounds.

11800 SW Military Lane. © **503/636-5613**. Free admission. Daily 8am–5pm. Bus: 35 or 36.

The Grotto—National Sanctuary of Our Sorrowful Mother   Although this forested 62-acre sanctuary is first and foremost a Catholic religious shrine (with a marble replica of Michelangelo's Pietà set in a shallow rock cave at the foot of a cliff), the gardens are quite beautiful. The gardens are at their best in the early summer and during the Christmas season, when the grounds are decorated with thousands of lights and a choral festival is held. An elevator ride to the top of the bluff offers panoramic views of the Cascade Range, the Columbia River, and Mount St. Helens. There are also a couple of chapels on the grounds, a gift shop, and a coffee shop. The Grotto is open to visitors of all faiths.

NE 85th Ave. and Sandy Blvd. © **503/254-7371**. www.thegrotto.org. Free admission (except during Christmas Festival of Lights: $6 adults, $3 children 3–12, free for children 2 and under); elevator $2. Open daily summer 9am–7:30pm, winter 9am–4pm, spring 9am–5:30pm. Closed Christmas and Thanksgiving. Bus: 12.

The World's Smallest Park

Don't blink as you cross the median strip on Naito Parkway at the corner of Southwest Taylor Street, or you might just walk right past **Mill Ends Park,** the smallest public park in the world.

Covering a whopping 452.16 square inches of land, this park was the whimsical creation of local journalist Dick Fagen. After a telephone pole was removed from the middle of Naito Parkway (then known as Front Ave.), Fagen dubbed the phone pole hole Mill Ends Park (Mill Ends, a lumber mill term, was the name of Fagen's newspaper column). The columnist, whose office looked down on the hole in the middle of Front Avenue, peopled the imaginary park with leprechauns and would often write of the park's goings-on in his column. On St. Patrick's Day 1976, it was officially designated a Portland city park. Rumor has it that despite its diminutive size, the park has been the site of several weddings (although the parks department has never issued a wedding permit for it).

OTHER IN-TOWN ATTRACTIONS

American Advertising Museum Like it or not, advertising is here to stay. In this fun and unusual little museum, you'll learn about its history, from the 1700s to the present, through displays on historic advertisements, celebrities, and jingles. Tapes of old TV commercials provide a popular trip down memory lane. Lots of 20th-century advertising icons are on display, and the most influential ads of the past century are chronicled in detail.

211 NW Fifth Ave. ✆ 503/226-0000. www.admuseum.org. Admission $5 adults, $4 seniors and children 4–12. Wed–Sun noon–5pm.

Portland Classical Chinese Garden This classically styled Chinese garden takes up an entire city block and is the largest of its type outside of China. The walls that surround these gardens in Portland's Chinatown separate the urban 21st century from the timeless Chinese landscape within. This landscape is designed to evoke the wild mountains of China and to create a tranquil oasis within an urban setting. The gardens are centered around a small pond, at one end of which stands a rock wall meant to conjure up the sort of images often seen in Chinese scroll paintings. Numerous pavilions, a small bridge, and a winding pathway provide ever-changing views of the gardens. With its many paved paths and small viewing pavilions, this garden has a completely different feel than the Japanese Garden. Try to visit as soon as the gardens open in the morning; when the crowds descend and the guided tours start circulating—well, so much for tranquillity. Be sure to stop and have a cup of tea and maybe a snack in the garden's tearoom.

NW Everett St. and NW Third Ave. ✆ 503/228-8131. Admission $6 adults, $5 seniors, $5 college students and children 6–18, free for children 5 and under. Apr 1–Oct 31 daily 9am–6pm; Nov 1–Mar 31 daily 10am–5pm.

24-Hour Church of Elvis/Where's the Art? *Finds* This is Portland's long-time temple of kitsch, the city's most bizarre attraction. Coin-operated art, a video psychic, cheap (though not legal) weddings, and other absurd assemblages, interactive displays, and kitschy contraptions (such as the Vend-O-Matic Mystery Machine with whirling doll heads) cram this second-floor oddity. As celebrity-spokesmodel/minister S.G. Pierce says, "the tour *is* the art form." If you pass the customer test, you can even buy a Church of Elvis T-shirt. Great fun if you're a fan of Elvis, tabloids, or the unusual; and if you've seen Elvis anytime in the past decade, a visit is absolutely mandatory.

720 SW Ankeny St. ℂ **503/226-3671.** www.churchofelvis.com. Free admission (with $1 purchase at gift shop). Flexible hours; almost always open on weekends. Any downtown bus.

6 Especially for Kids

In addition to the attractions listed below, the kids will especially enjoy the **Oregon Museum of Science and Industry,** which has lots of hands-on exhibits (see p. 92 for details), and the **Oregon Zoo** (see p. 95). From inside the zoo, it's possible to take a small train through Washington Park to the International Rose Test Garden, below which there is the **Rose Garden Children's Park,** a colorful play area for younger children. The **Salmon Street Springs fountain,** in downtown's Tom McCall Waterfront Park (at SW Naito Pkwy. and SW Salmon St.), is another fun place to take the kids. During hot summer months, there are always lots of happy kids playing in the jets of water that erupt from the pavement here. There are also big lawns in **Waterfront Park,** so the kids can run off plenty of excess energy.

CM2—Children's Museum 2nd Generation ⭐ *Kids* Located across the parking lot form the Oregon Zoo, this new children's museum opened in mid-2001. With much more space than the old museum, this "second generation" museum includes exhibits for children from 6 months to 13 years. Kids can experiment with gravity, act out fairy tales, or explore a magical forest. However, it is the Water Works exhibit that is likely to make the biggest splash with your kids. There are also six studios with changing exhibits and opportunities for exploring the visual, literary, and performing arts. Combined with the nearby zoo, this museum now makes for an easy all-day kid-oriented outing.

4015 SW Canyon Rd. ℂ **503/223-6500.** www.portlandcm2.org. Admission $5 adults and children, free for under 1 yr. Tues–Thurs 9am–5pm; Fri 9am–8pm; Sun 11am–5pm (open some school holiday Mon). Closed some national holidays. Bus: 63. MAX: Washington Park Station.

Oaks Park Amusement Center *Kids* What would summer be without the screams of happy thrill-seekers risking life and limb on a roller coaster? Covering more than 44 acres, this amusement park first opened in 1905 to coincide with the Lewis and Clark Exposition. Beneath the shady oaks for which the park is named, you'll find waterfront picnic sites, miniature golf, music, and plenty of thrilling rides. Check out the largest wood-floored roller-skating rink in the west where an organist still plays the Wurlitzer for the skaters.

East end of the Sellwood Bridge. ℂ **503/233-5777.** www.oakspark.com. Free admission; individual-ride tickets $1.50, limited-ride bracelet $9.75, deluxe-ride bracelet $12.25. Mid-June to Labor Day Tues–Thurs noon–9pm, Fri–Sat noon–10pm, Sun noon–7pm (separate hours for skating rink); May to mid-June and Sept (after Labor Day) Sat–Sun noon–7pm (weather allowing). Bus: 40.

7 Organized Tours
CRUISES

If you'd like to see the city from either the Columbia or the Willamette rivers, you've got plenty of options. Traditionalists will want to book a tour on the **Sternwheeler** *Columbia Gorge* ⭐ (ℂ **503/223-3928**), which offers sternwheeler cruises through Portland on the Willamette River between October and late June. During the summer months, this boat operates out of Cascade Locks on the Columbia River and does trips in the scenic Columbia Gorge. Although it's fun to see the city from the water, the summer trips beneath the towering cliffs of the Columbia Gorge are far more impressive—a definite must on a summertime visit to Portland. Two-hour cruises are $14.95 for adults and $8.95 for children. Call for information on brunch, dinner, and dance cruises.

If a modern yacht is more your speed, try the ***Portland Spirit*** (© 800/ 224-3901 or 503/224-3900; www.portlandspirit.com). This 75-foot yacht specializes in dinner cruises and seats 350 people on two decks. Lunch, brunch, and dinner cruises feature Northwest cuisine with views of the city skyline. Saturday nights the *Portland Spirit* becomes a floating nightclub with live bands or a DJ, and there are also Friday afternoon cocktail cruises in the summer. Call for reservations and schedule. Prices range from $15 to $52 for adults and $9 to $47 for children.

For high-speed tours up the Willamette River, there are the **Willamette Jet- boat Excursions** ★ (© 888/JETBOAT or 503/231-1532; www.jetboatpdx. com). The high-powered open-air boats blast their way from downtown Port- land to the impressive Willamette Falls at Oregon City. The 2-hour tours, which start at OMSI, are $25 for adults and $15 for children 4 to 11, free for 3 and under. Tours are offered from May to mid-October.

BUS TOURS

If you want to get a general overview of Portland, **Gray Line** (© 800/422-7042 or 503/285-9845) offers several half-day and full-day tours. One itinerary takes in the International Rose Test Garden and the grounds of Pittock Mansion; another stops at the Japanese Garden and the World Forestry Center. There are also tours up to see the waterfalls in the Columbia Gorge, to Mount Hood, and to the Oregon coast. Tour prices range from $27 to $47 for adults, and from $13.50 to $23.50 for children.

RAIL EXCURSIONS

While Portland is busy reviving trolleys as a viable mass transit option, the **Willamette Shore Trolley** ★ (© 503/222-2226) is offering scenic excursions along the Willamette River in historic trolley cars (including a double-decker) from the early part of this century. The old wooden trolleys rumble over trestles and through a tunnel as they cover the 7 miles between Portland and the pres- tigious suburb of Lake Oswego (a 45-min. trip). Along the way, you pass through shady corridors with lots of views of the river and glimpses into the yards of posh riverfront homes. In Lake Oswego, the trolley station is on State Street, between "A" Avenue and Foothills Road. In downtown Portland, the sta- tion is just south of the RiverPlace Athletic Club on Harbor Way (off Naito Pkwy. at the south end of Tom McCall Waterfront Park). The round-trip fare is $8 for adults, $7 for seniors, and $4 for children 3 to 12. Call for a schedule. They also do an annual Fourth of July fireworks run from Oaks Park on the east bank of the Willamette River, and a Christmas run to see the Holiday Parade of Ships.

WALKING TOURS

Peter's Walking Tours of Portland (© 503/665-2558 or 503/680-4296; famchausse@aol.com), led by university instructor Peter Chausse, are a great way to learn more about Portland. The walking tours of downtown take 2½ hours, cover about 1½ miles, and take in the city's fountains, parks, historic places, art, and architecture. Tours are by reservation and cost $10 for adults (children 12 and under free with a paying adult).

Two to three times a year, Sharon Wood Wortman, author of *The Portland Bridge Book,* offers a **Bridge Tour and Urban Adventure** that explores several Portland bridges. These tours are offered through the Outdoor Recreation Program of **Portland Parks and Recreation** (℗ 503/823-5132). Many other walking tours are also available through Portland Parks and Recreation.

The seamy underbelly of history is laid bare on **Portland Underground Tours** (℗ 503/622-4798), which head down below street level in the historic Old Town neighborhood. On these unusual tours, which are only for those who are steady on their feet and able to duck under pipes and joists and such, you'll hear tales of the days when Portland was known as one of the most dangerous ports on the Pacific Rim. Sailors were regularly shanghaied from bars and brothels in this area and a vast network of tunnels and underground rooms developed to support the shanghaiing business. Tours cost $10 and are offered on an irregular basis. Reservations are required.

8 Outdoor Pursuits

If you're planning ahead for a visit to Portland, contact **Metro Regional Parks and Greenspaces,** 600 NE Grand Ave., Portland, OR 97232-2736 (℗ 503/797-1850; www.metro-region.org), for its *Metro GreenScene* publication that lists tours, hikes, classes, and other outdoor activities and events being held in the Portland metro area.

BIKING

Portland is a very bicycle-friendly city, and you'll notice plenty of bikers on the streets. There are also lots of miles of paved bike paths around the city, and some good mountain biking areas as well. There aren't too many choices for rentals, but try **Fat Tire Farm,** 2714 NW Thurman St. (℗ 503/222-3276), where you can get a mountain bike for $40 a day. Straight up Thurman Street from the bike shop, you'll find the trail head for the **Leif Erickson Trail,** and old gravel road that is Forest Park's favorite route for cyclists and runners (the road is closed to motor vehicles); the trail is 12 miles long.

GOLF

If you're a golfer, don't forget to bring your clubs along on a trip to Portland. There are plenty of public courses around the area, and greens fees at municipal courses are as low as $21 for 18 holes on a weekday and $35 on weekends and holidays. Municipal golf courses operated by the Portland Bureau of Parks and Recreation include **Redtail Golf Course,** 8200 SW Scholls Ferry Rd. (℗ 503/646-5166); **Eastmoreland Golf Course,** 2425 SE Bybee Blvd. (℗ 503/775-2900), which is the second oldest golf course in the state (this one gets our vote for best municipal course); **Heron Lakes Golf Course,** 3500 N. Victory Blvd. (℗ 503/289-1818), a Robert Trent Jones design; and **Rose City Golf Course,** 2200 NE 71st Ave. (℗ 503/253-4744), on the site of a former country club.

If you want to tee off where the pros play, head west from Portland 20 miles to **Pumpkin Ridge Golf Club,** 12930 NW Old Pumpkin Ridge Rd. (℗ 503/647-4747), which has hosted the U.S. Women's Open. Greens fees are $120 ($135 with cart) and $65 after 3pm Monday through Thursday.

Impressions

While the people of Portland are not mercurial or excitable—and by Californians or people "east of the mountains" are even accused of being lymphatic, if not somnolent—they are much given . . . to recreation and public amusements.

—Harvey Scott, editor of the *Oregonian*, 1890

Also west of the city, on the south side of Hillsboro, you'll find the **Reserve Vineyards & Golf Club** *, 4805 SW 229th Ave., Aloha (℃ **503/649-8191;** www.reservegolf.com). Greens fees are $65 Monday through Thursday and $79 Friday through Sunday.

HIKING

Hiking opportunities in the Portland area are almost unlimited. For shorter hikes, you need not leave the city. Bordered by West Burnside Street on the south, Newberry Road on the north, St. Helens Road on the east, and Skyline Road on the west, **Forest Park** is the largest forested city park in the country. You'll find more than 50 miles of trails through this urban wilderness. One of our favorite access points is at the top of NW Thurman Street in northwest Portland. (After a hike, you can stop by one of the neighborhood brewpubs, an espresso bar, or bakery along NW 23rd or NW 21st Ave. for a post-exercise payoff.) The Wildwood Trail is the longest trail in the park and offers the most options for loop hikes along its length. For a roughly 2½-mile hike, head up Leif Erickson Drive to a left onto the Wild Cherry Trail to a right onto the Wildwood Trail to a right onto the Dogwood Trail, and then a right on Leif Erickson Drive to get you back to the trail head. There are also good sections of trail to hike in the vicinity of the Hoyt Arboretum. To reach the arboretum's visitor center, 4000 SW Fairview Boulevard (open daily 9am–3pm), drive west on West Burnside Street from downtown Portland and follow signs to the arboretum. You can get a trail map here at the visitor center.

About 5 miles south of downtown, you'll find **Tryon Creek State Park** on Terwilliger Road. This park is similar to Forest Park and is best known for its displays of trillium flowers in the spring. There are several miles of walking trails within the park, and a bike path to downtown Portland starts here.

You can buy or rent camping equipment from **REI Co-Op,** 1798 Jantzen Beach Center (℃ **503/283-1300**), or 7410 SW Bridgeport Rd., Tualatin (℃ **503/624-8600**). This huge outdoor recreation supply store also sells books on hiking in the area.

SEA KAYAKING

If you want to check out the Portland skyline from water level, arrange for a sea kayak tour through the **Portland River Company** *, 0315 SW Montgomery St. (℃ **888/238-2059** or 503/229-0551; www.portlandrivercompany.com), which operates out of the RiverPlace Marina at the south end of Tom McCall Waterfront Park. A 2½-hour tour that circles nearby Ross Island costs $35 per person. All-day trips on the lower Columbia River are also offered ($75 per person) and will get you off an urban river and into a wildlife refuge. This company also rents sea kayaks (to experienced paddlers) for $15 to $20 for the first hour and $10 to $15 per hour after that.

9 Spectator Sports

Tickets to most games, including those of the Trail Blazers, the Portland Winter Hawks, and the Portland Beavers, are sold through **Ticketmaster** (© **503/ 224-4400;** www.ticketmaster.com).

Tickets to events at the Rose Garden arena and Memorial Coliseum are also sold through the **Rose Quarter** box office (© **503/797-9617** for tickets; 503/321-3211 event information hot line; www.rosequarter.com). The Rose Garden arena is home to the Portland Trail Blazers and the Portland Winter Hawks and is the main focal point of Portland's **Rose Quarter.** This sports and entertainment neighborhood is still more an idea than a reality, but it does include the Rose Garden, Memorial Coliseum, and several restaurants and bars. To reach the Rose Garden or adjacent Memorial Coliseum, take the Rose Quarter exit off I-5. Parking is expensive, so you might want to consider taking the MAX light-rail line from downtown Portland.

AUTO RACING   Portland International Raceway, West Delta Park, 1940 N. Victory Blvd. (© **503/823-RACE**), hosts road races, drag races, motorcross and other motorcycle races, go-kart races, and even vintage-car races. February through October are the busiest months here.

BASEBALL   The Portland Beavers Baseball Club (© **503/553-5555;** www.pgepark.com), the AAA affiliate of the San Diego Padres, plays minor-league ball at the recently renovated PGE Park, SW 20th Avenue and Morrison Street. Tickets are $3.25 to $8.75.

BASKETBALL   The NBA's Portland Trail Blazers (© **503/231-8000** or 503/234-9291; www.nba.com/blazers) do well enough each year to have earned them a very loyal following. Unfortunately, they have a habit of not quite making it all the way to the top. The Blazers pound the boards at the Rose Garden arena. Call for current schedule and ticket information. Tickets are $10 to $127. If the Blazers are doing well, you can bet that tickets will be hard to come by.

10 Day Spas

If you'd rather opt for a massage than a hike in the woods, consider spending a few hours at a day spa. These facilities typically offer massages, facials, seaweed wraps, and the like. Portland day spas include **Aveda Lifestyle Store and Spa,** 5th Avenue Suites Hotel, 500 Washington St. (© **503/248-0615**); **Urbaca,** 120 NW Ninth Ave., Suite 101 (© **503/241-5030**); and **Salon Nyla—The Day Spa,** adjacent to the Embassy Suites hotel at 327 SW Pine St. (© **503/ 228-0389**). Expect to pay about $65 to $75 for a 1-hour massage and $150 to $435 for a multitreatment spa package.

11 Shopping

Portland has no sales tax, making it a popular shopping destination for Washingtonians, who cross the Columbia River to avoid paying their state's substantial sales tax.

THE SHOPPING SCENE

The **blocks around Pioneer Courthouse Square** are the heartland of upscale shopping in Portland. It's here that you'll find Nordstrom, NIKETOWN, Saks Fifth Avenue, Tiffany, Pioneer Place shopping mall, and numerous upscale boutiques and shops.

However, Portland's hippest shopping district is the **Nob Hill/Northwest neighborhood along NW 23rd Avenue beginning at West Burnside Street.** Here you'll find block after block of unusual boutiques as well as such chains as Gap, Urban Outfitters, and Pottery Barn.

For shops with a more down-to-earth, funky flavor, head out to the **Hawthorne District,** which is the city's counterculture shopping area (lots of tie-dye and imports).

In the **Pearl District,** of which NW Glisan Street and NW 10th Avenue are the center, you'll find the city's greatest concentration of art galleries.

Most small stores in Portland are open Monday through Saturday from 9 or 10am to 5 or 6pm. Shopping malls are usually open Monday through Friday from 9 or 10am to 9pm, Saturday from 9 or 10am to between 6 and 9pm, and Sunday from 11am until 6pm. Many department stores stay open past 6pm. Most art galleries and antiques stores are closed on Monday.

SHOPPING A TO Z
ANTIQUES

The **Sellwood** neighborhood (south of downtown at the east end of the Sellwood Bridge) is Portland's main antiques-shopping district, with about 30 antiques shops and antiques malls along 12 blocks of SE 13th Avenue. With its old Victorian homes and 19th-century architecture, Sellwood is an ideal setting for these shops. There are plenty of good restaurants in the area in case it turns into an all-day outing.

You'll also find three more large antiques malls (all under the same ownership) nearby on Milwaukie Boulevard: **Stars,** at 6717 SE Milwaukie Blvd. (℃ **503/235-9142**), and at 7027 SE Milwaukie Blvd. (℃ **503/239-0346**); and **Star & Splendid,** 7030 SE Milwaukie Blvd. (℃ **503/235-5990**).

ART GALLERIES

On the **first Thursday of the month,** galleries in downtown Portland schedule coordinated openings in the evening. Stroll from one gallery to the next, meeting artists and perhaps buying an original work of art.

A guide listing dozens of Portland galleries is available at galleries around the city.

General Art Galleries

Augen Gallery   When it opened 17 years ago, the Augen Gallery focused on internationally recognized artists such as Jim Dine, Andy Warhol, and David Hockney. Today, the gallery has expanded its repertoire to regional contemporary painters and printmakers as well. 817 SW Second Ave. ℃ **503/224-8182.** www.augengallery.com.

Blackfish Gallery   Artist-owned since 1979, the Blackfish is a large and relaxing space featuring contemporary images. Since this gallery is a cooperative, it doesn't have the same constraints as a commercial art gallery and thus can present more cutting-edge and thought-provoking work. 420 NW Ninth Ave. ℃ **503/224-2634.**

The Laura Russo Gallery   The focus here is on Northwest contemporary artists, showcasing talented emerging artists as well as the estates of well-known artists. Laura Russo has been on the Portland art scene for a long time and is highly respected. 805 NW 21st Ave. ℃ **503/226-2754.**

Margo Jacobsen Gallery   In the heart of the Pearl District, this gallery is where you'll find most of the crowds milling about on First Thursdays. Margo

Jacobsen promotes contemporary painters, printmakers, and photographers, with a focus on ceramics and glass. 1039 NW Glisan St. ℂ **503/224-7287.**

Pulliam Deffenbaugh Gallery This gallery represents a long list of both talented newcomers and masters from the Northwest. Solo shows and salon-style group shows are held here at the Pearl District location, and also at the Pulliam Deffenbaugh Broadway Gallery downtown at 507 SW Broadway (ℂ 503/228-8208). 522 NW 12th Ave. ℂ **503/228-6665.**

Quintana Galleries This large, bright space is virtually a small museum of Native American art, selling everything from Northwest Indian masks to contemporary paintings and sculptures by various Northwest coast Indian and Inuit artists. They also carry a smattering of Northwest and Southwest Indian antiquities. The jewelry selection is outstanding. Prices, however, are not cheap. 501 SW Broadway. ℂ **503/223-1729.**

Art Glass

The Bullseye Connection Located in the Pearl District, the Bullseye Connection is a large open exhibition and sales space for glass artists. Pieces sold here include sculptures, delightful glass jewelry, paperweights, and even marbles. There's even a Dale Chihuly chandelier of pink fruit-like objects on display. Workshops and lectures related to glassmaking are also offered. The **Bullseye Connection Gallery,** which is across the street at 300 NW 13th St. (ℂ **503/ 227-0222**), shows work of internationally acclaimed glass artists. 1308 NW Everett St. ℂ **503/227-2797.**

BOOKS

Major chain bookstores in Portland include **Barnes & Noble** at 1231 NE Broadway (ℂ **503/335-0201**) and 1720 Jantzen Beach Center (ℂ **503/ 283-2800**), and **Borders** at 708 SW Third Ave. (ℂ **503/220-5911**).

CRAFTS

For the largest selection of local crafts, visit the **Portland Saturday Market** (see "Markets," below), which is a showcase for local crafts.

Contemporary Crafts Gallery In business since 1937 and located in a residential area between downtown and the John's Landing neighborhood, this is the nation's oldest nonprofit art gallery showing exclusively artwork in clay, glass, fiber, metal, and wood. The bulk of the large gallery is taken up by glass and ceramic pieces in ongoing thematic exhibitions. There are also several cabinets of jewelry. 3934 SW Corbett Ave. ℂ **503/223-2654.**

Graystone Gallery This gallery in the Hawthorne district is full of fun and whimsical artwork and home furnishings, including paintings, jewelry, ceramics, and greeting cards. 3279 SE Hawthorne Blvd. ℂ **503/238-0651.**

Hoffman Gallery The Hoffman Gallery is on the campus of the Oregon College of Art and Craft, one of the nation's foremost crafts education centers since 1906. The gallery hosts installations and group shows by local, national, and international artists. The adjacent gift shop has a good selection of hand-crafted items. The grounds are serene and relaxing, and there is also a cafe. 8245 SW Barnes Rd. ℂ **503/297-5544.**

The Real Mother Goose This is Portland's premier fine crafts shop and one of the top such shops in the United States. It showcases only the very best contemporary American crafts, including imaginative ceramics, colorful art glass,

The City of Books

Portland's own **Powell's City of Books,** 1005 W. Burnside St. (✆ **503/ 228-4651** or 800/878-7323; www.powells.com), is the bookstore to end all bookstores. Powell's, which covers an entire city block three floors deep, claims to be the world's largest bookstore. Those books, roughly three-quarters of a million at any given time, are shelved side by side—well-thumbed old paperbacks next to the latest hardcover books—which is why browsing is what Powell's is all about.

Once inside the store, be sure to pick up a store map, which will direct you to the color-coded rooms. In the Gold Room, you'll find science fiction and mysteries. The Rose Room has books on ornithology, the outdoors, and sports, among other subjects, as well as children's books. In the Orange Room, there are books on cooking, gardening, business, and crafts. Serious book collectors won't want to miss a visit to the Rare Book Room.

One warning: If you haven't got at least an hour of free time, enter at your own risk. It's so easy to lose track of time at Powell's that many customers miss meals and end up in the store's in-house cafe.

Believe it or not, City of Books is even bigger than what you see here; it has several satellite stores. There's **Powell's Technical Bookstore,** 33 NW Park St. (✆ 503/228-3906); **Powell's Books for Cooks and Gardeners,** 3747 SE Hawthorne Blvd. (✆ **503/235-3802**); **Powell's Books on Hawthorne,** 3723 SE Hawthorne Blvd. (✆ **503/238-1668**); **Powell's Travel Store,** Pioneer Courthouse Square, SW Sixth Avenue and Yamhill Street (✆ **503/228-1108**); **Powell's Books in Beaverton,** at the Progress exit off Ore. 217 in Beaverton (✆ **503/643-3131**); and **Powell's Books at PDX,** Portland International Airport (✆ **503/249-1950**).

intricate jewelry, exquisite wooden furniture, and sculptural works. Hundreds of craftspeople and artists from all over the United States are represented here. There are also locations at Washington Square; Tigard (✆ **503/620-2243**); and Portland International Airport, Main Terminal (✆ **503/284-9929**). 901 SW Yamhill St. ✆ 503/223-9510. www.therealmothergoose.com. Also at Washington Square; Tigard (✆ 503/620-2243); and Portland International Airport, Main Terminal (✆ 503/284-9929).

Twist This large store has quite a massive selection of wildly colorful and imaginative furniture, crockery, glassware, and lamps, and also a limited but intense selection of handmade jewelry from artists around the United States. Pioneer Place, 700 SW Fifth Ave. ✆ 503/222-3137. Also at 30 NW 23rd Place (✆ 503/224-0334).

DEPARTMENT STORES

Meier and Frank Meier and Frank is a Portland institution and has been doing business here for more than 100 years. The flagship store on Pioneer Courthouse Square was built in 1898 and, with 10 stories, was at one time the tallest store in the Northwest. Today those 10 floors of consumer goods and great sales still attract crowds of shoppers. The store is open daily, with Friday usually the latest night. 621 SW Fifth Ave. ✆ 503/223-0512. Also at 1100 Lloyd Center (✆ 503/281-4797) and 9300 SW Washington Square Rd. in Tigard (✆ 503/620-3311).

Nordstrom Directly across the street from Pioneer Courthouse Square and a block away from Meier and Frank, Nordstrom is a top-of-the-line department store that originated in the Northwest and takes great pride in its personal service and friendliness. 701 SW Broadway. ✆ 503/224-6666. Also at 1001 Lloyd Center (✆ 503/287-2444) and 9700 SW Washington Square Rd. in Tigard (✆ 503/620-0555).

FASHION
Sportswear

Columbia Sportswear Company This flagship store is surprisingly low-key, given that the nearby Nike flagship store and the new REI in Seattle are designed to knock your socks off. Displays showing the Columbia line of outdoor clothing are rustic, with lots of natural wood. The most dramatic architectural feature of the store is the entryway, in which a very wide tree trunk seems to support the roof. 911 SW Broadway. ✆ 503/226-6800.

Columbia Sportswear Company Outlet Store *Value* This outlet store in the Sellwood neighborhood south of downtown and across the river sells well-made outdoor clothing and sportswear from one of the Northwest's premiere outdoor clothing manufacturers. You'll pay 30% to 50% less here than you will at the downtown flagship store (though the clothes will likely be last year's). 1323 SE Tacoma St. ✆ 503/238-0118.

The Jantzen Store Jantzen is another of Portland's famous sportswear manufacturers. The full line of attractive and innovative swimsuit styles are sold right here, and there are even occasional sales. 921 SW Morrison St. (in the Galleria). ✆ 503/221-1443. www.jantzen.com.

Nike Portland Factory Store *Value* The Nike outlet is one season behind the current season at NIKETOWN (see below), selling swoosh brand running, aerobic, tennis, golf, basketball, kids, and you-name-it sports clothing and accessories at discounted prices. 2650 NE Martin Luther King Jr. Blvd. ✆ 503/281-5901.

NIKETOWN Sure, you may have a NIKETOWN back home, but this one is the closest to Nike's headquarters in nearby Beaverton, which somehow makes it just a little bit special. Matte black decor, kinetic displays, and edgy music give NIKETOWN the feel of a sports museum or disco. A true shopping experience. 930 SW Sixth Ave. ✆ 503/221-6453.

Men's & Women's

Langlitz Leathers This family-run shop produces the Rolls Royce of leather jackets. Even though there may be a wait (the shop turns out only six handmade jackets a day), motorcyclists ride their Harleys all the way from the East Coast to be fitted. It's rumored that Jay Leno once bought a jacket here. 2443 SE Division St. ✆ 503/235-0959.

Norm Thompson Known throughout the country for its mail-order catalogs, Norm Thompson is a mainstay of the well-to-do in Portland. Classic styling for men and women is the name of the game here. 1805 NW Thurman St. ✆ 503/221-0764. Also at Portland International Airport (✆ 503/249-0170).

The Portland Pendleton Shop Pendleton wool is as much a part of life in the Northwest as forests and salmon. This company's fine wool fashions for men and women define the country-club look in the Northwest and in many other parts of the country. Pleated skirts and tweed jackets are de rigueur here, as are the colorful blankets that have warmed generations of Northwesterners through long chilly winters. 900 SW Fifth Ave. (entrance is actually on Fourth Ave. between Salmon and Taylor). ✆ 503/242-0037.

Women's Clothing

Byrkit   Byrkit specializes in natural fabric clothing of cotton, silk, rayon, and linen for women. The contemporary designs, including dresses, jumpers, and separates, are comfortable but still stylish. 2200 NE Broadway. (C) **503/282-3773.**

Changes   This shop specializes in handmade clothing, including hand-woven scarves, jackets, shawls, hand-painted silks, and other wearable art. 927 SW Yamhill St. (C) **503/223-3737.**

The Eye of Ra   Women with sophisticated tastes in ethnic fashions will want to visit this shop in The Water Tower at John's Landing shopping center. Silk and rayon predominate, and there's ethnic jewelry by creative designers. Ethnic furniture and home decor are also sold. 5331 SW Macadam Ave. (C) **503/224-4292.**

M. Sellin Ltd.   Located in the relaxed and low-key Hawthorne district, this shop carries women's "soft dressing" clothing made of natural fabrics with comfortable styling by designers such as Mishi and Amanda Gray. There's also a good selection of jewelry at reasonable prices. 3556 SE Hawthorne Blvd. (C) **503/239-4605.**

FOOD

The **Made in Oregon** shops offer the best selection of local food products. See "Gifts & Souvenirs," below, for details.

GIFTS & SOUVENIRS

For unique locally made souvenirs, your best bet is the **Portland Saturday Market** (see "Markets," below, for details).

Made in Oregon   This is your one-stop shop for all manner of made-in-Oregon gifts, food products, and clothing. Every product sold is either grown, caught, or made in Oregon. You'll find smoked salmon, filberts, jams and jellies, Pendleton woolens, and Oregon wines. All branches are open daily, but hours vary from store to store. 921 SW Morrison St. (in the Galleria). (C) **800/828-9673** or 503/241-3630. www.madeinoregon.com. Also at Portland International Airport ((C) **503/282-7827**); in Lloyd Center mall, SE Multnomah St. and SE Broadway ((C) **503/282-7636**); and in Old Town at 10 NW First Ave. ((C) **503/273-8354**).

JEWELRY

For some of the most creative jewelry in Portland, visit **Twist,** the **Graystone Gallery,** the **Hoffman Gallery,** the **Contemporary Crafts Gallery,** and the **Real Mother Goose.** See "Crafts," above.

MALLS & SHOPPING CENTERS

Lloyd Center   This large shopping mall in inner northeast Portland has five anchor stores and more than 200 specialty shops, including a Nordstrom and a Meier and Frank. A food court, ice-skating rink, and eight-screen cinema complete the mall's facilities. Bounded by SE Multnomah St., NE Broadway, NE 16th Ave., and NE Ninth Ave. (C) **503/282-2511.**

Pioneer Place   Just a block from Pioneer Courthouse Square, this is Portland's most upscale downtown shopping center. Anchored by a Saks Fifth Avenue, Pioneer Place is filled with stores selling designer fashions and expensive gifts. You'll also find the city's only Godiva chocolatier and Todai, a Japanese restaurant with a 160-foot sushi bar. 700 SW Fifth Ave. (between Third and Fifth aves.). (C) **503/228-5800.**

MARKETS

Portland Saturday Market   The Portland Saturday Market (held on both Sat and Sun) is arguably the city's single most important and best-loved event.

For years the Northwest has attracted artists and craftspeople, and every Saturday and Sunday nearly 300 of them can be found selling their creations here. In addition to the dozens of crafts stalls, you'll find ethnic and unusual foods, and lots of free entertainment. This is one of the best places in Portland to shop for one-of-a-kind gifts. The atmosphere is always cheerful, and the crowds are always colorful. Don't miss it. On Sunday, on-street parking is free. Under the west end of the Burnside Bridge (between SW First Ave. and SW Naito Pkwy.). ℂ **503/222-6072.** www.portlandsaturdaymarket.com. Open from the first weekend in Mar to Christmas Eve, Sat 10am to 5pm, Sun 11am to 4:30pm; closed Jan and Feb.

TOYS

Finnegan's Toys and Gifts   This is the largest toy store in downtown Portland. It'll have your inner child kicking and screaming if you don't buy that silly little toy you never got when you were young. 922 SW Yamhill St. ℂ **503/221-0306.** www.finneganstoys.com.

WINE

Oregon Wines on Broadway ·   This cozy wine bar/shop is located diagonally across from the Hotel Vintage Plaza in downtown Portland. Here you can taste some of Oregon's fine wines, including 30 different Pinot Noirs, as well as Chardonnays, Gewürztraminers and Washington state Cabernet Sauvignons and Merlots. 515 SW Broadway. ℂ **503/228-4655.**

12 Portland After Dark

Portland is the Northwest's number two cultural center (after Seattle, of course). The city's symphony orchestra, ballet, and opera are all well regarded, and the many theater companies offer classic and contemporary plays. If you're a jazz fan, you'll feel right at home—there's always a lot of live jazz being played around town. In summer, festivals move the city's cultural activities outdoors.

To find out what's going on during your visit, pick up a copy of *Willamette Week,* Portland's free weekly arts-and-entertainment newspaper. The *Oregonian,* the city's daily newspaper, also publishes lots of entertainment-related information in its Friday "A&E" section and also in the Sunday edition of the paper.

THE PERFORMING ARTS

For the most part, the Portland performing-arts scene revolves around the **Portland Center for the Performing Arts (PCPA),** 1111 SW Broadway (ℂ **503/248-4335**), which is comprised of five performances spaces in three different buildings. The **Arlene Schnitzer Concert Hall,** Southwest Broadway and Southwest Main Street, known locally as the Schnitz, is an immaculately restored 1920s movie palace that still displays the original Portland theater sign and marquee out front and is home to the Oregon Symphony. This hall also hosts popular music performers, lecturers, and many other special performances. Directly across Main Street from the Schnitz, at 1111 SW Broadway, is the sparkling glass jewel box known as the **New Theater Building.** This building houses both the **Newmark** and **Dolores Winningstad** theaters and **Brunish Hall.** The Newmark Theatre is home to Portland Center Stage, while the two theaters together host stage productions by local and visiting companies. Free tours of all three of these theaters are held Wednesdays at 11am, Saturdays every half hour between 11am and 1pm, and the first Thursday of every month at 6pm.

A few blocks away from this concentration of venues is the 3,000-seat **Keller Auditorium,** SW Third Avenue and SW Clay Street, the largest of the four halls and the home of the Portland Opera and the Oregon Ballet Theatre. The auditorium was constructed shortly after World War I and completely remodeled in the 1960s. In addition to the resident companies mentioned above, these halls host numerous visiting companies each year, including touring Broadway shows.

Note that PCPA's box office is open for ticket sales only for 2 hours before a show. At other times, tickets to PCPA performances and also performances at many other venues around the city, are sold through either **Ticketmaster** (© **503/224-4400;** www.ticketmaster.com), which has outlets at area G.I. Joe's and Meier and Frank stores, or **Fastixx** (© **800/992-TIXX** or 503/224-8499; www.fastixx.com), which has outlets at area Safeway stores. You can also purchase tickets to PCPA performances and other shows at **Ticket Central** (© **503/275-8358**), which is located at the **Portland Oregon Visitors Association (POVA) Information Center,** 701 SW Sixth Ave., Suite 1, in Pioneer Courthouse Square. This ticket office also sells day-of-show, half-price tickets to many area performances.

For much more daring and cutting edge performances, check out the calendar of the **Portland Institute for Contemporary Art (PICA),** 219 NW 12th Ave. (© **503/242-1419;** www.pica.org), which was created as a resource for exploring and supporting experimental art and new music in this city. PICA presents innovative performances by both well-known and less-established performance artists and musicians, as well as visual exhibitions focusing on contemporary trends in the regional, national, and international art scene. Call for a current schedule of performance events, which are held at various venues around town (tickets $16–$23).

One other performing arts venue worth checking out is **The Old Church,** 1422 SW 11th Ave. (© **503/222-2031;** www.oldchurch.org). Built in 1883, this wooden Carpenter Gothic church is a Portland landmark. It incorporates a grand traditional design, but was constructed with spare ornamentation. Today the building serves as a community facility, and every Wednesday at noon it hosts free lunchtime classical music concerts. There are also many other performances held here throughout the year.

OPERA & CLASSICAL MUSIC

Founded in 1896, the **Oregon Symphony** (© **800/228-7343** or 503/228-1353; www.orsymphony.org), which performs at the Arlene Schnitzer Concert Hall, 1111 SW Broadway (see above), is the oldest symphony orchestra on the West Coast. Under the expert baton of conductor James de Preist, the symphony has achieved national recognition and each year between September and June stages several series, including classical, pops, Sunday matinees, and children's concerts. Ticket prices range from $15 to $55 (seniors and students may purchase half-price tickets 1 hr. before a classical or pops concert; Mon nights there are $5 student tickets).

Each season, the **Portland Opera** (© **503/241-1802;** www.portlandopera.org), which performs at Keller Auditorium, SW Third Avenue and SW Clay Street (see above), offers five different productions that include both grand opera and light opera. The season runs September through May. Ticket prices range from $25 to $155.

Summer is the time for Portland's annual chamber music binge. **Chamber Music Northwest** (© **503/294-6400;** www.cmnw.org) is a 5-week-long series that starts in late June and attracts the world's finest chamber musicians. Performances are held at Reed College and Catlin Gable School (tickets $17–$33).

THEATER

Portland Center Stage (© **503/274-6588;** www.pcs.org), which holds performances at the Portland Center for the Performing Arts, 1111 SW Broadway (see above), is Portland's largest professional theater company. They stage a combination of six classic and contemporary plays during their September-to-April season (tickets $16–$44).

The play's the thing at **Tygres Heart Shakespeare Co.** (© **503/288-8400;** www.tygresheart.org), which performs at the Dolores Winningstad Theatre, 1111 SW Broadway (see above), and old Will would be proud. Tygres Heart remains true to its name and stages only works by the Bard himself. The three-play season runs September through May (tickets $11–$32).

If it's musicals you want, you've got a couple of options in Portland. At the Keller Auditorium, you can catch the **Portland Opera Presents the Best of Broadway** series (© **503/241-1802;** www.broadwayseries.com). Tickets range from around $15 to $69. For other Broadway classics, check the schedule of the **Musical Theatre Company** (© **503/916-6592** or 503/224-5411; www.themusicaltheatrecompany.com), a semiprofessional company that performs at the Eastside Performance Center, SE 14th Avenue and SE Stark Street. The season runs September through May (tickets $26–$30 for adults, $24–$28 for seniors, and $16 for students).

DANCE

Although the **Oregon Ballet Theatre** (© **888/922-5538** or 503/222-5538; www.obt.org), which performs at the Keller Auditorium and the Newmark Theatre (see above), is best loved for its sold-out performances each December of *The Nutcracker,* this company also stages the annual American Choreographers Showcase. This latter performance often features world premieres. Rounding out the season are performances of classic and contemporary ballets (tickets $5–$80).

PERFORMING ARTS SERIES

The **Museum After Hours** series at the **Portland Art Museum's North Wing,** 1119 SW Park Ave. (© **503/226-2811**), is a great place to catch some of the best local jazz, blues, rock, and folk bands. Performances are held October through April on Wednesday nights from 5:30 to 7:30pm, and admission is $6.

When summer hits, Portlanders like to head outdoors to hear music. The city's top outdoor music series is held at **Washington Park Zoo,** 4001 SW Canyon Rd. (© **503/226-1561;** www.oregonzoo.org), which brings in the likes of Bonnie Rait, John Prine, and Leo Kottke.

THE CLUB & MUSIC SCENE
ROCK, BLUES & FOLK

Aladdin Theater   This former movie theater now serves as one of Portland's main venues for touring performers such as Richard Thompson, the Buena Vista Social Club, and Brian Wilson. The very diverse musical spectrum represented includes blues, rock, ethnic, country, folk, and jazz. There are also regular singer-songwriter programs. 3017 SE Milwaukie Ave. © **503/233-1994.** www.showman.com. Tickets $10–$25.

Berbati's Pan   Located in Old Town, this is currently one of Portland's most popular rock clubs. A wide variety of acts play here, primarily the best of the local rock scene and bands on the verge of breaking into the national limelight. 231 SW Ankeny St. © **503/248-4579.** www.berbati.citysearch.com. Cover $5–$15.

Crystal Ballroom   The Crystal Ballroom first opened before 1920, and since then has seen performers ranging from early jazz musicians to James Brown, Marvin Gaye, and the Grateful Dead. The McMenamin Brothers (of local brewing fame) renovated the Crystal Ballroom several years back and refurbished its dance floor, which, due to its mechanics, feels as if it's floating. The ballroom now hosts a variety of performances and special events nearly every night of the week. **Lola's Room,** a smaller version of the Ballroom, is on the second floor and also has a floating dance floor. You'll find **Ringlers Pub** (a colorful brewpub) on the ground floor. 1332 W. Burnside St. © **503/225-0047** ext. 239 for box office, 503/ 225-5555 ext. 8811 for concert information. www.danceonair.com. Cover free–$28.

Roseland Theater & Grill   The Roseland Theater, though it isn't all that large, is currently Portland's premier live music club for touring national name acts. You might encounter the likes of the Neville Brothers, Tower of Power, or Steel Pulse. There's also a restaurant affiliated with the club. 8 NW Sixth Ave. © **503/219-9929.** Cover $5–$35.

JAZZ

Jazz De Opus   Located in the Old Town nightlife district, this restaurant/bar has long been one of Portland's bastions of jazz, with a cozy room and smooth sounds on the stereo. You can also catch live performances nightly by jazz musicians. 33 NW Second Ave. © **503/222-6077.** Cover $5 on weekends.

The Lobby Court   Hands down the most elegant old-world bar in Portland, the Lobby Court is in the city's most luxurious hotel. The Circassian walnut paneling and crystal chandeliers will definitely put you in the mood for a martini or single malt. Tuesday through Saturday, there's live jazz in the evening. In the Benson Hotel, 309 SW Broadway. © **503/228-2000.**

Typhoon! Imperial Lounge   Located off the lobby of downtown Portland's Imperial Hotel, this bar has live jazz Thursday through Saturday nights. Big windows fronting on the sidewalk let you check out the scene before venturing in. An eclectic array of musicians makes this place a bit different from other area jazz clubs. In the Imperial Hotel, 400 SW Broadway. © **503/224-8285.** No cover.

CABARET

Darcelle's XV   In business since 1967 and run by Portland's best-loved crossdresser, this cabaret is a campy Portland institution with a female-impersonator show that has been a huge hit for years. There are shows Wednesday through Saturday. 208 NW Third Ave. © **503/222-5338.** www.darcellexv.citysearch.com. Cover $10. Reservations recommended.

DANCE CLUBS

See also the listing for Saucebox, below, under "Bars"; this restaurant and bar becomes a dance club after 10pm, when a DJ begins spinning tunes.

Andrea's Cha-Cha Club   Located in the Grand Cafe and open on Wednesday through Saturday nights, this is Portland's premier dance spot for fans of Latin dancing. Whether it's cha-cha, salsa, or the latest dance craze from south of the border, they'll be doing it here. Lessons are available between 8:30 and 9:30pm. 832 SE Grand Ave. © **503/230-1166.** Cover $1–$3.

Bar 71   Located in the Old Town nightlife district, Bar 71 is a mixed-use sort of place. It offers DJ dancing Thursday through Saturday on the back patio, pool tables in front, and good bar food. It's the classiest of the Old Town bars. In summer, you can dance under the stars. 71 SW Second Ave. ℂ 503/241-0938. No cover before 9:30pm, $5 9:30–10pm, $10 after 10pm.

THE BAR & PUB SCENE
BARS
The Brazen Bean   What started out as a late-night coffeehouse is now a very hip cocktail and cigar bar with a fin-de-siècle European elegance in Northwest Portland. This is mainly a man's domain, but cigar-puffing women will appreciate it as well. 2075 NW Glisan St. ℂ 503/294-0636.

Jake's Famous Crawfish   In business since 1892, Jake's is a Portland institution and should not be missed (see the full review on p. 76). The bar is one of the busiest in town when the downtown offices let out. 401 SW 12th Ave. ℂ 503/226-1419.

McCormick and Schmick's Harborside Pilsner Room   Located at the south end of Tom McCall Waterfront Park overlooking the Willamette River and RiverPlace Marina, this restaurant/bar is affiliated with Hood River's Full Sail brewery and keeps 10 Full Sail brews on tap (plus 15 other area beers). The crowd is upscale, the view one of the best in town. (See p. 76 for a review of the restaurant.) 0309 SW Montgomery St. ℂ 503/220-1865. www.mccormickandschmicks.com.

¡Oba!   Currently one of the trendiest bars in Portland, this big Pearl District bar/nuevo Latino restaurant has a very tropical feel despite the warehouse district locale. After work, the bar is always packed with the stylish and the upwardly mobile. Don't miss the tropical-fruit margaritas! 555 NW 12th Ave. ℂ 503/228-6161.

Paragon   Dark and cavernous, this Pearl District warehouse makeover is among the hippest hangouts in town, and regulars like to dress to impress. Not so overdone that you can't recognize the space's industrial heritage, this place has a sort of Edward-Hopper-meets-the-21st-century feel. There's live music on Wednesday and Thursday nights and a DJ on Fridays and Saturdays. 1309 NW Hoyt St. ℂ 503/833-5060. www.paragonrestaurant.com.

Saucebox   Popular with the city's scene-makers, this downtown hybrid restaurant-bar is a large, dramatically lit dark box that can be very noisy. If you want to talk, you'd better do it before 10pm, when the DJ arrives to transform this place from restaurant into dance club. Great cocktails. 214 SW Broadway. ℂ 503/241-3393.

WINE BARS
Oregon Wines on Broadway   With just a handful of stools at the bar and a couple of cozy tables, this tiny place is the best spot in Portland to learn about Oregon wines. On any given night there will be 30 Oregon Pinot Noirs available by the glass, and plenty of white wines as well. 515 SW Broadway. ℂ 503/228-4655.

Southpark Seafood Grill & Wine Bar   With its high ceiling, long heavy drapes, halogen lights, and lively wall mural, the wine bar at Southpark (see the full dining review on p. 77) is a contemporary interpretation of a Parisian cafe from the turn of the last century. Very romantic. 901 SW Salmon St. ℂ 503/326-1300.

BREWPUBS
They're brewing beers in Portland the likes of which you won't taste in too many other places on this side of the Atlantic. This is the heart of the Northwest

Portland's Brewing Up a Microstorm

Espresso may be the drink that drives Portland, but when it's time to relax and kick back, **microbrewed beer** is often the beverage of choice around these parts. No other city in America has as large a concentration of brewpubs, and it was here that the craft brewing business got its start in the mid-1980s. Today, brewpubs can be found throughout the city, with cozy neighborhood pubs vying for business with big, polished establishments.

To fully appreciate what the city's craft brewers are concocting, it helps to have a little beer background. Beer has **four basic ingredients:** malt, hops, yeast, and water. The first of these, **malt,** is made from grains, primarily barley and wheat, which are roasted to convert their carbohydrates into the sugar needed to grow yeast. The amount of roasting the grains receive during the malting process determines the color and flavor of the final product. The darker the malt, the darker and more flavorful the beer or ale. There is a wide variety of malts, each providing its own characteristic flavor. **Yeast,** in turn, converts the malt's sugar into alcohol; there are many different strains of yeast that all lend different characters to beers. The **hops** are added to give beer its characteristic bitterness. The more "hoppy" the beer or ale, the more bitter it becomes. The Northwest is the nation's only commercial hop-growing region, with 75% grown in Washington and 25% grown in Oregon and Idaho.

Lagers, which are cold-fermented, are the most common beers in America and are made from pale malt with a lot of hops added to give them their characteristic bitter flavor. **Pilsner,** a style of beer that originated in the mid–19th century in Czechoslovakia, is a type of lager. **Ales,** which are the most common brews served at microbreweries, are made using a warm fermentation process and usually with more and darker malt than is used in lagers and pilsners. **Porters** and **stouts** get their characteristic dark coloring and flavor from the use of dark, even charred, malt.

To these basics, you can then add a few variables. **Fruit-flavored beers,** which some disparage as soda-pop beer, are actually an old European tradition and, when considering the abundance of fresh fruits in the Northwest, are a natural here. Also immensely popular in Portland are **hefe-weizens** (German-style wheat beers), which have a cloudy appearance, and IPAs **(Indian pale ales),** which are strong and hoppy. If you see a sign for **nitro beer** in a pub, it isn't referring to their explosive brews—it means they've got a keg charged with nitrogen instead of carbon dioxide. The nitrogen gives the beer an extra creamy head. (A nitro charge is what makes Guinness Stout so distinctive.) **Cask-conditioned ales,** served almost room temperature and with only their own carbon dioxide to create the head, are also gaining in popularity. Although some people find these brews flat, others appreciate them for their unadulterated character.

It all adds up to a lot of variety in Portland pubs. Cheers!

craft-brewing explosion, and if you're a beer connoisseur, you owe it to yourself to go directly to the source.

Brewpubs have become big business in Portland, and there are now glitzy upscale pubs as well as funky warehouse-district locals. No matter what vision you have of the ideal brewpub, you're likely to find your dream come true. Whether you're wearing bike shorts or a three-piece suit, there's a pub in Portland where you can enjoy a handcrafted beer, a light meal, and a convivial atmosphere.

With almost three dozen brewpubs in the Portland metropolitan area, the McMenamins chain is Portland's biggest brewpub empire. The owners of this empire think of themselves as court jesters, mixing brewing fanaticism with a Deadhead aesthetic. Throw in a bit of historic preservation and a strong belief in family-friendly neighborhood pubs and you'll understand why these joints are so popular.

Downtown

McMenamin's Ringlers Pub   With mosaic pillars framing the bar, Indonesian antiques, and big old signs all around, this cavernous place is about as eclectic a brewpub as you'll ever find. A block away are two associated pubs in a flat-iron building; one is below street level with a beer cellar feel and the other has walls of multipaned glass. These three pubs are the most atmospheric alehouses in town. 1332 W. Burnside St. ✆ **503/225-0627.** www.mcmenamins.com.

Tugboat Brewpub   This tiny brewpub on an alley-like street just off Broadway near The Benson hotel is just what a good local pub should be. With its picnic-table decor, it's decidedly casual, but the shelves of books lend the place a literary bent. Good brews, too. 711 SW Ankeny St. ✆ **503/226-2508.**

Northwest Portland

BridgePort Brewery and BrewPub   Located in the trendy Pearl District, Portland's oldest microbrewery was founded in 1984 and is housed in the city's oldest industrial building (where workers once produced rope for sailing ships). The ivy-draped old brick building has loads of character, just right for enjoying craft ales, of which there are usually four to seven on tap on any given night (including several cask-conditioned ales). The pub also makes great pizza. 1313 NW Marshall St. ✆ **888/834-7546** or 503/241-7179. www.bridgeport brew.com.

Portland Brewing Company's Brewhouse Tap Room and Grill   With huge copper fermenting vats proudly displayed and polished to a high sheen, this is by far the city's most ostentatious, though certainly not its largest, brewpub. We aren't particularly fond of the brews here, but Portland Brewing's MacTarnahan's Scottish-style amber ale does have some very loyal fans. 2730 NW 31st Ave. ✆ **503/228-5269.**

Rogue Ales Public House   This Pearl District pub is an outpost of a popular microbrewery headquartered in the Oregon coast community of Newport. Rogue produces just about the widest variety of beers in the state, and, best of all, keeps lots of them on tap at this pub. If you're a fan of barley-wine ale, don't miss their Old Crustacean. 1339 NW Flanders St. ✆ **503/241-3800.**

Southeast

The Lucky Labrador Brew Pub   With a warehouse-size room, industrial feel, and picnic tables on the loading dock out back, this brewpub is a classic southeast Portland local. The crowd is young, and dogs are welcome. (They don't even have to be Labs.) 915 SE Hawthorne Blvd. ✆ **503/236-3555.** www.luckylab.com.

Northeast & North Portland Pubs

Alameda Brewhouse   With its industrial chic interior, this high-ceilinged neighborhood pub brews up some of the most unusual beers in Portland. How about a rose-petal bock, a juniper berry porter, or a heather-flower ale made without hops? Some work, some don't, but fans of craft beers have to appreciate the willingness to experiment. 4765 NE Fremont St. ☎ 503/460-9025.

McMenamin's Kennedy School   Never thought they'd ever start serving beer in elementary school, did you? However, in the hands of the local McMenamins brewpub empire, an old northeast Portland school has been transformed into a sprawling complex complete with brewpub, beer garden, movie theater pub, a cigar-and-cocktails room, even a bed-and-breakfast inn. Order up a pint and wander the halls checking out all the cool artwork. 5736 NE 33rd Ave. ☎ 503/288-2192. www.mcmenamins.com.

Widmer Brewing and Gasthaus   Located in an industrial area just north of the Rose Garden arena, this place has the feel of a classic blue-collar pub. This is the brewery for Portland's largest craft brewing company, which is best known for its hefeweizen. German and American foods are served. 955 N. Russell St. ☎ 503/281-3333. www.widmer.com.

THE GAY & LESBIAN NIGHTLIFE SCENE
A DANCE CLUB

Embers Avenue   Though primarily a gay disco, Embers is also popular with straights. There are always lots of flashing lights and sweaty bodies until the early morning. Look for drag shows 6 nights a week; on Mondays, movies are shown on a giant-screen TV. 110 NW Broadway. ☎ 503/222-3082. Cover Fri–Sat $5, Sun–Thurs free.

BARS

The area around the intersection of **SW Stark Street and West Burnside Street** has the largest concentration of gay bars in Portland.

Eagle PDX   If leather and Levi's are your uniform, then you'll feel right at home in this dive bar. Loud rock music plays in the background, and it's popular with a young crowd. Long happy hours with good prices. 1300 W. Burnside St. ☎ 503/241-0105.

Scandal's & The Otherside Lounge   In business for more than 20 years, this bar/restaurant is at the center of the gay bar scene. There always seems to be some special event going on here. 1038 SW Stark St. ☎ 503/227-5887. www.scandals. citysearch.com.

13 A Side Trip to Oregon City

When the first white settlers began crossing the Oregon Trail in the early 1840s, their destination was Oregon City and the fertile Willamette Valley. At the time Portland had yet to be founded, and Oregon City, set beside powerful Willamette Falls, was the largest town in Oregon. However, with the development of Portland and the shifting of the capital to Salem, Oregon City began to lose its importance. Today it is primarily an industrial town, though one steeped in Oregon history and well worth a visit. To get here from downtown Portland, drive south on SW First Avenue and continue on SW Macadam Avenue, which is Ore. 43. Follow this road for roughly 12 miles to reach Oregon City. (It should take 30–45 min.)

Moments   **A Portland Original: The Theater Pub**

Portland brewpub magnates the McMenamin brothers have a novel way to sell their craft ales—in movie pubs. Although it's often hard to concentrate on the screen, it's always a lot of fun to attend a show. The movies are usually recent releases that have played the main theaters but have not yet made it onto video. Theaters include the **Bagdad Theater,** 3702 SE Hawthorne Blvd. (© **503/236-9234**), a restored classic Arabian Nights movie palace; the **Mission Theater,** 1624 NW Glisan St. (© **503/223-4527**), which was the first McMenamins theater pub; the **Kennedy School Theater,** 5736 NE 33rd Ave. (© **503/288-2192**), in a former elementary school; and the **Edgefield Theater,** 2126 SW Halsey St., Troutdale (© **503/ 492-4686**).

To get to Oregon City from Portland, you can take I-5 south to I-205 east or you can head south from downtown Portland on SW Riverside Drive and drive through the wealthy suburbs of Lake Oswego and West Linn. Once in Oregon City, your first stop should be just south of town at the **Willamette Falls overlook** on Ore. 99E. Though the falls have been much changed by industry over the years, they are still an impressive sight.

End of the Oregon Trail Interpretive Center   With its three Paul Bunyan–size wagons parked in the middle of Abernethy Green (the official end of the Oregon Trail), this interpretive center is impossible to miss. Inside the first of the giant wagons you'll find an exhibit hall, hands-on area, and gift shop. After looking around this first wagon, you'll then be led through the next one by costumed interpreters who explain the difficulties of provisioning for the overland trek. The third wagon houses a multimedia presentation based on three Oregon Trail diaries.

1726 Washington St. © **503/657-9336**. www.endoftheoregontrail.org. Admission $6.50 adults, $5.50 seniors, $4 children 5–12, free for children under 5. Mon–Sat 9am–5pm; Sun 10am–5pm. Tour hours vary with day and season.

McLoughlin House   Oregon City's most famous citizen, retired Hudson's Bay Company chief factor John McLoughlin helped found this mill town on the banks of the Willamette River in 1829. By the 1840s, immigrants were pouring into Oregon, and McLoughlin provided food, seeds, and tools to many. Upon retirement in 1846, McLoughlin moved to Oregon City, where he built what was at that time the most luxurious home in Oregon. Today McLoughlin's house is a National Historic Site and is furnished as it would have been in McLoughlin's days. Many of the pieces on display are original to the house.

713 Center St. © **503/656-5146**. www.mcloughlinhouse.org. Admission $4 adults, $3 seniors, and $2 children 6–17, free for under 6. Tues–Sat 10am–4pm; Sun 1–4pm. Closed Jan and major holidays.

The Willamette Valley: The Bread (& Wine) Basket of Oregon

For more than 150 miles, from south of Eugene to the Columbia River at Portland, the Willamette River (pronounced Wih-*lam*-it) flows between Oregon's two major mountain ranges. Tempered by cool moist air from the Pacific Ocean yet protected from winter winds by the Cascade Range, which lies between the valley and the ocean, the Willamette Valley enjoys a mild climate that belies its northerly latitudes. It was because of this relatively benign climate and the valley's rich soils that the region's first settlers chose to put down roots here. Today the valley is home to Oregon's largest cities, its most productive farmlands, the state capital, and the state's two major universities.

Despite the many hardships, families were willing to walk 2,000 miles across the continent for a chance at starting a new life in the Willamette Valley. The valley very quickly became the breadbasket of the Oregon country, and today, it still produces an agricultural bounty unequaled in its diversity. Throughout the year, you can sample the produce of this region at farms, fruit stands, and wineries. In spring, commercial fields of tulips and irises paint the landscape with bold swaths of color. In summer, there are farm stands near almost every town, and many farms will let you pick your own strawberries, raspberries, blackberries, peaches, apples, cherries, and plums. In the autumn, you can sample the filbert and walnut harvest, and at any time of year, you can do a bit of wine tasting at dozens of wineries.

1 The North Willamette Valley Wine Country

McMinnville: 38 miles SW of Portland, 26 miles NW of Salem

Were it not for Prohibition, wine connoisseurs might be comparing California wines to those of Oregon rather than vice versa. Oregon wines had already gained a national reputation back in the days when Oregon became one of the earlier states to vote in Prohibition. It would be a few years before more liberal California would outlaw alcohol, and in the interim, the Golden State got the upper hand. When Prohibition was rescinded, California quickly went back to wine production, but no one bothered to revive Oregon's wine potential until the 1970s. However, by then Napa Valley had popped the cork on its wine dominance. Perhaps someday Willamette Valley wineries will be as well known as those down in California, and for fans of Pinot Noir, those days have already arrived. Oregon's Pinot Noirs have gained such international attention that even some French wineries have planted vineyards here and begun producing their own Oregon wines.

The north Willamette Valley wine country begins in the town of Newberg and extends south to the Salem area. The majority of the region's wineries flank Ore. 99W, and a drive down this rural highway will turn up dozens of blue signs pointing to wineries within a few miles of the highway. To the south of Salem, there are more wineries in the Corvallis and Eugene areas, but these are dealt with in the appropriate sections of this chapter. To the north of Ore. 99W, there are still more wineries in Washington County, which is actually in the drainage of the Tualatin River, which flows into the Willamette. These latter wineries are included in this section.

The most important wine-growing areas within this region, and the areas that produce the best wines, are the Red Hills above the town of Dundee, the slopes outside the town of Carlton, and the Eola Hills northwest of Salem. In Dundee, you'll find the greatest concentration of good restaurants, while in McMinnville, the largest town in the area, you'll find plenty of hotel rooms and more good restaurants.

ESSENTIALS

GETTING THERE   You'll find the heart of wine country between Newberg and McMinnville along Ore. 99W, which heads southwest out of Portland.

VISITOR INFORMATION   Contact the **Greater McMinnville Chamber of Commerce,** 417 N. Adams St., McMinnville, OR 97128 (© **503/472-6196;** www.mcminnville.org), or the **Newberg Area Chamber of Commerce,** 115 N. Washington St., Newberg, OR 97132 (© **503/538-2014;** www.newberg.org).

FESTIVALS   The most prestigious festival of the year is the **International Pinot Noir Celebration,** P.O. Box 1310, McMinnville, OR 97128 (© **800/ 775-4762;** www.ipnc.org), held each year on the last weekend in July or first weekend in August. The 3-day event, which is so popular that tickets are sold on a lottery system, includes tastings, food, music, and seminars. Registration forms are mailed out in February each year and tickets are currently $795 per person.

TOURING THE WINERIES

Forget pretentiousness, grand villas, celebrity wineries, snobbish waiters, or high prices for tastings—this is not the Napa Valley. Oregon wineries are, for the most part, still small establishments. Even the new wineries that have been opening up right on Ore. 99W (and that seem calculated to provide beach-bound vacationers with a bit of distraction and some less-than-impressive wine for the weekend) are still small affairs compared to the wineries of Napa Valley. Although in recent years more and more "corporate" wineries have been opening with the sole purpose of producing high-priced Pinot Noir, many of the region's wineries are still family-owned and -operated and produce moderately priced wines.

Now forget about Cabernet Sauvignon and Zinfandel. The Willamette Valley just isn't hot enough to produce these two varietals. With the exception of southern Oregon wineries and a few Willamette Valley wineries that buy their grapes from warmer regions (southern Oregon, California, and Washington's Yakima Valley), Oregon wineries have, thankfully, given up on trying to produce Cabs and Zins to compete with those of California. The wines of the Willamette Valley are primarily the cooler climate varietals traditionally produced in Burgundy, Alsace, and Germany. Pinot Noir is the uncontested leader of the pack, with Pinot Gris running a close second. However, Gewürztraminer and Riesling are also produced, and, with the introduction of early ripening

Jugglers, dancers and an assortment of acrobats fill the street.

She shoots you a wide-eyed look as a seven-foot cartoon character approaches.

What brought you here was wanting the kids

to see something magical while they still believed in magic.

America Online Keyword: Travel

With 700 airlines, 50,000 hotels and over 5,000 cruise and vaca-

tion getaways, you can now go places you've always dreamed of.

WORLD'S LEADING TRAVEL WEB SITE, 5 YEARS IN A ROW." WORLD TRAVEL AWARDS

Travelocity.com
A Sabre Company
Go Virtually Anywhere.

I HAVE TO CALL THE TRAVEL AGENCY AGAIN. DARN, OUT TO LUNCH. NOW I HAVE TO CALL THE AIRLINE. I HATE CALLING THE AIRLINES. I GOT PUT ON HOLD AGAIN. "INSTRUMENTAL TOP-40" ... LOVELY. I HATE GETTING PUT ON HOLD. TICKET PRICES ARE ALL OVER THE MAP. HOW DO I DIAL INTERNA-TIONALLY? OH SHOOT, FORGOT THE RENTAL CAR. I'M STILL ON HOLD. THIS MUSIC IS GIVING ME A HEADACHE. WONDER IF SOMEONE ELSE HAS CHEAPER FLIGHTS. FORGET IT, CAN'T TAKE IT ANYMORE ... I'M HANGING UP

YAHOO! TRAVEL
100% MUZAK-FREE

Booking your trip online at Yahoo! Travel is simple. You compare the best prices. You click. You go have fun. Tickets, hotels, rental cars, cruises & more. Sorry, no muzak.

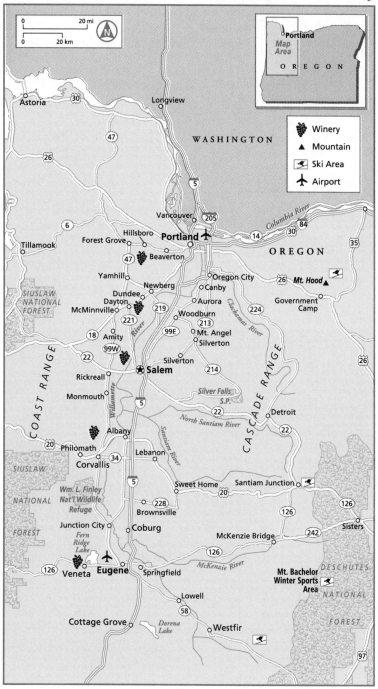

0 20 mi

0 20 km

N

Portland

Map
Area

OREGON

Winery
Mountain
Ski Area
Airport

Astoria

Longview

WASHINGTON

30

47

26

6

Tillamook

Vancouver

Columbia River

205

14

30

84

35

Hillsboro

Forest Grove

Portland

47

Beaverton

OREGON

Yamhill

Oregon City

26 Mt. Hood

Newberg

Canby

Government
Camp

Dundee

Aurora

Dayton

McMinnville

219

Woodburn

213

Clackamas River

224

SIUSLAW
NATIONAL
FOREST

221

River

99E

Mt. Angel

18 Amity

99W

Silverton

Silverton

26

Rickreall

Salem

214

Monmouth

Willamette

5

Silver Falls
S.P.

22

Detroit

COAST RANGE

North Santiam River

22

CASCADE RANGE

Albany

Santiam River

20

Philomath

Lebanon

SIUSLAW

34

Corvallis

5

NATIONAL

Sweet Home

Santiam Junction

20

126

FOREST

Wm. L. Finley
Nat'l Wildlife
Refuge

228

Brownsville

126

Sisters

Junction City

Fern
Ridge
Lake

Coburg

McKenzie Bridge

242

126

Veneta

Eugene

Springfield

McKenzie River

Mt. Bachelor
Winter Sports
Area

DESCHUTES

126

Lowell

NATIONAL

Cottage Grove

58

Dorena
Lake

Westfir

FOREST

97

Dijon-clone Chardonnay grapes, the region is finally beginning to produce Chardonnays that can almost compete with those of California. Other wines you'll likely encounter in this area include Müller-Thurgau (a usually off-dry white wine), Muscats (dessert wines) and sparkling wines (often made from Pinot Noir and Chardonnay grapes).

Wine country begins only a few miles west and southwest of Portland. Approaching the town of Newberg on Ore. 99W, you leave the urban sprawl behind and enter the rolling farm country of Yamhill County. These hills form the western edge of the Willamette Valley and provide almost ideal conditions for growing wine grapes. The views from these hills take in the Willamette Valley's fertile farmlands as well as the snowcapped peaks of the Cascades.

Between Newberg and Rickreall, you'll find more than two dozen wineries and tasting rooms that are open on a regular basis. There are concentrations of wineries in Dundee's Red Hills and in the Eola Hills northwest of Salem, and if you head north from Ore. 99W, you'll find another dozen or so wineries near Carlton, Yamhill, Hillsboro, and Forest Grove. Each of these groupings of wineries makes a good day's tasting route and has been organized here so that you can easily link them together as such.

Most, but not all, wineries maintain tasting rooms that are usually open between 11am or noon and 5pm. During the summer, most tasting rooms are open daily, but in other months they may be open only on weekends or by appointment. Wineries located right on Ore. 99W are usually open throughout the year. Many wineries also have a few picnic tables, so if you bring some goodies with you and then pick up a bottle of wine, you'll be set for a great picnic.

For anyone simply interested in tasting a little Oregon wine, the wineries along the highway are a good introduction. If you have a more than passing interest in wine, you'll want to explore the wineries that are located a few miles off Ore. 99W.

Many of the best wineries, however, are only open by appointment or on Memorial Day and Thanksgiving weekends. If you're serious about your wine, you might want to make appointments to visit some of these smaller wineries or plan a visit to coincide with Thanksgiving or Memorial Day. Oenophiles, especially Pinot Noir fans, are likely to uncover some rare gems and discover a few new favorite wineries this way.

At some wineries, you'll be asked to pay a tasting fee. However, most Oregon wineries do not charge for tastings unless they are offering reserve vintages or older "library" wines. Many wineries have celebrations, festivals, music performances, and picnics throughout the summer, and during these celebrations there is sometimes a fee to cover the cost of the appetizers and wine that are served. The Memorial Day and Thanksgiving weekend tastings usually carry a small fee.

For more information about the Oregon wine scene, including a calendar of winery events, pick up a copy of *Oregon Wine*, a monthly newspaper (available at area wine shops and wineries), or contact the **Oregon Wine Magazine,**

Tips **Taster's Tip**

Although few Oregon wineries have regularly scheduled winery tours, if you're interested and there is someone on hand to show you around, you're usually welcome to tour the facilities.

644 SE 20th Ave., Portland, OR 97214 (© **503/232-7607;** www.oregonwine press.com). The **Yamhill County Wineries Association,** P.O. Box 25162, Portland, OR 97298 (© **503/646-2985;** www.yamhillwine.com), publishes a free map and guide to the local wineries. You can pick up copies at almost any area winery.

THE YAMHILL COUNTY WINERIES
THE NEWBERG, DUNDEE & AURORA AREA

Argyle Winery   Located right on the highway in Dundee, this winery specializes in sparkling wines. Although wines can be had here for less than $20, these often seem a bit harsh. Bruts and Chardonnays are the specialty, and for these you'll pay a premium. Due to traffic congestion in Dundee, this winery is best visited when heading east on Ore. 99W.

691 Ore. 99W. © **503/538-8520.** www.argylewinery.com. Daily 11am–5pm.

Duck Pond Cellars   With its strategic location right on the highway, large parking lot, and tasting room full of gourmet food products and wine accessories, this winery aims to snag beach-bound traffic and on summer weekends the tasting room is often too crowded to be enjoyable. So far none of their wines have impressed us, but because they're so convenient to the highway, you might as well drop by and see if anything strikes your fancy.

23145 Ore. 99W. © **503/538-3199.** www.duckpondcellars.com. May–Oct daily 10am–5pm; Nov–Apr daily 11am–5pm. Closed Easter, Thanksgiving, Christmas, and New Year's Day.

Erath Vineyards ⭐   In business since 1972, Erath Vineyards, set high in the Red Hills of Dundee, was founded by Dick Erath, one of the pioneers of modern Oregon winemaking. A wide variety of wines is produced here and you can usually taste 10 or more during your visit to the tasting room. There's a pretty little public park, just right for a picnic, at the foot of the winery's driveway.

9409 NE Worden Hill Rd. © **800/539-9463** or 503/538-3318. www.erath.com. Daily 11am–5pm. In Dundee, go north on Ninth St., which becomes Worden Hill Rd.

Lange Winery ⭐   Good Pinot Noirs are the hallmark of this small winery, and although these usually cost $30 to $50, they are usually competitive with comparable premier Oregon Pinots. Lange also produces quite a few wines, mostly whites, in the under $20 range. The Pinots here are usually among the best in the state. We prefer the estate-grown Pinot Noirs.

18380 NE Buena Vista Rd., Dundee. © **503/538-6476.** www.langewinery.com. Wed–Mon 11am–5pm. Tasting fee $3. In Dundee, go north on Ninth St. and follow signs.

Ponzi Vineyards/Ponzi Wine Bar ⭐⭐   Ponzi Vineyards was one of the Oregon wine pioneers, and though it has its winery north of here near Beaverton, this tasting room/wine bar is a more convenient place to sample Ponzi wines. Expect excellent Pinot Gris and Chardonnay and be sure to sample the Arneis, an Italian varietal dry white wine that is aged in oak and is rarely planted in this area. Also don't miss the Vino Gelato, a dessert wine made from frozen grapes.

100 SW Seventh St. © **503/554-1500.** www.ponziwines.com. Daily 11am–5pm.

Rex Hill Vineyards   One of the oldest and largest wineries in Oregon, Rex Hill's setting is impressive. Inside the tasting room, you'll find antiques, contemporary art, and a large fireplace. Pinot Noirs are the main focus here, but Rex Hill also does respectable Pinot Gris, Sauvignon Blanc, Chardonnay, and Riesling.

30835 N. Hwy. 99W. © **503/538-0666.** www.rexhill.com. Daily 11am–5pm (Fri–Sun 10am–5pm in summer).

The Twice-A-Year Wineries

Harvest season aside, Memorial Day weekend and Thanksgiving weekend are the two most important weekends of the year in wine country. On these weekends, wineries often introduce their new releases and sometimes offer barrel tastings of wines that haven't yet been bottled. Many wineries offer live music, and most offer some sort of food, often exotic cheeses, to accompany the wines they are tasting.

Many of the area's best boutique wineries are *only* open to the public on these two weekends. So, if you're serious about wine, you won't want to pass up a Willamette Valley wine tour on one or the other of these holidays.

Area wineries open only Thanksgiving and/or Memorial Day weekend include the following wineries, most of which are located in Yamhill county. Head out to one of these wineries on either weekend and you can pick up a copy of that weekend's guide and map to open wineries. Once you've got a copy of the map in hand, you can pick and choose which wineries you'll want to visit.

Newberg, Dundee, Carlton & Yamhill Area

Adelsheim Vineyard, 22150 NE Calkins Lane, Newberg (© **503/538-3652**), one of Oregon's oldest wineries, now does several vineyard-designate wines.

Archery Summit, 18599 NE Archery Summit Rd., Dayton (© **503/864-4300;** www.archerysummit.com), produces Hearty Pinot Noirs reminiscent of Cabernet Sauvignon.

Beaux Frères, 15155 NE North Valley Rd., Newberg (© **503/537-1137**) offers a variety of expensive Pinot Noirs.

Belle Pente, 12470 NE Rowland Rd., Carlton (© **503/852-6389**), produces Pinot Noir, Pinot Gris, and Chardonnay at moderate prices.

Brick House Vineyards, 18200 Lewis Rogers Lane, Newberg (© **503/538-5136**), is an organic vineyard that produces Pinot Noir and Chardonnay, as well as a good Gamay Noir.

Cameron Winery, 8200 Worden Hill Rd., Dundee (© **503/538-0336**), produces the best nonvintage Pinot in the state (around $12). Open Thanksgiving weekend only.

St. Josef's Wine Cellar   Located a few miles north of Aurora toward Canby, this is one of the older wineries in the state, and with its half-timbered buildings has a very European feel. This winery is one of the few in the area that produces Cabernet Sauvignon, although these grapes are not always reliable here. The winery also does a sweet Gewürztraminer that's an excellent dessert wine.

28836 S Barlow Rd. © 503/651-3190. Tasting fee $1.50. June–Sept Wed–Sun noon–5pm; Oct–Dec and mid-Feb to May Sat–Sun 11am–5pm. Closed Jan to mid-Feb. From Aurora, go north on Ore. 99E to a right on Barlow Rd.

Sokol Blosser Winery   Another of the big Oregon wineries, Sokol Blosser sits high on the slopes above the west end of Dundee. Off-dry whites are a strong point here, and the Evolution No. 9, a blend of 10 different grapes, shouldn't be

Carlo & Julian Vineyard and Winery, 1000 E. Main St., Carlton (© **503/ 852-7432**), produces Sauvignon Blanc and some very drinkable and reasonably priced Pinot Noir.

Chehalem, 31190 NE Veritas Lane, Newberg (© **503/538-4700**), produces a range of wines that includes Cerise (a Gamay Noir/Pinot Noir blend) and good Pinot Noir.

Ken Wright Cellars, 236 N. Kutch St., Carlton (© **800/571-6825** or 503/852-7070; www.kenwrightcellars.com), is one of the region's top Pinot Noir producers. Open Thanksgiving weekend only.

Patricia Green Cellars, 15225 NE North Valley Rd., Newberg (© **503/ 554-0821**), produces small amounts of Pinot Noir, Sauvignon Blanc, and Pinot Gris. Patricia Green first made a name for herself as the winemaker at Torii Mor.

McMinnville & Amity Area

The Eyrie Vineyards, 935 E. Tenth Ave., McMinnville (© **503/472-6315**), is one Oregon's oldest wineries and produced the Willamette Valley's first Pinot Noir and Chardonnay, and America's first Pinot Gris.

Panther Creek Cellars, 455 N Irvine Rd., McMinnville (© **503/472-8080**), is known for its excellent Pinot Noir and Chardonnay but also is one of the few Oregon wineries to produce Melón, a wine made from Muscadet grapes.

Tempest Vineyards, 6000 Karla's Rd., Amity (© **503/835-2600**), produces Pinot Noir and Chardonnay, but also does several aperitif wines.

Youngberg Hill Vineyards, 10660 SW Youngberg Hill Rd., McMinnville (© **503/472-2727** or 888/657-8668), is affiliated with a B&B and makes an excellent base of operations for exploring this region.

Hillsboro Area

Beran Vineyards, 30088 SW Egger Rd., Hillsboro (© **503/628-1298**), is a small winery producing only premium estate-bottled Pinot Noir.

Raptor Ridge, 29090 SW Wildhaven Lane, Scholls (© **503/887-5595**; www.raptorridge.com), produces several different bottlings of Pinot Noir each year (we like the Shea Vineyards wines), as well as Chardonnay and Pinot Gris.

missed. A walk-through showcase vineyard provides an opportunity to learn about the growing process.

5000 Sokol Blosser Lane. © 503/864-2282. www.sokolblosser.com. Tasting fee $3. Daily 11am–5pm. West of Dundee off Ore. 99W.

Torii Mor Winery ⊛   With the Japanese-inspired name (torii means "gate" in Japanese) and gardens, you might expect this winery to produce *sake*, but instead they limit their production primarily to high-end Pinot Noir. Their better Pinot Noirs tend to be in the $50 range and new winemaker Joe Dobbes, something of a celebrity on the Oregon wine scene, is making sure that the winery continues to produce some of the best Pinots in the state.

18325 NE Fairview Dr. ✆ **503/434-1439.** www.toriimorwinery.com. Tasting fee $3. May–Nov Sat–Sun noon–5pm. In Dundee, go north on Ninth St. (which becomes Worden Hill Rd.), and turn right on Fairview Rd.

THE MCMINNVILLE, AMITY & DAYTON AREA

For a selection of area wines (several of which can be tasted on any given day), visit **Noah's–A Wine Bar,** 525 NE Third St., McMinnville (✆ **503/434-2787**), or, west of McMinnville on Ore. 18, the **Oregon Wine Tasting Room,** 19702 SW Ore. 18, Sheridan (✆ **503/843-3787**), which is adjacent to the Lawrence Gallery.

Amity Vineyards ⭐   This was one of the earlier wineries in Oregon and is one of the few wineries in the state producing Gamay Noir wine. Amity also produces unsulfited Pinot Blanc and Pinot Noir from organically grown grapes. Its late-harvest and dessert wines are a strong point. Amity also operates the Oregon Wine Tasting Room (✆ **503/843-3787**) at the Lawrence Gallery near Sheridan and the Oregon Wine Tasting Room Too (✆ **503/965-7369**) in Pacific City.

18150 Amity Vineyards Rd., Amity. ✆ **503/835-2362.** www.amityvineyards.com. Feb–Dec 23 daily noon–5pm. Closed Dec 24–Jan 31. In Amity, go east on Rice Lane.

Kristin Hill Winery ⭐   "Méthode champenoise" sparkling wines are a specialty here and make this winery well worth a visit. The Fizzy Lizzy, a cherry-infused dry sparkling wine, is one of Kristin Hill's most popular wines.

3330 SE Amity-Dayton Hwy., Amity. ✆ **503/835-0850.** Mar–Dec daily noon–5pm; Jan–Feb Sat–Sun noon–5pm. Closed Thanksgiving, Christmas, and New Year's Day. Just north of Amity at the junction with Ore. 233.

Yamhill Valley Vineyards ⭐   Located west of McMinnville near Sheridan, this winery is set on a 150-acre estate in the foothills of the Coast Range. Pinot Noirs are the strong point here and prices for younger Pinots are often quite reasonable (under $20). The Chardonnay here represents an especially good deal, and good Pinot Blancs and dry Rieslings are also produced. This is one of our favorite area wineries.

16250 Oldsville Rd. ✆ **503/843-3100.** www.yamhill.com. Mid-Mar to Memorial Day weekend Sat–Sun 11am–5pm; Memorial Day weekend–Thanksgiving weekend daily 11am–5pm.

THE YAMHILL & CARLTON AREA

In the town of Carlton, you'll find **The Tasting Room,** 105 W. Main St. (✆ **503/852-6733**), which specializes in wines from wineries that are not usually open to the public, which makes this an absolute must if you can't be around on Memorial Day or Thanksgiving weekend. Most wines featured here are from wineries in the immediate vicinity of Carlton.

Chateau Benoit ⭐   Set amid nearly 100 acres of vines and located high on a hill with one of the best views in the area, this winery has a large and impressive tasting room and does quite a few respectable white wines, most of which sell for less than $20. Dry Gewürztraminers and Müller-Thurgaus are among the more reliable dry whites here. The winery also produces decent Pinot Noir, as well as good Chardonnay from Dijon-clone vines.

6580 NE Mineral Springs Rd. ✆ **800/248-4835** or 503/864-2991. www.chateaubenoit.com. Daily 10am–5pm. Take Ore. 99W to Lafayette and go north on Mineral Springs Rd.

Cuneo Cellars ⭐⭐   Big reds are the specialty of this winery. Winemaker Gino Cuneo's Cana's Feast Cabernet-Merlot blend is a favorite. Cabernet Sauvignon, Pinot Noir, and even Nebbiolo all get the same treatment. If you like assertive red wines, don't miss this small winery.

750 Lincoln Rd. ✆ **503/835-2782.** Apr–Nov Fri–Sun noon–5pm. Located just off Ore. 47 on the north side of town.

Laurel Ridge Winery ⭐⭐ With its wide variety of wines, Laurel Ridge is a surefire spot to please a carload of different wine palates. Laurel Ridge has long been known for its excellent sparkling wines and Sauvignon Blanc, but also does some good inexpensive Pinot Noirs. A couple of different ports are also available.

13301 NE Kuehne Rd., Carlton. ✆ 503/852-7050. Daily 11am–5pm. From Carlton, drive east on Main St., which becomes Hendricks Rd. and then curves around to the north to become Kuehne Rd.

Willakenzie Estate ⭐ Situated on a 400-acre estate above the Chehalem Valley, this winery produces primarily Pinot Noir, Pinot Gris, Pinot Blanc, and Chardonnay in its gravity-fed facility. There's a nice picnic area with good views.

19143 NE Laughlin Rd., Yamhill. ✆ 888/953-9463 or 503/662-3280. www.willakenzie.com. Memorial Day–Labor Day daily noon–5pm.

THE WASHINGTON COUNTY WINERIES
THE HILLSBORO & BEAVERTON AREA

Cooper Mountain Vineyards ⭐ Now nearly surrounded by wealthy suburbs, this mountaintop winery is one of the few in the state that uses only organic grapes. The Pinot Gris is moderately priced and quite tasty as are the Chardonnays, which go light on the oak. Pinot Noirs are decent and for those who like a light wine, there is a Pinot Blanc that makes a great picnic wine.

9480 SW Grabhorn Rd., Beaverton. ✆ 503/649-0027. Feb–Dec daily noon–5pm; Jan Mon–Fri noon–5pm. From Ore. 217 on the west side of Portland, take Ore. 210 (Scholls Ferry Rd.) west approximately 5 miles, turn right on Tile Flat Rd. and right again on Grabhorn Rd.

Lion Valley Vineyards ⭐⭐ This small winery does very good Pinot Noirs in the $16 to $25 range. Although serious Burgundy drinkers sometimes find the Pinots here to be a bit too untraditional, we find them very drinkable. Worth seeking out.

35040 SW Unger Rd., Cornelius. ✆ 503/628-5458. www.lionvalley.com. Sat–Sun noon–5pm. Take Ore. 219 south 5 miles from Hillsboro, then go 3 miles west on SW Unger Rd.

Oak Knoll Winery ⭐ Although the only grape they actually grow here is a Niagara, from which they make a fruity but very drinkable wine, Oak Knoll manages each year to acquire some of the best grapes from area vineyards, and from these the winery usually succeeds in producing some good wines. Oak Knoll's Frambrosia is a delicious raspberry dessert wine.

29700 SW Burkhalter Rd., Hillsboro. ✆ 503/648-8198. Daily 11am–5pm. From Hillsboro, go south on Ore. 219 and turn left on Burkhalter Rd.

Ponzi Vineyards ⭐ Although Ponzi's tasting room/wine bar on Ore. 99W in Dundee is more convenient for most people touring wine country, it is also possible to taste wines here at the winery. Though there are no views here, the quiet setting and old shade trees make this an ideal spot for a picnic. See the listing above for information on wines produced by this pioneering Oregon winery.

14665 SW Winery Lane, Beaverton. ✆ 503/628-1227. www.ponziwines.com. Mon–Fri 11am–5pm; Sat–Sun noon–5pm. Closed Thanksgiving, Christmas, and New Year's Day. From Ore. 217 on the west side of Portland, take Ore. 210 (Scholls Ferry Rd.) west 4½ miles to a left on Vandermost Rd.

THE GASTON & FOREST GROVE AREA

Although Gaston is little more than a wide spot in the road, it is home to a great little wine and sandwich shop. **24° Brix,** 108 Mill St. (✆ **503/985-3434**) specializes in good local wines for under $20. Several of the wines carried by this shop are from tiny wineries that are never open to the public. (By the way, the Brix is the scale by which sugar in grapes is measured.)

David Hill Winery ⚑   This winery, up a gravel road, overlooks the forested foothills of the Coast Range and has its tasting room in a picturesque farmhouse. Here you'll usually find more than a dozen wines available for tasting. The sparkling wine and dessert wines (including a port) are particularly noteworthy. For the most part, wines here are very reasonably priced ($10–$15 range).

46350 David Hill Rd. ☏ **877/992-8545** or 503/992-8545. www.davidhillwinery.com. Tues–Sun noon–5pm. West of Forest Grove off Ore. 8.

Elk Cove Vineyards ⚑   Located in the hills above the community of Gaston, this is another of the state's larger wineries. La Sirene table wines, available both in red and white, are unusual blends that are quite balanced and drinkable. Their Roosevelt Pinot Noir, although expensive, can be very good, and the dessert wines are delicious.

27751 NW Olson Rd., Gaston. ☏ **503/985-7760.** www.elkcove.com. Daily 11am–5pm. Closed Thanks-giving, Christmas Eve, Christmas, and New Year's Day. From Ore. 47 in Gaston, go west on Olson Rd.

Kramer Vineyards   Located a little farther along the same road as Elk Cover Vineyards, this small winery does a decent Chardonnay. Don't miss the rasp-berry wine; it's the absolute essence of berries—a perfect summer dessert wine. Prices are fairly reasonable. There are numerous special events here throughout the year.

26830 NW Olson Rd., Gaston. ☏ **503/662-4545.** www.kramerwine.com. June–Sept daily noon–5pm; Mar–May and Oct–Dec Fri–Sun noon–5pm. Closed Easter, Thanksgiving, and Christmas. From Ore. 47 in Gaston, go west on Olson Rd.

Montinore Vineyards ⚑   This is another of Oregon's big wineries, and as at other large Oregon wineries, the wines are somewhat lacking, though prices are generally reasonable. Exceptions include reasonably priced Pinot Noirs, Chardonnays, and their late-harvest Riesling (which isn't too sweet). The setting, with an old farmhouse that looks straight out of the antebellum South, is quite picturesque.

3663 SW Dilley Rd. ☏ **503/359-5012.** www.montinore.com. Jan–Mar Sat–Sun noon–5pm; Apr–Dec daily 11am–5pm. Closed major holidays. South of Forest Grove off Ore. 47 at Dilley.

Shafer Vineyard Cellars ⚑   Small enough that the owners still work the tasting room but large enough to have a dozen or more wines available for tast-ing on any given day, this winery is strong on white wines, which it sells at very reasonable prices. Expect good Müller-Thurgaus and Gewürztraminers, and the Rieslings are also very consistent.

6200 NW Gales Creek Rd. ☏ **503/357-6604.** Mar–May Sat–Sun 11am–5pm; June–Dec Thurs–Mon 11am–5pm. Closed Jan–Feb. From Forest Grove, go 4½ miles west on Ore. 8.

Tualatin Estate Vineyards ⚑   Under the same ownership as the huge Willamette Valley Vineyards, this off-the-beaten-path winery is worth seeking out. Although Tualatin Estate does a respectable Pinot Noir, the winery is perhaps best known for its semi-sparkling Muscat dessert wine. You can also expect good Riesling late harvest Gewürztraminer.

10850 NW Seavey Rd. ☏ **503/357-5005.** Mar–Dec Sat–Sun noon–5pm. Closed Easter, Thanksgiving, Christmas, and Jan–Feb. From Forest Grove, go west on Ore. 8, turn north on Thatcher Rd. and then west on Clapshaw Hill Rd.

Finds Sake It to Me, Baby

When you've had it with peppery Pinot Noir, crisp Pinot Gris, and oaky Chardonnay, why not try a little sake? In Forest Grove you'll find **Saké One Brewery,** 820 Elm St. off Ore. 47 (© **503/357-7056;** www.sakeone.com), one of North America's few sake breweries. However, this Japanese-style rice wine is unlike any you've likely tasted before. This is premium sake and is meant to be served cold, not hot, which is the traditional way to serve premium sake in Japan. To make things even more unusual, this sake brewery also bottles several very untraditional flavored sakes that are made with citrus, hazelnut, Asian pear, and black raspberry flavoring. Think sake latte and you've got a pretty good idea of what these rice wines are like. The tasting room is open Saturdays from noon to 5pm, excluding major holidays.

THE MARION & POLK COUNTY WINERIES
THE EOLA HILLS

Some people claim the best Pinot Noirs in Oregon come from the Eola Hills northwest of Salem. Why not decide for yourself?

Bethel Heights Vineyards Set high on a hill and surrounded by more than 50 acres of grapes, Bethel Heights primarily produces Chardonnays and Pinot Noirs. Their less expensive Pinot Noirs can be good buys, and while their best Chardonnays are around $20, they're very good.

6060 Bethel Heights Rd. NW. © 503/581-2262. www.bethelheights.com. June–Aug Tues–Sun 11am–5pm; Mar–May and Sept–Dec Sat–Sun 11am–5pm. Closed Dec 24–Feb. From Ore. 221 in Lincoln, take Zena Rd. west and turn right on Bethel Heights Rd.

Cristom Vineyards With a beautiful setting high in the Eola Hills, this winery is an ideal place for a picnic. The Chardonnays, from both estate-grown grapes and grapes grown elsewhere in the region, are quite good and fall in the $20 price range. Cristom is one of the few wineries in the region producing a Viognier wine, which has a Riesling-like nose, but is peppery like a Gewürztraminer.

6905 Spring Valley Rd. NW. © 503/375-3068. www.cristomwines.com. Apr–May and Oct–Nov Fri–Sun 11am–5pm; June–Sept Tues–Sun 11am–5pm. Closed Dec–Mar. From Ore. 221 in Lincoln, take Zena Rd. west and turn right on Spring Valley Rd. or take Spring Valley Rd. west from Ore. 221 north of Lincoln.

Redhawk Vineyard Best known for its "Grateful Red" Pinot Noir, Redhawk brings a welcome dose of humor to wine making and wine tasting. Other noteworthy vintages include Chateau Mootom (with a cow on the label), Great White, and Punk Floyd (with an alien punk rocker on the label). There are also plenty of serious wines available. Most table wines run $7 to $12. Definitely not for wine snobs.

2995 Michigan City Rd. NW. © 503/362-1596. Apr–Nov daily noon–5pm; Dec–Mar Mon–Fri noon–5pm. 3 miles north of Ore. 22 off Ore. 221.

Witness Tree Vineyard Named for a tree used by surveyors in the 19th century, this unpretentious winery produces estate-grown Chardonnays and Pinot Noirs. In a region of high-priced Pinots, Witness Tree is noteworthy for offering very drinkable bottles at around $20 (though they also produce pricier vintage select Pinots).

7111 Spring Valley Rd. NW. ✆ **503/585-7874.** www.witnesstreevineyard.com. June–Aug Tues–Sun 11am–5pm; Mar–May and Sept–Dec Sat–Sun 11am–5pm. Closed Jan–Feb. From Ore. 221 in Lincoln, take Zena Rd. west and turn right on Spring Valley Rd. or take Spring Valley Rd. west from Ore. 221 north of Lincoln.

THE RICKREALL & DALLAS AREA

Chateau Bianca Winery ✺✺   This family-run winery does a wide range of wines, most of which are quite excellent, as one would expect from a family that brought its winemaking skills over from Germany. The Pinot Noirs here are good values, with bottles usually available in both the $10 and $20 range. The dry Riesling here is proof that a good German-style wine is just as good as the much-touted Burgundian-style wines so prevalent in Oregon. A good sparkling wine is also available. The winery has a B&B.

17485 Ore. 22, Dallas. ✆ **503/623-6181.** Feb–May and Nov–Dec daily 11am–5pm; June–Oct daily 10am–6pm. Closed Jan. On Ore. 22 about 10 miles west of Rickreall and Ore. 99W.

Eola Hills Wine Cellars ✺   Well known in the area for its Sunday brunches, this winery on the outskirts of Rickreall offers everything from Cabernet Sauvignon to Zinfandel—almost all at reasonable prices. Eola Hills is able to provide a wide variety of well-priced wines because they bring their grapes from as far away as California.

501 S. Pacific Hwy., Rickreall. ✆ **503/623-2405.** Daily 11am–5pm. On Ore. 99W between Rickreall and Monmouth.

Flynn Vineyards ✺   This winery is known primarily for its sparkling wines, and they do both a Brut (75% Pinot Noir and 25% Chardonnay) and a Blanc de Blanc (100% Chardonnay), both of which are quite good and usually sell for less than $20. The tasting room is in the winery's aging room, and you can observe the steps involved in the classic *méthode champenoise.* They also do decent, inexpensive Chardonnays and Pinot Noirs.

2200 W. Pacific Hwy., Rickreall. ✆ **503/623-8683.** www.flynnvineyards.com. Sat–Sun 11am–5pm. Closed Easter, Christmas Eve, Christmas, and New Year's Day. On Ore. 99W north of Rickreall.

Oak Grove Orchards Winery/Stevens Cellars ✺   This casual little winery on the west side of the Eola Hills specializes in dessert wines, particularly various types of Muscat wines. If you're a fan of Muscats, don't pass up an opportunity to stop here.

6090 Crowley Rd., Rickreall. ✆ **503/364-7052.** Tues–Sun noon–6pm. From Ore. 99W between Amity and Rickreall, go east on Crowley Rd. or the road on the north side of Flynn Vineyards.

Van Duzer Vineyards ✺   Producing primarily Pinot Noir, Pinot Gris, and Chardonnay in the Burgundian style, this winery is built on the side of an oak-shaded knoll with a commanding view across the valley to the Eola Hills. The tasting room is small and only a few wines are available at any given time.

11975 Smithfield Rd. ✆ **503/623-6420.** Mar–Dec daily 11am–5pm. North of Rickreall off Ore. 99W; take graveled Smithfield Rd. 3 miles west.

OTHER WINE COUNTRY ACTIVITIES

You can also see the wine country from the air on a hot-air balloon ride with **Vista Balloon Adventures** (✆ **800/622-2309** or 503/625-7385; www.vista balloon.com), which charges $160 to $185 per person for a 1-hour flight (with hot breakfast and sparkling wine toast). Alternatively, between March and October, you can opt for a flight over the region in a glider. Contact **Cascade Soaring,** McMinnville Airport (✆ **503/472-8805**), which offers a variety of flights ranging in duration from 15 to 55 minutes and in price from $40 to $160. Gliders carrying one or two passengers are used.

Want to see wine country from a saddle? Give the **Wine Country Farms Arabian Horseback Riding,** 6855 Breyman Orchards Rd. (© **503/864-3178**), a call. They offer 2-hour horseback rides for $40.

Seven miles south of Newberg off Ore. 219, on the banks of the Willamette River, is **Champoeg State Park** (pronounced Sham-*poo*-ee) (© **503/ 678-1251**). The park includes a campground, a bike path, a picnic area, a historic home, a log cabin, and a visitor center that traces Champoeg's history from its days as an Native American village up through its pioneer farming days. Park admission is $3.

Howard Hughes's famous "Spruce Goose" flying boat has finally come to roost at the **Evergreen Aviation Museum** ✦✦, 3685 NE Three Mile Lane, McMinnville (© 503/434-4180; www.sprucegoose.org). Although designed during World War II as a flying troop transport that wouldn't have to worry about attacks from German U-boats, the Spruce Goose wasn't completed until 1947, at which point it was no longer needed. The plane flew only one time, with Howard Hughes at the controls. The massive wooden plane rests in the company of many other, smaller planes. Among these are a Ford Trimotor, a P-51 Mustang, a Spitfire, a MiG-15 UTI Midget, and a replica of the Wright Brothers' 1903 plane. By the way, the term "Spruce Goose" is actually a misnomer; most of the plane is made of birch. Admission is $9 adults, $7 seniors, $5 students, and free for children 5 and under. Open daily from 9am to 5pm. Closed Thanksgiving, Christmas, and New Year's Day.

THE AURORA COLONY

An interesting chapter in Oregon pioneer history is preserved 13 miles south of Oregon City in the town of Aurora, founded in 1855 as a Christian communal society. Similar to such better-known communal experiments as the Amana Colony and the Shaker communities, the Aurora Colony lasted slightly more than 20 years. Today Aurora is a National Historic District and the large old homes of the community's founders have been restored. Many of the old commercial buildings now house antiques stores. You can learn the history of Aurora at the **Old Aurora Colony Museum,** Second and Liberty streets (© **503/678-5754**). Between April and October, the museum is open Tuesday through Saturday from 10am to 4pm and on Sunday from noon to 4pm; from March to mid-April and mid-October to December, the museum is open Friday and Saturday from 10am to 4pm and Sunday from noon to 4pm (open Jan and Feb by appointment only). Admission is $3.50 for adults, $3 for seniors, and $1.50 for children 6 to 18.

Tips **The Grape Escape**

If you're interested in learning more about Oregon wines, contact **Grape Escape** (© **503/283-3380;** www.grapeescapetours.com), which offers an in-depth winery tour of the Willamette Valley. All-day tours include stops at several wineries, appetizers, lunch, and dessert, and pickup and drop-off at your hotel ($85 per person). For people with less time, there are half-day afternoon trips that take in two or three wineries ($60 per person).

SHOPPING IN THE AREA

If you're interested in picking up some local art or crafts, there are several places worth visiting. West of McMinnville near Sheridan, you'll find the **Lawrence Gallery,** Ore. 18 (© **503/843-3633**). This large art gallery features regional artists and has a sculpture garden and a water garden. Right across the street, you'll find the **Fire's Eye Gallery,** Ore. 18 (© **503/843-9797**), with more whimsical, colorful artwork than the Lawrence Gallery.

If you enjoy shopping for antiques and collectibles, check out the **Lafayette Schoolhouse Antique Mall,** 784 Ore. 99W, Lafayette (© **503/864-2720**), housed in a 1910 schoolhouse and filled with more than 100 dealers. Lafayette is 6 miles east of McMinnville on Ore. 99W.

To stock up on local jams, wines, and other gourmet food items, visit **Your Northwest,** Ore. 99W and Seventh Street, Dundee (© **503/554-8101**). This little shop is crammed full of all manner of foods and Northwest crafts. **Firestone Farms,** 18400 N. Hwy. 99W (© **503/864-2672;** www.firestonefarms. com), just west of Dundee, also sells a wide selection of local produce, wines, and gourmet foods. If you like chocolate, you might want to head down to Amity and stop in at the **Brigittine Monastery,** 23300 Walker Lane (© **503/ 835-8080;** www.brigittine.org), known for its heavenly fudge. The fudge and truffles are on sale at the guest reception area, which is open daily from 9am to 5:30pm (closed 10:30am–1:30pm Sun).

WHERE TO STAY
THE NEWBERG & DUNDEE AREA

Partridge Farm Bed & Breakfast ⭑   This old yellow farmhouse feels secluded even though it's right on busy Ore. 99W and gets a bit of traffic noise. Shade trees, beautiful gardens, berry hedges, and fruit trees give Partridge Farm a relaxing country atmosphere that, on a sunny summer afternoon, begs to be enjoyed with a glass of wine and a good book. Inside, there's a hint of French country sophistication. The one room and two suites are all quite large and are furnished with period antiques.

4300 E. Portland Rd., Newberg, OR 97132. © 503/538-2050. 3 units. $70–$90 double; $90–$110 suite. Rates include full breakfast. MC, V. *In room:* A/C.

Springbrook Hazelnut Farm ⭑⭑   Only 20 miles from Portland, this 70-acre working farm is a convenient rural getaway for anyone who craves a slower-paced vacation. The four craftsman-style buildings are listed on the National Register of Historic Places and include the main house with its two rooms and a suite, a carriage house, and a cottage. Original artwork abounds in the boldly decorated, colorful main house. Both of the main buildings overlook the farm's pond and lovely back garden, and there are also tennis courts and a swimming pool. Through the hazelnut orchard is Rex Hill Vineyards, and there's also a small winery operating here on the farm. The little white cottage, with its antique fireplace mantle, fir floors, and tiled bathroom overlooks the farm's pond and a meadow that's filled with daffodils in the spring.

30295 N. Ore. 99W, Newberg, OR 97132. © 800/793-8528 or 503/538-4606. www.nutfarm.com. 5 units. $105 double; $190 suite; $200 cottage; $175 carriage house. Rates include full breakfast. No credit cards. **Amenities:** Outdoor pool; access to nearby health club. *In room:* Coffeemaker, hair dryer, iron, no phone.

Willamette Gables Riverside Estate ⭑⭑ *(Finds*   The banks of Oregon's Willamette River may not be where you'd expect to find a southern plantation home, but nonetheless, here it is. Designed as a reproduction of a home in Natchez, Mississippi, this secluded and tranquil B&B is authentic in almost every detail and is as elegant an inn as you'll find anywhere in the region. The views of the river from the breakfast room will start your day out just right. The inn is close to Champoeg State Park, about midway between Aurora and Newberg, and there's a winery not too far away.

10323 Schuler Rd., Aurora, OR 97002. ☎ 503/678-2195. www.willamettegables.com. 5 units. $135–$155 double. Rates include full breakfast. MC, V. *In room:* No phone.

Wine Country Farm ☆   Located high in the hills between Dundee and Lafayette, this B&B has one of the best views in the area, a wine tasting room, and 5 acres of grapevines. When this 1910 farmhouse was renovated and converted into a B&B, the owners even gave the facade the look of a French farmhouse. Although the decor is nothing fancy, two of the rooms have good views, as do the breakfast room and the deck that runs the entire length of the house. The Courtyard Room and the Vineyard Suite are the two best choices here. A croquet lawn and horseshoe pit provide traditional rural recreational activities when guests aren't out wine tasting. Horseback riding is also available, and some rooms have TVs and VCRs.

6855 Breyman Orchards Rd., Dayton, OR 97114. ☎ 800/261-3446 or 503/864-3446. Fax 503/864-3109. www.winecountryfarm.com. 7 units. $95–$135 double; $135 suite. Rates include full breakfast. MC, V. **Amenities:** Jacuzzi; sauna; bikes; massage. *In room:* A/C.

THE MCMINNVILLE AREA

Best Western Vineyard Inn Motel ☆   This modern hotel was the first in the area to actively cater to the growing numbers of oenophiles who are touring Oregon's wine country. Purple and lavender are the predominant colors here, and there are wine posters throughout the hotel. The guest rooms are very comfortable, and most are quite spacious.

2035 S. Hwy. 99W, McMinnville, OR 97128. ☎ 800/285-6242 or 503/472-4900. Fax 503/434-9157. 65 units. $90–$117 double. Rates include continental breakfast. AE, DC, DISC, MC, V. **Amenities:** Indoor pool; exercise room; Jacuzzi; coin-op laundry. *In room:* A/C, TV, fridge, coffeemaker, hair dryer, iron.

Mattey House ☆   This restored 1892 Queen Anne Victorian farmhouse sits on 10 acres of farmland behind 1½ acres of grapevines. This is a grand old house, and up on the second floor, you'll find a tiny balcony overlooking the vineyard. It's the perfect spot for a glass of wine in the afternoon. Guest rooms are decorated in country Victorian style, with antique beds. The Riesling Room, with its claw-foot bathtub, is our favorite.

10221 NE Mattey Lane, McMinnville, OR 97128. ☎ 503/434-5058. Fax 503/434-6667. www.matteyhouse. com. 4 units. $100–$130 double. Rates include full breakfast. MC, V. *In room:* No phone.

McMenamins Hotel Oregon ☆☆   This restored historic hotel in downtown McMinnville is operated by a Portland-based chain of brewpubs, nightclubs, and unusual hotels that are all filled with interesting artwork. Guest rooms here are done in a simple, classic style, with antique and reproduction furniture. The corner kings with private baths and big windows on two sides are the nicest rooms; however, most rooms here have shared bathrooms. Offsetting this inconvenience is the hotel's genuinely historic feel. What make the Hotel Oregon imminently recommendable are its ground-floor brewpub/dining room and its rooftop bar and deck overlooking McMinnville and the Yamhill Valley. There are also a couple of good restaurants within a few blocks.

310 NE Evans St., McMinnville, OR 97128. ☎ 888/472-8427 or 503/472-8427. Fax 503/435-3141. www.hoteloregon.com. 42 units (6 with private bathroom). $75–$110 double with shared bathroom; $95–$125 double with private bath. Rates include full breakfast. AE, DISC, MC, V. **Amenities:** Restaurant (American), 2 lounges. *In room:* A/C.

Youngberg Hill Vineyards & Inn ★★ Set on a 50-acre farm that includes 12 acres of vineyards, this is the quintessential wine country inn. A long gravel driveway leads to the large, modern structure atop a hill with commanding views of the Willamette Valley, snow-capped Cascades peaks, and the Coast Range. Large decks wrap around both floors of the inn, and some of the rooms have their own fireplaces. Big breakfasts, often using produce from the farm, get visitors off to a good start each morning. Pull up a chair on the porch, pour a glass of the inn's own Pinot Noir, gaze out over the rolling hills, and you'll probably start thinking about cashing in the mutual funds to start a vineyard of your own.

10660 SW Youngberg Hill Rd., McMinnville, OR 97128. © 888/657-8668 or 503/472-2727. Fax 503/ 472-1313. www.youngberghill.com. 7 units. $135–$159 double; $179–$239 suite. Rates include full breakfast. MC, V. **Amenities:** Massage. *In room:* A/C, hair dryer.

THE FOREST GROVE AREA

McMenamins Grand Lodge ★★ Housed in a former Masonic retirement home, this sprawling lodge is part of a local microbrewery chain and has a decidedly countercultural feel. Although only one of the rooms here has a private bath, there are plenty of well-appointed bathrooms, and most rooms do have sinks. There's also lots of colorful works of art incorporated into the design of the building. However, the main attractions here are the brewpub, beer garden, and numerous small lounges scattered around the main building. The lodge is surrounded by huge lawns and is close to more than half a dozen wineries.

3505 Pacific Ave., Forest Grove, OR 97116. © 877/922-9533 or 503/992-9533. www.thegrandlodge.com. 77 units (1 with private bathroom). $50–$90 double with shared bathroom; $150–$200 double with private bathroom. Rates include full breakfast. AE, DISC, MC, V. **Amenities:** 2 restaurants (American), 5 lounges; soaking pool; day spa; massage. *In room:* No phone.

THE EOLA HILLS

Bethel Heights Farm Bed & Breakfast ★★ Set high on a hill overlooking the Willamette Valley, the Coast Range, and the distant Cascades (including Mt. Jefferson), this inn is in the middle of a 20-acre farm and vineyard. Outside the front door are a rock garden, small pond, and gazebo, while down the hill and into the oak woods, you'll find a much larger farm pond. Inside, all is spotless and modern. The two rooms have outstanding views west to the Coast Range. One has a patio, the other a balcony. The gourmet breakfasts include homemade jams and syrups and homemade pastries. If you're in the area specifically to do a bit of wine touring, there is no better location than this contemporary inn in the middle of the Eola Hills wine region.

6055 Bethel Heights Rd. NW, Salem, OR 97304. © 503/364-7688. Fax 503/371-8365. www.oregon-b-and-b. com. 2 units. $95 double. DISC, MC, V. *In room:* No phone.

WHERE TO DINE
THE NEWBERG & DUNDEE AREA

The Dundee Bistro ★★ NORTHWEST Located in the same building as the Ponzi Wine Bar and the Your Northwest gift shop, this chic eatery would fit right in in Portland's hip Pearl District. It's quite popular with people touring the area wineries. The menu is relatively short and changes on a regular basis. However, the emphasis is on fresh regional ingredients, which translates into the likes of roasted fennel soup, pork loin with dried-cherry sauce, chanterelle ravioli with hazelnut brown butter, or prosciutto and fresh fig pizza.

100-A SW Seventh St., Dundee. © 503/554-1650. Reservations recommended. Main courses $9.50–$24. AE, MC, V. Mon–Thurs 11:30am–8:30pm; Fri–Sat 11:30am–9:30pm; Sun noon–7pm.

Red Hills Provincial Dining ★★ FRENCH/CONTINENTAL/NORTH-WEST   Located in a 1920s craftsman bungalow, this restaurant sums up the Oregon wine country appeal with both its setting and its food. The dinner menu changes regularly, and you can be sure it will always include plenty of fresh local produce, as well as Northwest meats and seafoods. The menu draws on a variety of European influences and can be counted upon to include the likes of champagne chicken, grilled eggplant torte, veal saltimbocca, or seafood in saffron-herb broth. There's a very good selection of wines available (local wines are featured), and dishes are calculated to pair well with the wines of the region.

276 Hwy. 99W, Dundee. ✆ 503/538-8224. Reservations recommended. Main courses $18.50–$26. MC, V. Tues–Sat 11:30am–2pm and 5–9pm; Sun 5–9pm.

Tina's ★★ CONTINENTAL/NORTHWEST   Despite its rather small and nondescript building right on the highway in Dundee, Tina's has long been one of the Yamhill County wine country's premier restaurants. The menu changes regularly and usually has around half a dozen entrees and fewer appetizers. However, a balance between the traditional (grilled rib-eye steak with portobello mushrooms and hand-cut fries) and the less familiar (pan-roasted duck breast with corn soufflé and green-peppercorn sauce), keeps diners content. There are usually almost as many desserts available as there are entrees, and the wine selection, of course, emphasizes local wines.

760 Hwy. 99W. ✆ 503/538-8880. Reservations recommended. Dinner $18–$28. AE, DISC, MC, V. Daily 5–9pm.

THE AMITY & DAYTON AREA

The Joel Palmer House ★★★ FRENCH/NORTHWEST   If you love mushrooms in all their earthy guises, then, in this downtown Dayton restaurant, you will find your culinary Nirvana. Chef/owner Jack Czarnecki is a man obsessed with mushrooms, and nearly every dish has mushrooms in it. Start your meal with the extraordinary wild mushroom soup made with suillis mushrooms, then move on to the elk with juniper berries and black chanterelles, the beef Stroganoff with wild mushrooms and Oregon white truffles, or the (mushroom-free) crab cakes. Also mushroom-free, the rack of lamb with a Pinot-hazelnut sauce is a quintessential wine country entree. The extensive wine list features Oregon wines. Don't miss an opportunity to sample the rich, unique chocolate-lavender ice cream should it be available. The restaurant is in a house built in the 1850s and is quite formal. Mushroom lovers will be in good hands if they opt for the "Mushroom Madness" prix fixe dinner.

600 Ferry St., Dayton. ✆ 503/864-2995. www.joelpalmerhouse.com. Reservations highly recommended. Main courses $17.50–$25.50; prix fixe $52. AE, DC, DISC, MC, V. Tues–Fri 11:30am–2pm and 5–9pm; Sat 5–9pm. Closed mid-Feb to mid-Mar.

THE MCMINNVILLE AREA

For casual and inexpensive meals, try the **McMenamins Pub,** Hotel Oregon, 310 NE Evans St. (✆ 503/472-8427), which serves decent pub fare, plus good microbrews and regional wines. More pub fare, microbrews, and local wines can also be had at the **Golden Valley Brewery & Pub,** 980 E. Fourth St. (✆ 503/472-2739). For espresso, drop by **Union Block Coffee,** 403 NE Third St. (✆ 503/472-0645) or **Cornerstone Coffee Roasters,** 216 NE Third St. (✆ 503/472-6622).

The Fresh Palate Cafe ★ SEAFOOD/NORTHWEST   This casual spot is popular both with people touring the wine country and those headed to or from the beach. Good choices include crab cakes, crab-stuffed portobello mushrooms, and a sandwich made with hazelnut-crusted salmon. There are usually a half dozen or so daily specials. Because this is the best place for miles around, there is usually a wait for a table on summer weekends. If the weather is nice, try to get a table on the deck.

19706 SW Ore. 18 (between McMinnville and Sheridan). ☎ 503/843-4400. Reservations recommended on weekends. Main courses $15–$17. AE, MC, V. Mon–Tues 11am–3pm; Wed–Sun 11am–7pm.

Nick's Italian Café ☆☆ NORTHERN ITALIAN   There's nothing in Nick's narrow storefront windows to indicate that this is one of the best restaurants in the region. However, when you step through the door and are immediately confronted by the rich tones of carved and polished wood, you'll know that this is someplace special. Each evening, there's a fixed-price five-course dinner. (A la carte is also available.) Dinner might start with an avocado topped with bay shrimp and sauce Louis, followed by a salad of tomatoes, mozzarella, and basil. From there you might move on to an antipasti, and then minestrone soup. For the entree, there's always a choice between three dishes—say, grilled salmon, pork loin with cider-pear compote and mushroom-bacon risotto, or garlic-marinated shrimp with balsamic-Gorgonzola butter and horseradish mashed potatoes. If you still have room after all that, there are desserts such as tiramisu, chocolate brandy torte, and crème brûlée.

521 E. Third St. ☎ 503/434-4471. Reservations recommended. 5-course fixed-price dinner $35–$37. AE, MC, V. Tues–Thurs 5:30–9pm; Fri–Sat 5:30–10pm; Sun 5–8pm.

THE CARLTON & YAMHILL AREA

Caffé Bisbo ☆☆ ITALIAN   This family-run restaurant in downtown Carlton is small and has a short menu, but each dish is lovingly prepared by chef Claudio Bisbocci. If you're lucky, you just might find Claudio's pesto lasagna on the day's menu, but even if you don't, the lasagna with homemade noodles is always excellent. The chicken cacciatore, bathed in olives and olive oil, is also good. However, the very best comes last—Caffé Bisbo's tiramisu is absolutely heavenly.

214 Main St., Carlton. ☎ 503/852-7248. Reservations required for dinner. Main courses $5–$10 lunch, $16–$26 dinner. MC, V. Thurs–Sat 11:30am–2pm and 5–9pm.

IN THE GASTON & FOREST GROVE AREA

If you're up in the northern end of wine country and need light lunch, drop by **24° Brix**, 108 Mill St., Gaston (☎ 503/985-3434), a small sandwich shop and wine-tasting room that does focaccia sandwiches and sells breads, pastries, and cheeses as well.

EN ROUTE TO THE BEACH

It used to be almost impossible to get beach-bound traffic on Ore. 18 west of McMinnville to stop for anything, but that was before the **Spirit Mountain Casino** (☎ 800/760-7977; www.spiritmountain.com) opened in the town of Grand Ronde and became the most popular casino in Oregon. These days a lot of the traffic on this highway isn't even going to the beach, it's headed straight to this large, glitzy temple of luck.

2 Salem & the Mid-Willamette Valley

47 miles S of Portland, 40 miles N of Corvallis, 131 miles W of Bend, 57 miles E of Lincoln City

Though it's the state capital, the third largest city in the state, and home to Willamette University, Salem feels more like a small Midwestern college town than a Pacific Rim capital. Founded by a Methodist missionary, the city still wears its air of conservatism like a minister's collar. No one has ever accused Salem of being too raucous or rowdy. Even when both the school and the legislature are in session, the city barely seems charged with energy. The quiet conservatism does, however, give the city a certain charm that's not found in the other cities of the Willamette Valley. Though there are some interesting museums and the state capitol building to be visited here, it is the countryside surrounding Salem that is the real attraction. Within 20 to 25 miles of Salem, you'll find the Oregon Garden, Silver Falls State Park (one of the most beautiful state parks in Oregon), wineries, commercial flower fields, and several quaint small towns (Silverton, Mt. Angel, Independence, and Monmouth) that conjure up the Willamette Valley's pioneer past.

Salem's roots date from 1834, when Methodist missionary Jason Lee, who had traveled west to convert the local Indians, founded Salem, making it the first American settlement in the Willamette Valley. In 1842, 1 year before the first settlers crossed the continent on the Oregon Trail, Lee founded the Oregon Institute, the first school of higher learning west of the Rockies. In 1857, the first textile mill west of the Mississippi opened here, giving Salem a firm industrial base. However, despite all these historic firsts, Oregon City and Portland grew much faster and quickly became the region's population centers. Salem seemed doomed to backwater status until 1859, when Oregon became a state and Salem was chosen to become the state capital.

ESSENTIALS

GETTING THERE   Salem is on I-5 at the junction of Ore. 22, which heads west to connect with Ore. 18 from Lincoln City and southeast to connect with U.S. 20 from Bend.

Amtrak has passenger rail service to Salem. The station is at 13th Street between Leslie and Bellevue streets.

VISITOR INFORMATION   Contact the **Salem Convention & Visitors Association,** 1313 Mill St. SE, Salem, OR 97301 (© **800/874-7012** or 503/ 581-4325; fax 503/581-4540; www.scva.org). For more information on the Silverton area, contact the **Silverton Chamber of Commerce,** 426 Water St. (P.O. Box 257), Silverton, OR 97381 (© **503/873-5615;** www.silvertonor.com).

GETTING AROUND   Car rentals are available from **Hertz, Budget,** and **Enterprise.** If you need a taxi, contact **Yellow Cab** (© **503/362-2411**); fares start at $2.20 for flag drop and then $1.80 per mile. Public bus service throughout the Salem area is provided by **Salem Area Transit** (© **503/588-BUSS**), which goes by the name of Cherriots.

FESTIVALS   Two of the biggest events of the year in Salem are the **Oregon State Fair** (© **800/833-0011** in Oregon or 503/947-3247), which is held from late August to Labor Day, and the **Salem Arts Festival** (© **503/581-2228;** www.salemartfestival.org), which is the largest juried art fair in Oregon and is held the third weekend in July.

Each year on the second weekend after Labor Day, the town of Mt. Angel is the site of the huge **Mt. Angel Oktoberfest** ⊛ (© **503/845-9440;** www. oktoberfest.org). With polka bands from around the world, beer and wine gardens, German food, and dancing in the streets, this is just about the biggest party in the state.

SALEM
SEEING THE SIGHTS

Though it is sometimes easy to forget, Salem is a river town. On the western edge of downtown, you'll find Salem's Riverfront Park, which features a state-of-the-art playground, amphitheater, carousel, and meandering pathways. It is also home to the A.C. Gilbert Discovery Village (see below). The park also is the site of the dock for the *Willamette Queen* (℃ **503/371-1103;** www.willamettequeen.com), a paddlewheeler that cruises the Willamette River. Cruises range from basic 1-hour outings to lunch, brunch, dinner, and even murder-mystery cruises. Prices range from $10 ($5 children 12 and under) for a 1-hour cruise to $35 for a 2-hour dinner or brunch cruise ($20.50 for children 12 and under). Seniors receive a 10% discount.

Also worth a visit is Willamette University's Martha Springer Botanical Garden and Rose Garden, located near the gymnasium in the southeast corner of the campus. Here you'll find a rose garden full of modern hybrids and heirloom roses, a Japanese garden, an alpine rock garden, and an English perennial garden.

Bush Barn Art Center ⊕ The Salem Art Association's Bush Barn Art Center includes a sales gallery as well as exhibition spaces that feature changing art exhibits. The focus is on local and regional artists, and the quality is quite high. Each year on the third weekend in July, Bush's Pasture Park is the site of the Salem Art Fair and Festival, one of the most popular art festivals in the Northwest.

Bush and High sts. ℃ **503/581-2228.** www.salemart.org. Free admission. Tues–Fri 10am–5pm; Sat–Sun noon–5pm. Closed major holidays.

Bush House Museum ⊕ Set at the top of a shady hill in the 100-acre Bush's Pasture Park, this imposing Italianate Victorian home dates back to 1878. Inside, you can see the original furnishings, including 10 fireplaces and the original wallpaper. At the time it was built, this home had all the modern conveniences—indoor plumbing, gaslights, and central heating. Also on the grounds is Oregon's oldest greenhouse conservatory.

600 Mission St. SE. ℃ **503/363-4714.** www.salemart.org. Admission $4 adults, $3 students and seniors, $2 children 6–12. May–Sept Tues–Sun noon–5pm; Oct–Apr Tues–Sun 2–5pm. Closed major holidays.

Hallie Ford Museum of Art ⊕⊕ This is the second largest art museum in Oregon and features collections of Native American baskets, and Northwest, European, and Asian art. The first-floor galleries are devoted to contemporary art and feature changing exhibitions. Upstairs, you'll find one gallery filled with more than 70 Native American baskets, the finest collection of such baskets in the state. Other galleries contain artifacts ranging from an ancient Egyptian coffin mask to 19th-century Chinese porcelain.

700 State St. ℃ **503/370-6855.** www.willamette.edu/museum_of_art/. Admission $3 adults, $2 seniors and students, free for children under 13. Tues–Sat 10am–5pm.

Historic Deepwood Estate ⊕ Set on 5½ acres of English-style gardens and woodlands, this Queen Anne Victorian home is a delicate jewel box of a house. Although the house, with its many stained-glass windows, golden-oak moldings, and numerous lightning rod–topped peaked roofs and gables, was built in 1894, the gardens weren't added until the 1930s and were designed by the Northwest's first women-owned landscape architecture firm.

1116 Mission St. SE. ℃ **503/363-1825.** www.oregonlink.com/deepwood/. Admission $4 adults, $3 seniors and students, $2 children 6–12. Grounds daily dawn–dusk; guided house tours May–Sept Sun–Fri noon–5pm, Oct–Apr Wed–Thurs and Sat noon–5pm.

Mission Mill Museum 👶👶 The sprawling red Thomas Kay Woolen Mill, a water-powered mill built in 1889, is one of the most fascinating attractions in Salem. (The Salem Visitors Information Center on site also makes this the best place to start a tour of the state capital.) The restored buildings house exhibits on every stage of the wool-making process, and in the main mill building, the water-driven turbine is still in operation, producing electricity for the buildings. Also on these neatly manicured grounds are several other old structures (including the Jason Lee House, which was built by Salem's founder in 1841 and is the oldest frame house in the Northwest), a cafe, and a collection of interesting shops. The Marion County Historical Society Museum, also on the grounds, houses exhibits on the history of the area with a particularly interesting section on the local Kalapuyan Indians.

1313 Mill St. SE. 📞 503/585-7012. www.missionmill.org. Admission $6 adults, $5 seniors, $4 children. Mon–Sat 10am–5pm. Closed major holidays.

Oregon State Capitol Where's the dome? That's the first thing that strikes most visitors to the Oregon State Capitol, which looks as if builders forgot to complete the building. However, it was actually designed without a dome, and consequently, the building, which opened in 1938, has a stark appearance (not unlike that of a mausoleum). If you look closer, though, you'll recognize the pared down lines of Art Deco design aesthetics in this building. *The Oregon Pioneer,* a 23-foot-tall gilded statue, tops this Greek revival building of white Italian marble. Outside the building, there are numerous sculptures and attractive gardens; inside, there are murals of historic Oregon scenes. Tours of the capitol are available during the summer. There are also changing art exhibits and videos about the history of the building and the state.

900 Court St. NE. 📞 503/986-1388. Free admission. Building Mon–Fri 7:30am–5:30pm, Sat 9am–4pm, Sun noon–4pm; tours offered mid-June to Labor Day Mon–Fri 9am–4pm, Sat 9am–3pm, Sun noon–3pm. Closed national holidays.

A NEARBY STATE PARK & TWO WILDLIFE REFUGES

North of Salem 8 miles you'll find **Willamette Mission State Park** (📞 503/393-1172), which preserves the site of the first settlement in the Willamette Valley. It was here that Methodist missionary Jason Lee and four assistants established their first mission in 1834. Today, there are 8 miles of walking, biking, and horseback-riding paths through the park, which is also home to the largest black cottonwood tree in the country. Horseback rides are offered Saturday and Sunday during the summer for $20 per person for a 1-hour ride (reservations recommended; 📞 503/393-1611).

If it's bird-watching that interests you, there are two national wildlife refuges in the area that are excellent places to observe ducks, geese, swans, and raptors. Ankeny National Wildlife Refuge is 12 miles south of Salem off I-5 at exit 243. Basket Slough National Wildlife Refuge is northwest of the town of Rickreall on Ore. 22, which passes through the north end of downtown Salem. Fall through spring are the best times of year for birding here. For more information, contact the **William L. Finley National Wildlife Refuge** (📞 541/757-7236).

ESPECIALLY FOR KIDS

In addition to the two attractions listed below, the younger ones will likely enjoy a ride on **Salem's Riverfront Carousel** 👶, 101 Front St. NE (📞 503/540-0374), which is a modern carousel with 42 hand-carved horses. The carousel has its own building in Riverfront Park and is within walking distance of A.C Gilbert Discovery Village.

During the summer, the carousel operates Monday through Thursday from 10am to 7pm, Friday and Saturday from 10am to 9pm, and Sunday from 11am to 6pm; other months the carousel closes up to 2 hours earlier. Rides are $1.

A.C. Gilbert Discovery Village ⚘ *Kids*   Known as the "man who saved Christmas," Salem's A.C. Gilbert may not be familiar to most people, but the toy he invented, the Erector Set, certainly is. Erector Sets have inspired generations of budding engineers, and it was during World War I that Gilbert saved Christmas. It seems Congress wanted to turn his toy factory into a munitions factory, but after taking Erector Sets to Congress, he convinced the solons that America needed to prime its next generation of inventors just as much as it needed to prime its war machine. Here, in two Queen Anne Victorian homes, a few other small historic buildings, and a half-acre outdoor play/recreation center, the 21st century's inventors can let loose their own creative energies. Among the many interactive exhibits here, there are plenty of Erector Set constructions, a bubble room, a Maasai village, an ancient forest, and an optical illusion room.

116 Marion St. NE. ℂ 503/371-3631. www.acgilbert.org. Admission $4 adults and children over 3, $3 seniors, free for children 2 and under. Mon–Sat 10am–5pm; Sun noon–5pm.

Enchanted Forest *Kids*   Classic children's stories come to life at this amusement park for kids. In addition to Storybook Land, English Village, and a mining town, there's a haunted house, a bobsled run, a log-flume ride, and a comedy theater. Rides cost extra. Adjacent to Enchanted Village is **Thrill-Ville USA** (ℂ **503/363-4095**), a small amusement park with a roller coaster, water slides, and other rides and activities. It's open in summer from 11am to 6pm; rides cost $2 to $3 and an all-day water-slide pass is $10.

8462 Enchanted Way SE., Turner. ℂ 503/363-3060 or 503/371-4242. www.enchantedforest.com. Admission $6.95 adults, $6.50 seniors, $6.25 children 3–12. Mar 15–31 daily 9:30am–6pm; Apr and Sept Sat–Sun 9:30am–6pm; May–Labor Day daily 9:30am–6pm. Closed Oct–Mar 14. Take I-5 7 miles south of Salem to Exit 248.

SILVERTON

Set in the foothills of the Cascade Range, Silverton is a quaint community on the banks of Silver Creek. The creekside setting gives the town something of the feel of an old New England mill town. Although the area's major attractions are Silver Falls State Park and The Oregon Garden, the downtown is also worth a stroll, and a pedestrian covered bridge leads to a pleasant, shady park.

WATERFALLS AND DISPLAY GARDENS

The Oregon Garden ⚘⚘   The Oregon Garden, which opened to the public in the summer of 2000, is one of the largest public display gardens in the Northwest. Nursery plants are currently Oregon's leading crop and are shipped all over the country, and the Oregon Garden was created to showcase the state's horticultural heritage and the wide variety of plants grown in Oregon's commercial plant nurseries. When they mature, the gardens here will be world-class, and even now many of the gardens are quite impressive. The dream is to make this into an Oregon equivalent of Victoria, British Columbia's, famed Butchart Gardens, and actually, with 60 acres of plantings in the first phase, the gardens are already much larger. In addition to an incredible array of plantings, the numerous gardens include several water features and ponds, terraced gardens, a sensory garden, a children's garden, and a native oak grove. During the summer months, there are concerts held in the garden's amphitheater. The Oregon Garden is also home to the Gordon House, a Frank Lloyd Wright home that is currently undergoing renovation and reconstruction. There are free guided walking tours of the garden and tours by electric tram ($2).

879 W. Main St., Silverton. © 877/674-2733 or 503/874-8100. www.oregongarden.org. Admission $6 adults, $5 seniors and students 14–17, $3 children 8–13. Summer daily 9am–6pm; winter daily 9am–3pm. Closed Thanksgiving, Christmas, and New Year's Day.

Silver Falls State Park ★★   Located 26 miles east of Salem on Ore. 214, this is the largest state park in Oregon and one of the most popular. Hidden in the lush canyons and dark old-growth forests of this park are 10 silvery waterfalls ranging in height from 27 to 177 feet. The trails are some of the most enjoyable in the state and can usually be hiked any time of year. Although the best hike is the 7-mile loop trail that links all of the falls, shorter hikes are also possible. You can even walk behind South, Lower South, and North falls. You can spend an afternoon or several days exploring the park. Camping (for reservations, call **Reservations Northwest** © **800/452-5687**), swimming, picnicking, bicycling, and horseback riding are all popular activities. Guided **horseback rides** are available from Memorial Day to Labor Day ($25 for a 1-hr. ride). For reservations, call © **503/873-3890.**

15 miles southeast of Silverton on Ore. 214. © 503/873-8681. www.oregonstateparks.org. Admission $3 per car. Daily dawn–dusk.

OTHER AREA ATTRACTIONS & ACTIVITIES
While in Silverton, be sure to wander around town and admire the many murals. Local artists who display their work at the **Lunaria Gallery,** 216 E. Main St. (© **503/873-7743**), painted some of these. Also worth a visit is the **Silver Creek Gallery,** 119A N. Water St. (© **503/873-6767**), featuring works by regional artists and jewelry designed by the gallery's owners. If you want to learn more about local history, drop by the **Silverton Country Museum,** 428 S. Water St. (© **503/873-4766**). The museum is open Thursday and Sunday from 1 to 4pm, and admission is $1 for adults and 50¢ for children.

WHERE TO DINE
For a quick pick-me-up, try the **Silver Creek Coffee House,** 111 N. Water St. (© **503/874-9600**), which has a deck overlooking Silver Creek.

Silver Grille Cafe & Wines ★★ BISTRO FRENCH This classy little restaurant in an old storefront is a welcome outpost of urban culinary aesthetics in this small town. The menu emphasizes fresh organically grown produce and hormone-free meats. A recent summer menu included a cooling gazpacho, albacore tuna cakes, salmon with morel sauce, and lavender-poached peach tart. Wine is also a very important part of a meal here, as the wine bottles around the dining room, the wine quotes on the front windows, and a small wine shop give away.

206 E Main St. © 503/873-4035. www.silvergrille.com. Main courses $16–$22; 4-course prix fixe dinner $35. AE, MC, V. Wed–Sun 4–9pm.

MT. ANGEL
Mt. Angel is best known as the site of Oregon's most popular Oktoberfest celebration, but should you be here any other time of year beside the second weekend after Labor Day, you might want to visit the **Mount Angel Abbey** (© **503/845-3303;** www.mtangel.edu), which stands atop a 300-foot bluff on the edge of town and has peaceful gardens, an architecturally interesting library designed by famous Finnish architect Alvar Aalto, and a collection of rare books. Established by Benedictine monks in 1882, the Abbey has a gift shop and offers

tours by appointment. The abbey is also the site of the annual **Abbey Bach Festival** (✆ **503/845-332**), which takes place each year on the last Wednesday, Thursday, and Friday in July and sells out shortly after tickets go on sale in March.

WHERE TO DINE

Mt. Angel Brewing Company ✦ AMERICAN/GERMAN   In an old potato warehouse that now looks surprisingly like a Munich beer hall, this brewpub serves a wide variety of microbrew ales and everything from German sausages to pizza. Smoked meats and hot entrees cooked over wood are a specialty.

210 N. Monroe St. ✆ 503/845-9624. www.mtangelbrewing.com. Main courses $6–$17. MC, V. Sun–Thurs 11am–8:30pm (9:30pm in summer); Fri–Sat 11am–9:30pm (10:30pm in summer).

MONMOUTH

Jensen Arctic Museum ✦✦ (Finds)   Although Monmouth may seem an unlikely location for a museum dedicated to the natural and cultural history of the Arctic, it is here that the museum's founder lived while working with Alaskan Eskimo peoples. The core of the museum's exhibits is Dr. Jensen's personal collection, but over the years, the museum has become a repository for more than 60 other collections. Though small, this museum has fascinating displays, including a parka made from cormorant feathers, salmon-skin mukluks, a waterproof seal-intestine jacket, and woven-baleen baskets.

590 W. Church St., Monmouth. ✆ 503/838-8468. Admission $2 adults, $1 children. Wed–Sat 10am–4pm.

BROOKS

Antique Powerland Museum   Dedicated to the preservation of old farm equipment and related items, this sprawling open-air museum is home to lots of old tractors and steam-driven mills. For the kids, there's a miniature railroad. This museum is best known as the site of the annual Great Oregon Steamup, held each year on the last weekend in July and the first weekend in August. Also on the grounds is the Pacific **Northwest Truck Museum** (✆ **503/463-8701; www.pacifnwtruckmuseum.org**), open on weekends throughout the summer.

3995 Brooklake Rd. NE, Brooks. ✆ 503/393-2424. www.antiquepowerland.com. Admission $2. Apr–Oct daily 10am–6pm; Nov–Mar daily 10am–4pm.

WINE TOURING

For information on the many wineries west and northwest of Salem, see "The North Willamette Valley Wine Country" section earlier in this book.

St. Innocent Winery ✦   This winery produces very drinkable white wines as well as some good Pinot Noirs. It is also one of the few wineries in the state to produce sparkling wines.

1360 Tandem Ave. NE. ✆ 503/378-1526. www.stinnocentwine.com. Sat–Sun noon–5pm.

Willamette Valley Vineyards ✦✦   Willamette Valley Vineyards, one of the largest wine producers in the state, sits high on a hill overlooking the Willamette Valley, and with its huge facility and fabulous views, it's about as close to a Napa Valley wine-tasting experience as you'll find in Oregon. With nearly 20 wines usually available for tasting and three separate labels available, Willamette Valley manages to produce wines to please almost every palate. Be sure to try the reserve wines, for which there is a small tasting fee. There are monthly jazz concerts here most of the year and numerous other special events. Good Chardonnays and Pinot Noirs.

8800 Enchanted Way SE, Turner. ✆ 800/344-9463 or 503/588-9463. www.wvv.com. Daily 11am–6pm. Take exit 248 or 244 off I-5.

Blossom Time

Each year between mid-May and early June, the countryside around Salem bursts into color as commercial iris fields come into bloom. During blossom time, the two biggest growers open their farms up to the public. **Cooley's Gardens,** 11553 Silverton Rd. NE (© **503/873-5463**), with approximately 250 acres and more than 3 million irises, is the world's largest bearded iris grower. This farm is open daily from 8am to 7pm between mid-May and early June. To reach the gardens, take the Market Street exit and drive east to Lancaster Road; at Lancaster, turn left and drive north to Silverton Road where you make a right turn. It's less than 10 miles on Silverton Road. **Schreiner's Iris Gardens,** 3625 Quinaby Rd. NE, Salem (© **503/393-3232**), the nation's largest retail iris grower, has more than 200 acres of irises and is an equally impressive sight. To reach Schreiner's, take the Brooks exit (exit 263) off I-5 north of Salem, drive east to Portland Road, turn right and continue south to Quinaby Road. Also in the area are **Adelman Peony Gardens,** 5690 Brooklake Rd. NE (© **503/393-6185;** www.peonyparadise.com), which has more than 100 varieties of peonies in bloom between early May and mid-June. They're open daily from 9am to 7pm during blossom time. From the Brooks exit, go east on Brooklake Road.

From late March to late April, you can see more than 90 acres of tulips in bloom at **Wooden Shoe Bulb Company,** 33814 S. Meridian Rd., Woodburn (© **800/711-2006** or 503/634-2243). Throughout the blossom season, there are wooden shoe–making seminars, hot-air balloon rides, vintage car shows, live music, and lots of other activities.

WHERE TO STAY

A Creekside Inn, The Marquee House *Value* Fans of old movies will want to make this their address in Salem. All the rooms are named for well-known movies and are furnished to reflect the movie theme. We like the Topper Room with its black-tie theme and the Blazing Saddles Room with its Wild West decor. This B&B is located on a narrow lane in a quiet residential neighborhood and has Mill Creek running through the backyard. The gardens are quite impressive.

333 Wyatt Ct. NE, Salem, OR 97301. © 800/949-0837 or 503/391-0837. Fax 503/391-1713. www.marqueehouse.com. 5 units (3 with private bathroom). $65 double with shared bathroom, $75–$95 double with private bathroom. Rates include full breakfast. DC, DISC, MC, V. *In room:* A/C.

Phoenix Inn Of Salem's many corporate business hotels, the modern Phoenix Inn is one of the best and is popular with both legislators and business travelers. The rooms are quite large and well designed for both business and relaxation. The top-end rooms also have whirlpool tubs.

4370 Commercial St. SE, Salem, OR 97302. © 800/445-4498 or 503/588-9220. Fax 503/585-3616. www.phoenixinn.com. 89 units. $69–$119 double. Rates include continental breakfast. AE, DISC, MC, V. Pets accepted ($10 fee). **Amenities:** Indoor pool; Jacuzzi; exercise room. *In room:* A/C, TV, dataport, fridge, coffeemaker, hair dryer, iron, free local calls.

WHERE TO DINE
SALEM

If you have a sweet tooth, you won't want to miss **Gerry Frank's Konditorei,** 310 Kearney St. SE (© **503/585-7070**), which has an amazing selection of extravagant cakes and pastries. For a good cup of espresso (or a sandwich), head to **The Beanery,** 220 Liberty St. NE (© **503/399-7220**). If you're looking for a microbrew and a burger, try **Ram Restaurant & Big Horn Brewery,** 515 12th St. SE (© **503/363-1904**). For Sunday brunch, consider **Eola Hills Wine Cellars,** 501 S. Pacific Hwy., Rickreall (© **503/623-2405;** www.eolahillswinery .com), which serves gourmet omelets, pan-fried oysters, pasta, Belgian waffles, sparkling wine, and more for $15.95. Reservations recommended.

Alessandro's 120 ★★ ITALIAN   The ever-popular Alessandro's is in an older downtown building that, with its wooden floors, exposed brick walls, and player piano has both a historic and a romantic feel. Alessandro's menu includes dishes in a wide range of prices, though the set menus are a bit pricey. Sauces are made fresh daily from the finest ingredients, including fresh herbs and the best of Northwest seafood. The wine list features moderately priced Italian and Oregon wines. The restaurant has a full bar, which is very popular with Salem's moneyed set and politicos.

120 Commercial St. NE. © 503/370-9951. www.alessandros120.com. Reservations recommended. Main courses $9.50–$23; fixed-price dinners $32–$43; lunch $6.50–$10. AE, DISC, MC, V. Mon–Thurs 11:30am–2pm and 5:30–9pm; Fri 11:30am–2pm and 5:30–10pm; Sat 5:30–10pm.

Court Street Dairy Lunch ★ *Finds* BURGERS   In business since the 1920s, the Court Street Dairy Lunch is the quintessential small-town diner and a Salem institution. Burgers and sandwiches "just like Mom used to make" are the attraction. The specialties of the house are the ranch burger and ranch dog, marionberry pie, and chocolate malts.

347 Court St. © 503/363-6433. Meals $3–$7. AE, MC, V. Mon–Fri 6am–2pm.

DaVinci Ristorante ★★ ITALIAN   Competing directly with Alessandro's for the title of reigning upscale Italian restaurant in Salem, DaVinci abounds in early-20th-century ambience, with a pressed-tin ceiling and lots of oak and exposed brick. Wonderful aromas greet you as you step through the door of this casual yet elegant restaurant in a restored downtown building. Dishes range from simple fare to more creative, contemporary Italian. Be sure to start a meal with the prawns wrapped in prosciutto. From there you might move on to capellini with lobster or beef tenderloin with portobello mushroom. There's live jazz or classical music nightly, and the restaurant is popular with Salem politicos.

180 High St. SE. © 503/399-1413. Reservations recommended. Main courses $14–$24. AE, DISC, MC, V. Mon–Thurs 4:30–9:30pm; Fri–Sat 5–10:30pm; Sun 5–8pm.

Morton's Bistro Northwest ★★ AMERICAN REGIONAL   This romantic little bistro serves up the most imaginative meals in Salem. The menu changes regularly depending on the whim of the chef, the availability of ingredients, and even the weather. On a recent evening, flavors ranged from the subtle scents of ale-steamed clams to the fiery flavors of penne diablo made with shrimp and andouille sausage. Other standouts included a jerked pork tenderloin with mango-cilantro salsa and hazelnut-crusted oysters.

1128 Edgewater St. W. © 503/585-1113. Reservations recommended. Main courses $15–$23. MC, V. Tues–Sat 5–10pm.

Rudy's at Salem Golf Club ★★   This reproduction of an antebellum southern plantation home has an classic feel. Though the menu may not break new ground, it is varied and reliable, and locals praise the traditional atmosphere. Keep an eye out for the crab cakes, which might be served with a red-pepper sauce. The steaks and prime rib are local favorites.

2025 Golf Course Rd. S. ✆ 503/399-0449. Reservations recommended. Main courses $6–$11 lunch, $8–$20 dinner. DISC, MC, V. Daily 6:30am–9:30pm.

SALEM AFTER DARK

The Oregon Symphony performs in Salem between September and May, with concerts at Smith Auditorium on the campus of Willamette University. For more information, contact the **Oregon Symphony Association in Salem** (✆ **503/364-0149**). Classical music lovers can also catch the **Salem Chamber Orchestra;** for ticket information, contact the Mid-Valley Arts Council, Salem Center Mall, 401 Center St. NE, Suite 1156 (✆ **503/364-7474**). There are regularly scheduled performances by touring companies at the historic **Elsinore Theater,** 170 High St. SE (✆ **503/375-3574** or 503/581-8810; www.elsinore theatre.com). Since 1954, **Pentacle Theatre,** 324 52nd Ave. NW (✆ **503/ 364-7121;** www.pentacletheatre.org) located in the West Salem hills, has been bringing live theater to the state capital; for ticket information, contact the Mid-Valley Arts Council, Salem Center Mall, 401 Center St. NE, Suite 1156 (✆ **503/364-7474**).

3 Corvallis & Albany

40 miles S of Salem, 45 miles N of Eugene, 55 miles E of Newport

In Latin, Corvallis means "heart of the valley," and that is exactly where this college town is located. Set in the middle of the Willamette Valley and surrounded by farmlands, Corvallis is home to Oregon State University (OSU), a noted center for agricultural research. Life in this town revolves around the university, but the lively downtown, with its riverfront setting, makes this a pleasant base for exploring nearby wine country and the historic town of Albany. Numerous walking and bicycling paths add to the appeal of a stay here.

In addition to being home to OSU, Corvallis is at the center of the Willamette Valley's grass seed fields. Area farms produce much of the nation's (and the world's) grass-seed crop. Visitors should note that in late summer, after the seed has been harvested, the remaining stubble has traditionally been burned. The field burnings, which have been scaled back in recent years, still can blanket the valley with dense black smoke, making driving quite difficult along certain roads. So, don't be too alarmed if you encounter smoky skies in the area in August.

Nearby Albany, 13 miles northeast, was a prosperous town in territorial days. Located on the banks of the Willamette River, the town made its fortune as a shipping point in the days when the river was the main transportation route for the region. More than 500 historic homes make Albany the best-preserved historic town in the state.

ESSENTIALS

GETTING THERE   Albany is on I-5 at the junction with U.S. 20, which heads east to Bend and west to Newport. Corvallis is 12 miles west of I-5 at the junction of U.S. 20, Ore. 99W, and Ore. 34.

VISITOR INFORMATION Contact the **Corvallis Convention & Visitors Bureau,** 420 NW Second St., Corvallis, OR 97330 (© **800/334-8118** or 541/757-1544; www.visitcorvallis.com), or the **Albany Convention & Visitors Association,** 250 Broadalbin St. NW, Suite 110 (P.O. Box 965), Albany, OR 97321 (© **800/526-2256** or 541/928-0911; www.albanyvisitors.com).

GETTING AROUND Public bus service around the Corvallis area is provided by the **Corvallis Transit System** (© **541/757-6998;** www.ci.corvallis.or.us/pw/cts). Adult fare is 50¢.

FESTIVALS **DaVinci Days** (© **800/334-8118;** www.davinci-days.org), held each year in mid-July, is Corvallis's most fascinating festival. The highlight of this celebration of art, science, and technology is the **Kinetic Sculpture Race** in which competitors race homemade, people-powered vehicles along city streets, through mud, and down the Willamette River. Prizes are given for engineering and artistry. Another offbeat celebration, the **Shrewsbury Renaissance Faire** (© **541/929-4897;** www.shrewfaire.com), is held each year in Philomath in early September. The **World Championship Timber Carnival,** held annually on the Fourth of July, is Albany's biggest celebration. This festival attracts logging contestants from around the world.

EXPLORING OFF-CAMPUS CORVALLIS

The tree-shaded streets of downtown Corvallis are well worth a wander. Here you'll find lots of interesting shops, as well as the stately **Benton County Courthouse,** 120 NW Fourth Street, built in 1888 and still in use today. A few blocks away, you'll find the **Corvallis Arts Center,** 700 SW Madison Ave. (© **541/754-1551**), which is housed in an old church and schedules changing exhibits of works by regional artists. The gift shop has a good selection of crafts. The center is open Tuesday through Sunday from noon to 5pm; admission is free. Downtown borders the Willamette River, and at press time, the waterfront was undergoing a major renovation. Part of the renovation will include the addition of river-viewing decks and riverfront plazas along the paved multi-use path that parallels the river at this point.

EXPLORING HISTORIC ALBANY

Albany is a hidden jewel right on I-5 that is often overlooked because the only thing visible from the interstate is a smoke-belching wood-pulp mill. Behind this industrial screen lies a quiet town that evokes days of starched crinolines and straw boaters. Throughout the mid– to late 19th century, Albany prospered, shipping agricultural and wood products down river to Oregon City and Portland. Though every style of architecture popular during that period is represented in downtown Albany's historic districts, it is the town's many elegant Victorian homes that are the most compelling. Each year, on the last Saturday of July, many of the historic homes are opened to the public for a **Summer Historic Homes Tour,** and on the third Sunday in December, homes are opened for a **Christmas Parlour Tour.** For a guide to the historic buildings, and information on the tours, contact the **Albany Convention & Visitors Association.**

Among the town's more noteworthy buildings are two sparkling white 1890s churches—the **Whitespires Church** and **St. Mary's Church**—both built in the Gothic revival style. The **Monteith House,** 518 Second Ave. SW (© **541/928-0911**), built in 1849, is the town's oldest frame building. The house is open from mid-June to mid-September Wednesday through Saturday from noon to 4pm; admission is free.

Tips **Beaver Believers**

The Oregon State University NCAA football team has been on a roll the past few years, and in 2000, was ranked fourth nationally. This ranking landed the team in the New Year's Day Fiesta Bowl, where the Beavers trounced Notre Dame making "Beaver Believers" of fans all across Oregon. Check on ticket availability by contacting the **OSU Beaver Ticket Office** (© **800/GO-BEAVS** or 541/737-4455).

To learn more about Albany's past, stop in at the **Albany Regional Museum,** 136 Lyon St. SW (© **541/967-7122**). It's open Monday through Saturday from noon to 4pm. Admission is by donation.

The most educational and entertaining way to delve into Albany's past is by attending one of the living history dinner theater programs presented by **Flinn's Tours,** 222 W. First Ave. (© **800/636-5008** or 541/928-5008; www.flinns. com). Vaudeville shows, tales of women's lives in pioneer days, and murder mysteries currently play at this downtown theater, which doubles as a tearoom. There are several special programs at Christmas.

While touring the historic districts, you can stop in at more than a dozen antiques stores, most of which are on First and Second avenues downtown.

WINE TOURING

The Corvallis area is about the upper limit of Cabernet Sauvignon production in Oregon, so if you aren't headed down to southern Oregon but want to sample an Oregon Cabernet, you might want to stop by some of the area wineries. **Springhill Cellars,** 2920 NW Scenic Dr., Albany (© **541/928-1009**), which produces excellent Pinot Noir and Pinot Gris, is one of our favorite small wineries in the state and is open only by appointment.

Airlie Winery ✦ This winery is quite a distance from the main wine-touring routes, but its setting in a narrow valley surrounded by forested hills is idyllic. There's a large pond and a covered picnic area, making it a good place to stop for lunch. They produce a wide variety of wines, but their Müller-Thurgaus and Gewürztraminers are highlights.

15305 Dunn Forest Rd., Monmouth. © 503/838-6013. www.airliewinery.com. Mid-Mar to mid-Dec Sat–Sun noon–5pm. Closed Jan–Feb. From Ore. 99W between Corvallis and Monmouth, go 7 miles west on Airlie Rd., turn left on Maxfield Creek Rd. and continue another 3 miles.

Bellfountain Cellars ✦✦ At the end of a long driveway in a remote heat pocket of the Coast Range foothills, Bellfountain is a family operation producing exceptional wines. Because this little valley has such a long growing season, Bellfountain is able to ripen Cabernet Sauvignon grapes, which, however, are sometimes bottled as red table wine when they don't meet winemaker Rob Mommsen's high standards. A good spot for a picnic.

25041 Llewellyn Rd., Corvallis. © 541/929-3162. www.proaxis.com/~winemaker/. Apr–Oct Fri–Sun noon–6pm; Nov–Mar Fri–Sun noon–5pm. Closed Dec 24–Jan 31. From Corvallis, go south on Ore. 99W, then go west on Llewellyn Rd. and watch for the sign west of the Fern Rd. intersection.

Tyee Wine Cellars ✦ Tyee Wine Cellars is on a 460-acre farm established in 1885, and the tasting room is in an old milking barn from the days when this was a dairy farm. Although Tyee does a decent, peppery Pinot Noir, their real strength lies in the consistency of their whites—Pinot Gris, Pinot Blanc,

Chardonnay, and Gewürztraminer all tend to be dry and light. Be sure to walk the 1½-mile trail through farm and forest.

26335 Greenberry Rd., Corvallis. ✆ 541/753-8754. www.tyeewine.com. Apr–Dec Sat–Sun noon–5pm. Closed Jan–Mar. From Corvallis, go 7 miles south on Ore. 99W and then 2½ miles west on Greenberry Rd.

A COVERED BRIDGE TOUR

If you're a fan of covered bridges, you won't want to pass up an opportunity to drive the back roads east of Albany. Here you'll find nine wooden covered bridges dating mostly from the 1930s. For a map to these covered bridges, contact the **Albany Convention & Visitors Association.** A tenth covered bridge, the Irish Bend Bridge, can be found in Corvallis on a pedestrian/bicycle path on the west side of the university campus.

OUTDOOR ACTIVITIES

If you're a bird-watcher, the **William L. Finley National Wildlife Refuge** (✆ **541/757-7236**), 12 miles south of Corvallis on Ore. 99W, is a good place to add a few more to your list. This refuge has three short, easy hiking trails that provide the region's best glimpse of what the Willamette Valley looked like before the first settlers arrived.

For superb views of the valley and a moderately strenuous hike, head west 16 miles from Corvallis on Ore. 34 to **Mary's Peak,** the highest peak in the Coast Range. A road leads to the top of the mountain, but there is also a trail that leads from the campground up through a forest of old-growth noble firs to the meadows at the summit. For more information, contact the **Siuslaw National Forest,** 4077 SW Research Way (P.O. Box 1148) Corvallis, OR 97339 (✆ **541/750-7000;** www.fs.fed.us/r6/siuslaw).

WHERE TO STAY
IN CORVALLIS

Hanson Country Inn ✮ Situated atop a knoll on the edge of town and surrounded by 5 acres of fields and forests, this B&B feels as if it's out in the country, yet is within walking distance of the university. The Dutch colonial-style farmhouse was built in 1928 and features loads of built-in cabinets, interesting woodwork, and lots of windows. The decor is in a pastel country motif, and two of the rooms have large balconies. The two-bedroom cottage, ideal for families, sits behind the main house and is tucked back in the trees.

795 SW Hanson St., Corvallis, OR 97333. ✆ 541/752-2919. 4 units (including a cottage). $95–$145 double. Rates include full breakfast. AE, DISC, MC, V. Take Western Blvd. to West Hills Rd.; Hanson St. is on the right just past the fork onto West Hills Rd. **Amenities:** Guest laundry. In room: A/C, TV.

Super 8 Motel ✮ It may seem hard to believe that a Super 8 Motel could be one of the best accommodations in town, but Corvallis just doesn't have too many places to stay. This budget motel has a great location on the bank of the Willamette River only a few blocks from downtown.

407 NW Second St., Corvallis, OR 97330. ✆ 800/800-8000 or 541/758-8088. Fax 541/758-8267. 101 units. $59–$77 double. Rates include continental breakfast. AE, DC, DISC, MC, V. **Amenities:** Indoor pool; Jacuzzi; coin-op laundry. In room: A/C, TV, dataport, free local calls.

IN ALBANY

Brier Rose Inn ✮ This turreted Queen Anne–style Victorian B&B is on a busy corner in the heart of Albany's historic district and surprisingly is the only historic B&B in town. With its balconies, bay windows, curving porches, stained glass, and numerous styles of siding, it's a classic example of Victorian excess. Common areas are filled with period antiques, though the guest rooms are more simply furnished.

206 Seventh Ave. SW, Albany, OR 97321. © 888/848-4395 or 541/926-0345. http://cmug.com/~brierroseinn/. 5 units (4 with private bathroom). $59–$79 double with shared bathroom; $89–$125 double with private bathroom. Rates include full breakfast. AE, MC, V.

WHERE TO DINE
IN CORVALLIS

When you just have to have a jolt of java and a pastry, drop by **New Morning Bakery,** 219 SW Second St. (© **541/754-0181**). If you're looking for some picnic fare stop by **Great Harvest Bread Co.,** 134 SW First St. (© **541/ 754-9960**). For microbrews and pub fare, try **McMenamins,** 420 NW Third St. (© **541/758-6044**).

Big River ⭐⭐ INTERNATIONAL   This modern American bistro is one of our favorite Corvallis restaurants, especially when we're dining out with a lot of friends or family members. Housed in a renovated warehouse-like space across the street from the Willamette River, this big, lively place serves everything from designer brick-oven pizzas to Asian-inspired pastas to Cuban pork loin to various smoked chicken dishes. The owners of this restaurant have a commitment to fresh local produce (often organic), local wines, Oregon-caught seafood (when possible), and organic meats. The rustic breads are baked here on the premises. Though this is a big space, you probably won't be able to miss the case full of tempting desserts.

101 Jackson St. © **541/757-0694.** www.bigriverrest.com. Reservations for 8 or more only. Main courses $14–$22. AE, DC, DISC, MC, V. Mon–Thurs 11am–2pm and 5–10pm; Fri 11am–2pm and 5pm–midnight; Sat 5pm–midnight.

Le Bistro ⭐⭐ *Finds* FRENCH   This minimally decorated restaurant focuses on country French preparations, and with surprisingly low prices, manages to attract students as well as local high-tech employees. Although there are daily specials, the main menu offers no surprises, just down-home French country cooking. Among other dishes, you'll find coq au vin and pork medallions with a light mustard *velouté.* The restaurant is only half a block from the river and the waterfront pathway.

150 SW Madison Ave. © **541/754-6680.** www.lebistro.com. Reservations recommended. Main courses $9.25–$18. MC, V. Tues–Sat 4:30–9:30pm.

Nearly Normal's ⭐ VEGETARIAN/INTERNATIONAL   Nearly Normal's is your basic college-town vegetarian hippie cafe serving up filling portions that span the globe. Look for anything from pad Thai to garlic-Gorgonzola ravioli. If it's sunny out, try to get a seat out back in the patio area planted with apple trees and kiwi vines. As often as possible, ingredients are organically grown. Good iced teas in summer.

109 NW 15th St. © **541/753-0791.** Reservations for 8 or more only. Main courses $3.60–$9. No credit cards. Mon–Fri 8am–9pm; Sat 9am–9pm (in winter Mon–Wed 8am–8pm).

Sweet's Bar-B-Que ⭐ BARBECUE   Barbecue joints seem to be springing up all over the place lately, and in Corvallis, everyone knows that Sweet's is the place. Boasting "old-school taste," this downtown joint not only does succulent ribs, but also barbecued chicken, beef brisket, and hot links. True barbecue fanatics can get a full rack of ribs or a four-meat combo dinner. All the usual side orders (baked beans, coleslaw, potato salad, corn) are available. Wash it all down with a Northwest microbrew.

225 SW Fourth St. © **541/754-3663.** www.sweetsbbq.com. Main courses $5.50–$17.50. DISC, MC, V. Mon–Thurs 10am–9pm; Fri–Sat 11am–10pm.

IN ALBANY

For a good cup of coffee, try **Boccherini's Coffee & Tea House,** 208 SW First Ave. (© **541/926-6703**). For quick deli meals there's the **Wine Depot & Deli,** Two Rivers Market, 300 Second Ave. (© **541/967-9499**). If it's a good pint of ale and some pub food you crave, check out **Wyatt's Eatery & Brewhouse,** 211 NW First Ave. (© **541/917-3727**).

Novak's Hungarian Restaurant ⭐ *(Finds)* HUNGARIAN   From the outside, Novak's looks as if it could be a car-repair garage. However, as soon as you walk through the door you're hit with gracious Hungarian hospitality. The tongue-twisting dishes on the menu challenge the long-held belief that Eastern European cuisine means meat and potatoes. More often than not, Hungarian pearl noodles or fresh bread accompany dishes here. The homemade pork sausage is very good, though the chicken paprika, in its creamy red sauce, is probably the restaurant's most popular dish.

2835 Santiam Hwy. SE. © 541/967-9488. Reservations recommended. Main courses $8.25–$16.45. AE, DISC, MC, V. Sun–Fri 11am–9pm; Sat 4–9pm.

4 Eugene & Springfield

40 miles S of Salem, 71 miles N of Roseburg, 61 miles E of Florence

Although Eugene, with more than 100,000 residents, is the second-largest city in Oregon, tie-dyed T-shirts are more common than silk ties on downtown streets. This laid-back character is due in large part to the presence of the University of Oregon, the state's liberal arts college. On the university's tree-shaded 250-acre campus you'll find an art museum, a natural-history museum, and a science museum. Adding to the city's diverse cultural scene is the grandiose, glass-gabled **Hult Center for the Performing Arts.**

Eugene has for years been home to liberal-minded folks who adopted alternative lifestyles. At the **Saturday Market,** a weekly outdoor craft market, you can see the works of many of these colorful and creative spirits.

Throw in a couple of beautiful riverfront parks with miles of bike paths, numerous excellent restaurants, brewpubs, nearby wineries, and proximity to both mountains and coast, and you have a great base for exploring a good chunk of the state.

ESSENTIALS

GETTING THERE   Eugene is located just off I-5 at the junction with I-105, which connects Eugene and Springfield, and Ore. 126, which leads east to Bend and west to Florence. Ore. 58 leads southeast from Eugene to connect with U.S. 97 between Klamath Falls and Bend. Ore. 99W is an alternative to I-5.

The **Eugene Airport,** Mahlon Sweet Field, 28855 Lockheed Dr. (© **541/ 682-5430;** www.eugeneairport.com) is 9 miles northwest of downtown off Ore. 99W. America West Express, Horizon Air, and United/United Express fly here. There's nonstop service to Portland, Seattle, San Francisco, Los Angeles, Denver, and Phoenix.

Amtrak (© **800/USA-RAIL**) passenger trains stop in Eugene. The station is at East Fourth Avenue and Willamette Street.

VISITOR INFORMATION   Contact the **Convention & Visitors Association of Lane County Oregon,** 115 W. Eighth Ave., Suite 190 (P.O. Box 10286), Eugene, OR 97440 (© **800/547-5445** or 541/484-5307; www.visitlane county.org).

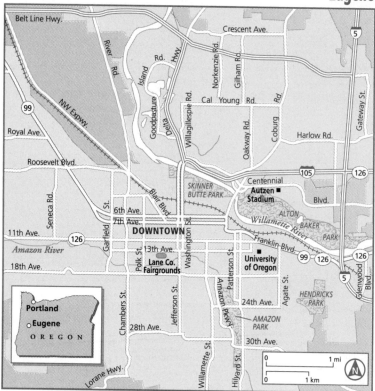

GETTING AROUND Car rentals are available at the Eugene airport from **Avis, Budget, Hertz,** and **National.** If you need a taxi, contact **Yellow Cab** (📞 **541/343-7711**); fares are $2 at flag drop and then $2 per mile. **Lane Transit District (LTD)** (📞 **541/687-5555;** www.ltd.org) provides public transit throughout the metropolitan area and out to a number of nearby towns including McKenzie Bridge; some routes do not run on Sunday. You can pick up bus-route maps and other information at the **LTD Customer Service Center** at the corner of 11th Avenue and Willamette Street. LTD fares are $1 for adults, 50¢ for seniors and youths 5 to 18.

FESTIVALS Eugene's two biggest and most important music festivals are the **Oregon Bach Festival** (📞 **541/682-5000;** www.oregonbachfestival.com) and the **Oregon Festival of American Music** (📞 **541/687-6526;** www.ofam.org). The former is just what its name implies and is held the last week in June and the first week in July. The latter is a celebration of everything from blues to gospel to jazz and is held in August. Most performances for both festivals are held at the Hult Center in downtown Eugene. The **Eugene Celebration** (📞 **541/681-4108**), held the third weekend in September, is a 3-day celebration that includes a wacky parade and the crowning of the annual Slug Queen. In mid-July, all the region's hippies, both young and old, show up in nearby Veneta for the **Oregon Country Fair** ★★ (📞 **541/343-4298;** www.oregon countryfair.org), a showcase for alternative music and unusual crafts. Also of note is **Junction City's Scandinavian Festival** (📞 **541/998-9372**), which celebrates the region's Scandinavian heritage and is held each year on the second weekend in August. Junction City is 14 miles northwest of Eugene.

SEEING THE SIGHTS
MUSEUMS & HISTORIC BUILDINGS

Maude Kerns Art Center ⭐ The works of contemporary local, regional, and national craftspeople are the subjects of changing exhibits at this small gallery.

1910 E. 15th Ave. 📞 541/345-1571. www.mkartcenter.org. Admission $3 suggested donation. Mon–Fri 10am–5:30pm; Sat noon–4pm.

Oregon Air and Space Museum This museum focuses on the history of aviation in Oregon. Numerous aircraft, including a World War I Fokker triplane, an F-4 Phantom, an F-86 Sabre Jet, and a Russian YAK-50, are on display.

90377 Boeing Dr. 📞 541/461-1101. www.oasm.org. Admission $5 adults, $4 seniors, $3 children 13–18, $2 children 6–12, free for 5 and under. Wed–Fri and Sun noon–4pm, Sat 11am–4pm.

Shelton-McMurphey-Johnson House ⭐ Built in 1888, this ornate Queen Anne Victorian home stands on the south slope of Skinner Butte on the north edge of downtown Eugene and was long referred to as the Castle on the Hill. Tours of the beautiful old home focus on the families that lived here over the century that it was a private residence.

303 Willamette St. 📞 541/484-0808. www.smjhouse.org. Admission $3 adults, $1 children under 12. Tues, Thurs, and Sun 1–4pm.

Springfield Museum In a renovated 1908 Pacific Power & Light building, you'll find historical artifacts of the region's industrial, logging, and agricultural heritage. The collection of old photos is very evocative. There are also interesting temporary exhibits, often of contemporary art.

590 Main St. 📞 541/726-3677. www.springfieldmuseum.com. Admission $1 adults. Tues–Fri 10am–5pm; Sat noon–5pm.

University of Oregon Museum of Art An extensive Asian art collection and exhibits of contemporary art are the main focus here. At press time, however, this museum was under renovation and not scheduled to reopen until spring 2003.

1430 Johnson Lane. 📞 541/346-3027. www.uoma.oregon.edu. Call for new hours and admission prices. East of 14th Ave. and Kincaid St. on the U of O campus.

University of Oregon Museum of Natural History ⭐ This small museum is housed in a building designed to vaguely resemble a traditional Northwest Coast Indian longhouse. The ancient peoples and even more ancient animals that once roamed the Northwest are the main focus of the museum's exhibits. However, there are also exhibits focusing on traditional cultures of Papua New Guinea and on pre-Columbian ceramics from western Mexico. Geology, botany, and archaeology topics also get plenty of display time here.

1680 E. 15th Ave. 📞 541/346-3024. http://natural-history.uoregon.edu. Admission $2 suggested donation. Tues–Sun noon–5pm.

Willamette Science & Technology Center (WISTEC) *Kids* With loads of cool hands-on exhibits, this is the place to bring the kids to teach them about science. This building also houses the Lane Education Service District Planetarium.

2300 Leo Harris Pkwy. 📞 541/682-7888. www.wistec.org. Admission $4 adults, $3 seniors and children 3–17. Wed–Fri noon–5pm; Sat–Sun 11am–5pm.

The Bridges of Lane County

Today, there are more than 50 covered bridges in Oregon. The oldest covered bridge is the Drift Creek Bridge near Lincoln City, which dates from 1914, and the newest (a pedestrian bridge in Silverton) dates to as recently as 2000. Built of wood and covered to protect them from the rain and extend their life, the covered bridges of Oregon are found primarily in the Willamette Valley, where early farmers needed safe river and stream crossings to get their crops to market. The highest concentration of covered bridges is found in Lane County, which stretches from the crest of the Cascade Range all the way to the Pacific Ocean and is home to 20 covered bridges.

You can get a map and guide to Lane County's covered bridges from the **Convention & Visitors Association of Lane County Oregon,** 115 W. Eighth Ave., Suite 190 (P.O. Box 10286), Eugene, OR 97440 (② **800/ 547-5445** or 541/484-5307; www.visitlanecounty.org).

PARKS & GARDENS

Alton Baker Park, on the north bank of the Willamette River, is Eugene's most popular park and offers jogging and biking trails. Across the river, **Skinner Butte Park** on the north side of downtown Eugene has more paved paths. Nearby are the **Owen Memorial Rose Gardens.** At the **Mount Pisgah Arboretum,** 33735 Seavey Loop Rd. (② **541/747-1504**), south of town, you can hike 7 miles of trails through meadows and forests. There are good views along the way, but watch out for poison oak. Set beneath towering fir trees high on a hill overlooking the city, **Hendricks Park and Rhododendron Garden,** 1800 Skyline Blvd. (② **541/687-5324**), is one of the prettiest parks in the city, especially in the spring when the rhododendrons bloom. There are free public tours of the garden on Sundays at 1pm between early April and late May. You'll find this park in southeast Eugene off Franklin Boulevard (U.S. 99). Take Walnut Street to Fairmount Boulevard and then turn east on Summit Avenue. If you're crazy about rhododendrons (as so many Northwesterners are), be sure to schedule a visit to **Greer Gardens,** 1280 Goodpasture Island Rd. (② **541/686-8266;** www.greergardens.com), one of the Northwest's most celebrated nurseries.

WINE TOURING

Eugene is at the southern limit of the Willamette Valley wine region, and there are a half dozen wineries within 30 miles of the city.

Chateau Lorane ★★ In a wooded setting overlooking a lake, Chateau Lorane produces a greater variety of wines than just about any other winery in the state. Many of these you won't find at other Oregon wineries, and several are made from organic grapes. Some of the more unusual include a Viognier, a Flora (this grape is a cross between a Gewürztraminer and a Semillon), an organic Marechal Foch (and a late harvest wine from this same grape), and several meads, including a huckleberry mead. They also do a good Pinot Noir for around $20.

27415 Siuslaw River Rd., Lorane. ② **541/942-8028.** www.chateaulorane.com. June–Sept daily noon–5pm; Oct–Dec and Mar–May Sat–Sun noon–5pm. Closed Jan–Feb. Take Ore. 126 west to Veneta and go south through Crow to Lorane.

Hinman Vineyards–Silvan Ridge ⭐⭐ If you happen to enjoy sweet wines, you'll definitely want to drop by this winery. The semi-sparkling Muscat here is outstanding, the perfect dessert wine. Hinman also does respectable Merlots and Cabernet Sauvignons with grapes from southern Oregon, and the Pinot Gris, Chardonnay, and Riesling tend to be quite good. All in all, one of the best and most reliable wineries in the state.

27012 Briggs Hill Rd., Eugene. ℂ **541/345-1945.** www.silvanridge.com. Daily noon–5pm. Closed Thanksgiving, Dec 24–Jan 1. Take Ore. 126 west to Veneta and go south through Crow, west on Territorial Hwy., and north on Briggs Hill Rd.

King Estate ⭐ Set in an idyllic hidden valley southwest of Eugene, this is one of the largest wineries in the state. The winery, part of an 850-acre estate, is surrounded by 235 acres of vineyards and features a huge, château-like facility. The tasting room, however, is one of the smallest in the state. This winery feels more like a corporate endeavor than a work of love, and the wines are generally not among the state's better wines. However, if you want to tour a winery, this is one of the best to visit.

80854 Territorial Rd. ℂ **800/884-4441** or 541/942-9874. www.kingestate.com. June–Sept daily noon–5pm; Oct–May Sat–Sun noon–5pm. Take Ore. 126 west to Veneta and go south through Crow almost to Lorane.

LaVelle Vineyards ⭐ Consistently good white wines (fruity but not too sweet) are the hallmark here. The Pinot Gris (especially the green label vintages, which are put through malo-lactic fermentation) and Riesling are usually quite good. Special events are held throughout the summer, including first Sunday music performances. LaVelle also has a tasting room in downtown Eugene at the Fifth Street Public Market, 296 E. Fifth Ave. (ℂ **541/338-9875**). This latter facility is a good place to start a wine tour of the area.

89697 Sheffler Rd., Elmira. ℂ **541/935-9406.** www.lavelle-vineyards.com. Vineyard: Memorial Day–Oct daily noon–6pm; Nov–May Sat–Sun noon–5pm. Eugene Tasting Room: Sun–Wed 11am–6pm; Thurs–Sat 11am–9pm. Closed Thanksgiving, Christmas, New Year's Day. Off Ore. 126 west of Eugene.

Secret House Vineyards Winery ⭐ This small, casual winery is known for its many special events, including the Wine and Blues Festival on the second weekend of August. Chardonnay, Pinot Noir, and Riesling wines are produced, but the sparkling wines are what make this winery noteworthy.

88324 Vineyard Lane, Veneta. ℂ **541/935-3774.** www.secrethousewinery.com. Daily 11am–5pm. Closed Thanksgiving, Christmas, New Year's Day. Off Ore. 126 west of Eugene.

OUTDOOR ACTIVITIES

Eugene has long been known as Tracktown, USA, and if you want to follow in the footsteps of Steve Prefontaine, there are plenty of routes around town for doing some running. At the Convention & Visitors Association of Lane County Oregon (see above), you can pick up a map of area running trails. These jogging routes include the popular **Pre's Trail,** a 3.87-mile system of loops in Alton Baker Park, which is just across the Willamette River from downtown Eugene. When the university's track team isn't practicing, it's also possible to run the track at the University of Oregon's **Hayward Field,** where Pre and other Eugene runners have trained. You'll find Hayward Field off Agate Street in the southeast corner of the campus. Runners may also want to drop by the **Nike Store,** Fifth Street Public Market, 248 E Fifth Ave. (ℂ **541/342-5155**), which has an interesting exhibit about Steve Prefontaine, Bill Bowerman, and Phil Knight, who together laid the foundations for Nike's later success.

Go Ducks!

The University of Oregon's Ducks football team had an outstanding season in 2000, finishing seventh in the nation, which landed the team in the San Diego Holiday Bowl (which the Ducks won). Tickets sell out quickly, but if you're a fan, contact the **UO Athletic Ticket Office** (© **800/WEB FOOT** or 541/346-4461; www.goducks.com).

With two rivers, the McKenzie and the Willamette, flowing through the area, it isn't surprising that Eugene has quite a few water-oriented activities. You can rent canoes and kayaks at **Oregon River Sports,** 1640 W. Seventh Ave. (© **888/790-PADL** or 541/334-0696; www.oregonriversports.com), which has its canoe path rental facility beside the Kowloon Restaurant, 2222 Centennial Blvd. Rates range from $20 to $55 per day. See the "The Santiam Pass, McKenzie Pass & McKenzie River" section of chapter 8 for information on rafting the nearby McKenzie River.

Eugene is Oregon's best bicycling city; to see why, rent a bike at **High Street Bicycles,** 535 High St. (© **541/687-1775**), located only a couple of blocks from the city's extensive riverside network of bike paths. Rates start at $5 per hour or $20 per day. Another great place for a bike ride is the paved Row River Trail, which starts in the nearby town of Cottage Grove and follows an abandoned railroad grade past Dorena Lake.

Golfers have plenty of Eugene options, including the **Emerald Valley Golf Club,** 83301 Dale Kuni Rd., Creswell (© **541/895-2174**), a championship public course with views of the Willamette River; **Fiddler's Green Golf Center,** 91292 Hwy. 99 N (© **541/689-8464**), an 18-hole par-three course; **Laurelwood Golf Club,** 2700 Columbia St. (© **541/687-5321**), a 9-hole city-owned course; and the **Riveridge Golf Course,** 3800 N. Delta Hwy. (© **541/345-9160**), which is on the Willamette River.

SHOPPING

You can shop for one-of-a-kind crafts at Eugene's **Saturday Market** (© **541/686-8885**), which covers more than two downtown blocks beginning at the corner of Eighth Avenue and Oak Street. The bustling market was founded in 1970 and is something of a bastion of hippie crafts. There are also food vendors, fresh produce, and live music. The market, held April through November, takes place on Saturdays between 10am to 5pm.

Other days of the week, you can explore the **Market District,** a 6-block area of restored buildings that houses unusual shops, galleries, restaurants, and nightclubs. The **Fifth Street Public Market,** 296 E. Fifth St. (© **541/484-0383**), at the corner of Fifth Avenue and High Street, is the centerpiece of the area. In this shopping center, you'll find **New Twist** (© **541/342-8686**), selling fine crafts and wildly artistic jewelry; **French Quarter** (© **541/343-8904**), selling fine linens; **Destinations** (© **541/302-0787**), a travel store; and **The Nike Store** (© **541/342-5155**). Directly across Fifth Avenue is the **5th & Pearl building,** which houses a couple of restaurants and a few more shops. **Station Square,** a block west on Fifth Avenue, is a modern upscale mall designed to look like an old train station. Also nearby is **Down to Earth,** 532 Olive St. (© **541/342-6820**), a fascinating garden and housewares shop housed in an old granary building.

If you're interested in art, there is a monthly **First Friday Artwalk** during which downtown art galleries have openings and stay open late. For information, contact the **Lane Arts Council**, 44 W Broadway Suite 304 (© **541/485-2278;** www.lanearts.org).

WHERE TO STAY

Best Western New Oregon Motel ★ *Value*   Located across the street from the university campus, this Best Western is a convenient and fairly economical choice. Although the motel looks a bit old from the outside, guest rooms are in good shape. The abundance of recreational amenities is another plus here.

1655 Franklin Blvd., Eugene, OR 97403. © 800/528-1234 or 541/683-3669. Fax 541/484-5556. www.bestwestern.com/neworegonmotel. 128 units. $72–$88 double. AE, DC, DISC, MC, V. Pets accepted. **Amenities:** Indoor pool; exercise room; Jacuzzi; sauna; coin-op laundry; laundry service; dry cleaning. *In room:* A/C, TV, dataport, fridge, coffeemaker, hair dryer, iron.

The Campbell House ★★   Only 2 blocks from the Market District and set at the base of Skinner's Butte overlooking the city, this large Victorian home was built in 1892 and now offers luxury, convenience, and comfort. The guest rooms here vary considerably in size and price. Breakfasts are served in a cheerful room with a curving wall of glass. Several of the guest rooms on the first floor have high ceilings, and on the lower level there's a pine-paneled room with a fishing theme and another with a golf theme. The upstairs rooms have plenty of windows, and in the largest room you'll find wood floors and a double whirlpool tub. A separate carriage house contains some of the inn's most luxurious and most thoughtfully designed rooms.

252 Pearl St., Eugene, OR 97401. © 800/264-2519 or 541/343-1119. Fax 541/343-2258. www.campbellhouse.com. 18 units. $86–$386 double. AE, DC, DISC, MC, V. Rates include full breakfast. **Amenities:** Access to nearby health club; concierge; massage; laundry service; dry cleaning. *In room:* A/C, TV, dataport, fridge, hair dryer, iron.

Hilton Eugene & Conference Center ★★   This is Eugene's only downtown corporate high-rise convention hotel, and it caters primarily to business travelers and conventioneers. However, with the Hult Center for the Performing Arts next door and dozens of restaurants and cafes within a few blocks, it's also a good choice if you want to take in a show or explore downtown Eugene. Try to get a room on an upper floor so you can enjoy the views. The restaurant just off the lobby features a Northwest fishing theme and serves moderately priced meals.

66 E. Sixth Ave., Eugene, OR 97401. © 800/937-6660 or 541/342-2000. Fax 541/342-6661. www.eugene.hilton.com. 272 units. $99–$186 double; $175–$325 suite. AE, DC, DISC, MC, V. Pets accepted ($25 per day). **Amenities:** Restaurant (Northwest), lounge; indoor pool; exercise room and access to nearby health club; Jacuzzi; sauna; concierge; car-rental desk; courtesy airport shuttle; salon; room service; laundry service; dry cleaning; concierge-level rooms. *In room:* A/C, TV, dataport, coffeemaker, hair dryer, iron.

McKenzie View ★★ *Finds*   This country inn set on 6 acres of woodlands overlooks the McKenzie River. Beautiful perennial and cutting gardens surround the inn, and there are decks and a gazebo. The inn itself is an expansive contemporary home that is comfortably furnished (neither overdone nor so full of antiques that guests feel uncomfortable). Three of the rooms are quite large (two are suites) and have views of the river through large windows. The smallest room doesn't have a river view, but it is quite economical. Avid gardeners will love this place. The inn is about a 15- to 20-minute drive from downtown Eugene.

34922 McKenzie View Dr., Springfield, OR 97478. © 888/MCK-VIEW or 541/726-3887. Fax 541/726-6968. www.mckenzie-view.com. 4 units. Apr–Oct $90–$250 double; Nov–Mar $75–$200 double. Rates include full breakfast. AE, DISC, MC, V. **Amenities:** Access to nearby health club. *In room:* A/C, dataport, hair dryer.

The Secret Garden ★★ *Finds*   This B&B is housed in a former sorority house, previously the home of Eugene pioneer Alton Baker. Today, the large inn features European and Asian art and antiques. Guest rooms are beautifully and tastefully decorated. One of our favorites is the Scented Garden, which has floor lamps made from Tibetan horns and a gorgeous sitar on display. And yes, there is a secret garden, a unique outdoor room with living walls concealing a whirlpool tub.

1910 University St., Eugene, OR 97403. ℭ **888/484-6755** or 541/484-6755. Fax 541/431-1699. www. secretgardenbbinn.com. 10 units. May–Oct $115–$235 double; Nov–Apr $105–$215 double. Rates include full breakfast. AE, MC, V. **Amenities:** Access to nearby health club; Jacuzzi. *In room:* A/C, TV, fridge, hair dryer, iron.

Valley River Inn ★★   Although this lushly landscaped low-rise hotel boasts an envious location on the bank of the Willamette River, the rates are aimed at expense accounts and not vacationers. If you can get any sort of substantial discount, this might be a good choice. The hotel is only a few minutes' drive from downtown and the university, and is adjacent to Eugene's largest shopping mall. All the rooms are large and have a balcony or patio, but the riverside rooms have the best views. Sweetwater's Restaurant has a long wall of glass overlooking the river and serves primarily Northwest cuisine.

1000 Valley River Way, Eugene, OR 97401. ℭ **800/543-8266** or 541/687-0123. Fax 541/683-5121. www. valleyriverinn.com. 257 units. $129–$220 double; $250–$400 suite. AE, DC, DISC, MC, V. Pets accepted. **Amenities:** Restaurant (Northwest), lounge; outdoor pool; exercise room, access to nearby health club; Jacuzzi; sauna; bike rental; concierge; room service; laundry service; dry cleaning; concierge-level rooms. *In room:* A/C, TV, dataport, coffeemaker, hair dryer, iron.

WHERE TO DINE

For rustic breads, breakfast pastries, and desserts, drop by the **Palace Bakery,** 844 Pearl St. (ℭ **541/484-2435**), which is an offshoot of the popular Zenon Café. For espresso, drop by **Cafe Paradiso,** 115 W. Broadway (ℭ **541/484-9933**), one of Eugene's most popular coffeehouses.

EXPENSIVE

Adam's Place ★★ NORTHWEST   Downtown on the pedestrian mall, Adam's Place conjures up an old English inn and is one of the most elegant dining establishments in the city. The menu is short and changes frequently, but on a recent summer evening the appetizer menu included an unusual yam and sweet chili bisque as well as *mieng kum,* a Thai dish of spinach leaves wrapped around an assortment of ingredients that you assemble yourself. Entree flavors tend to be simple, yet creative, emphasizing subtle flavors and perfect preparation. Salmon might be served in a saffron-leek court bouillon, and rack of lamb might be crusted in herbs and garlic and served with a caramelized-onion demiglace. In the summer, you can dine under the stars out on the patio. Several nights each week there is live jazz.

30 E. Broadway. ℭ **541/344-6948.** Reservations recommended. Main courses $16–$27. www.adamsplace restaurant.com. AE, MC, V. Sun–Thurs 3:30–9pm; Fri–Sat 3:30–10pm.

Chanterelle ★★ CONTINENTAL   This small continental restaurant is in one of downtown Eugene's many restored industrial buildings. There are few surprises on the menu, just tried-and-true recipes such as escargots bourguignon, oysters Rockefeller, tournedos of beef, and steak Diane. All are prepared with reliable expertise and served graciously. Game meats such as emu, moose, and buffalo are also sometimes on the menu. A long wine list offers plenty of choices.

207 E. Fifth St. ℭ **541/484-4065.** Reservations highly recommended. Main courses $17–$24. AE, DC, MC, V. Tues–Thurs 5–10pm; Fri–Sat 5–11pm. Closed Mar 14–Apr 5 and Aug 16–Sept 8.

Marché ★★ MEDITERRANEAN   Marché, located in the Fifth Street Public Market, is a quintessential urban American bistro, and, with its hip decor, tiny (but popular) bar, patio, and display kitchen with a few settings for solo diners, the restaurant pulls in a wide range of customers, from couples on dates to pre-theater parties and even families. The menu, though at times a bit pretentious, is as creative as you'll find in Eugene and preparations are fairly reliable. As often as possible, ingredients are organic and non-GMO (genetically modified). There's an extensive wine list with plenty of reasonably priced wine, plus plenty of wines by the glass as well.

296 E. Fifth Ave. ✆ 541/342-3612. www.marcherestaurant.com. Reservations recommended. Main courses $14.50–$25.50. AE, DISC, MC, V. Mon–Thurs 11:30am–10pm; Fri–Sat 11:30am–11pm; Sun 10am–10pm.

MODERATE

The LocoMotive ★★ VEGETARIAN   Eugene has long been a magnet for counterculture types, so it should come as no surprise that the city has an excellent gourmet vegetarian restaurant. (Think white tablecloths not hippie hangout.) Across the street from the Fifth Street Public Market and adjacent to the railroad tracks, this restaurant not only serves excellent vegetarian fare influenced by the cuisines of the world, but also uses organic ingredients as often as possible. A recent menu included vegetarian paella, a corn-and-cheese tart, and a portobello mushroom sautéed in wine sauce. Desserts, ranging from an organic blueberry pie (in season) to apples poached in red wine and calvados, are worth saving room for. Keep an eye out for the unforgettable lavender ice cream.

291 E. Fifth Ave. ✆ 541/465-4754. Reservations recommended. Main courses $13–$14. MC, V. Wed–Thurs 5–9pm; Fri–Sat 5–10pm.

Zenon Café ★★ (Value) INTERNATIONAL   Zenon has long been the city's top outpost for cutting-edge cookery. If you've read about it in the latest *Gourmet* or *Bon Appétit,* you'll probably find it on the menu here. The setting is fairly stark, though with some raw wood for warmth, but the menu, which changes daily, is long and emphasizes East Indian and Middle Eastern flavors. You're almost assured of finding something you've never tried before. Before you ever reach your table, though, you'll have to run the gamut of the dessert case, which usually flaunts about 20 irresistible cakes, pies, tortes, and other pastries.

898 Pearl St. ✆ 541/343-3005. Main courses $5.75–$17. MC, V. Sun–Thurs 8am–11pm; Fri–Sat 8am–midnight.

INEXPENSIVE

Mona Lizza/West Brothers Bar-B-Que ★★ (Value) BARBECUE/ITALIAN   With two restaurants and a brewpub under one roof, this place may have a split personality, but it sure keeps Eugene's residents happy. Though you can't get barbecue on the Mona Lizza side or Italian on the West Brothers side, you can get the same good Eugene City Brewery beers at either restaurant. Mona Lizza's offers primarily wood-oven pizzas and pasta, while West Brothers serves up half a dozen types of barbecue including Carolina pork shoulder and Memphis baby back pork ribs. The dessert case just inside the front door of Mona Lizza may have you thinking about a salad instead of a big plate of pasta. For decor, there are Mona Lisa paintings in contemporary poses and, at West Brothers, photos of barbecue joints around the country. Both places are pretty casual.

830 and 844 Olive St. Mona Lizza ✆ 541/345-1072. West Brothers ✆ 541/345-4026. www.west-bros. com. Main courses $7.50–$18. AE, DC, DISC, MC, V. Daily 11:30am–11:30pm.

EUGENE AFTER DARK

With its two theaters and nonstop schedule, the **Hult Center for the Performing Arts,** One Eugene Center, Seventh Avenue and Willamette Street (© **541/682-5000;** www.hultcenter.org), is the heart and soul of this city's performing arts scene. The center's huge glass gables are an unmistakable landmark, and each year this sparkling temple of the arts puts together a first-rate schedule of performances by the Eugene Symphony, the Eugene Ballet Company, the Eugene Opera, and other local and regional companies, as well as visiting companies and performers. During the summer, the center hosts the Oregon Bach Festival and the Oregon Festival of American Music. Summer concerts are also held at the **Cuthbert Amphitheater** in Alton Baker Park.

To find out what's happening, pick up a copy of the free *Eugene Weekly,* which is available at restaurants and shops around town.

BREWPUBS

In addition to the places listed below, you'll find plenty of microbreweries in Eugene. These include the **High Street Brewery & Cafe,** 1243 High St. (© 541/345-4905); the **East 19th Street Cafe,** 1485 E. 19th St. (© 541/342-4025); **Steelhead Brewing Co.,** 199 E. Fifth Ave. (© 541/686-2739); and the **Wild Duck Restaurant & Brewery,** 169 W. Sixth Ave. (© 541/485-3825).

NIGHTCLUBS & BARS

Adam's Place ⭐   This downtown restaurant and jazz bar has been giving Jo Federigo's a run for its money of late, and some of the same musicians show up at both places. 30 E. Broadway. © **541/344-6948.**

Jo Federigo's Café & Bar ⭐   Housed in a historic granary building, Jo Federigo's is both a popular restaurant and Eugene's favorite jazz club. Live music nightly. 259 E. Fifth Ave. © **541/343-8488.**

Oregon Electric Station ⭐⭐   This building dates from 1914, and with a wine cellar in an old railroad car, lots of oak, and a back bar that requires a ladder to access all the various bottles of premium spirits, it's the poshest bar in town. 27 E. Fifth Ave. © **541/485-4444.**

Wild Duck Music Hall ⭐   For great rock and reggae from around the region and the country, check out this brewpub. 169 W. Sixth Ave. © **541/485-3825.** www.wildduckbrewery.com.

WOW Hall ⭐⭐   The historic Woodmen of the World Hall now serves as a sort of community center for the performing arts and hosts an eclectic array of concerts and performances by alternative bands. 291 W. Eighth Ave. © **541/687-2746.**

6

The Oregon Coast

Extending from the mouth of the Columbia River in the north to California's redwood country in the south, the Oregon coast is a shoreline of stunning natural beauty. Yes, it's often rainy or foggy, and yes, the water is too cold and rough for swimming, but the coastline more than makes up for these shortcomings with its drama and grandeur. Wave-pounded rocky shores; dense, dark forests; lonely lighthouses; rugged headlands—these set this shoreline apart.

In places, the mountains of the Coast Range rise straight from the ocean's waves to form rugged, windswept headlands that still bear the colorful names given them by early explorers—Cape Foulweather, Cape Blanco, and Cape Perpetua. With roads and trails that scale these heights, these capes provide ideal vantage points for surveying the wave-washed coast. Miles of sandy beaches stretch between the rocky headlands. In fact, on the central coast there's so much sand that dunes rise as high as 500 feet.

Wildlife viewing opportunities here are outstanding. From the beaches and the waters just offshore rise countless haystack rocks, rocky islets, monoliths, and other rock formations that serve as homes to sea birds, sea lions, and seals. Harbor seals loll on isolated sand spits, and large colonies of Steller's sea lions lounge on rocks and docks, barking incessantly and entertaining people with their constant bickering. The best places to observe sea lions are at Sea Lion Caves north of Florence and at Cape Arago State Park outside of Coos Bay. Hundreds of gray whales also call these waters home, and each year thousands more can be seen during their annual migrations. Twice a year, in late winter and early spring, gray whales migrate between the Arctic and the waters off Baja California. They pass close by the coast and can be easily spotted from headlands such as Tillamook Head, Cape Meares, Cape Lookout, and Cape Blanco. In coastal meadows, majestic elk graze contentedly, and near the town of Reedsport, the Dean Creek meadows have been set aside as an elk preserve. It's often possible to spot 100 or more elk grazing here. The single best introduction to the aquatic flora and fauna of the Oregon coast is Newport's Oregon Coast Aquarium, where you can learn more about the myriad animals and plants that inhabit the diverse aquatic environments of the Oregon coast.

Rivers, bays, and offshore waters are also home to some of the best **fishing** in the country. The rivers, though depleted by a century of overfishing, are still home to salmon, steelhead, and trout, most of which are now hatchery raised. Several charter-boat marinas up and down the coast offer saltwater-fishing for salmon and bottom fish, and few anglers return from these trips without a good catch. **Crabbing** and **clamming** are two other productive coastal pursuits that can turn a trip to the beach into a time for feasting.

To allow visitors to enjoy all the beauties of the Oregon coast, the state has created nearly 80 state parks, waysides, recreation areas, and scenic viewpoints between Fort Stevens State Park in the north and McVay Rock

Value The Cost of the Coast

State parks, county parks, national-forest recreation areas, outstanding natural areas—along the Oregon coast, there are numerous state and federal access areas that now charge day-use fees. You can either pay these fees as you encounter them or purchase an Oregon Pacific Coast Passport for $10. These passes are good for 5 days, and get you into all state and federal parks and recreation areas along the coast. (However, you'll still have to pay campsite fees.) A $35 annual pass is also available. Passports are available at most state parks that charge a day-use fee. For more information contact **Oregon State Parks Information Center** (© 800/551-6949).

State Recreation Site in the south. Among the more popular activities at these parks are kite flying and beach-combing (but not swimming; the water is too cold).

As we've already mentioned, it rains a lot here. Bring a raincoat, and don't let a little moisture prevent you from enjoying one of the most beautiful coastlines in the world. In fact, the mists and fogs add an aura of mystery to the coast's dark, forested mountain slopes. Contrary to what you might think, the hot days of July and August are not always the best time to visit. When it's baking inland, the coast is often shrouded in fog. The best months to visit tend to be September and October, when the weather is often fine and the crowds are gone.

1 Astoria

95 miles NW of Portland; 20 miles S of Long Beach, WA; 17 miles N of Seaside

Astoria, situated on the banks of the Columbia River just inland from the river's mouth, is the oldest American community west of the Mississippi. More a river town than a beach town, Astoria's greatest attraction lies in its hillsides of restored Victorian homes and the scenic views across the Columbia to the hills of southwestern Washington. The combination of historical character, scenic vistas, a lively arts community, and some interesting museums make this one of the most intriguing communities on the Oregon coast. Although it still has seamy sections of waterfront, the town has been busy over the past few years developing something of a tourist-oriented waterfront character.

Astoria's Euro-American history got its start in the winter of 1805–06 when Lewis and Clark built a fort near here and established an American claim. Five years later, in 1811, fur traders working for John Jacob Astor arrived at the mouth of the Columbia River to set up a fur-trading fort that was named Fort Astoria. During the War of 1812, the fort was turned over to the British, but by 1818 it reverted to American hands. When the salmon-canning boom hit in the 1880s, Astoria became a bustling little city—the second largest in Oregon—and wealthy merchants began erecting the ornate, Victorian-style homes that today give Astoria its historic character.

ESSENTIALS

GETTING THERE   From Portland, take U.S. 30W. From the north or south, take U.S. 101.

VISITOR INFORMATION   Contact the **Astoria-Warrenton Area Chamber of Commerce,** 111 W. Marine Dr. (P.O. Box 176), Astoria, OR 97103 (© 800/875-6807 or 503/325-6311; www.oldoregon.com).

FESTIVALS The **Astoria Regatta,** held each year in early August, is the city's biggest festival and includes lots of sailboat races. As part of the festival, you can catch a performance of the Astor Street Opry Company's *Shanghaied in Astoria,* a musical melodrama staged at the Old Finnish Meat Market under the big bridge (✆ **503/325-6104**). This usually runs from mid-July to late August.

DELVING INTO ASTORIA HISTORY

Columbia River Maritime Museum ★★ The Columbia River, the second-largest river in the United States, was the object of centuries of exploration in the Northwest, and since its discovery in 1792, has been essential to the region. This boldly designed museum, built to resemble waves on the ocean, tells the story of the river's maritime history. High seas and constantly shifting sands make this one of the world's most difficult rivers to enter, and displays of shipwrecks, light-houses, and historical lifesaving missions testify to the danger. Fishing, naviga-tion, and naval history are also subjects of museum exhibits. Docked beside the museum and open to visitors is the lightship *Columbia,* the last seagoing light-house ship to serve on the West Coast. The museum is currently undergoing a $5-million renovation and expansion that should be done by spring of 2002.

1792 Marine Dr. ✆ **503/325-2323**. www.crmm.org. Admission $5 adults, $4 seniors, $2 children 6–17. Daily 9:30am–5pm. Closed Thanksgiving, Christmas.

Flavel House Museum ★ The Flavel House, owned and operated by the Clatsop County Historical Society, is the grandest and most ornate of Astoria's many Victorian homes. This Queen Anne–style Victorian mansion was built in 1885 by Capt. George Flavel, who made his fortune operating the first pilot service over the Columbia River Bar and was Astoria's first millionaire. When constructed, this house was the envy of every Astoria resident. The high-ceilinged rooms are filled with period furnishings that accent the home's superb construction, and throughout the house there is much ornate woodwork.

441 Eighth St. ✆ **503/325-2203**. Admission $5 adults, $2.50 children 6–17. May–Sept daily 10am–5pm; Oct–Apr daily 11am–4pm.

Fort Clatsop National Memorial ★★ During the winter of 1805–06, Meriwether Lewis, William Clark, and the other members of the Corps of Dis-covery camped at a spot near the mouth of the Columbia River. They built a log stockade and named their encampment Fort Clatsop after the local Clatsop Indians who had befriended them. Today's Fort Clatsop is a replica of Lewis and Clark's winter encampment and is built near the site of the original fort. The 50-foot-by-50-foot compound contains seven rooms, each of which is furnished much as it may have been during Lewis and Clark's stay. From late spring to Labor Day, park rangers clad in period clothing give demonstrations of activities such as flintlock use, buckskin preparation, and candle making. In the visitor center you can learn more about the history of the area.

Off U.S. 101, 5 miles southwest of Astoria. ✆ **503/861-2471**. www.nps.gov/focl. Admission $3 per person or $5 per car. Labor Day to mid-June daily 8am–5pm; mid-June to Labor Day daily 8am–6pm. Closed Christmas.

Heritage Museum Housed in Astoria's former city hall, this small museum chronicles the history of Astoria and surrounding Clatsop County. Native American and pioneer artifacts and historic photos comprise the main exhibits, but there is also an exhibit on the many saloons that filled this town in the late 19th century.

1618 Exchange St. ✆ **503/325-2203**. Admission $3 adults, $2 seniors, $1 children 6–17. Summer daily 10am–5pm; off-season daily 11am–4pm.

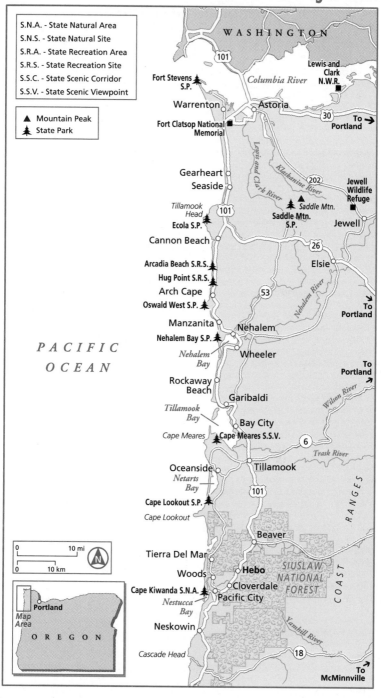

The Northern Oregon Coast

S.N.A. - State Natural Area
S.N.S. - State Natural Site
S.R.A. - State Recreation Area
S.R.S. - State Recreation Site
S.S.C. - State Scenic Corridor
S.S.V. - State Scenic Viewpoint

▲ Mountain Peak
🌲 State Park

WASHINGTON

101

Columbia River

Lewis and Clark N.W.R.

Fort Stevens S.P.

Warrenton

Astoria

30

To Portland

Fort Clatsop National Memorial

Lewis and Clark River

Klaskanine River

202

Jewell Wildlife Refuge

Gearheart

Seaside

Tillamook Head

101

Saddle Mtn.

Saddle Mtn. S.P.

Jewell

Ecola S.P.

Cannon Beach

26

Arcadia Beach S.R.S.

Elsie

Hug Point S.R.S.

Arch Cape

53

Oswald West S.P.

Nehalem River

Manzanita

Nehalem

To Portland

Nehalem Bay S.P.

Wheeler

Nehalem Bay

Rockaway Beach

To Portland

Garibaldi

Wilson River

Tillamook Bay

Bay City

Cape Meares

Cape Meares S.S.V.

6

Oceanside

Tillamook

Trask River

Netarts Bay

101

Cape Lookout S.P.

R A N G E S

Cape Lookout

Beaver

PACIFIC OCEAN

Tierra Del Mar

Woods

Hebo

SIUSLAW NATIONAL FOREST

Cape Kiwanda S.N.A.

Cloverdale

Pacific City

Nestucca Bay

C O A S T

Neskowin

Yamhill River

0   10 mi
0   10 km

N

18

To McMinnville

Portland

Map Area

Cascade Head

O R E G O N

OTHER ASTORIA ACTIVITIES & ATTRACTIONS

Atop Coxcomb Hill, which is reached by driving up 16th Street and following the signs and painted "column" markings on the road, you'll find the **Astoria Column.** Built in 1926, the column is patterned after Trajan's Column in Rome and stands 125 feet tall. On the exterior wall of the column, a mural depicts the history of the area. There are 164 steps up to the top of the column, and on a clear day the view makes the climb well worth the effort. The column is open daily from dawn to dusk and admission is free. On the way to the Astoria Column, stop by **Fort Astoria,** on the corner of 15th and Exchange streets. A log blockhouse and historical marker commemorate the site of the trading post established by John Jacob Astor's fur traders.

There are several places in downtown where you can linger by the riverside atop the docks that once comprised much of the city's waterfront. Stop by the **Sixth Street Viewing Dock,** where there is a raised viewing platform as well as a fishing dock. From here you can gaze out at the massive Astoria-Megler Bridge, stretching for more than 4 miles across the mouth of the river. Also keep an eye out for sea lions. The best way to see the waterfront is aboard the restored 1913 streetcar operated by **Astoria Riverfront Trolley.** This streetcar operates daily from Memorial Day to Labor Day (and weekends in Oct), and rides are $1. If you'd like to see the waterfront from an offshore perspective, you can book a river cruise by **Tiki Charters** (© **503/325-7818**). Cruises of the Astoria waterfront are $20 per person, and trips upriver through the inside passage to Cathlamet are $80 per person.

Right in downtown Astoria, you'll find one of the most unusual wineries in the state. **Shallon Winery,** 1598 Duane St. (© **503/325-5978;** www.shallon. com), specializes in fruit wines, but it is the unique whey wines that are winemaker Paul van der Veldt's greatest achievement. The Cran du Lait, made with local cranberries and whey from the Tillamook cheese factory, is surprisingly smooth and drinkable. Also look for the amazing chocolate-orange wine, a thick nectar that will make a chocoholic of anyone.

If you'd like to see what local artists are up to, stop by the **Pacific Rim Gallery,** 1 12th St. (© **503/325-5450**), which also has an espresso bar and cafe. For more regional art, visit the **RiverSea Gallery,** 1160 Commercial St. (© **503/325-1270**). Right next door, the **Hide & Silk Co.,** 1164 Commercial St. (© **503/325-2766**), sells handmade clothing made of natural fabrics. Should you find yourself in need of an umbrella, stop by **Let It Rain,** 1124 Commercial St. (© **800/998-0773** or 503/325-7728), which has one of the largest selections of umbrellas in the Northwest.

OUTDOOR ACTIVITIES

Fort Stevens State Park (© **503/861-1671**), 8 miles from Astoria at the mouth of the Columbia, preserves a fort that was built during the Civil War to protect the Columbia River and its important port cities. Though Fort Stevens had the distinction of being the only mainland military reservation to be fired on by the Japanese, the fort was deactivated after World War II. Today the fort's extensive grounds include historic buildings and gun emplacements, a museum housing military artifacts, miles of bicycle paths and beaches, and a campground and picnic area. Admission is $3. At the north end of the park, you can climb to the top of a viewing tower and get a good look at the South Jetty, which was built to make navigating the mouth of the Columbia easier. Also within the park you can see the wreck of the *Peter Iredale,* one ship that did not make it safely over the sandbars at the river's mouth. You can rent bikes from **Bikes & Beyond,** 1089 Marine Dr. (© **503/325-2961**).

If you're interested in exploring the waters of the Astoria area, you can rent a kayak from **Pacific Wave Ltd.,** 21 U.S. 101, Warrenton (© **503/861-0866;** www.pacwave.net), which also offers classes and guided tours.

Several charter-fishing boats operate out of nearby Warrenton. Arrange trips through **Tiki Charters** (© **503/325-7818**) and **Charlton Deep Sea Charters** (© **503/861-2429**). Expect to pay $70 to $75 per person.

A few miles outside of town on Ore. 30, bird-watchers will find a roadside viewing platform overlooking the marshes of the **Twilight Creek Eagle Sanctuary.** Take Burnside Road off Ore. 30 between the John Day River and Svenson.

WHERE TO STAY

Clementine's Bed and Breakfast ✦✦
Across the street from the Flavel House Museum, this eclectic little inn built in 1888 in the Italianate Victorian style, is filled with Asian arts and antiques, and surrounded by beautiful flower gardens. Rooms vary considerably in size. Two have their own little balconies, and several have expansive views of the river and town. The two suites are quite large and are great for families. With backgrounds in music and river guiding on the Colorado River, innkeepers Judith and Cliff Taylor keep guests informed about what there is to see and do in the area.

847 Exchange St., Astoria, OR 97103. © **800/521-6801** or 503/325-2005. Fax 503/325-7056. www. clementines-bb.com. 7 units. $70–$135 double; $135 suite (lower rates Oct 16–May 15). AE, DISC, MC, V. 2-night minimum on summer weekends. Pets accepted in suites ($15). **Amenities:** Jacuzzi; sauna. *In room:* Hair dryer, no phone.

Crest Motel ✦
Located a few miles from downtown Astoria, the Crest Motel sits high on a hillside overlooking the town and the river. The views, congenial atmosphere, and comfortable refurbished rooms have made this motel immensely popular. Keep in mind that the lower-priced rooms have no views— and since the views are the main reason to stay here, it's worth a bit of a splurge for a better room even if you're on a tight budget. The deluxe-view rooms are very large and have sliding glass doors and a patio or balcony. The Jacuzzi is in a gazebo overlooking the river.

5366 Leif Erickson Dr. (about 2 miles east of town on U.S. 30), Astoria, OR 97103. © **800/421-3141** or 503/325-3141. Fax 503/325-3141. www.crest-motel.com. 40 units. $55.50–$107.50 double. AE, DC, DISC, MC, V. Pets accepted. **Amenities:** Jacuzzi; coin-op laundry. *In room:* TV, dataport, fridge, coffeemaker, iron.

Officer's Inn Bed and Breakfast ✦ *Finds*
Housed in the former Fort Stevens officers' quarters built in 1905, this sprawling 8,000-square-foot B&B is just around the corner from the Fort Stevens Museum and about a 10-minute drive from Astoria. The inn captures the essence of small-town America with its long front porch overlooking the old parade grounds. Inside, you'll find simple, classic decor. However, it is the perfectly preserved pressed-tin ceilings of the parlors and dining rooms that are the inn's finest feature. Guest rooms vary in size and come with king, queen, or double beds. There are even two rooms set up for families. Any time of year, but especially in spring and fall, you might see elk grazing in the field behind the inn.

540 Russell Place, Hammond, OR 97121. © **800/377-2524** or 503/861-2524. www.moriah.com/officersinn. 8 units. $79–$99 double. MC, V. *In room:* No phone.

Rosebriar Hotel ✦
Originally built as a private home in 1902, the Rosebriar became a convent in the 1950s, then was renovated and turned into a small

> **Tips   Plan Ahead—Campground Reservations**
>
> For information on **camping** in area state parks, call the state parks infor-
> mation line at © 800/551-6949. To make a camping reservation, contact
> **Reservations Northwest,** 2501 SW First St. (P.O. Box 500), Portland, OR
> 97207 (© **800/452-5687** or 503/731-3411; www.oregonstateparks.org).

1920s-style hotel in the 1990s. Ornate wainscoting, scrollwork ceilings, and lots
of wood trim show the quality of workmanship that went into this home. The
grand old Georgian mansion sits high above the river and street, with commanding views from the two front rooms. The carriage-house cottage has its
own fireplace, whirlpool tub, and private patio.

636 14th St., Astoria, OR 97103. © 800/487-0224 or 503/325-7427. http://astoria-usa.com/rosebriar.
11 units. June–Sept $75–$169 double; Oct–May $65–$118 double. Rates include full breakfast. 2-night
minimum on weekends. AE, DC, DISC, MC, V. *In room:* TV.

CAMPGROUNDS
Fort Stevens State Park, on the beach at the mouth of the Columbia River, is
one of the largest and most popular state park campgrounds on the Oregon
coast. For reservations, contact **Reservations Northwest** (© **800/452-5687;**
www.oregonstateparks.org).

WHERE TO DINE
In addition to the restaurants listed below, you might want to check out **Joseph-
son's,** 106 Marine Dr. (© **800/772-3474** or 503/325-2190), a local seafood-
smoking company that sells smoked salmon by the pound and has a take-out
deli counter with clam chowder, smoked seafood on rolls, and more. If you're
looking for some local ale, stop by **The Wet Dog Cafe,** 144 11th St. (© **503/
325-6975**), the town's only brewpub. For espresso, a quick lunch, or a light dinner, head to **T. Paul's Urban Café,** 1119 Commercial St. (© **503/338-5133**).

Columbian Café ⊗ *Finds* VEGETARIAN/SEAFOOD   With offbeat and
eclectic decor, this tiny place looks a bit like a cross between a college hangout
and a seaport diner, and indeed the clientele reflects this atmosphere. There are
only three or four booths and a lunch counter, and the cafe's reputation for good
vegetarian fare keeps the seats full. Crepes are the house specialty and come with
a variety of fillings, including avocado, tomato, and cheese, or curried bananas.
Dinner offers a bit more variety, with an emphasis on seafood, and there are
always lots of specials. Even the condiments here, including pepper jelly and
garlic jelly, are homemade.

1114 Marine Dr. © 503/325-2233. Breakfast or lunch $4–$9; dinner $8–$18.50. No credit cards. Mon–Tues
8am–2pm; Wed–Thurs 8am–2pm and 5–9pm; Fri 8am–2pm and 5–10pm; Sat 9am–2pm and 5–10pm; Sun
9am–2pm. (Dining hours may change with the season.)

Gunderson's Cannery Cafe ★ SEAFOOD/NORTHWEST   Housed in a
restored salmon cannery, this restaurant provides a more contemporary dining
alternative than nearby Pier 11. You get the same views and are just as likely to
see sea lions, but the food is a bit more creative. For nightly specials, the chef
draws upon world cuisines for inspiration; and on the main menu, you'll also find
international influences in such dishes as pan-Asian salmon and Mediterranean
halibut. The crab and shrimp cakes are perennial favorites. Lunches are mostly
sandwiches (the panini are our favorites), salads, and good chowder.

Sixth St. on the Columbia River. © 503/325-8642. Reservations recommended. Main courses lunch $5–$12, dinner $8–$25. AE, DC, DISC, MC, V. Mon 11am–3pm; Tues–Thurs 11am–8pm; Fri–Sat 11am–9pm.

Home Spirit ★★ *Finds* INTERNATIONAL   Housed in a restored Victorian home, this place is both a bakery and cafe and, in the evening, Astoria's finest restaurant. Each night there is a different prix-fixe menu offering a choice of four different entrees. A meal might start with fresh corn soup or peanut bisque followed by a pear and hazelnut salad with blue cheese or a salad of melon, mint, and cucumber. Among the entrees you might encounter spicy chicken vindaloo, salmon in sweet red curry, stuffed Cajun pork chops, or artichoke and sweet corn lasagna. Can you say eclectic? This is just the sort of unexpectedly delightful place that makes Astoria such a hidden gem of a town to explore.

1585 Exchange St. © 503/325-6846. Reservations recommended. Main courses $16–$19. Tues 9am–3pm; Wed–Sat 9am–3pm and 5:30–8pm.

Pier 11 Feed Store Restaurant ★ SEAFOOD   Originally a freight depot for river cargo and one of the few buildings in town that was not destroyed by a fire in 1922, Pier 11 now houses a few small shops and this popular, though touristy, seafood restaurant. Nearly everyone gets a great view of the river through the restaurant's wall of glass, and if you're lucky, you might spot some seals or sea lions frolicking just outside. Although most of the seafood dishes served here come deep-fried, there are some alternatives, little neck clams steamed with garlic and butter and an unusual halibut baked in blue cheese sauce. Be sure to say hello to Cecil the sea serpent.

At the foot of Tenth and Eleventh sts. © 503/325-0279. Reservations recommended. Main dishes lunch $4.25–$12; dinner $12–$21.75. AE, DC, DISC, MC, V. Mon–Sat 11am–9pm; Sun 9am–9pm (until 10pm nightly in summer).

Someplace Else ★ INTERNATIONAL   Each day Someplace Else serves an international dish, such as Thai prawn curry with pineapple or French roast chicken with grapes. The owner has traveled to the places from which she draws her recipes, but since her family is from Sicily, the menu has a decidedly southern Italian slant. Some of the dishes are more successful than others. Homey treatments of pastas such as ravioli are satisfying, and sliced tomatoes with onions and anchovies make a tasty salad. This is a cozy neighborhood place popular with the locals for the nightly international specials, but even if you're only in town for one night you'll probably enjoy it.

965 Commercial St. © 503/325-3500. www.pacifier.com/~someplac. Reservations recommended. Main courses $4.75 lunch, $6.75–$14 dinner. AE, DISC, MC, V. Wed–Sun 11:30am–2pm and 4–9pm.

2 Seaside

17 miles S of Astoria, 79 miles W of Portland, 7 miles N of Cannon Beach

Seaside is the northern Oregon coast's favorite family vacation destination. Although the town is one of the oldest beach resorts on the coast (dating from 1899) and is filled with quaint historic cottages and tree-lined streets, it is better known for its miniature golf courses, bumper boats, video arcades, and souvenir shops.

This is not the sort of place most people imagine when they dream about the Oregon coast, and if you're looking for a quiet, romantic weekend getaway, don't head here. As one of the closest beaches to Portland, crowds and traffic are a way of life on summer weekends. The town is also a very popular conference site, and several of the town's largest hotels cater primarily to this market (and have the

Biking the Oregon Coast

The Oregon coast is one of the nation's best-known bicycle tour routes, ranking right up there with the back roads of Vermont, the Napa Valley, and the San Juan Islands. Cyclists will find breathtaking scenery, interesting towns, parks and beaches to explore, wide shoulders, and well-spaced places to stay. You can stay in campgrounds (all state park campgrounds have hiker/biker campsites) or hotels. If you can afford it, an inn-to-inn pedal down this coast is the way to go; as you slowly grind your way up hill after hill, you'll appreciate not having to carry camping gear.

The entire route, from Astoria to California, covers between 368 and 378 miles (depending on your route) and includes a daunting 16,000 total feet of climbing. Although most of the route is on U.S. 101, which is a 55-mph highway for most of its length, the designated coast route leaves the highway for less crowded and more scenic roads whenever possible.

During the summer, when winds are generally out of the northwest, you'll have the wind at your back if you ride from north to south. In the winter (when you'll likely get very wet), you're better off riding from south to north to take advantage of winds out of the southwest. Planning a trip along the coast in winter is not advisable; even though there is less traffic, winter storms frequently blow in with winds of up to 100 mph.

For a map and guide to bicycling the Oregon coast, contact the **Oregon Bicycle Map Hot Line** (✆ **503/986-3556**). You might also want to get a copy of the *Umbrella Guide to Bicycling the Oregon Coast* (Epicenter Press, 1990), by Robin Cody.

outrageous rates to prove it). However, the nearby community of Gearhart, which has long been a retreat for wealthy Portlanders, is as quiet as any town you'll find on this coast.

ESSENTIALS

GETTING THERE　Seaside is on U.S. 101 just north of the junction with U.S. 26, which connects to Portland.

VISITOR INFORMATION　Contact the **Seaside Chamber of Commerce,** 7 N. Roosevelt (P.O. Box 7), Seaside, OR 97138 (✆ **800/444-6740** or 503/738-3097; www.seasideor.com).

FESTIVALS　The weekend before Labor Day weekend, the **Hood to Coast Run** celebration is held in Seaside.

ENJOYING THE BEACH & SEASIDE'S OTHER ATTRACTIONS

Seaside's centerpiece is its 2-mile-long beachfront **Promenade** (or Prom), built in 1921. At the west end of Broadway, the Turnaround divides the walkway into the North Prom and the South Prom. Here a bronze statue marks the official end of the trail for the Lewis and Clark expedition. South of this statue on

Lewis & Clark Way between the Promenade and Beach Drive, 8 blocks south of Broadway, you'll find the **Lewis and Clark Salt Works,** a reconstruction of a fire pit used by members of the famous expedition. During the winter of 1805–06, while the expedition was camped at Fort Clatsop near present-day Astoria, Lewis and Clark sent several men southwest 15 miles to a good spot for making salt from seawater. It took three men nearly 2 months to produce 4 bushels of salt for the return trip east. Five kettles were used for boiling seawater, and the fires were kept stoked 24 hours a day.

History is not what attracts most people to Seaside, though. Miles of **white-sand beach** begin just south of Seaside at the foot of the imposing Tillamook Head and stretch north to the mouth of the Columbia River. Though the waters here are quite cold and only a few people venture in farther than knee-deep, there are lifeguards on duty all summer, one reason Seaside is popular with families. At the south end of Seaside beach is one of the best surf breaks on the north coast. You can rent a board and wetsuit at **Cleanline Surf,** 719 First Ave. (© **503/738-7888**). A complete rental package runs $35 a day for adults, $25 for kids. You can also rent body boards here.

However, because of the cold water, kite flying, beach cycling, and other nonaquatic activities prove far more popular than swimming or surfing. All over town there are places that rent in-line skates, four-wheeled bicycles called surreys, and three-wheeled cycles (funcycles) for pedaling on the beach. The latter are the most popular and the most fun, but can really be used only when the tide is out and the beach is firm enough to pedal on. Skates rent for about $8 an hour, cycles go for between $10 and $15 an hour, and multipassenger surreys rent for between $15 and $36 an hour. Try **Wheel Fun Rentals** at 407 S. Holladay Dr. (© **503/738-8447**).

If you prefer hiking over cycling, head south of town to the end of Sunset Boulevard, where you'll find the start of the **Tillamook Head Trail,** which leads 6 miles over the headland to Indian Beach in **Ecola State Park.** This trail goes through shady forests of firs and red cedars with a few glimpses of the Pacific along the way.

Golfers can play a round at the **Seaside Golf Club,** 451 Ave. U (© **503/738-5261**), **The Highlands at Gearhart,** 1 Highlands Rd. (© **503/738-5248**), or the recently renovated and redesigned **Gearhart Golf Links,** on North Marion Street in Gearhart (© **503/738-3538**). Expect to pay between about $18 and $45 for 18 holes.

The **Seaside Aquarium,** 200 N. Promenade (© **503/738-6211**), where you can feed seals, is popular. Admission is $6 for adults and $3 for children. Kids will also enjoy the gaudily painted **carousel** at the Seaside Town Center Mall at 300 Broadway.

WHERE TO STAY
IN SEASIDE

The Gilbert Inn ★★ One block from the beach and 1 block south of Broadway, on the edge of both the shopping district and one of Seaside's old residential neighborhoods, the Gilbert Inn is a big yellow Queen Anne–style Victorian house with a pretty little yard. Alexander Gilbert, who had this house built in 1892, was once the mayor of Seaside, and he built a stately home worthy of someone in such a high position. Gilbert made good use of the plentiful fir trees of the area; the interior walls and ceilings are constructed of tongue-and-groove fir planks. The current owners, Dick and Carole Rees, have decorated the house in country French decor that enhances the Victorian ambience.

341 Beach Dr., Seaside, OR 97138. ℭ **800/410-9770** or 503/738-9770. Fax 503/717-1070. www.gilbertinn. com. 10 units. $89–$115 double; $105–$125 suite. 2-night minimum on weekends, 3-night on minimum on holiday weekends. Rates include full breakfast. AE, DISC, MC, V. **Amenities:** Access to nearby health club. *In room:* TV.

Riverside Inn Bed & Breakfast (★ (Value) The Riverside Inn is an oasis amid the traffic and commercial businesses on busy Holladay Drive. Beautiful gardens frame the restored 1907 home and its attached cottages, and the Necanicum River flows through the backyard. All the guest rooms here are a bit different, with antique country decor and an emphasis on fishing collectibles. The Captain's Quarters room, way up on the third floor, features a skylight directly over the bathtub and has the feel of a well-appointed artist's garret. Another of our favorites is the Old Seaside, a two-room unit with its own private deck. There is also a sprawling multilevel deck in back of the inn that allows guests to enjoy the riverside location. If you're planning a long stay, there are some rooms with kitchenettes. This is one of the best values on the northern Oregon coast.

430 S. Holladay Dr., Seaside, OR 97138. ℭ **800/826-6151** or 503/738-8254. Fax 503/738-7375. www. riversideinn.com. 11 units. $60–$100 double. Rates include full breakfast. AE, DISC, MC, V. *In room:* TV, no phone.

IN GEARHART
Gearhart by the Sea (★ (Kids) Although this four-story condominium hotel isn't the most attractive building on the coast (stark cement exterior), with the Gearhart Golf Links directly across the street, it is ideal for golfers. Condos all have full kitchens, fireplaces, and ocean views; but the two-bedroom units (good for families) have the best views. The beach is a bit farther than the golf course, and across the sand dunes.

1157 N. Marion Ave. (P.O. Box 2700), Gearhart, OR 97138. ℭ **800/547-0115** or 503/738-8331. Fax 503/738-0881. www.gearhartresort.com. 100 condos. $126–$148 1-bedroom; $158–$194 2-bedroom. AE, DISC, MC, V. Pets accepted ($10 per night). **Amenities:** Restaurant (Northwest), lounge; 2 indoor pools; 18-hole golf course; Jacuzzi. *In room:* TV, kitchen, coffeemaker.

Gearhart Ocean Inn (★ (Value) This old motor-court-style motel offers modest and economical accommodations that have been renovated with the sort of care usually reserved for historic homes. A taupe exterior with white trim gives the two rows of wooden buildings a touch of sophistication, and roses and Adirondack chairs add character to the grounds, though a wide expanse of gravel parking lot does detract somewhat from the effect. The rooms all have lots of character and have been decorated in a mix of country cute and casual contemporary. Some rooms have kitchens.

67 N. Cottage St. (P.O. Box 2161), Gearhart, OR 97138. ℭ **800/352-8034** or 503/738-7373. Fax 503/717-8008. www.gearhartoceaninn.com. 11 units. $45–$109 double. AE, DC, DISC, MC, V. Pets accepted ($10 fee). *In room:* TV, fridge, coffeemaker.

WHERE TO DINE
If you're looking for a quick meal, some picnic food, or something to take back and cook in your room, drop by the old-timey **Bell Buoy Crab Co.,** 1800 S. Roosevelt St. (ℭ **503/738-2722**), which sells not only cooked Dungeness crabs, but award-winning chowder, smoked salmon, fresh seafood, and shrimp or crab melts.

IN SEASIDE
Vista Sea Café (★ PIZZA/SANDWICHES Whether you're in the mood for pizza or soup and a sandwich, you can't go wrong here. High-backed antique

booths and big windows that let in plenty of sunshine in the summer make this a cheerful spot. Whatever you do, don't leave without trying the clam chowder, which is served with delicious homemade beer bread. On the pizza menu you'll find creations such as pesto pizza and veggie and blue-cheese pizza.

150 Broadway. ✆ **503/738-8108.** Pizzas $12–$24; sandwiches $6–$8. MC, V. Summer daily 11:30am–10pm (open fewer days and shorter hours in winter).

IN GEARHART

Pacific Way Cafe and Bakery ⋆ *Finds* SANDWICHES/NORTHWEST
This former mom-and-pop grocery store is in the center of Gearhart. The vintage interior of the restaurant harkens to the 1930s. At lunch, there are appetizing sandwiches and salads. In the evening, try the grilled scallops and prawns over grilled polenta, good Dungeness crab cakes with red-pepper aioli, or spicy seafood stew. There's an adjacent bakery open Saturday and Sunday from 8am to 1pm.

601 Pacific Way, in Gearhart. ✆ **503/738-0245.** Main dishes $7.25–$23.50. MC, V. Thurs–Mon 11:30am–3:30pm and 5–9pm.

3 Cannon Beach ⋆⋆⋆

7 miles S of Seaside, 112 miles N of Newport, 79 miles W of Portland

When most people dream of a vacation on the Oregon coast, chances are they're thinking of a place such as **Cannon Beach:** weathered cedar-shingle buildings, picket fences behind drifts of nasturtiums, quiet gravel lanes, interesting little art galleries, and massive rock monoliths rising from the surf just off the wide sandy beach. If it weren't for all the other people who think Cannon Beach is a wonderful place, this town would be perfect. However, Cannon Beach is suffering from its own quaintness and the inevitable upscaling that ensues when a place begins to gain national recognition. Once the Oregon coast's most renowned artists' community, Cannon Beach is now going the way of California's Carmel—lots of upscale shopping tucked away in utterly tasteful little plazas along a neatly manicured main street. Despite the crowds, however, it still has a village atmosphere, and summer throngs and traffic jams can do nothing to assault the fortress-like beauty of the rocks that lie just offshore.

ESSENTIALS

GETTING THERE   Cannon Beach is on U.S. 101 just south of the junction with U.S. 26.

VISITOR INFORMATION   Contact the **Cannon Beach Chamber of Commerce,** 207 N. Spruce St. (P.O. Box 64), Cannon Beach, OR 97110 (✆ **503/436-2623;** www.cannonbeach.org).

GETTING AROUND   The **Cannon Beach Shuttle,** which provides free van service up and down the length of town, operates daily with seasonal hours. Watch for signed shuttle stops. Donations for the ride are accepted.

FESTIVALS   Each year in late April, the **Puffin Kite Festival** fills the skies over Cannon Beach with colorful kites and features stunt kite-flying exhibitions. In early June, the **Sand Castle Day** contest turns the beach into one vast canvas for sand sculptors from all over the region, and in early November, the **Stormy Weather Arts Festival** celebrates the arrival of winter storms. On summer Sunday afternoons, the **Concerts in the Park** series stages free concerts in a variety of musical styles at City Park on the corner of Second and Spruce streets.

HITTING THE BEACH

Ecola State Park ⟨⟨ (© **503/368-5154**), just north of the town of Cannon Beach, marks the southernmost point that Lewis and Clark explored on the Oregon coast. The park offers the most breathtaking vantage point from which to soak up the view of Cannon Beach, Haystack Rock, and the Tillamook Rock Lighthouse. The park also has several picnic areas perched on bluffs high above the crashing waves and a trail that leads 6 miles over Tillamook Head to Seaside. The 1-mile stretch of trail between the main bluff-top picnic area and Indian beach is particularly rewarding, passing through old-growth forests and offering good views of the ocean and beaches far below. The day use fee is $3 per vehicle.

Kite flying and beachcombing are the most popular Cannon Beach pastimes. However, you can also enjoy the beach a variety of other ways. Guided horseback rides to Cove Beach and Haystack Rock are offered by **Sea Ranch Stables,** 415 Fir St. (no phone), which is at the north entrance to Cannon Beach. Rides cost $35, and you must drop by the stables and make a reservation.

Another great way to see the beach is from a funcycle, a three-wheeled beach cycle. These cycles allow you to ride up and down the beach at low tide. Funcycles can be rented from **Manzanita Fun Merchants,** 1160 S. Hemlock St. (© **866/436-1880** or 503/436-1880), and **Mike's Bike Shop,** 248 N. Spruce St. (© **503/436-1266**) for about $8 for an hour and a half. Mountain bikes are also available for rent from Mike's.

Three miles south of town is **Arcadia Beach Wayside** ⟨, one of the prettiest little beaches on the north coast; and another mile farther south you'll find **Hug Point State Recreation Site** ⟨, which has picnic tables, a sheltered beach, and the remains of an old road that was cut into the rock face of this headland. **Oswald West State Park** ⟨⟨, 10 miles south of Cannon Beach, is one of our favorites of all the parks on the Oregon coast. A short paved trail leads to a driftwood-strewn cobblestone beach on a small cove. Headlands on either side of the cove can be reached by hiking trails that offer splendid views. The waves here are popular with surfers. There's also a walk-in campground.

EXPLORING THE TOWN

For many Cannon Beach visitors, **shopping** is the town's greatest attraction. In the heart of town, along Hemlock Street, you'll find dozens of densely packed

---

⸢ *Fun Fact* **Cannon Beach Trivia**

- **Cannon Beach** was named for several cannons that washed ashore after the warship *Shark* wrecked on the coast north of here.
- The most photographed monolith on the Oregon coast is **Haystack Rock,** which rises 235 feet above the water.
- The offshore rocks are protected nesting grounds for sea birds. Watch for **tufted puffins,** something of a Cannon Beach mascot.
- Tillamook Rock is the site of the **Tillamook Rock Lighthouse** (aka "Terrible Tilly"), which was subject to huge storm waves that occasionally sent large rocks crashing through the light, 133 feet above sea level. The lighthouse was decommissioned in 1957 and is now used as a columbarium (a vault for the interment of the ashes of people who have been cremated).

small shops and galleries offering original art, fine crafts, unusual gifts, and casual fashions. Galleries worth seeking out include **Jeffrey Hull Gallery,** 172 N. Hemlock St. (© **503/436-2600**), specializing in Oregon coast landscapes; **The White Bird Gallery,** 251 N. Hemlock St. (© **503/436-2681**), a respectable gallery for contemporary work; and **Northwest by Northwest Gallery,** 239 N. Hemlock St. (© **503/436-0741**). South of downtown, you'll find **Icefire Glassworks,** 116 E. Gower St. (© **503/436-2359**), a glassblowing studio. Across the street from this studio is the **Cannon Beach Arts Association Gallery,** 1064 S. Hemlock St. (© **503/436-0744**), which mounts shows in a wide variety of styles not usually seen in other Cannon Beach galleries (which tend to be heavy on beach landscapes).

WHERE TO STAY

If you're heading here with the whole family or plan to stay a while, consider renting a house, a cottage, or an apartment. Offerings range from studio apartments to large luxurious oceanfront houses, and prices span an equally wide range. Contact **Cannon Beach Property Management** (© **503/436-2021;** www.cbpm.com) or **Arch Cape Property Services** (© **503/436-1607;** www.archcaperental.com) for more information.

Cannon Beach Hotel Lodgings ⋆   Although not in the town's best location (there are parking lots all around), this hotel manages to capture Cannon Beach's spirit economically. A white picket fence, green shutters, and cedar-shingle siding, give the hotel plenty of character, while inside you'll find attractively furnished rooms that vary in size and price. The best rooms are those with fireplaces and whirlpool tubs, and two of these have partial ocean views. Rooms are also rented in two other nearby buildings, with some of these rooms being more luxurious than those here.

1116 S. Hemlock St. (P.O. Box 943), Cannon Beach, OR 97110. © **800/238-4107** or 503/436-1392. www.cannonbeachhotel.com. 26 units. June to mid-Sept $85–$165 double. Mid-Sept to Oct and mid-Mar to May $59–$139 double. Nov to mid-Mar $49–$125 double. Rates include continental breakfast (for rooms in hotel only). AE, DC, DISC, MC, V. **Amenities:** Restaurant (Northwest); room service. *In room:* TV.

Hallmark Resort ⋆ *(Kids)*   Situated on a bluff at the south end of town and with a head-on view of Haystack Rock, the Hallmark appeals to both families and couples on romantic getaways, and the wide range of rates reflects the variety of rooms available. The lowest rates are for nonview standard rooms, and the highest rates are for oceanfront two-bedroom suites. In between these extremes are all manner of rooms, studios, and suites. The best values are the limited-view rooms, many of which have fireplaces and comfortable chairs set up to take in what little view there might be. Some rooms also have kitchens.

1400 S. Hemlock St. (P.O. Box 547), Cannon Beach, OR 97110. © **888/448-4449** or 503/436-1566. Fax 503/436-0324. www.hallmarkinns.com. 142 units. May–Sept $99–$289 double; $164–$319 suite. Oct–Apr $59–$209 double; $99–$219 suite. AE, DC, DISC, MC, V. Pets accepted ($5 per night). **Amenities:** 2 indoor pools; exercise room; Jacuzzi; sauna; massage; coin-op laundry. *In room:* TV, fridge, coffeemaker, hair dryer, iron.

St. Bernards ⋆⋆ *(Finds)*   If you can't find time in your schedule for that trip to France this year, a stay at St. Bernard's will provide a reasonable facsimile. Although the setting, just off U.S. 101 between Cannon Beach and Manzanita, won't convince you that you're in Provence, the building itself is as grand a manor house as any in France. Incorporating elements from castles and châteaux, this inn is straight out of a fairy tale. European antiques and original art fill the house, which has tile floors and an abundance of tapestry-cloth furnishings. Each of the rooms fulfills a different fantasy of the perfect romantic escape. There is the

circular Tower room, with its own soaking tub; the Gauguin, filled with reproductions of paintings by you-know-who; and the Tapestry room, with a stained-
glass ceiling and an ocean view from the soaking tub. Lavish, multicourse
breakfasts are served in the conservatory, and evening social hour is usually held
by the fireplace. So luxurious is this place that the fact that you aren't right on the
beach doesn't even seem to matter.

3 E. Ocean Rd. (P.O. Box 102), Arch Cape, OR 97102. © **800/436-2848** or 503/436-2800. Fax 503/436-1206.
www.st-bernards.com. 7 units. $139–$199 double. Rates include full breakfast. AE, MC, V. **Amenities:** Exercise room; sauna; concierge; massage. *In room:* TV/VCR, fridge, dataport, hair dryer, iron.

The Sea Sprite ★ (Finds
This collection of suites and studios is in the
Tolovana Park area south of Cannon Beach, and it's a great choice for families
even though it's been around for quite a few years. All rooms have kitchens and
most have woodstoves. However, it's the views of Haystack Rock that convince
most people that the Sea Sprite is aging gracefully. These are housekeeping units,
so you'll have to pick up after yourself and make your own bed.

280 Nebesna St. (P.O. Box 933), Cannon Beach, OR 97110. © **866/828-1050** or 503/436-2266. Fax 503/
436-0715. www.seasprite.com. 6 units. $110–$200 double. Lower rates in off-season. DISC, MC, V.
Amenities: Guest laundry. *In room:* TV/VCR, kitchen, fridge, coffeemaker.

Stephanie Inn ★★★
The Stephanie Inn is the most classically romantic inn
on the Oregon Coast—the perfect place for an anniversary or other special
weekend away. With flower boxes beneath the windows and neatly manicured
gardens by the entry, the inn is reminiscent of New England's country inns, but
the beach out the back door is definitely of Pacific Northwest origin. Inside, the
lobby feels warm and cozy with its river-rock fireplace, huge wood columns, and
beamed ceiling. The guest rooms, all individually decorated, are equally cozy,
and most have double whirlpool tubs and gas fireplaces. The higher you go in
the three-story inn, the better the views and the more spacious the outdoor
spaces (patios, balconies, and decks). A bounteous breakfast buffet is served each
morning, and there is also a complimentary afternoon wine gathering. Creative
four-course prix-fixe dinners ($39.95) are served in the evening. (Reservations
are required.)

2740 S. Pacific St. (P.O. Box 219), Cannon Beach, OR 97110. © **800/633-3466** or 503/436-2221. www.
stephanie-inn.com. 50 units. $169–$359 double; $379–$449 suite. Rates include full breakfast. AE, DC, DISC,
MC, V. Children 12 and over are welcome. **Amenities:** Restaurant (Northwest); access to nearby health club;
courtesy shopping shuttle; room service; massage. *In room:* A/C, TV/VCR, coffeemaker, hair dryer.

The Waves/The Argonauta Inn/White Heron Lodge ★★
Variety is the
name of the game in eclectic Cannon Beach, and The Waves plays the game
better than any other accommodation in town. This lodge, only a block from
the heart of town, consists of more than 4 dozen rooms, suites, cottages, and
beach houses at The Waves and two other jointly managed lodges, The
Argonauta Inn and the White Heron Lodge. The Garden Court rooms (with no
ocean views) are the least expensive. Our favorites, however, are the cottages of
The Argonauta Inn. Surrounded by beautiful flower gardens in the summer,
these old oceanfront cottages capture the spirit of Cannon Beach. For sybarites
and romantics, there are fireplaces in some rooms and whirlpool spas overlooking the ocean. If you want to get away from the crowds, ask for an apartment at
the White Heron Lodge. The Waves itself offers contemporary accommodations, some of which are right on the beach and have great views.

188 W. Second St. (P.O. Box 3), Cannon Beach, OR 97110. © **800/822-2468** or 503/436-2205. Fax 503/
436-1490. www.thewavesmotel.com. 55 units. $99–$325 double. 3-night minimum July–Aug; 2-night

minimum on weekends Sept–June. DISC, MC, V. **Amenities:** Access to nearby health club; Jacuzzi; coin-op laundry. *In room:* TV/VCR, kitchen, coffeemaker, hair dryer, iron.

CAMPGROUNDS

Despite the fact that **Oswald West State Park,** which is south of Cannon Beach and has the only area state park campground, has only walk-in campsites, the sites are closer together than those at most car campgrounds. Don't say I didn't warn you if the guy in the next campsite keeps you up all night with his snoring. At the north end of town, the **Sea Ranch R.V. Park,** 415 Fir St. (P.O. Box 214), Cannon Beach, OR 97110 (✆ **503/436-2815;** www.cannon-beach.net/ searanch), offers sites for RVs and tents. The campground is green and shady and is right across the street from the road to Ecola State Park. Rates range from $19 to $24 per night. You can also try **Wright's for Camping,** P.O. Box 213, Cannon Beach, OR 97110 (✆ **503/436-2347;** www.wrightsforcampping. com), which is set back in the trees on the inland side of the road at the second Cannon Beach exit off U.S. 101 and charges $19 for campsites. At either of these, you'll need to make reservations at least a month in advance for summer weekends.

WHERE TO DINE

If you've got a weakness like ours for good bakeries, check out **Grain & Sand Baking,** 1064 S. Hemlock St. (✆ **503/436-0120**). For good locally brewed beer, visit **Bill's Tavern & Brewhouse,** 188 N. Hemlock St. (✆ **503/436-2202**).

Bistro Restaurant ✿✿ NORTHWEST   If you're looking for atmosphere and good food, this is the place. Bistro Restaurant is set back a bit from the street behind a small garden and down a brick walkway. Step through the door and you'll think you've just walked into a French country inn. Stucco walls, old prints of flowers, and fresh flowers on the tables are the only decor this tiny place can afford without growing cramped. Dining choices here include exquisitely prepared seafood dishes such as sautéed oysters, grilled salmon, and seafood stew. There's live music on Friday and Saturday evenings, and even a tiny bar.

263 N. Hemlock St. ✆ **503/436-2661.** Reservations highly recommended. Main courses $18.75–$21.75. MC, V. Daily 4–9:30pm. Closed Tues in winter.

Kalypso ✿✿ REGIONAL/INTERNATIONAL   Along with the Bistro Restaurant, this is one of the few places in town where people get dressed up, but you don't have to. Decor in this small and quiet restaurant is pleasantly minimal, with twinkle lights and colorful walls. There's a patio out back, but not much of a view. For starters, there's crab cakes or chicken satay with Thai-style peanut dipping sauce. For entrees, we prefer to stick with the fish dishes, which have interesting accompaniments and sauces (miso-glazed salmon, petrale sole with Scandinavian shrimp sauce). Razor clams that come crusted with sesame seeds and wasabi vinaigrette, and Pacific snapper with a spicy Creole sauce are a couple of standouts.

140 N. Hemlock St. ✆ **503/436-1585.** Reservations recommended. Main courses $16–$24. MC, V. Summer daily 5–9pm (closed Mon other months).

EN ROUTE TO OR FROM PORTLAND

If you'd like to see a large herd of **Roosevelt elk,** watch for the Jewell turnoff about 37 miles before reaching Cannon Beach on U.S. 26. From the turnoff, continue 10 miles north following the wildlife-viewing signs to the **Jewell Meadows Wildlife Area** ✿✿ (✆ **503/755-2264**) where there's a large meadow frequented in the cooler months by up to 300 elk. Although November through

March are the best months to see the elk, September and October are rutting season and, at this time, big bulls can often be heard bugling and seen locking antlers. Although summer is not usually a reliable time for seeing the elk, in June, you may see elk cows with calves. During the winter, the elk are provided with supplemental hay to keep the herd healthy, and it is possible to assist in the daily feeding. Participants are taken out into the meadows on a flatbed trailer loaded with hay, which is then tossed out to the expectant elk. To participate, however, you'll need to call on the morning of December 1 to make your reservation. (Weekends fill up the fastest.)

Twelve miles past the U.S. 26 turnoff for Jewell, you'll find **Saddle Mountain State Natural Area** ⋆⋆, which is a favorite day hike in the area. A strenuous 2½-mile trail leads to the top of Saddle Mountain, from which there are breathtaking views up and down the coast. In the spring, rare wildflowers are abundant along this trail. The trail is steep and rocky, so wear sturdy shoes or boots and carry water.

WHERE TO DINE

Camp 18 Restaurant ⋆ AMERICAN   There is no better place than this combination restaurant and logging museum to learn how logging was done in the days before clear-cutting. The restaurant is in a huge log lodge with lots of chain-saw art, axes for door handles, and a hollowed-out stump for a hostess desk. The restaurant's 85-foot-long ridge pole, the log beam that runs along the inside of the peak of the roof, is the largest of its kind in the country and weighs 25 tons. There is also a pair of stone fireplaces and lots of old logging photos. After tucking into logger-size meals (don't miss the marionberry cobbler), you can wander the grounds studying old steam logging equipment. A gift shop sells logging-oriented souvenirs. Oh, and the food? Basic steak and seafood, mostly fried, with a few pasta and chicken dishes thrown in.

In Elsie 22 miles east of Seaside on U.S. 26. © 503/755-1818. Main courses $6–$10 lunch, $12–$21 dinner. AE, DISC, MC, V. Daily 7am–9pm.

4 Tillamook County

75 miles W of Portland, 51 miles S of Seaside, 44 miles N of Lincoln City

Tillamook is a mispronunciation of the word *Killamook*, which was the name of the Native American tribe that once lived in this area. The name is now applied to a county, a town, and a bay. Although this is one of the closest stretches of coast to Portland, it is not a major destination because there are no large beachfront towns in the area. The town of Tillamook, which lies inland from the Pacific at the south end of Tillamook Bay, is the area's commercial center, but it is the surrounding farmland that has made the biggest name for Tillamook County. Ever since the first settlers arrived in Tillamook in 1851, dairy farming has been the mainstay of the economy, and large herds of contented cows graze in the area's fragrant fields. These cows provide the milk for the Tillamook County Creamery Association's cheese factory, which turns out a substantial share of the cheese consumed in Oregon. With no beaches to attract visitors, the town of Tillamook has managed to turn its dairy industry into a tourist attraction. No, this isn't the cow-watching capital of Oregon, but the town's cheese factory is now one of the most popular stops along the Oregon coast, annually attracting more than 800,000 visitors.

There are a few beachside hamlets in the area that offer a variety of accommodations, activities, and dining options. Tillamook is also the starting point for the scenic Three Capes Loop, which links three state parks and plenty of great coastal scenery.

ESSENTIALS

GETTING THERE   Tillamook is on U.S. 101 at the junction with Ore. 6, which leads to Portland.

VISITOR INFORMATION   For more information on the area, contact the **Tillamook Chamber of Commerce,** 3705 U.S. 101 N., Tillamook, OR 97141 (© **503/842-7525;** www.tillamookchamber.org); or the **Nehalem Bay Area Chamber of Commerce,** P.O. Box 601, Wheeler, OR 97147 (© **503/368-5100;** www.nehalembaychamber.com).

MANZANITA

As the crowds have descended on Cannon Beach, people seeking peace and quiet, and a slower pace have migrated south to the community of Manzanita. Located south of Neahkanie Mountain, Manzanita enjoys a setting similar to Cannon Beach but without the many haystack rocks. There isn't much to do here except walk on the beach and relax, which is exactly why most people come here.

The beach at Manzanita stretches for 5 miles from the base of Neahkanie Mountain to the mouth of the Nehalem River and is a favorite of both surfers and sailboarders. The latter have the option of sailing either in the oceanfront waves or in the quieter waters of Nehalem Bay, which is just across Nehalem Spit from the ocean. Access to both the bay and the beach is provided at **Nehalem Bay State Park** (© **503/368-5154**), which is just south of Manzanita and encompasses all of Nehalem Spit. The park, which includes a campground (and an airstrip), has a 2-mile paved bike path, a horse camp, and horse trails. The day-use fee is $3. Out at the south end of the spit, more than 50 harbor seals can often be seen lounging on the beach. To reach the seal area requires a 5-mile round-trip hike. Alternatively, you can take a brief seal-watching boat excursion through **Jetty Fishery** (see below).

If you absolutely must do something while you're here, try renting a beach bike from **Manzanita Fun Merchants,** 186 Laneda Ave. (© **866/436-1880** or 503/368-6606). The low-slung, three-wheel beach bikes are a great way to explore the beach, and they cost $8 for an hour and a half. You could also play a round of golf on the meandering fairways of the nine-hole **Manzanita Golf Course,** Lake View Drive (© **503/368-5744**), which charges $14 for nine holes. Or take a romantic horseback ride along the beach with **Pearl Creek Stables** (© **503/368-5267**). Rates are $40 per person and reservations are necessary.

WHERE TO STAY

If you want to rent a vacation house in Manzanita, contact **Manzanita Rental Company,** 32 Laneda Ave. (P.O. Box 162), Manzanita, OR 97130 (© **800/579-9801** or 503/368-6797; www.manzanitarentals.com).

Coast Cabins ★★ (Finds   These four modern cabins are set back a ways from the beach but are the most impressive cabins on the entire coast. Done in a sort of modern interpretation of Scandinavian cabins, these accommodations are designed as romantic getaways for couples. Two of the cabins are tall, two-story structures, and the second-floor bedrooms have walls of windows. The cabin interiors are well designed and artfully decorated, with such touches as Tibetan carpets, original art, and unusual lighting fixtures. Now, imagine the burnished glow of the cabins' cedar exteriors accented by lovely terraced perennial gardens, and you'll have an idea of just how the perfect getaway on the Oregon coast should look.

635 Laneda Ave. (P.O. Box 88), Manzanita, OR 97130. (C) **503/368-7113.** www.coastcabins.com. 4 units. $90–$135 double. MC, V. *In room:* TV, kitchen.

The Inn at Manzanita ★★   Searching for an unforgettably romantic spot for a weekend getaway? This is it. Right in the heart of Manzanita and within steps of a couple of good restaurants, the Inn at Manzanita is a great place to celebrate a special event. Double whirlpool tubs sit between the fireplace and the bed in every room, and most rooms have balconies that look out through shady pines to the ocean. The weathered cedar-shingle siding blends unobtrusively with the natural vegetation, and the grounds are planted with beautiful flowers for much of the year.

67 Laneda Ave. (P.O. Box 243), Manzanita, OR 97130. (C) **503/368-6754.** Fax 503/368-5941. www.neahkahnie. net. 13 units. $120–$160 double (lower off-season midweek rates available). 2-night minimum on weekends and July 1–Labor Day, 3 nights on some holidays. MC, V. No children accepted. **Amenities:** Massage. *In room:* TV/VCR, fridge, coffeemaker, hair dryer.

WHERE TO DINE

For lattes and the latest news, head to **Manzanita News & Espresso,** 500 Laneda Ave. ((C) **503/368-7450**).

Blue Sky Café ★★ NORTHWEST   Although the Blue Sky Café is a casual place, it is also one of the best restaurants on the coast. The menu changes with the seasons and so keeps current with both the freshest ingredients and the latest food trends. A recent menu included delicious and unusual chickpea cakes served with cilantro-coconut chutney, as well as a spicy Mexican cheese fondue (*queso fundido*). Entrees show influences from around the globe. The Salmon might be prepared Greek-style with a tzatziki marinade and cucumber-tomato salad, or an assortment of seafood might be prepared in a paella with saffron rice. There is usually a vegetarian or vegan offering as well. For dessert, who could pass up sweet potato pecan pie with bourbon crème anglaise?

154 Laneda Ave. (C) 503/368-5712. Reservations highly recommended. Main courses $11–$25. No credit cards. Summer Mon–Sat 5:30–9:30pm; Sun 9am–2pm and 5:30–9:30pm (closed Mon–Tues off season).

WHEELER

Located on Nehalem Bay, this wide spot in the road has long been popular for crabbing and fishing. However, in recent years it has also become a favorite sea-kayaking locale. The marshes of the bay provide plenty of meandering waterways to explore, and several miles of the Nehalem River can also be easily paddled if the tides are in your favor. There are two places in town where you can rent a kayak: **Nehalem Bay Kayak Co.,** 395 Hwy. 101 ((C) **877/KAYAKCO** or 503/368-6055; www.nbkayak.com), and **Wheeler on the Bay Lodge & Marina,** 580 Marine Dr. ((C) **800/469-3204** or 503/368-5858). Rates range from around $12 to $21 per hour and from $32 to $38 per day; higher rates are for double kayaks.

If you're interested in trying your hand at crabbing, contact **Jetty Fishery** ((C) **800/821-7697** or 503/368-5746; www.jettyfishery.com), located just south of Wheeler at the mouth of the Nehalem River. They rent boats and crab rings and offer dock crabbing. The folks here also offer a ferry service ($5 per person) across the river to Nehalem Bay State Park, where you can often see dozens of harbor seals lying out on the beach. Interestingly enough, the seals will let people get a lot closer in a motorized boat than in a kayak. You can also sometimes see seals close up if you sit on the jetty rocks at nearby Neadonna, which is just south of Jetty Fishery.

WHERE TO STAY

The Nehalem River Inn ⭐ *(Finds)*   The Oregon coast is not just about beaches and rocky headlands, it's also about meandering tidal rivers, and this country inn is set on one. Situated a couple of miles off U.S. 101 between Nehalem and Wheeler, the inn is a hideaway par excellence, with its own restaurant and wines bottled under its own label. Accommodations range from the cozy Kingfisher Room to the two-room Riverside Cottage; all have fireplaces and decks or views of the river and mountains. The cottage has a private spa on its deck and the Cormorant's Watch has a whirlpool tub. The inn rents kayaks to guests and has a riverside hot tub.

34910 Hwy. 53 (P.O. Box 421), Nehalem, OR 97131. © 800/368-6499 or 503/368-7708. Fax 503/355-2301. www.river-inn.com. 5 units. $89–$149 double. AE, DISC, MC, V. **Amenities:** Restaurant (Northwest), lounge; Jacuzzi; kayak rentals; concierge; room service. *In room:* TV, coffeemaker, hair dryer, iron.

Wheeler on the Bay Lodge ⭐   Located right on the shore of Nehalem Bay, this is a great spot for a romantic weekend. One of our favorite rooms on the coast, the Honeymoon room, has walls of glass looking onto the bay, a private deck, a fireplace, and, best of all, a whirlpool tub with great views. Six of the rooms have spas, and most of these have water views. All the rooms sport distinctive decor: a "Mess O' Trout" string of lights, bold sunflower patterns, tropical fish motifs, for example.

580 Marine Dr. (P.O. Box 580), Wheeler, OR 97147. © 800/469-3204 or 503/368-5858. www.mkt-place. com/wheeler. 10 units. $75–$125 double. AE, DISC, MC, V. **Amenities:** Kayak rentals; massage. *In room:* TV/VCR, fridge, coffeemaker.

CAMPGROUNDS

At **Nehalem Bay State Park,** there are yurts as well as plenty of campsites. To make reservations, contact **Reservations Northwest** (© **800/452-5687;** www. oregonstateparks.org).

WHERE TO DINE

If you like smoked salmon, don't miss **Karla's Smokehouse** ⭐, 2010 U.S. 101 N. (© **503/355-2362**), which is at the north end of nearby Rockaway Beach and sells some of the best smoked fish and oysters on the coast. Karla's is open daily from 9am to 5pm in summer, but is only open on weekends in the winter.

Nehalem Dock Restaurant ⭐ AMERICAN   With a pleasant deck on the Nehalem River, this casual restaurant is a great place for lunch if you are exploring the area. It also makes a good sunset dinner spot. Tasty sandwiches and local seafood are the mainstays. It's a fun destination to paddle to if you rented a kayak in nearby Wheeler.

35815 Hwy. 101, Nehalem. © 503/368-5557. Main courses $10–$17. DISC, MC, V. Mon–Thurs 11:30am–3pm and 4–8pm; Fri–Sat 11:30am–3pm and 4–9pm; Sun 11:30am–3pm and 4–8pm.

The Nehalem River Inn Restaurant ⭐⭐ *(Finds)* NORTHWEST   Set on the bank of the Nehalem River, this restaurant, part of a secluded little country inn, serves some of the best food on the Oregon coast. The menu is contemporary and relies heavily on wild ingredients and organic produce. Although it changes with the seasons, you might start your meal with shell-baked scallops with wild sea greens or a salad of wild sorrel and organic greens. For an entree, try the tasty roulade of salmon stuffed with crab, shrimp, and spinach, or pan-fried pork tenderloin medallions with grilled figs and wild mushrooms. For dessert? How about raspberry-peach melba or lemon mousse tart with wild huckleberies and lemon sauce? The inn's wines are produced for them at Eola Hills Winery, and tastings are available daily.

34910 Hwy. 53 (less than 3 miles off U.S. 101). ℂ **800/368-6499** or 503/368-7708. Reservations highly recommended. Main courses $13.50–$24.50. AE, DISC, MC, V. Thurs–Mon 6–10pm.

Treasure Café ★ *Finds* BREAKFAST/INTERNATIONAL This hidden jewel serves the best breakfasts on the Oregon coast. Located in a tiny cottage a block off U.S. 101 in Wheeler, the Treasure Cafe has views of Nehalem Bay and Neahkanie Mountain from its small front deck. Breakfasts here attract locals as well as tourists, but the locals all know that the fries are so good they're worth ordering by themselves. If you have a sweet tooth, put in your order for a schnecken cinnamon roll as soon as you show up. (They go fast.) If you want a full breakfast, don't miss the oysters and eggs or the omelet made with house-smoked salmon. Dinner, served on weekends in the summer, features fresh local ingredients and international touches. Although reservations aren't taken, they'll give you a walkie-talkie to carry around town while you wait for a table.

92 Rorvik St. ℂ **503/368-7740**. www.treasurecafe.com. Breakfast $4.50–$8.50; main courses $13–$17. No credit cards. Wed–Fri 9am–1pm; Sat–Sun 8am–1pm. Dinner served Fri–Sat in summer 6–9pm.

GARIBALDI

Named (by the local postmaster) in 1879 for Italian patriot Giuseppi Garibaldi, this little town is at the north end of Tillamook Bay and is the region's main sportfishing and crabbing port. If you've got an urge to do some salmon or bottom fishing, this is the place to book a trip. Try **Troller Charters** (ℂ **503/ 322-3666**), **Siggi-G Ocean Charters** (ℂ **503/322-3285**), or **Kerri Lin Charters** (ℂ **503/355-2439**). Rates are around $65 to $70 for a full day of salmon fishing. Deep-sea halibut fishing will run you about $140 to $150 per day.

Some of these companies also offer **whale-watching** and **bird-watching** trips, and **Troller Charters** (ℂ **503/322-3666**) offers quick trips (known as ocean eco-tours) around Tillamook Bay for about $10 per person per hour (with a $60 minimum). At the **Garibaldi Marina,** 300 Mooring Basin Rd. (ℂ **503/ 322-3312**), you can rent boats, tackle, and crab rings, if you want to do some fishing or crabbing on your own.

Garibaldi is also where you'll find the depot for the **Fun Run Express** (ℂ **800/ 685-1719**), an excursion train that runs along some of the most scenic portions of this section of coast. The train usually runs weekends during the summer. Call to see if it's on track when you visit.

TILLAMOOK

Tillamook has long been known as one of Oregon's foremost dairy regions, and Tillamook cheese is ubiquitous in the state. So it's no surprise that the **Tillamook Cheese Factory,** on U.S. 101 just north of Tillamook (ℂ **503/842-4481; www.tillamookcheese.com**), is the most popular tourist attraction in town. Not only can visitors observe the cheese-making process (cheddars are the specialty), but there's also a large store where all manner of cheeses and other edible gifts are available. The factory is open daily from 8am to 8pm in summer and 8am to 6pm in winter.

If the Tillamook Cheese Factory seems too crowded for you, head back toward town a mile and you'll see the **Blue Heron French Cheese Company,** 2001 Blue Heron Dr. (ℂ **503/842-8281**), which is on the same side of U.S. 101 as the Tillamook Cheese Factory. Located in a big old dairy barn with a flagstone floor, this store stocks the same sort of comestibles as the Tillamook Cheese Factory, though the emphasis here is on brie (which, however, is not made locally). Farm animals make this a good stop for kids. Blue Heron is open daily from 8am to 8pm in summer and 9am to 5pm in winter.

A hangar built during World War II for a fleet of navy blimps is 2 miles south of town off U.S. 101 and lays claim to being the largest freestanding wooden building in the world. Statistics bear this out: It's 250 feet wide, 1,100 feet long, and 170 feet high. The blimp hangar now houses the **Tillamook Naval Air Station Museum,** 6030 Hangar Rd. (© 503/842-1130), which contains a respectable collection of old planes, including a P-51 Mustang, a B-25 Mitchell, an F4U Corsair, and a PBY-5A Catalina. The museum is open from Memorial Day to Labor Day daily from 9am to 6pm; other months daily from 10am to 5pm. Admission is $9.50 for adults, $8.50 for seniors, $5.50 for youths 13 to 17, and $2 for children 7 to 12.

You can go up in a small plane to see this section of the coast and may even see whales. Contact **Tillamook Air Tours** (© 503/842-1942; www.oregon flyer.com), offering tours in a restored 1942 Stinson Reliant V-77 plane and a 1928 Travel Air open cockpit 2-passenger biplane. Flights start at $50 per person.

Anglers interested in going after salmon or steelhead in Tillamook Bay or area rivers should contact **Fishing Oregon** (© 503/842-5171; www.fish-oregon. com), or **Ted Wade River Guide Service** (© 503/245-0206).

WHERE TO DINE

If you need to stock up your larder for the beach house or are on your way back from a weekend at the beach, don't miss an opportunity to stop in at **Bear Creek Artichokes** (© 503/398-5411), which is located 11 miles south of Tillamook on U.S. 101. This is one of the only commercial artichoke farms in Oregon and usually has fresh artichokes throughout the summer and fall. The farm stand has lots of other great produce, as well as jams, mustards, and salsas. The display gardens offer a pleasant break from driving.

THE THREE CAPES SCENIC LOOP

The **Three Capes Scenic Loop** begins just west of downtown Tillamook and leads past Cape Meares, Cape Lookout, and Cape Kiwanda. Together these capes offer some of the most spectacular views on the northern Oregon coast. All three capes are state parks, and all make great whale-watching spots in the spring or storm-watching spots in the winter. To start the loop, follow Third Street out of town and watch for the right turn for Cape Meares State Scenic Viewpoint. This road will take you along the shore of Tillamook Bay and around the north side of Cape Meares, where the resort town of Bayocean once stood. Built early in this century by developers with a dream to create the Atlantic City of the West, Bayocean was constructed at the end of a sand spit that often felt the full force of winter storms. When Bayocean homes began falling into the ocean, folks realized that this wasn't going to be the next Atlantic City. Today there's no sign of the town, but the long sandy beach along the spit is a great place for a walk and a bit of bird-watching.

Just around the tip of the cape, you'll come to **Cape Meares State Scenic Viewpoint,** which is the site of the **Cape Meares Lighthouse.** The lighthouse is open to the public and houses a small museum. The views from atop this rocky headland are superb. Continuing around the cape, you come to the residential community of **Oceanside,** from where you have an excellent view of the **Three Arch Rocks** just offshore. The beach at Oceanside is a popular spot and is often protected from the wind in the summer. Oceanside is a popular lunch stop for people doing the Three Capes Loop.

Three miles south of Oceanside, you'll come to tiny **Netarts Bay,** which is known for its excellent clamming and crabbing. Continuing south, you come to **Cape Lookout State Park** ⚐⚐, which has a campground, picnic areas, beaches, and several miles of hiking trails. The most breathtaking trail leads 2½ miles out to the end of Cape Lookout, where, from several hundred feet above the ocean, you can often spot gray whales in the spring and fall.

Cape Kiwanda ⚐⚐, which lies just outside the town of Pacific City, is the last of the three capes and is preserved as Cape Kiwanda State Natural Area. At the foot of the cape's sandstone cliffs, you'll find sand dunes and tide pools, and it's possible to scramble up a huge sand dune to the top of the cape for dramatic views of this rugged piece of shoreline. At the base of the cape is the staging area for Pacific City's beach-launched dory fleet. These flat-bottomed commercial fishing boats are launched from the beach and plow through crashing breakers to get out to calmer waters beyond. When the day's fishing is done, the dories roar into shore at full throttle and come to a grinding stop as high up on the beach as they can. This is Oregon's only such fishing fleet and is celebrated each year during the annual Dory Derby on the third weekend in July.

The beach at the base of Cape Kiwanda is also one of the north coast's best surfing spots, and the high sand dune behind the beach has perfect conditions for paragliding. **Over the Hill Paragliding** (ⓒ **503/667-4557;** www.overthehillparagliding.com) and the **Hang Gliding and Paragliding School of Oregon** (ⓒ **503/223-7448**) offer paragliding classes here.

If you'd like to do a bit of horseback riding in the area, contact **Into the Sunset** (ⓒ **503/965-6326**).

WHERE TO STAY
In Oceanside

House on the Hill Motel ⚐ *Finds*   Set 250 feet above Oceanside's beach on a promontory jutting into the ocean, this motel boasts one of the most spectacular settings on the Oregon coast. However, with too much asphalt parking lot around the buildings, the grounds leave a bit to be desired. The motel is a collection of two-story buildings, several of which look like truncated A-frames. Rooms are large and the views are just stunning, with the Three Arch Rocks directly offshore. In many rooms you can even lie in bed and soak up the views. With cliffs dropping off from the edge of the property, this is not a good choice for families with small children. Note that this is a no-smoking motel.

1816 Maxwell Mountain Rd. (P.O. Box 187), Oceanside, OR 97134. ⓒ **503/842-6030.** www.houseonthehillmotel.com. 16 units. May–Oct $85–$150 double. Nov–Apr $65–$135 double. DISC, MC, V. No pets accepted. *In room:* TV, fridge, coffeemaker.

Oceanside Inn ⚐ *Value*   Located right next door to Roseanna's Oceanside Café (see "Where to Dine," below), this restored older inn sits at the top of a steep stairway down to the beach and has five rooms with ocean views. Of these, room 6 is our favorite. It's up on the second floor and has three walls of windows to take in the great views. This room also has a whirlpool tub, and at $85 it is a real bargain for the area. If you opt for an economical room without a view, you can still hang out on the large deck that's perched high above the beach. This place isn't fancy, but it is comfortable.

1440 Pacific Ave. NW, Oceanside, OR 97134. ⓒ **800/347-2972** or 503/842-2961. 9 units. $65–$100 double. MC, V. *In room:* TV/VCR, kitchen.

In Pacific City

Inn at Cape Kiwanda 🐾🐾 *Finds*   For many years Pacific City was a sleepy little fishing village, but all that changed with the opening of the Inn at Cape Kiwanda several years ago. Although it's across the street from the beach (and Cape Kiwanda State Natural Area), this modern cedar-shingled three-story hotel has one of the best views on the Oregon coast: Directly offshore rises Haystack Rock, a huge jug-handled monolith. Since a great view isn't quite enough, the hotel was designed with luxurious, contemporary rooms, all of which have balconies and fireplaces. A few have whirlpool tubs, and there is also a very luxurious suite. The corner rooms are our favorites. The inn is affiliated with the Pelican Pub & Brewery, which is right across the street, and on the inn's ground floor there is an art gallery and an espresso bar that also sells wine and books.

33105 Cape Kiwanda Dr., Pacific City, OR 97135. ©️ **888/965-7001** or 503/965-7001. Fax 503/965-7002. www. innatcapekiwanda.com. 35 units. $109–$199 double; $189–$259 suite. AE, DISC, MC, V. **Amenities:** Restaurant (brewpub), lounge; exercise room; massage; guest laundry. *In room:* TV/VCR, minibar, coffeemaker, hair dryer.

CAMPGROUNDS

Cape Lookout State Park is the largest campground along the Three Capes Loop. For reservations, contact **Reservations Northwest** (©️ **800/452-5687;** www.oregonstateparks.org). **Whalen Island County Park,** on the south side of Sand Lake just off Sand Lake Road, is a smaller and less crowded alternative (though it's not right on the ocean).

WHERE TO DINE
In Oceanside

Roseanna's Oceanside Café 🐾 SEAFOOD/INTERNATIONAL   When you're the only restaurant in town, you can't help staying busy, but Roseanna's is such a Scenic Loop legend that people come from miles around to eat here and don't seem to mind long waits to get a table. What brings them are the reliable meals and the view of the beach and offshore rocks. Lunch prices are reasonable, with such offerings as a full-flavored cioppino soup or oyster sandwich. Angels on horseback (oysters wrapped in bacon and broiled) is one of our favorite appetizers. Entrees offer a choice of shellfish or fish with a choice of sauces (apricot-ginger glaze, aioli, or spicy garlic-chili, for example). The wait for a table can be long, so if you just want a quick snack, there are bar stools at the front counter.

1490 Pacific Ave. ©️ **503/842-7351**. Main courses $6–$12 lunch, $7–18.25 dinner. MC, V. Daily 10:30am–9pm (may close 1 hr. earlier in winter).

In Pacific City

For tasty baked goods and lunches, stop in at **The Grateful Bread Bakery & Restaurant,** 34805 Brooten Rd. (©️ **503/965-7337**), with tables both inside and out on a deck. If you enjoy good books, coffee, and wine, you'll appreciate **Migrations,** a small shop located on the ground floor of the Inn at Cape Kiwanda, 33105 Cape Kiwanda Dr. (©️ **503/965-4661**).

Pelican Pub & Brewery 🐾 PUB FOOD   With massive Haystack Rock looming just offshore and the huge dune of Cape Kiwanda just up the beach, this brewpub claims the best view of any in Oregon. The pub is right on the beach and even has its own beach volleyball court. There's a good selection of brews, including Tsunami Stout and our personal favorite, the Doryman's Dark Ale. Sandwiches, burgers, fish-and-chips, and pizzas are the menu mainstays here, but the steamed clams served with barley bread made from beer grain are divine. Kids are welcome, and the beach location makes this a great spot for lunch or dinner if you're hanging out on the beach all day.

33180 Cape Kiwanda Dr. © **503/965-7007.** Main courses $8–$17. AE, DISC, MC, V. Sun–Thurs 8am–9pm; Fri–Sat 8am–10pm. Later closing times in the summer.

The Riverhouse ⭐ AMERICAN   This tiny place is built on the bank of the Nestucca River and has great river views out its many windows. Because there is nothing but forest across the river, the Riverhouse feels as if it's miles out in the country, though it is only a few blocks from Pacific City's main intersection and a couple more from the beach. With a timeless roadside diner feel and a casual, friendly atmosphere, this place has the feel of someplace that time and contemporary fads have passed by. Although burgers and sandwiches are the order of the day at lunch, the dinner menu features prawns in a creamy wine sauce; fresh fish amandine; halibut basted with butter, lemon pepper, and dill; filet mignon, and crepes Florentine.

Brooten Rd. © **503/965-6722.** Main courses $7–$15 lunch, $7–20 dinner. MC, V. Sun–Thurs 11am–9pm; Fri–Sat 11am–10pm (closes 1 hr. earlier in winter).

NESKOWIN

The quaint little community of Neskowin is nestled at the northern foot of Cascade Head, 12 miles north of Lincoln City. Inland families have spent their summers in these tiny cottages and tree-lined lanes for decades. Quiet vacations are the rule in Neskowin, where you'll find only condominiums and rental houses. The beach is accessible at **Neskowin Beach State Recreation Site,** which faces Proposal Rock, a tree-covered haystack rock bordered by Neskowin Creek.

In Neskowin, you'll also find two nine-hole golf courses. The **Hawk Creek Golf Course,** 48480 U.S. 101 (© **503/392-4120),** plays up the valley of Hawk Creek with mountains rising on three sides. The greens fee is $14 for nine holes. Across the highway, in a wide flat area, is the **Neskowin Beach Golf Course,** Hawk Avenue (© **503/392-3377),** which isn't quite as scenic and charges the same price ($12.50).

If you're interested in art, check out the **Hawk Creek Gallery,** 48460 U.S. 101 S. (© **503/392-3879),** which is open in the summer and features the paintings of Michael Schlicting, a master watercolorist.

Just to the south of Neskowin is rugged, unspoiled **Cascade Head.** Rising 1,770 feet from sea level, this is one of the highest headlands on the coast, and it creates its own weather: rain falls here more than 180 days a year. Lush forests of Sitka spruce and windswept cliff-top meadows thrive in this rainy climate and are home to such a diverse flora and fauna that the Nature Conservancy purchased much of the land here. Trails onto Cascade Head start about 2 miles south of Neskowin. The Nature Conservancy's preserve has been set aside primarily to protect the habitat of the rare Oregon silverspot butterfly; the upper trail is closed from January 1 to July 15 due to the timing of the butterflies' life cycle. However, a lower trail, reached from Three Rocks Road (park at Knight Park and walk up Savage Rd. to the trail head) is open year-round.

On the south side of Cascade Head, you'll find the **Sitka Center for Art and Ecology,** Neskowin Coast Foundation, P.O. Box 65, Otis, OR 97368 (© **541/994-5485;** www.sitkacenter.org), which runs summer classes on subjects such as writing, painting, ecology, and ceramics.

WHERE TO STAY

In addition to the condominium resort listed here, there are numerous vacation cottages and beach houses for rent in Neskowin. Contact **Sea View Vacation Rentals,** P.O. Box 1049, Pacific City, OR 97135 (© **503/965-7888;** www. wcn.net/seaview), or **Grey Fox Vacation Rentals,** P.O. Box 364, Neskowin, OR 97149 (© **503/392-4355;** www.oregoncoast.com). Rates range from about $90 to $300 per night. The first company also rents homes in nearby Pacific City and Tierra del Mar.

Neskowin Resort 🦝 Most units at this condominium resort have views of Proposal Rock, and the views, combined with the tranquillity of Neskowin, set this place apart from hotels in nearby Lincoln City. Most of the units have kitchens, making it a popular choice with families. Hawk Creek runs along the back of the resort, and just across the parking lot is a good little cafe. The views from the rooms here are among the best on the Oregon coast. Over the past couple of years, about a dozen condos here have been remodeled, and these are worth requesting.

48990 U.S. 101 S. (P.O. Box 447), Neskowin, OR 97149. © **503/392-4850.** Fax 503/392-4264. 30 condos. July 1–Sept 15 $49–$139 double; $165–$325 4–6 people; $275–$325 2- to 3-bedroom town house. Sept 16–June 30 $35–$79 double; $89–$249 4–6 people; $219–$249 2- to 3-bedroom town house. No credit cards. Pets accepted. **Amenities:** Restaurant (American). *In room:* TV, fridge, coffeemaker.

5 Lincoln City/Gleneden Beach

88 miles SW of Portland, 44 miles S of Tillamook, 25 miles N of Newport

Lincoln City is not really a city, but a collection of five small towns that stretch for miles along the coast. Over the years these towns grew together as this became the most popular beach destination for vacationers, especially families, from Portland and Salem. Today there's no specific downtown area, and though there may be more motel rooms here than anywhere else on the Oregon coast, there's little to distinguish most of the thousands of rooms. However, families looking for a long beach and steady winds for flying kites will enjoy Lincoln City. Motel rates here, though often high for what you get, are generally better than those in beach towns that are longer on charm, and you'll find an abundance of vacation homes for rent. Likewise, restaurants catering to big families and small pocketbooks proliferate. Such restaurants purvey hot meals rather than haute cuisine, and you can eat your fill of seafood without going broke.

Once referred to as "20 miracle miles," Lincoln City is no longer the miracle it once was. Miracle miles have become congested urban sprawl, and a summer weekend in Lincoln City can mean coping with bumper-to-bumper traffic. Not surprisingly, many have come to think of this as "20 miserable miles." If at all possible, come during the week or during the off-season to avoid the crowds.

Once you get off U.S. 101, though, Lincoln City has neighborhoods as charming as any on the coast. It is also here, in the Gleneden Beach area just south of Lincoln City, that you'll find the coast's most prestigious resort. Also in this area are some of Oregon's best art galleries and some interesting artists' studios.

ESSENTIALS

GETTING THERE   Ore. 22 from Salem merges with Ore. 18 before reaching the junction with U.S. 101. From Portland, take Ore. 99W to McMinnville and then head west on Ore. 18.

VISITOR INFORMATION For more information on the area, contact the **Lincoln City Visitor and Convention Bureau,** 801 SW U.S. 101, Lincoln City, OR 97367 (✆ **800/452-2151** or 541/994-8378; www.oregoncoast.com).

GETTING AROUND Car rentals are available from **Robben Rent-A-Car** (✆ **800/305-5530** or 541/994-5530). If you need a taxi, contact **Lincoln Cab Co.** (✆ **541/996-2003**). Public bus service between the Rose Lodge on Ore. 18 and Newport, south of Lincoln City, is provided by **Lincoln County Transit** (✆ **541/765-2177,** ext. 4900) but is available on weekdays only.

FESTIVALS Annual **kite festivals** include the Spring Kite Festival in early May and the Fall International Kite Festival in early October. In addition, Lincoln City hosts the annual **Cascade Head Music Festival** in mid- to late June, and in August there's the annual **Sandcastle Building Contest.** On the nearby Siletz Indian Reservation, the **Nesika Illahee,** the annual Siletz Pow Wow takes place on the second weekend in August.

ENJOYING THE BEACH & THE OUTDOORS

Lincoln City's 7½-mile-long **beach** is its main attraction. However, cold waters and constant breezes conspire to make swimming a pursuit for Polar Bear Club members only. The winds, on the other hand, make this beach the best kite-flying spot on the Oregon coast. If you didn't bring your own kite, you can buy one at **Catch the Wind,** 266 SE U.S. 101 (✆ **541/994-9500**). Among the better beach-access points are the D River State Wayside on the south side of the river and the Road's End State Wayside up at the north end of Lincoln City. Road's End is also a good place to explore some tide pools. You'll find more tide pools on the beach at Northwest 15th Street and at Southwest 32nd Street.

Adding to the appeal of Lincoln City's beach is **Devil's Lake,** which drains across the beach by way of the D River, the world's shortest river. Formerly called Devil's River (Christians didn't like the name), the D River is only 120 feet long, flowing from the outlet of Devil's Lake, under U.S. 101 and across the beach to the Pacific Ocean. Boating, sailing, water-skiing, windsurfing, swimming, fishing, and camping are all popular Devil's Lake activities. Access points on the west side of the lake include **Devil's Lake State Park (West),** NE Sixth Street (✆ **541/994-2002**), which has a campground, and **Regatta Grounds Park** and **Holmes Road Park,** both of which are off West Devil's Lake Road and have boat ramps and picnic tables. On the east side you'll find **Devil's Lake State Park (East)** 2 miles east on East Devil's Lake Road and **Sand Point Park** on View Point Lane near the north end of East Devil's Lake Road. Both of these parks have picnic tables and swimming areas. If you don't have your own boat, you can rent canoes, kayaks, paddleboats, aquabikes, and various motorboats at **Blue Heron Landing,** 4008 W. Devil's Lake Rd. (✆ **541/994-4708**). Rates range from $10 an hour for a kayak up to $40 an hour for a runabout or pontoon boat. You'll also find bumper boats here at Blue Heron Landing.

If you're a gardener or enjoy visiting public gardens, schedule time to visit the **Connie Hansen Garden,** 1931 NW 33rd St. (✆ **541/994-6338**). This cottage garden was created over a 20-year period and abounds in primroses, irises, and rhododendrons, making it a great place to visit in the spring. The gardens are staffed on Tuesday and Saturday from 10am to 2pm, but the garden is always open to the public. Call for directions.

Golfers have two options. The top choice is the Scottish-inspired (though solidly Northwestern in character) **Salishan Golf Links** ★, on U.S. 101 in Gleneden Beach (✆ **541/764-3632**), which charges $65 for 18 holes of golf in

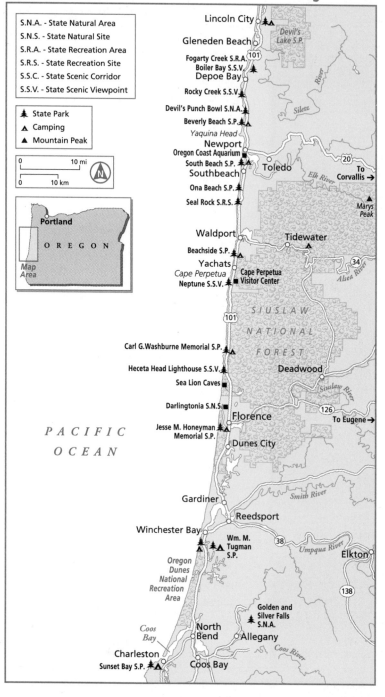

The Central Oregon Coast

S.N.A. - State Natural Area
S.N.S. - State Natural Site
S.R.A. - State Recreation Area
S.R.S. - State Recreation Site
S.S.C. - State Scenic Corridor
S.S.V. - State Scenic Viewpoint

🌲 State Park
△ Camping
▲ Mountain Peak

0   10 mi
0   10 km

Portland
O R E G O N
Map
Area

PACIFIC
OCEAN

Lincoln City
Gleneden Beach
Fogarty Creek S.R.A.
Boiler Bay S.S.V.
Depoe Bay
Rocky Creek S.S.V.
Devil's Punch Bowl S.N.A.
Beverly Beach S.P.
Yaquina Head
Newport
Oregon Coast Aquarium
South Beach S.P.
Southbeach
Ona Beach S.P.
Seal Rock S.R.S.
Waldport
Beachside S.P.
Yachats
Cape Perpetua
Neptune S.S.V.
Cape Perpetua
Visitor Center
Carl G.Washburne Memorial S.P.
Heceta Head Lighthouse S.S.V.
Sea Lion Caves
Darlingtonia S.N.S.
Florence
Jesse M. Honeyman
Memorial S.P.
Dunes City
Gardiner
Reedsport
Winchester Bay
Wm. M.
Tugman
S.P.
Oregon
Dunes
National
Recreation
Area
Golden and
Silver Falls
S.N.A.
North
Bend
Allegany
Charleston
Sunset Bay S.P.
Coos Bay
Coos
Bay

Devil's
Lake S.P.
101
Siletz
River
20
To
Corvallis →
Toledo
Elk River
Marys
Peak
Tidewater
34
Alsea River
101
S I U S L A W
N A T I O N A L
F O R E S T
Deadwood
Siuslaw River
126
To Eugene →
Smith River
38
Umpqua River
Elkton
138
Coos River

the summer months. This resort course is a longtime Oregon coast favorite. Otherwise, it's the **Lakeside Golf & Fitness Club,** 3245 Club House Dr. (© **541/994-8442**), which charges $35 to $40 for 18 holes.

If you want to challenge the waves, you can rent a wetsuit, surfboard, or body board at the **Oregon Surf Shop,** 4933 SW U.S. 101 (© **541/996-3957**).

Hikers should head inland approximately 10 miles to **Drift Creek Falls Trail** ⋆, which leads through coastal forest to a 240-foot-long suspension bridge above a 75-foot-tall waterfall. From the bridge you have a bird's-eye view not only of the falls but of the treetops as well. It's 1¼ miles in to the bridge and the route is moderately difficult. To find the trail head (Northwest Forest Pass is required), head east from U.S. 101 on Drift Creek Road, which is just north of the Westin Salishan lodge at the south end of Lincoln City. Turn right onto South Drift Creek Road and then left onto Forest Road 17 (not Anderson Creek Rd.) and continue 10 miles on this single-lane road.

INDOOR PURSUITS

These days the hottest thing in town is the **Chinook Winds Casino,** 1777 NW 44th St. (© **888/CHINOOK;** www.chinookwindscasino.com), a massive gambling palace run by the Confederated Tribes of Siletz Indians and located right on the beach at the north end of town. The casino offers bingo, blackjack, poker, slot machines, and keno. There's plenty of cheap food, as well as a video-game room for the kids. Big-name entertainers (Bill Cosby, B.B. King, Loretta Lynn, and Ray Charles) help attract folks who might not otherwise consider visiting a casino.

You can catch live jazz at **Eden Hall,** 6675 Gleneden Beach Loop Rd. (© **541/764-3826**), a big club and restaurant just south of the Westin Salishan Lodge.

The casino may actually be second in popularity to the **Factory Stores @ Lincoln City,** 1500 SE East Devils Lake Rd. (© **888/SHOP333** or 541/996-5000; www.shoplincolncity.com), which is on the corner of U.S. 101.

Lincoln City has a surprising number of interesting art galleries and artists' studios. At the north end of town, the first gallery you'll come to is the **Ryan Gallery,** 4270 N. U.S. 101 (© **541/994-5391**). Right in the heart of Lincoln City's main business strip, watch for the **Earthworks Gallery,** 620 NE U.S. 101 (© **541/557-4148**), which emphasizes ceramic and glass art, but also carries a variety of other fine crafts. Gardening enthusiasts will also want to visit **Garden Art & Gifts,** 3001 SW U.S. 101 (© **541/994-2660**), a store full of beautiful garden accessories and garden-oriented art.

South of Lincoln City proper, you'll find the impressive **Freed Gallery,** 6119 SW U.S. 101 (© **541/994-5600**), which has an excellent selection of art glass and ceramic work, as well as sculptures and paintings in a wide variety of styles. Just off U.S. 101, north of the Westin Salishan, you'll find **Alder House III,** 611 Immonen Rd. (no phone; www.alderhouse.com), the oldest glassblowing studio in Oregon. The shop and studio are open daily from 10am to 5pm between

---

(**Fun Fact** **Finders Keepers**

Each year between October and late May, Lincoln City hides more than 2,000 art-glass balls, similar to the much-prized Japanese hand-blown glass fishing floats that sometimes drift ashore on this coast. Look above the high-tide line for the colorful globes of glass. Some are hidden each week.

March and November. Also on Immonen Road (which is just north of the Westin Salishan) is **Mossy Creek Pottery** (© 541/996-2415), with an eclectic selection of porcelain and stoneware by Oregon potters. Also not to be missed by art collectors is the **Gallery at Salishan** (© 800/764-2318), which is in the Marketplace at Salishan shopping plaza opposite the entrance to the Westin Salishan Lodge.

WHERE TO STAY

In addition to the town's many hotels and motels, Lincoln City has plenty of vacation rental houses and apartments offering good deals, especially for families. For information, contact **Horizon Rentals** (© 800/995-2411 or 541/994-2226; www.horizonrentals.com) or **Pacific Retreats** (© 800/473-4833; www.pacificretreats.com). Rates generally range from around $100 up to $250 nightly for houses for anywhere from 4 to 12 people.

EXPENSIVE

The Inn at Spanish Head 🐾🐾   Located toward the south end of Lincoln City, this hotel is the only high-rise hotel on the Oregon coast, but you'd never know it from the parking lot. From the entry, the hotel appears to be only two stories tall. What isn't readily apparent is that the lobby is on the ninth floor (there are eight stories below the parking-lot level) due to the fact that the hotel is built into a steep cliff that rises up from the beach. This is a condominium resort and all the rooms are individually owned, which means there's a different decor in every room. However, the furnishings are reliably comfortable. All the rooms have an ocean view, and there are large suites for families. The hotel's restaurant and lounge, on the 10th floor, provides a dizzying view and fresh seafood.

4009 SW U.S. 101, Lincoln City, OR 97367. © 800/452-8127 or 541/996-2161. Fax 541/996-4089. www. spanishhead.com. 126 units. $155–$175 double; $245 suite. Lower rates in winter. AE, DC, DISC, MC, V. Free valet parking. **Amenities:** Restaurant (seafood); lounge; outdoor pool; exercise room; Jacuzzi; 2 saunas; game room; room service; massage; babysitting; coin-op laundry. *In room:* TV/VCR, dataport, kitchen/kitchenette, fridge, coffeemaker, hair dryer.

The O'dysius Hotel 🐾🐾   Although it seems a bit out of place, this hotel offers the sort of luxury you would expect from a downtown Portland historic hotel—with a beach right across the street. Traditional European styling dominates, and the lobby, with its antique furniture, has the feel of a very luxurious living room. It's here that the hotel serves its complimentary afternoon wine. Guest rooms have lots of nice touches, including slate entries, down comforters, Art Nouveau lamps, gas fireplaces, and VCRs. All the rooms have ocean views, and some have balconies. If you enjoy luxury but aren't into the golf-resort scene, this is definitely the place for you.

120 NW Inlet Court, Lincoln City, OR 97367. © 800/869-8069 or 541/994-4121. Fax 541/994-8160. www. odysius.com. 30 units. $149–$192 double; $209–$311 suite. Rates include continental breakfast. AE, DISC, MC, V. Pets accepted. **Amenities:** Access to nearby health club; concierge; massage. *In room:* TV/VCR, dataport, hair dryer, iron.

The Westin Salishan Lodge 🐾🐾🐾 *Kids*   The largest and most luxurious resort on the coast, the Salishan Lodge is nestled amid towering evergreens on a hillside at the south end of Siletz Bay. Because the resort is almost half a mile from the beach and on the inland side of U.S. 101, it's more of a golf resort than a beach resort. There are also plenty of activities for kids, and an extensive network of walking paths meanders through the resorts 760-acre grounds. Guest rooms come in three sizes. Whichever size you opt for, try to get a second-floor room. Most of these have cathedral ceilings and stone fireplaces. For breathtaking views, you'll have to shell out top dollar for a deluxe or premier room. The Salishan Dining Room is the most upscale restaurant on the entire coast (see p. 189 for details).

7760 U.S. 101, Gleneden Beach, OR 97388. © **888/725-4742** or 541/764-2371. Fax 541/764-3681. www.salishan.com. May–Oct $179–$289 double. Nov–Apr $99–$249 double. AE, DC, DISC, MC, V. Pets accepted ($25). **Amenities:** 3 restaurants (Northwest, American), lounge; indoor pool; 18-hole golf course; 1 outdoor and 3 indoor tennis courts; exercise room; Jacuzzi; sauna; children's programs; game room; concierge; business center; room service; massage; babysitting; laundry service; dry cleaning. *In room:* TV, dataport, minibar, coffeemaker, hair dryer, iron.

MODERATE

Siletz Bay Lodge ⭐   Located at the south end of Lincoln City right on Siletz Bay, this modern motel is a good choice for both families and couples. Although the motel isn't on the ocean, it is on a driftwood-strewn beach that has quiet waters that are perfect for kids, and across the bay you can often see harbor seals lounging on the beach. About half of the standard rooms have balconies. Spa rooms and spa suites are also available if you happen to be in town for a romantic getaway.

1012 SW 51st St. (P.O. Box 952), Lincoln City, OR 97367. © **888/430-2100** or 541/996-6111. Fax 541/996-3992. www.siletzbaylodge.com. 44 units. Summer $98–$145 double; $145 suite. Off-season $69–$125 double; $125 suite. Rates include continental breakfast. 3-night minimum on holidays. AE, DISC, MC, V. **Amenities:** Jacuzzi. *In room:* TV, dataport, coffeemaker, hair dryer.

CAMPGROUNDS

There's a campground at **Devil's Lake State Park,** just off U.S. 101 north of the D River. To make reservations, contact **Reservations Northwest** (© **800/452-5687;** www.oregonstateparks.org).

WHERE TO DINE

If you're looking for some good smoked salmon or smoked oysters, stop by **Mr. Bill's Village Smokehouse,** 2981 SW U.S. 101 (© **888/MR-BILLS** or 503/994-4566). For a good cup of espresso, visit **Café Roma,** 1437 NW U.S. 101 (© **541/994-6616**).

EXPENSIVE

Bay House ⭐⭐ NORTHWEST   With a big wall of glass overlooking the Siletz Bay and Salishan Spit, the Bay House, between Lincoln City and Gleneden Beach, provides fine dining and dramatic sunsets (and good bird-watching if you're interested). There are snowy linens on the tables, and service is gracious. The menu here changes seasonally but always shows influences from Asia (seared scallops with pineapple chutney, pan-fried oysters in Asian broth) and the Mediterranean (grilled salmon with fennel slaw and blood-orange reduction, pork tenderloin with brandy, apple, fennel, sparkling cider, and toasted hazelnuts). Lately the restaurant has faltered on some of its seafood dishes, but the few meat dishes continue to be reliable.

5911 SW Hwy. 101. © **541/996-3222.** Reservations recommended. Main courses $18–$28. AE, DISC, MC, V. May–Sept Sun–Fri 5:30–9pm; Sat 5–9pm. Closed Mon–Tues Oct–Apr.

Blackfish Café ⭐⭐   Near the north end of Lincoln City, this restaurant has a big reputation for such a casual and unpretentious spot. At lunch, as well as dinner, care is taken with all the preparations. The grilled shrimp or scallop "martinis" (basically just seafood cocktails) make great starters, although the flatbread platter is good for parties of four or more. The menu includes everything from fish-and-chips and burgers to citrus-marinated breast of duck and pork loin with smoked-onion mashed potatoes. Keep an eye out for any dish served with the Asian slaw, which is the most unusual slaw you may ever taste. Lunches just might be the best on the entire coast.

2733 NW Hwy. 101. ℂ 541/996-1007. www.blackfishcafe.com. Reservations recommended. Main courses $6–$13 lunch, $11–$19 dinner. AE, DISC, MC, V. Wed–Thurs and Sun–Mon 11:30am–3pm and 5–9pm; Fri–Sat 11:30am–3pm and 5–10pm.

Chez Jeanette ✶✶ FRENCH/NORTHWEST   With the Westin Salishan in the neighborhood, Gleneden Beach is the Oregon coast's poshest destination. It's not surprising, then, that this little French place is one of the most expensive restaurants on the coast. Housed in a quaint little cottage tucked under the trees, Chez Jeanette does a commendable job of duplicating the feel of a French country inn and is the perfect spot for a romantic dinner. Although there is always plenty of seafood on the menu, wild game is also a specialty. The venison tenderloin is a good choice, and there are seafood specials nightly. You'll find Chez Jeanette south of Salishan Lodge on a side road leading to Gleneden Beach.

7150 Gleneden Beach Loop, Gleneden Beach. ℂ 541/764-3434. Reservations highly recommended. Main courses $24–$30. MC, V. Daily 5:30–8 or 8:30pm.

The Dining Room at Salishan Lodge ✶✶✶ NORTHWEST   The Westin Salishan Lodge boasts one of the coast's best restaurants. The menu is as creative as any around and can hold its own with popular restaurants in Portland. The menu changes regularly to take advantage of the ever-changing offerings of fresh Northwest ingredients. Expect plenty of seafood-based appetizers such as oysters on the half shell (with apple-quince salsa, habanero-honey aioli, and champagne mignonette), or Dungeness crab cakes with balsamic-port glaze and lemon-walnut aioli. The main courses are more evenly split among meats and seafood. Try the elk loin with honey-ginger demi-glace, squash purée, and wheat-berry-pancetta risotto. Lots of windows assure every diner a view of the lush, tranquil forest outside. Service is professional and unobtrusive, and the wine cellar, with more than 15,000 bottles, is legendary.

U.S. 101, Gleneden Beach. ℂ 541/764-2371. Reservations highly recommended. Main courses $26–$38. AE, DC, DISC, MC, V. Daily 5–9pm.

MODERATE

Kyllo's Seafood Grill ✶ SEAFOOD   Providing a lively "beach party" atmosphere on a family-oriented beach, Kyllo's is housed in an architecturally striking contemporary building with concrete floors and walls, a big copper fireplace, plenty of deck space, and walls of glass to take in the view of the D River and the ocean. If all this sounds like you're going to be paying for the atmosphere, think again. Prices for such dishes as large and tasty crab cakes, halibut with lemon-garlic butter, or Cajun-style pan-fried oysters are quite reasonable. You'll almost definitely have to wait for a table if you come here on a summer evening.

1110 NW First Court. ℂ 541/994-3179. Main courses $8–$22. AE, DISC, MC, V. Sun–Thurs 11am–9pm; Fri–Sat 11am–10pm.

INEXPENSIVE

Otis Café ✶ *Finds* AMERICAN   If you've ever seen the determination with which urbanites flock to the beach on summer weekends, you can understand what a feat it is to get cars to stop before they've got sand in the treads of their tires. This tiny roadside diner 5 miles north of Lincoln City and 4 miles shy of the beach manages to do just that with its black bread, cinnamon rolls, and fried red potatoes. The homemade mustard and killer salsa are also favorites. Pies—marionberry, strawberry/rhubarb, or walnut—have crusts to be savored only by people unconcerned with cholesterol and are memorable even in a region of numerous perfect pies. Expect a line out the screen door. Otis made national news back in 1999 when the whole town was put up for sale for $3 million.

Ore. 18, Otis. © 541/994-2813. Breakfast, lunch, and dinner $4–$10. AE, DISC, MC, V. June–Sept daily 7am–9pm; Oct–May Mon–Thurs 7am–3pm, Fri–Sun 7am–9pm.

6 Depoe Bay

13 miles S of Lincoln City, 13 miles N of Newport, 70 miles W of Salem

Depoe Bay calls itself the smallest harbor in the world. Though it covers only 6 acres, it's home to more than 100 fishing boats. As fascinating as the harbor itself is the narrow channel, little more than a crack in the coastline's solid rock wall, that leads into Depoe Bay. During stormy seas, it's almost impossible to get in or out of the harbor safely.

Shell mounds and kitchen middens around the bay indicate that Native Americans long called this area home. In 1894, the U.S. government deeded the land surrounding the bay to a Siletz Indian known as Old Charlie Depot, who had taken his name from an army depot at which he had worked. Old Charlie later changed his name to DePoe, and when a town was founded here in 1927, it took the name Depoe Bay. Though most of the town is a bit off the highway, you'll find a row of garish souvenir shops right on U.S. 101, which sadly mar the beauty of this rocky section of coast. Among these shops are several family restaurants and charter-fishing and whale-watching companies.

ESSENTIALS

GETTING THERE   From the north, the most direct route is Ore. 99W/18 to Lincoln City and then south on U.S. 101. From the south take U.S. 20 from Corvallis to Newport and then go north on U.S. 101.

VISITOR INFORMATION   Contact the **Depoe Bay Chamber of Commerce,** 70 NE U.S. 101 (P.O. Box 21), Depoe Bay, OR 97341 (© **541/765-2889;** www.stateoforegon.com).

FESTIVALS   Memorial Day is time for the **Fleet of Flowers,** during which local boats carry flower wreaths out to sea in memory of loved ones. In mid-September, the town holds its annual **Salmon Bake,** which is a great opportunity to enjoy some traditionally prepared salmon. Contact the Chamber of Commerce for details.

DEPOE BAY ACTIVITIES & ATTRACTIONS

Aside from watching the boat traffic passing in and out of the world's smallest harbor, the most popular activity here, especially when the seas are high, is watching the **spouting horns** across U.S. 101 from Depoe Bay's souvenir shops. Spouting horns, which are similar to blowholes, can be seen all along the coast, but nowhere are they more spectacular than here. These geyser-like plumes occur in places where water is forced through narrow channels in basalt rock. As the channels become more restricted, the water shoots skyward under great pressure and can spray 60 feet into the air. If the surf is really up, the water can carry quite a ways, and more than a few unwary visitors have been soaked.

Boiler Bay State Scenic Viewpoint, a mile north of Depoe Bay, is a good picnic spot and a good spot from which to search for gray whales. There are also tide pools among the rocks in some small coves here. Although the beach itself is not accessible from the state park pull-off, about midway between Boiler Bay and Fogarty Creek, which is a mile north of here, there's a trail that leads down to the beach. At **Fogarty Creek State Recreation Area,** you'll find a beautiful little cove with basalt cliffs at one end and a creek flowing across the beach. The parking area is on the east side of U.S. 101.

South of Depoe Bay, U.S. 101 winds through scenes of rugged splendor, passing several small, picturesque coves. Just south of town, **Rocky Creek State Scenic Viewpoint,** with windswept lawns, picnic tables, and great views of buff-colored cliffs and spouting horns, is a good picnic spot. In a few more miles you'll come to the **Otter Crest State Scenic Viewpoint** on Cape Foulweather. Named by Capt. James Cook in 1778, the cape was his first glimpse of land after leaving the Sandwich Islands (Hawaii). The cape frequently lives up to its name, with winds often gusting to more than 100 miles per hour. However, the views are quite stupendous. Keep an eye out for the sea lions that sun themselves on offshore rocks near Cape Foulweather. Although the Otter Crest Scenic Loop is no longer open due to a landslide that closed part of the road, there is a historic building now used as a gift shop that provides a protected glimpse of the sea from atop Cape Foulweather.

At the south end of the Otter Crest Scenic Loop, you'll find an overlook at **Devil's Punchbowl State Natural Area** ★★. The overlook provides a glimpse into a collapsed sea cave that during high tides or stormy seas becomes a churning cauldron of foam. Adjacent to Devil's Punchbowl, in a small cove, you'll find the **Marine Gardens,** where numerous tide pools can be explored at low tide. From this cove, you can also explore inside the Devil's Punchbowl. South of Devil's Punchbowl State Natural Area lies **Beverly Beach State Park,** which has a large campground and is a popular surfing spot.

If you're interested in **sportfishing** or **whale-watching** ★★, contact **Tradewinds** (✆ **800/445-8730** or 541/765-2345), at the north end of the bridge; **Joan-E Charters** (✆ **800/995-FUNN** or 541/765-2222), at the south end of the bridge; or **Dockside Charters** (✆ **800/733-8915** or 541/765-2545), down by the marina. Whale-watching trips run about $13, and fishing trips run $55 for 5 hours up to $165 for a day of halibut or tuna fishing.

WHERE TO STAY

Channel House ★★   Perched above the narrow, cliff-bordered channel into tiny Depoe Bay is the Channel House, one of the coast's most luxurious and strikingly situated small inns. A contemporary building with lots of angles and windows, the Channel House has large rooms, and the gas fireplaces and private decks with whirlpool tubs make it one of the most romantic inns on the coast. You can sit and soak as fishing boats navigate their way through the channel below you.

35 Ellingson St., Depoe Bay, OR 97341. ✆ **800/447-2140** or 541/765-2140. Fax 541/765-2191. www. channelhouse.com. 12 units. $90–$110 double oceanview; $190 oceanfront; $250–$270 suite. Rates include continental breakfast. AE, DISC, MC, V. No children accepted. *In room:* TV, fridge, hair dryer.

Inn at Arch Rock ★ *(Finds*   You just won't find a better view from any hotel on the Oregon coast. This collection of renovated Cape Cod–style buildings sits above the cliffs on the north side of Depoe Bay. You can sit in your room and watch the waves crashing against the rocks or walk down a flight of stairs to a tiny beach. Guest rooms have a simple, modern cottage decor, and most have big windows, microwaves, and coffeemakers. Out on the lawns overlooking the ocean you'll find white Adirondack chairs. The inn is just around the corner from the Tidal Raves restaurant.

P.O. Box 1516, Depoe Bay, OR 97341. © **800/767-1835** or 541/765-2560. www.innatarchrock.com. 13 units. $49–$149 double; $149–$259 suite/cottage. Lower rates in winter. AE, DISC, MC, V. Pets accepted ($10 per night). *In room:* TV/VCR, fridge, coffeemaker, hair dryer, iron.

Inn at Otter Crest ★★ Few hotels on the Oregon coast boast as spectacular a setting as the Inn at Otter Crest, one of the region's top resorts. If you want to get away from it all and enjoy a bit of forest seclusion on the beach, there's no better spot. The inn's numerous weathered-cedar buildings are surrounded by 35 acres of forests and beautifully landscaped gardens on a rocky crest above a secluded cove. Trails meander through the woods and lead down to the nearby Devil's Punchbowl and Beverly Beach State Park. Most rooms have excellent ocean views through a wall of glass that opens onto a balcony. Our favorites are the loft suites, which have fireplaces, kitchens, and high ceilings. Service is rather casual, in keeping with Northwest attitudes, and you'll have to leave your car in a parking lot that's somewhat removed from the guest rooms. (Staff will shuttle you around in golf carts.)

301 Otter Crest Loop Rd. (P.O. Box 50), Otter Rock, OR 97369. © **800/452-2101** or 541/765-2111. Fax 541/765-2047. www.ottercrest.com. 130 units. $89–$149 double; $189–$309 suite. 2-night minimum on holidays and weekends in July–Aug. AE, DISC, MC, V. **Amenities:** Restaurant (Northwest), lounge; outdoor pool; 2 tennis courts; exercise room; Jacuzzi; sauna; guest laundry. *In room:* TV, fridge, coffeemaker.

The Surfrider ★ Though it has been around for many years and is nothing fancy, this low-rise motel just north of Depoe Bay claims an enviable location and view and has long been a family favorite. It's hidden from the highway, which gives it a secluded feel, and there are great views from the open bluff-top setting. You can choose between basic motel rooms and rooms with fireplaces, kitchens, or whirlpool tubs. At the foot of a long staircase is the wide beach of Fogarty Creek State Recreation Area, which is on a pretty little cove. The dining room and lounge have great views of this cove.

3115 NW U.S. 101 (P.O. Box 219), Depoe Bay, OR 97341. © **800/662-2378** or 541/764-2311. Fax 541/764-4634. www.surfriderresort.com. 42 units. Mid-June to Sept 30 $79–$124 double. Lower rates in off-season. AE, DC, DISC, MC, V. **Amenities:** Restaurant (American), lounge; indoor pool; Jacuzzi; sauna; massage; coin-op laundry. *In room:* TV/VCR, dataport, fridge, coffeemaker, hair dryer.

WHERE TO DINE

At the **Siletz Tribal Smokehouse,** on U.S. 101 south of the bridge (© **800/828-4269** or 541/765-2286), you can buy smoked salmon and other seafood. The Smokehouse is run by the Confederated Tribes of the Siletz and is a great place to buy picnic fixings as you head out to the beach.

Tidal Raves ★★ (Finds) SEAFOOD With bright, uncluttered decor and big windows for taking in the wave-carved sandstone cliffs outside, Tidal Raves has the most dramatic restaurant setting on the Oregon coast. Located at the north end of Depoe Bay's strip of tourist shops, this place has had folks raving for years now. On days when the surf is up, it's hard to take your eyes off the wave-pounded cliffs outside the window. The menu offers plenty of straightforward seafood, but it also includes some creative preparations such as oysters Santa Fe and Thai grilled tiger shrimp. For light eaters, there are small portions of many menu favorites.

279 NW U.S. 101. © **541/765-2995.** Reservations highly recommended (4–5 days in advance for summer weekends). Main courses $7–$19.50. AE, DISC, MC, V. Daily 11am–9pm.

7 Newport

23 miles S of Lincoln City, 58 miles W of Corvallis, 24 miles N of Yachats

As Oregon coast towns go, Newport has a split personality. Dockworkers unloading fresh fish mingle with vacationers licking ice-cream cones, and both fishing boats and pleasure craft ply the waters of the bay. The air smells of fish and shrimp, and freeloading sea lions doze on the docks while they wait for their next meal from the processing plants along the waterfront. Directly across the street, art galleries and souvenir shops stand side by side. Across Yaquina Bay from the waterfront, you'll find the Oregon Coast Aquarium (the coast's top tourist attraction) and the Hatfield Marine Science Center. If you're looking for a balance of the old and the new on the Oregon coast, Newport is the place.

Newport got its start in the late 1800s as both an oystering community and one of the earliest Oregon beach resorts, and many of the old cottages and historic buildings can still be seen. Although the town's Nye Beach area has the feel of a 19th-century resort, the downtown bay front is, despite its souvenir shops, galleries, and restaurants, still a working port and home to the largest commercial fishing fleet on the Oregon coast. Oysters are also still important to the local economy and are raised in oyster beds along Yaquina Bay Road east of town.

Though in recent years it has come close to matching the overdevelopment of Lincoln City, this fishing port on the shore of Yaquina Bay still manages to offer a balance of industry, history, culture, beaches, and family attractions.

ESSENTIALS

GETTING THERE   Newport is on U.S. 101 at the junction with U.S. 20, which leads to Corvallis. **Lincoln County Transit** (© 541/265-4900) provides bus service from Lincoln City in the north and Yachats in the south.

VISITOR INFORMATION   Contact the Greater **Newport Chamber of Commerce,** 555 SW Coast Hwy., Newport, OR 97365 (© **800/262-7844** or 541/265-8801; www.newportchamber.org).

GETTING AROUND   Public bus service is provided by **Lincoln County Transit** (© 541/265-4900), which operates north to Lincoln City and south to Yachats. If you need a taxi, call **Yaquina Cab** (© 541/265-9552).

FESTIVALS   In late July each year, the music of composer Ernest Bloch, who once lived in this area, is celebrated during the **Ernest Bloch Music Festival** (© **541/265-ARTS**). In February, there's the **Seafood and Wine Fest;** contact the Newport Chamber for information.

FINS AND FLIPPERS

Hatfield Marine Science Center ⭐ (Kids)   Before the Oregon Coast Aquarium was built, Newport was already known as a center for marine science research. This facility, though primarily a university research center, also contains displays that are open to the public. Exhibits, although not quite as impressive as those at the Oregon Coast Aquarium, highlight current topics in marine research and include an octopus aquarium and a "touch" tank. Interpretive exhibits explain life in the sea. A worthwhile adjunct to a visit to the Oregon Coast Aquarium.

2030 Marine Science Dr. © **541/867-0100.** www.hmsc.orst.edu. Admission by donation. Memorial Day–Oct 1 daily 10am–5pm; Oct 1–Memorial Day Thurs–Mon 10am–4pm.

Oregon Coast Aquarium ⭐⭐⭐ (Kids)   Considered one of the top aquariums in the country, the Oregon Coast Aquarium focuses on sea life native to the

Oregon coast. There are so many fascinating displays that it's easy to spend the better part of a day here. The stars are the playful sea otters, but the clown-faced tufted puffins, which are kept in a walk-through aviary, are big favorites as well. The sea lions sometimes rouse from their naps to put on impromptu shows, and the lucky visitor even gets a glimpse of a giant octopus with an arm span of nearly 20 feet. Artificial waves surge in a tank that reproduces, on a speeded-up scale, life in a rocky intertidal zone. And so far, you haven't even made it to the indoor aquarium displays. Currently one of the most fascinating exhibits here is a walk-through deep-sea shark tank featuring a 200-foot-long acrylic walkway. You'll also find "At the Jetty," a 35,000-gallon tank that spotlights salmon and the issues surrounding their continued survival in the Northwest. Other indoor exhibits focus on various coastal habitats and the life-forms that inhabit them. There are examples of sandy beaches, rocky shores, salt marshes, kelp forests, and even the open ocean, where diaphanous jellyfish drift lazily on the currents. Because this is the most popular attraction on the Oregon coast, lines to get in can be very long. Arrive early if you're visiting on a summer weekend.

2820 SE Ferry Slip Rd. © 541/867-3474. www.aquarium.org. Admission $10.25 adults, $9.25 seniors and children 13–18, $6.25 children 4–12. Memorial Day–Labor Day daily 9am–6pm; Labor Day–Memorial Day daily 10am–5pm. Closed Christmas.

SEEING THE LIGHTS

Newport is home to two historic lighthouses, which are just 3 miles apart. The **Yaquina Bay Lighthouse** began operation in 1871 but in 1874 was replaced by the **Yaquina Head Lighthouse.** The latter was supposed to be built on Cape Foulweather farther to the north, but heavy seas made it impossible to land there. Instead, the light was built on Yaquina Head, and so powerful was the light that it supplanted the one at Yaquina Bay.

At 93 feet tall, the **Yaquina Head Lighthouse,** 3 miles north of Newport, is the tallest lighthouse on the Oregon coast and is still a functioning light. The lighthouse, open to the public whenever volunteers are available to man it (usually daily noon–4pm in summer), lies within the **Yaquina Head Outstanding Natural Area** (© 541/574-3100). Adjacent to the lighthouse, you'll find the **Yaquina Head Interpretive Center,** which houses displays covering everything from the life of lighthouse keepers and their families to the sea life of tide pools. Cormorants and pigeon guillemots can be seen roosting on the steep slopes, and harbor seals lounge on the rocks. In early winter and spring, you may spot gray whales migrating along the coast. On the cobblestone beach below the lighthouse, you can explore tide pools at low tide, and there is even a wheelchair-accessible tide-pool trail in a cove that once was the site of a rock quarry. Admission to Yaquina Head is $5 per car.

The older of the two lighthouses, **Yaquina Bay Lighthouse,** is now part of Yaquina Bay State Park, 846 SW Government St. (© 541/265-5679), which can be found just north and west of the Yaquina Bay Bridge. This 1871 lighthouse is the oldest building in Newport, and it is unusual in that the light is in a tower atop a two-story wood-frame house. The building served as both home and lighthouse, and supposedly is haunted. The lighthouse is open from mid-May to the end of September daily from 11am to 5pm; from October to mid-May, it's open daily from noon to 4pm.

BEACHES

Beaches in the Newport area range from tiny rocky coves to long, wide stretches of sand perfect for kite flying. Right in town, north and west of the Yaquina Bay

Bridge, you'll find the **Yaquina Bay State Park,** which borders on both the ocean and the bay. North of Newport is **Agate Beach,** which was once known for the beautiful agates that could be found there. However, sand now covers the formerly rocky beach, hiding the stones from rock hunters. This beach has a stunning view of Yaquina Head. Two miles south of Newport, you'll find **South Beach State Park,** a wide sandy beach with picnic areas and a large campground (that also rents yurts).

Six miles south of Newport, you'll find **Ona Beach State Park,** a sandy beach with a picnic area under the trees. Beaver Creek, a fairly large stream, flows through the park and across the beach to the ocean. Another 2 miles south will bring you to **Seal Rock State Recreation Site,** where a long wall of rock rises from the waves and sand and creates numerous tide pools and fascinating nooks and crannies to explore.

THE BAYFRONT

The Bayfront is tourist central for Newport. Here you'll find ice-cream parlors, saltwater taffy stores, chowder houses, and souvenir shops. However, it is also home to commercial fishermen, seafood processing plants, and art galleries. The waters of the Bayfront are also home to numerous sea lions, which love to sleep on the floating docks adjacent to Undersea Gardens. From the adjacent pier, you can observe the sea lions at close range. Their bickering and barking makes for great free entertainment.

As one of the coast's most popular family vacation spots, Newport has all the tourist traps one would expect. Billboards up and down the coast advertise the sorts of places that kids demand to be taken to. Tops on this list are **Ripley's Believe It or Not** and the **Wax Works Museum.** Across the street from these you'll find **Undersea Gardens,** where a scuba diver feeds fish in a large tank beneath a boat moored on the Bayfront. All three attractions are on the Bayfront and share the same address and phone number: Mariner Square, 250 SW Bay Blvd. (© **541/265-2206;** www.marinersquare.com). Admission for each is $6.95 for adults, $3.95 for children; or $15.90 for adults and $9.90 for children to visit all three attractions.

Adults will likely be more interested in the Bayfront's numerous art galleries. **Breach the Moon Gallery,** 434 SW Bay Blvd. (© **541/265-9698**), features art glass and art with ocean and whale themes. Nearby is **Oceanic Arts,** 444 SW Bay Blvd. (© **541/265-5963**), which sells interesting crafts, including wind chimes and lots of ceramics. The **Wood Gallery,** 818 SW Bay Blvd. (© **541/265-6843**), specializes in wooden items, including boxes and musical instruments.

The Bayfront is also the place to arrange **whale-watching tours** and **fishing trips.** Whale-watching tours are offered throughout the year by **Marine Discovery Tours,** 345 SW Bay Blvd. (© **800/903-BOAT** or 541/265-6200; www.marinediscovery.com), which charges $22 for a 2-hour cruise. You can charter a fishing boat on the Bayfront at **Bayfront Charters,** 890 SE Bay Blvd. (© **800/828-8777** or 541/265-7558; www.bayfrontcharters.com); or **Newport Tradewinds,** 653 SW Bay Blvd. (© **800/676-7819** or 541/265-2101; www. newporttradewinds.com). Salmon, tuna, halibut, and bottom fish can all be caught off the coast here depending on the season. Fishing trips cost anywhere from $60 to $150. These last two companies also offer whale-watching trips; tickets for these are about $20.

Newport claims to be the Dungeness crab capital of the world, and if you'd like to find out if this claim is true, you can rent crab rings and boats at

Sawyer's Landing, 4098 Yaquina Bay Rd. (© **541/265-3907**), for $37.50 for 3 hours or $50 for the whole day.

NYE BEACH

Newport was one of the earliest beach vacation destinations in Oregon, and it was in Nye Beach that the first hotels and vacation cottages were built. Today this neighborhood, north of the Yaquina Bay Bridge along the beach, is slowly being renovated and has both historic and hip hotels, good restaurants, some interesting shops, and, of course, miles of sandy beach. There's public parking at the turnaround on Beach Drive.

The works of local and regional artists are showcased at the **Newport Visual Arts Center,** 777 NW Beach Dr. (© **541/265-6540**). The center is open Tuesday through Sunday: April through September from noon to 4pm and October through March from 11am to 3pm. Just a few blocks away, the **Newport Performing Arts Center,** 777 W. Olive St. (© **541/265-ARTS;** www.coastarts. org/pac), hosts local and nationally recognized performers throughout the year and also runs a film series. Tickets run $6 to $50.

At the **Newport Fine Arts Gallery,** 316 NW Coast St. (© **541/574-8445**), you can see cutting-edge art unusual for the coast. At the **Nye Beach Gallery,** 715 NW Third St. (© **541/265-3292**), you'll find the nature-oriented sculptures of Lon Bruselback, as well as an interesting selection of wines and specialty cheeses for sale. A block away, **Toujours,** 704 NW Beach Dr. (© **541/ 574-6404**), sells natural-fiber women's clothes. On this same street, you'll find several other interesting gift shops.

OTHER NEWPORT ACTIVITIES & ATTRACTIONS

If you'd like to delve into local history, stop by the **Oregon Coast History Center,** 545 SW Ninth St. (© **541/265-7509**), which consists of two historic buildings—the Burrows House and the Log Cabin. The Burrows House was built in 1895 as a boardinghouse and now contains exhibits of Victorian household furnishings and fashions. The Log Cabin houses Siletz Indian artifacts from the area, as well as exhibits on logging, farming, and maritime history. The museum is open Tuesday through Sunday, June through September from 10am to 5pm and October through May from 11am to 4pm. Admission is free.

In the community of Seal Rock, 10 miles south of Newport, you'll find **Triad Gallery** (© **541/563-5442**) at 5667 NW U.S. 101, which has an eclectic array of fine arts and crafts and is the most strikingly designed art gallery on the Oregon coast.

WHERE TO STAY
EXPENSIVE

Newport Belle Bed & Breakfast ★★ *Finds* This 100-foot-long modern stern-wheeler is one of the most unusual B&Bs on the Oregon coast and is docked in the Newport Marina in Yaquina Bay not far from the Oregon Coast Aquarium. The guest rooms (staterooms) here are small, as you'd expect on any boat, but they all have big windows, private bathrooms, and wood floors. A parlor on the main deck serves as a gathering space.

P.O. Box 685, South Beach, OR 97366. © **800/348-1922** or 541/867-6290. Fax 541/867-6291. www. NewportBelle.com. 5 units. $125–$145 double. Rates include full breakfast. 2-night minimum on weekends and during summer. AE, DC, MC, V. No children accepted. *In room:* No phone.

Starfish Point ★★ North of town in a grove of fir trees on the edge of a cliff, the Starfish Point condominiums are our favorite rooms in the area. Each of the six condos has two bedrooms and two baths spaced over two floors. Between the two floors you'll find a cozy sitting area in an octagonal room that's almost all windows. This little sunroom is in addition to the spacious living room with its fireplace and stereo. The bathrooms here are extravagant affairs with two-person whirlpool tubs and skylights or big windows. A path leads down to the beach, and to the north is Yaquina Head, one of the coast's picturesque headlands. You're a ways out of town here, so you might want to cook your own meals and savor the solitude.

140 NW 48th St., Newport, OR 97365. ℂ 541/265-3751. Fax 541/265-3040. www.newportnet.com/starfishpoint. 6 units. $155–$190 for 2–6 people. Off-season rates available. 2-night minimum on weekends. AE, DISC, MC, V. Pets accepted ($7.50 per day). *In room:* TV, kitchen, fridge, coffeemaker.

MODERATE

Elizabeth Street Inn ★
Located in the Nye Beach area and walking distance from Yaquina Bay State Park, this is one of Newport's newest beachfront hotels, and with its stone foundation wall, cedar-shingle facade, and white trim, it has a classic beachy feel. There's nautical theme throughout and all rooms have ocean views, balconies, and fireplaces; some also have whirlpool tubs. The hotel is perched up on a bluff above the beach, and there are several good restaurants within walking distance.

232 SW Elizabeth St. (P.O. Box 1342), Newport, OR 97365. ℂ 877/265-9400 or 541/265-9400. Fax 541/265-9551. www.elizabethstreetinn.com. 74 units. $89–$189 double. Rates include continental breakfast. AE, DISC, MC, V. **Amenities:** Indoor pool; exercise room; Jacuzzi. *In room:* TV, fridge, coffeemaker, hair dryer.

Nye Beach Hotel & Café ★ (Value)
Located on the same block as the literary Sylvia Beach Hotel, the Nye Beach has adopted the visual and performing arts as its theme; and has resident tropical birds. The wide-open combination lobby and dining room has the feel of an urban loft space, though the beach is just outside. A funky urban chic pervades this hotel, appealing most to young urbanites for whom there are very few hip beach retreats on the Oregon coast. Although all the guest rooms have balconies and ocean views, room decor diverges wildly from that of most oceanfront hotels in the area. Bent-willow love seats, tubular metal bed frames, old movie and theater posters, and Indonesian masks add up to a decidedly eclectic style. The best rooms are the oceanfront spa rooms with gas fireplaces ($115–$150 per night). The restaurant in the lobby serves mostly snacks and simple meals.

219 NW Cliff St., Newport, OR 97365. ℂ 541/265-3334. Fax 541/265-3622. www.nyebeach.com. 18 units. $65–$150 double. AE, DISC, MC, V. **Amenities:** Restaurant (International), lounge. *In room:* TV, fridge.

Sylvia Beach Hotel ★★ (Finds)
This eclectic four-story cedar-shingled hotel pays homage to literature and is one of the Oregon coast's most famous lodgings. The guest rooms are named for different authors, and in each you'll find memorabilia, books, and decor that reflect their lives, times, and works. The Agatha Christie Room, the hotel's most popular, seems full of clues, while in the Edgar Allan Poe Room, a pendulum hangs over the bed and a stuffed raven sits by the window. Among the writers represented are Tennessee Williams, Colette, Ernest Hemingway, Mark Twain, Jane Austen, F. Scott Fitzgerald, Emily Dickinson, and even Dr. Seuss. If you happen to be allergic to cats, you'll want to pass on this inn since there is one in residence. The Tables of Content restaurant downstairs is a local favorite (see p. 198). Hot wine is served in the library at 10pm each evening.

267 NW Cliff St., Newport, OR 97365. ℂ 888/SYLVIAB or 541/265-5428. Fax 541/574-8204. www.sylviabeachhotel.com. 20 units. $63–$158 double. Rates include full breakfast. 2-night minimum on weekends. AE, MC, V. **Amenities:** Restaurant (Northwest). *In room:* No phone.

Tyee Lodge ★★ Just south of Yaquina Head, this oceanfront bed-and-breakfast sits atop a high bluff surrounded by tall trees. Guest rooms are large and all have good ocean views, as do the living and dining rooms. Although the first floor of the inn dates back more than 50 years, the upper floor, which houses all the guest rooms, was added on much more recently, a complete interior renovation has given the entire house a very fresh and modern look. There are gas fireplaces in all the rooms. In the breakfast room, you'll find a telescope for whale-watching, and on cooler days, a fireplace warms the living room.

4925 NW Woody Way, Newport, OR 97365. © 888/553-8933 or 541/265-8953. www.tyeelodge.com. 5 units. $100–$140 double. Rates include full breakfast. AE, DISC, MC, V. **Amenities:** Concierge. *In room:* No phone.

CAMPGROUNDS

North of Newport you'll find **Beverly Beach State Park,** which is known for its good surfing and has campsites and yurts. South of town at the mouth of Yaquina Bay, is **South Beach State Park** (© **541/867-4715**), one of the biggest state-park campgrounds on the coast. It also has yurts and campsites, but we prefer Beverly Beach. To make reservations at either campground, contact **Reservations Northwest** (© **800/452-5687;** www.oregonstateparks.org).

WHERE TO DINE

For an espresso, a slice of pizza, or a good panini sandwich, drop by **Panini Bakery,** 232 NW Coast St. (© **541/265-5033**), which is in the Nye Beach neighborhood.

MODERATE

April's at Nye Beach ★★ MEDITERRANEAN Located in the historic Nye Beach neighborhood, this restaurant provides an alternative to the Tables of Content restaurant across the street. Popular with a hip crowd as well as patrons of the nearby Newport Center for the Performing Arts, the restaurant dishes up good contemporary Italian fare amid artistic surroundings. The afternoon light here is fabulous, so try to schedule your dinner for sunset (and ask for a table with an ocean view). There's an excellent selection of regional wines at reasonable prices.

749 NW Third St. © 541/265-6855. Reservations recommended. Main courses $12–$20. DISC, MC, V. Tues–Sun 5–9pm. Closed in Jan.

Canyon Way Restaurant & Bookstore ★★ NORTHWEST/INTERNA-TIONAL Located just up the hill from Bay Boulevard (and off the main tourist drag), this big pink building is a combination restaurant, bookstore, and gift shop and has long been a Newport favorite. With a very extensive lunch menu and some of Newport's best food at dinner, Canyon Way is a good bet throughout the day. For dinner you might start with crab cakes with caper rémoulade or prawns-and-snow pea risotto and then move on to hazelnut-crusted lingcod, sesame-coated oysters, or New Orleans bouillabaisse. At lunch, although you'll find simple meals such as fish-and-chips, Szechuan shrimp and shrimp in pesto cream sauce are also available. Early dinners ($12.50), served between 5 and 6pm, are a good deal.

1216 SW Canyon Way. © 541/265-8319. Reservations recommended. Main courses $4.25–$14 lunch, $15–$23 dinner. DISC, MC, V. Tues–Thurs 11am–3pm and 5:30–9pm; Fri–Sat 11am–3pm and 5:30–9:30pm (sometimes longer hours in summer).

Tables of Content ★★ *Finds* INTERNATIONAL Located in the Sylvia Beach Hotel, this restaurant serves delicious and very reasonably priced four-course dinners. Although on any given night you'll have limited choices, if you enjoy creative cookery and eclectic combinations, you'll leave happy. Expect dishes such as mushroom sauté, Greek salad, salmon dijonnaise, and black-bean cakes.

Sylvia Beach Hotel, 267 NW Cliff St. ✆ 541/265-5428. www.sylviabeachhotel.com. Reservations required. Fixed-price 4-course dinner $17.95. AE, MC, V. Seatings Sun–Thurs 7pm; Fri–Sat 6 and 8:30pm.

INEXPENSIVE

Lighthouse Deli & Fish Company ✪ DELI
If you're looking for the best fish-and-chips on the Oregon coast, be sure to sample the offerings at this little roadside stand near the Oregon Coast Aquarium. You can get salmon and chips, halibut and chips, oysters and chips, shrimp and chips, or the basic house fish-and-chips, which is made with whatever fresh inexpensive fish is available that day. Okay, so the chips aren't the best, but the fish is very lightly battered, which lets its flavor shine through. They also do smoked salmon and tuna.

3650 SW Coast Hwy. ✆ 541/867-6800. www.lighthousedeli.com. Main dishes $5–$9.50. AE, DISC, MC, V. Daily 8am–8pm.

Mo's ✪ SEAFOOD
Established in 1942, Mo's has become such an Oregon coast institution that it has spawned five other restaurants up and down the coast. Clam chowder is what made Mo's famous, and you can get it by the bowl, by the cup, or family style. *Be forewarned, though:* Some people think this clam chowder is the best and others think it's awful. (We'd put it somewhere in between the two extremes.) Basic seafood dinners are fresh, large, and inexpensive, and the seafood-salad sandwiches are whoppers. There are also such dishes as cioppino, oyster stew, and slumgullion (clam chowder with shrimp). Expect a line out the door.

657 SW Bay Blvd. ✆ 541/265-2979. www.moschowder.com. Complete dinner $7.50–$11.50. AE, DISC, MC, V. Daily 11am–9pm.

Rogue Ales Public House ✪ PUB FOOD
This microbrewery's fresh ales, of which there can be as many as a dozen on tap, not only are delicious to drink, but also end up in a number of this pub's most popular dishes. The clams are steamed in ale; the English bangers are served with Golden Ale mustard; and even the dough for the garlic bread is made with ale. There's a second Rogue brewpub across the bay near the Oregon Coast Aquarium at 2320 OSU Dr. (✆ 541/867-3660). The main pub also has some apartments that can be rented on a nightly basis. (One-bedrooms are $80 and two-bedrooms are $120 for 1 night; lower rates for 3 nights or more.)

748 SW Bay Blvd. ✆ 541/265-3188. www.rogue.com. Sandwiches $4.75–$11.50; pizzas $8–$21. AE, DC, DISC, MC, V. Daily 11am–11:30pm (beer until 2am).

8 Yachats

26 miles S of Newport, 26 miles N of Florence, 138 miles SE of Portland

Located on the north side of 800-foot-high Cape Perpetua, the village of Yachats (pronounced *Yah*-hots) is known as something of an artists' community. When you get your first glimpse of the town's setting, you, too, will likely agree that there's more than enough beauty here to inspire anyone to artistic pursuits. Yachats is an Alsi Indian word meaning "dark waters at the foot of the mountains," and that sums up perfectly the setting of this small community, one of the few on the Oregon coast that could really be considered a village. The tiny Yachats River flows into the surf on the south edge of town, and to the east stand steep, forested mountains. The shoreline on which the town stands is rocky, with little coves here and there where you can find agates among the pebbles paving the beach. Tide pools offer hours of exploring, and in winter, storm waves create a spectacular show. Uncrowded beaches, comfortable motels, and one of the coast's best restaurants add up to a great spot for a quiet getaway.

ESSENTIALS

GETTING THERE   From the north, take Ore. 34 west from Corvallis to Waldport and then head south on U.S. 101. From the south, take Ore. 126 west from Eugene to Florence and then head north on U.S. 101.

VISITOR INFORMATION   Contact the **Yachats Area Chamber of Commerce,** 241 U.S. 101 (P.O. Box 728), Yachats, OR 97498 (© **800/929-0477** or 541/547-3530; www.yachats.org).

YACHATS AREA ACTIVITIES & ATTRACTIONS

Looming over tiny Yachats is the impressive bulk of 800-foot-high Cape Perpetua, the highest spot on the Oregon coast. Because of the cape's rugged beauty and diversity of natural habitats, it has been designated the **Cape Perpetua Scenic Area** 😊😊😊. The **Cape Perpetua Interpretive Center** (© **541/547-3289**) is on a steep road off U.S. 101 and houses displays on the natural history of the cape and the Native Americans who harvested its bountiful seafood for thousands of years. The visitor center is open daily from 9am to 5pm between Memorial Day and Labor Day. Admission is $5 per vehicle. Within the scenic area are 18 miles of hiking trails, tide pools, ancient forests, scenic overlooks, and a campground. During the summer, guided hikes are offered. If you're here on a clear day, be sure to drive to the top of the cape for one of the finest vistas on the coast. Waves and tides are a year-round source of fascination along these rocky shores, and Cape Perpetua's tide pools are some of the best on the coast. There's good access to the tide pools at the pull-off at the north end of the scenic area. However, it is the more dramatic interactions of waves and rocks that attract most people to walk the oceanside trail here: At the **Devil's Churn,** a spouting horn caused by waves crashing into a narrow fissure in the basalt shoreline sends geyser-like plumes of water skyward, and waves boil through a narrow opening in the rocks.

Right in Yachats, **Smelt Sands State Recreation Site** has a three-quarter-mile trail along a rocky stretch of coastline. Along the route of the trail, there are little pocket beaches (where smelts spawn) and tide pools. At the north end of the trail, a wide, sandy beach stretches northward. Just across the bridge at the south end of town, you'll find another good beach access.

Between April and October each year, **fishing** in Yachats takes on an unusual twist. It's during these months that thousands of smelts, sardine-like fish, spawn in the waves that crash in the sandy coves just north of Yachats. The fish can be caught using a dip net, and so popular are the little fish that the town holds an annual **Smelt Fry** each year on the second Saturday in July.

Gray whales also come close to shore near Yachats. You can see them in the spring from Cape Perpetua, and throughout the summer several take up residence at the mouth of the Yachats River. South of Cape Perpetua, Neptune State Wayside at the mouth of Cummins Creek, and Strawberry Hill Wayside are other good places to spot whales, as well as sea lions, which can be seen lounging on the rocks offshore at Strawberry Hill.

A couple of historic buildings in the area are also worth a visit. Built in 1927, the **Little Log Church by the Sea,** on the corner of Third and Pontiac streets, is now a museum housing displays on local history. Nine miles up Yachats River

Road, you'll find a **covered bridge** that was built in 1938 and is one of the shortest covered bridges in the state.

The Yachats area has several crafts galleries, the most interesting of which is **Earthworks Gallery,** 2222 U.S. 101 N. (© **541/547-4300**), located north of town and focusing on glass and ceramic art.

WHERE TO STAY

In addition to the hotels listed below, plenty of rental homes are available in Yachats. Contact **Ocean Odyssey,** P.O. Box 491, Yachats, OR 97498 (© **800/ 800-1915** or 541/547-3637; www.ocean-odyssey.com), or **Yachats Village Rentals,** 230 Aqua Vista Loop (P.O. Box 44), Yachats, OR 97498 (© **888/ 288-5077** or 541/547-3501). Rates range from around $105 to $215 per night.

Overleaf Lodge ⭐⭐   Overlooking the rocky shoreline at the north end of Yachats, this small hotel offers some of the most luxurious and tastefully decorated rooms on the central coast. Built in a sort of modern interpretation of the traditional Victorian beach cottage, the lodge caters primarily to couples seeking a romantic escape. Guest rooms all have ocean views, and most have patios or balconies. For a truly memorable stay, book one of the Restless Waters rooms, which have whirlpool tubs overlooking the crashing waves below. If you don't want to spring for one of these rooms, you can still curl up in a sunny little window nook beside your balcony and watch the waves in relative comfort. Many rooms also have fireplaces. Throughout the hotel you'll find artwork by Oregon artists.

2055 U.S. 101 N., Yachats, OR 97498. © 800/338-0507 or 541/547-4880. Fax 541/547-4888. www. overleaflodge.com. 42 units. Late June to mid-Sept $130–$200 double; $225–$230 suite. Mid-Sept to late June $90–$200 double; $225–$230 suite. Rates include continental breakfast. AE, DISC, MC, V. **Amenities:** Exercise room; room service; massage; guest laundry. *In room:* TV, dataport, fridge, coffeemaker, hair dryer, iron.

Shamrock Lodgettes ⭐ *Finds*   This collection of classic log cabins at the mouth of the Yachats River bewitched us the first time we saw it. Spacious lawns and old fir trees give the rustic cabins a relaxed old-fashioned appeal that just begs you to kick back and forget your cares. Each log cabin has a tile entry, hardwood floors, a kitchenette, a stone fireplace, and a big picture window that takes in a view of either the beach or the river. Otherwise, they're pretty basic. The motel rooms are more up-to-date and also have fireplaces and views. Some rooms have whirlpool tubs.

105 U.S. 101 S. (P.O. Box 346), Yachats, OR 97498. © 800/845-5028 or 541/547-3312. Fax 541/547-3843. www.shamrocklodgettes.com. 19 units (including 6 cabins). $75–$100 double; $96–$118 cabin for 2. AE, DISC, MC, V. Pets accepted ($5). **Amenities:** Exercise room; Jacuzzi; sauna. *In room:* TV, fridge, coffeemaker.

CAMPGROUNDS

Beachside State Park is just north of Yachats on U.S. 101, but we don't particularly recommend it. To make reservations, contact **Reservations Northwest** (© **800/452-5687;** www.oregonstateparks.org). For exploring the rugged Cape Perpetua area, the Forest Service's **Cape Perpetua Campground,** in a wooded setting set a little way back from the water, is your best option.

WHERE TO DINE

The **Yachats Crab & Chowder House,** 131 U.S. 101 (© **541/547-4132**), makes unusual chowders such as smoked salmon or Dungeness crab chowder, along with the traditional New England style.

The Drift Inn ⭐ *Finds* AMERICAN/NORTHWEST   This unprepossessing place right on U.S. 101 in the center of Yachats may seem at first glance to be little more than a modern tavern (albeit a tavern with big windows, wooden booths, and polished wood floors), but looks can be deceiving. The Drift Inn actually has a split personality. Sure there's the standard beer-and-burgers menu, but at dinner, there are specials such as tuna kabobs marinated in lime and coconut milk; sirloin steak with cherry liquor, Merlot, and mushrooms; and salmon topped with a sauté of hazelnuts, mushrooms, and blackberries.

124 U.S. 101. ℂ 541/547-4477. Main courses $6.50–$17. MC, V. Daily 11am–10pm.

La Serre ⭐⭐ NORTHWEST   For years, La Serre has served up the best food in the area, and although the greenhouse setting is attractive, if you're like us, you'll be immediately distracted by the dessert table just inside the front door. Hanging from the ceiling are lots of plants and old Japanese glass fishing floats (the sort that occasionally wash up on the shores of this coast). Be sure to start your meal with an order of the clam puffs (a blend of clams, herbs and cream cheese baked in puff pastry). The entree menu includes an excellent fisherman's stew, which is basically a cioppino with so much fish, shrimp, clams, crab, and oysters in it that you don't know where to start. We also like the charbroiled prawns. The desserts, including tiramisu and berry cobbler, are as good as they look, plus there are also great homemade ice creams and sorbets.

Second Ave. and Beach St. ℂ 541/547-3420. Reservations highly recommended. Main courses $13.50–$25. AE, MC, V. Mon and Wed–Sun 5–9pm. Closed Jan.

SOUTH TO FLORENCE

More wide sandy beaches can be found south of Yachats at (in order from north to south) Stonefield Beach State Recreation Site, Muriel O. Ponsler Memorial Wayside, and Carl G. Washburne Memorial State Park. The latter offers 2 miles of beach, hiking trails, and a campground.

The next park to the south, **Heceta Head Lighthouse State Scenic Viewpoint,** offers the most breathtaking setting. Situated on a small sandy cove, the park has a stream flowing across the beach and several haystack rocks just offshore. As the new park name implies, the park is also home to **Heceta Head Lighthouse,** the most photographed lighthouse on the Oregon coast. On summer weekends, volunteers lead guided tours of the lighthouse. Heceta (pronounced Huh-*see*-tuh) Head is a rugged headland that's named for Spanish explorer Capt. Bruno Heceta. The old lighthouse keeper's home is now a bed-and-breakfast (see below).

Another 7 miles south is the **Darlingtonia Botanical Gardens,** a small botanical preserve protecting a bog full of *Darlingtonia californica* plants, insectivorous pitcher plants also known as cobra lilies. You'll find this interesting preserve on Mercer Lake Road.

At more than 300 feet long and 120 feet high, **Sea Lion Caves** ⭐⭐, 91560 U.S. 101 (ℂ **541/547-3111;** www.sealioncaves.com), 1 mile south of Heceta Head Lighthouse, is the largest sea cave in the United States. The cave was discovered in 1880, and since 1932 it has been one of the most popular stops along the Oregon coast. The cave and a nearby rock ledge are the only year-round mainland homes for Steller's sea lions, hundreds of which reside here throughout the year. This is the larger of the two species of sea lion that frequent this coast, and bulls can weigh almost a ton. The sea lions spend the day lounging and barking up a storm, and the bickering of the adults and antics of the pups are always entertaining. Although at any time of year you're likely to find quite a few of the sea lions here, it is during the fall and winter that the majority of the sea lions move into the cave. Today, a combination of stairs, pathways, and an elevator leads down from the bluff-top gift shop to a viewpoint in the cave wall. The best time to visit is late in the afternoon, when the sun shines directly into the cave and the crowds of people are smaller. Admission $6.50 adults, $4.50 children 6 to 15. Daily from 8am in July through August, 9am other months; closes 1 hour before darkness in the cave.

WHERE TO STAY

Heceta Head Lightstation ★★ Thanks to a spectacular setting on a forested headland, the Heceta Head Lighthouse is the most photographed lighthouse on the Oregon coast. Although you can't spend the night in the lighthouse itself, you can stay in the former lighthouse keeper's home, a white-clapboard Victorian building high atop an oceanfront bluff and set behind a picket fence. Because the house is a national historic site, it has been preserved much the way it might have been when it was active. Breakfasts are elaborate seven-course meals that last at least an hour. This is one of the most popular B&Bs on the coast, so you'll need to book your room 2 to 3 months in advance for a weekday stay and 5 to 6 months in advance for a weekend stay. Oh, and by the way, it's haunted.

92072 U.S. 101 S., Yachats, OR 97498. ☏ 541/547-3696. www.hecetalighthouse.com. 5 units (1 with private bathroom). $135–$150 double with shared bathroom; $250 double with private bathroom. Rates include full breakfast. MC, V. *In room:* No phone.

Ocean Haven ★ *Value* Rustic and cozy, the Ocean Haven is a great place to hole up with family or friends. Opt for either the North View or the South View room, and you'll find yourself with two walls of glass overlooking the ocean. When the weather's good, you're only a short walk from the beach and some of the best tide pools around; when it's stormy, watch the waves from your room. (Binoculars are provided.) The Shag's Nest cottage is the lodge's most popular room. This private elfin cottage, located across the grass from the main lodge and perched on the edge of the bluff, allows you to lie in bed gazing out to sea with a fire crackling in the fireplace. A minimum stay may apply, and there are a few house rules, but if you're looking for a good value, great views, and rooms that are a little bit unusual, this is the place. All rooms but one have kitchens.

94770 U.S. 101, Yachats, OR 97498. ☏ 541/547-3583. www.oceanhaven.com. 7 units. $70–$100 double. MC, V. *In room:* Fridge, no phone.

Sea Quest Bed and Breakfast ★★ Set on a low bluff above the beach, this sprawling contemporary inn is about as luxurious a place as you'll find on the central Oregon coast. Privacy and romance are high priorities here, and all rooms have private entrances, ocean views, and whirlpool tubs. The convivial great room on the second floor has expansive views. There's also a huge deck. Miles of beach stretch on either side of the inn.

95354 Hwy. 101, Yachats, OR 97498. ☏ 800/341-4878 or 541/547-3782. www.seaq.com. 5 units. $150–$280 double. 2-night minimum on weekends. MC, V. *In room:* No phone.

Ziggurat Bed & Breakfast ★★ If you like contemporary styling, this is your best bet on the coast. Located 6½ miles south of Yachats on a wide, flat stretch of beach beside a salmon stream, the Ziggurat is an architectural gem—a four-story pyramidal contemporary home. The interior is every bit as breathtaking. A maze of rooms and stairways lead to the two huge first-floor suites, the larger of which covers more than 700 square feet. In these fascinating spaces you'll find slate floors, walls of windows, spacious bathrooms, private saunas, and contemporary furnishings—in short, they're the most stunning rooms on the coast. Up at the apex of the pyramid is the third room, which has a half bathroom in the room plus a full bathroom two flights below. This room has two decks and the best views in the house.

95330 U.S. 101 S., Yachats, OR 97498. ℂ 541/547-3925. www.newportnet.com/ziggurat. 3 units. $165 double. Rates include full breakfast. No credit cards. **Amenities:** Exercise room. *In room:* No phone.

CAMPGROUNDS
Just south of Cape Perpetua, there are a couple of campgrounds within Siuslaw National Forest. **Rock Creek Campground** is tucked back in the woods along a pretty creek and is a good choice for tenters and anyone who dislikes crowds. **Carl G. Washburne Memorial State Park** is the area's state park option and is one of only a few coastal state parks that do not take reservations. Campsites are across the highway from a pretty beach just north of Heceta Head.

9 Florence & the Oregon Dunes National Recreation Area

50 miles S of Newport, 50 miles N of Coos Bay, 60 miles W of Eugene

Florence and the Oregon Dunes National Recreation Area, which stretches south of town for almost 50 miles, have long been a popular summer vacation spot for Oregon families. The national recreation area is the longest unbroken, publicly owned stretch of coastline on the Oregon coast, and within its boundaries are 14,000 acres of dunes, some of which stand more than 500 feet tall.

Within this vast area of shifting sands, which is the largest area of sand dunes on the West Coast, there are numerous lakes both large and small, living forests, and skeletal forests of trees that were long ago "drowned" beneath drifting sands. Many area lakes are ringed with summer homes and campgrounds, and it is these lakes that are the primary destination of many vacationers. Consequently, water-skiing and fishing are among the most popular activities, followed by riding off-road vehicles (ORVs) through the sand dunes.

The Umpqua River divides the national recreation area is roughly at its midway point, and on its banks you'll find the towns of Gardiner, Reedsport, and Winchester Bay, each of which has a very distinct character. Gardiner was founded in 1841 when a Boston merchant's fur-trading ship wrecked near here. An important mill town in the 19th century, Gardiner has several stately Victorian homes. Reedsport is the largest of these three communities and is the site of the Umpqua Discovery Center, a museum focusing on the history and natural history of this region. The town of Winchester Bay is almost at the mouth of the Umpqua River and is known for its large fleet of charter-fishing boats.

Florence is one of the few towns on the Oregon coast with historic character. Set on the banks of the Siuslaw River, it is filled with restored wooden commercial buildings that house restaurants and interesting shops. The charm of this neighborhood is all the more appealing when compared to the unsightly sprawl of U.S. 101.

ESSENTIALS
GETTING THERE Florence is on U.S. 101 at the junction with Ore. 126 from Eugene. Gardiner, Reedsport, and Winchester Bay are all on U.S. 101 at or near the junction with Ore. 38 from Elkton, which in turn is reached from I-5 by taking either Ore. 99 from Drain or Ore. 138 from Sutherlin.

VISITOR INFORMATION   For more information on the dunes, contact the **Oregon Dunes National Recreation Area,** 855 U.S. 101, Reedsport, OR 97467 (© **541/271-3611;** www.fs.fed.us/r6/siuslaw/oregondunes). This visitor center is open in summer Monday through Friday from 8am to 4:30pm and Saturday from 10am to 4pm, and November through May it's open Monday through Friday from 8am to 4:30pm.

For more information on Florence, contact the **Florence Area Chamber of Commerce,** 270 U.S. 101, Florence, OR 97439 (© **800/524-4864** or 541/997-3128; www.florencechamber.com).

THE OREGON DUNES NATIONAL RECREATION AREA

The first Oregon dunes were formed between 12 and 26 million years ago by the weathering of inland mountain ranges. Though the dunes are in constant flux, they reached their current size and shape about 7,000 years ago after the massive eruption of the Mount Mazama volcano, which emptied out the entire molten-rock contents of the mountain, and in the process created the caldera that would become Crater Lake.

Water currents and winds are factors responsible for the dunes. Currents move the sand particles north each winter and south each summer, while constant winds off the Pacific Ocean blow the sand eastward, piling it up into dunes that are slowly marching east. Over thousands of years, the dunes have swallowed up forests, leaving some groves of trees as remnant tree islands.

Freshwater trapped behind the dunes has formed numerous **freshwater lakes,** many of which are now ringed by campgrounds and vacation homes. These lakes are popular for fishing, swimming, and boating. The largest of the lakes lie outside the national recreation area and are, from north to south, Woahink Lake, Siltcoos Lake, Tahkenitch Lake, Clear Lake, Eel Lake, North Tenmile Lake, and Tenmile Lake. Smaller lakes that are within the recreation area include Cleawox Lake, Carter Lake, Beale Lake, and Horsfall Lake. Traditionally, these lakes have been in a constant state of flux; however, with the construction of homes around their shores, the lakes must be maintained at their current shape and size.

European beach grass is playing an even greater role in changing the natural dynamics of this region. Introduced to anchor sand dunes and prevent them from inundating roads and river channels, this plant has been much more effective than anyone ever imagined. Able to survive even when buried under several feet of sand, European beach grass has covered many acres of land and formed dunes in back of the beach. These dunes effectively block sand from blowing inland off the beach, and as winds blow sand off the dunes into wet, low-lying areas, vegetation takes hold, thus eliminating areas of former dunes. Aerial photos have shown that where once 80% of the dunes here were open sand, today only 20% are. It is predicted that within 50 years, these dunes will all have been completely covered with vegetation and will no longer be the barren, windswept expanses of sand seen today. In an attempt to restore at least a small area of the dunes and to eliminate European beach grass from this much-visited area, the National Guard engineers bulldozed 50 acres of dunes near the Dunes Overlook in 1998.

There are numerous options for exploring the dunes. **Jessie M. Honeyman Memorial State Park** 👭 (© **541/997-3641**), 3 miles south of Florence, is a unique spot with a beautiful forest-bordered lake and towering sand dunes. The park offers camping, picnicking, hiking trails, and access to Cleawox and Woahink lakes. On Cleawox Lake, there is a swimming area and a boat-rental facility. The dunes adjacent to Cleawox Lake are used by off-road vehicles.

The easiest place to get an overview of the dunes is at the **Dunes Overlook,** 10 miles south of Florence. Here you'll find viewing platforms high atop a forested sand dune that overlooks a vast expanse of bare sand. Another easy place from which to view the dunes is the viewing platform on the Taylor Dunes Trail, which begins at the **Carter Lake Campground,** 7½ miles south of Florence. It is an easy half-mile walk to the viewing platform.

If you want to wander among these Saharan sand dunes, there are several places to try. If you have time only for a quick walk in the sand, head to **Carter Lake Campground,** where you can continue on from the Taylor Dunes viewing platform. The beach is less than a mile beyond the viewing platform, and roughly half this distance is through dunes. From this same campground, you can hike the **Carter Dunes Trail.** The beach is 1½ miles away through dunes, forest, and meadows known as a deflation plain. A 3½-mile loop trail leads from the **Dunes Overlook** (see above) out to the beach by way of Tahkenitch Creek, a meandering stream that flows through the dunes and out to the ocean. Another mile south of the Dunes Overlook, you'll find the **Tahkenitch Trailhead,** which accesses an 8-mile network of little-used trails that wander through dunes, forest, marshes, and meadows. However, for truly impressive dunes, the best route is the **Umpqua Dunes Trail** ★★, which has its trail head a half mile south of **Eel Creek Campground** (which is 10½ miles south of Reedsport). This 2½-mile round-trip trail leads through an area of dunes 2 miles wide by 4 miles long. Don't get lost!

About 30% of the sand dunes are open to **off-road vehicles (ORVs),** and throngs of people flock to this area to roar up and down the dunes. If you'd like to do a little off-roading, you can rent a miniature dune buggy from **Sandland Adventures,** 85366 U.S. 101 S. (✆ 541/997-8087; www.sandland.com), 1 mile south of Florence (this company has a little amusement park as well); or **Sand Dunes Frontier** (✆ 541/997-3544), 4 miles south of Florence. Both companies also offer guided tours of the dunes in a variety of vehicles. Down at the southern end of the recreation area, you can rent vehicles or take tours from **Spinreel Dune Buggy Rentals,** 67045 Spinreel Dr. (✆ 541/759-3313; www.spinreel.com), located just off U.S. 101, about 9 miles south of Reedsport; or **Pacific Coast Recreation,** 4121 U.S. 101 (✆ 541/756-7183), located 5 miles north of North Bend. The latter company operates its tours in World War II military surplus transport vehicles. The tours cost about $12 for adults and $8 for children. Off-road vehicles rent for about $30 to $40 per hour.

If you'd rather avoid the dune buggies and ORVs, stay away from the dunes between the South Jetty area (just south of Florence) and Siltcoos Lake; the area adjacent to Umpqua Lighthouse State Park just south of Winchester Bay; and the area from Spinreel Campground south to the Horsfall Dune & Beach Access Road, which is just north of the town of North Bend.

Currently there is a $5-per-car day-use fee within the recreation area. If you just want to stop at the Dunes Overlook, there is a $1 fee.

OTHER ACTIVITIES & ATTRACTIONS
IN THE FLORENCE AREA

Florence's **Old Town,** on the north bank of the Siuslaw River, is one of the most charming historic districts on the Oregon coast. The restored wood and brick buildings capture the flavor of a 19th-century fishing village, many of them housing interesting shops, galleries, and restaurants.

Westward Ho! (✆ 541/997-9691), a half-scale replica of an 1850s stern-wheeler, conjures up pioneer days. Regular cruises cost $14 for adults, $10 for

---

Fun Fact **Iditarod in the Sand?**

The area's most unusual annual event is the **Dune Musher's Mail Run,** which takes place each year in March and attracts dogsled teams from all over the United States and Canada. Teams race from Horsfall Beach near Coos Bay all the way to Florence, with miniteams of three or four dogs covering 55 miles in 3 days, and full-size teams of 5 to 12 dogs covering 72 miles in 2 days. For this race, dogsleds with fat tires (instead of skids) are used. Racers carry special commemorative envelopes that are canceled at both Horsfall Beach and Florence. For more information, contact Beverly Meyers at ✆ **541/269-1269.**

---

children 4 to 12; the dinner cruise is $33 to $36. The *Westward Ho!* leaves from a dock on the Old Town waterfront and operates daily between April and mid-October.

If you'd like to ride a horse along the beach, head north to **C&M Stables,** 90241 U.S. 101 N. (✆ **541/997-7540**), which is located 8 miles north of Florence and offers rides either on the beach and through the dunes or into the coast range. Shorter rides last 1½ to 2 hours, and prices range from about $30 to $38.

If you want to get on or in the water, you can rent surfboards, body boards, sea kayaks, canoes, and scuba-diving equipment from **Central Coast Watersports,** 1560 Second St. (✆ **800/789-DIVE** or 541/997-1812), which also offers lessons.

If golf is your sport, try the 18-hole **Sandpines Golf Course,** 1201 35th St. (✆ **541/997-1940**), which plays through dunes and pine forest and is one of Oregon's most popular courses. You'll pay $30 to $50 for 18 holes. Or you can try the 18-hole **Ocean Dunes Golf Links,** 3345 Munsel Lake Rd. (✆ **800/468-4833** or 541/997-3232), which also plays through the dunes and charges $28 to $35 for 18 holes.

IN THE REEDSPORT AREA

In downtown Reedsport on the Umpqua River waterfront, you can visit the **Umpqua Discovery Center,** 409 Riverfront Way (✆ **541/271-4816;** harborside.com/~discover). This modern museum contains displays on the history and ecology of the area. It's open in summer, daily from 9am to 5pm; in winter, daily from 10am to 4pm. Admission is $5 for adults, $3 for children 6 to 15. Outside the discovery center, you'll find an observation tower that is sometimes a good place to do a little bird-watching.

At the **Dean Creek Elk Viewing Area** 🦌, 1 mile east of town on Ore. 38, you can spot 120 or more elk grazing on 1,000 acres of meadows that have been set aside as a preserve. In summer, the elk tend to stay in the forest, where it's cooler.

In Winchester Bay, you can visit the historic **Umpqua River Lighthouse.** The original lighthouse was at the mouth of the Umpqua River and was the first lighthouse on the Oregon coast. It fell into the Umpqua River in 1861 and was replaced in 1894 by the current lighthouse. Adjacent to the lighthouse is the **Visitors Center & Museum,** 1020 Lighthouse Rd. (✆ **541/271-4631**), which is housed in a former coast-guard station and contains historical exhibits and an information center. Here at the museum, you can arrange to join a tour of the lighthouse. Tours are offered in the summer Wednesday through Sunday between 10am and 4pm; call for tour schedule other months.

Across the street from the lighthouse is a **whale-viewing platform.** (The best viewing months are Nov–June.) Also nearby is the very pretty **Umpqua Lighthouse State Park,** the site of the 500-foot-tall sand dunes that are the tallest in the United States. The park offers picnicking, hiking, and camping amid forests and sand dunes.

WHERE TO STAY
IN FLORENCE

Driftwood Shores Resort & Conference Center ⚡ *Kids*   Several miles north of Florence's Old Town district, this is the only oceanfront lodging in the area. It's popular year-round, so book early. The rooms vary in size and amenities, but all have ocean views and balconies. Most also have kitchens, and the three-bedroom suites are as large as many vacation homes. The hotel's restaurant has ocean views from every table.

88416 First Ave., Florence, OR 97439-9112. ℭ **800/422-5091** or 541/997-8263. Fax 541/997-5857. www. driftwoodshores.com. 136 units. $82–$228 double; $194–$275 suite. AE, DC, DISC, MC, V. **Amenities:** Restaurant (American), lounge; indoor pool; Jacuzzi; coin-op laundry. *In room:* TV, coffeemaker, hair dryer, iron.

The Edwin K Bed & Breakfast ⚡⚡   Located only 2 blocks from Old Town Florence, this 1914 home is one of the most luxurious B&Bs on the coast. The four upstairs rooms are the most spacious, and two overlook the Siuslaw River, which is just across the street and has a huge sand dune rising up on its far shore. One of these two front rooms has a claw-foot tub on a raised tile platform beside the bed; the other has a double whirlpool tub. Other rooms, although not as plush, are still comfortable. Breakfasts are lavish formal affairs.

1155 Bay St. (P.O. Box 2687), Florence, OR 97439. ℭ **800/8-EDWIN-K** or 541/997-8360. Fax 541/997-1424. www.edwink.com. 6 units. May–Oct $85–$125 double. Lower rates other months. Rates include full breakfast. DISC, MC, V. *In room:* No phone.

River House Motel ⚡   Overlooking the Siuslaw River drawbridge and sand dunes on the far side of the river, the River House is only 1 block from the heart of Florence's Old Town district. This modern motel offers comfortable and attractive rooms, most of which have views and balconies. The largest and most expensive have double whirlpool tubs. All of the riverfront rooms were redone recently and are worth requesting.

1202 Bay St., Florence, OR 97439. ℭ **877/997-3933** or 541/997-3933. www.riverhouseflorence.com. 40 units. Summer $69–$120 double. Lower rates off-season. AE, DC, DISC, MC, V. **Amenities:** Access to nearby health club; Jacuzzi; coin-op laundry. *In room:* TV, coffeemaker.

CAMPGROUNDS

North of Florence are the first of this region's many campgrounds, **Sutton** and **Alder Dune,** both of which are operated by the Forest Service. Just outside Florence at the Siuslaw River's north jetty is the relatively quiet **Harbor Vista County Park** (ℭ **541/997-5987**); with nice campsites and day-use areas it's an alternative to crowded Honeyman State Park. South of Florence, you'll find 13 Forest Service campgrounds and 3 state park campgrounds within the Oregon Dunes National Recreation Area. With two lakes, swimming, canoeing, sand dunes, and shady forests **Jesse M. Honeyman Memorial State Park,** just a few miles south of Florence, is one of the most popular state parks in Oregon and stays full throughout the summer. Just south of here you'll find the Siltcoos Recreation Area, where **Lagoon Campground** and **Waxmyrtle Campground** are the better choices. **Carter Lake Campground,** on a popular swimming and boating lake, is another quiet choice in this area. The **Tahkenitch**

Campground, however, is probably the best choice in the area. It's set in the forest on the edge of the dunes. South of Reedsport and Winchester Bay, you'll find **William M. Tugman State Park,** at the south end of Eel Lake. **Eel Creek Campground,** adjacent to the Umpqua Dunes, is a quiet choice down at the southern end of the national recreation area. For reservations at the state park campgrounds, contact **Reservations Northwest** (© **800/452-5687;** www. oregonstateparks.org). National-forest campgrounds in the area that accept reservations are Carter Lake, Eel Creek, Tahkenitch, and Tyee. For reservations, call the **National Recreation Reservation Service** (© **800/280-2267** or 877/ 444-6777; www.reserveusa.com).

WHERE TO DINE
IN FLORENCE

When you need a good cup of espresso, stop in at **Siuslaw River Coffee Roasters,** 1240 Bay St. (© **541/997-3443**). To enjoy sunset over the Siuslaw River with a glass of wine, drop by **Grape Leaf,** 1368 Bay St. (© **541/997-1646**), a wine bar with a deck out back.

Bridgewater Seafood Restaurant ⊛ AMERICAN/SEAFOOD   Located in a restored building in Old Town, this eclectic eatery combines a Wild West storefront facade with a tropical interior complete with wicker furniture and potted plants. In the summer there's patio dining, and any time of year the lounge area is a cozy place to wait out the rain. The menu is long and includes everything from jambalaya and turkey enchiladas to pasta, burgers, and chowders.

1297 Bay St. © 541/997-9405. Reservations recommended. Main courses $7–$18. AE, DISC, MC, V. Daily 8:30am–8:30pm (shorter hours in the off-season).

International C-Food Market ⊛ *Kids* SEAFOOD   Located on a dock on the old waterfront, this restaurant also happens to be a fish-processing facility, which means the seafood served here is as fresh as you'll find anywhere on the coast. The warehouse-like space has loads of windows providing views of the river, and interesting undersea murals on every wall that doesn't have a window. The steamed Manila clams here are excellent. Order up a pot and be sure to ask for some "tiger's milk," a drink made from the clam broth, lemon juice, Tabasco sauce, and cracked pepper. After this, you can hardly go wrong. The crab cakes are another good bet and, together with the steamed clams, make a great meal. With burgers and fries, plus a separate kids' menu, this is a good family choice.

1498 Bay St. © 541/997-7978. Reservations recommended. Main courses $7–$26. DISC, MC, V. Daily 11am–10pm (winter daily 11am–8pm).

IN WINCHESTER BAY

If you're craving some smoked salmon or other fish, drop by **Sportsmen's Cannery & Smokehouse,** 182 Bayfront Loop, Winchester Bay (© **541/271-3293**).

Bayfront Bistro ⊛ AMERICAN   Although the menu is none too French at this cozy little place in the Salmon Harbor Marina area, the Bayfront does a respectable job of conjuring up the atmosphere of a Parisian bistro. Be sure to order oysters, which come from right here in the Umpqua River. You can get them on the half shell, poached, in stew, as shooters, in burgers, or as an entree. Friday and Saturday nights are prime-rib nights, but you could still start with an oyster appetizer. There's a modest selection of Oregon wines and microbrews. At lunch, simple sandwiches dominate. The clam chowder is pretty good, too.

208 Bayfront Loop, Winchester Bay. © 541/271-9463. www.bayfrontbistro.com. Reservations recommended. Main courses $5.25–$10 lunch, $9–$17 dinner. AE, MC, V. Daily 11am–9pm (closes at 8pm in winter).

Café Français ⭐ *Finds* COUNTRY FRENCH   With flower boxes in the windows and fine linens on the tables, this place is a world away from the family restaurants that line the roads in this area. (Nothing here is deep-fried—amazing!) The menu consists of a handful of daily specials, which might include pork loin with a port wine reduction, scallops in garlic-ginger cream sauce, or duck in an orange essence. There is a good selection of wines from Oregon, France, and California. For a starter, you can usually opt for escargot, oysters on the half shell, or stuffed mushrooms.

U.S. 101, Winchester Bay. ② 541/271-9270. Reservations recommended. Main courses $20–$24. MC, V. Wed–Sun 5–10pm.

10 The Coos Bay Area

85 miles NW of Roseburg, 48 miles S of Florence, 24 miles N of Bandon

With a population of around 35,000, the Coos Bay area, consisting of the towns of Coos Bay, North Bend, and Charleston, is the largest urban center on the Oregon coast. Coos Bay and North Bend are the bay's commercial center and have merged into a single large town, while nearby Charleston maintains its distinct character as a small fishing port.

As the largest natural harbor between San Francisco and Puget Sound, Coos Bay has long been an important port. Logs, wood chips, and wood products are the main export, but with the controversy over raw log shipments to Japan and the continuing battle to save old-growth forests in the Northwest, Coos Bay's days as a timber-shipping port may be numbered. In response to the economic downturn of the port, the bay area has been gearing up to attract both more tourists and more industry. In downtown Coos Bay, there is an attractive waterfront boardwalk, complete with historical displays, and what was once a huge lumber mill is now the site of the equally large Mill Resort & Casino.

Even if it isn't the most beautiful town on the Oregon coast, Coos Bay has a lot of character and also quite a few tourist amenities, including several good restaurants, moderately priced motels, and even a few B&Bs. However, what makes Coos Bay a town not to be missed is its proximity to a trio of state parks that are among the most beautiful on the coast.

ESSENTIALS
GETTING THERE   From the north, take Ore. 99 from just south of Cottage Grove. This road becomes Ore. 38. At Reedsport, head south on U.S. 101. From the south, take Ore. 42 from just south of Roseburg.

The North Bend–Coos Bay Municipal Airport is served by **Horizon Air** (② 800/547-9308).

VISITOR INFORMATION   Contact the **Bay Area Chamber of Commerce & Visitor Bureau,** 50 E. Central Ave., Coos Bay, OR 97420 (② 800/824-8486 or 541/269-0215; www.oregonbayareachamber.com). North of the city of Coos Bay off U.S. 101, there's the **North Bend Information Center,** 1380 Sherman St., N. Bend, OR 97459 (② 541/756-4613).

GETTING AROUND   If you need a taxi, contact **Coos Yellow Cab** (② 541/267-3111). Car rentals are available in the Coos Bay area from **Hertz** and **Enterprise Rent-a-Car.**

The Southern Oregon Coast

S.N.A. - State Natural Area
S.N.S. - State Natural Site
S.R.A. - State Recreation Area
S.R.S. - State Recreation Site
S.S.C. - State Scenic Corridor
S.S.V. - State Scenic Viewpoint

State Park
Camping
Mountain Peak

Oregon Dunes National Recreation Area

Golden and Silver Falls State Park

North Bend
Allegany
Coos Bay

Coos River

Charleston

Coos Bay

Sunset Bay S.P.
Shore Acres S.P.
Cape Arago S.P.

101

0   10 mi
0   10 km

Bullards Beach S.P.

Coquille

Bandon
Face Rock S.S.V.
Bandon S.N.A.

Coquille River

East Fork Coquille River

Myrtle Point

PACIFIC OCEAN

Bennet Butte

South Fork Coquille River

COAST RANGES

42

Langlois

Cape Blanco
Cape Blanco S.P.
Sixes

Port Orford

WILD ROGUE WILDERNESS AREA

KLAMATH MTNS.

Humbug Mtn. S.P.

101

Agness

Rogue River

Nesika Beach

Silver River

Gold Beach

SISKIYOU

Illinois River

Cape Sebastian S.S.C.
Cape Sebastian

NATIONAL

Pearsoll Peak

Pistol River
Pistol River S.S.V.
Samuel H. Boardman S.S.C.

Pistol River

FOREST

KALMIOPSIS

Bosley Butte

Chetco River

WILDERNESS

AREA

Cape Ferrelo
Harris Beach S.P.
Brookings Harbor

Alfred A. Loeb S.P.

Illinois River S.P.

199

SISKIYOU NATIONAL FOREST

Portland
OREGON
Map Area

Smith River

CALIFORNIA

138

Coos Bay

A TRIO OF STATE PARKS & MORE

Southwest of Coos Bay you'll find three state parks and a county park that preserve some of the most breathtaking shoreline in the Northwest. The three parks are connected by an excellent day hike trail.

Start your exploration of this beautiful stretch of coast by heading southwest on the Cape Arago Highway. In 12 miles you'll come to **Sunset Bay State Park** ⚓ (ⓒ **541/888-4902** or 800/551-6949). This park has one of the few beaches in Oregon where the water actually gets warm enough for swimming (although folks from warm-water regions may not agree). Sunset Bay is almost completely surrounded by sandstone cliffs, and the entrance to the bay is quite narrow, which means the waters here stay fairly calm. Picnicking and camping are available, and there are lots of tide pools to explore.

Another 3 miles brings you to **Shore Acres State Park** ⚓⚓ (ⓒ **541/ 888-3732** or 800/551-6949), once the estate of local shipping tycoon Louis J. Simpson, who spent years developing his gardens. His ships would bring him unusual plants from all over the world, and eventually the gardens grew to include a formal English garden and a Japanese garden with a 100-foot lily pond. The gardens and his home, which long ago was torn down, were built atop sandstone cliffs overlooking the Pacific and a tiny cove. Rock walls rise up from the water and have been sculpted by the waves into unusual shapes. During winter storms, wave-watching is a popular pastime here. The water off the park is often a striking shade of blue, and **Simpson Beach,** in the little cove, just might be the prettiest beach in Oregon. A trail leads down to this beach.

Cape Arago State Park ⚓⚓ (ⓒ **541/888-4902** or 800/551-6949) is the third of this trio of parks. Just offshore from the rugged cape lie the rocks and small islands of Simpson Reef, which provide sunbathing spots for hundreds of seals (including elephant seals) and sea lions. Their barking can be heard from hundreds of yards away, and though you can't get very close, with a pair of binoculars you can see the seals quite well. The best viewing point is at **Simpson Reef Viewpoint.** On either side of the cape are coves with quiet beaches, although the beaches are closed from March 1 to June 30 to protect young seal pups. Tide pools along these beaches offer hours of fascination during other months.

Also in the vicinity of these three state parks, you'll find **Bastendorff Beach County Park** (ⓒ **541/888-5353**), north of Sunset Bay at the mouth of Coos Bay, which offers a long, wide beach that's popular with surfers.

Four miles down Seven Devils Road from Charleston, you'll find the **South Slough National Estuarine Research Reserve** (ⓒ **541/888-5558;** www. southsloughestuary.com). An interpretive center (open 8:30am–4:30pm, daily in summer and Mon–Fri other months) set high above the slough provides background on the importance of estuaries. South Slough is in the process of being restored after many years of damming, diking, and reclamation of marshlands by farmers. A hiking trail leads down to the marshes, and there is good canoeing and sea kayaking.

OTHER AREA ACTIVITIES & ATTRACTIONS

Charleston is the bay area's charter-fishing marina. If you'd like to do some sportfishing, contact **Bob's Sport Fishing** (ⓒ **800/628-9633** or 541/888-4241; www.bobssportfishing.com) or **Betty Kay Charters** (ⓒ **800/752-6303** or 541/888-9021). Expect to pay around $60 for a 5-hour bottom-fishing trip and $150 for a 12-hour halibut-fishing trip.

In addition to all the outdoor recreational activities around the bay area, there are also a few museums. The **Coos Art Museum,** 235 Anderson Ave., Coos Bay

---

Fun Fact **Oregon Myrtlewood**

At Coos Bay you enter **myrtlewood** country. The myrtle tree grows only along a short section of coast in southern Oregon and northern California and is prized by woodworkers for its fine grain and durability. A very hard wood, it lends itself to all manner of platters, bowls, goblets, sculptures, and whatever. All along the south coast, you'll see myrtlewood factories and shops where you can see how the raw wood is turned into finished pieces. South of Coos Bay, watch for **The Oregon Connection** (© 800/255-5318 or 541/267-7804), which is right on U.S. 101. This is one of the bigger myrtlewood factories. The **Real Oregon Gift**, 3955 U.S. 101 (© 541/756-2220), 5 miles north of North Bend, is another large factory and showroom. Six miles south of Bandon on U.S. 101, watch for **Zumwalt's Myrtlewood Factory** (© 541/347-3654), which has a good selection and prices, and, about a mile farther south, **Pacific Myrtlewood** (© 541/347-2200).

(© 541/267-3901; www.coosart.org), is a highly regarded little museum that hosts changing exhibits in a wide variety of styles and media. It's open Tuesday through Friday from 10am to 4pm and Saturday from 1 to 4pm; admission is by $2.50 donation.

Part of the renovation of the Coos Bay waterfront has been the construction of **The Mill Resort & Casino,** 3201 Tremont Ave., North Bend (© 800/953-4800 or 541/756-8800; www.themillcasino.com). Here you can play slot machines, blackjack, poker, and bingo. There are several restaurants and a lounge.

WHERE TO STAY

Coos Bay Manor Bed & Breakfast Inn ✪   Built in the colonial style in 1912, this restored home in a quiet residential neighborhood in downtown Coos Bay is your best bet in the area if you're looking for a bed-and-breakfast. The guest rooms are large and vary from a Victorian room full of ruffles and lace to the masculine Cattle Baron's Room, which has bear and coyote rugs.

955 S. Fifth St., Coos Bay, OR 97420. © 800/269-1224 or 541/269-1224. www.virtualcities.com. 5 units (3 with private bathroom). $79 double with shared bathroom, $100 double with private bathroom. Rates include full breakfast. AE, DISC, MC, V. Pets accepted ($10 per animal). **Amenities:** Bikes; laundry service. *In room:* TV, dataport, fridge, hair dryer, iron.

Edgewater Inn ✪   This is Coos Bay's only waterfront hotel, and though the water it faces is only a narrow stretch of the back bay, you can sometimes watch ships in the harbor. The guest rooms are large, and the deluxe rooms are particularly well designed and spacious, with a breakfast bar and an extra large TV. Other deluxe rooms have in-room spas. Most rooms also have balconies overlooking the water (and industrial areas).

275 E. Johnson Ave., Coos Bay, OR 97420. © 800/233-0423 or 541/267-0423. Fax 541/267-4343. www.edgewater-inns.com. 82 units. $75–$120 double. Rates include continental breakfast. AE, DC, DISC, MC, V. Pets accepted ($8 per day). **Amenities:** Outdoor pool; exercise room; Jacuzzi; sauna; dry cleaning. *In room:* A/C, TV, dataport, fridge, coffeemaker, hair dryer, iron.

CAMPGROUNDS

About 12 miles outside Coos Bay, you'll find **Sunset Bay State Park** (see p. 212 for more information). To make a reservation, contact **Reservations Northwest** (© 800/452-5687; www.oregonstateparks.org). **Bastendorff Beach County**

Park (© 541/888-5353), north of Sunset Bay at the mouth of Coos Bay, is an alternative to the frequently full Sunset Bay State Park campground.

WHERE TO DINE

Blue Heron Bistro 🐦 INTERNATIONAL   A casual cafe, espresso bar, deli, and international restaurant are what you'll find at the Blue Heron in the heart of downtown Coos Bay. Add one of the largest assortments of imported beers on the coast, and you have the sort of place that's perfect for lunch, dinner, or just a quick bite over a periodical from the restaurant's extensive library. Items range from German bratwurst to oysters with Cajun cream sauce to pizzas and pastas.

100 Commercial Ave., Coos Bay. © 541/267-3933. Reservations recommended for parties of 6 or more. Main courses $5–$8.50 lunch, $8.50–$16 dinner. AE, DISC, MC, V. July–Aug daily 11am–10pm; Sept–June Mon–Sat 11am–9pm.

Portside 🐦 (Kids SEAFOOD   Charleston is home to Coos Bay's charter and commercial fishing fleets, so it's no surprise that it's also home to the area's best seafood restaurant. This restaurant has been in business for almost 40 years and has developed quite a reputation. Check the daily fresh sheet to see what just came in on the boat. Preparations tend toward traditional continental dishes, of which the house specialty is a bouillabaisse Marseillaise that's just swimming with shrimp, red snapper, lobster, crab legs, butter clams, prawns, and scallops. The restaurant overlooks the boat basin and is popular with families.

8001 Kingfisher Dr., Charleston. © 541/888-5544. www.portsidebythebay.com. Reservations recommended. Main courses $11.50–$30. AE, DC, MC, V. Daily 11:30am–11pm.

11 Bandon

24 miles S of Coos Bay, 85 miles W of Roseburg

Once known primarily as the cranberry capital of Oregon (you can see the cranberry bogs south of town along U.S. 101), Bandon is now better known as an artists' colony. It's also set on one of the most spectacular pieces of coastline in the state. Just south of town, the beach is littered with boulders, monoliths, and haystack rocks that seem to have been strewn by some giant hand. Sunsets are stunning—it's easy to see why artists have been drawn here.

Just north of town the Coquille River empties into the Pacific, and at the river's mouth stands a picturesque lighthouse. The lighthouse was one of only a handful of Bandon buildings to survive a fire in 1936. Even though most buildings downtown date only from the 1930s, Bandon has a quaint seaside village atmosphere.

ESSENTIALS

GETTING THERE   From Roseburg, head west on Ore. 42 to Coquille, where you take Ore. 42S to Bandon, which is on U.S. 101.

VISITOR INFORMATION   Contact the **Bandon Chamber of Commerce,** 300 SE Second St. (P.O. Box 1515), Bandon, OR 97411 (© **541/347-9616;** www.bandon.com).

FESTIVALS   Bandon is the cranberry capital of Oregon, and each year in September the impending harvest is celebrated with the **Bandon Cranberry Festival.** Other festivals include the **Seafood and Wine Festival** held over Memorial Day weekend and the **Festival of Lights,** held each year during the Christmas season.

OUTDOOR ACTIVITIES

Head out of Bandon on Beach Loop Road, and you'll soon see why the rocks are a big draw. Wind and waves have sculpted monoliths along the shore into contorted spires and twisted shapes. The first good place to view the rocks and get down to the beach is at **Coquille Point,** at the end of 11th Street. Here you'll find a short, paved interpretive trail atop a bluff overlooking the beach, rock monoliths, and river mouth. There's also a long staircase leading down to the beach. From here you can see Table Rock and the Sisters. From the **Face Rock Viewpoint** you can see the area's most famous rock, which resembles a face gazing skyward. Nearby stand a dog, a cat, and kittens. A trail leads down to the beach from the Viewpoint, so you can go out and explore some of the rocks that are left high and dry by low tide. South of the rocks, along a flat stretch of beach backed by dunes, there are several beach access areas, all of which are within **Bandon State Natural Area.**

Across the river from downtown Bandon, you'll find **Bullards Beach State Park** (© **541/347-2209**). Within the park are beaches, a marsh overlook, hiking and horseback-riding trails, a picnic area, a campground, and a boat ramp. Fishing, crabbing, and clamming are all very popular. In the park you'll also find the 1896 **Coquille River Lighthouse.** This lighthouse is one of the only lighthouses to ever be hit by a ship—in 1903 an abandoned schooner plowed into the light. In December the lighthouse is decorated with Christmas lights. Between May and October, tours of the lighthouse are generally offered daily from 10am to 4pm.

At Bandon, as elsewhere on the Oregon coast, **gray whales** migrating between the Arctic and Baja California, Mexico, pass close to the shore and can often be spotted from land. The whales pass Bandon between December and February on their way south and between March and May on their way north. Gray days, and early mornings, before the wind picks up, is the best time to spot whales. Coquille Point, at the end of 11th Street, and the bluffs along Beach Loop Road are the best vantage points.

More than 300 species of birds have been spotted in the Bandon vicinity, making this one of the best sites in Oregon for **bird-watching.** The **Oregon Islands National Wildlife Refuge,** which includes 1,400 rocks and islands off the state's coast, includes the famous monoliths of Bandon. Among the birds that nest on these rocks are rhinoceros auklets, storm petrels, gulls, and tufted puffins. These latter birds, with their large colorful beaks, are the most beloved of local birds, and their images show up on all manner of local souvenirs. The **Bandon Marsh National Wildlife Refuge,** at the mouth of the Coquille River, is another good spot for bird-watching. In this area you can expect to see grebes, mergansers, buffleheads, plovers, and several birds of prey.

Anglers can head offshore for bottom fish, salmon, tuna, and halibut with **Port O' Call,** 155 First St. (© **541/347-2875**), which charges $55 to $150 for a fishing trip. If you're interested in exploring the Coquille River, you can rent a sea kayak from **Adventure Kayak,** 315 First St. (© **541/347-3480**), which also offers kayak tours during the summer months. Boats rent for $24 to $30 for the first 2 hours, and tours are $35. If you'd rather ride a horse down the beach, contact **Bandon Beach Riding Stables** (© **541/347-3423**), on Beach Loop Drive south of Face Rock. A 1-hour ride is $30.

With the opening in 1999 of the world-class **Bandon Dunes Golf Course,** 57744 Round Lake Dr. (© **888/345-6008** or 541/347-4380; www.bandondunes golf.com), a classic Scottish-style links course and Oregon's only oceanfront golf course, Bandon became a major golfing destination. The course has been compared to Pebble Beach and St. Andrews and is notorious for its blustery winds. The summer greens fee are $120 for resort guests and $150 for nonguests ($70 for your second 18 holes). This is a walking course, and no golf carts are allowed; but caddies are available for an additional $35.

If that's out of your price range, there is always the **Bandon Face Rock Golf Course,** 3295 Beach Loop Dr. (© **541/347-3818**), which offers a scenic nine holes not far from the famous Face Rock. The greens fee is $10 for nine holes.

OTHER AREA ACTIVITIES & ATTRACTIONS

The **West Coast Game Park** ✦, 7 miles south of Bandon on U.S. 101 (© **541/347-3106;** www.gameparksafari.com), bills itself as America's largest wild-animal petting park and is a must for families. Depending on what young animals they have at the time of your visit, you might be able to play with a leopard, tiger, or bear cub. It's open daily from 9am to 7pm in summer, with shorter hours other months; call for hours. Admission is $10 for adults, $9 for seniors, $8 for children 7 to 12, $5 for children 2 to 6.

Shopping is one of Bandon's main attractions, and in **Old Town Bandon,** just off U.S. 101, you'll find some interesting shops and galleries. A couple of galleries sell artworks by regional artists. One of the better ones is the **Bandon Glass Art Studio** at 240 U.S. 101 (© **541/347-4723**), a short walk across the highway from Old Town. Here you can watch glass direct from the furnace being made into the paperweights or fluted glass bowls the gallery sells.

At the **Bandon Cheese Factory,** located on U.S. 101 in the middle of town (© **800/548-8961**), you can watch cheese being made, try some samples, and maybe pick up some fixings for a picnic on the beach. A few blocks away, **Cranberry Sweets,** on the corner of First Street and Chicago Avenue (© **541/347-9475**), sells 200 varieties of handmade candies, some with, some without cranberries. At **Faber Farms,** 519 Morrison Rd. (© **541/347-1166**), a working cranberry farm, you can see how cranberries are grown and sample a variety of cranberry products. If you visit in October, you'll be there for the harvest. To reach the farm, drive 1½ miles north of Florence, turn east on Morrison Road, and continue another mile.

WHERE TO STAY

Bandon Dunes Golf Resort ✦✦✦ Although this is one of the most tasteful and luxurious accommodations on the Oregon coast, the emphasis is so entirely on the golf course that anyone not interested in the game will feel like an interloper. However, if golf is your game then you'll love this place. The lodge sits up on the dunes and looks out over the fairways to the Pacific. Rooms are also available in what are called "Lily Pond Cottages," not really cottages but rather multi-unit buildings arranged around a pretty little pond. These rooms don't have the golf course views, but they are very comfortable.

57744 Round Lake Dr., Bandon, OR 97411. © **888/345-6008** or 541/347-4380. www.bandondunesgolf. com. 68 units. $165–$275 double; $650–$850 suite. AE, DC, DISC, MC, V. **Amenities:** Restaurant (Northwest), 2 lounges; 2 18-hole golf courses; exercise room; Jacuzzi; sauna; business center; massage; babysitting; dry cleaning. *In room:* TV, coffeemaker, iron, safe.

Best Western Inn at Face Rock Resort ✦✦ About a mile south of Face Rock, this modern hotel is Bandon's original golf resort, and is adjacent to the nine-hole Bandon Face Rock Golf Course. Guest rooms here are the best on Beach Loop Drive, and there are plenty of recreational facilities. Although the hotel is across the street from the beach, many of the rooms have ocean views. The views from the hotel restaurant aren't nearly as good as at the nearby Lord Bennett's Restaurant. A short path leads down to the beach.

3225 Beach Loop Dr., Bandon, OR 97411. ℂ **800/638-3092** or 541/347-9441. Fax 541/347-2532. www. facerock.net. 76 units. Mid-June to mid-Sept $105–$205 double. Mid-Sept to mid-June $70–$180 double. AE, DC, DISC, MC, V. Pets accepted. **Amenities:** Restaurant (American), lounge; indoor pool; exercise room; Jacuzzi; sauna; bike rentals; room service; coin-op laundry. *In room:* TV, coffeemaker.

Lighthouse Bed and Breakfast ⭐

Located on the road that leads to the mouth of the Coquille River, this riverfront B&B has a view of the historic Bandon Lighthouse, and, with its weathered cedar siding, large decks, and small sunroom, is the quintessential beach house. Guest rooms range from a small room with the private bath across the hall to a spacious room with views of the ocean and lighthouse, a wood-burning stove, and a double whirlpool tub overlooking the river. Both the beach and Old Town Bandon are within a very short walk.

650 Jetty Rd. SW (P.O. Box 24), Bandon, OR 97411. ℂ **541/347-9316**. www.lighthouselodging.com. 5 units. $110–$185 double. MC, V. *In room:* A/C, hair dryer.

Sunset Motel ⭐ (Value

Dozens of Bandon's famous monoliths rise from the sand and waves in front of this motel, making sunsets from the Sunset truly memorable. The rooms, with their dated furnishings and paneled walls, aren't nearly as good as the views, however. You'll find everything from economy motel rooms to contemporary condos, rustic cabins, and classic cottages. If you want modern accommodations, opt for the Vern Brown addition rooms; and if you want something rustic and private, try to get one of the cottages. The adjacent Lord Bennet Restaurant has *the* view in Bandon.

1865 Beach Loop Rd. (P.O. Box 373), Bandon, OR 97411. ℂ **800/842-2407** or 541/347-2453. www. sunsetmotel.com. 70 units. May 15–Oct 15 $52–$175 double. Oct 16–May 14 $40–$175 double. AE, DISC, MC, V. Pets accepted ($10 per night). **Amenities:** Restaurant (seafood), lounge; Jacuzzi; concierge; business center; coin-op laundry. *In room:* TV, dataport, coffeemaker, free local calls.

CAMPGROUNDS

Bullards Beach State Park, across the Coquille River from downtown Bandon, has 190 campsites and 13 yurts for rent. To make reservations, call **Reservations Northwest** (ℂ **800/452-5687;** www.oregonstateparks.org).

WHERE TO DINE

When it's time for espresso, stop in at **Rayjen Coffee Company,** 365 Second St. SE (ℂ **541/347-1144**), in a cottage on the edge of Old Town. **Bandon Gourmet,** 92 Second St. (ℂ **541/347-3237**), is a great place for a gourmet sandwich and fresh baked breads and pastries. For a quick meal of incredibly fresh fish-and-chips, you can't beat **Bandon Fish Market,** 249 First St. (ℂ **541/347-4282**), which is right on the waterfront and has a few picnic tables.

Bandon Boatworks ⭐ SEAFOOD

Directly across the Coquille River from the historic Bandon Lighthouse, this large seafood restaurant has a view similar to Harp's (see below), though the menu is more traditional and the atmosphere not as romantic. But the views are great: you can watch the waves crashing on the jetties at the mouth of the river while you dine on shrimp scampi or steak and lobster. Fish-and-chips, burgers, and sandwiches predominate on the lunch menu. There's also a seniors' menu.

275 Lincoln Ave. SW. ℂ **541/347-2111**. Reservations recommended both lunch and dinner. Main courses $6–$10 lunch, $12–$25 dinner. AE, DISC, MC, V. Mon–Sat 11:30am–9pm; Sun 11am–8:30pm.

Stormy Weather

"And the weather at the coast this weekend will be high winds and heavy rain, as another storm front moves in off the Pacific Ocean." This sort of forecast would keep most folks cozily at home, but in Oregon, where storm-watching has become a popular winter activity, it's the equivalent of "Surf's up!"

Throughout the winter, Oregon's rocky shores and haystack rocks feel the effects of storms that originate far to the north in cold polar waters. As these storms slam ashore, sometimes with winds topping 100 mph, their huge waves smash against the rocks with breathtaking force, sending spray flying. The perfect storm-watching days are those rare clear days right after a big storm, when the waves are still big but the sky is clear. After a storm is also the best time to go beachcombing—it's your best chance to find the rare hand-blown Japanese glass fishing floats that sometimes wash ashore on the Oregon coast.

Among the **best storm-watching spots** on the coast are the South Jetty at the mouth of the Columbia River in Fort Stevens State Park, Cannon Beach, Cape Meares, Depoe Bay, Cape Foulweather, Devil's Punchbowl on the Otter Crest Scenic Loop, Seal Rock, Cape Perpetua, Shore Acres State Park, Cape Arago State Park, Face Rock Viewpoint outside Bandon, and Cape Sebastian.

Some of the **best lodgings** for storm-watching are the Inn at Otter Crest north of Depoe Bay, the Channel House in Depoe Bay, the Cliff House in Waldport, the Adobe Motel Resort in Yachats, and the Sunset Motel in Bandon. The coast's **best restaurants** for storm-watching are Tidal Raves in Depoe Bay, the dining room of the Adobe Motel Resort in Yachats, and Lord Bennett's Restaurant in Bandon.

Harp's On The Bay ★★ SEAFOOD/AMERICAN   Harp's, located in a restored historic building on the Coquille River, is the most sophisticated and romantic restaurant in Bandon. Although casual dress is certainly acceptable (as are families with children), it's a place where people are more likely to dress for dinner. Ask for a table with a view of the Coquille Light House. There's no easy-listening music or fried food here, but there is some of the best clam chowder on the Oregon coast. House-made pasta with garlic and olive oil comes with entrees such as halibut charbroiled with an unusual spicy pistachio sauce or grilled oysters.

480 First St. SW. ℂ **541/347-9057.** Reservations recommended. Main courses $8–$25. AE, DC, DISC, MC, V. Tues–Sun 5–9pm.

Lord Bennett's Restaurant and Lounge ★★ AMERICAN   Lord Bennett's is the only restaurant in Bandon that overlooks this town's bizarre beachscape of contorted rock spires and sea stacks, and this alone makes it a must for a meal. This place isn't as casual as the Bandon Boatworks or as attractive a setting as Harp's (see above), but the sunsets are unforgettable. Since sunsets come late in the day in the summer, you might want to eat a late lunch the day you plan to come here. We suggest starting dinner with some crab cakes before moving on to such main courses as New York steak with peppercorns or lamb chops with a hazelnut crust. There's a decent wine list, and the desserts are both beautiful and delicious.

1695 Beach Loop Dr., next to the Sunset Motel. ☎ **541/347-3663.** Reservations recommended. Main courses $6–$10 lunch, $13–$22 dinner. AE, DISC, MC, V. Daily 11am–3pm and 5–9pm.

12 The Southern Oregon Coast

Port Orford: 27 miles S of Bandon, 79 miles N of Crescent City, 95 miles W of Grants Pass
Gold Beach: 54 miles N of Crescent City, Calif.; 32 miles S of Port Orford
Brookings/Harbor: 26 miles N of Crescent City, 35 miles S of Gold Beach

The 60-mile stretch of coast between Port Orford and the California state line is perhaps the most beautiful stretch of the entire Oregon coast, yet because of its distance from major metropolitan areas, it is relatively little visited.

Port Orford, anchoring the northern end, is today little more than a wide spot in the road, yet it is the oldest town on the coast other than Astoria. Named by Captain George Vancouver on April 5, 1792, this natural harbor in the lee of Port Orford Heads became the first settlement right on the Oregon coast when, in 1851, settlers and soldiers together constructed Fort Orford. A fort was necessary due to hostilities with the area's native population. Eventually the settlers fled inland, crossing the Siskiyou Mountains.

Although the first settlers made camp here because there was something of a natural harbor, these days the area's fishing fleet is hauled out of the water nightly by a large crane. Working out of this tiny port are a fishing fleet and sea-urchin harvesting industry.

Cape Blanco, located just north of Port Orford and discovered and named by Spanish explorer Martín de Aguilar in 1603, once made an even grander claim than Port Orford when it was heralded as the westernmost point of land in the lower 48. Today, that claim has been laid to rest by Cape Flattery, Washington, and Cape Blanco now only claims to be the westernmost point in Oregon.

In 19th-century California, gold prospectors had to struggle through rugged mountains in search of pay dirt, but here in Oregon they could just scoop it up off the beach. The black sands at the mouth of the Rogue River were high in gold, and it was this gold that gave the Gold Beach its name. The white settlers attracted by the gold soon came in conflict with the local Rogue River (or TuTuNi) Indians. Violence erupted in 1856, but within the year the Rogue River Indian Wars had come to an end and the TuTuNis were moved to a reservation.

The TuTuNis had for centuries found the river to be a plentiful source of salmon, and when the gold played out, commercial fishermen moved in to take advantage of the large salmon runs. The efficiency of their nets and traps quickly decimated the local salmon population, and a hatchery was constructed to replenish the runs.

Brookings and Harbor compose the southernmost community on the Oregon coast. Because of the warm year-round temperatures, this region is known as the Oregon Banana Belt, and you'll see palm trees and other cold-sensitive plants thriving in gardens around town. Farms south of town grow nearly all of the Easter lilies sold in the United States. Other plants that thrive in this climate include coast redwoods, Oregon myrtles, and wild azaleas. Dividing the sister towns of Brookings and Harbor is the Chetco River, one of the purest and most beautiful rivers in the state.

ESSENTIALS

GETTING THERE   There is no convenient way to get to this stretch of coast. Coming from the north, the nearest highway connection to I-5 is Ore. 42 from Roseburg to Bandon. Coming from the south, you must either follow U.S. 101 north through California or take U.S. 199 southwest from Grants Pass and then continue north on U.S. 101. There is also a narrow, winding road over the mountains to Gold Beach from Galice (near Grants Pass).

VISITOR INFORMATION   For more information on Port Orford, contact the **Greater Port Orford North Curry Chamber of Commerce** (P.O. Box 637), Battle Rock Park, U.S. 101 S., Port Orford, OR 97465 (© **541/ 332-8055;** www.portorfordoregon.com). For information on the Gold Beach area, contact the **Gold Beach Visitor's Center & Chamber of Commerce,** 29279 Ellensburg Ave., Suite 3, Gold Beach, OR 97444 (© **800/525-2334** or 541/247-7526; www.goldbeach.org). For more information on the Brooking area, contact the **Brookings-Harbor Chamber of Commerce,** 16330 Lower Harbor Rd. (P.O. Box 940), Brookings, OR 97415 (© **800/535-9469** or 541/469-3181; www.brookingsor.com).

THE PORT ORFORD AREA

Cape Blanco is now preserved as **Cape Blanco State Park** (© **541/332-6774**), where you'll find miles of beaches and hiking trails through windswept meadows, a campground, and picnic areas. This high headland is also the site of the **Cape Blanco Lighthouse,** which is the oldest continuously operating lighthouse in Oregon. Not far from the lighthouse is the **Hughes House Museum,** a restored Eastlake Victorian home that was built in 1898 and is furnished with period antiques. It's open April through October only, Thursday through Monday from 10am to 3:30pm.

For a good view of Port Orford and this entire section of coast, drive up to the **Port Orford Heads Wayside,** which is located on the northern edge of town and has a short trail out to an overlook. The route to the wayside is well marked. Right in town, you can visit **Battle Rock Park** and learn the history of the rock refuge that rises out of Port Orford's beach. If you want to walk the beach, this is a good one, as is the beach at **Paradise Point State Recreation Site** just north of town.

Right in town you'll find several art galleries. Among our favorites are **Cook Gallery,** 705 Oregon St. (© **541/332-0045**), which features beautiful handcrafted wood furniture and sculptures, as well as prints and ceramics, and **Laughing Baskets,** 330 W. Fifth St. (© **541/332-4101**), featuring baskets made from sea grass.

Six miles south of Port Orford, you'll find **Humbug Mountain State Park** (© **541/332-6774**), where Humbug Mountain rises 1,756 feet from the ocean. A pretty campground is tucked into the forest at the base of the mountain, and a trail leads to the summit.

About 12 miles south of Port Orford is a place the kids aren't going to let you pass by. The **Prehistoric Gardens,** 36848 U.S. 101 S. (© **541/332-4463;** www.prehistoricgardens.com), is a lost world of life-size dinosaur replicas. Though they aren't as realistic as those in *Jurassic Park,* they'll make the kids squeal with delight. The gardens are open in the summer daily from 8am to dusk; other months, call for hours. Admission is $6 for adults, $5 for seniors and youths 12 to 18, $4 for children 4 to 11.

WHERE TO STAY

The Castaway ✪ *(Value)*　On a hill high above Port Orford harbor and commanding a sweeping panorama of the southern Oregon coast, this modest motel is far more comfortable than it appears from the outside. All the rooms take in the extraordinary view, and most have comfy little sunrooms from which to gaze off to sea. The rooms are quite large and well maintained, and some have kitchenettes. Out back there is a lawn with a few benches overlooking the harbor.

P.O. Box 844, Port Orford, OR 97465. ℂ 541/332-4502. Fax 541/332-9303. www.castawaybythesea.com. 13 units. $45–$80 double. Lower rates in off-season. DISC, MC, V. Pets accepted ($5 per night). **Amenities:** Massage. *In room:* TV, kitchen/kitchenette, fridge, coffeemaker.

Home by the Sea ✪　Set high atop a bluff overlooking the beach and Battle Rock, this contemporary B&B has large guest rooms (and a downstairs living room) with some of the best views on the coast. The inn is a block off U.S. 101 and within walking distance of several restaurants and art galleries.

444 Jackson St. (P.O. Box 606), Port Orford, OR 97465. ℂ 541/332-2855. www.homebythesea.com. 2 units. $95–$105 double. Rates include full breakfast. MC, V. **Amenities:** Courtesy beach shuttle; guest laundry. *In room:* TV, fridge.

CAMPGROUNDS

Cape Blanco State Park is the most popular camping spot in this area, and reservations aren't accepted for campsites. However, there are some basic cabins here that can be reserved through **Reservations Northwest** (ℂ **800/452-5687;** www.oregonstateparks.org).

THE GOLD BEACH AREA

Although there is of course a beach at Gold Beach, it is not really the area's main attraction. That distinction goes to the **Rogue River,** which empties into the Pacific here at the town of Gold Beach. This is the most famous fishing and rafting river in the state. You can tour the river in powerful hydrojet boats that use water jets instead of propellers and have a very shallow draft, which allows them to cross rapids and riffles only a few inches deep. Along the way you may see deer, black bear, river otters, and bald eagles. A running narration covers the river's colorful history. Three different trips are available, ranging in length from 64 to 104 miles. Two companies operate these trips. **Rogue River Mail Boat Trips** (ℂ **800/458-3511** or 541/247-7033; www.mailboat.com) leaves from a dock a quarter mile upriver from the north end of the Rogue River Bridge. **Jerry's Rogue Jets** (ℂ **800/451-3645** or 541/247-4571) leaves from the Port of Gold Beach on the south side of the Rogue River Bridge. Fares range from $30 to $75 for adults and $12 to $35 for children.

Fighting salmon and steelhead are what have made the Rogue River famous, and if you'd like to hire a guide to take you to the best **fishing** holes, you have plenty of options. Some guides to check out include **Rogue River Outfitters** (Craig Hughson) (ℂ **541/451-4498**) and **Russell McCall Guide Service** (ℂ **541/247-2061**). Or call the fishing and referral line at Curry Guides Association (ℂ **800/775-0886** or 541/247-3476; www.curryguides.com). A full day will cost around $150 per person. Clamming and crabbing can also be quite productive around Gold Beach.

Jerry's Rogue River Museum (ℂ 541/247-4571), at the Port of Gold Beach and affiliated with Jerry's Jet Boat Tours, is the more modern and informative of the town's two museums. It focuses on the geology and cultural and natural history of the Rogue River. It's open daily in summer from 8am to 9pm and daily in the off season from about 9am to 6pm; admission is free. At the diminutive **Curry County Historical Museum,** 29410 Ellensburg Ave. (© **541/247-6113**), you can learn more about the history of the area and see plenty of Native American and pioneer artifacts. The museum is open June through September, Tuesday through Saturday from noon to 4pm; the rest of the year, on Saturday from noon to 4pm. Admission is by donation.

Golfers can play a round at **Cedar Bend Golf Course,** 34391 Squaw Valley Rd. (© **541/247-6911**), 12 miles north of Gold Beach off U.S. 101. If you'd like to go horseback riding, contact **Hawk's Rest Ranch** (© **541/247-6423**) in Pistol River, 10 miles south of Gold Beach. Expect to pay between $20 and $45 for a 1- to 2-hour ride.

Hikers have an abundance of options. At the **Schrader Old-Growth Trail,** 10 miles up Jerry's Flat Road/South Bank Rogue Road near the Lobster Creek Campground, you can hike through an ancient forest and see for yourself the type of majestic trees that so many people in the Northwest are fighting to save. In this same area, you'll also find the **Myrtle Tree Trail.** Along this short trail, you'll find the world's largest myrtle tree, which is 88 feet tall and 42 feet in circumference. For more information on hiking in the Gold Beach area, contact the **Siskiyou National Forest,** Gold Beach Ranger District, 29279 Ellensburg Ave., Gold Beach, OR 97444 (© **541/247-3600;** www.fs.fed.us/r6/siskiyou).

THE ROGUE COAST

Gold Beach itself is a wide sandy beach, but just a few miles to the south, the mountains once again march into the sea, creating what many say is Oregon's single most spectacular section of coastline. Though it's only 30 miles from Gold Beach to **Brookings,** you can easily spend the whole day making the trip. Along the way are numerous viewpoints, picnic areas, hiking trails, and beaches.

The **Oregon Coast Trail,** which extends (in short sections) from California to Washington, has several segments both north and south of Gold Beach. The most spectacular sections of this trail are south of town at Cape Sebastian and in Samuel H. Boardman State Scenic Corridor.

The first place you'll come to as you drive south from Gold Beach is **Turtle Rock Wayside,** just south of town. Although this is little more than a roadside pull-off, it does have a nice view. The next place to stop is at **Cape Sebastian** ★★, which is 5 miles south of Gold Beach. This headland towers 700 feet above the ocean and between December and March is a good vantage point for whale-watching. A 2-mile trail leads from the parking area out to the end of the cape, and continues down to the beach at Hunter's Cove. This little visited spot is one of the best places on the south coast for a hike.

Another 2 miles south on U.S. 101, you come to **Meyers Creek** ★★, which is at the **Pistol River State Scenic Viewpoint.** Here you can get a closer look at some of the rugged monolithic rock formations scattered on the beach that make this coastline so breathtaking. This is the most popular windsurfing and surfing beach on the south coast and is also a good clamming beach. About 2 miles farther south, you'll come to the sand dunes at the mouth of Pistol River.

South of Pistol River you enter the **Samuel H. Boardman State Scenic Corridor,** which has numerous viewpoints, **beaches** ★, picnic areas, and stretches of hiking trail. About 6 miles south of the Pistol River, you come to **Arch Rock Viewpoint** ★, a picnic area with a stunning view of an offshore monolith that has been carved into an arch by the action of the waves. Two miles beyond this, you come to the **Natural Bridge Viewpoint.** These two arches were formed when a sea cave collapsed. In 2 more miles you cross the

Thomas Creek Bridge, which at 345 feet high is the highest bridge in Oregon. In a little more than a mile, you come to **Whalehead Beach Viewpoint,** where a pyramidal rock just offshore bears a striking resemblance to a spy-hopping whale. There's a better view of Whalehead Rock half a mile south.

In another 1½ miles you'll come to **House Rock Viewpoint,** which offers sweeping vistas to the north and south. At **Cape Ferrelo Viewpoint** and **Lone Ranch Viewpoint** just to the south, you'll find a grassy headland. Just south of here, watch for the **Rainbow Rock Viewpoint,** which has a panorama of a stretch of beach strewn with large boulders. Three more miles brings you to **Harris Beach State Park** (✆ **541/469-2021**), the last stop along this coast. Here you'll find picnicking and camping and a good view of **Goat Island,** which is the Oregon coast's largest island.

WHERE TO STAY

Inn at Nesika Beach ⍟   Located 5½ miles north of Gold Beach, this modern Victorian-style inn is set on a bluff above the beach and has expansive ocean views from its many windows. All four guest rooms have whirlpool tubs and feather beds, making this one of the coziest and most romantic lodgings on the south coast. Three of the guest rooms also have gas fireplaces, and two have private decks. Hardwood floors throughout the three-story inn provide a classic feel. Guests are served a sumptuous, large breakfast each morning.

33026 Nesika Rd., Gold Beach, OR 97444. ✆ **541/247-6434.** www.moriah.com/nesika. 4 units. $125–$160 double. Rates include full breakfast. No credit cards. *In room:* No phone.

Ireland's Rustic Lodges ⍟ *Finds*   The name sums it all up—rustic cabins set amid shady grounds that are as green as Ireland (and beautifully landscaped, too). Though there are some modern motel rooms here, they just can't compare to the quaint old cabins, which have stone fireplaces, paneled walls, and unusual door handles made from twisted branches. Built in 1922, the cabins are indeed rustic and are not for those who need modern comforts. The mature gardens surrounding the cabins are beautiful any time of year but particularly in late spring.

29330 Ellensburg Ave. (P.O. Box 774), Gold Beach, OR 97444. ✆ **541/247-7718.** Fax 541/247-0225. www. irelandsrusticlodges.com. 40 units (including 9 cottages and 3 houses). $55–$95 double. Lower rates off-season. AE, DISC, MC, V. Pets accepted. *In room:* TV.

Jot's Resort ⍟⍟ *Kids*   Stretching along the north bank of the Rogue River, Jot's has a definite fishing orientation and is very popular with families. The resort offers a wide variety of room sizes and rates, but every room has a view of the water and the Rogue River Bridge. The deluxe rooms are the most attractively furnished, while the condos are the most spacious (some have spiral staircases that lead up to loft sleeping areas). The dining room and lounge offer reasonably priced meals. Fishing guides and deep-sea charters can be arranged, and there is a boat dock and marina if you happen to have your own boat with you.

94360 Waterfront Loop (P.O. Box 1200), Gold Beach, OR 97444. ✆ **800/367-5687** or 541/247-6676. Fax 541/ 247-6716. www.jotsresort.com. 140 units. Summer $85–$95 double; $135–$325 suite/condo. Off-season $50–$75 double; $100–$225 suite/condo. AE, DC, DISC, MC, V. Pets accepted ($10 per night). **Amenities:** Restaurant (American), lounge; indoor and outdoor pools; exercise room; Jacuzzi; sauna; fishing-boat rentals; activities desk; business center; babysitting; coin-op laundry. *In room:* TV, dataport, coffeemaker, hair dryer, iron.

Tu Tu Tun Lodge ⍟⍟⍟   Tu Tu Tun Lodge, located 7 miles up the Rogue River from Gold Beach, is the most luxurious lodging on the south coast, and it can hold its own against any luxury lodge in the country. In fact, Tu Tu Tun has developed a national reputation for its sophisticated styling and its idyllic setting. The main lodge building incorporates enough rock and natural wood to give it a rustic feel without sacrificing any modern comforts, and the immense fireplace in the lounge is the center of activity. On warm days, the patio overlooking the river is a great spot for relaxing and sunning, and on cold nights logs crackle in a fire pit. The guest rooms are large and beautifully furnished with slate-topped tables and tile counters. Each room has a private patio or balcony, and should you get an upstairs room, you'll have a high ceiling and an excellent river view. Some rooms also come with fireplaces or outdoor soaking tubs. The dining room overlooks the river and serves four-course fixed-price dinners ($45.50) focusing on Northwest cuisine. For those heading out on the river, box lunches are available. Fishing guides and boat rentals can be arranged, and the lodge has its own dock.

96550 N. Bank Rogue Rd., Gold Beach, OR 97444. © **800/864-6357** or 541/247-6664. Fax 541/247-0672. www.tututun.com. 20 units (including 2 houses). $140–$235 double; $210–$260 suite; $235–$335 house. Lower rates in winter. DISC, MC, V. **Amenities:** Restaurant (Northwest), lounge; outdoor lap pool; 4-hole pitch-and-putt golf course; sea kayaks for guest use; game room; concierge; activities desk; 24-hr. room service; massage; babysitting; laundry service. *In room:* Dataport, fridge, hair dryer, iron.

CAMPGROUNDS

Up the Rogue River between Gold Beach and Agness, you'll find two campgrounds: **Lobster Creek** and **Quosatana.** A third, **Illahee,** is another 6 miles past Agness, though not on the river. At Foster Bar, above Agness, there is an unofficial campground right on the river.

WHERE TO DINE

The best meals in Gold Beach are served in the dining room at **Tu Tu Tun Lodge** (see "Where to Stay," above for details).

Nor'wester Seafood 🍴 SEAFOOD/STEAK   Simply prepared fresh seafood and large portions are the mainstay of the menu at this dockside restaurant, which has long been the best place in town. Fish-and-chips are good, and the steak-and-seafood combinations are popular choices for big appetites; but we prefer such dishes as pasta and shrimp with a tapenade sauce or salmon with a glaze made from sake, cayenne, ginger, and soy sauce. From the second-floor dining room, you can watch fishing boats on the Rogue River. The port is at the north end of town.

Port of Gold Beach. © **541/247-2333.** Reservations for 5 or more people only. Main courses $14–$23. AE, MC, V. Daily 5–9pm.

THE BROOKINGS AREA

The Chetco River is known throughout Oregon as one of the best salmon and steelhead rivers in the state. It is also one of the prettiest rivers and offers opportunities for swimming, rafting, and canoeing. One interesting way to experience the Chetco River is on a combination backpacking and paddling trip with **Wilderness Canyon Adventures** (© **888/517-1613** or 541/247-6924; www.wilderness-canyon-ex.com), which offers several different types of trips from a day of paddling to multiday paddling/hiking trips. Rates for a 1-day paddling trip range from $80 to $95. For information on hiking in the area, which includes the high country of the Kalmiopsis Wilderness, contact the **Chetco Ranger District,** 555 Fifth St., Brookings, OR 97415 (© **541/469-2196**).

If you want to head out to sea to do your fishing, contact **Tidewind Sportfishing** (© **800/799-0337** or 541/469-0337), which operates out of Harbor and offers both salmon- and bottom-fishing trips for $65 to $80 per person, as well as whale-watching excursions ($25 per person).

The area's botanical attractions are one of the most interesting reasons to pay a visit to the Brookings area. Not far from town, you can see old-growth myrtle trees (from which the ubiquitous myrtlewood souvenirs of the south coast are made) at **Alfred A. Loeb State Park,** 8 miles up the Chetco River from Brookings on North Bank Road. Myrtle (*Umbellularia californica*) occurs naturally only along the southern Oregon and Northern California coasts. The Brookings area is the northernmost range of the giant coast redwoods (*Sequoia sempervirens*), and just beyond Loeb State Park, you'll come to one of the largest stands of coast redwoods in Oregon. Here, the 1.2-mile **Redwood Nature Trail** loops past numerous big trees. This nature trail is connected to Loeb State Park via the three-quarter-mile Riverview Trail. The region's wild azaleas, celebrated each year over Memorial Day weekend, come into bloom in May. The best place to see them is at **Azalea Park** near the south end of Brookings.

To learn the history of the area, drop by the **Chetco Valley Historical Museum,** 15461 U.S. 101 S. (© **541/469-6651**), which is located south of town just off the highway. The museum is in the oldest standing house in the area (built in 1857), and out front is the nation's largest Monterey cypress tree. The museum is open from mid-March to October, Thursday through Sunday from noon to 4pm, and admission is $1.

One of the more unusual places to visit in the area is the **Brandy Peak Distillery,** Tetley Road (© **541/469-0194**), which is located north of Brookings off U.S. 101. (Take Carpenterville Rd. for several miles up into the hills and then go right on Tetley Rd. and immediately right into the distillery.) This microdistillery produces varietal marc brandies (unaged brandies), as well as barrel-aged brandies, grappas, and pear brandy. All are produced in small wood-fired pot stills. The distillery is open for tours and tastings Tuesday through Saturday from 1 to 5pm between March and early January and by appointment the rest of the year. If you want to be absolutely sure you'll find someone in, call before you come.

WHERE TO STAY

Best Western Beachfront Inn ⋆   On the edge of the modern marina in Brooking's sister town of Harbor (on the south side of the Chetco River), the Beachfront Inn is the only oceanfront accommodation in this area. Most rooms are fairly large and all have ocean views, balconies, microwaves, and refrigerators. The more expensive rooms also have whirlpool tubs with picture windows over them. There is an outdoor pool and a whirlpool.

16008 Boat Basin Rd. (P.O. Box 2729), Harbor, OR 97415. © **800/468-4081** or 541/469-7779. Fax 541/469-0283. 102 units. $84–$170 double. AE, DC, DISC, MC, V. Pets accepted. **Amenities:** Outdoor pool; access to nearby health club; Jacuzzi. *In room:* TV, fridge, coffeemaker.

Chetco River Inn & Lavender Bee Farm ⋆⋆ *Finds*   Set on 35 very secluded acres on the banks of the Chetco River, this contemporary B&B caters to nature lovers and anglers and makes a great weekend retreat. However, in order to get away, you'll first have to find the lodge, which is 17 miles from town up North Bank Road (the last bit on gravel). The lodge makes use of alternative energy, yet is luxurious and filled with antiques. The Siskiyou National Forest surrounds the property, and hiking, swimming (there are lots of great swimming holes), and stargazing are popular pastimes. If you don't feel like leaving the woods, you can arrange to have meals at the lodge.

21202 High Prairie Rd., Brookings, OR 97415. © **541/670-1645** or 800/327-2688 (Mon–Fri 9am–5pm). www.chetcoriverinn.com. 6 units (including 1 cottage). $125–$145 double. Rates include full breakfast. MC, V. **Amenities:** Massage. *In room:* No phone.

South Coast Inn Bed & Breakfast 🌟🌟   This 1917 craftsman bungalow was designed by the famous San Francisco architect Bernard Maybeck and is filled with the sort of beautiful architectural details that characterized the Arts and Crafts movement. The inn's most spacious guest room is dedicated to Maybeck. Two of the guest rooms have good views, and the cottage, across the garden from the main house, offers a more private setting. Guests have use of a large living room full of antiques (including an old grand piano), where a fire often crackles in the stone fireplace, although the weather never gets very cold.

516 Redwood St., Brookings, OR 97415. ℂ **800/525-9273** or 541/469-5557. Fax 541/469-6615. www. southcoastinn.com. 5 units (including 1 cottage). $89–$109 double. Rates include full breakfast. AE, DISC, MC, V. **Amenities:** Exercise room; Jacuzzi; sauna; concierge. *In room:* A/C, TV/VCR, dataport, hair dryer, iron.

CAMPGROUNDS

The best base for exploring the scenic wonders of Samuel H. Boardman State Scenic Corridor is **Harris Beach State Park,** on the beach just north of Brookings. Up the North Bank Chetco River Road out of Brookings, you'll find **Loeb State Park,** which is set amid redwood and myrtle trees along the banks of the beautiful Chetco River. A bit farther up the Chetco is the Forest Service's **Little Redwood Campground,** which is the site of a very popular swimming hole.

WHERE TO DINE

If it's pizza you're craving, **Wild River Pizza Company,** 16279 U.S. 101 S., just south of Brookings (ℂ **541/469-7454**), turns out a crispy one, accompanied by their own microbrews. For smoked salmon, head south of town to **The Great American Smokehouse & Seafood Co.,** 15657 U.S. 101 S. (ℂ **541/469-6903**), which sells a wide variety of smoked and canned seafood and also has a sit-down restaurant. Locals swear by **The Hungry Clam,** at the Port of Brookings-Harbor (ℂ **541/469-2526**), for fish-and-chips.

Chive's 🌟🌟 NORTHWEST   If you've just reached Oregon from California and are looking for your first bite of Northwest cuisine, this gem of a restaurant is a great place to stop. Leaded glass and art by local artists on the walls make it a bit upscale for Brookings, but you can still show up in jeans and a T-shirt to try the salad with pear, endive, and watercress dressed with goat cheese and walnuts; roast breast of pheasant with soft polenta; or crisp salmon cakes with lemon-caper beurre blanc. Dishes are artistically presented, and there are always interesting daily specials. Dessert is a high point of a meal here in more ways than one; such dishes as a sabayon (zabaglione) with marsala wine or a bread pudding with a Jack Daniel's sauce shouldn't be served to minors. There's also a good selection of reasonably priced wines.

1025 Chetco Ave. ℂ **541/469-4121.** Reservations recommended. Main courses $14–$22. MC, V. Feb–Dec Wed–Sun 5–9pm.

7

The Columbia Gorge

The Columbia Gorge, which begins just a few miles east of Portland and stretches for nearly 70 miles along shores of the Columbia River, is a dramatic landscape of mountains, cliffs, and waterfalls created by massive floods. Flanked by national forests and snow-covered peaks on both the Oregon and Washington sides of the Columbia River, the Gorge is as breathtaking a landscape as you will find anywhere in the West. The fascinating geology, dramatic vistas, and abundance of recreational opportunities make it a premier vacation destination almost any month of the year. Not only are there waterfalls, trails, and some of the world's best windsurfing, but there are also fascinating museums, resort hotels, historic B&Bs, and even wineries. Between 1913 and 1922, a scenic highway (one of the first paved roads in the Northwest) was built through the Gorge, and in 1986 much of the area was designated the Columbia Gorge National Scenic Area in an attempt to preserve the gorge's spectacular and unique natural beauty.

The Columbia River is older than the hills. It's older than the mountains, too, and this explains why this river flows not from the mountains but through them. Although the river's geologic history dates back 40 million years or so, it was a series of recent events, geologically speaking, that gave the Columbia Gorge its very distinctive appearance. About 15,000 years ago, toward the end of the last Ice Age, huge dams of ice far upstream

collapsed and sent floodwaters racing down the Columbia. As the floodwaters swept through the Columbia Gorge, they were as much as 1,200 feet high. Ice and rock carried by the floodwaters helped the river to scour out the sides of the once gently sloping valley, leaving behind the steepwalled gorge that we know today. The waterfalls that elicit so many oohs and aahs are the most dramatic evidence of these great floods.

The vast gorge that the Columbia River has formed as it slices through the mountains is a giant bridge between the rain-soaked forests west of the Cascades and the desert-dry sagebrush scrublands of central Oregon. This change in climate is caused by moist air condensing into snow and rain as it passes over the crest of the Cascades. Most of the air's moisture falls on the western slopes, so the eastern slopes and the land stretching for hundreds of miles beyond lie in a rain shadow. Perhaps nowhere else on earth can you so easily witness this rain-shadow effect. It's so pronounced that as you come around a bend on I-84 just east of Hood River, you can see dry grasslands to the east and dense forests of Douglas fir over your shoulder to the west. In between the two extremes lies a community of plants that's unique to the Columbia Gorge, and springtime here brings colorful displays of wildflowers.

In North America, the Columbia River is second only to the Mississippi in the volume of water it carries to the sea, but more than just water flows through the Columbia Gorge. As the only break over the entire length of the Cascade Range, the Gorge acts as a massive natural wind tunnel. During the summer, the sun bakes the lands east of the Cascades, causing the air to rise. Cool air from the west side then rushes up the river, whipping through Hood River with near gale force at times. These winds, blowing against the downriver flow of water, set up ideal conditions for windsurfing on the Columbia. The reliability of the winds, and the waves they kick up, has turned Hood River, once an ailing lumber town, into the Aspen of windsurfing.

For centuries the Columbia River has been an important route between the maritime Northwest and the dry interior. Lewis and Clark canoed down the river in 1805, and pioneers followed the Oregon Trail to its shores at The Dalles. It was here at The Dalles that many pioneers transferred their wagons to boats for the dangerous journey downriver to Oregon City. The set of rapids known as The Dalles and the waterfalls of the Cascades were the two most dangerous sections of the Columbia Gorge, so towns arose at these two points to transport goods and people around the treacherous waters. Locks and a canal helped circumvent the two sections of white water, but today the rapids of the Columbia lie flooded beneath the waters behind the Bonneville and The Dalles Dams. The ease of navigating the river today has dimmed the importance of the Cascade Locks and The Dalles, two river towns steeped in the history of the Gorge.

1 The Columbia Gorge National Scenic Area ✶✶✶

Columbia Gorge: Begins 18 miles E of Portland

Stretching from the Sandy River in the west to the Deschutes River in the east, the Columbia Gorge National Scenic Area is one of the most breathtakingly dramatic places in the United States. Carved by floods of unimaginable proportions and power, this miles-wide canyon is flanked on the north by Mount Adams and on the south by Mount Hood, both of which rise more than 11,000 feet high. With its diaphanous waterfalls, basalt cliffs painted with colorful lichens, and dark forests of Douglas firs rising up from the banks of the Columbia River, the Gorge is a year-round recreational area where hiking trails lead to hidden waterfalls and mountain-top panoramas, mountain-bike trails meander through the forest, and windsurfers race across wind-whipped waters.

The Columbia Gorge National Scenic Area is also as controversial as it is beautiful. Over the years since this area received this federal designation, the fights over the use of private land within the Gorge have been constant. The pressure to develop this scenic marvel of the Northwest has been unrelenting, as land owners throughout the Gorge have fought against restrictions on development. To find out more about protecting the Gorge, contact the **Friends of the Columbia Gorge** (© 503/241-3762; www.gorgefriends.org), which, each spring, offers numerous guided wildflower hikes.

ESSENTIALS

GETTING THERE   I-84 and the Historic Columbia River Highway both pass through the Gorge on the Oregon side of the Columbia.

VISITOR INFORMATION   Contact the **Columbia River Gorge National Scenic Area,** 902 Wasco Ave., Suite 200, Hood River, OR 97031 (© 541/386-2333; www.fs.fed.us/r6/columbia). There's also a **Forest Service Information**

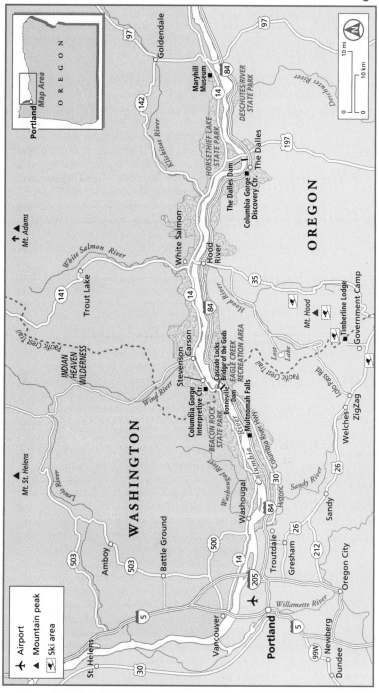

Center (© 503/695-2372) at Multnomah Falls Lodge (take the Historic Columbia River Hwy. or the Multnomah Falls exit off I-84) and another in the lobby of **Skamania Lodge,** 1131 SW Skamania Lodge Dr. (© **509/427-2528**), in Stevenson, Washington.

LEARNING ABOUT THE GORGE & ITS HISTORY

Columbia Gorge Interpretive Center 𝔸𝔸   Focusing on the Gorge's early Native American inhabitants and the development of the area by white settlers, this museum is the best introduction to the Columbia Gorge. Exhibits contain historical photographs by Edward Curtis and other photos that illustrate the story of portage companies and paddlewheelers that once operated along this stretch of the Columbia River. A relic you can't miss is a 37-foot-high replica of a 19th-century fish wheel, which gives an understanding of how salmon runs have been threatened in the past and the present. Displays also frankly discuss other problems that the coming of civilization brought to this area. A slide program tells the history of the formation of the Gorge, and when the volcanoes erupt, the floor in the theater actually shakes from the intensity of the low-volume sound track. When it's not cloudy, the center has an awesome view of the south side of the Gorge.

990 SW Rock Creek Dr., Stevenson. © 509/427-8211. www.columbiagorge.org. Admission $6 adults, $5 seniors and students, $4 children 6–12, free for children 5 and under. Daily 10am–5pm. Closed Thanksgiving, Christmas, and New Year's Day.

A DRIVING TOUR

Though I-84 is the fastest road through the Columbia Gorge, it is not the most scenic route. The Gorge is well worth a full day's exploration and is best appreci-ated at a more leisurely pace on the **Historic Columbia River Highway** 𝔸𝔸, which begins 16 miles east of downtown Portland at the second Troutdale exit off I-84. Opened in 1915, this highway was a marvel of engineering at the time and, by providing access to automobiles, opened the Gorge to casual visits.

At the western end of the historic highway, you'll find **Lewis & Clark State Park,** which is near the mouth of the Sandy River. This park is popular with anglers and Portlanders looking to cool off in the Sandy River during the hot summer months. There is also a rock-climbing area within the park.

The first unforgettable view of the Gorge comes at the **Portland Women's Forum State Scenic Viewpoint,** which may also be your first encounter with the legendary Columbia Gorge winds. To learn more about the historic highway and how it was built, stop at the nearby **Vista House** (© **503/695-2230;** www.vistahouse.com), 733 feet above the river on **Crown Point.** Inside this historic 1916 building, which underwent renovations in 2001, there are inform-ative displays, including old photos. However, most visitors can't concentrate on the exhibits, preferring to gaze at the some 30 miles of breathtaking views.

From Crown Point, the historic highway drops down into the Gorge and passes several picturesque **waterfalls.** The first of these is 249-foot **Latourell Falls** 𝔸, a diaphanous wisp of a waterfall cascading over basalt cliffs stained lime-green by lichen. A 2¼-mile loop trail leads from this waterfall up to the smaller Upper Latourell Falls. East of these falls, you'll come to Shepherd's Dell Falls, Bridalveil Fall, Mist Falls, and Wahkeena Falls, all of which are either right beside the road or a short walk away. If you're interested in a longer hike, there are trails linking several of the falls. However, for spectacular views, you can't beat the steep 4.4-mile round-trip hike to Angels Rest. The well-signposted trail head for this hike is on the historic highway near the community of Bridal Veil.

Multnomah Falls 🎯🎯🎯 is the largest and the most famous waterfall along this highway, and the state's most visited natural attraction. At 620 feet from the lip to the lower pool, it's the tallest waterfall in Oregon and the fourth tallest in the United States. An arched bridge stands directly in front of the falls part way up. This bridge is part of a steep paved trail that leads from the foot of the falls up to the top. From the top of the falls, other trails lead off into the **Mount Hood National Forest.** The historic Multnomah Falls Lodge has a restaurant, snack bar, and gift shop, as well as a **National Forest Interpretive Center** (📞 **503/695-2372**) with information on the geology, history, and natural history of the Gorge.

East of Multnomah Falls, the scenic highway passes by **Oneonta Gorge** 🎯🎯, a narrow rift in the cliffs. Through this tiny gorge flows a stream that serves as a pathway for anyone interested in exploring upstream to **Oneonta Falls.** Less than a half mile east of Oneonta Gorge, you'll come to **Horsetail Falls.** From these roadside falls, a trail leads uphill to Upper Horsetail Falls. The trail then passes behind the upper falls and continues another 2 miles to Triple Falls, passing above Oneonta Gorge along the way.

If you'd like to escape the crowds and see a little visited waterfall, watch for Frontage Road on your right just before the historic highway merges with I-84. Drive east for 2 miles to a gravel parking area at the trail head for **Elowah Falls** 🎯🎯. These 289-foot-tall falls are set in a beautiful natural amphitheater less than a mile from the road. Just be aware that this parking area is subject to car break-ins; don't leave any valuables in your car.

Just after the two highways merge, you come to the exit for **Bonneville Lock and Dam** (📞 **541/374-8820**). The **Bradford Island Visitors Center** has exhibits on the history of this dam, which was built in 1927. One of the most important features of the dam is its fish ladder, which allows adult salmon to return upriver to spawn. Underwater windows let visitors see fish as they pass through the ladder. Visit the adjacent **Bonneville Fish Hatchery** to see how trout, salmon, and sturgeon are raised before being released into the river. A **Sturgeon Viewing Center** 🎯🎯 allows you to marvel at several immense sturgeons through an underwater viewing window. At this same exit off I-84 (and at Eagle Creek), you'll find access to a section of the **Historic Columbia River Highway State Trail,** a paved multi-use trail that connects the town of Cascade Locks with Bonneville Dam. This trail incorporates abandoned sections of the Historic Columbia River Highway and is open to hikers and bikers. Near the trail head for this trail you'll also find the trail head for **Wahclella Falls** 🎯, a little-visited, yet very picturesque waterfall tucked back in a side canyon. The trail is less than a mile and is relatively flat.

Beyond the dam is Eagle Creek, the single best spot in the Gorge for a hike. The **Eagle Creek Trail** 🎯🎯 leads past several waterfalls, and if you have time for only one hike in the Gorge, it should be this one. You'll also find a campground and picnic area here.

Not far beyond Eagle Creek is the **Bridge of the Gods,** which connects Oregon and Washington at the site where, according to a Native American legend, once stood a natural bridge used by the gods. Geologists now believe that the legend is based in fact; there is evidence that a massive rock slide may have once blocked the river at this point.

Just beyond the Bridge of the Gods is **Cascade Locks.** It was at this site that cascades once turned the otherwise placid Columbia River into a raging torrent that required boats to be portaged a short distance downriver. The Cascade

Locks were built in 1896 and allowed steamships to pass unhindered. The locks made traveling between The Dalles and Portland much easier, but the completion of the Columbia River Scenic Highway in 1915 made the trip even easier by land. With the construction of the Bonneville Lock and Dam, the cascades were flooded, and the locks became superfluous.

There are two small museums here at the locks. The **Cascade Locks Historical Museum,** Port Marina Park (© **541/374-8535**), which is housed in the old lock tender's house, includes displays of Native American artifacts and pioneer memorabilia, as well as the Northwest's first steam engine. The museum is open May through September, Monday through Friday from noon to 6pm and Saturday and Sunday from 10am to 6pm. Admission is by donation.

The **Port of Cascade Locks Visitors Center,** which has displays on river travel in the past, is also the ticket office for the **Sternwheeler** *Columbia Gorge* ★★ (© **541/374-8427** or 503/223-3928), which makes regular trips on the river all summer. These cruises provide a great perspective on the Gorge. Fares for the 2-hour scenic cruises are $14.95 for adults and $8.95 for children; dinner, lunch, breakfast, brunch, and other special cruises run $32.95 to $54.95 for adults and $19.95 to $36.95 for children.

Should you decide not to take the historic highway and stay on I-84, you may want to stop at **Rooster Rock State Park,** especially if it's a hot summer day. This park has a long sandy beach, and in a remote section of the park there's even a clothing-optional beach. From I-84 there's also easy access to Multnomah Falls, the main attraction of the Historic Columbia River Highway.

Another option is to cross to the Washington side of the Columbia River and take Wash. 14 east from Vancouver. This latter highway actually provides the most spectacular views of both the Columbia Gorge and Mount Hood. If you should decide to take this route, be sure to stop at **Beacon Rock State Park** ★★ (© **509/427-8265**), which has as its centerpiece an 800-foot-tall monolith that has a trail (mostly stairways and catwalks) leading to its summit. At one time there was talk of blasting the rock apart to build jetties at the mouth of the river. Luckily, another source of rock was used, and this amazing landmark continues to guard the Columbia. If you want to make better time, you can cross back to Oregon on the Bridge of the Gods. Continuing east on the Washington side of the river, you'll come to Stevenson, site of the above-mentioned Columbia Gorge Interpretive Center.

Beyond Stevenson, you come to the town of Carson, where you can avail yourself of the therapeutic waters of the **Carson Hot Springs Resort** (© **800/607-3678** or 509/427-8292), located just north of town. It's open daily from 7:30am to 7:30pm; charges are $12 for a soak that includes a postsoak wrap and $55 for an hour's massage. The resort has been in business since 1897 and looks every bit its age. However, it's just this old-fashioned appeal that keeps people coming back year after year. Some very basic hotel rooms ($35–$45) and cabins ($45–$60) are also available. If you're looking for natural hot springs, the folks here can give you directions to some that are nearby.

WINDSURFING & OTHER ACTIVITIES

If you want to launch your sailboard along this stretch of the Gorge, try **Rooster Rock State Park,** near the west end of the Gorge, or **Viento State Park,** just west of Hood River. Both parks are right off I-84 and are well marked.

If you're interested in hiring a fishing guide, contact **Page's Northwest Guide Service** (© **866/760-3370** or 503/760-3373; www.fishinoregon.net), which will take you out for salmon, steelhead, walleye, and sturgeon on the Columbia or Willamette Rivers, on Nehalem or Tillamook Bays or on other area waters ($135 per person, per day). **Reel Adventures** (© **877/544-REEL** or 503/ 622-5372; www.donsreeladventures.com) offers a similar fishing-guide service ($150 per person, per day).

Prefer to be on dry land? You can go horseback riding at **Mountain Shadow Ranch,** 690 Herman Creek Rd. (© **541/374-8592**), which is located on the outskirts of Cascade Locks. Expect to pay $30 for a 1-hour ride and $55 for a 2-hour ride. Reservations are required.

WHERE TO STAY

Best Western Columbia River Inn ⋆   At the foot of the Bridge of the Gods—ideal for exploring the Gorge—this modern motel has splendid views from its river-view rooms. Many of the rooms also have small balconies, although nearby railroad tracks can make them a bit noisy. Luckily, rooms are well insulated against train noises. For a splurge, try a spa room.

735 WaNaPa St. (P.O. Box 580), Cascade Locks, OR 97014. © **800/595-7108** or 541/374-8777. Fax 541/ 374-2279. www.gorge.net/cri. 63 units. $64–$124 double. Rates include continental breakfast. AE, DC, DISC, MC, V. Pets accepted ($10 fee). **Amenities:** Indoor pool; exercise room; Jacuzzi; coin-op laundry. *In room:* A/C, TV, dataport, fridge, coffeemaker, hair dryer, iron.

Dolce Skamania Lodge ⋆⋆⋆   Boasting the most spectacular vistas of any hotel in the Gorge, Skamania Lodge is also the only golf resort around. However, it is also well situated whether you brought your sailboard, hiking boots, or mountain bike. The interior decor is classically rustic with lots of rock and natural wood, and throughout the hotel there are Northwest Indian art and artifacts on display. Huge windows in the lobby have superb views of the Gorge. Of course, the riverview guest rooms are more expensive than the forestview rooms (which overlook more parking lot than forest), but these rooms are well worth the extra cost. There are also rooms with fireplaces available. At press time, the lodge was planning to add 59 new rooms.

P.O. Box 189, Stevenson, WA 98648. © **800/221-7117** or 509/427-7700. www.dolce.com/skamania. 253 units. $169–$199 double; $239–$385 suite (lower rates in winter). AE, DC, DISC, MC, V. **Amenities:** Restaurant (Northwest); lounge; indoor pool; 18-hole golf course; 2 tennis courts; exercise room; Jacuzzi; sauna; bike rentals; children's programs; activities desk; business center; room service; massage; babysitting; laundry service. *In room:* A/C, TV, dataport, minibar, coffeemaker, hair dryer, iron.

McMenamins Edgefield ⋆ *Finds*   B&Bs don't usually have more than 100 rooms, but this is no ordinary inn. Ideally situated for exploring the Columbia Gorge and Mount Hood, this flagship of the McMenamin microbrewery empire is the former Multnomah County poor farm. Today, the property includes not only tastefully decorated guest rooms with antique furnishings, but a brewery, a pub, a beer garden, a restaurant, a movie theater, a winery, a wine-tasting room, a distillery, a golf course, a cigar bar in an old shed, and extensive gardens. With so much in one spot, this makes a great base for exploring the area. The beautiful grounds give this inn the feel of a remote retreat, though you are still within a 30 miles of Portland.

2126 SW Halsey St., Troutdale, OR 97060. © **800/669-8610** or 503/669-8610. Fax 5-3/492-7750. www. mcmenamins.com. 114 units (101 with shared bathroom), 24 hostel beds. $85–$105 double with shared bathroom; $115–$130 double with private bathroom; $20 hostel bed per person. Rates include full breakfast (not included with hostel). AE, DISC, MC, V. **Amenities:** 3 restaurants (Northwest, American), 6 lounges; 18-hole par-3 golf course; exercise room and access to nearby health club; Jacuzzi; sauna; business center; massage. *In room:* No phone.

CAMPGROUNDS

Camping in the Gorge isn't quite the wonderful experience you might think. With an interstate highway and a very active railway line paralleling the river on the Oregon side and another railroad and a secondary highway on the Washington side, the Gorge tends to be quite noisy. However, there are a few camping options between Portland and Hood River, and these campgrounds do what they can to minimize the traffic noises. **Ainsworth State Park,** 3½ miles east of Multnomah Falls, has showers, and the RV sites are quite nice. At exit 41 off I-84, there is **Eagle Creek Campground,** the oldest campground in the National Forest system and popular for its access to the Eagle Creek Trail. In Cascade Locks you'll find the **Cascade Locks Marina Park,** a campground that is little more than a lawn with some picnic tables. At exit 51 off of I-84, there is **Wyeth Campground,** a U.S. Forest Service campground on the bank of Gordon Creek. Over on the Washington side of the Columbia River, there is also first-come, first-served camping at **Beacon Rock State Park,** which is located 7 miles west of the Bridge of the Gods. Because it is tucked back away from the highway and railroad tracks, this is just about the quietest campground in the gorge.

WHERE TO DINE

The area's best place to eat is the dining room of the Skamania Lodge (see above).

Black Rabbit Restaurant ★★ NORTHWEST/REGIONAL AMERICAN This casual-yet-upscale restaurant is located on the grounds of the McMenamins Edgefield (reviewed above). It is the ideal place to stop for dinner on the way back to Portland after a day of exploring the Gorge. Start with the crab cakes or calamari (perhaps accompanied by a glass of Edgefield wine) and then move on to the seared ahi tuna with smoked chili-mango relish or braised lamb shanks cooked in honey and red wine. If you aren't in the mood for a formal dinner, there is also a less expensive and less formal brewpub here.

McMenamins Edgefield, 2126 SW Halsey St., Troutdale. ⓒ 503/492-3086. Main courses $12.75–$19.50. AE, DISC, MC, V. Mon–Sat 7–11:15am, 11:30am–2:30pm, and 5–10pm; Sun 7am–1:15pm and 5–10pm.

Multnomah Falls Lodge ★ AMERICAN Built in 1925 at the foot of Multnomah Falls, the historic Multnomah Falls Lodge may be the most touristy place to eat in the entire Gorge, but the setting is excellent and the food isn't half bad. Breakfast, when the crowds haven't yet arrived, is one of the best times to eat here. Try the grilled salmon or trout and eggs. At dinner, stick with the prime rib or Yankee pot roast. For a peek at the falls, try to get a table in the conservatory room or, in summer, out on the patio.

50,000 Historic Columbia River Hwy. (or I-84, exit 31). ⓒ 503/695-2376. Main courses $10–$17. AE, DISC, MC, V. Daily 8am–9pm.

Tad's Chicken 'n Dumplins ★ (Finds AMERICAN Located on the banks of the Sandy River at the western end of the Historic Columbia Gorge Highway, this rustic restaurant has been in business more than 50 years and, as its name implies, specializes in all-American chicken and dumplings. Sure you can get a steak, pan-fried oysters, or salmon, but you'd be remiss if you passed up this opportunity to fill up on this restaurant's namesake dish. Try to get a seat on the enclosed back porch, which overlooks the river. If you're coming here after dark, just watch for the classic neon sign out front.

1325 E. Historic Columbia River Hwy., Troutdale. ⓒ 503/666-5337. Call ahead wait list recommended. Main courses $11–$22. AE, MC, V. Mon–Sat 5–11pm; Sun 2–10pm.

2 Hood River: The Windsurfing Capital of the Northwest

62 miles E of Portland, 20 miles W of The Dalles, 32 miles N of Government Camp

They used to curse the winds in Hood River. Each summer, hot air rising over the desert to the east sucks cool air up the Columbia River Gorge from the Pacific, and the winds howl through what is basically a natural wind tunnel. The winds are incessant and gusts can whip the river into a tumult of whitecaps.

But things change, and ever since the first person pulled into town with a sailboard, Hood River has taken to praying for wind. Hood River is now the windsurfing capital of America, which has given this once ailing lumber town a new lease on life. People come from all over the world to catch the "nuclear" winds that howl up the Gorge. In early summer the board-heads roll into town in their "Gorge-mobiles," the 1990s equivalent of surfers' woodies, and start listening to the wind reports. They flock to riverside parks on both the Oregon and Washington sides of the Columbia, unfurl their sails, zip up their wet suits, and launch themselves into the melee of hundreds of other like-minded souls shooting back and forth across a mile of windswept water. High waves whipped up by gale-force winds provide perfect launching pads for rocketing skyward. Aerial acrobatics such as flips and 360° turns are common sights. The latest rage is kiteboarding, which replaces the sail with a kite, and allows even more radical maneuvers and higher speeds than windsurfing. Even if you're not into this fast-paced sport, you'll get a vicarious thrill from watching the board-heads going for airtime.

Until recently, Hood River was pretty much a one-trick town, but sometimes the winds just aren't accommodating and even board-heads can get bored sitting on shore waiting for conditions to improve. The town has become something of an outdoor sports mecca, with a rapidly developing reputation for excellent mountain biking, white-water kayaking and rafting, paragliding, rock climbing, hiking, skiing, and snowboarding. In other words, Hood River is full of active people.

Hood River does not exist on sports alone, however; and outside town, in the Hood River Valley, are apple and pear orchards, wineries, and vineyards. Hood River also claims one of the best hotels in the state and several good restaurants. Most of the town's old Victorian and craftsman houses have been restored, giving Hood River a historic atmosphere to complement its lively windsurfing scene.

ESSENTIALS

GETTING THERE   Hood River is on I-84 at the junction with Ore. 35, which leads south to connect with U.S. 26 near the community of Government Camp.

Amtrak offers passenger-rail service to the town of Bingen, Washington, just across the Columbia River from Hood River. The station is at the foot of Walnut Street.

VISITOR INFORMATION   Contact the **Hood River County Chamber of Commerce,** 405 Portway Ave., Hood River, OR 97031 (© **800/366-3530** or 541/386-2000; www.hoodriver.org), near the river at exit 63 off I-84.

FESTIVALS   The Hood River Valley Blossom Festival is held in mid-April and celebrates the flowering of the valley's pear and apple trees. In mid-October the Hood River Valley Harvest Fest at the Hood River Expo Center and the Autumn Fest in Parkdale take place.

WINDSURFING & OTHER OUTDOOR ACTIVITIES ★★★

If you're here to ride the wind or just want to watch, head to the Columbia Gorge Sailpark at Hood River Marina, the nearby Event Site, or The Hook, all of which are accessible via exit 63 off I-84. Across the river in Washington, try the fish hatchery (The Hatchery), west of the mouth of the White Salmon River, or Swell City, a park about 4 miles west of the bridge. If you're a windsurfer, you'll find all kinds of windsurfing-related shops in downtown Hood River. Classes are available through the **Rhonda Smith Windsurfing School** (© 541/386-WIND; http://windsurf.gorge.net/rhondas) and **Gorge Wind Guide Service** (© 541/490-4401; www.windguide.com).

When there isn't enough wind for sailing, you can go rafting on the White Salmon River just across the bridge from Hood River. Companies offering raft trips include **Zoller's Outdoor Odysseys** (© 800/366-2004; www.zooraft.com) and **AAA Rafting** (© 800/866-RAFT or 509/493-2511). The river-rafting season runs March through October, and a half-day trip will cost around $60 per person.

Mountain biking is also very popular, and Hood River bike shops can direct you to some fun area rides. Check at **Discover Bicycles,** 205 Oak St. (© 541/386-4820), or **Mountain View Cycles,** 411 Oak St. (© 541/386-2453), both of which rent bikes. Expect to pay between $5 and $12 per hour and between $25 and $60 per day.

If fly-fishing is your passion, drop by the **Gorge Fly Shop,** 201 Oak St. (© 541/386-6977; www.gorgeflyshop.com), which can not only fill all your angling needs and point you to where the fish are biting, but also offer guided fly-fishing trips in the area.

Hikers have their choice of trails in Mount Hood National Forest (see "Mount Hood: Skiing, Hiking & Scenic Drives," in chapter 8), the Columbia Gorge (see earlier in this chapter), or across the river (head up Wash. 141 to Mt. Adams). At 12,276 feet in elevation, Mount Adams is the second-highest peak in Washington. For more information on hiking on Mount Adams, contact the **Gifford Pinchot National Forest,** Mt. Adams Ranger District, 2455 Wash. 141, Trout Lake, WA 98650 (© 509/395-3400).

THE FRUIT LOOP (EXPLORING THE HOOD RIVER VALLEY)

Before windsurfing took center stage, the Hood River Valley was known as one of Oregon's top fruit-growing regions, and today the valley is still Oregon's top apple and pear grower. From blossom time (Apr) to harvest season (Sept and Oct), the valley offers quiet country roads to explore. Along the way you'll find numerous farm stands, wineries, museums, and interesting shops that reflect the valley's rural heritage. Pick up a brochure called *Guide to Local Farm Stands/Fruit Loop Hood River County* at the Hood River County Chamber of Commerce visitor center (see "Visitor Information," above).

Be sure to start your tour of the Hood River Valley by stopping at **Panorama Point,** off of Ore. 35 just south of town (follow the signs). This hilltop park provides a splendid view of the valley's orchards with Mount Hood looming in the distance.

In the fall, fruit stands pop up along the roads around the valley. **Smiley's Red Barn,** Ore. 35 and Ehrck Hill Road (© 541/386-9121), and **Rasmussen Fruit & Flower Farm,** 3020 Thomsen Rd. (© 541/386-4622)—two of the biggest and best farm stands in the valley—are adjacent to one another off Ore. 35 about 6 miles south of Hood River. Also not to be missed is the nearby

River Bend Country Store, 2363 Tucker Rd. (© **541/386-8766**), where you can stock up on seasonal and organic produce and other homemade specialties. The 3-pound fruit pies here are legendary. You'll find the store west of Smiley's and Rasmussen's on the opposite side of the valley. Also in the valley are numerous orchards and farms where you can pick your own fruit. Keep an eye out for U-PICK signs.

The Hood River Valley also grows quite a few acres of wine grapes. You can visit several wineries in the area and taste the local fruit of the vine. West of town, off Country Club Road (take Oak St./Cascade St. west from downtown), you'll find two wineries. **Flerchinger Vineyards and Winery,** 4200 Post Canyon Dr. (© **541/386-2882**), produces a good Riesling as well as Pinot Gris, Chardonnay, Petit Syrah, and a Cabernet-Merlot blend. **Hood River Vineyards,** 4693 Westwood Dr. (© **541/386-3772**), makes excellent fruit wines, including a d'Anjou pear wine that tastes like a grape wine. They also produce an excellent Zinfandel port. Across the Columbia River in Washington, near the town of Husum (take Wash. 141 north from White Salmon), you'll find **Wind River Cellars,** 196 Spring Creek Rd., Husum (© **509/493-2324**), with a wide range of reds and whites.

The little hamlet of Parkdale, at the south end of the Fruit Loop, is home to the fascinating little **Hutson Museum,** 4967 Baseline Rd. (© **541/352-6808**), which houses lapidary, archaeology, and anthropology collections, of which the rock collection and exhibits of Native American artifacts are a highlight. The museum is open Wednesday through Friday from 11am to 2pm and Saturday and Sunday from 11am to 5:30pm. Also in Parkdale you'll find the **Elliot Glacier Public House,** 4945 Baseline Rd. (© **541/352-1022**), a brewpub with a great view of Mount Hood from the picnic tables out back.

Any time between late March and late December, but especially during fruit-blossom time, the **Mount Hood Railroad** (© **800/872-4661**) offers a great way to see the Hood River Valley. The diesel locomotives operated by this scenic railroad company depart from the historic 1911 Hood River depot and pull restored Pullman coaches on 4-hour excursions. The train winds its way up the valley to Parkdale, where you can get a snack at a cafe or visit the Hutson Museum. Fares are $22.95 for adults, $20.95 for seniors, and $14.95 for children 2 to 12. In July and August, the train runs daily except Monday. The schedule varies with the season, so call ahead to make a reservation. There are also regularly scheduled dinner, brunch, and other specialty excursions. Reservations are recommended.

OTHER ATTRACTIONS IN HOOD RIVER

Hood River County Historical Museum   Down by the river at Port Marina Park (take exit 63 off I-84), you'll find this small museum, with exhibits of Native American artifacts from this area. There are also displays on pioneer life, but many visitors find the museum's windsurfing exhibit most compelling.

Port Marina Park. © **541/386-6772.** Admission by donation. Apr–Aug Mon–Sat 10am–4pm, Sun noon–4pm; Sept–Oct daily noon–4pm.

International Museum of Carousel Art ★ *Kids*   Carousel fans won't want to miss this fun little museum. Although there isn't an actual working carousel on the premises, there are 135 carousel animals on display, which makes this the largest such collection in the country. The museum also houses a working 1917 Wurlitzer band organ and exhibits on various aspects of carousel history and art. The owners of the collection have assisted in the restoration of numerous historic carousels around the country.

304 Oak St. ℂ **541/387-4622**. www.carouselmuseum.com. Admission $5 adults, $4 seniors and students, $2 children under 10. Wed–Sun noon–4pm (shorter hours in winter).

SHOPPING

In downtown Hood River, drop in at the community-sponsored, nonprofit **Columbia Art Gallery**, 207 Second St. (ℂ **541/386-4512**). If you're an avid cook, you'll want to stop in at **Annz Panz,** 315 Oak St. (ℂ **541/387-2654**), a large and well-stocked cookware store with a cafe and espresso counter. The First Friday of each month, downtown galleries and shops are open from 5 to 8pm with local artists on hand to sell their work and demonstrate their skills. Between mid-May and mid-October, you can sample local produce at downtown **Hood River's Saturday Market** on Cascade Avenue between Fifth and Seventh streets between 9am and 3pm.

WHERE TO STAY

If you're looking for a bed-and-breakfast and those below are full, call **Roomfinder** (ℂ **541/386-6767;** www.moriah.com/hoodriverbba), a free service provided by the Hood River Bed & Breakfast Association.

Best Western Hood River Inn ★★   As the only area hotel located right on the water (there's a dock and private beach), the Best Western is popular with windsurfers. The convention hotel atmosphere (crowds of corporate types busily networking) is somewhat constraining, but if you like comfort and predictability, this is a good bet. The Riverside Grill serves dependable meals with a bit of Northwest imagination and a great view across the river.

1108 E. Marina Way, Hood River, OR 97031. ℂ **800/828-7873** or 541/386-2200. Fax 541/386-8905. www.hoodriverinn.com. 149 units. June–Sept $89–$124 double, $160–$180 suite; Oct–May $74–$99 double, $119–$140 suite. AE, DC, DISC, MC, V. Pets accepted ($12 per night). **Amenities:** Restaurant (American/Northwest), lounge; outdoor pool; exercise room; Jacuzzi; watersports-equipment rentals; bike rentals; business center; room service; coin-op laundry; dry cleaning. *In room:* A/C, TV, dataport, fridge, coffeemaker, hair dryer, iron.

Columbia Gorge Hotel ★★   Just west of Hood River off I-84 and in business since shortly after 1915, this little oasis of luxury offers a genteel atmosphere that was once enjoyed by Rudolph Valentino and Clark Gable. With its yellow-stucco walls and red-tile roofs, this hotel would be at home in Beverly Hills, and the hotel gardens could hold their own in Victoria, British Columbia. However, despite the attractive furnishings and gardens, it is almost impossible to notice anything but the view from the windows. The hotel is perched more than 200 feet above the river on a steep cliff. Guest rooms are all a little different, with a mixture of antique and classic furnishings. There are canopy beds, brass beds, and even some hand-carved wooden beds. Unfortunately, many of the rooms are rather cramped, as are the bathrooms, most of which have older fixtures. However, some rooms have soaking tubs and fireplaces.

4000 Westcliff Dr., Hood River, OR 97031. ℂ **800/345-1921** or 541/386-5566. Fax 541/387-5414. www.columbiagorgehotel.com. 39 units. $169–$279 double. Rates include multicourse breakfast. AE, DC, DISC, MC, V. Pets accepted with $25. **Amenities:** Restaurant (Northwest/Continental), lounge; concierge; room service; massage. *In room:* A/C, TV, dataport, hair dryer, iron, safe.

Hood River Hotel ★   Built in 1913 and located in downtown Hood River, this hotel boasts a casual elegance and is an economical alternative to the pricey Columbia Gorge Hotel. Canopy beds, ceiling fans, and oval floor mirrors give the rooms a classic feel. Most third-floor rooms have skylit bathrooms, which makes them our favorites. (These are also the only rooms with air-conditioning, which you'll appreciate in the summer.) The river-view rooms are the most expensive, and there are suites with full kitchens as well. The hotel's casual dining room serves good Italian meals. Light sleepers should be aware of the railroad tracks behind the hotel.

102 Oak Ave., Hood River, OR 97031. ✆ **800/386-1859** or 541/386-1900. Fax 503/386-6090. www.hoodriverhotel.com. 41 units. $49–$119 double; $95–$165 suite. Rates include continental breakfast. AE, DC, DISC, MC, V. Pets accepted ($15 per day). **Amenities:** Restaurant (Italian), lounge; exercise room; Jacuzzi; sauna; room service. In room: TV.

Inn at the Gorge ✿

Though this bed-and-breakfast is housed in a 1908 Victorian home, it's still a casual sort of place catering primarily to windsurfing enthusiasts. Each of the three suites has a kitchenette. The sunny Garden Suite, with its claw-foot tub, is our favorite. There's also a storage area for windsurfing and skiing gear. The innkeepers can steer you to the best spots for your skill level.

1113 Eugene St., Hood River, OR 97031. ✆ **541/386-4429.** www.innatthegorge.com. 5 units. $85–$105 double. Rates include full breakfast. MC, V. In room: A/C, TV, fridge.

Meredith Motel ✿ (Finds)

Fans of retro 1950s styling won't want to miss this economical choice at the western edge of Hood River. (Take exit 62 and drive west on Westcliff.) The vintage motel has been completely remodeled, and all the rooms now have 1950s lamps, vintage phones, and retro furnishings reminiscent of the 1950s. As if that weren't enough, the hotel is perched on the edge of a cliff above the Columbia River, and big picture windows put you face-to-face with the Gorge in all its grandeur.

4300 Westcliff Dr., Hood River, OR 97031. ✆ **541/386-1515.** Fax 541/356-3968. http://lodging.net/meredith. 21 units. $49–$79 double. AE, DC, DISC, MC, V. Rates include continental breakfast. Pets accepted ($12 per day). In room: A/C, TV, dataport.

The Mosier House Bed & Breakfast ✿✿ (Finds)

This beautifully restored Victorian home is in the small town of Mosier, 5 miles east of Hood River. The views of the Columbia Gorge from the inn's front porch are unforgettable. Inside, you'll find wood floors and period antiques. Although the four rooms with shared bathrooms are all fairly small, they have the feel of an authentic vintage travelers' hotel. One of the shared bathrooms has a claw-foot tub, as does the room with the private bathroom. All in all, this inn manages to capture a bygone era without being overly frilly or self-consciously romantic, and it makes an excellent base for exploring the eastern end of the Columbia Gorge.

704 Third Ave. (P.O. Box 476), Mosier, OR 97040. ✆ **541/478-3640.** www.mosierhouse.com. 5 units (1 with private bathroom). $85–$100 double with shared bathroom; $125 double with private bathroom. Rates include full breakfast. MC, V. In room: No phone.

Vagabond Lodge ✿ (Kids)

If you've got a banker's tastes but a teller's vacation budget, you can take advantage of the Vagabond Lodge's proximity to the Columbia Gorge Hotel and enjoy the latter's gardens and restaurant without breaking the bank. Actually, the back rooms at the Vagabond are some of the best in Hood River simply for their views. (Some have balconies.) However, this motel's grounds are also quite attractive. There are lots of big old oaks and evergreens, and natural rock outcroppings have been incorporated into the motel's landscaping. If you're in the mood for a splurge, ask for one of the suites. (Some have fireplaces, others whirlpool tubs.) A playground and lots of grass make this a good choice for families.

4070 Westcliff Dr., Hood River, OR 97031. ✆ **541/386-2992.** Fax 541/386-3317. www.vagabondlodge.com. 42 units. $45–$76 double; $77–$86 suite. AE, DC, MC, V. Pets accepted. In room: A/C, TV.

CAMPGROUNDS

Area campgrounds include **Toll Bridge Park,** on Ore. 35, 17 miles south of town, and **Tucker Park,** on Tucker Road (Ore. 281) just a few miles south of town. Both of these county parks are both on the banks of the Hood River. Farther south, you'll find the **Robinhood Campground** and the **Sherwood Campground,** two national-forest campgrounds also on the banks of the Hood River. (These campgrounds are favored by mountain bikers.) Eight miles west of Hood River off I-84 is **Viento State Park,** which gets quite a bit of traffic noise both from the interstate and from the adjacent railroad tracks. Eleven miles east of town, you'll find **Memaloose State Park,** which has the same noise problems. These two state parks are popular with windsurfers.

WHERE TO DINE

When you just have to have a bagel, the **Hood River Bagel Co.,** 13 Oak St. (© **541/386-2123**), is the best place in town. For espresso and a pastry or a slice of pizza, try **Andrew's Pizza & Bakery,** 107 Oak St. (© **541/386-1448**). **Holstein's Coffee Co.,** 12 Oak St. (© **541/386-4115**), is a good place for a latte. The best restaurant in town is the dining room at the **Columbia Gorge Hotel** (see "Where to Stay" above for details).

The Mesquitery 🍴 STEAK/SEAFOOD   Located in the uptown district of Hood River, the Mesquitery is a small and cozy grill with a rustic interior. As the name implies, mesquite grilling is the house specialty. Chicken and ribs are most popular, but you can also get a sirloin steak or grilled fish. At lunch there are sandwiches made with grilled meats. If you aren't that hungry, this is a good place to put together a light meal from such a la carte dishes as shrimp burritos, fish tacos, and fettuccine pesto.

1219 12th St. © 541/386-2002. Main courses $9–$17. AE, DISC, MC, V. Wed–Fri 11:30am–2pm and 4:30–9:30 or 10pm; Sat–Tues 4:30–9:30 or 10pm.

North Oak Brasserie 🍴🍴 ITALIAN   Located below street level, this dark, romantic place is one of the few formal, fine-dining restaurants in town and is under the same management as Stonehedge Inn. The emphasis here is on traditional and creative Italian food and good wine. If you don't have to worry about your cholesterol, be sure to opt for the roasted garlic and brie soup. The butternut ravioli with caramelized onions is a slightly sweet pasta dish that's a hit with both vegetarians and meat-eaters.

113 Third Ave. © 541/387-2310. Reservations recommended. Main courses lunch $6–$8, dinner $17–$20. AE, DISC, MC, V. Daily 11am–2pm and 5–9pm; Fri–Sat 11am–2pm and 5–10pm.

Santacroces' 🍴 *Finds* ITALIAN   Located adjacent to a large lumber mill south of Hood River up the Hood River Valley, this casual little place is part tavern and part great little Italian place. The pizzas here have a legendary reputation as the best for many miles around. If you're not in the mood for pizza, consider anything with the homemade spicy Italian sausage. Although the menu leans toward pasta dishes, keep an eye out for the pork *capperi,* which consists of thinly sliced pork filets in a caper-and-onion sauce.

4780 Hwy. 35. © 541/354-2511. Reservations recommended. Main courses $10–$18. DISC, MC, V. Wed–Sun 4–9pm (June–Sept 4–10pm).

Sixth Street Bistro 🍴🍴 AMERICAN/INTERNATIONAL   Just a block off Oak Street toward the river, the Sixth Street Bistro has an intimate little dining room and patio on the lower floor and a lounge with a balcony on the second floor. Each has its own entrance, but they share a menu. There are numerous international touches, such as chicken satay, pad Thai, and hummus, and also juicy burgers and interesting pasta dishes, including house-made ravioli that changes daily. You'll find seasonal specials and vegetarian dishes as well.

509 Cascade Ave. ✆ 541/386-5737. Reservations recommended. Main courses $9–$20. MC, V. Daily 11:30am–10pm.

Stonehedge Inn ☆☆ CONTINENTAL   Built as a summer vacation home in 1898, the Stonehedge Inn is in the woods west of downtown Hood River down a long gravel driveway off Cascade Drive. When you finally find the restaurant, you'll feel as though you've arrived at a remote Maine lodge. Inside the inn, there's a small lounge with a bar taken from an old tavern, and several dining rooms, all of which feel genuinely old-fashioned. Although the entree menu sticks to traditional continental dishes such as steak Diane, rack of lamb, and chicken cordon bleu, you'll find some more creative offerings, such as grilled goat cheese with roasted garlic or seared ahi tuna on the appetizer menu. Whatever you order, be sure to save room for the unusual bread pudding. New owners are upgrading the restaurant and have added a huge patio dining area.

3405 Cascade Dr. ✆ 541/386-3940. Reservations recommended. Main courses $10–$27. AE, DISC, MC, V. Daily 5–8 or 9pm.

HOOD RIVER AFTER DARK

Big Horse Brew Pub ☆   Located in a vertiginous old house above downtown, this brewpub usually has a good selection of brews and food, and the views from the third floor can't be beat. 115 State St. ✆ **541/386-4411.**

Full Sail Tasting Room & Pub   Full Sail brews some of the most consistently flavorful and well-rounded beers and ales in the Northwest and has developed a loyal following. You have to walk right past the brewery to get to the pub, which is at the back of an old industrial building a block off Hood River's main drag. Big windows look out over the river. 506 Columbia St. ✆ 541/386-2247.

Hood River Wine & Internet Bar ☆   For an upscale alternative to the local brewpub scene, drop by this cozy downtown wine bar and sample some Oregon wines. Occasionally there is live music. 106 Third St. ✆ 541/386-3239.

EAST OF HOOD RIVER: WILDFLOWERS & VIEWS

East of Hood River, you'll find two more sections of the Historic Columbia River Highway (Ore. 30), one of which is open only to hikers and bikers. The other is open to automobiles. The former section, located between Hood River and Mosier and known as the **Historic Columbia River Highway State Trail** (✆ **800/551-6949**) was abandoned when I-84 was built and two tunnels on this section of the old highway were filled in. After the tunnels were re-excavated in order to open up this stretch as a 4½-mile paved trail, a rock catchment had to be built along part of the route leading up to the tunnels from the west. Although the trail receives some traffic noise from I-84, it is a fascinating and easy hike or bike ride. To reach the western trail head, head east out of downtown Hood River and continue east on Old Columbia River Drive. For the eastern trail head, take exit 69 off I-84 and then take the first left. Starting from this latter trail head makes for a much shorter hike. However, the main visitor center for the trail is at the western trail head. There is a $3 fee to use the trail.

The second stretch of the old highway, beginning at exit 69 off I-84 and stretching from Mosier to The Dalles, climbs up onto the Rowena Plateau, where sweeping vistas take in the Columbia River, Mount Hood, and Mount Adams. Between March and May the wildflowers are some of the best in the state. The best place to see the flowers is at the Nature Conservancy's **Governor Tom McCall Preserve** (© 503/230-1221). On spring weekends there are usually volunteers on hand guiding wildflower walks through the preserve.

3 The Dalles

128 miles W of Pendleton, 85 miles E of Portland, 133 miles N of Bend

The Dalles (rhymes with "the pals"), a French word meaning "flagstone," was the name given to this area by early-19th-century French trappers. These early explorers may have been reminded of stepping stones or flagstone-lined gutters when they first gazed upon the flat basalt rocks that forced the Columbia River through a long stretch of rapids and cascades here. These rapids, which were a barrier to river navigation, formed a natural gateway to western Oregon.

For more than 10,000 years, Native Americans inhabited this site because of the ease with which salmon could be taken from the river as it flowed through the tumultuous rapids. The annual fishing season at nearby Celilo Falls was a meeting point for tribes from all over the West. Tribes would come to fish, trade, and stockpile supplies for the coming winter.

White settlers, the first of whom came to The Dalles as missionaries in 1838, were latecomers to this area. However, by the 1840s, a steady flow of pioneers was passing through the region, which was effectively the end of the overland segment of the Oregon Trail. Pioneers who were headed for the mild climate and fertile soils of the Willamette Valley would load their wagons onto rafts at this point and float downriver to the mouth of the Willamette and then up that river to Oregon City.

By the 1850s, The Dalles was the site of an important military fort and had become a busy river port. Steamships shuttled from here to Cascade Locks on the run to Portland. However, the coming of the railroad in 1880, and later the flooding of the river's rapids, reduced the importance of The Dalles as a port town. Today, the city serves as the eastern gateway to the Columbia Gorge and, as such, is the site of the Columbia Gorge Discovery Center.

ESSENTIALS

GETTING THERE   The Dalles is on I-84 at the junction of U.S. 197, which leads south to Antelope, where it connects with U.S. 97.

Amtrak passenger trains stop across the Columbia River from The Dalles in Wishram, Washington. The station is at the west end of Railroad Avenue.

VISITOR INFORMATION   Contact **The Dalles Area Chamber of Commerce,** 404 W. Second St., The Dalles, OR 97058 (© **800/255-3385** or 541/ 296-2231; www.thedalleschamber.com).

LEARNING ABOUT THE GORGE

Columbia Gorge Discovery Center/Wasco County Historical Museum ⋆

These two museums, housed in one building on the outskirts of The Dalles, serve as the eastern gateway to the Columbia Gorge. In the museum building, constructed to resemble a Northwest Native American longhouse, you'll find exhibits on the geology and history of the Gorge. Among the most fascinating exhibits is a film of Native Americans fishing at Celilo Falls before the rising waters behind The Dalles Dam flooded the falls. The museum's star attraction, however, is a 33-foot-long river model with flowing water. On the surrounding museum grounds, there is a **Living History Park,** where on summer weekends interpreters discuss

Native American traditions and pioneer experiences. There is also a short nature trail that leads past a small pond.

5000 Discovery Dr. © 541/296-8600. www.gorgediscovery.org. $6.50 adults, $5.50 seniors, $3 children 6–16. Daily 10am–6pm. Closed Thanksgiving, Christmas, and New Year's Day.

EXPLORING THE DALLES

Long before settlers arrived in The Dalles, Lewis and Clark's expedition stopped here. The site of their camp is called **Rock Fort** and is one of their only documented campsites. The historic site is west of downtown, near The Dalles's industrial area. Go west on West Second Street, turn right on Webber Street West, turn right again onto First Trail Road and continue east for about a half mile.

Some of The Dalles's most important historic buildings can be seen at the **Fort Dalles Museum,** 500 W. 15th St. (© **541/296-4547**), at the corner of Garrison Street. Established in 1850, Fort Dalles was the only military post between Fort Laramie and Fort Vancouver. By 1867, the fort had become unnecessary, and after several buildings were destroyed in a fire, it was abandoned. Today, several of the original buildings, including a Carpenter-Gothic officers' home, are still standing. Though small, this is the oldest history museum in Oregon. April through September, the museum is open daily from 11am to 5pm; call for hours in other months. Admission is $3, free for children 18 and under.

Not far from the Fort Dalles Museum, at **Sorosis Park,** there's a good view of The Dalles, the Columbia River, and Mount Adams. To reach this park, drive 1 block west from the museum and turn left on Trevitt Street, which becomes Scenic Drive. Continue on this latter street to the park.

Within a decade of the establishment of Fort Dalles, this community became the county seat of what was the largest county ever created in the United States. Wasco County covered 130,000 square miles between the Rocky Mountains and the Cascade Range. The old **Wasco County Courthouse,** 410 W. Second St. (© **541/296-4798**), a two-story wooden structure built in 1859, has been preserved, and the inside looks much as it did when it was a functioning courthouse. June through August, it's open Monday, Tuesday, Friday, and Saturday from 10am to 4pm; April, May, September, and October, it's open from 11am to 3pm (closed other months). Admission is free.

The Dalles's other historic landmark is a much more impressive structure. **St. Peter's Landmark Church** (© **541/296-5686**), at the corner of West Third and Lincoln streets, is no longer an active church, but its 176-foot-tall steeple is a local landmark. The church was built in the Gothic Revival style in 1897, and a 6-foot-tall rooster symbolizing The Dalles tops its spire. The church is open Tuesday through Friday from 11am to 3pm and Saturday and Sunday from 1 to 3pm.

If you're interested in learning more about the history and the historic buildings of The Dalles, pick up a copy of the historic walking tours brochure at the chamber of commerce. As you explore The Dalles, also keep an eye out for the city's many **historical murals.**

At the east of town rises **The Dalles Lock and Dam** (© **541/296-9778**), which provides both irrigation water and electricity. The dam, which was completed in 1957, stretches for 1½ miles from the Oregon shore to the Washington shore. One of the main reasons this dam was built was to flood the rapids that made this section of the Columbia River impossible to navigate. Among the numerous rapids flooded by the dam were Celilo Falls, which, for thousands of years before the dam was built, was the most important salmon-fishing area in the Northwest. Each year thousands of Native Americans would gather here to catch and smoke salmon, putting the dried fish away for the coming winter. The traditional method of catching the salmon was to use a spear or a net on the end of a long pole. Men would build precarious wooden platforms out over the river and catch the salmon as they tried to leap up the falls. You can still see traditional Native American fishing platforms near the Shilo Inn here in The Dalles. The dam's **visitor center** has displays on both the history of the river and the construction of the dam, and a small train takes visitors on free guided tours of the fish ladder and powerhouse. These tours are offered June through Labor Day daily from 9am to 6pm. To reach the visitor center, take exit 87 off I-84 and turn right on Northeast Frontage Road. Other months, you can take a self-guided tour Monday through Friday between 9am and 5pm. During these times of year, take exit 88 of I-84.

EAST OF THE DALLES

In the vicinity of the two attractions listed here, you'll also find three wineries. **Maryhill Winery,** 9774 Hwy. 14, Maryhill (© **877/627-9445;** www.maryhill winery.com) has the best view of any winery in the Northwest and also produces some very good wines. **Cascade Cliffs Vineyard & Winery,** Milepost 88.6, Hwy. 14, Wishram (© **509/767-1100**), is set at the foot of 400-foot-tall basalt cliffs and produces, among other wines, Nebbiolo and Barbera. **Marshal's Winery,** 150 Oak Creek Rd., Dallesport (© **509/767-4633**), which is located 2 miles up a gravel road, is a tiny family-run winery that produces some of Washington's smoothest Cabernet Sauvignons and Merlots, as well as some unusual sweet wines.

Horsethief Lake State Park *(Finds* Located between The Dalles Dam and Wishram on Wash. 14, Horsethief Lake is a popular fishing area and campground. However, long before the area was designated a state park, this was a gathering ground for Native Americans, who fished for salmon at nearby Celilo Falls. The park isn't far from the famous Celilo Falls, which were, before being inundated by the waters behind The Dalles Dam, the most prolific salmon-fishing area in the Northwest. Each year for thousands of years Native Americans would gather here from all over the Northwest. These Native Americans drew petroglyphs on rocks that are now protected within this park. The most famous of these is Tsagaglalal ("she who watches"), a large face that gazes down on the Columbia River. Due to past vandalism, the only way to see this and other park petroglyphs is on ranger-led walks held on Friday and Saturday mornings at 10am. Reservations for these walks should be made at least 2 to 3 weeks in advance.

Wash. 14. © 509/767-1159. Free admission. Apr–Oct daily 6:30am–dusk. Closed Nov–Mar.

Maryhill Museum of Art *(Finds* After the Gorge itself, this museum, located across the river in Washington and about 20 miles east of The Dalles, is the most important attraction in the vicinity of The Dalles—don't miss it. Maryhill houses a collection of Rodin sculptures, Native American artifacts, Russian icons, Fabergé artifacts, miniature French fashions, and 19th-century American and European paintings. The museum is fascinating both for its superb collections and for its remote and spectacular setting high above the Columbia River. The lush grounds surrounding the museum have sculptures, picnic tables, and plenty of shade trees, making them an ideal spot for a picnic. (There's also a cafe.)

35 Maryhill Museum Dr. (Wash. 14). © 509/773-3733. www.maryhillmuseum.org. Admission $7 adults, $6 seniors, $2 children 6–12. Mar 15–Nov 15 daily 9am–5pm. Closed Nov 16–Mar 14.

OUTDOOR ACTIVITIES

East of town 17 miles, you'll find the **Deschutes River State Recreation Area** (© **541/739-2322**), which is at the mouth of the Deschutes River and is the eastern boundary of the Columbia Gorge National Scenic Area. The park has several miles of hiking trails, and an old railway right-of-way that parallels the Deschutes River for 25 miles has been turned into a gravel mountain-biking and horseback-riding trail. This trail is fairly flat and passes through some spectacular canyon scenery. There is also a campground in the park.

If you're interested in fishing for sturgeon, steelhead, or salmon in the area, contact **Young's Fishing Service** (© **800/270-7962** or 541/296-5371; www. FishYFS.com), which offers trips on the Columbia, Deschutes, and John Day rivers. Expect to pay around $135 to $155 per day.

WHERE TO STAY

Shilo Inn The Dalles ⚐   The Shilo Inn is a couple of miles from downtown and has the most dramatic setting of any lodging in the area. The motel is set on the banks of the Columbia River at the foot of The Dalles Dam and is adjacent to the Native American ghost town of Lone Pine. The rooms are typical motel units, and it's definitely worth spending a little extra for a river-view room. The dining room and lounge offer moderately priced meals and views of the river.

3223 Bret Clodfelter Way, The Dalles, OR 97058. © **800/222-2244** or 541/298-5502. Fax 541/298-4673. www. shiloinns.com. 112 units. $65–$99 double. AE, DC, DISC, MC, V. Pets accepted ($10 per night). **Amenities:** Restaurant (American); lounge; outdoor pool; exercise room; Jacuzzi; sauna; coin-op laundry; dry cleaning. *In room:* A/C, TV, fridge, coffeemaker, hair dryer, iron.

CAMPGROUNDS

If you're looking for someplace to pitch a tent or park an RV, try **Deschutes River State Recreation Area,** 17 miles east of The Dalles off I-84. For reservations, contact **Reservations Northwest/Reserve America** (© **800/452-5687;** www.oregonstateparks.org/reserve.html). On the Washington side of the gorge, there is camping at **Horsethief Lake State Park** (no reservations), near the community of Dallesport (take U.S. 197 north to Wash. 14 east).

WHERE TO DINE

Bailey's Place ⚐ PRIME RIB/CONTINENTAL   Located in the 1865 Edward French house, this restaurant is The Dalles' best fine-dining establishment. The prime rib au jus is a local legend. The kitchen also does a respectable job on seafood, but if you only come here once go for the prime rib. There's a good selection of reasonably priced wines.

515 Liberty St. © **541/296-6708.** Reservations recommended. Main courses $8–$20. AE, DISC, MC, V. Tues–Thurs 4:30–9pm; Fri–Sat 4:30–9:30pm.

Baldwin Saloon Historic Restaurant & Bar ⚐ AMERICAN/CONTINENTAL   Built in 1876, the Baldwin Saloon has one of the few remaining cast-iron facades in town and is one of the only restaurants in The Dalles with much historic character. Brick walls, wooden booths, and a high ceiling (high enough for a loft with a piano) add to the old-time feel, as do the collections of late-19th-century landscape paintings and large bar nudes. The menu is pretty straightforward and simple. There's live piano music on Friday and Saturday nights. A macabre aside: The building was once a warehouse for coffins.

First and Court sts. © **541/296-5666.** Reservations accepted only for parties of 6 or more. Main courses $5.75–$19. MC, V. Mon–Sat 11am–9pm (until 10pm in summer).

8

The Cascades

From the schussing of January and the kayaking of April to the wildflowers of August and the splashes of fall foliage in October, Oregon's Cascade Range is a year-round recreational magnet. Stretching from the Columbia Gorge in the north to California in the south, the Cascades are a relatively young volcanic mountain range with picture-perfect, snowcapped volcanic peaks rising above lush green forests of evergreens. The Cascade's volcanic heritage sets this mountain range apart from others in the West, and throughout these mountains, signs of past volcanic activity are evident. Crater Lake, formed after a massive volcanic eruption, is the most dramatic evidence of the Cascades' fiery past. But you can also see evidence of volcanic activity in the cones of Mount Hood and Mount Jefferson, and in the lava fields of McKenzie Pass.

As spectacular as this volcanic geology is, however, it is not what draws most people to these mountains. The main attraction is the multitude of outdoor sports available. Crystal-clear rivers, churned into white water as they cascade down from high in the mountains, provide numerous opportunities for rafting, kayaking, canoeing, and fishing. High mountain lakes hold hungry trout, and throughout the summer, lakeside campgrounds stay filled with anglers. The Pacific Crest Trail winds the entire length of the Cascades, but it is the many wilderness areas scattered throughout these mountains that are the biggest draw for day hikers and backpackers. At lower elevations, mountain bikers find miles of national-forest trails to enjoy. In winter, skiers and snowboarders flock to more than half a dozen ski areas and countless miles of cross-country ski trails—and because winter lingers late in the high Cascades, the ski season here is one of the longest in the country. Skiing often begins in mid-November and continues on into April and even May and June at Mount Bachelor. In fact, on Mount Hood, high-elevation snowfields atop glacial ice allow a year-round ski season that attracts Olympic ski teams for summer training.

The Cascades also serve as a dividing line between the lush evergreen forests of western Oregon and the dry, high desert landscapes of eastern Oregon. On the western slopes, Douglas firs and western red cedars dominate, while on the east side, the cinnamon-barked ponderosa pine is most common. These trees have been the lifeblood of the Oregon economy for much of this century, and with few virgin forests left in the state, the fight to protect the last old-growth forests has been long and litigious. Today, visitors to the Cascades will be confronted at nearly every turn by the sight of clear-cuts scarring the mountainsides, yet it is still possible to find groves of ancient trees beneath which to hike and camp.

The Cascades

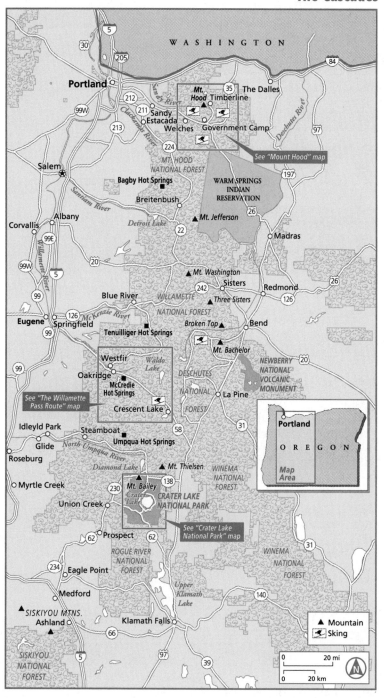

WASHINGTON

Portland

Mt. Hood
Timberline
The Dalles

Sandy
Estacada
Welches
Government Camp

See "Mount Hood" map

MT. HOOD
NATIONAL FOREST

Bagby Hot Springs

WARM SPRINGS
INDIAN
RESERVATION

Breitenbush

Salem

Corvallis

Albany

Mt. Jefferson

Detroit Lake

Madras

Mt. Washington

Sisters

Redmond

Blue River

WILLAMETTE

Three Sisters

Eugene
Springfield

NATIONAL FOREST

Broken Top

Bend

Tenuilliger Hot Springs

Mt. Bachelor

NEWBERRY
NATIONAL
VOLCANIC
MONUMENT

Westfir

Waldo
Lake

DESCHUTES

Oakridge

McCredie
Hot Springs

La Pine

*See "The Willamette
Pass Route" map*

Crescent Lake

NATIONAL

FOREST

Idleyld Park

Steamboat

Umpqua Hot Springs

Glide

North Umpqua River

Roseburg

Diamond Lake

Mt. Thielsen

WINEMA

Myrtle Creek

Mt. Bailey

NATIONAL

Crater
Lake

CRATER LAKE
NATIONAL PARK

FOREST

Union Creek

Prospect

*See "Crater Lake
National Park" map*

Eagle Point

ROGUE RIVER
NATIONAL
FOREST

WINEMA

Upper
Klamath
Lake

NATIONAL

Medford

FOREST

SISKIYOU MTNS.
Ashland

Klamath Falls

SISKIYOU
NATIONAL
FOREST

Portland

O R E G O N

Map
Area

▲ Mountain
Sking

0   20 mi

0   20 km

1 Mount Hood: Skiing, Hiking & Scenic Drives ⋆⋆⋆

60 miles E of Portland, 46 miles S of Hood River

At 11,235 feet, Mount Hood, a dormant volcano, is the tallest mountain in Oregon. Fewer than 60 miles east of downtown Portland, it is also the busiest mountain in the state. Summer and winter, people flock here in search of cool mountain air filled with the scent of firs and pines. Campgrounds, hiking and mountain-biking trails, trout streams and lakes, downhill ski areas, and cross-country ski trails all provide ample opportunities for outdoor recreational activities on Mount Hood.

With five downhill areas and many miles of cross-country trails, the mountain is a ski bum's dream come true. One of the country's largest night-skiing areas is here, and at Timberline you can ski right through the summer. And because even those with a moderate amount of mountain-climbing experience can reach the summit fairly easily, it's also the most climbed major peak in the United States.

One of the first settlers to visit Mount Hood was Samuel Barlow, who, in 1845, had traveled the Oregon Trail and was searching for an alternative to taking his wagon train down the treacherous waters of the Columbia River. Barlow blazed a trail across the south flank of Mount Hood, and the following year opened his trail as a toll road. The **Barlow Trail,** though difficult, was cheaper and safer than rafting down the river. The trail is now used for hiking and mountain biking.

During the Great Depression, the Works Progress Administration employed skilled craftsmen to build the rustic **Timberline Lodge** at the tree line on the mountain's south slope. Today, the lodge is a National Historic Landmark and is the main destination for visitors to the mountain. Its views of Mount Hood's peak and of the Oregon Cascades to the south are superb and should not be missed.

Don't expect to have this mountain all to yourself, though. Because of its proximity to Portland, Mount Hood sees a lot of visitors throughout the year, and on snowy days the road back down the mountain from the ski areas can be bumper to bumper and backed up for hours. Also keep in mind that you'll need to have a Sno-Park Permit in the winter (available at ski shops around the area) and a Northwest Forest Pass to park at trail heads in the summer (available at ranger stations, visitor centers, and a few outdoors-oriented shops).

ESSENTIALS

GETTING THERE   Mount Hood is reached by taking U.S. 26 east from Portland (take exit 16A off I-84) or Ore. 35 from Hood River. These two highways meet just east of the town of Government Camp, which is the main tourist town on the mountain. The Lolo Pass Road is a gravel road that skirts the north and west sides of the mountain connecting these two highways.

VISITOR INFORMATION   For more information on Mount Hood, contact the **Mount Hood Information Center,** 65000 E. Hwy. 26, Welches, OR 97067 (© **888/622-4822** or 503/622-4822; www.mthood.org), or the **Mount Hood Ranger District,** 6780 Ore. 35 S., Mount Hood–Parkdale, OR 97041 (© **541/352-6002**).

SUMMER ON THE MOUNTAIN

In snow-free months most visitors are heading to historic **Timberline Lodge** (see "Where to Stay" below). Besides having a fabulous view of Mount Hood,

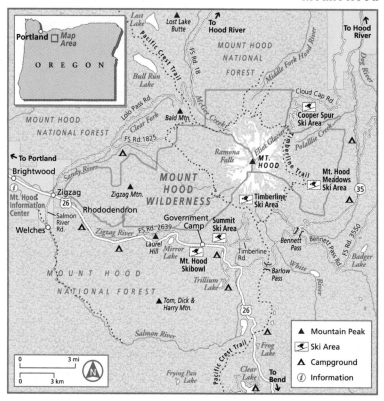

the lodge is surrounded by meadows that burst into bloom in July and August. Here you'll find the 41-mile-long **Tamolitch Pool** ♣, which circles the mountain. If you just have time for a short hike, head west from the lodge on this trail rather than east. The route east passes through dusty ash fields and then drops down into the hot, barren White River Valley. You'll find snow here year-round, and there's even summer skiing at the **Timberline Ski Area.** The lift-accessed ski slopes are high above the lodge on the Palmer Glacier and are open only in the morning. In summer, you can ride the lift even if you aren't skiing.

In summer, you can also ride the lift at **Mt. Hood SkiBowl Summer Action Park,** 8700 E. Hwy. 26 (© **503/222-2695**), where there are mountain-biking trails, hiking trails, an alpine slide (sort of a summertime bobsled run), and numerous other rides and activities.

One of the most popular and most enjoyable hikes on Mount Hood is the trail to **Mirror Lake** ♣, which, as its name implies, reflects the summit of Mount Hood in its waters. The trail is fairly easy and is good for families with young children. If you want to add a bit more challenge, you can continue to the summit of Tom, Dick & Harry Mountain, the backside of which in winter serves as the Mt. Hood SkiBowl. The view from the summit is superb, and in late summer there are huckleberries along the trail. You'll find the trail head right on U.S. 26 just before you reach Government Camp.

The east side of the mountain, accessed by Ore. 35 from Hood River, is much drier and less visited than the south side. Here on the east side, you'll find good hiking trails in the vicinity of **Mount Hood Meadows,** where the wildflower displays in late July and August are some of the best on the mountain. The loop trail past Umbrella and Sahalie falls is particularly enjoyable. Also on this side of the mountain, you'll find the highest segment of the Timberline Trail. This section of trail climbs up Cooper Spur ridge from historic Cloud Cap Inn (no longer open to the public.) The close-up views of the mountain and the distant views of eastern Oregon's dry landscape make this one of our favorite hiking destinations on Mount Hood. To reach the trail head, follow signs off Ore. 35 for Cooper Spur and Cloud Cap. On the east side of Ore. 35, off Forest Service Road 44, you'll also find the best **mountain-biking trails** in the area. Among these are the Surveyor's Ridge Trail and the Dog Mountain Trail.

If you're interested in a little adventure and an alternative route from the west side of the mountain to the Hood River area, try exploring the gravel **Lolo Pass Road,** which is usually in good enough condition for standard passenger cars. Be sure to have a Forest Service map (available from the **Mount Hood Information Center,** 65000 E. Hwy. 26, Welches, OR 97067; © **888/622-4822** or 503/622-4822), since roads out here are not well marked and it's easy to get lost. Branching off from the Lolo Pass Road are several smaller roads that lead to some of the best hiking trails on Mount Hood. Also off the Lolo Pass Road, you'll find **Lost Lake,** one of the most beautiful (and most photographed) lakes in the Oregon Cascades. When the water is still, the view of the mountain and its reflection in the lake is positively sublime. Here you'll find campgrounds, cabins, picnic areas, good fishing, and hiking trails that lead both around the lake and up a nearby butte.

If you're interested in a more strenuous mountain experience, the Mount Hood area offers plenty of mountain- and rock-climbing opportunities. **Timberline Mountain Guides,** P.O. Box 1167, Bend, OR 97709 (© **541/ 312-9242;** www.timberlinemtguides.com), leads summit climbs on Mount Hood. They also offer snow, ice, and rock-climbing courses. A 2-day Mount Hood mountaineering course with summit climb costs $375.

WINTER ON THE MOUNTAIN

Although snowpacks that can be slow to reach skiable depths and frequent mid-winter rains make the ski season on Mount Hood unpredictable, in an ordinary year the regular ski season runs from around Thanksgiving right through March or April. Add to this the summer skiing on the Palmer Glacier at Timberline Ski Area, and you have the longest ski season in the United States. There are five ski areas on Mount Hood, though two of these are tiny operations that attract primarily beginners and families looking for an economical way to all go schussing together. For cross-country skiers, there are many miles of marked ski trails, some of which are groomed.

The single most important thing to know about skiing anywhere in Oregon is that you'll have to have a **Sno-Park Permit.** These permits, which sell for $3.50 a day or $15.50 for the season, allow you to park in plowed parking areas on the mountain. You can get permits at ski shops in Sandy and Hood River and at a few convenience stores.

Mt. Hood SkiBowl (© **503/272-3206;** 503/222-2695 for snow report; www.skibowl.com), located in Government Camp on U.S. 26, the closest ski area to Portland, offers 1,500 vertical feet of skiing and has more expert slopes than any other ski area on the mountain. SkiBowl is also the largest lighted ski area in the country. Adult lift ticket prices range from $18 for midweek night skiing to $31 for a weekend all-day pass. Call for hours of operation.

Timberline Ski Area (© **503/272-3311** for information; 503/222-2211 for snow report; www.timberlinelodge.com) is the highest ski area on Mount Hood and has one slope that is open throughout the summer. This is the site of the historic **Timberline Lodge.** Adult lift ticket prices range from $18 for night skiing to $37 for an all-day pass. Call for hours of operation.

Mount Hood Meadows 👍👍 (© **503/337-2222;** 503/227-7669 for snow report; www.skihood.com), 12 miles northeast of Government Camp on Ore. 35, is the largest ski resort on Mount Hood, with more than 2,000 skiable acres, 2,777 vertical feet, and a wide variety of terrain. This is the closest Mount Hood comes to having a destination ski resort, and it is here that you'll find the most out-of-state skiers. Lift ticket prices range from $18 for night skiing to $41 for a weekend all-day pass. Call for hours of operation.

If you're interested in **cross-country skiing,** there are plenty of trails. For views, head to the **White River Sno-Park,** east of Government Camp. The trails at **Glacier View Sno-Park,** across U.S. 26 from Mount Hood SkiBowl, are good for beginner and intermediate skiers. The mountain's best-groomed trails are at the **Mount Hood Meadows Nordic Center** ($10 trail pass) on Ore. 35 and at **Teacup Lake** (small donation requested), which is across the highway from the turnoff for Mount Hood Meadows. Teacup Lake is maintained by a local ski club and has the best system of groomed trails on the mountain. In the town of Sandy and at Government Camp are numerous ski shops that rent cross-country skis.

WHERE TO STAY
ON THE MOUNTAIN

Falcon's Crest Inn 👍 This sprawling chalet-style lodge tucked into the trees on the edge of Government Camp is your best bet on Mount Hood for a B&B within walking distance of the ski slopes. Both suites, one of which is done up in a Mexican theme, have whirlpool tubs (one outside on a deck), and though a bit incongruous in this mountain setting, the Safari Room, with its deck and view of the ski slopes, is a great choice. The inn also serves elegant six-course dinners for $39.95 (Cornish game hen, stuffed pork loin, beef Wellington) by reservation.

87287 Government Camp Loop Hwy. (P.O. Box 185), Government Camp, OR 97028. © **800/624-7384** or 503/272-3403. Fax 503/272-3454. www.falconscrest.com. 5 units. $95–$125 double; $169–$179 suite. AE, DC, DISC, MC, V. **Amenities:** Restaurant (Continental); massage.

Mt. Hood Inn 👍 At the west end of Government right on the highway, this modern budget hotel doesn't have a lot of character, but adjacent Mt. Hood Brew Pub makes this a great place to stay if you enjoy craft beers. Pine furnishings give the guest rooms here a contemporary rustic feel. The king spa rooms, with two-person whirlpool tubs beside the king-size beds, are definitely the best rooms, but they're somewhat overpriced. Other rooms have refrigerators and microwaves.

87450 E. Government Camp Loop, Government Camp, OR 97028. © **800/443-7777** or 503/272-3205. www.mthoodinn.com. 55 units. $149–$169 double. Rates include continental breakfast. AE, DC, DISC, MC, V. Pets accepted ($5). **Amenities:** Jacuzzi; coin-op laundry. *In room:* TV.

Timberline Lodge 👍👍 Constructed during the Great Depression of the 1930s as a WPA project, this classic alpine ski lodge overflows with craftsmanship. The grand stone fireplace, huge exposed beams, and wide plank floors of the lobby impress every first-time visitor. Woodcarvings, imaginative wrought-iron fixtures, hand-hooked rugs, and handmade furniture complete the rustic picture. Rooms vary in size considerably, and the smallest lack private bathrooms. All rooms, however, feature the same rustic furnishings. Unfortunately, room windows are not very large, but you can always visit the Ram's Head lounge for a better view of Mount Hood.

Timberline, OR 97028. ℭ **800/547-1406** or 503/622-7979. Fax 503/622-0710. www.timberlinelodge.com. 70 units (10 without bathroom). $75 double with shared bathroom, $115–$225 double with private bathroom. AE, DISC, MC, V. Snow-park permit required in winter, but hotel will provide guests with one. **Amenities:** 2 restaurants (Northwest, American), 2 lounges; small outdoor pool; Jacuzzi; sauna; children's ski programs; coin-op laundry. *In room:* TV, dataport, hair dryer, iron, safe.

AT THE BASE OF THE MOUNTAIN
The Resort at the Mountain 𝒞𝒞 This golf resort is set in a large clearing
in the dense woods at the base of Mount Hood. It's a bit of a drive to Timberline or Government Camp and the area's hiking trails and ski areas, but if a round of golf in a gorgeous setting sounds tempting, this is one of your best choices. Beautifully landscaped grounds incorporating concepts from Japanese garden design hide the resort's many low-rise buildings and make this a tranquil woodsy retreat. The guest rooms are large and have either a balcony or a patio. Special closets for ski gear are available in some rooms. The main lodge has a formal dining room, while a more casual dining room overlooks the golf course. In addition to amenities listed below, there are horseshoe pits, croquet and lawn bowling courts, volleyball and badminton courts, nature trails, and a pro shop.

68010 E. Fairway Ave., Welches, OR 97067. ℭ **800/669-7666** or 503/622-3101. Fax 503/622-2222. www. theresort.com. 160 units. June–Sept $129–$179 double, $199–$249 suite; Oct–May $99–$139 double, $159–$199 suite. AE, DC, DISC, MC, V. **Amenities:** 2 restaurants (Northwest, American), 2 lounges; outdoor pool; 27-hole golf course; 4 tennis courts; exercise room; Jacuzzi; bike rentals; business center; room service; massage; coin-op laundry; dry cleaning. *In room:* TV/VCR, dataport, coffeemaker, hair dryer, iron.

NORTHEAST OF THE MOUNTAIN
The Inn at Cooper Spur 𝒞 𝒞Value If you want to get away from it all, try this
surprisingly remote lodge in the off-season. (During ski season it can be difficult to get a reservation.) The inn consists of a main building and a handful of modern log cabins—these are the more enjoyable rooms. The cabins have two bedrooms and a loft area reached by a spiral staircase. There are also rooms with full kitchens. The inn's restaurant serves decent, reasonably priced meals. At the end of the day you can soak yourself in one of the inn's whirlpool spas.

10755 Cooper Spur Rd., Mount Hood, OR 97041. ℭ **541/352-6692.** Fax 541/352-7551. http://business. gorge.net/cooperspurinn. 15 units (including 6 cabins). $90–$110 double; $172–$226 cabin or suite. AE, DISC, MC, V. **Amenities:** Restaurant (American); tennis court; Jacuzzi. *In room:* TV.

Mt. Hood Bed & Breakfast 𝒞 Located on a 42-acre working farm on the
northeast side of Mount Hood, this B&B offers a quiet escape. As an added bonus, you're only minutes away from a small ski area, and the mountain's major ski areas are less than 30 minutes away. We recommend either the Mount Hood or the Mount Adams rooms, both of which have views of their respective mountains. Guests can spend time in a barn that has a tennis court and basketball court.

8885 Cooper Spur Rd., Parkdale, OR 97041. ℭ **800/557-8885** or 541/352-6885. www.mthoodbnb.com. 4 units (2 with private bathroom). $110–$135 double. Rates include full breakfast. DISC, MC, V. **Amenities:** Tennis court. *In room:* TV/VCR.

WHERE TO DINE
ON THE MOUNTAIN

Cascade Dining Room 🅰🅰 NORTHWEST   It may seem a bit casual from the lobby and there are no stunning views of Mount Hood even though it's right outside the window, but the Cascade Dining Room is by far the best restaurant on Mount Hood. The menu changes regularly, but for appetizers, we recommend the Swiss-style thin-sliced air-dried beef and fire-roasted oysters. Main courses might include grilled prosciutto-wrapped halibut, smoked cumin-lime chicken, or rack of lamb with polenta crust. There are also always several interesting vegetarian offerings. There's a good wine selection, and desserts showcase a variety of local seasonal ingredients such as raspberries, pears, and apples.

In Timberline Lodge, Timberline. ⓒ 503/622-0700. Reservations highly recommended on weekends. Main courses lunch $9–$11.50, dinner $16–$35. AE, DISC, MC, V. Summer 8–10am, noon–2pm, and 5–9pm. Hours may vary other seasons.

Mt. Hood Brew Pub 🅰 PUB FOOD   This brewpub on the edge of Government Camp is affiliated with Timberline Lodge and offers good microbrews and pub food (sandwiches, salads, pasta, pizzas), as well as comfort food such as meatloaf with garlic mashed potatoes. There are at least six beers on tap (including cask-conditioned ales and a couple of daily choices on the nitro taps), and a large selection of Northwest wines.

87304 E. Government Camp Loop. ⓒ 503/272-3724. www.mthoodbrewing.com. Main courses $7–$14. AE, DISC, MC, V. Sun–Thurs noon–10pm; Fri–Sat noon–11pm.

AT THE BASE OF THE MOUNTAIN

Calamity Jane's 🅰 *Finds* BURGERS   What, you ask, is a $12.25 hamburger? Well, at Calamity Jane's, it's a 1-pound pastrami-and-mushroom cheeseburger. If you think that's outrageous, wait until you see the other burgers listed on the menu. There's the peanut-butter burger, the George Washington burger (with sour cream and sweet pie cherries), the hot-fudge-and-marshmallow burger—even an unbelievably priced inflation burger. Not all the burgers at this entertaining and rustic eatery are calculated to turn your stomach—some are just plain delicious. There are even pizza burgers. This place is just east of Sandy on U.S. 26.

42015 U.S. 26, Sandy. ⓒ 503/668-7817. Burgers $4.25–$12.25. AE, DISC, MC, V. Sun–Thurs 11am–9pm (until 10pm in summer); Fri–Sat 11am–10pm.

The Rendezvous Grill 🅰🅰 MEDITERRANEAN   Right on U.S. 26 in Welches, this casual, upscale restaurant is a great choice for dinner on your way back to Portland. Although the emphasis is on the Mediterranean, other flavors also show up in the guise of sake-glazed salmon and crab and shrimp cakes with chipotle aioli. The grilled steak with Whidbey's port, shiitake mushrooms, and blue cheese sauce is a must for steak fans.

67149 E. U.S. 26, Welches. ⓒ 503/622-6837. www.rendezvousgrill.com. Reservations recommended. Main courses lunch $7.50–$10, dinner $15–$20. AE, DISC, MC, V. Daily 11:30am–9pm.

2 The Santiam Pass, McKenzie Pass & McKenzie River

Santiam Pass: 82 miles SE of Salem, 40 miles NW of Bend; McKenzie Pass: 77 miles NE of Eugene, 36 miles NW of Bend

As the nearest recreational areas to both Salem and Eugene, the Santiam Pass, McKenzie Pass, and McKenzie River routes are some of the most popular in the state. Ore. 22, which leads over Santiam Pass, is also one of the busiest routes to the Sisters and Bend areas in central Oregon. Along these highways are some of the state's best white-water-rafting and fishing rivers, some of the most popular and most beautiful backpacking areas, and good downhill and cross-country skiing. In the summer, the Detroit Lake recreation area is the main attraction along Ore. 22 and is a favorite of water-skiers and lake anglers. In winter, it's downhill and cross-country skiing at Santiam Pass that brings people up this way.

Ore. 126, on the other hand, follows the scenic McKenzie River and is favored by white-water rafters and drift-boat anglers fishing for salmon and steelhead. Several state parks provide access to the river. During the summer, Ore. 126 connects to Ore. 242, a narrow road that climbs up and over McKenzie Pass, the most breathtaking pass in the Oregon Cascades.

ESSENTIALS

GETTING THERE   Santiam Pass is a year-round pass and is reached by Ore. 22 from Salem, U.S. 20 from Albany, and Ore. 126 from Eugene. McKenzie Pass is on Ore. 242 and lies to the south of Santiam Pass. It can be reached by all the same roads that lead to Santiam Pass, but it is closed during in winter.

VISITOR INFORMATION   For more information on outdoor recreation in this area, contact the **Detroit Ranger Station,** HC73, Box 320, Mill City, OR 97360 (© **503/854-3366**); the **McKenzie Ranger Station,** 57600 McKenzie Hwy., McKenzie Bridge, OR 97413 (© **541/822-3381**); or the **Blue River Ranger Station,** P.O. Box 199, Blue River, OR 97413 (© **541/822-3317**). Also check the website of the Willamette National Forest (www.fs.fed.us/ r6/willamette). For more general information, contact the **McKenzie River Chamber of Commerce,** P.O. Box 1117, Leaburg, OR 97489 (© **800/ 318-8819** or 541/896-3330; www.el.com/to/mckenzierivervalley), which operates a visitor center at the old Leaburg fish hatchery on Leaburg Lake east of Springfield on the McKenzie Highway.

ALONG THE SANTIAM PASS HIGHWAY

Detroit Lake is the summertime center of activity on this route, with fishing and water-skiing the most popular activities. North of the lake, you'll find the **Breitenbush Hot Springs Retreat and Conference Center** (© **503/854-3314;** www.breitenbush.com), a New Age community/retreat center that allows day use of its hot springs by advance reservation. The fee is between $8 and $15 per person, and vegetarian meals are available. Breitenbush offers massage, yoga, meditation classes, and a wide range of other programs focusing on holistic health and spiritual growth.

At Santiam Pass, you'll find the **Hoodoo Ski Area** (© **541/822-3337** for snow report, or 541/822-3799; www.hoodoo.com), which was scheduled to add a new lodge in the winter of 2001–02 and has been busily upgrading over the past few years. The ski area has five chair lifts and 29 runs for all levels of experience. Lift tickets are $28 to $30 for adults and $20 to $23 for children. Night skiing is available. Here you'll also find the **Hoodoo Nordic Center,** which has almost 10 miles (16km) of groomed cross-country ski trails and charges $8 for a trail pass. Also in the Santiam Pass area, you'll find several Sno-Parks. The Maxwell, Big Springs, and Lava Lake East Sno-Parks access the best trails in the area.

UP THE MCKENZIE RIVER

The McKenzie River is one of Oregon's most popular white-water-rafting rivers, and the cold blue waters challenge a wide range of experience levels. **Oregon**

Whitewater Adventures (© 800/820-RAFT or 541/746-5422; www.oregon whitewater.com), **McKenzie River Adventures** (© **800/832-5858** or 541/ 822-3806), and **Jim's Oregon Whitewater** (© **800/254-JIMS** or 541/ 822-6003; www.raft2fish.com) all offer half- and full-day trips. Expect to pay around $55 for a half day of rafting and $75 to $90 for a full day. For a tamer white-water experience, try the pontoon platform boats of **McKenzie Pontoon & Raft Trips** (© 541/741-1905).

If you're interested in seeing this area by bike, contact **Oregon Adventures** (© **541/984-1433;** www.oregon-adventures.com), which offers a variety of bike rides, both road and trail, for $45 to $55 for a half-day ride and $85 for a full-day mountain-bike ride. This company can also arrange rafting trips, guided hikes, and even skydiving.

Surprisingly, the McKenzie River town of Blue River is home to one of the best golf courses in Oregon. **Tokatee Golf Club,** 54947 McKenzie Hwy., Blue River (© **800/452-6376** or 541/822-3220; www.tokatee.com), gets consistently high ratings and has a spectacular setting with views of snowcapped Cascade Peaks and lush forests. Greens fee is $37 for 18 holes.

Off Ore. 126, between the towns of Blue River and McKenzie Bridge, you'll find the turnoff for the **Aufderheide National Scenic Byway** (Forest Service Rd. 19). This road meanders for 54 miles through the foothills of the Cascades, first following the South Fork McKenzie River (and Cougar Reservoir) and then following the North Fork of the Middle Fork Willamette River, which offers excellent fly-fishing and numerous swimming holes. At the south end of Cougar Reservoir, you'll find a trail that leads to the very popular **Terwilliger Hot Springs.** The southernmost stretch of this road is the most scenic portion and passes through a deep, narrow gorge formed by the North Fork of the Middle Fork Willamette River. Along the route, you'll find several hiking trails. At the southern end of the scenic byway is the community of Westfir, which is the site of the longest covered bridge in Oregon.

Between the turnoff for McKenzie Pass and the junction of Ore. 126 and U.S. 20, you'll find some of the Cascades' most enchanting water features. Southernmost of these is **Belknap Resort and Hot Springs** (© 541/822-3512), where, for $4.50 an hour or $8.50 a day, you can soak in a hot mineral swimming pool. Just north of Trail Bridge Reservoir, on a side road off the highway, a 4-mile round-trip hike on a section of the McKenzie River Trail leads to the startlingly blue waters of the **Tamolitch Pool** ★★. This pool is formed when the McKenzie River wells up out of the ground after flowing underground for 3 miles. Five miles south of the junction with Ore. 20, you'll come to two picturesque waterfalls, **Sahalie Falls** and **Koosah Falls.** Across the highway from these falls is **Clear Lake,** the source of the McKenzie River. This spring-fed lake truly lives up to its name, and a rustic lakeside resort rents rowboats so you can get out on the water and see for yourself. Be sure to hike the trail on the east side of the lake; it leads to the turquoise waters of **Great Springs,** which is connected to the lake by a 100-yard stream.

One of the most breathtaking sections of road in the state begins just east of **Belknap Hot Springs.** Ore. 242, which is open only in the summer, is a narrow, winding road that climbs up through forests and lava fields to **McKenzie Pass** ★★, from which there's a sweeping panorama of the Cascades and some of the youngest lava fields in Oregon. An observation building made of lava rock provides sighting tubes so that you can identify all the visible peaks, and a couple of trails will lead you out into this otherworldly landscape. In autumn, this road has some of the best fall color in the state. On the west side of the pass, the short **Proxy Falls** trail leads through old lava flows to a waterfall that in late summer has no outlet stream. The water simply disappears into the porous lava.

WHERE TO STAY

Belknap Lodge & Hot Springs ♠ Finds
On the banks of the McKenzie River, this lodge is one of the most enjoyable mountain retreats in the state. Extensive lawns and perennial gardens have been planted, turning this clearing in the forest into a burst of color in the summer. Guest rooms vary in size, but all have comfortable modern furnishings. Some also have whirlpool tubs or decks overlooking the roaring river. Water from the hot springs, which are on the far side of the river and reached by a footbridge, is pumped into two small pools. The cabins are more rustic than the lodge rooms. The lodge also has sites for tents and RVs ($19–$20).

59296 N. Belknap Springs Rd. (P.O. Box 2001), McKenzie Bridge, OR 97413. © **541/822-3512.** Fax 541/ 822-3327. 24 units. $55–$110 cabin; $85–$110 double; $145–$185 suite. Rates for lodge include continental breakfast. MC, V. **Amenities:** 2 hot springs–fed outdoor pools. *In room:* No phone.

Holiday Farm Resort ♠ Finds
This beautifully situated and recently renovated getaway is a collection of white cottages perched on the edge of the McKenzie River. The setting under the big trees is as idyllic as you'll find in Oregon. Holiday Farm started out as a stagecoach stop and has been around long enough to have hosted U.S. President Herbert Hoover. Two dining rooms, including one beside the river, together serve three meals a day. Guests have 800 feet of riverfront to enjoy and two private lakes for fishing and swimming.

54455 McKenzie River Dr., Blue River, OR 97413. © **800/823-3715** or 541/822-3715. www.holidayfarmresort. com. 16 units. $125–$150 cottage. AE, MC, V. **Amenities:** Restaurant (International), lounge; babysitting. *In room:* Kitchen, no phone.

Log Cabin Inn ♠
Situated on 6½ acres in the community of McKenzie Bridge, this log lodge was built in 1906 after the original 1886 lodge (a stage-coach stop) burned to the ground. Today, you can stay in rustic cabins, all but one of which have their own fireplaces. The one cabin without a fireplace does, however, have a kitchen, which the others do not. Although the one duplex log cabin has cramped rooms, it has a lot of woodsy character. There are also large teepees ($45 per night) that sleep up to six people for anyone interested in camping. The lodge's restaurant is renowned for its high-quality meals, which include such game as wild boar, venison, and buffalo (see p. 257 for details).

56483 McKenzie Hwy., McKenzie Bridge, OR 97413. © **800/355-3432** or 541/822-3432. Fax 541/822-6183. www.logcabininn.com. 8 cabins. $90–$110 cabin for 2–4 people. 2-night minimum stay on weekends Apr–Oct. DISC, MC, V. **Amenities:** Restaurant (American), lounge; massage. *In room:* Coffeemaker.

CAMPGROUNDS

There are several campgrounds along the McKenzie River on Ore. 126. Of these, the **Delta Campground,** set under huge old-growth trees between Blue River and McKenzie Bridge, is one of the finest. If you are up this way to hike, mountain bike, or do some flat-water canoeing, there is no better choice than Clear Lake's **Coldwater Cove Campground** on Ore. 126 just south of Santiam Pass junction. South of here on Ore. 126, the **Trail Bridge Campground** makes a good alternative to Coldwater Cove. Along the popular McKenzie Pass Highway (Ore. 242), you'll find **Scott Lake Campground, Alder Springs Campground,** and **Lava Lake Campground.**

Along the Aufderheide National Scenic Byway, you'll find several camp-grounds. **Cougar Crossing,** toward the north end of the scenic byway, is the closest campground to Terwilliger Hot Springs. South of here you'll find **Frissell Crossing, Homestead,** and **French Pete,** all of which are on the banks of the South Fork of the McKenzie River. Toward the south end of this road is **Kiahanie Campground,** which is on the North Fork of the Middle Fork of the Willamette River and is popular with fly anglers.

WHERE TO DINE

For burgers, try the **Vida Cafe,** milepost 26 (© **541/896-3289**), or, at milepost 38, the **Finn Rock Store and Grill,** 50660 McKenzie Hwy. (© **541/822-3299**), which has a deck beside the river. For some of the best pies in the state, stop at the **Village Cafe/Mom's Pies,** 49647 McKenzie Hwy., Vida (© **541/822-3891**).

Log Cabin Inn ✍ AMERICAN   If you've been searching for the quintessen-tial Cascades dining experience, this is it. This log-cabin restaurant has been in business since 1906, and serves mountain classics such as pan-fried trout and charbroiled venison medallions. In the warmer months, the big veranda, sur-rounded by colorful flower gardens, is the place to eat. For only $10.95, Sunday brunch here is a great deal, and at lunch other days of the week, keep an eye out for wild game stew. Top it all off with some marionberry cobbler.

56483 McKenzie Hwy., McKenzie Bridge. © 541/822-3432. Main courses lunch $8–$10, dinner $15–$21. DISC, MC, V. Mon–Sat noon–2pm and 5–8pm; Sun 10am–1pm and 5–8pm. Reduced hours in winter.

3 The Willamette Pass Route

Oakridge: 41 miles SE of Eugene; Willamette Pass: 68 miles SE of Eugene

Ore. 58, which connects Eugene with U.S. 97 north of Crater Lake, is the state's fastest and straightest route over the Cascades. However, this is not to imply that there isn't anything along this highway worth slowing down for. Flanked by two wilderness areas, Waldo Lake and Diamond Peak, and three major lakes, Waldo, Odell, and Crescent, Ore. 58 provides access to a wide range of recreational activities, chief among which are mountain biking, fishing, and boating in sum-mer and both downhill and cross-country skiing in winter.

The sister towns of Oakridge and Westfir are the only real towns on this entire route and are the only places where you'll find much in the way of services. West-fir is also the southern terminus of the Aufderheide National Scenic Byway, which winds through the Cascade foothills to just outside the town of McKenzie Bridge on Ore. 126. For information on this scenic drive, see above.

ESSENTIALS

GETTING THERE   Ore. 58 begins just south of Eugene off I-5 and stretches for 92 miles to U.S. 97.

VISITOR INFORMATION   For more information on recreational activities in this area, contact the **Middle Fork Ranger Station,** 46375 Hwy. 58, Westfir, OR 97492 (© **541/782-2291**). For other information, contact the **Oakridge/Westfir Chamber of Commerce,** P.O. Box 217, Oakridge, OR 97463 (© **541/782-4146;** www.oakridgechamber.com).

WHAT TO SEE & DO: HOT SPRINGS TO SNOW SKIING

In the Willamette National Forest outside the logging town of Oakridge are miles and miles of great **mountain-biking trails** that have turned the Oakridge area into one of Oregon's top mountain-biking regions. Stop by the ranger station in Westfir to get maps and information on riding these trails. One of the most scenic rides is the 22-mile trail around Waldo Lake. You'll also find trails at Willamette Pass Ski Area, where the cross-country ski trails are great for biking.

If you're keen to soak in some natural hot springs, you'll find some right beside Ore. 58 about 10 miles east of Oakridge. **McCredie Hot Springs** are neither the hottest nor the most picturesque springs in the state, and with traffic noise and crowds, they aren't the most pleasant either. But if you want a quick soak without having to go wandering down gravel roads, they do the trick.

Just before reaching Willamette Pass, you'll see signs for **Salt Creek Falls,** which are well worth a stroll down the short trail to the falls overlook. At 286 feet high, these are the second-highest falls in the state. Longer hiking trails also lead out from the falls parking area.

Also just before Willamette Pass is the turnoff for Forest Service Road 5897, which leads 10 miles north to **Waldo Lake,** one of the purest lakes in the world. The lake, which is just over a mile high, covers 10 square miles and is 420 feet deep. When the waters are still, it is possible to see more than 100 feet down into the lake. Because this is such a large lake, and because there are reliable afternoon winds, it is popular for sailboating and windsurfing. Powerboaters, canoeists, and sea kayakers also frequent the lake. There are several campgrounds along the east shore of the lake, while the west shore abuts the Waldo Lake Wilderness Area. The 22-mile loop trail around the lake is popular with mountain bikers and backpackers, but shorter day hikes, particularly at the south end, are rewarding. The mosquitoes here are some of the worst in the state, so before planning a trip up here, be sure to get a bug report from the Middle Fork Ranger Station.

Just over Willamette Pass lie two more large lakes. **Odell Lake** is best known by anglers who come to troll for kokanee salmon and Mackinaw trout. However, it's also a good windsurfing lake, and each July it hosts the Pioneer Cup Canoe Races. Although the waters never exactly get warm, **Crescent Lake** is the area's best for swimming, notably at Symax Beach, on the lake's northeast corner.

At **Willamette Pass Ski Area** (✆ **541/345-SNOW;** www.willamettepass. com), 69 miles southeast of Eugene on Ore. 58, you'll find 29 downhill runs and 12 miles (20km) of groomed cross-country trails. The ski area is open daily from around Thanksgiving to mid-April. Night skiing is available on Friday and Saturday nights from late December to March. Adult lift tickets are $32 per day.

WHERE TO STAY

Odell Lake Lodge ✦   This rustic cabin resort is pretty basic, but the location is great. At the east end of Odell Lake just off Ore. 58, the lodge is set beneath tall trees beside the lake. Most popular in the summer, when fishing is the sport of choice, the lodge also stays open through the winter and has its own network of groomed cross-country ski trails. The lodge rooms are generally rather small, but the economical prices keep them filled. The cabins vary in size from tiny one-bedroom buildings to one with four bedrooms. All the cabins have wood stoves and kitchens, and about half overlook the water. In summer, the lodge's marina rents fishing boats (and tackle), canoes, rowboats, and sailboats. The lodge also rents mountain bikes and cross-country skis. Several of the cabins have been recently remodeled, so try to get one of these.

P.O. Box 72, Crescent Lake, OR 97425. ✆ **541/433-2540.** www.odelllakeresort.com. 19 units (including 12 cabins). $48–$62 double; $80–$235 cabin. Pets accepted ($5 per day). DISC, MC, V. **Amenities:** Restaurant (American); watersports equipment rentals; bike rentals. *In room:* No phone.

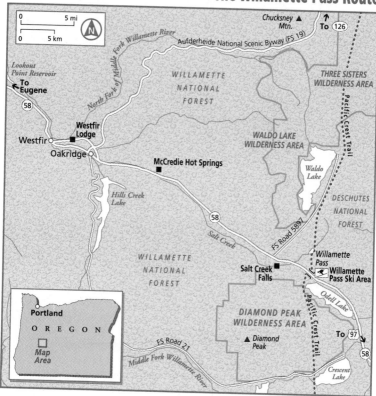

Westfir Lodge ⍟ Set at the southern end of the Aufderheide National Scenic Byway, this inn makes an excellent base for exploring both the McKenzie River to the north and the Willamette Pass area to the east. The inn is housed in what was once the company headquarters for a long-gone lumber mill and has a very Victorian feel inside and beautiful flower gardens outside. Directly across the street is the longest covered bridge in Oregon. Although all the rooms have private bathrooms, only four of these are actually in the room itself; others are across the hall from the guest room. An eclectic assemblage of antiques and artifacts from the innkeepers' world travels fills the guest rooms and many public rooms.

48365 First St., Westfir, OR 97492. ℂ **541/782-3103.** Fax 541/782-3103. 8 units. $50–$90 double. Rates include full breakfast. No credit cards. *In room:* A/C.

CAMPGROUNDS

On Waldo Lake, the **North Waldo Campground,** with its swimming area and boat launch, should be your first choice. Second choice on the lake should be **Islet Campground** or **Shadow Bay Campground** at the south end of the lake. If you have a boat, you can camp at primitive campsites along the west shore of the lake. **Gold Lake Campground,** just west of Willamette Pass on FS Road 500, is a quiet spot on a pretty fly-fishing-only lake that allows no motorboats. Just over Willamette Pass, there are several campgrounds on Odell Lake. **Odell Creek Campground** at the east end of the lake is the quietest campground on this lake.

WHERE TO DINE

Most people heading up this way plan to be self-sufficient when mealtime rolls around, whether they're camping or staying in a cabin. If you don't happen to have a full ice chest, you'll find a couple of pizza places, a Mexican restaurant, and a couple of espresso places in Oakridge. Although none of these is particularly memorable, they're the only places to get a meal other than in the dining room of the Odell Lake Lodge or the pizza place at the Willamette Pass Ski Area.

4 The North Umpqua–Upper Rogue River Scenic Byway

Diamond Lake: 76 miles E of Roseburg, 80 miles NE of Medford

Ore. 138, which heads east out of Roseburg and leads to Diamond Lake and the north entrance to Crater Lake National Park, is one of the state's most scenic highways. Along much of its length, the highway follows the North Umpqua River, which is famed among fly anglers for its fighting steelhead and salmon. As far as we're concerned, this deep aquamarine stream is the most beautiful river in Oregon and is well worth a visit even if you don't know a wooly bugger from a muddler minnow. Between Idleyld Park and Toketee Reservoir, you'll find numerous picnic areas, boat launches, swimming holes, and campgrounds.

As Ore. 138 approaches the crest of the Cascades, it skirts the shores of Diamond Lake, which though not even remotely as beautiful as nearby Crater Lake is still a major recreational destination. The lake, which is almost a mile in elevation, is set at the foot of jagged Mount Thielsen, a spire-topped pinnacle known as the "lightning rod of the Cascades." The lake offers swimming, boating, fishing, camping, hiking, biking, and, in winter, snowmobiling and skiing. Just beyond Diamond Lake is the north entrance to Crater Lake National Park.

The 24-mile-long Ore. 230 connects the Diamond Lake area with the valley of the upper Rogue River at the community of Union Creek. Although this stretch of the Rogue is not as dramatic as the North Umpqua or the lower Rogue River, it has its charms, including a natural bridge, a narrow gorge, and some grand old trees.

ESSENTIALS

GETTING THERE The North Umpqua River is paralleled by Ore. 138, which connects Roseburg, on I-5, with U.S. 97, which parallels the Cascades on the east side of the mountains. This highway leads to the north entrance of Crater Lake National Park.

VISITOR INFORMATION For information on recreational activities in this area, contact the **North Umpqua Ranger District,** 18782 N. Umpqua Hwy., Glide, OR 97443 (© **541/496-3532**); or the **Diamond Lake Ranger District,** 202 Toketee RS Rd., Idleyld Park, OR 97447 (© **541/498-2531**). Also check the websites of the **Rogue National Forest** (www.fs.fed.us/r6/rogue) and the **Umpqua National Forest** (www.fs.fed.us/r6/umpqua).

WHAT TO SEE & DO: FLY-FISHING, RAFTING & A WATERFALL

Oregon abounds in waterfalls and white-water rivers, but in the town of Glide, 12 miles east of Roseburg, you'll find the only place in the state where rivers collide. At the interesting **Colliding Rivers Viewpoint,** the North Umpqua River rushing in from the north slams into the white water of the Little River, which flows from the south, and the two rivers create a churning stew. However, this phenomenon is really only impressive during times of winter rains or during spring snowmelt season.

The most celebrated portion of the river is the 31-mile stretch from Deadline Falls, in Swiftwater Park to Soda Springs Dam. This stretch of river is open to fly angling only. Between June and October, you can often see salmon and steelhead leaping up Deadline Falls, which has a designated salmon-viewing area down a short trail on the south bank of the river. For fly-fishing needs and advice, stop in at the **Blue Heron Fly Shop,** 109 Hargis Lane, Idleyld Park (© **541/496-0448**), which is just off Ore. 138, or **Steamboat Inn,** 42705 North Umpqua Hwy. (© **541/498-2230**) in Steamboat. If you want to hire a guide to take you out fishing on the North Umpqua River, try **Jerry Q. Phelps** (© **541/672-8324**). Expect to pay between $150 and $250 per day.

If you'd rather just paddle the river in a kayak or raft, contact **North Umpqua Outfitters** (© **888/789-7152** or 541/673-4599; www.nuorafting.com) or **Oregon Ridge and River Excursions** (© **888/454-9696** or 541/496-3333; http://rafting.rosenet.net), offering trips of varying lengths. Rates are around $90 to $95 for a full day and $65 to $75 for a half day. Oregon Ridge and River Excursions also offers half-day and full-day guided mountain-bike rides ($55 and $75), daylong, flat-water canoe tours ($90), as well as multiday tours.

At the turnoff for Toketee Reservoir, you'll find the trail head for the half-mile hike to **Toketee Falls** ☞. This double cascade plummets 120 feet over a wall of columnar basalt and is one of the most picturesque waterfalls in the state. The viewing area is on a deck built around a large old tree and perched out on the edge of a cliff. Also in this same area, past the Toketee Lake Campground, you'll find **Umpqua Hot Springs,** which are down a short trail. These natural hot springs perch high above the North Umpqua River on a hillside covered with mineral deposits. For longer hikes, consider the many segments of the 79-mile **North Umpqua Trail,** which parallels the river from just east of Glide all the way to the Pacific Crest Trail. The lower segments of this trail are also popular mountain-biking routes.

At **Diamond Lake,** just a few miles north of Crater Lake National Park, you'll find one of the most popular mountain recreation spots in the state. In summer, the popular and somewhat run-down **Diamond Lake Resort** is the center of area activities. Here you can rent boats, swim at a small beach, and access the 10½-mile paved hiking/biking trail that circles Diamond Lake.

Near the community of Union Creek, west of the Crater Lake National Park on Ore. 62, are the Rogue River Gorge and a small natural bridge formed by a lava tube. The gorge, though only a few feet wide in places, is quite dramatic and has an easy trail running alongside.

In winter, Diamond Lake Resort serves as the region's main snowmobiling destination, but it also serves as a base camp for downhill skiers heading out with **Mount Bailey Snowcats** (© **800/446-4555;** www.mountbailey.com), which provides access to untracked snow on the slopes of nearby Mount Bailey. A day of snowcat-skiing will cost you $200. Cross-country skiers will find rentals and groomed trails at **Diamond Lake Resort.** There are also many more miles of marked, but not groomed, cross-country ski trails in the area; the more interesting trails are found at the south end of the lake. Snowmobile rentals and tours are also available. For more information on these activities, contact **Diamond Lake Resort** (© **800/733-7593**).

WHERE TO STAY & DINE

Prospect Historical Hotel/Motel ☞ (Finds)   This combination historic hotel/modern motel is in the tiny hamlet of Prospect, 30 miles from Crater Lake's Rim Village. The 1889 hotel is a big white building with a wraparound porch, and although the small rooms have few furnishings, their country styling lends them a bit of charm. If you stay in one of these rooms, you'll get air conditioning and continental breakfast. The motel rooms are much larger and have TVs, telephones, and coffeemakers; some also have kitchenettes. The elegant dining room, which is open May through September, serves good, simple food, including potpie, grilled salmon, filet mignon, and chicken Dijon.

391 Mill Creek Dr., Prospect, OR 97536. © 800/944-6490 or 541/560-3664. Fax 503/560-3825. www. prospecthotel.com. 24 units. $50–$90 double. DC, DISC, MC, V. Pets accepted. **Amenities:** Restaurant (American). *In room :* A/C, TV, coffeemaker.

Steamboat Inn ★★   Roughly midway between Roseburg and Crater Lake, this inn on the banks of the North Umpqua River is by far the finest lodging on the river. Although the lodge appeals primarily to anglers, the beautiful gardens, luxurious guest rooms, and gourmet meals also attract a fair number of people looking for a quiet getaway in the forest and a base for hiking and biking. If you aren't springing for one of the suites, which have their own soaking tubs overlooking the river, your best bet will be a streamside rooms, misleadingly referred to as cabins. These have gas fireplaces and open onto a long deck that overlooks the river. The hideaway cottages are more spacious but don't have river views and are half a mile from the lodge (and the cozy dining room). Dinners ($40) are multicourse affairs and are open to the public by reservation. There's a fly-fishing shop on the premises.

42705 N. Umpqua Hwy., Steamboat, OR 97447-9703. © 800/840-8825 or 541/498-2230. Fax 541/498-2411. www.thesteamboatinn.com. 19 units (including 5 cottages and 4 houses). $140 cabin; $180–$185 cottages and houses; $260 suites. MC, V. Closed Jan–Feb. **Amenities:** Restaurant (Northwest). *In room:* Hair dryer.

CAMPGROUNDS

Along the North Umpqua River between Idleyld Park and Diamond Lake, you'll find the Bureau of Land Management's **Susan Creek Campground,** the most upscale public campground along the North Umpqua. (It even has hot showers.) The large **Horseshoe Bend Campground,** near Steamboat, is popular with rafters and kayakers on weekends and has well-separated campsites, big views of surrounding cliffs, and access to the North Umpqua Trail. **Toketee Lake Campground,** at Toketee Reservoir, is situated back from the lake, but there are a few sites on the river.

Diamond Lake has three U.S. Forest Service campgrounds—Diamond Lake, Broken Arrow, and Thielsen View—with a total of 450 campsites. Here you'll also find the **Diamond Lake RV Park** (© 541/793-3318).

Southwest of the Crater Lake National Park on Ore. 62, you'll find **Farewell Bend Campground,** which is set amid big trees on the Rogue River. The next campgrounds are **Union Creek** and **Natural Bridge,** both of which are also along the Rogue River. North of Ore. 62 on Ore. 230, you'll find the **Hamaker Campground,** on a pretty bend in the Rogue River with big trees and meadows across the river.

5 Crater Lake National Park ★★★

71 miles NE of Medford, 83 miles E of Roseburg, 57 miles N of Klamath Falls

At 1,932 feet deep, Crater Lake is the deepest lake in the United States (and the seventh deepest in the world). But depth alone is not what has made this one of the most visited spots in the Northwest. Ever since a prospector searching for gold

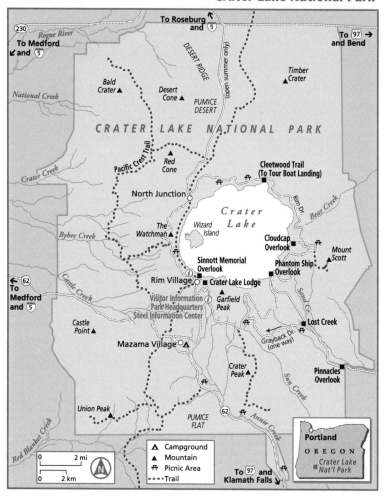

stumbled on the high mountain lake in 1853, its sapphire-blue waters have mesmerized visitors. In 1902, the lake and its surroundings became a national park.

The crater (or more accurately, a caldera) that holds the serene lake was born in an explosive volcanic eruption 7,700 years ago. When the volcano, now known as Mount Mazama, erupted, its summit (thought to have been around 12,000 ft. high) collapsed, leaving a crater 4,000 feet deep. It has taken thousands of years of rain and melting snow to create the cold, clear lake, which today is surrounded by crater walls nearly 2,000 feet high.

The drive into the park winds through forests that offer no hint of the spectacular sight lying hidden among these mountains. With no warning except the signs leading to Rim Village, you suddenly find yourself gazing down into a vast bowl of blue water. Toward one end of the lake, the cone of Wizard Island rises from the lake. This island is the tip of a volcano that has been building slowly since Mount Mazama's last eruption.

ESSENTIALS

GETTING THERE   If you're coming from the south on I-5, take exit 62 in Medford and follow Ore. 62 for 75 miles. If you're coming from the north, take Exit 124 in Roseburg and follow Ore. 138. From Klamath Falls, take U.S. 97 north to Ore. 62. In winter, only the south entrance is open. Due to deep snowpack, the north entrance usually doesn't open until sometime in late July.

VISITOR INFORMATION   For more information, contact **Crater Lake National Park,** P.O. Box 7, Crater Lake, OR 97604 (© **541/594-2211;** www. nps.gov/crla).

ADMISSION   Park admission is $10 per vehicle.

SEEING THE HIGHLIGHTS

After your first breathtaking view of the lake, you may want to stop by one of the park's two visitor centers. The **Steel Information Center** is between the south park entrance and the Rim Village, which is where you'll find the smaller and less thorough **Rim Village Visitor Center.** Though the park is open year-round, in winter, when deep snows blanket the region, only the road to Rim Village is kept clear. During the summer (roughly beginning in late June), the **Rim Drive** 🏵🏵 provides many viewpoints along its 39-mile length.

Narrated boat trips 🏵🏵 around the lake are the park's most popular activity. These tours last 1¾ hours and begin at Cleetwood Cove, at the bottom of a very steep 1-mile trail that descends 700 feet from the rim to the lakeshore. Before deciding to take a boat tour, be sure you're in good enough physical condition to make the steep climb back up to the rim. Bring warm clothes because it can be quite a bit cooler on the lake than it is on the rim. A naturalist on each boat provides a narrative on the ecology and history of the lake, and all tours include a stop on Wizard Island. Tours are offered from late June to mid-September and cost $19.25 for adults and $11 for children 11 and under.

Of the many miles of **hiking trails** within the park, the mile-long Cleetwood Trail is the only trail that leads down to the lakeshore. It's a steep and tiring hike back up from the lake. The trail to the top of Mount Scott, although it's a rigorous 2½-mile hike, is the park's most rewarding. Shorter trails with good views include the 0.8-mile trail to the top of the Watchman, which overlooks Wizard Island, and the 1.7-mile trail up Garfield Peak. The short Castle Crest Wildflower Trail is best hiked in late July or early August. Backpackers can hike the length of the park on the Pacific Crest Trail (PCT) or head out on a few other trails that lead into more remote, though less scenic, corners of the park.

Other summertime park activities include children's programs, campfire ranger talks, history lectures, and guided walks. To find out about these, check in *Crater Lake Reflections,* a free park newspaper given to all visitors when they enter the park.

In winter, **cross-country skiing** is popular on the park's snow-covered Rim Drive and in the backcountry. At Rim Village, you'll find several miles of well-marked ski trails, affording some of the best views in the state, weather permitting. Skiers in good condition can usually make the entire circuit of the lake in 2 days but must be prepared to camp in the snow. Spring, when the weather is warmer and there are fewer severe storms, is actually the best time to ski around the lake.

WHERE TO STAY & DINE

Crater Lake Lodge 🏵🏵   Perched on the edge of the rim overlooking Crater Lake, this lodge is the finest national-park lodge in the Northwest. Not only are the views breathtaking, but also the amenities are modern without sacrificing the rustic atmosphere (a stone fireplace and ponderosa pine-bark walls in the lobby). Slightly more than half of the guest rooms overlook the lake, and although most rooms have modern bathrooms, eight have claw-foot bathtubs. The very best rooms are the corner rooms on the lake side of the lodge. The lodge's dining room provides a view of both Crater Lake and the Klamath River basin. Reservations are hard to come by. Plan as far in advance possible.

Mailing address: 1211 Ave. C, White City, OR 97503. ☏ **541/830-8700.** Fax 541/830-8514. www.crater-lake.com. 71 units. $120–$175 double. MC, V. Closed mid-Oct to mid-May. **Amenities:** Restaurant (Northwest), lounge. *In room:* No phone.

Mazama Village Motor Inn 🐾   Though the Mazama Village Motor Inn isn't on the rim of the crater, it's just a short drive away and should be your second choice of lodgings on a Crater Lake vacation. The modern motel-style guest rooms are housed in 10 steep-roofed buildings that look much like traditional mountain cabins. A laundry, gas station, and general store make Mazama Village a busy spot in the summer.

Mailing address: 1211 Ave. C, White City, OR 97503. ☏ **541/830-8700.** Fax 541/830-8514. www.crater-lake.com. 40 units. $101 double. MC, V. Closed Nov–May. *In room:* Coffeemaker, no phone.

CAMPGROUNDS

Tent camping and RV spaces are available on the south side of the park at the **Mazama Campground,** where there are 200 sites ($15.50–$17 per night). This campground is open May through October. There are also 16 tent sites available at **Lost Creek Campground** ($10 per night) on the park's east side. This campground is open June through September. Reservations are not accepted at either campground. For information on campgrounds outside the park, see "Campgrounds" in "The North Umpqua–Upper Rogue River Scenic Byway" section above.

9

Southern Oregon

Stretching from the California state line in the south to a little way north of Roseburg, Southern Oregon is a mountainous region that has far more in common with Northern California than it has with the rest of Oregon. Dominating the region are the Siskiyou Mountains, a jumble of rugged peaks and rare plants that serve as a link between the Cascades and the Coast Range.

It was gold that first brought European settlers to this area, and it was timber that kept them here. The gold is all played out now, but the legacy of the gold-rush days, when stagecoaches traveled the rough road between Sacramento and Portland, can be seen in picturesque towns such as Jacksonville and Oakland.

Although Southern Oregon is a long drive from the nearest metropolitan areas, it is relatively easy to plan a multiday trip from San Francisco, Portland, or Seattle. From Ashland, the southernmost city in the region, it's a 6-hour trip to either Portland or San Francisco.

Ashland is renowned for its **Oregon Shakespeare Festival,** which attracts tens of thousands of theatergoers annually. The festival, which now stretches through most of the year, has turned a sleepy mill town into a facsimile of Tudor England. Not to be outdone, the nearby historic town of **Jacksonville** ✿ offers performances by internationally recognized musicians and dance companies throughout the summer.

However, the performing arts aside, it is rugged beauty and the outdoors that draw most people to the region. **Crater Lake National Park,** Oregon's only national park, hides within its boundaries a sapphire jewel formed by the massive eruption of Mount Mazama less than 7,000 years ago. In this same area rise two of the most fabled **fly-fishing** rivers in the country. Ever since Zane Grey wrote of the fighting steelhead trout and salmon of the Rogue and Umpqua Rivers, flyfishers have been casting their lines in hopes of hooking a few of these wily denizens of the Cascade Range's cold waters. (For information on Crater Lake and the North Umpqua River, see chapter 8.)

1 Ashland & the Oregon Shakespeare Festival

285 miles S of Portland, 50 miles W of Klamath Falls, 350 miles N of San Francisco

With new cocktail bars and upscale restaurants, live jazz in the clubs and cafes, more art galleries than ever before, and day spas that take advantage of Ashland's famed Lithia Springs mineral waters, Ashland is growing ever more cosmopolitan. Sure, this is still a small town 6 hours by car from the nearest metropolitan area, but more than half a century of staging Shakespeare plays has turned it into Oregon's preeminent arts community.

It all started on the Fourth of July 1935. In a small Ashland theater built as part of the Chautauqua movement, Angus Bowmer, an English professor at

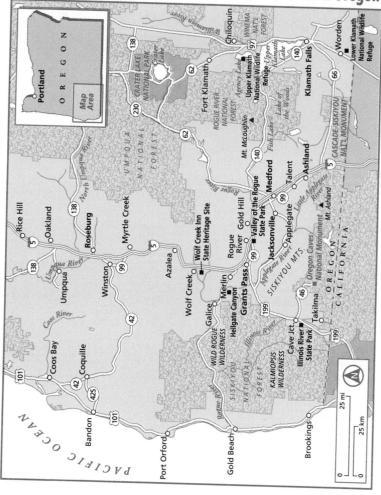

Southern Oregon University, was staging a performance of Shakespeare's *As You Like It.* The Depression had dashed any hopes local businessman Jesse Winburne had of turning Ashland, a quiet mill town in the rugged Siskiyou Mountains, into a mineral-springs resort. However, before the Depression struck, Winburne had managed to construct beautiful **Lithia Park.** Luckily, neither man's love's labor was lost, and today their legacies have turned the town into one of the Northwest's most popular destinations.

Each year more than 300,000 people attend performances of the **Oregon Shakespeare Festival,** a 9-month-long repertory festival that was born of Bowmer's love of the Bard. Though Ashland never became a mineral-springs resort, Lithia Park, through which still flow the clear waters of Winburne's dreams, is the town's centerpiece. Surrounding the town are mountains and forests that also offer a wealth of outdoor recreational activities, so there's still plenty to do when the stages are quiet and dark. This is one of the best little arts towns in America, so be prepared to fall in love.

> ⌒Tips **For Your Information**
>
> In addition to the sources of information listed in each individual city section, you can get information on all of southern Oregon by contacting the following regional tourism associations: **Southern Oregon Visitors Association,** P.O. Box 1645, Medford, OR 97501-0731 (© **800/448-4856;** www. sova.org), and the **Southern Oregon Reservation Center,** P.O. Box 477, Ashland, OR 97520 (© **800/547-8052** or 541/488-1011; www.sorc.com), which mainly provides information and reservations for area theater, attractions, and lodging.

ESSENTIALS

GETTING THERE   Ashland is located on I-5. From the east, Ore. 66 connects Ashland with Klamath Falls.

The nearest airport is the **Rogue Valley International–Medford Airport** in Medford, which is served by Horizon/Alaska Airlines and United Airlines. A taxi from the airport to Ashland will cost around $16.

VISITOR INFORMATION   Contact the **Ashland Chamber of Commerce,** 110 E. Main St. (P.O. Box 1360), Ashland, OR 97520 (© **541/482-3486;** www.ashlandchamber.com).

GETTING AROUND   If you need a taxi, call **Yellow Cab** (© **541/ 482-3065**). Car-rental companies with offices at the Rogue Valley International Airport are Avis, Budget, Hertz, and National. **Rogue Valley Transportation District** (© **541/779-2877**) provides public bus service in the Ashland area.

FESTIVALS   The month-long Yuletide **Holiday Festival of Lights** held each year in December is Ashland's other big annual festival.

THE OREGON SHAKESPEARE FESTIVAL

The raison d'être of Ashland, the Oregon Shakespeare Festival is an internationally acclaimed theater festival with a season that stretches from February to October. The season typically includes four works by Shakespeare plus eight other classic or contemporary plays. These plays are performed in repertory, with as many as four staged on any given day.

The festival complex, often referred to as "the bricks" because of its brick courtyard, is in the center of town and contains three theaters. The visually impressive outdoor **Elizabethan Theatre,** modeled after England's 17th-century Fortune Theatre, is used only in the summer and early fall. The **Angus Bowmer Theatre** is the festival's largest indoor theater. By the 2002 season, the festival should have its state-of-the-art **New Theatre** up and running. This theater replaces the Black Swan, which for many years was a venue for contemporary and experimental plays.

In addition to the plays, there are **backstage tours.** (Tickets are $10 for adults and $7.50 for children, with lower prices in spring and fall.) Throughout the festival season there are also talks and special performances. The opening of the Elizabethan Theatre is celebrated each June in Lithia Park with the elaborate Feast of Will.

For more information and upcoming schedules, contact the **Oregon Shakespeare Festival,** 15 S. Pioneer St. (P.O. Box 158), Ashland, OR 97520 (© **541/ 482-4331;** www.osfashland.org). Ticket prices range from $28 to $56; children's

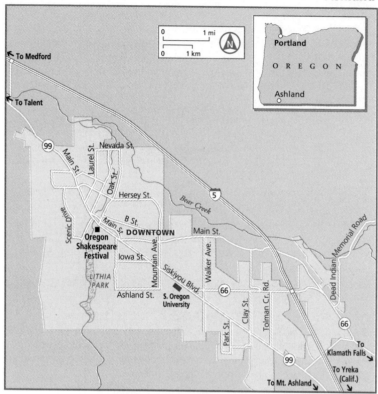

and preview tickets are less expensive. In spring and fall, all ticket prices are discounted 25%.

EXPLORING ASHLAND & ITS SURROUNDINGS

The **Schneider Museum of Art,** 1250 Siskiyou Blvd. (© **541/552-6245;** www.sou.edu/sma), on the campus of the Southern Oregon University, mounts art exhibits of a quality you'd expect in a museum in a major city. The museum is open Tuesday through Saturday from 10am to 4pm (until 7pm on first Fri of each month).

Ashland's first claim to fame was its healing mineral waters, and today you can still relax and be pampered at one of the city's day spas. **Ashland Springs Spa & Boutique,** 236 E. Main St. (© **541/552-0144**), **The Phoenix,** 2425 Siskiyou Blvd. (© **541/488-1281**), and **Atrium Center for Body Therapies,** 51 Water St. (© **541/488-4088**), all offer various body treatments, skin care, and massages.

Long before Shakespeare came to town, this was farm country, and if you'd like to pay a visit to a first-class farm stand, head over to Talent, where you'll find **MeadowBrook Farm,** 6731 Wagner Creek Rd. (© **541/535-2688**). Step into the past at this National Historical Landmark and organic farm. There are flower and herb gardens and a renovated barn, and you can have a picnic on the grounds. To reach the farm, take Rapp Road west from Ore. 99 in Talent.

WINE TOURING

Ashland Vineyards   Grapes used in the wines here are organically grown on the surrounding vineyards. Best for white wines such as Chardonnay and dry Sauvignon Blanc.

2775 E. Main St. ✆ 541/488-0088. www.winenet.com. 50¢ per taste. Apr–Oct Tues–Sun 11am–5pm; Nov–Dec and Mar Tues–Sat 11am–5pm; Jan by appt. Closed Dec 23–Mar 1. From I-5, take exit 14, drive east and follow signs.

Paschal ✿✿   This is the newest winery in the region and at press time was just finishing its tasting room. Although they don't yet produce very many varietals here (Chardonnay, Pinot Gris, Cabernet Sauvignon, Syrah-Cabernet blend), the vineyards are planted with a wider variety of grapes. Within the next few years look for Viognier and Merlot as well.

1122 Suncrest Rd., Talent. ✆ 800/446-6050. www.paschalwinery.com. Tues–Sun 10am–6pm. From Ore. 99 north of Ashland, take W. Valley View Rd. and turn left onto Suncrest Rd.

Weisinger's ✿   Just south of town, this family-owned winery has a great view over the hills and valleys. Dry whites are a strong point, though if you like tannins you may like Weisinger's Merlot and Petite Pompadour, a Bordeaux-style blend of Cabernet Franc, Merlot, Malbec, and Cabernet Sauvignon.

3150 Siskiyou Blvd. ✆ 800/551-WINE or 541/488-5989. www.weisingers.com. May–Oct daily 10am–6pm; Nov–Apr Wed–Sun 11am–5pm. Take Ore. 99 (Siskiyou Blvd.) south from downtown Ashland.

ENJOYING THE GREAT OUTDOORS

A memorable part of your visit will be a long, leisurely stroll through beautiful **Lithia Park.** This 100-acre park follows the banks of Ashland Creek starting at the plaza. Shade trees, lawns, flowers, ponds, fountains, and, of course, the babbling brook are reminiscent of an English garden.

Summertime thrill-seekers shouldn't pass up the chance to do some **white-water rafting** ✿ on the Rogue or Klamath River while in southern Oregon. Several companies offer trips between April and October. Try **Noah's River Adventures,** 53 N. Main St. (✆ 800/858-2811 or 541/488-2811; www.noahsrafting.com), or **The Adventure Center,** 40 N. Main St. (✆ 800/444-2819 or 541/488-2819; www.raftingtours.com), both of which have trips lasting from half a day to 5 days. Prices range from $69 for a half-day trip per person to about $119 to $250 for a full day, depending on the length and type of the trip. The former company also offers salmon- and steelhead-fishing trips, and the latter offers downhill bike rides from the top of Mount Ashland.

Mountain bikes ($10 per hr. or $45 per day) can be rented at **Bear Creek Bicycles,** 1988 Hwy. 99N (✆ 541/488-4270), and the folks at this shop can point you in the direction of good rides. The Bear Creek path is a great, easy choice.

Miles of **hiking trails,** including the Pacific Crest Trail, can be found up on Mount Ashland in the Siskiyou Rogue River National Forest. Another stretch of the Pacific Crest Trail lies within the newly designated **Cascade-Siskiyou National Monument,** which is located south and east of Ashland. This monument was created to preserve an area of outstanding botanical diversity, but is limited in its recreational opportunities. For more information, contact the Medford office of the **Bureau of Land Management** (✆ 541/618-2200).

Horseback riding is available at **Mountain Gate Stables,** 4399 Ore. 66 (✆ 541/482-8873). Rides start at $25 for 1 hour (two-person minimum).

In the winter there's good downhill and cross-country **skiing** at **Mt. Ashland Ski Area,** 15 miles south of Ashland (© **541/482-2897** for information or **541/482-2754** for snow report; www.mtashland.com). Day-lift tickets for adults range from about $23 to $27. You can rent cross-country skis and pick up ski-trail maps at **Ashland Outdoor Store,** 37 Third St. (© **541/488-1202**).

SHOPPING

Ashland has the best shopping in southern Oregon. Interesting and unusual shops line East Main Street, so when the curtains are down on the stages, check the windows of downtown.

Art galleries abound in Ashland, and on the first Friday of the month, many are open late. One of our favorites for contemporary art is the **Hanson Howard Gallery,** 82 N. Main St. (© **541/488-2562**). Right on the plaza, be sure to check out the **Ashland Hardwood Gallery,** 17 N. Main St. (© **877/723-6766;** www.hardwoodgallery.com), which is filled with fascinating works of art in wood. **Davis & Cline,** 525 A St., Ste. 1 (© **541/482-2069**), which is located in the historic Railroad District about 8 blocks from the plaza, is another of our favorite contemporary art galleries here in town. This gallery even sells Dale Chihuly art glass. And for a gallery of wearable art, stop by **The Web-sters,** 11 N. Main St. (© **541/482-9801**), a knitting and weaving store carrying beautiful sweaters, woven jackets, and accessories. At **Footlights Theatre Gallery,** 240 E. Main St. (© **541/488-5538;** www.footlightsgallery.com), you'll find a wall of posters available for purchase, from *Amadeus* to *West Side Story.* For a well-rounded selection of wines and other gourmet treats, you can't beat the **Chateaulin Wine Shoppe,** 52 E. Main St. (© **541/488-9463**), which is located next door to Chateaulin restaurant.

WHERE TO STAY

It seems Shakespeare and B&Bs go hand in hand. At last count, there were more than 30 bed-and-breakfasts in town. If your reason for coming to Ashland is to attend the Shakespeare Festival and you plan to stay at a B&B, you'll find it most convenient to choose an inn within walking distance of the theaters. By doing so, you'll also be within walking distance of the town's best restaurants and shopping and won't have to deal with finding a parking space before the show. For a comprehensive list of Ashland inns, contact **Ashland's Bed & Breakfast Network,** P.O. Box 1051, Ashland, OR 97520-0048 (© **800/944-0329;** www.abbnet.com).

If all you're looking for is a clean, comfortable room for the night, the **Super 8 Motel—Ashland,** 2350 Ashland St., Ashland, OR 97520 (© **800/800-8000** or 541/482-8887), is the most reliable bet in town and charges $50 to $69 double.

IN TOWN

Ashland Springs Hotel ★★ *Finds*   First opened in 1925, this nine-story historic hotel underwent a complete renovation between 1998 and 2000 and is now one of the finest hotels between Portland and San Francisco. In the light-filled lobby there are cases full of Victorian-era natural history displays, and on the mezzanine overlooking the lobby, tea is served on the weekends. Guest rooms are luxuriously appointed and beds sport crisp white linens, feather pillows, and down comforters. Although all the rooms have large windows, the corner rooms are worth requesting, as are rooms facing east over the city and the valley. Be sure to notice the fascinating collection of pressed plants that is on display behind the reception desk, in the elevator, and in guest rooms. The hotel's Elfinwood restaurant is an elegant Mediterranean-inspired space, while the casual Bulls-Eye Bistro takes old board games as its decorative theme.

212 E. Main St., Ashland, OR 97520. © 800/325-4000 or 541/488-1700. Fax 541/488-1701. www.westcoast hotels.com. 70 units. Mid-May to early Oct $119–$189 double; early Oct to mid-May $79–$129 double. Rates include full breakfast. AE, DISC, MC, V. **Amenities:** 2 restaurants (Northwest, American), lounge; affiliated adjacent full-service spa; concierge; room service; laundry service; dry cleaning. *In room:* A/C, TV, dataport, fridge, hair dryer, iron.

Best Western Bard's Inn ⌒ If you prefer motels to B&Bs and want to be within walking distance of downtown, the Bard's Inn should be your first choice in Ashland. This motel's best feature is that it's only 2 blocks from the festival theaters. The rooms are large and comfortable, and those in the new annex have patios or balconies, though they get a bit of traffic noise. The older rooms have all been refurbished.

132 N. Main St., Ashland, OR 97520. © 800/528-1234 or 541/482-0049. Fax 503/488-3259. www. bestwestern.com. 91 units. Mid-May to mid-Oct $119–$179 double. Mid-Oct to mid-May $72–$134 double. Rates include continental breakfast. AE, DC, DISC, MC, V. **Amenities:** Small outdoor pool; Jacuzzi. *In room:* A/C, TV, fridge, coffeemaker, hair dryer, iron.

Coolidge House ⌒⌒ Located right on busy North Main Street only 3 blocks from the theaters, this 1875 Victorian sits high above the street on a hill with commanding views across the valley. Although this is one of the oldest homes in Ashland inside you'll find not only interesting antiques, but also some decidedly modern amenities. Guest suites have sitting rooms and large luxurious bathrooms, most of which come with either a whirlpool tub or a claw-foot tub. The Parlor Suite, with its draped window seat, is the inn's most romantic room. However, if views and space are what you seek, opt for the Sun Suite or the Grape Arbor. There is a pleasant patio in the back garden.

137 N. Main St., Ashland, OR 97520. © 800/655-5522 or 541/482-4721. www.coolidgehouse.com. 6 units. Apr–Oct $150–$185 double. Nov–Mar $85–$120 double. Rates include full breakfast. 2-night minimum on weekends Apr–Oct. MC, V. *In room:* A/C, no phone.

The Palm ⌒ 𝘝𝘢𝘭𝘶𝘦 Although about a mile's drive or walk from the theaters of the Shakespeare Festival, this old, but recently upgraded motor court is an excellent value. The collection of little Cape Cod cottages is surrounded by colorful perennial gardens, and there's even a tiny swimming pool on the grounds. All the old cottages have been completely redone and have a classic cottage feel. Some rooms have kitchens.

1065 Siskiyou Blvd., Ashland, OR 97520. © 877/482-2635 or 541/482-2636. www.palmcottages.com. 13 units. $69–$95 double. MC, V. **Amenities:** Outdoor pool. *In room:* A/C, TV, dataport.

Peerless Hotel ⌒⌒ Located in the historic Railroad District 7 blocks from the festival theaters, this restored 1900 brick boarding house is one of Ashland's most interesting lodgings. With the feel of a small historic hotel rather than a B&B, the Peerless is filled with antiques and an eclectic array of individually decorated guest rooms. Of these, the West Indies suite, with its balcony, double whirlpool tub, and view of Ashland, is by far the most luxurious. However, all other rooms feature lush fabrics, unusual murals, stenciling, and tile work that add up to unexpected luxury. Most rooms have either a whirlpool tub or a claw-foot tub. (One even has two side-by-side claw-foot tubs.) The hotel's restaurant is one of the finest in Ashland (see below for details).

243 Fourth St., Ashland, OR 97520. © 800/460-8758 or 541/488-1082. www.peerlesshotel.com. 6 units. Early June–early Nov $125–$170 double; $195–$210 suite. Early Nov to mid-Feb $70–$130 double; $135–$180 suite. Mid-Feb to early June $95–$130 double; $160–$180 suite. Rates include full breakfast.

AE, DISC, MC, V. **Amenities:** Restaurant (Northwest), lounge; access to nearby health club; room service. *In room:* A/C, TV, minibar.

The Winchester Country Inn ★★   With its massive old shade trees, English tea gardens, and elegant, international restaurant (see "Where to Dine," below for details), the Winchester is Ashland's premier historic inn. Though it styles itself as a country inn, it's actually right in town within a few blocks of the theaters. The rooms are very comfortably furnished with antiques and modern bath fixtures, including sinks built into old bureaus in some rooms. We prefer the upstairs rooms, which get quite a bit more light than those on the ground floor. There are also rooms in the building next door. If you want a bit more space, six suites are available, two of which are in the old carriage house. The suites also come with TVs and VCRs. A decanter of sherry in each room is a welcome touch. Throughout the year, special events are held here, including murder-mystery weekends and Christmas Dickens feasts.

35 S. Second St., Ashland, OR 97520. ✆ 800/972-4991 or 541/488-1113. Fax 541/488-4604. www. winchesterinn.com. 18 units. $110–$150 double; $130–$215 suite. Rates include full breakfast. AE, DISC, MC, V. **Amenities:** Restaurant (International); access to nearby health club. *In room:* A/C, dataport, hair dryer, iron.

OUT OF TOWN

Country Willows ★★   Just outside town and surrounded by 5 acres of rolling hills and pastures, the Country Willows B&B offers the tranquillity of a farm only minutes from Ashland's theaters and excellent restaurants. If you're looking for a very special room, consider the Sunrise Suite, which is in a renovated barn behind the main house: it has pine paneling, a high ceiling, a king-size bed, a gas fireplace, and, best of all, an old-fashioned tub for two with its very own picture window and skylight. Rooms in the restored farmhouse are smaller, but some offer excellent views across the valley. Ducks, geese, and goats call the farm home, and there's a 2-mile hiking trail that starts at the back door. You'll also find a pool and whirlpool on the grounds.

1313 Clay St., Ashland, OR 97520. ✆ 800/WILLOWS or 541/488-1590. Fax 541/488-1611. www. willowsinn.com. 9 units. Mar–Oct $110–$155 double; $175–$225 suite. Nov–Feb $88–$124 double; $140–$180 suite. Rates include full breakfast. AE, DISC, MC, V. **Amenities:** Outdoor pool; access to nearby health club; Jacuzzi; bikes; concierge. *In room:* A/C, dataport, hair dryer, iron.

Mt. Ashland Inn ★★   Located on 160 acres on the side of Mount Ashland, this massive log home commands distant panoramas from its forest setting, and though the inn is only 15 minutes from downtown Ashland, you're in a different world up here. The Pacific Crest Trail, which stretches from Canada to Mexico, passes through the front yard, and just a few miles up the road is the Ski Ashland ski area. Whether you're in the area for an active vacation or a few nights of theater, this lodge makes a very special base of operations. The decor is straight out of an Eddie Bauer catalog, and in one guest bathroom there's a stone wall with a built-in waterfall. The Sky Lakes Wilderness Suite, which is on the top floor and has views of Mount Shasta is the best room in the house. In the winter, the inn has cross-country skis, snowshoes, and sleds for the use of the guests.

550 Mt. Ashland Rd., Ashland, OR 97520. ✆ 800/830-8707 or 541/482-8707. www.mtashlandinn.com. 5 units. $135–$200 suite. Rates include full breakfast. DISC, MC, V. **Amenities:** Jacuzzi; sauna; bikes. *In room:* Fridge, hair dryer, iron, microwave.

WHERE TO DINE

If you're headed to the theater after dinner, let your wait staff know. They will usually do whatever they can to make sure you aren't late! For a light post-theater meal, try Chateaulin (see below).

EXPENSIVE

Chateaulin ★★ FRENCH   Located just around the corner from the festival theaters, this has long been one of the finest restaurants in town. Exposed brick walls and old champagne bottles give Chateaulin a casually elegant appearance that's accented by Art Nouveau touches and dark-wood furnishings. The menu is almost as traditional as the decor; you can start your meal with escargots or house paté and then move on to rack of lamb. A separate bar menu (items are $6–$10) caters to smaller or après-theater appetites. The restaurant's award-winning wine list features French wines, as well as lots of hard-to-find wines from Oregon, Washington, and California. For visitors on a budget, there is a more affordable and contemporary prix-fixe menu that changes weekly. There's also an attached wine and gourmet-foods store for classy picnic fare.

50 E. Main St. ✆ 541/482-2264. www.chateaulin.com. Reservations recommended. Main courses $15–$29. AE, DISC, MC, V. June–Oct daily 5–9:30pm; Nov–May Wed–Sun 5:30–9pm. Bar open until midnight.

Firefly ★★ INTERNATIONAL   Located on the third floor of a building right on the plaza, Firefly has for several years now been one of Ashland's trendier restaurants, and is a big hit with visitors from San Francisco, Seattle, and Portland. The food here tends to be complex and beautifully presented, as you might expect from the hefty prices, and preparations follow the latest trends in high-end fusion foods. Currently, you'll find interesting combinations such as venison medallions with blueberry bread pudding and cognac demi-glace; pineapple-glazed confit of duck with an asparagus spring roll and coconut risotto; Gorgonzola and goat cheese ravioli with black truffles, grilled artichokes, and balsamic-soaked bread. There always seems to be an eclectic selection of desserts here. Plenty of wines by the glass and a good bar menu also make this a good spot for a fast, light meal.

23 N. Main St. ✆ 541/488-3212. www.fireflyrestaurant.com. Reservations recommended. Main courses $18–$29. AE, DISC, MC, V. Summer Tues–Sun 5–8:30pm; winter Wed–Sun 5–8pm.

Monet ★★ FRENCH   For fine French cuisine with an emphasis on lighter, more contemporary preparations, it's hard to beat Monet. Owned and operated by chef Pierre Verger, Monet has been in business for more than a decade, a testament to the popularity and quality of the restaurant's Gallic cuisine. Be sure to start with the smoked salmon wrapped around avocado mousse and served with a lemon-lime vinaigrette. From there, you've got plenty of good choices, including filet mignon with a port-and-truffle sauce. For lighter appetites, there are always several interesting salads and an excellent French onion soup. Vegetarians can choose from several dishes. Though the big white house (across the street from the Winchester Inn) looks rather plain from the outside, inside you'll find a somewhat formal and impeccably set dining room. On warm days, you may want to dine in the garden surrounded by many of the same flowers that grow in Monet's famous garden in France.

36 S. Second St. ✆ 541/482-1339. www.mind.net/monet. Reservations recommended. Main courses $17–$26. MC, V. June–Oct Tues–Sun 5:30–8:30pm; Nov–Dec and Feb–Apr Tues–Sat 5:30–8:30pm. Closed Jan.

New Sammy's Cowboy Bistro ★★ *Finds* NORTHWEST   Unmarked yet unmistakable, New Sammy's is a tiny shack of a place in nearby Talent. If it weren't for the fact that the building looks as if the owners got their paint at a Sherwin Williams going-out-of-business sale, you wouldn't even notice it. Be bold. Open the door. Things look different inside.

The menu is as imaginative as the exterior paint job, and everything is as fresh as it gets, with lots of organic produce from local growers and delicious rustic breads. Meats are antibiotic- and hormone-free, and for dessert there's a choice of several homemade ice creams and fresh fruits. This is a mom-and-pop operation (Mom cooks and Pop serves), and tables are frequently reserved several weeks in advance; so be sure to call ahead for a reservation.

2210 S. Pacific Hwy., Talent. ☎ 541/535-2779. Reservations highly recommended. Main courses $18–$35; 4-course menu $37. MC, V. Feb–Oct Thurs–Sun 5–9pm; Nov–Jan Fri–Sat 5–9pm.

The Peerless Restaurant ★★ PAN ASIAN/CONTINENTAL   With its

Hawaiian/tropical decor, this upscale restaurant a few blocks from the plaza seems decidedly out of place in the southern Oregon hills, but good food is good food no matter where it's served. The Peerless is actually two restaurants in one: a very formal gourmet dining room and a more casual (though only slightly less expensive) bistro. There's also a garden patio for summertime alfresco dining. Because The Peerless is out of Ashland's restaurant mainstream, it tends to work just a little bit harder to satisfy its customers. In the bistro, dinner might include a shrimp spring roll with spicy mango-ginger sauce for a starter, and caramelized salmon with orange-shoyu glaze for an entree. In the fine-dining wing, you might start with a duck *foie gras* or baked escargot followed by roasted rabbit or a wild mushroom crusted Alaskan halibut. For a truly decadent dinner, top it all off with a Grand Marnier or chocolate soufflé.

265 Fourth St. ☎ 541/488-6067. Reservations recommended. Bistro $14–$26; fine dining $21–$32. AE, DC, DISC, MC, V. June–Oct daily 5–9pm; Apr–May closed Sun; Nov–Mar closed Sun–Mon.

Primavera Restaurant & Gardens ★★ MEDITERRANEAN/REGIONAL

Housed in a former church and in business for more than a decade, Primavera serves an eclectic menu that focuses primarily on Mediterranean flavors. With both a full dinner menu and a bistro menu, there's enough variety to satisfy any budget. The menu changes regularly and is limited to a few choice treatments of beef (filet with Gorgonzola horseradish butter), chicken (breast baked with white wine, tomatoes, and kalamata olives), and fish (salmon baked in parchment), as well as a vegetarian dish. The produce used is largely organic, and the restaurant makes its own breads and ice cream. In keeping with Ashland's theatrical theme, this restaurant has adopted a very dramatic decor, with rich colors, soft lighting, and theatrically lit paintings inspired by old Ballet Russe posters. A handsome garden at the back is a fine place to dine before attending a summertime performance. In keeping with the atmosphere, you might want to dress up.

241 Hargadine St. ☎ 541/488-1994. Reservations recommended in summer. Main courses $15.50–$24; bistro menu $8.50–$13. AE, MC, V. Summer Wed–Thurs and Sun 5–8:30pm; Fri–Sat 5–9pm. Closed Jan to mid-Feb and Wed fall–spring.

The Winchester Inn ★★ INTERNATIONAL   Located on the ground floor

of Ashland's premier in-town country inn, this restaurant melds a historic Victorian setting with an eclectic international menu that visits such far-flung culinary destinations as China, Mexico, Greece, and the Mediterranean. Starters here tend toward such delectable preparations as Dungeness crab tarts made with goat cheese or baked brie in a peppernut crust served with apple-pear chutney. Teng dah beef, the inn's signature French-Vietnamese dish, is an unusual treatment of filet mignon, marinated in soy sauce and flavored with lemon zest, nutmeg, and anise. Sunday brunch is the perfect way to finish a weekend of theater before heading home. The dining rooms overlook the inn's English tea gardens, and in summer there is dining on the porch and deck as well. During the Christmas season, there are special Dickens feasts here.

35 S. Second St. ℂ 541/488-1115. www.winchesterinn.com. Reservations highly recommended. Main courses $16.50–$25; Sun brunch $9–$11.50. AE, DISC, MC, V. Summer Mon–Thurs 5–8pm; Fri–Sat 5:30–8:30pm; Sun 9:30am–12:30pm (brunch) and 5–8pm. Closed Mon from mid-Oct to Mar.

MODERATE

Cucina Biazzi 𝒢𝒢 TUSCAN   The owners have transformed this Ashland bungalow on the edge of downtown into a cozy Italian cottage, with romantic touches including lace curtains and candlelight. The menu here, inspired by available seasonal ingredients, changes every week or two, but you might find that the antipasto course is a salad of Tuscan white beans, mushrooms, marinated artichokes, asiago cheese, and other tempting ingredients. The pasta course might include bow-tie pasta with basil and pistachio pesto or spaghetti with clams, Tuscan-style. For a main course, you usually have a choice of a chicken, fish, veal, or steak dish. For a switch on the American norm, the salad course comes last here (but before dessert—save room). There's a low-walled patio if you want to dine alfresco. Service is excellent.

568 E. Main St. ℂ 541/488-3739. Reservations recommended in summer. 4-course fixed-price dinner $22–$30. MC, V. Daily 5:30–8:30pm; hours may be shorter in winter.

Kat Wok 𝒢 PACIFIC RIM   With the sort of clever ambience you'd find in a hip new restaurant in Portland or Seattle, Kat Wok is a prime example of Ashland's increasingly cosmopolitan atmosphere. If you happen to enter from "the bricks," you'll think you've stumbled onto a theater's backstage. Each table is dramatically lit, and there are tables on a catwalk-like mezzanine (hence the name). Kat Wok is popular with people of all ages who come here for light Asian-style cuisine, such as a pear salad with roasted chicken, sesame-crusted pork medallions, or Szechwan green beans. Later in the evening, Kat Wok becomes a nightclub with live music.

62 E. Main St. ℂ 541/482-0787. Reservations recommended. Main courses $12–$17. AE, MC, V. Summer Sun–Mon 5–8pm; Tues–Thurs 5–9pm; Fri–Sat 11:30am–2:30pm and 5–9pm. Closed Mon in other months.

Plaza Café 𝒢 𝒱𝒶𝓁𝓊ℯ REGIONAL AMERICAN   Located on the plaza in downtown Ashland, this cafe has an upscale urban atmosphere with a high ceiling and art on the brick walls. It's practically next door to Quinz (see below) but more informal. We enjoy the coconut-lime poached halibut with Chinese vegetables and the delicious black tiger shrimp kabob with peanut sauce. Salads, such as a warm spinach salad, are generous and fresh, featuring local organic produce. Prices here (including wine) are quite reasonable, and brunch is served on Sunday. There's also creekside seating out in back of the restaurant.

47 N. Main St. ℂ 541/488-2233. Reservations recommended. Main courses $7–$15. DISC, MC, V. Mon–Thurs 11am–10pm; Fri–Sat 11am–11pm; Sun 9am–10pm.

Quinz 𝒢𝒢 MEDITERRANEAN   With its colorful decor, convenient location on the plaza, and prompt service, Quinz is a good place to stop for reasonably priced Mediterranean-influenced food. The menu is fairly long and includes plenty of options for light eaters as well as the famished. You can get anything from grilled Italian sausage with polenta to maple barbecue-glazed pork loin. Don't-miss dishes include the Catalan-style saffron risotto, the Moroccan lamb meatballs in cumin-coriander tomato sauce, and the souvlaki. The indecisive should consider the substantial antipasti platter for two. It's enough for a light meal (especially if you have dessert).

29 N. Main St. ☎ **541/488-5937**. Reservations recommended. Small plates $5–$9, large plates $13–$17. DISC, MC, V. Daily 5:30–9pm.

INEXPENSIVE

If you're in need of a latte and a muffin, head to **The Beanery,** 1602 Ashland St. (☎ 541/488-0700), which, though a bit removed from downtown, is the locals' favorite coffeehouse. For salads and pizzas in a cafe atmosphere, there's **Lela's Bakery and Café,** 258 A St. (☎ **541/482-1702**).

Ashland Bakery Cafe ✿ INTERNATIONAL   You'll find this cafe right in the hub of downtown Ashland. It's usually mobbed at breakfast with people reading newspapers and sipping coffee while patiently waiting for smoked salmon or tofu scrambles, or basil-and-cheese omelets. At lunch or dinner it's a good place for a quick sandwich, pizza, or pasta dish. Top it off with a giant cookie from the bakery case.

38 E. Main St. ☎ **541/482-2117**. Breakfast, sandwiches, and main courses $7–$10. MC, V. Mon–Tues 7:30am–3pm; Wed–Sun 7:30am–8pm.

ASHLAND AFTER DARK

The Oregon Shakespeare Festival may be the main draw, but Ashland is overflowing with talent. From experimental theater to Broadway musicals, the town sees an amazing range of theater productions. To find out what's going on while you're in town, pick up a free copy of *Sneak Preview.* If you've had enough Shakespeare, check out the performance calendars of the **Oregon Cabaret Theatre,** First and Hargadine streets (☎ **541/488-2902**), a professional dinner theater; or the **Theatre Arts Department of Southern Oregon University,** 1250 Siskiyou Blvd. (☎ **541/552-6346**), which stages well-regarded student productions.

2 Jacksonville & Medford: After the Gold Rush

16 miles N of Ashland, 24 miles E of Grants Pass

Jacksonville is a snapshot from southern Oregon's past. After the Great Depression it became a forgotten backwater, and more than 80 buildings from its glory years as a gold-boom town in the mid-1800s were left untouched. The entire town has been restored, thanks to the photos of pioneer photographer Peter Britt, who moved to Jacksonville in 1852 and operated the first photographic studio west of the Rockies. His photos of 19th-century Jacksonville have provided preservationists with invaluable 100-year-old glimpses of many of the town's historic buildings. Britt's name has been attached to the **Britt Festivals,** another southern Oregon cultural binge that rivals the Oregon Shakespeare Festival in its ability to stage first-rate entertainment.

Though thousands of eager gold-seekers were lured into California's Sierra Nevada by the **gold rush** of 1849, few struck it rich. Many of those who were smitten with gold fever and were unwilling to give up the search for the mother lode headed out across the West in search of golder pastures. At least two prospectors hit pay dirt in the Siskiyou Mountains of southern Oregon in 1851, at a spot that would soon be known as Rich Gulch. Within a year Rich Gulch had become the site of booming Jacksonville, and within another year the town had become the county seat and commercial heart of southern Oregon. Over the next half century, Jacksonville developed into a wealthy town with brick commercial buildings and elegant Victorian homes. However, in the 1880s, the railroad running between Portland and San Francisco bypassed Jacksonville in favor of an easier route 5 miles to the east. It was at this spot that the trading town of **Medford** began to develop.

Despite a short rail line into Jacksonville, over the years more and more business migrated to the main railway in Medford. Jacksonville's fortunes began to decline, and by the time of the Depression, residents were reduced to digging up the streets of town for the gold that lay there. In 1927, the county seat was moved to Medford, and Jacksonville was left with its faded grandeur and memories of better times.

Off the beaten path, forgotten by developers and modernization, Jacksonville inadvertently preserved its past in its buildings. In 1966, the entire town was listed on the National Register of Historic Places, and Jacksonville, with the aid of Britt's photos, underwent a renaissance that has left it a historical showcase. Together the Britt Festivals and Jacksonville's history combine to make this one of the most fascinating towns anywhere in the Northwest.

ESSENTIALS

GETTING THERE Medford is right on I-5, 30 miles north of the California state line, and Jacksonville is 5 miles west on Ore. 238.

Horizon/Alaska Airlines and United Airlines serve **Rogue Valley International–Medford Airport,** at 3650 Biddle Rd., Medford.

VISITOR INFORMATION Contact the **Jacksonville Chamber of Commerce,** 185 N. Oregon St. (P.O. Box 33), Jacksonville, OR 97530 (℃ **541/ 899-8118;** www.jacksonvilleoregon.org), or the **Medford Visitor & Convention Bureau,** 101 E. Eighth St., Medford, OR 97501 (℃ **800/469-6307** or 541/779-4847; www.visitmedford.org).

THE BRITT FESTIVALS & OTHER AREA PERFORMANCES

Each summer between early June and mid-September, people gather several nights a week for folk, pop, country, jazz, and classical music concerts; theater; and modern dance performances. The Britt Festivals are a celebration of music and the performing arts featuring internationally renowned performers. The setting for the performances is an amphitheater on the grounds of Britt's estate. Located only a block from historic California Street, the ponderosa pine–shaded amphitheater provides not only a great setting for the performances, but a view that takes in distant hills and the valley far below.

Both reserved and general-admission tickets are available for most shows. If you opt for a general-admission ticket, arrive early to claim a prime spot on the lawns behind the reserved seats—and be sure to bring a picnic. For information, contact the festival at P.O. Box 1124, Medford, OR 97501 (℃ **800/88-BRITT** or 541/773-6077; www.brittfest.org). Tickets range from $12 to $68.

Not wanting to lose out to its better-known neighbors, Medford recently renovated an old downtown theater and christened it the **Craterian Ginger Rogers Theater,** 23 S. Central Ave. (℃ **541/779-3000**), in honor of the famous dancer who lived in the area after her retirement. The theater stages everything from performances by the Rogue Opera (℃ **541/608-6400**) to touring Broadway shows and classical music performances.

When the Britt Festivals have closed up shop for the year, you can still catch Dixieland jazz at the annual **Medford Jazz Jubilee,** which is held in early October. For information, call ℃ **800/599-0039** or 541/770-6972.

MUSEUMS & HISTORIC HOMES

With more than 80 buildings listed on the National Register of Historic Places, Jacksonville boasts that it's the most completely preserved historic town in the nation. Whether or not this claim is true, there are certainly enough restored old buildings to make the town a genuine step back in time. Along California Street you'll find restored brick commercial buildings that now house dozens of interesting shops, art galleries, and boutiques. On the side streets you'll see the town's many Victorian homes.

Beekman House   At the 1876 Beekman House, history comes alive as actors in period costume portray the family of an early Jacksonville banker. The 19th-century Beekman Bank, 101 W. California St., is also open to the public.

470 E. California St. ℂ **541/773-6536**. Beekman House, $3 adults, $2 seniors and children 6–12; Beekman Bank, free admission. Beekman House, Memorial Day–Labor Day daily 1–5pm. Beekman Bank, year-round.

Butte Creek Mill   In nearby Eagle Point, you can visit Oregon's only operating water-powered flour mill. The Butte Creek Mill was built in 1873, and its millstones are still grinding out flour. After looking around at the workings of the mill, you can stop in at the mill store and buy a bag of flour or cornmeal. Next door, the **Oregon General Store Museum** has a fascinating collection of antique items representing a 19th-century grocery store. Ask at the Mill and someone may take you over for a look. Also on this same block is the **Eagle Point Historical Museum** (ℂ **541/826-4166**), in case you want to learn more about local history. It's open during the summer Tuesday through Saturday from noon to 4pm and other times by appointment. The Antelope covered bridge is also here in Eagle Point.

402 N. Royal Ave., Eagle Point. ℂ **541/826-3531**. Free admission. Mon–Sat 9am–5pm.

Jacksonville Museum of Southern Oregon History   In order to get some background on Jacksonville, make this museum your first stop in town. Housed in the 1883 county courthouse, the museum has displays on the history of Jacksonville, including 19th-century photos by Peter Britt. The price of admission also includes the adjacent Children's Museum, housed in the former jail.

206 N. Fifth St. ℂ **541/773-6536**. Admission $3 adults, $2 seniors and children 6–12. Wed–Sat 10am–5pm; Sun noon–5pm.

Southern Oregon History Center   Located in downtown Medford, this is the headquarters for the Southern Oregon Historical Society, which stages changing exhibits pertaining to the history of this region.

106 N. Central Ave. ℂ **541/773-6536**. www.sohs.org. Free admission. Mon–Fri 9am–5pm.

MORE TO SEE & DO

Pears and roses both grow well in the Jacksonville and Medford area, and these crops have given rise to two of the country's best-known mail-order businesses. **Harry and David's Country Village**, 1314 Center Dr. (ℂ **877/322-8000**), is the retail outlet of a fruit company specializing in mail-order Fruit-of-the-Month Club gift packs. You'll find the store just 1 mile south of Medford at exit 27 off I-5. You can tour the Harry and David's packinghouse and then wander through the store in search of bargains. Associated with this store is the **Jackson and Perkins rose test garden** and mail-order rose nursery.

Each year in early autumn, the Jacksonville Boosters Club sponsors a **homes tour** that allows glimpses into many of Jacksonville's most lovingly restored old homes. Contact the Jacksonville Chamber of Commerce for details.

There are lots of great stores in Jacksonville, and one of our favorites is the **GeBzz Gallery,** 150 S. Oregon St. (© **541/899-7535**), which carries a diverse selection of contemporary art works.

OUTDOOR ACTIVITIES

Rafting and **fishing** on the numerous fast-flowing, clear-water rivers of southern Oregon are two of the most popular sports in this region, and Medford makes a good base for doing a bit of either, or both. **Arrowhead River Adventures** (© **800/227-7741** or 541/830-3388; www.arrowheadadventures.com) and **River Trips Unlimited** (© **800/460-3865** or 541/779-3798; www.rogue fishing.com) offer both rafting and fishing. **Rogue Excursions Unlimited** (© **541/826-6222;** www.fishandraft.com) offers fishing. A day of rafting will cost around $85 to $120, and fishing trips cost about $150 per person per day (with a minimum of two people).

If you're here in the spring, you can catch the colorful **wildflower displays** at Table Rocks. These mesas are just a few miles northeast of Medford, and because of their great age and unique structure, they create a variety of habitats that allow the area to support an unusual diversity of plants. For more information, contact the **Bureau of Land Management,** Medford District Office (© **541/770-2200**).

Information on **hiking** and **backpacking** is available from the **Rogue River National Forest,** 333 W. Eighth St. (P.O. Box 520), Medford, OR 97501 (© **541/858-2200;** www.fs.fed.us/r6/rogue).

For a different perspective on this region, try a **hot-air balloon ride** with **Oregon Adventures Aloft** (© **800/238-0700** or 541/582-1574).

WINE TOURING

You can taste local wines at the **Valley View Vineyard,** 100 Upper Applegate Rd. (© **800/781-WINE** or 541/899-8468), or their in-town tasting room at **Anna Maria's,** 125 W. California St., Jacksonville (© **541/899-1001**). Valley View is known for its red wines but also produces good dry whites. The Cotes du Rogue, a blend of Syrah, Zinfandel, Cabernet, and Merlot, is particularly tasty.

Wine connoisseurs also won't want to miss perusing the wine racks at the **Jacksonville Inn Wine Shop,** 175 E. California St., Jacksonville (© **541/899-1137**), where you might find a bottle of 1811 Tokay Essencia for $5,500 or a bottle of Chateau Lafite-Rothschild for $1,500. Oregon wines (and beef jerky) can also be tasted at the **Gary R. West Tasting Room,** 690 N. Fifth St., Jacksonville (© **541/899-1829**).

WHERE TO STAY
IN JACKSONVILLE

Historic Orth House/The Teddy Bear Inn ★★   This 1880 Italianate brick house stands behind majestic old shade trees 1 block from busy California Street. The picket fence, an old buggy in the side yard, and inviting front porch bring back small-town America and slower times. Inside, the glowing woodwork, pressed-tin ceilings, and antique furnishings conjure up the 19th century. Don't miss the inn's extensive collection of teddy bears and antique toys. One of our favorite rooms is romantic Josie's Room with its in-room claw-foot tub. Keep an eye out for deer in the yard.

105 W. Main St. (P.O. Box 1437), Jacksonville, OR 97530-1437. © **800/700-7301** or 541/899-8665. Fax 541/899-9146. www.orthbnb.com. 3 units. May–Oct $135–$150 double; $190 suite. Nov–Apr $95–$125 double; $125 suite. Rates include full breakfast. DISC, MC, V. **Amenities:** Bike. *In room:* A/C.

Jacksonville Inn 🐸🐸   In the heart of the town's historic business district in a two-story brick building, the Jacksonville Inn is best known for its gourmet restaurant. Upstairs, however, there are eight antiques-filled rooms that offer traditional elegance mixed with modern amenities (hair dryers, irons and ironing boards, and refrigerators). Rooms are elegantly furnished and several have exposed brick walls that conjure up the inn's past. (Part of the inn was built in 1861.) Room 1, with its queen-size canopy bed and whirlpool tub for two, is the most popular. If you're looking for more privacy and greater luxury, consider the cottages, which are a couple of blocks away and have whirlpool tubs, steam showers, and entertainment centers.

175 E. California St. (P. O. Box 359), Jacksonville, OR 97530. ⓒ **800/321-9344** or 541/899-1900. Fax 541/899-1373. www.jacksonvilleinn.com. 11 units (including 3 cottages). $125–$169 double; $225–$350 cottage. Rates include full breakfast. AE, DC, DISC, MC, V. **Amenities:** Restaurant (Northwest/Continental), lounge. *In room:* A/C, fridge, hair dryer, iron.

The McCully House 🐸🐸   Built in 1861, the McCully House is one of the oldest buildings in Oregon that is currently being used as an inn, and with its classic, symmetrical lines and simple pre-Victorian styling, it looks as if it could easily be an 18th-century New England inn. If you like being steeped in local history, this is Jacksonville's best choice. In the McCully Room, you'll even find the original black-walnut master bedroom furnishings. Surrounding the inn, and enclosed by a white picket fence, is a formal rose garden with an amazing variety of roses. The inn houses one of Jacksonville's finest restaurants, and the downstairs parlors now serve as dining rooms. However, in summer, most people prefer to eat outside in the garden. Breakfasts are served in a cheery sunroom that overlooks the less formal back garden and patio.

240 E. California St., Jacksonville, OR 97530. ⓒ **800/367-1942** or 541/899-1942. www.mccullyhouseinn. com. 3 units. May–Sept $125 double. Oct–Apr $105 double. Rates include full breakfast. AE, DC, DISC, MC, V. **Amenities:** Restaurant (New American), lounge. *In room:* A/C, no phone.

The Stage Lodge 🐸   Jacksonville has several bed-and-breakfast inns, but it's short on moderately priced motels. Filling the bill in the latter category is a motel designed to resemble a 19th-century stage stop, with gables, clapboard siding, and turned-wood railings along two floors of verandas. These details allow the lodge to fit right in with all the original buildings in town. The rooms are spacious and comfortable and have a few nice touches such as ceiling fans, TV armoires, and country decor.

830 N. Fifth St. (P.O. Box 1316), Jacksonville, OR 97530. ⓒ **800/253-8254** or 541/899-3953. www. stagelodge.com. 27 units. $78–$88 double. Lower rates Oct–Apr. AE, DISC, MC, V. *In room:* A/C, TV.

TouVelle House Bed & Breakfast 🐸   This inn sits at the top of a 1½-acre hilly yard on the edge of town, but only 2 blocks from downtown and the Britt Festivals amphitheater. Built in 1916, the three-story craftsman-style home is one of the largest historic homes in town. The wood-paneled great room with its large stone fireplace is a favorite gathering spot for guests, especially in the cooler months. There is also a hot tub and an outdoor swimming pool. If you don't want to climb a lot of stairs, ask for the Judge's Chamber, the only guest room on the ground floor. The third-floor Pendleton Suite, with its claw-foot tub, and the second-floor Garden Suite, with its Roman tub for two, are favorites. A gourmet three-course breakfast is served each morning.

455 N. Oregon St. (P.O. Box 1891), Jacksonville, OR 97530. ⓒ **800/846-8422** or 541/899-8938. Fax 541/899-3992. www.touvellehouse.com. 6 units. May–Oct $135–$140 double. Nov–Apr $90–$99 double. AE, DISC, MC, V. **Amenities:** Outdoor pool; bikes. *In room:* A/C, hair dryer, iron.

IN MEDFORD

In addition to the B&B listed below, you'll find dozens of inexpensive chain motels clustered along I-5.

Under the Greenwood Tree ★★   Located just west of Medford and taking its name from the 300-year-old oaks that shade the front yard, this B&B offers a step back in time to the days of iced tea on the veranda, croquet on the lawn, and stolen kisses behind the barn. Romance is the name of the game here, with beds piled with plump pillows and lace curtains swaying in the summer breezes. During the summer, fresh-cut flower arrangements fill the house. The guest rooms are furnished with antiques, and two have separate sitting rooms. Throughout the house you'll find antique quilts and Oriental carpets, which give the inn a touch of country class. Out back there is a huge deck that overlooks the inn's 10 acres of land and its gazebo, garden, and barns, all of which you can explore. A three-course breakfast and afternoon tea are served by innkeeper Renate Ellam, a Cordon Bleu–trained chef.

3045 Bellinger Lane, Medford, OR 97501. © **541/776-0000.** www.greenwoodtree.com. 5 units. $125–$145 double. Rates include full breakfast. V. Pets accepted by arrangement. **Amenities:** Exercise room and access to nearby health club; bikes; concierge; massage. *In room:* A/C, dataport, hair dryer, iron.

IN THE APPLEGATE VALLEY

Applegate Lodge ★★ *(Finds)*   Situated on the bank of the Applegate River 16 miles outside Jacksonville, this lodge boasts one of the prettiest settings in southern Oregon and is a masterpiece of woodworking, with burnished woods (including rare fiddleback redwood paneling) and unique wooden details throughout. The high-ceilinged great room with a river-rock fireplace features a wall of glass looking out on the river, and across the length of the lodge is a deck where you can sit and listen to the music of the water. The guest rooms are all very large, and several of them have loft sleeping areas. Lots of peeled log furniture gives the inn a solidly western feel. Right next door and under the same ownership is the ever-popular Applegate River Ranch House (see "Where to Dine" below for details). The river here is great for swimming.

15100 Ore. 238, Applegate, OR 97530. © **541/846-6690** or 541/846-6408. www.applegateriverlodge.com. 7 units. $125–$145 double (10% off in winter). DISC, MC, V. Pets accepted. **Amenities:** Restaurant (steak/seafood), lounge; Jacuzzi; massage. *In room:* A/C.

WHERE TO DINE
IN JACKSONVILLE

In addition to the establishments mentioned below, **Good Bean Coffee,** 165 S. Oregon St. (© **541/899-8740**), is *the* place for a cup of espresso. **MacLevin's Whole Foods Saloon,** 150 W. California St. (© **541/899-1251**), will pack up a deli-style picnic for a Britt performance (or any other occasion).

Bella Union Restaurant & Saloon ★ ITALIAN/AMERICAN   For casual dining or someplace to just toss back a cold beer or sip an Italian soda, the Bella Union is Jacksonville's top choice. The lounge hearkens back to the days when the Bella Union was one of Jacksonville's busiest saloons, and in the back of the building is a garden patio. However, it's the main dining room up front that's most popular. Old wood floors, storefront windows, and exposed brick walls conjure up images of gold miners out on the town. Meals range from pizzas and pastas to a delicious house chicken that's marinated in Gorgonzola and walnut pesto.

170 W. California St. © **541/899-1770.** At dinner, call ahead to be placed on wait list. Main courses $7–$16. AE, MC, V. Mon–Fri 11:30am–10pm; Sat 11am–10pm; Sun 10am–10pm; lounge until midnight daily.

Gogi's Restaurant ★★ REGIONAL AMERICAN With an ambience somewhere between the casual atmosphere of Bella Union and the formality of the Jacksonville Inn Dinner House, this relatively new restaurant on the Jacksonville scene is a gleaming and comfortable little bistro. The small plates, such as roasted garlic with olives and goat cheese or oysters on the half shell with Asian slaw, make good choices for sharing around the table. Other tasty standouts include spicy flank steak with roasted peppers, corn, and smoked Gouda cheese, and rack of lamb in a pistachio-almond crust with Cabernet sauce.

235 W. Main St. ℂ 541/899-8699. Reservations recommended. Main courses $14–$20. DISC, MC, V. Tues–Sun 5–9pm.

Jacksonville Inn Dinner House ★★ *Value* CONTINENTAL/MEDITERRANEAN Old-world atmosphere, either in the cozy and cave-like downstairs or in the airier upstairs dining room, sets the mood for reliable continental fare. Together the cuisine and the decor attract well-heeled families and retirees that favor familiar dishes perfectly prepared, such as rack of lamb, veal scaloppini, or prime rib. The bistro menu is lighter and leans toward Mediterranean influences, with such dishes as eggplant lasagna and roasted garlic pasta. Pears are a mainstay of the local economy and show up frequently in both entrees and desserts. The inn's wine shop gives diners access to a cellar boasting more than 1,500 wines.

175 E. California St. ℂ 541/899-1900. Reservations recommended. Main courses lunch $7–$11, dinner $16–$24. DISC, MC, V. Sun 10am–2pm (brunch) and 5–8:45pm; Mon 5–9:45pm; Tues–Sat 11:30am–2pm and 5–9:45pm. Bistro menu served daily 2pm–closing.

McCully House Inn ★★ NEW AMERICAN The McCully House is one of the oldest homes in Jacksonville, and though the dining rooms have plenty of historic atmosphere, the beautiful gardens are the place to dine on a summer evening. Try the salmon cakes with lemon-caper aioli, followed by pork tenderloin with balsamic-glazed apples or rosemary-pesto rack of lamb. Although the menu leans a bit toward steaks, fresh fish is also a strong point and the Dijon-crusted salmon is a favorite. You can also get boxed meals to go if you are heading to a Britt Festival performance and want to take a picnic with you. The wine list includes reasonably priced Oregon and Washington wines.

240 E. California St. ℂ 541/899-1942. www.mccullyhouseinn.com. Main courses lunch $3–$8, dinner $13–$24. AE, DC, DISC, MC, V. Wed–Sat 11:30am–2:30pm and 5–9pm; Sun 10am–3pm and 5–9pm.

IN MEDFORD
Samovar Restaurant ★ *Finds* RUSSIAN/UKRAINIAN Russian posters on the wall plus friendly owners give this place character, and it's clear that the food is prepared according to old family recipes. At this unexpected find in downtown Medford, bakery products made with whole grains, fresh produce, and low-fat poultry and meats are the mainstay ingredients for dishes such as a bracing and delicious borscht with cabbage, tomatoes, and beets (and topped with sour cream, of course). Other Russian and Middle Eastern favorites are blintzes, *piroshki* (flaky dough pies stuffed with cheese or meat), stuffed cabbage, and skewered kabobs of lamb or chicken. To top off your meal, tortes and pastries are available from the bakery to eat in or take out.

101 E. Main St., Medford. ℂ 541/779-4967. Reservations recommended on weekends. Main courses $13–$17; lunch $6–$8. MC, V. Tues–Sat 11am–3pm and 5–9pm.

IN THE APPLEGATE VALLEY
Applegate River Ranch House ★ *Finds* STEAK/SEAFOOD With a deck overlooking the beautiful Applegate River, the location here just can't be beat.

We like to enjoy the view with a plate of succulent oak-wood-broiled mushrooms and a glass of crisp Chardonnay. From the chicken to various cuts of beef, anything broiled over the local red-oak wood is delicious. We like to top it all off with a piece of the "hula" pie.

15100 Hwy. 238, Applegate. ⓒ **541/846-6690**. www.applegateriverlodge.com. Reservations recommended in summer and on weekends. Main courses $7.50–$22. MC, V. Wed–Mon 5–9pm.

3 The Klamath Falls Area: Bird-Watching & Native American Artifacts

65 miles E of Ashland, 60 miles S of Crater Lake

Unless you are an avid bird watcher or are looking for a cheap place to stay close to Crater Lake National Park, you won't find too much to attract you to the Klamath Falls area. However, this region, a wide, windswept expanse of lakes and high desert just north of the California line, has a history of human presence that stretches back more than 14,000 years. The large lakes in this dry region have long attracted a wide variety of wildlife (especially waterfowl), which once provided a food source for the area's Native American population. The prehistoric residents of the region lived on the banks of the Klamath Basin's lakes and harvested fish, birds, and various marsh plants. Today, two local museums exhibit extensive collections of Native American artifacts that have been found in this area.

Upper Klamath Lake and adjacent Agency Lake have shrunk considerably over the years as shallow, marshy areas have been drained to create pastures and farmland. Today, however, as the lake's native fish populations have become threatened and migratory bird populations in the region have plummeted, there is a growing movement to restore some of the region's drained marshes to more natural conditions. Although large portions of the area are now designated as national wildlife areas that offer some of the best bird-watching in the Northwest, farming and ranching are still considered the primary use of these wildlife lands. The conflict between local farmers and environmentalists came to a head during the dry summer of 2001 in which there was insufficient water in the area to provide for the various needs of farmers and fishermen, bald eagles, and endangered species of fish.

The region's shallow lakes warm quickly in the hot summers here, and, partly because of the excess nutrients in the waters from agricultural runoff, they support large blooms of blue-green algae. Although the algae blooms deprive the lake's fish of oxygen, they provide the area with its most unusual agricultural activity. The harvesting and marketing of Upper Klamath Lake's blue-green algae as a dietary supplement has become big business throughout the country as people have claimed all manner of health benefits from this chlorophyll-rich dried algae.

ESSENTIALS

GETTING THERE Klamath Falls is on U.S. 97, which leads north to Bend and south to I-5 near Mount Shasta in California. The city is also connected to Ashland by the winding Ore. 66 and to Medford by Ore. 140, which continues east to Lakeview in eastern Oregon. The **Klamath Falls Airport,** 6775 Arnold Ave. (ⓒ **541/883-5372;** www.klamathfallsairport.com) is served by Horizon/Alaska Airlines from Portland. Amtrak's *Coast Starlight* trains stop here en route between San Francisco and Portland.

VISITOR INFORMATION   For more information on the region, contact the **Klamath County Department of Tourism,** 507 Main St., Klamath Falls, OR 97601 (© **800/445-6728** or 541/884-0666; www.klamathcountytourism.com).

GETTING AROUND   Rental cars are available at Klamath Falls Airport from Budget, Enterprise, and Hertz.

DELVING INTO LOCAL HISTORY

In addition to the two museums listed here, you might want to drive by the historic **Ross Ragland Theater,** 218 N. Seventh St. (© **888/627-5484** or 541/884-5483; www.rrtheater.org), an impressive Art Deco theater in downtown Klamath Falls. The theater stages a wide variety of performances throughout the year.

Favell Museum of Western Art and Indian Artifacts ★★ Finds   Anyone

with an interest in Native American artifacts or Western art will be fascinated by a visit to this unusual museum, considered one of the best Western museums in the country. On display are thousands of arrowheads (including one made from fire opal), obsidian knives, spear points, stone tools of every description, baskets, pottery, and even ancient shoes and pieces of matting and fabric. Though the main focus is on the Native Americans of the Klamath Basin and Columbia River, there are artifacts from Alaska, Canada, other regions of the United States, and Mexico. Few museums anywhere in the country have such an extensive collection on display, and the cases of artifacts can be overwhelming, so take your time. The other half of the museum's collection is Western art by more than 300 artists, including 13 members of the famous Cowboy Artists of America association. Paintings, bronzes, photographs, dioramas, and woodcarvings capture the Wild West in realistic, romantic, and even humorous styles. There is also the world's largest publicly displayed miniature gun collection.

125 W. Main St. © **541/882-9996.** Admission $4 adults, $3 seniors, $2 children 6–16. Mon–Sat 9:30am–5:30pm.

Klamath County Museum ★   More Native American artifacts, this time

exclusively from the Klamath Lakes area, are on display in this museum, while a history of the Modoc Indian Wars chronicles the most expensive campaign of the American West. Also of particular interest are the early-20th-century photos by local photographer Maud Baldwin. In addition, there's an extensive collection of stuffed birds.

1451 Main St. © **541/883-4208.** Admission $2 adults, $1 seniors and students. Tues–Sat 9am–5pm.

BIRD-WATCHING & OTHER OUTDOOR ACTIVITIES

In this dry region between the Cascades and the Rocky Mountains, there are few large bodies of water, so the lakes and marshes of the Klamath Basin are a magnet for birds. White pelicans, great blue herons, sandhill cranes, egrets, geese, ducks, grebes, bitterns, and osprey can all be seen in the area at different times of year. However, the main attraction for many human visitors is the annual winter gathering of bald eagles. In the winter the region is home to as many as 500 bald eagles, making this the largest concentration of bald eagles in the Lower 48. Each winter morning, starting about 30 minutes before sunrise, as many as 100 eagles can be seen heading out to the marshes from their roosting areas in the **Bear Valley National Wildlife Refuge** near the town of Worden, 11 miles south of Klamath Falls. To find the eagle-viewing area, drive south out of Klamath Falls on U.S. 97 through the community of Worden and almost to the California state line. Turn west onto the Keno-Worden Road, and, just after the railroad tracks, turn left onto a dirt road. Follow this road for a half mile or so and pull off on the shoulder. Now start scanning the skies for eagles heading east to the marshlands. For more information on bird-watching in the area, contact the **Klamath Basin National Wildlife Refuges,** 4009 Hill Rd., Tulelake, CA 96134 (𝄐 **530/667-2231;** www.klamathnwr.org).

The easiest way to get out on the waters of Klamath Lake is on an excursion aboard the *Klamath Belle* (𝄐 **541/883-4622;** www.klamathbelle.com), a replica paddlewheeler that operates out of the Running Y Resort Marina. There are both family "Ice Cream Social" cruises ($12.50 adults and seniors, $4 children 5–14) and dinner and brunch cruises ($39.95 adults, $35 seniors, $29.50 children 5–14).

If, on the other hand, you want to get out and paddle yourself around one of the local lakes, check out the **Upper Klamath Canoe Trail,** which begins near the junction of Ore. 140 and West Side Road northwest of Klamath Falls. The canoe trail wanders through marshlands on the edge of Upper Klamath Lake. For more information, contact the **Winema National Forest,** Klamath Ranger District, 1936 California Ave., Klamath Falls, OR 97601 (𝄐 **541/885-3400;** www.fs.fed.us/r6/winema). Canoes and kayaks can be rented at the adjacent **Rocky Point Resort,** 28121 Rocky Point Rd. (𝄐 **541/356-2287**), for $20 for half a day.

Horseback rides are available through the **Running Y Horse Stables,** 5115 Running Y Rd. (𝄐 **541/850-5691**), which charges $27 for a 1-hour ride, $37 for a 1½-hour ride, and $50 for a 2 hour ride. Pony rides are also available.

Northwest of Klamath Falls about 35 miles on Ore. 140, you'll find the region's main mountain recreation area. Here, in the vicinity of **Lake of the Woods** and **Fish Lake,** you'll find, in summer, the fun High Lakes mountain-bike trail, which leads through a rugged lava field. Also in the area is the hiking trail to the summit of Mount McLoughlin. In winter, this same area has cross-country ski trails. There are rustic cabin resorts and campgrounds on both Lake of the Woods and Fish Lake.

WHERE TO STAY

Rocky Point Resort 𝄐 (Finds)   This rustic fishing resort on the west shore of Upper Klamath Lake is the sort of place that conjures up childhood memories of summer vacations by the lake. Neither the rooms nor the cabins are anything special, but the setting is bewitching. Shaded by huge old ponderosa pine trees and partly built atop the rocks for which this point is named, the resort has a great view across the waters and marshes of the Upper Klamath National Wildlife Refuge. Green lawns set with Adirondack chairs go right down to the water, where there is a small boat-rental dock. The rustic restaurant and lounge boast the best views on the property. The Upper Klamath Lake canoe trails originate here, and the bird-watching is excellent, but fishing is still the most popular pastime. The resort also has tent and RV sites.

28121 Rocky Point Rd., Klamath Falls, OR 97601. 𝄐 **541/356-2287.** Fax 541/356-2222. www.rockypoint oregon.com. 9 units. $55 double; $89–$109 cabin. MC, V. Pets accepted in cabins ($2 per night). **Amenities:** Restaurant (American); lounge; watersports rentals; coin-op laundry. *In room:* No phone.

Running Y Ranch Resort 𝄐𝄐   Located northwest of town off Ore. 140, this golf resort and time-share condominium community is built close to the shore of Upper Klamath Lake amid ponderosa pines. Although remote, it is almost as luxurious as any of the central Oregon resorts in the Bend and Sisters areas. The hotel has a mountain-lodge feel, though guest rooms are fairly standard in their decor. Some rooms, however, do have balconies. Dining options here at the resort are limited to a restaurant at the golf course and a snack bar across the parking lot from the hotel. With an Arnold Palmer–designed golf course, the resort is obviously aiming primarily to attract golfers. However, horseback riding, bicycling on paved and gravel trails, and canoeing through a wetland area under restoration are other options.

5115 Running Y Rd., Klamath Falls, OR 97601. © **888/850-0275.** Fax 541/850-5593. www.runningy.com. 81 units. May 15–Oct 15 $121–$132 double; $184–$242 suite. Oct 16–May 14 $91–$102 double; $184–$195 suite. Rates include continental breakfast. AE, DC, DISC, MC, V. Pets accepted. **Amenities:** 2 restaurants (Northwest/German, American), lounge; indoor pool; 2 tennis courts; health club; spa; Jacuzzi; sauna; water-sports rentals; bike rentals; horseback riding; children's programs; concierge; massage. *In room:* A/C, TV/VCR, dataport, coffeemaker, hair dryer, iron.

CAMPGROUNDS

Along Ore. 140 between Klamath Falls and Medford are several national-forest campgrounds. On Fish Lake, **Fish Lake Campground** and **Doe Point Campground** are in nice locations, but they both get a lot of traffic noise. Just west of Fish Lake on F.S. 37, the **North Fork Campground** provides a quieter setting on a trout stream and a scenic mountain-bike trail. **Sunset Campground** and **Aspen Point Campground** on Lake of the Woods are popular in summer with the boat-fishing and water-skiing crowd. The latter campground is near Great Meadow Recreation Area, has a swimming beach, and is right on the High Lakes mountain-bike trail.

WHERE TO DINE

For dinner with the best view in the area, make a reservation at the **Rocky Point Resort** (see above), which is 30 minutes outside Klamath Falls and is open nightly in summer and on weekends in spring and fall.

4 Grants Pass & the Rogue River Valley

63 miles S of Roseburg, 40 miles NW of Ashland, 82 miles NE of Crescent City

"It's the climate," proclaims a sign at the entrance to Grants Pass, and with weather almost as reliably pleasant as California's, the town has become a popular base for outdoor activities of all kinds. The Rogue River runs through the center of town, so it's not surprising that most local recreational activities revolve around the waters of this famous river. Grants Pass is located at the junction of I-5 and U.S. 199 and is the last large town in Oregon if you're heading over to the redwoods, which are about 90 miles southwest on the northern California coast. About the same distance to the northeast, you'll find Crater Lake National Park, so Grants Pass makes a good base if you're trying to see a lot of this region in a short time.

The city is slowly reviving its few blocks of historic commercial buildings, and it's worth wandering down Southwest G Street to see what's new along the historic blocks.

ESSENTIALS

GETTING THERE   Grants Pass is at the junction of I-5 and U.S. 199. The **Rogue Valley International–Medford Airport,** 3650 Biddle Rd. (© **541/ 776-7222**), Medford, is served by Horizon/Alaska Airlines and United Airlines.

VISITOR INFORMATION   Contact the **Grants Pass Visitors & Convention Bureau,** 1995 NW Vine St., Grants Pass, OR 97526 (© **800/547-5927** or 541/476-7717; www.visitgrantspass.org).

FESTIVALS **Boatnik,** held Memorial Day weekend, is Grants Pass's biggest annual festival and includes jet boat and hydroplane races on the Rogue River, as well as lots of festivities at Riverside Park.

OUTDOOR ACTIVITIES

Grants Pass is midway between the source and the mouth of the Rogue River and is an ideal base for river-oriented activities. The Rogue, first made famous by Western novelist and avid fly-fisherman Zane Grey, is now preserved for much of its length as a National Wild and Scenic River. Originating in Crater Lake National Park, the river twists and tumbles through narrow gorges and steep mountains as it winds its way to the coast at Gold Beach. The most famous section of the river is 250-foot-deep **Hellgate Canyon,** where the river narrows and rushes through a cleft in the rock. The canyon can be seen from an overlook on Merlin-Galice Road, which begins at exit 61 off I-5. From I-5, it's about 10 miles to the canyon overlook.

Several area companies offer **river trips** of varying length and in a variety of watercraft. You can spend the afternoon paddling the Rogue in an inflatable kayak or several days rafting the river with stops each night at riverside lodges. If you have only enough time for a short trip on the river, we'd recommend a jet-boat trip up to Hellgate Canyon, which, as we mentioned above, is the most scenic spot on this section of the river. **Hellgate Jetboat Excursions,** 966 SW Sixth St., Grants Pass (© 800/648-4874 or 541/479-7204; www.hellgate.com), operates four different jet-boat trips, with adult ticket prices ranging from $26 to $49.

Local **white-water-rafting** companies offer half-day, full-day, and multiday trips, with the multiday trips stopping either at rustic river lodges or at campsites along the riverbanks. Area rafting companies include **Rogue Wilderness,** (© 800/336-1647 or 541/479-9554; www.wildrogue.com); **Galice Resort,** 11744 Galice Rd., Merlin (© 541/476-3818; www.galice.com); **Orange Torpedo Trips,** 209 Merlin-Galice Rd., Merlin (© 800/635-2925; www.orange torpedo.com); and **Rogue River Raft Trips,** Morrison's Lodge, 8500 Galice Rd., Merlin (© 800/826-1963 or 541/476-3825; www.rogueraft.com). Expect to pay around $45 for a half day and $65 to $69 for a full day. Three-day lodge or camping trips are in the $520 to $560 range.

At several places near Merlin, you can rent rafts and kayaks of different types and paddle yourself downriver. Try **White Water Cowboys,** 209 Merlin-Galice Rd., Merlin (© 541/479-0132; www.orangetorpedo.com); **Galice Resort Store,** 11744 Galice Rd., Merlin (© 541/476-3818; www.galice.com); or **Ferron's Fun Trips** (© 800/404-2201 or 541/474-2201; www.roguefuntrips. com). Rental rates range from $20 to $30 for inflatable kayaks and from $50 to $60 for paddle rafts.

If **fishing** is your passion, the steelhead and salmon of the Rogue River already haunt your dreams. To make those dreams a reality, you'll want to hire a guide to take you where the fish are sure to bite. Good local guide services include Rogue Wilderness (mentioned above); **Rogue Excursions Unlimited** (© 541/826-6222; www.fishandraft.com), which charges $250 per boat with two clients; and **Geoff's Guide Service** (© 541/474-0602), which charges $90 per person per day.

OTHER THINGS TO SEE & DO

Though most people visiting Grants Pass are here to enjoy the mountains and rivers surrounding the town, history buffs can pick up a free map of the town's historic buildings at the Tourist Information Center. Two small art museums—the

Grants Pass Museum of Art, 229 SW G St. (© **541/479-3290**), and the **Wiseman Gallery,** 3345 Redwood Hwy., at Rogue Community College (© **541/956-7339**)—offer changing exhibits of classic and contemporary art by local and national artists.

Wildlife Images Rehabilitation and Education Center 🐾, 11845 Lower River Rd. (© **541/476-0222;** www.wildlifeimages.org), is dedicated to nurturing injured birds of prey and other wild animals back to health and then releasing them back into the wild, if possible. The center is 13 miles south of Grants Pass and is open for tours daily by reservation only. Admission is by donation. One of the best things about this place is that you can get closer to the animals than you can in a zoo.

Riverside Park, in the center of town, is a popular place to play, especially in the warmer months when people come to cool off in the river.

About midway between Medford and Grants Pass and about 6 miles off I-5 (take exit 40), you'll find one of Oregon's most curious attractions: the **Oregon Vortex and House of Mystery,** 4303 Sardine Creek Rd., Gold Hill (© **877/3VORTEX** or 541/855-1543; www.oregonvortex.com). Straight out of "Ripley's Believe It or Not," this classic tourist trap is guaranteed to have the kids, and many adults, oohing and aahing in bug-eyed amazement at the numerous strange phenomena that defy the laws of physics. People grow taller as they recede. You, and the trees surrounding the House of Mystery, lean toward magnetic north rather than stand upright. Seeing is believing—or is it? Open March through May and September through mid-October, daily from 9am to 5pm; June through August, daily from 9am to 6pm (closed mid-Oct through Feb). Admission is $7.50 for adults, $6.50 for seniors, $5.50 for children 5 to 11.

Fourteen miles north of Grants Pass in Sunny Valley, you'll find the **Applegate Trail Interpretive Center,** 500 Sunny Valley Loop, Sunny Valley (© **888/411-1846** or 541/472-8545; www.rogueweb.com/interpretive). This small museum documents the little-known Applegate Trail, which was an alternative to the Oregon Trail. To find the museum, take exit 71 off I-5 and go 2 blocks east. The museum is open daily from 10am to 5pm and admission is $5.95 for adults, $4.95 for seniors and children 13 to 18.

WHERE TO STAY
IN TOWN

Riverside Inn Resort ⭐⭐ Located in downtown Grants Pass, the Riverside Inn is right on the bank of the Rogue River. A weathered wood exterior and cedar-shingle roof give the two-story inn a bit of Northwest flavor, though the setting between two busy bridges is not exactly idyllic. Luckily, a park across the river means the views from most rooms are quite pleasant. The inn sprawls over 3 blocks, and rooms vary in age and quality. Our favorites are the fireplace rooms in the west section and the whirlpool river-view suites. Though the river-view rooms are a bit more expensive than nonview rooms, they're certainly worth the price. Avoid the rooms near the road, which can be quite noisy. The inn's restaurant and lounge offer a great view of the river and some of the best meals in town. Jet-boat tours to Hellgate Canyon leave from the resort.

971 SE Sixth St., Grants Pass, OR 97526. © **800/334-4567** or 541/476-6873. Fax 541/474-9848. www.riverside-inn.com. 174 units. $69–$99 standard double; $99–$119 river-view double; $125–$350 suite. Lower rates Nov–Mar. AE, DC, DISC, MC, V. Pets accepted ($15). **Amenities:** Restaurant (American), lounge; 2 outdoor pools; access to nearby health club; day spa; 2 Jacuzzis; room service; massage; babysitting; dry cleaning. *In room:* A/C, TV, dataport, coffeemaker.

OUTSIDE OF TOWN

Morrison's Rogue River Lodge ☆☆   If you're in the area to do a bit of fishing or rafting, we can think of no better place to stay than at Morrison's. Perched on the banks of the Rogue, this fishing lodge epitomizes the Rogue River experience. The main lodge is a massive log building that's rustic yet comfortable, with a wall of glass that looks across wide lawns to the river. All the rooms have been recently redecorated, and though there are B&B–style accommodations in the main lodge, the cabins seem more appropriate in this setting. The spacious cabins stand beneath grand old trees, and all have good views of the river. Fireplaces will keep you warm and cozy in the cooler months. The dining room serves surprisingly creative four-course dinners ($27–$34). Fishing and rafting trips are the specialty here, but, in addition to amenities listed below, there is also a private beach.

8500 Galice Rd., Merlin, OR 97532. ✆ **800/826-1963** or 541/476-3825. Fax 541/476-4953. www.morrisons lodge.com. 13 units. $180–$320 double. Rates include 2–3 meals per day. DISC, MC, V. Closed Dec–Apr. **Amenities:** Restaurant (Northwest); lounge; outdoor pool; putting green; 2 tennis courts; concierge; business center; room service (breakfast only); coin-op laundry. *In room:* A/C, TV, fridge, coffeemaker.

Pine Meadow Inn–A Garden Retreat ☆☆   Situated between a meadow and a pine forest on 9 acres of land near the Rogue River, this modern farmhouse B&B is secluded, yet close to town. The tranquil setting, with a hot tub and koi pond in the backyard, makes it easy to slow down and relax. The guest rooms are all furnished with antiques and fresh flowers. Two rooms have mountain views, while the other two overlook the gardens and forest. Breakfasts often feature fresh organic produce from the inn's own gardens. The inn is located close to the Wild and Scenic stretch of the Rogue River and makes a good base if you are planning on doing some rafting or fishing.

1000 Crow Rd., Merlin, OR 97532-9718. ✆ **800/554-0806** or 541/471-6277. Fax 541/471-6277. www. pinemeadowinn.com. 4 units. Apr–Oct $90–$120 double. Nov–Mar $80–$100 double. Rates include full breakfast. AE, DISC, MC, V. **Amenities:** Jacuzzi. *In-room:* A/C, hair dryer, iron.

Weasku Inn ☆☆ *Finds*   Set on the bank of the Rogue River just below the Savage Rapids Dam, this log lodge built in 1924 was once *the* area fishing lodge. That was back in the days when Clark Gable, Carole Lombard, Walt Disney, Zane Grey, Bing Crosby, and Herbert Hoover used to stay here. Today, after a total renovation, the lodge is once again the sort of place where such luminaries would feel comfortable. Guest rooms, on the second floor of the old log lodge, are spacious and modern and have interesting details such as bent-willow furnishings and coiled-rope lamps. The riverside cabins are in a modern lodge style with whirlpool tubs, fireplaces, and private decks. Set beneath towering trees a few miles out of Grants Pass, this inn is one of the most memorable lodgings in the state, the quintessential mountain/fishing lodge. In addition to breakfast, guests are treated to a complimentary wine-and-cheese reception each evening.

5560 Rogue River Hwy., Grants Pass, OR 97527. ✆ **800/4-WEASKU** or 541/471-8000. Fax 541/471-7038. www.weasku.com. 17 units. $110–$175 double; $195–$295 suite/cabin. Rates include continental breakfast. AE, DC, DISC, MC, V. **Amenities:** Access to nearby health club; massage; babysitting; dry cleaning. *In room:* A/C, TV, dataport, fridge, coffeemaker, hair dryer, iron.

Wolf Creek Inn ☆ *Finds*   Originally opened in 1883 on the old stagecoach road between Sacramento and Portland, the Wolf Creek Tavern is a two-story clapboard building with wide front verandas along both floors. Today the inn, which is 25 miles north of Grants Pass and just off I-5, is the oldest hotel in Oregon and is owned and managed by the Oregon State Parks and Recreation

Division. The interior is furnished in period antiques dating from the 1870s to the 1930s. On a winter's night there's no cozier spot than by the fireplace in the downstairs "ladies parlor." The guest rooms are small and comfortably furnished, much as they might have been in the early 1900s. Meals are available in the inn's dining room. All in all, this inn has a genuinely timeless feel.

100 Front St. (P.O. Box 6), Wolf Creek, OR 97497. © 541/866-2474. www.oregonstateparks.org. 8 units. $75–$100 double (lower rates in winter). Rates include full breakfast in summer, continental breakfast in winter. MC, V. **Amenities:** Restaurant (American). *In room:* No phone.

CAMPGROUNDS

Along the Rogue River east of Grants Pass, you'll find the very busy **Valley of the Rogue State Park** (© 541/582-1118) just off I-5 near the town of Rogue River. West of Grants Pass, there are several county-operated campgrounds, of which **Indian Mary Park,** near Galice on Merlin-Galice Road in the Hellgate Canyon area, is the nicest. Near Indian Mary Park, you'll also find the **Almeda Park,** which is close to the Grave Creek trail head of the Rogue River Trail.

WHERE TO DINE

If all you need is a pizza and a microbrew, try **Wild River Brewing & Pizza Co.,** 595 NE E St. (© 541/471-RIVR). Alternatively, check out the same company's **Wild River Pub,** 533 NE F St. (© 541/474-4456). For espresso drinks and light meals, try the fun atmosphere at **Coffee Cartel,** 405 NE 7th St. (© 541/955-8573). **The Cake Shop,** 215 Galice Rd., Merlin (© 541/479-0188), is open only Friday through Sunday; but if you happen to be there during that time, it's worth a stop for the Wisconsin cheese rolls. **Morrison's Rogue River Lodge,** 8500 Galice Rd., Merlin (© 541/476-3825), serves the best meals on the river. For nonguests, dinners are $22 to $32. Reservations are required. See above for details.

Hamilton River House ★REGIONAL AMERICAN   If you're eager to soak up as much Rogue River atmosphere as you can while you're in Grants Pass, be sure to have a meal at this restaurant right on the banks of the river. Three levels of decks outside provide plenty of seating in pleasant weather, and even if you have to eat inside, there are big windows that let you gaze out at the water. Oven-roasted trout and rotisserie chicken are two of the best choices. For dessert, try one of the cheesecakes. The lively bar really gets hopping on weekends when there's live jazz.

1936 Rogue River Hwy. © 541/479-3938. Reservations recommended. Main courses $7.50–$15. AE, DISC, MC, V. Sun–Thurs 4–9pm; Fri–Sat 4–10pm.

The Laughing Clam ★SEAFOOD/PUB FARE   Located in a historic building in the historic G Street neighborhood, this pub is furnished in "shabby chic" and sports a bar that came around Cape Horn by ship a long time ago. They serve up tasty salads, sandwiches, and pastas, and there are also plenty of meatless and seafood selections to accompany a microbrew or glass of Oregon wine. We really like the curried coconut prawns and calamari with spicy chili mayonnaise.

121 SW G St. © 541/479-1110. Main courses $6–$20. DISC, MC, V. Mon–Thurs 11am–9pm; Fri–Sat 11am–10pm; Sun noon–9pm.

Summer Jo's Farm, Garden & Restaurant ★★ *Finds* STEAK/SEAFOOD Out in the country on an organic farm growing flowers, herbs, and vegetables, this casual restaurant provides a glimpse of the good life, Grants Pass style. If you like gardens, you'll especially enjoy a meal here in high summer when the gardens are bursting with life and color. Lunch (popular with groups and often crowded) is served inside or outside on the lawn. The cafe uses organically grown herbs and produce from the surrounding farm. With the exception of the creative vegetarian cuisine, dishes tend toward the traditional. And with both chef and sous chef hailing from the Culinary Institute of America, the preparation is impeccable.

2315 Upper River Rd. Loop. 𝄢 **541/476-6882.** Reservations recommended. Main courses $7–$17. AE, MC, V. Tues–Thurs 11am–3pm; Fri–Sat 11am–3pm and 5–9pm. Closed Jan. Drive west on G St. and look for the sign; it's 1½ miles from downtown Grants Pass.

5 Oregon Caves National Monument & the Illinois Valley

Cave Junction: 30 miles SW of Grants Pass, 56 miles NE of Crescent City

For many people, U.S. 199 is simply the road to the redwoods from southern Oregon. However, this remote stretch of highway passes through the Illinois Valley and skirts the Siskiyou Mountains, two areas that offer quite a few recreational activities. The Illinois River, which flows into the Rogue River, is an even wilder river than the Rogue, and experienced paddlers looking for real whitewater adventures often run its Class V waters. Because the Siskiyou Mountains are among the oldest in Oregon, they support a unique plant community. These mountains are also known for their rugged, rocky peaks, which, though not very high, can be very impressive.

ESSENTIALS

GETTING THERE   Cave Junction is on U.S. 199 between Grants Pass and the California state line. Oregon Caves National Monument is 20 miles outside Cave Junction on Ore. 46.

VISITOR INFORMATION   For more information on this area, contact the **Illinois River Valley Visitor Center,** 201 Caves Hwy., Cave Junction, OR 97523 (𝄢 **541/592-2631**).

EXPLORING THE CAVES

Oregon Caves National Monument 𝄐   High in the rugged Siskiyou Mountains, a clear mountain stream cascades through a narrow canyon, and here stands one of southern Oregon's oldest attractions. Known as the marble halls of Oregon and first discovered in 1874, the caves, which stretch for 3 miles under the mountain, were formed by water seeping through marble bedrock. The slight acidity of the water dissolves the marble, which is later redeposited as beautiful stalactites, stalagmites, draperies, soda straws, columns, and flowstone. Guided tours of the caves take about 1½ hours, and up above ground there are several miles of hiking trails that start near the cave entrance. During the summer, there are also candlelight tours of the cave at the end of the day. To reach the monument, take Ore. 46 out of Cave Junction and follow the signs.

19000 Caves Hwy. 𝄢 **541/592-2100.** www.nps.gov/orca. Admission $7.50 adults, $5 children 6–11. Cave tours mid-Mar to late May and Labor Day–early Dec daily 10am–4pm; late May–late June daily 9am–5pm; late June daily 9am–6:30pm.

OTHER THINGS TO SEE & DO IN THE ILLINOIS VALLEY

The Illinois River, when it isn't raging through rock-choked canyons, creates some of the best **swimming holes** in the state. Try the waters at Illinois River State Park, just outside Cave Junction, or ask at the **Illinois Valley Ranger District,** 26568 Redwood Hwy., Cave Junction, OR 97523 (𝄢 **541/592-2166**), for directions to other good swimming holes in the area. At this ranger station, you can also pick up information and directions for **hiking trails** in the Siskiyous, where the 180,000-acre Kalmiopsis Wilderness is a destination for backpackers.

WINE TOURING

The Cave Junction area is one of the warmest regions of Oregon and consequently produces some of the best Cabernet Sauvignons and Merlots in the state. This is about as far south as you can get and still claim to be producing Oregon wines—just a few more miles and you're in California (though it's still a long way to Napa Valley).

Bridgeview ✿ Best known for its distinctive blue bottles, Bridgeview is one of the three largest wineries in the state and produces primarily inexpensive white wines for the masses. This place is not for wine snobs, but for those who enjoy a pleasant glass of wine with dinner. The tasting room boasts an idyllic setting beside a large pond that is stocked with trout. (Don't forget to feed them.) Whites are usually under $10, while most reds tend to be around $20.

4210 Holland Loop Rd. ✆ 877/273-4843 or 541/592-4688. Daily 11am–5pm. From Cave Junction, go east on Ore. 46 and turn right on Holland Loop Rd.

Foris ✿ Full-bodied and complex red wines are the hallmark of Foris Vineyards Winery. The Marechal Foch, Pinot Noir, and Cabernet Sauvignon/ Merlot/Cabernet Franc blend are all outstanding. They also do very good Chardonnay, a popular and inexpensive Pinot Gris, and even a port.

654 Kendall Rd. ✆ 800/843-6747 or 541/592-3752. www.foriswine.com. Daily 11am–5pm. Closed major holidays.

WHERE TO STAY

Oregon Caves Chateau ✿ A narrow road winds for 20 miles south from Cave Junction into the Siskiyou National Forest, climbing through deep forests before finally coming to an end in a narrow, steep-walled canyon. At the very head of this canyon stands the Oregon Caves Chateau, a rustic six-story lodge built in 1934. Huge fir beams support the lobby ceiling, and two marble fireplaces beckon. (It can be cool here any time of year.) About the only thing that's missing from this alpine setting is a view. (Because the lodge is in a wooded canyon, there are no sweeping vistas.) The guest rooms have rather unattractive furnishings and don't live up to the promise of the rest of the building. However, if you spend your time exploring the caves, hiking the hills, or lounging in the lobby, you'll hardly notice. A 1930s-style soda fountain (an absolute classic) serves burgers, shakes, and other simple meals, while in the main dining room steak and seafood dinners are available.

20000 Caves Hwy. (P.O. Box 1278), Cave Junction, OR 97523. ✆ 541/592-3400. Fax 541/592-3800. www. visitoregoncaves.com. 20 units. $95 double; $125–$135 suite. AE, DC, DISC, MC, V. Pets accepted. **Amenities:** 2 restaurants (steak/seafood, American). *In room:* No phone.

Out 'n' About Treehouse Treesort ✿ *Finds* This is by far the most unusual accommodation in southern Oregon: a complex of treehouses. Michael Garnier, the owner, fought for years with county officials over whether the treehouses were safe. The county finally agreed to let the treetop cottages remain, much to the delight of the many people who have stayed here. Choices include a Tree Room Schoolhouse, the Swiss Family Complex (complete with swinging bridge to the kids' room), the Peacock Perch, the Cabintree (actually a landlocked cabin), and the Treeplex, which consists of two "treepis" and a "Cavaltree" fort (big hit with kids). The Tree Room Schoolhouse has a bathroom and the

Treezebo has a toilet and sink. Despite the address, Out 'n' About is actually located in the community of Takilma.

300 Page Creek Rd., Cave Junction, OR 97523. © **800/200-5484** or 541/592-2208. www.treehouses.com. 7 units. $80–$150 double. Rates include continental breakfast. No credit cards. Pets accepted ($15 per day). **Amenities:** Outdoor pool; tour desk. *In room:* Fridge, no phone.

CAMPGROUNDS

Although there are no campgrounds in Oregon Caves National Monument, there are a couple of national-forest campgrounds nearby. On the road to the national monument, you'll find **Grayback Campground** and **Cave Creek Campground,** both of which are in forest settings on creek banks.

WHERE TO DINE

Wild River Brewing & Pizza Company 🅖 *Finds* PIZZA/DELI   If you're a fan of microbrewery ales, a pleasant surprise awaits you in the crossroads community of Cave Junction. This very casual combination pizza parlor and deli also happens to be a respectable little brewery specializing in British ales. The rich and flavorful ales go great with the pizzas, several of which are made with locally made sausage. And for fans of the unusual, there's a pizza with smoked sausage and sauerkraut and another with avocado and sprouts.

249 N. Redwood Hwy. © **541/592-3556.** www.wildriverbrewing.com. Sandwiches $4–$5.50; pizzas $4–$20. DISC, MC, V. Mon–Sat 11am–10pm; Sun noon–9pm.

6 The Roseburg Area: Lions & Tigers & Wineries

68 miles N of Grants Pass, 68 miles S of Eugene, 83 miles W of Crater Lake National Park

Although primarily a logging mill town, Roseburg is set at the mouth of the North Umpqua River and, consequently, is well situated for exploring one of the prettiest valleys in Oregon. The surrounding countryside bears a striking resemblance to parts of northern California, so it should come as no surprise that there are a half dozen wineries in the area. The hills south of town look a bit like an Africa savanna, which may be why the Wildlife Safari park chose to locate here. Today this drive-through wildlife park is one of the biggest attractions in southern Oregon. In downtown Roseburg, you'll find numerous old Victorian homes, and a drive through these old neighborhoods will be interesting for fans of late-19th-century architecture.

WHAT TO SEE & DO: LOCAL HISTORY & A WILDLIFE PARK

Douglas County Museum of History & Natural History 🅖   South of town at the Douglas County Fairgrounds, you'll find this surprisingly well-designed museum. It is housed in an unusual, large building that resembles an old mining structure or mill. Inside are displays on the history and natural history of the region. Pioneer farming and mining displays interpret the settlement of the region, but it's the very large elk that really grabs people's attention. Interesting traveling exhibits often show up here, so it's worth checking to see what is scheduled.

123 Museum Dr. (exit 123 off I-5). © **541/957-7007.** www.co.douglas.or.us/museum. $3.50 adults, $1 children 4–17. Mon–Fri 9am–5pm; Sat 10am–5pm; Sun noon–5pm.

Wildlife Safari 🅖🅖 *Kids*   This 600-acre drive-through nature park is home to wild animals from around the world. You'll come face-to-face with curious bears, grazing gazelles and zebras, ostriches, and even lumbering elephants and rhinos.

You can also visit the educational center or attend an animal show. Convertibles are not allowed in the lion or bear enclosures, but rental cars are available.

Off Ore. 42, just outside Winston (south of Roseburg). ✆ 800/355-4848 or 541/679-6761. www.rosenet. net/tourism/wildlife_safari.html. Admission $14.50 adults, $11.50 seniors, $8.50 children 4–12, free for children 3 and under. Summer daily 9am–7pm; spring and fall daily 9am–5pm; winter daily 9am–4pm.

THE NEARBY HISTORIC TOWN OF OAKLAND

About 15 miles north of Roseburg is the historic town of Oakland, which is listed on the National Register of Historic Places. Though the town was founded in the 1850s, most of the buildings here date from the 1890s. A stroll through town soaking up the atmosphere is a pleasant way to spend a morning or an afternoon. You can pick up a self-guided walking-tour map at the **Oakland Museum,** 130 Locust St. (✆ **541/459-4531**), which is housed in an 1893 brick building and contains collections of historic photos, old farm tools, household furnishings, and clothing from Oakland's past. Admission is by donation, and the museum is open daily from 1 to 4pm.

WINE TOURING

The Roseburg area is home to half a dozen wineries, all of which are located within a few miles of I-5.

Callahan Ridge Winery   The tasting room at this winery is housed in a beautifully weathered old barn set in a grove of shady oak trees. Red wines, including Zinfandel and a Cabernet-Merlot blend, are strong points, but they also do very good Riesling and white Zinfandel. With the exception of the dessert wines, most bottles are $10 or less.

340 Busenbark Lane. ✆ **541/673-7901.** www.callahanridge.com. Mon–Sat 11am–5pm. From Roseburg, go west on Garden Valley Rd., and turn left on Melrose Rd.

Girardet Wine Cellars ⭐   Although this winery is unique in Oregon for producing such obscure wines as Baco Noir and Seyval Blanc, Girardet is best known for its big, bold red wines, which include the unusual Marechal Foch.

895 Reston Rd. ✆ **541/679-7252.** www.girardet.com. Apr–Oct daily 11am–5pm; Nov–Mar Mon–Sat 11am–5pm. Closed Dec 20–Jan 30 and major holidays. Take Ore. 42 (exit 119) west from I-5 south of Roseburg and turn right on Reston Rd. before reaching Tenmile.

Henry Estate Winery   This winery on the bank of the Umpqua River produces primarily white wines. Grapes are grown on a special trellising system known as a Scott Henry trellis, named for the winery's founder and now used all over the world.

Ore. 9 west of Umpqua. ✆ **800/782-2686** or 541/459-5120. www.henryestate.com. Daily 11am–5pm. Closed major holidays. From exit 136 off I-5 at Sutherlin, go west on through Umpqua and cross the Umpqua River.

Hillcrest Vineyards   This winery is worth seeking out if for no other reason than that it is Oregon's oldest continuously operating winery producing wines from vinifera (European) grapes. Vineyards here were first planted in 1961. The winemaker here believes in releasing his wines when they're ready to drink, so expect to find wines several years older than those at other area wineries.

240 Vineyard Lane. ✆ **800/736-3709.** www.hillcrestwine.com. Daily 11am–5pm. From Roseburg, go west on Garden Valley Rd., and turn left on Melrose Rd., right on Doerner Rd., right onto Elgarose Rd., and left onto Vineyard Lane.

La Garza Cellars   This small winery just off I-5 is very convenient if you just want to make a quick foray into the world of Oregon wines. They specialize in

Cabernet Sauvignon but also do a dry Riesling. The reserve Cabs, though pricey (up around $40), can be excellent, and they are among the best Oregon Cabernets you'll find.

491 Winery Lane. ℂ 541/679-9654. June–Sept daily 11am–5pm. Call for off-season hours. South of Roseburg, take exit 119 off I-5 and go west ½ mile.

WHERE TO STAY
IN ROSEBURG

Holiday Inn Express ✿   Although located just off I-5, this modern economy hotel also happens to sit on the banks of the Umpqua River, and every room has a balcony and a view of the river. The Jacuzzi is set in a gazebo amid green lawns between the hotel building and the river. Downtown Roseburg and a couple of good restaurants are a short walk away.

375 W. Harvard Blvd., Roseburg, OR 97470. ℂ 800/HOLIDAY or 541/673-7517. Fax 541/673-8331. 100 units. $74–$139 double. Rates include continental breakfast. AE, DC, DISC, MC, V. Pets accepted ($5 fee). **Amenities:** Indoor pool; exercise room; Jacuzzi; business center; guest laundry. *In room:* A/C, TV, dataport, coffeemaker, hair dryer, iron.

WHERE TO DINE
IN ROSEBURG

Dino's Ristorante Italiano ✿ ITALIAN   With its brick walls and shelves and shelves of wine bottles (both Northwest and imported) lining the back of the restaurant, Dino's has the feel of a well-stocked wine cellar. Dino, the restaurant's owner and the ultimate Italian host, is also a winemaker, producing decent wines at his own winery, the DeNino Estate Umpqua River Winery. Yes, this is a place for wine lovers, but it's also a good (and romantic) place to assuage your Italian food cravings with the likes of portobello-and-ricotta ravioli or lasagna *Bolognese*.

404 SE Jackson St. ℂ 541/673-0848. Main courses $7–$19. MC, V. Tues–Thurs 5–9pm; Fri–Sat 5–10pm.

McMenamins Roseburg Station Pub & Brewery ✿ PUB   Another jewel in the McMenamins brewpub crown, the Roseburg Station Pub is a good example of the way McMenamins breathes new life into historic buildings. This authentic restoration of an old train station celebrates Roseburg's rail culture and is a casual place for dinner and a microbrew. An eclectic collection of chandeliers decorates the 16-foot ceiling, and street signs from around the world punctuate the room. Original features such as the dark wainscoting have been restored to their former elegance. A straightforward menu features burgers, sandwiches, and house-specialty Terminator stout chili. Be sure to accompany your meal with one of the craft ales for which the McMenamins pubs are famous.

700 Sheridan St. ℂ 541/672-1934. www.mcmenamins.com. Main courses $4.25–$12.25. AE, DISC, MC, V. Daily 11am–1am.

IN OAKLAND

Tolly's ✿ *Kids* SODA FOUNTAIN/REGIONAL AMERICAN   Since 1964, folks from all over the region have been stopping in Tolly's to have dinner or just a root-beer float or sundae. Housed in a storefront on Locust Street, Tolly's is both an elegant restaurant and an old-fashioned soda fountain. You can hop onto a stool at the counter and sip a cold malted milk shake in a tall glass, or linger over a dinner of steak or perfectly prepared salmon. Check out the case for deliciously decadent desserts. Attached to the restaurant are both an antiques shop and an art gallery.

115 Locust St., Oakland. ℂ 541/459-3796. Reservations recommended for dinner. Main courses lunch $6.50–$12, dinner $15–$27. AE, DC, MC, V. Mon–Tues 9am–5pm; Wed–Fri 9am–9pm; Sat–Sun 8am–9pm.

NORTH OF ROSEBURG: A SERIOUS ICE-CREAM STOP

Consider yourself very lucky if you happen to be driving north from Roseburg on I-5 on a hot summer day. Respite from the heat lies just off the interstate at the Rice Hill exit ramp, at legendary **K&R Drive Inn** (© **541/849-2570**), where every scoop of ice cream you order is actually a double scoop! Consider this before you order two scoops of rocky road. The K&R is open daily from 10am to 9pm in summer, daily from 10:30am to 8pm in winter.

10

Central Oregon

On the west side of the Cascade Range, rain is as certain as death and taxes. But cross the invisible dividing line formed by the mountains and you leave the deluge behind. Central Oregon basks under blue skies nearly 300 days of the year—in fact, it gets so little rain that parts of the region are considered high desert. Such a natural attraction is a constant enticement to Oregonians living west of the Cascades. In summer, they head to central Oregon for hiking, fishing, rafting, and camping, and in winter they descend on the ski slopes of Mount Bachelor, Oregon's best ski resort.

"Central Oregon" does not so much refer to a geographical area as to a recreational region, and it doesn't actually lie in the central part of the state. The Cascade Range is responsible for a rain-shadow effect, creating a distinct and visible dividing line between the wet west side and the dry east side. Ponderosa pines rather than Douglas firs and western red cedars dominate the eastern foothill forests of this region. Farther east, where there is even less annual rainfall, juniper and sagebrush country takes over. It is this classically Western environment that has in part led to the adoption of a Wild West theme in the town of Sisters, which is filled with false-fronted buildings and covered wooden sidewalks.

On closer inspection, however, it becomes evident that it is more than just a lack of rainfall that sets this region apart. Central Oregon's unique volcanic geography provides the scenic backdrop to the region's many recreational activities. Obsidian flows, lava caves, cinder cones, pumice deserts—these are the sorts of features that make the central Oregon landscape unique.

Despite the dryness of the landscape here, water is the region's primary recreational draw. The Deschutes River is the state's most popular rafting river and is fabled among fly anglers for its wild red-side rainbow trout and its steelheads. West of Bend, a scenic highway loops past a dozen or so lakes, each with its own unique character and appeal. Closer to Bend, the Deschutes River cascades over ancient lava flows, forming impressive waterfalls that are favorite destinations of area hikers.

However, for solitude and scenic grandeur, most hikers and backpackers head out from Bend and Sisters into the Three Sisters Wilderness, which encompasses its snow-clad namesake peaks. Outside the wilderness, there are also many miles of mountain-biking trails that have made the Bend and Sisters areas the best mountain-biking destination in the state.

Although the open slopes of Mount Bachelor ski area attract the most visitors in the winter, the area also has many miles of cross-country ski trails, including the state's finest Nordic center (at Mt. Bachelor, of course). Snowmobiling is also very popular.

1 North Central Oregon & the Lower Deschutes River

Maupin: 95 miles N of Bend, 100 miles E of Portland, 40 miles S of The Dalles

Dominated by two rivers—the Deschutes and the John Day—north central Oregon is the driest, most desert-like part of this region. It is also the closest sunny destination for rain-soaked Portlanders.

Hot springs, canyon lands, and some of the best rafting and fishing in the state are the main draws in this part of central Oregon. For many visitors, the high-desert landscape is a fascinating change from the lushness of the west side of the Cascades. For others it is just too bleak and barren. But there is no denying that the Deschutes River is the busiest river in the state. Rafters and anglers descend en masse throughout the year, but especially in summer, to challenge the rapids and the red sides under sunny skies.

Even if the Deschutes is not your destination, this region has several unusual attractions that make it worthwhile for a weekend's exploration. First and foremost of these is the Kah-Nee-Ta Resort, which, with its proximity to Portland and its warm-spring swimming pool, is a powerful enticement after several months of gray skies and constant drizzle west of the Cascades.

Not far from the resort, in the town of Warm Springs, is a fascinating modern museum dedicated to the cultures of Northwest Native Americans. A forgotten page of pioneer days can be found at nearby Shaniko, a ghost town that once made it big as a wool-shipping town. Much older history, up to 40 million years of it, is laid bare in the three units of the John Day Fossil Beds National Monument. If the stark hills of the national monument don't give you enough sense of being in the desert, be sure to visit The Cove Palisades State Park, where three steep-walled canyons have been flooded by the waters of Lake Billy Chinook.

ESSENTIALS

GETTING THERE   Maupin, which is the staging site for most rafting and fishing trips on the lower Deschutes River, is at the junction of U.S. 197, the main route from The Dalles south to Bend, and Ore. 216, which connects to U.S. 26 east of Mount Hood.

VISITOR INFORMATION   For more information on this area, contact the **Greater Maupin Area Chamber of Commerce,** P.O. Box 220, Maupin, OR 97037 (© **541/395-2599**).

RAFTING, FISHING & OTHER AQUATIC ACTIVITIES

Flowing through a dry sagebrush canyon lined with basalt cliffs, the lower Deschutes River, from the U.S. 26 bridge outside Warm Springs down to the Columbia River, is one of the most popular stretches of water in Oregon. This section of the river provides lots of Class III rapids, and 1-day **rafting trips** here are very popular. However, at almost 100 miles in length, the lower Deschutes also provides several options for multiday rafting trips.

Popular 1-day splash-and-giggle trips are offered by dozens of rafting companies and usually start just upstream from Maupin and end just above the impressive Sherar's Falls. Some companies also offer 2- and 3-day trips. Rafting companies operating on the lower Deschutes River include **All Star Rafting** (© **800/ 909-7238** or 541/395-2201; www.asrk.com), which also rents rafts and offers kayaking lessons; **Imperial River Company** (© **800/395-3903** or 541/ 395-2404; www.deschutesriver.com), which operates a bed-and-breakfast inn for rafters in Maupin; and **Rapid River Rafters** (© **800/962-3327** or 541/382-1514;

www.rapidriverrafters.com). Expect to pay around $75 to $90 for a day trip up to around $350 for a 3-day trip.

If you're just passing through the region but would like to catch a glimpse of some of the lower Deschutes River's more dramatic sections, you can visit **Sherar's Falls,** which are at the Sherar Bridge on Ore. 216 between Tygh Valley and Grass Valley. Native Americans can sometimes be seen dip-netting salmon from the waters of these falls, which can also be reached by following the river road north from Maupin for 8 miles. Just west of Sherar Bridge, you'll also find **White River Falls State Park,** where more waterfalls can be seen.

The stretch of the Deschutes River from Pelton Dam to the Columbia River is one of Oregon's most legendary stretches of **fishing** water and is managed primarily for wild steelhead and the famed red-side rainbow trout. Together these two types of fish provide fly anglers with nearly year-round action. From the mouth of the river upstream to several miles above Maupin, there are several good access points. Fly-fishing supplies and equipment rentals are available in Maupin at the **Deschutes Canyon Fly Shop,** 599 S. Hwy. 197, Maupin (✆ 541/395-2565; www.flyfishingdeschutes.com).

South of Madras 12 miles you'll find one of the most unlikely settings in the state. **Lake Billy Chinook,** an artificial lake created by the construction of Round Butte Dam in 1964, now fills the canyons of the Metolius, Crooked, and Deschutes Rivers and seems lifted straight out of the canyon lands of Arizona or Utah. Here, nearly vertical basalt cliffs rise several hundred feet above the lake waters, and sagebrush and junipers cling to the rocky hillsides. The lake is most popular with water-skiers and anglers who come to fish for kokanee (landlocked sockeye salmon) and bull trout (also known as dolly vardens). However, **The Cove Palisades State Park** (✆ 541/546-3412), which is on the south shore, offers easy 3-hour sea-kayak tours of the lake. These tours are offered throughout the year, and the schedule varies with the seasons (more tours in summer, fewer in winter). Tours cost $10 in a single kayak, $17 in a double kayak, and reservations are recommended. At the state park, you'll also find boat ramps, a marina, campgrounds, picnic areas, and swimming beaches. There are even houseboats for rent (see below), and at the marina you'll find a restaurant atop a hill overlooking the lake. The park day-use fee is $3.

A NATIVE AMERICAN HERITAGE MUSEUM

The Museum at Warm Springs ★★ *Finds*   For thousands of years the Warm Springs, Wasco, and Paiute tribes have inhabited this region, part of which is today the Confederated Tribes of the Warm Springs Reservation, and adapted to its environment. It is the history of these peoples that is presented in this impressive modern museum. Over the decades prior to the opening of the museum, the tribes amassed an outstanding collection of regional Native American artifacts, which now form the core of the museum's collection. To better display these artifacts, various styles of traditional houses have been reconstructed at the museum and serve as backdrops for displays on everything from basketry and beadwork to fishing and root gathering. There are new temporary exhibits every 3 months, including exhibitions of Native American artwork.

2189 U.S. 26, Warm Springs. ✆ 541/553-3331. Admission $6 adults, $5 seniors, $4.50 students, $3 children 5–12. Daily 9am–5pm.

A GHOST TOWN & A FOSSIL EXCURSION

Between 1900 and 1911, **Shaniko** was the largest wool-shipping center in the country, and it claims to have been the site of the last range war between cattle

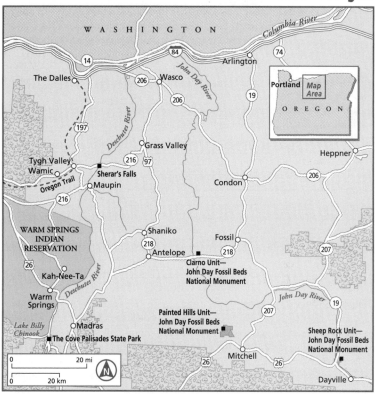

ranchers and sheepherders. However, when the railroad line from the Columbia River down to Bend bypassed Shaniko, the town fell on hard times. Eventually, when a flood washed out the railroad spur into town, Shaniko nearly ceased to exist. Today the false-fronted buildings and wooden sidewalks make this Oregon's favorite and liveliest ghost town. Antiques shops, a wedding chapel, and a historic hotel make for a fun excursion or overnight getaway.

The **John Day Fossil Beds National Monument,** HCR 82, Box 126, Kimberly, OR 97848 (© **541/987-2333;** www.nps.gov/joda), consisting of three individual units separated by as much as 85 miles, preserves a 40-million-year fossil record which indicates that this region was once a tropical or subtropical forest. From tiny seeds to extinct relatives of the rhinoceros and elephant, an amazing array of plants and animals has been preserved in one of the world's most extensive and unbroken fossil records.

To see fossil leaves, twigs, branches, and nuts in their natural state, visit the **Clarno Unit,** 23 miles southeast of Shaniko and U.S. 97. Here ancient mudflows inundated a forest, and today these ancient mudflows appear as eroding cliffs, at the base of which a quarter-mile trail leads past numerous fossils. Although you can't collect fossils in the national monument, you can dig them up behind the Wheeler High School in the small town of **Fossil,** 20 miles east of the Clarno Unit. From the Clarno Unit, it is an 85-mile drive on Ore. 218 and Ore. 19 to the national monument's **Sheep Rock Unit,** which is the site of the monument **Visitor Center.** Here you can get a close-up look at numerous fossils and sometimes watch a paleontologist at work. The visitor center is open daily in summer from 9am to 5pm (closed weekends and holidays Thanksgiving–Feb). Just north of the visitor center you'll pass **Blue Basin,** where there's an interpretive trail.

From the Sheep Rock Unit, the monument's **Painted Hills Unit,** along the John Day River near Mitchell, is another 30 miles west on U.S. 26. You won't see any fossils here, but you will see strikingly colored rounded hills that are favorites of photographers. The weathering of volcanic ash under different climatic conditions created the bands of color on these hills.

WHERE TO STAY & DINE

In addition to the resort and the historic hotel listed below, you'll find three modern log cabins for rent on the shore of Lake Billy Chinook at **The Cove Palisades State Park.** These cabins rent for $65 per night for up to five people ($45 Oct–Apr) and are right beside the water. For reservations, call **Reservations Northwest** (© 800/452-5687 or 503/731-3411). Houseboats are also available for rent at Lake Billy Chinook. Contact **Cove Palisades Marina** (© 541/546-3521, or in winter 541/504-9117; www.covepalisadesmarina.com), for about $1,995 to $2,195 per week in summer (lower rates in spring and fall), or **Lake Billy Chinook Houseboats,** P.O. Box 40, Culver, OR 97734 (© 541/546-2939), for $1,050 to $2,045 per week.

Imperial River Company   Popular primarily with people heading out rafting on the Deschutes River, this lodge may not be your classic B&B, but it is the most comfortable place for many miles around. Guest rooms, all of which have private entrances, sport Oregon themes and have handmade quilts on the beds. The river-view rooms are the best and have whirlpool tubs. Dinner is available, and meals feature organically grown herbs and vegetables. Imperial River Company also offers a wide variety of rafting trips.

304 Bakeoven Rd., Maupin, OR 97037. © 800/395-3903 or 541/395-2404. www.deschutesriver.com. 12 units. $65–$110 double. Rates include full breakfast. AE, DISC, MC, V. **Amenities:** Restaurant (American/Northwest); Jacuzzi. *In room:* A/C.

Kah-Nee-Ta High Desert Resort & Casino 𝓡𝓡 *(Kids)*   Only 120 miles from Portland and set in a remote high-desert canyon, Kah-Nee-Ta Resort, operated by the Confederated Tribes of the Warm Springs Reservation, is the closest sunny-side resort to rain-soaked Portland. The main attraction here is the resort's huge warm-springs-fed main swimming pool (fed by the spring for which the Warm Springs Reservation is named). Because Kah-Nee-Ta offers a wide range of activities and accommodations, it is particularly popular with families, who tend to stay in the resort's large and modern mountain-lodge-style "Village" rooms, which are located beside the main pool. Couples tend to opt for rooms in the main lodge, which is set high on a hillside adjacent to the Indian Head Casino. Down by the main pool, you'll also find teepees and RV sites. The resort has been remodeling its lodge rooms, and the newest rooms are in the west wing. The main dining room has a great view and serves creative Northwest dishes. During the summer, there is a Saturday night traditional salmon bake followed by Native American dancing.

P.O. Box K, Warm Springs, OR 97761. © 800/554-4786 or 541/553-1112. www.kahneetaresort.com. 169 units (plus 20 teepees). $130–$150 double; $180–$370 suite; $70 teepee (for 3 people). AE, DC, DISC, MC, V. **Amenities:** 2 restaurants (American/Northwest, American), lounge, casino; 2 outdoor pools; 18-hole golf course and miniature golf; 2 tennis courts; 2 exercise rooms; full-service spa; 3 Jacuzzis; sauna; kayak rentals and white-water-rafting trips; fishing-rod rentals; bike rentals; horseback riding; children's programs; game room; courtesy resort shuttle; massage; coin-op laundry. *In room:* A/C, TV, coffeemaker, hair dryer, iron.

Tips **Travelers' Tip**

For reservations at Forest Service campgrounds, contact the **National Recreation Reservation Service** (© **800/280-CAMP** or www.reserveusa.com), which charges a $9 reservation fee. These sites can be reserved up to 8 months in advance.

Shaniko Historic Hotel ⭐ *Finds* This restored and recently renovated two-story brick hotel is a surprisingly solid little place in a ghost town full of glorified shacks. However, don't start thinking that this is a fancy B&B; it's not. Most rooms are fairly small and simply furnished, but guests don't seem to mind. No one comes out here to be pampered; they come for a bit of rustic Wild West atmosphere, and that's exactly what they get. The faded elegance hints at the wealth that once made the fortunes of area sheep ranchers, and the covered wooden sidewalk out front conjures up images of the Wild West.

Fourth and E sts., Shaniko, OR 97057. © **800/483-3441** or 541/489-3441. Fax 541/489-3441. www. shaniko.com. 18 units. $66 double. Rates include full breakfast. MC, V. Closed Nov–Apr. **Amenities:** Restaurant (American), lounge. *In room:* No phone.

CAMPGROUNDS

Downriver from Sherar's Falls, there are many undeveloped campsites along the Deschutes River. At Lake Billy Chinook, west of U.S. 97 between Madras and Redmond, there are several campgrounds. The most developed are the two at **The Cove Palisades State Park.** Reservations can be made through **Reservations Northwest** (© **800/452-5687;** www.oregonstateparks.org). Farther west, up the Metolius arm of the reservoir on F.S. Road 64, you'll find the Forest Service's primitive **Perry South Campground.** A little bit farther west is the **Monty Campground,** which is the lowermost campground on the Metolius River's free-flowing waters.

2 The Sisters Area

108 miles SE of Salem, 92 miles NE of Eugene, 21 miles NW of Bend

Lying at the eastern foot of the Cascades, the small Western-themed town of Sisters takes its name from the nearby Three Sisters mountains, which loom majestically over the town. Ponderosa pine forests, aspen groves, and wide meadows surround Sisters, giving it a classic Western setting that the town has cashed in on in recent years. Modern buildings sport false fronts and covered sidewalks, though the predominantly pastel color schemes are more 1990s than 1890s.

Once just someplace to stop for gas on the way to Bend, Sisters is now a destination in itself. A few miles outside of town is the Black Butte Resort, one of the state's finest golf resorts, and also nearby is the tiny community of Camp Sherman, which has been a vacation destination for nearly a century. Sisters has also become Oregon's llama capital, with numerous large llama ranches around the area.

ESSENTIALS

GETTING THERE Sisters is at the junction of U.S. 20 (which connects I-5 near Corvallis with Bend), Ore. 126 (which links Redmond with Eugene), and Ore. 242 (the McKenzie Pass scenic highway). Horizon Airlines and United Express serve **Redmond Municipal Airport,** 20 miles east of Sisters.

VISITOR INFORMATION   Contact the **Sisters Area Chamber of Commerce,** 164 N. Elm St. (P.O. Box 430), Sisters, OR 97759 (✆ **541/549-0251;** www.sisterschamber.com).

FESTIVALS   During the annual **Sisters Outdoor Quilt Show** on the second Saturday in July, buildings all over town are hung with quilts. The **Sisters Rodeo,** held the second weekend of June, also attracts large crowds.

ENJOYING THE OUTDOORS

Although shopping may be the number one recreational activity right in Sisters, the surrounding lands are the town's real main attraction. Any month of the year, you'll find an amazing variety of possible activities within a few miles of town. Northwest in the community of Camp Sherman is one of the area's top outdoor attractions, the springs that form the **headwaters of the Metolius River.** Cold, crystal-clear waters bubble up out of the ground and, within only a few hundred yards, produce a full-blown river.

FLY-FISHING   If you need some fly-fishing supplies or want to hire a guide to take you out on the local waters, try **The Fly Fisher's Place,** 151 W. Main Ave. (✆ **541/549-3474**). The folks here can guide you to the best **fly-fishing** spots on the Deschutes, McKenzie, and Crooked Rivers.

GOLFING   At **Black Butte Ranch** (✆ **800/399-2322** or 541/595-1500; www. blackbutteranch.com), west of Sisters, you'll find two courses surrounded by ponderosa pines and aspens ($32–$65 greens fee). At **Eagle Crest** (✆ **541/923-4653;** www.eagle-crest.com), east of Sisters, you get a more desert-like experience with junipers and sagebrush surrounding the fairways ($35–$65 greens fees). There are great views at both resorts. However, the best golf value in the area is the **Crooked River Ranch Golf Course,** 5010 Clubhouse Rd., Crooked River Ranch (✆ **800/ 833-3197** or 541/923-6343; www.crookedriverranch.com), which is northwest of Redmond off U.S. 97 and plays through and alongside a spectacular canyon ($25–$30 greens fees).

HIKING   West and south of Sisters, several excellent scenic trails lend themselves to both day hikes and overnight trips. Many of these trails lead into the Mount Washington, Mount Jefferson, and Three Sisters wilderness areas. Near Camp Sherman, you can hike to the summit of Black Butte for 360° views or hike along the spring-fed Metolius River. Farther west off U.S. 20, you'll find trails leading up to the base of craggy Three Fingered Jack. South of town there are trail heads leading into the Three Sisters Wilderness. (The Chambers Lakes area is particularly scenic.) The hike up Tam McArthur Rim is another good one if you're looking for spectacular views. Stop by the **Sisters Ranger Station** (✆ **541/549-7700**) at the west end of town for information and trail maps.

To the east of Sisters outside the town of Terrebonne, there are several miles of very scenic hiking trails within **Smith Rock State Park** (✆ **800/551-6949** or 541/548-7501). The park's 400-foot crags and the meandering Crooked River provide the backdrops for hikes through high desert scrublands. Hiking trails lead through the canyon and up to the top of the rocks. The view of the Cascades framed by Smith Rock is superb.

HORSEBACK RIDING   If Sisters has put you in a cowboy state of mind, you can saddle up a palomino and go for a ride at **Black Butte Stables** (✆ **541/ 595-2061;** www.oregoncowboy.com), which has stables at and near Black Butte Ranch west of Sisters. These stables offer a variety of rides, with an hour ride costing $30.

Central Oregon

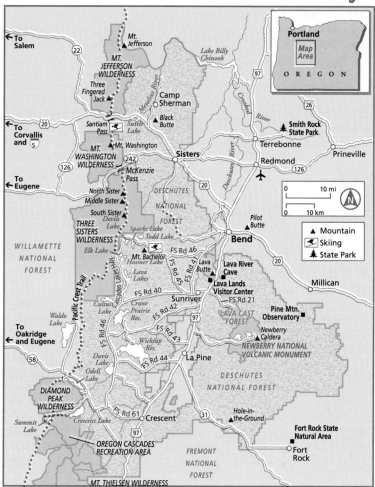

MOUNTAIN BIKING   Sisters makes an excellent base for mountain bikers, who will find dozens of miles of trails of all skill levels within a few miles of town. In fact, one easy ride, the Sisters Bike Trail, starts only a few blocks south of downtown's many shops at the Village Green Park on Elm Street. Other fun rides include the Butte Loops Trail around Black Butte and the strenuous Green Ridge Trail. Stop by the **Sisters Ranger Station** (✆ **541/549-7700**) at the west end of town for information and trail maps. You can rent bikes in town at **Eurosports,** 182 E. Hood Ave. (✆ **541/549-2471**), for about $15 per day.

ROCK CLIMBING   Located east of Terrebonne, **Smith Rock State Park** is one of central Oregon's many geological wonders. Jagged rock formations tower above the Crooked River here and attract rock climbers from around the world. A couple of shops in the area cater primarily to climbers. If you want to learn how to climb, contact **First Ascent Climbing Services** (✆ **800/325-5462** or 541/548-5137; www.goclimbing.com), which offers classes ($190 for an all-day class).

OTHER AREA ATTRACTIONS

Rail-travel enthusiasts might consider an excursion on the **Crooked River Railroad Company Dinner Train,** 4075 NE O'Neil Rd., Redmond (© **541/548-8630;** www.crookedriverrailroad.com). The 38-mile, approximately 3-hour rail excursion travels from Redmond to Prineville and back. Restored dining cars are the setting for dinners or brunches that may feature train-robbery or murder-mystery themes. Fares are $59 to $71 for adults and $38 for children 4 through 12. Reservations are required.

Fans of folk art should be sure to stop by the **Petersen Rock Gardens,** 7930 SW 77th St., Redmond (© **541/382-5574**), 9 miles north of Bend just off U.S. 97. This 4-acre folk-art creation consists of buildings, miniature bridges, terraces, and tiny towers all constructed from rocks. The gardens, built between 1935 and 1952 by a Danish immigrant farmer, are open daily from 9am to dusk; admission is $3 adults, $1.50 children 12 to 16, and 50¢ children 6 to 11.

Reindeer Ranch at Operation Santa Claus (© **541/548-8910;** www.oscreindeer.com), 2 miles west of Redmond on Ore. 126, is the largest reindeer ranch in the United States and is home to more than 100 reindeer. It's open daily and admission is free.

WHERE TO STAY

Black Butte Ranch ☆☆☆ (Kids   Located 8 miles west of Sisters on former ranch lands, the Black Butte Ranch resort community has the most breathtaking mountain views of any of Central Oregon's resorts. It's also the first resort you come to after crossing to the east side of the Cascades, and a stay here lets you avoid the traffic congestion in Bend. With its aspen-ringed meadows and expansive views, this is as beautiful a spot as you'll find in central Oregon. Add a pair of golf courses, 16 miles of paved biking/jogging paths, and lots of recreational activities and you have a nearly perfect family vacation resort. The only drawback is that you're a long way from Mount Bachelor's ski slopes in winter (though the slopes at Hoodoo Ski Area are nearby). The condos and homes are set amid open lawns between the forest and the meadows, and most have fireplaces and kitchens. Large decks and sliding glass doors let you enjoy the views no matter what the weather. In the resort's main dining room, which serves good steaks and Northwest cuisine, large windows provide nearly every table with a view of the mountains or adjacent lake.

13653 Hawks Beard Rd. (P.O. Box 8000), Black Butte Ranch, OR 97759. © 800/452-7455 or 541/595-6211. Fax 541/595-2077. www.blackbutteranch.com. 97 units. May–Sept $90–$120 double, $142–$350 condo or home; Oct–Apr $75–$110 double, $132–$350 condo or home (2- to 6-night minimums in July and Aug). AE, DC, DISC, MC, V. **Amenities:** 2 restaurants (American), lounge; 4 outdoor pools; 2 18-hole golf courses; 20 tennis courts; exercise room; Jacuzzi; canoe and paddleboat rentals; bike rentals; horseback riding; children's programs; game room. *In room:* TV, dataport, coffeemaker.

Conklin's Guest House ☆☆   Surrounded by meadows and with an unobstructed view of the mountains, Conklin's B&B is an excellent choice for anyone who has become enamored of Sisters' Western charm. The inn's country decor fits right in with the town, and a duck pond and a trout pond provide a bit of a farm feel. There's even a swimming pool, and breakfast is served in a tile-floored sunroom. Our favorite room has a big old claw-foot tub surrounded by windows that look out to the Cascades. This room also has its own little balcony.

69013 Camp Polk Rd., Sisters, OR 97759. © 800/549-4262 or 541/549-0123. Fax 541/549-4481. www.conklinsguesthouse.com. 5 units. June–Dec $90–$150 double; Jan–May $70–$130 double. Rates include full breakfast. No credit cards. **Amenities:** Outdoor pool; exercise room; massage; laundry service. *In room:* No phone.

Eagle Crest Resort ⚐ Less than 20 miles east of Sisters, on the banks of the Deschutes River, is another sprawling resort that attracts sun worshipers and golfers. The landscape is much drier here than around Sisters and is dominated by scrubby junipers that give Eagle Crest the feel of a desert resort. The rooms overlook the golf course rather than the mountains, which should give you an idea of most guests' priorities. Facilities here are geared primarily toward owners of homes and condos, so if you aren't a buyer, you may feel a bit left out. Also, the location is quite a bit out of the mainstream of Central Oregon outdoor recreational activities and is removed from the shopping and other attractions in Sisters and Bend. Plan on either staying put or doing quite a bit of driving. The resort's main restaurant is located on the opposite side of the golf course from the main building, so you'll have to walk or drive. The menu and decor are both very traditional. In addition to amenities listed below, there is an extensive network of jogging trails.

P.O. Box 1215, Redmond, OR 97756. ☎ 800/682-4786 or 541/923-2453. Fax 541/923-1720. www. eagle-crest.com. 300 units. $61–$109 double; $84–$145 suite; $119–$309 town house. AE, DC, DISC, MC, V. **Amenities:** 3 restaurants (International, American); lounge; 4 pools (1 indoor); 3 golf courses and 1 putting course; 6 tennis courts (2 indoor); racquetball courts; health club; full-service spa; Jacuzzi; sauna; bike rentals; horseback riding; children's programs; game room; concierge; massage; laundry service; dry cleaning. *In room:* A/C, TV, dataport, coffeemaker, hair dryer, iron.

Metolius River Resort ⚐⚐ *Finds* Despite the name, this hardly ranks as a resort. However, it is perfect for those seeking peace and quiet or a romantic getaway. Set on the banks of the crystal-clear, spring-fed Metolius River 14 miles west of Sisters, the contemporary cedar-shingled two-story cabins are exceptional, offering modern amenities and styling with a bit of a rustic feel. Peeled-log beds, wood paneling, river-stone fireplaces, and green roofs give the cabins a quintessentially Western appeal. Although the Metolius River is legendary as the most difficult trout-fishing stream in Oregon, the cabins here are particularly popular with trout anglers. Not far away, you'll find the springs of the Metolius, where the river comes welling up out of the ground.

25551 SW F.S. Rd. 1419, Camp Sherman, OR 97730. ☎ 800/81-TROUT. Fax 541/595-6281. www. metolius-river-resort.com. 11 cabins. $180 double. 2- to 3-night minimum. MC, V. **Amenities:** Restaurant (Northwest). *In room:* TV/VCR, dataport, kitchen, fridge, coffeemaker, hair dryer.

CAMPGROUNDS

About a dozen Forest Service campgrounds are strung out along F.S. Road 14 north of Camp Sherman. All of these campgrounds are on the banks of the river and are most popular with anglers. The first of these, the **Camp Sherman Campground,** is only a half mile north of Camp Sherman. South of Sisters, at the end of F.S. Road 16, there are three campgrounds at or near Three Creek Lake. For reservations, contact the **National Recreation Reservation Service** (☎ **800/280-CAMP** or www.reserveusa.com).

WHERE TO DINE

No visit to Sisters is complete without a stop at the **Sisters Bakery,** 251 E. Cascade St. (☎ **541/549-0361**), for marionberry pastries and bear claws. For meals with a view of the mountain, you can't beat the **Restaurant at Black Butte Ranch** (see "Where to Stay," above).

Bronco Billy's Ranch Grill and Saloon ⚐ STEAK/SEAFOOD/MEXICAN Located in the old Hotel Sisters building (no longer a hotel), Bronco Billy's serves up good old-fashioned Wild West grub in the form of belt-loosening platters of barbecued ribs, steaks, and green-chili burgers. Step through the swinging saloon doors leading from the dining room to the bar and you'll find genuine Western decor, including a various trophy animal heads on the walls.

190 E. Cascade St. ✆ **541/549-7427.** Reservations recommended. Main courses $9–$20. MC, V. May–Oct daily 11:30am–9 or 10pm; Nov–Apr Mon–Fri 3–9 or 10pm, Sat–Sun 11:30am–9 or 10pm.

Kokanee Café ★★ (Finds) NORTHWEST   This out-of-the-way place, located about 14 miles west of Sisters adjacent to the Metolius River Resort in Camp Sherman, is one of the best restaurants in the region. The interior of the log building is contemporary rustic with an open-beamed ceiling and a wrought-iron chandelier, and out back there's a deck under the ponderosa pines. The menu is short and includes fresh trout (our favorite), lamb chops with mint sauce, and grilled duck breast with marionberry sauce. There are also daily specials, often seafood prepared in whatever style is currently the rage. The always-interesting dessert menu includes Oregon hazelnut cheesecake and Northwest berry pie. Lots of reasonably priced wines are available by the bottle or glass, with the emphasis on Oregon wines.

25551 SW F.S. Rd. 1419, Camp Sherman. ✆ **541/595-6420.** Reservations highly recommended. Main courses $7.50–$22. MC, V. Apr–May and Oct to mid-Nov Thurs–Sun 5–9pm; mid-June to Sept daily 5–9pm. Closed mid-Nov to Mar.

3 Bend & Sunriver: Skiing, Hiking, Fishing, Mountain Scenery & More

160 miles SE of Portland, 241 miles SW of Pendleton

Situated on the banks of the Deschutes River, Bend is the largest city east of the Oregon Cascades, and the surrounding area has more resorts than any other region in the state. To understand why a small town on the edge of a vast high desert could attract so many vacationers, just look to the sky. It's blue. And the sun is shining. For the webfoots who spend months under gray skies west of the Cascades, that's enough of an attraction.

However, Bend doesn't end with sunny skies. It is also home to Mount Bachelor, the biggest and best ski area in the Northwest. Several other mountains—the Three Sisters and Broken Top among them—provide a breathtaking backdrop for the city, and their pine-covered slopes, many lakes, and trout streams attract hikers, mountain bikers, and anglers. A lively downtown area filled with interesting shops, excellent restaurants, and attractive Drake Park (which is named for the city's founder, A. M. Drake, and not for the ducks that are the park's major attraction) complements the outdoor offerings of the area.

ESSENTIALS

GETTING THERE   Bend is at the junction of U.S. 97, which runs north and south, and U.S. 20, which runs east to west across the state. From the Portland area, the most direct route is by way of U.S. 26 to Madras and then south on U.S. 97.

Horizon Airlines and United Express serve **Redmond Municipal Airport,** 16 miles north of Bend. **CAC Transportation** (✆ **800/847-0157** or 541/389-7469) operates a shuttle between Portland and Bend, with stops at the Redmond Airport, Sisters, and Sunriver. There are also taxis operating from the Redmond Airport.

VISITOR INFORMATION   Contact the **Bend Visitor & Convention Bureau,** 63085 N. Hwy. 97, Bend, OR 97701 (✆ **800/949-6086** or 541/382-8048; www.visitbend.org).

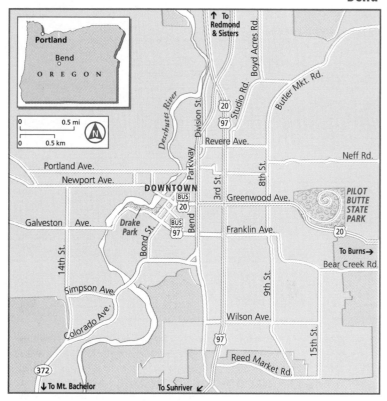

GETTING AROUND   Car rentals are available from **Avis, Budget,** and **Hertz.** If you need a taxi, call **Owl Taxi Service** (℮ **541/382-3311**).

FESTIVALS   The **Cascade Festival of Music** (℮ **888/545-7435** or 541/383-2202), held the last week in August in Drake Park, is Bend's biggest festival.

EXPLORING THE BEND AREA

If you'd like to have a guide show you around the area, contact **Wanderlust Tours** (℮ **800/962-2862** or 541/389-8359; www.empnet.com/wanderlust), which offers trips to many of the region's natural attractions. Rates range from $32 to $45.

The High Desert Museum ⭐⭐⭐ *Kids*   Bend lies on the westernmost edge of the Great Basin, a region that stretches from the Cascade Range to the Rocky Mountains and is often called the high desert. Through the use of historical exhibits, live animal displays, and reconstructions of pioneer buildings, this combination museum and zoo, one of the finest in the Northwest, brings the cultural and natural history of the region into focus. In the main building is a walk-through timeline of Western history, as well as a fascinating exhibit on the region's Plateau Indians. The natural history of the region comes alive in the Desertarium, where live animals of the region can be observed in a very natural setting. Outside, frolicking river otters and slow-moving porcupines are the star attractions, but the new birds of prey center is just as interesting. A pioneer homestead and a forestry exhibit with a steam-driven sawmill round out the

Moments **Seeing Stars**

Central Oregon's clear skies not only provide the region with abundant sunshine but also allow the stars to shine brightly at night. At two area observatories you can get a closer look at those stars. At the small **Pine Mountain Observatory** (© 541/382-8331; http://pmo-sun.uoregon. edu), 35 miles east of Bend off U.S. 20, you can gaze at the stars and planets through 15- and 24-inch telescopes. Admission is a $3 suggested donation, and the observatory is open Memorial Day weekend through September on Friday and Saturday nights from 8pm (also open Sun of 3-day weekends).

In the resort community of Sunriver, south of Bend, the **Sunriver Nature Center & Observatory** (© 541/598-4406; www.sunrivernaturecenter.org), which can be found by following the signs through Sunriver, has summer and fall star-gazing programs Tuesday through Sunday nights between 9 and 11pm. Admission is $6 for adults and $4 for children. There are also daytime solar viewing programs here.

outdoor exhibits. Informative talks are scheduled throughout the day. The museum's cafe is a good place for lunch.

59800 S. Hwy. 97. © 541/382-4754. www.highdesert.org. Admission $8.50 adults, $7.50 students and seniors, $4 children 5–12. Daily 9am–5pm (Wed until 8pm in summer). Closed Thanksgiving, Christmas, New Year's Day. Take U.S. 97 3½ miles south of Bend.

EXPLORING CENTRAL OREGON'S VOLCANIC LANDSCAPE

From snow-covered peaks to lava caves, past volcanic activity and geologic history are visible everywhere around Bend. For a sweeping panoramic view of the Cascade Range, head up to the top of **Pilot Butte** at the east end of Greenwood Avenue. From the top of this cinder cone, you can see all of the Cascades' major peaks—from Mount Hood to Mount Bachelor—every one of which is volcanic in origin.

To the south of Bend lies a region of relatively recent volcanic activity that has been preserved as the **Newberry National Volcanic Monument.** The best place to start an exploration of the national monument is at the **Lava Lands Visitor Center,** 58201 S. Hwy. 97 (© 541/593-2421), 11 miles south of Bend and open from about April through October. Here you can learn about the titanic forces that sculpted this region. An interpretive trail outside the center wanders through a lava flow at the base of 500-foot-tall **Lava Butte** 🐾, an ominous black cinder cone, and a road leads to the top. From the summit of the cinder cone you have an outstanding view of the Cascades. A $5 Northwest Forest Pass is necessary to visit the Lava Lands Visitor Center. If you don't already have one, you can purchase one here. As you leave the parking lot of the Lava Lands Visitor Center, the side road (F.S. Road 9702) to the right leads to the trailhead for the impressive **Benham Falls** 🐾🐾, which are a three-quarter-mile walk from the trail head. Be sure to bring mosquito repellant if you visit the falls during the summer.

A mile to the south, you'll find the **Lava River Cave,** which is actually a long tube formed by lava flows. The cave is more than a mile long and takes about an hour to explore. Admission is $3 for adults and $2.50 for children 13 to 17, plus $2 for lantern rentals. When lava flowed across this landscape, it often inundated pine forests, leaving in its wake only molds of the trees. At **Lava Cast Forest,** 9 miles down a very rough road off U.S. 97 south of Lava River Cave, a paved trail leads past such molds. Continuing farther south on U.S. 97 will bring you to the turnoff for the **Newberry Caldera** area, the centerpiece of the monument. Covering 500 square miles, the caldera contains Paulina and East Lakes, both of which are popular with boaters and anglers, and numerous volcanic features, including an astounding flow of obsidian. Today there are rental cabins and campgrounds within the national monument, and 150 miles of hiking trails.

HITTING THE SLOPES & OTHER WINTER SPORTS

If downhill skiing is your passion, you probably already know about the fabulous skiing conditions and myriad runs of **Mount Bachelor Ski & Summer Resort** ★★★ (© **800/829-2442;** www.mtbachelor.com), 22 miles west of Bend on the Cascades Lakes Highway. With a 3,100-foot vertical drop, 70 runs, 11 lifts, and skiing November through July, it's no wonder this place is so popular. All-day lift tickets are $42 to $45 for adults, $35 to $37 teenagers 13 to 18, $24 to $26 for children 7 to 12, and free for children 6 and under. The ski area's **Super Shuttle** ($3 each way) operates to and from Bend and leaves from the corner of Colorado Avenue and Simpson Street, where there's a large parking lot.

Cross-country skiers will also find plenty of trails to choose from. Just be sure to stop by a ski shop and buy a **Sno-Park** permit before heading up to the cross-country trail heads, the best of which are along the Cascades Lakes Highway leading to Mount Bachelor ski area. At the ski area itself, there are 35 miles (56km) of groomed trails. Passes to use these trails are $12 to $13 for adults and $5.25 to $5.50 for children. Ski shops abound in Bend, and nearly all of them rent both downhill and cross-country equipment. If you're heading to Mount Bachelor, you can rent equipment there, or try the **Powder House,** 311 SW Century Dr. (© **541/389-6234**), on the way out of Bend heading toward Mount Bachelor.

If you've had enough skiing, how about a **dogsled ride?** At **Oregon Trail of Dreams** (© **800/829-2442;** www.sleddogrides.com) you can take a 1-hour dogsled ride and then learn about the care of sled dogs. Rates are $60 for adults, $30 for children under 80 pounds. All-day and overnight trips are also available.

Easy 1½- to 2-hour **snowshoe walks** are led by ranger-naturalists on weekends and holidays starting from the **West Village Ski & Sport Building** at Mount Bachelor. For more information call © **541/383-4771.**

SUMMER ACTIVITIES

Both hiking and mountain biking are available at **Mount Bachelor** (© **541/382-2442**) in the summer, when a chair lift operates to the 9,065-foot top of the mountain; the fare is $10 for adults, $9 for seniors, $6 for children 7 to 12, and free for children 6 and under. From here you may either ride the chair or hike down. Mountain-bike rentals are available at the base of the mountain.

FISHING If fishing is your passion, you've come to the right place. The Deschutes River flows right through downtown Bend, and good trout waters can be found both upstream and downstream from town. The lakes of the Cascade Lakes Highway west of Bend are, however, the most popular fishing destinations in the area. Of these, Hosmer Lake (a catch-and-release fly-fishing-only lake), and Crane Prairie and Wickiup reservoirs, which are known for their trophy trout, are among the most fabled area fishing spots. If you're not familiar with these rivers and lakes, you may want to hire a guide to show you where to hook a big one. Try contacting **Garrison's Fishing Guide Service** (© 541/ 593-8394; www.garrisonguide.com) or **Fishing on the Fly** (© 800/952-0707 or 541/389-3252). Expect to pay between $150 and $165 for a day of fishing. Fly-fishing supplies are available at **The Fly Box,** 1293 NE Third St. (© 541/ 388-3330).

GOLF   For many of central Oregon's visitors, Bend's abundance of sunshine means only one thing—plenty of rounds of golf at area's 25 golf courses. Of the resort courses in the area, the three courses at **Sunriver** (© 800/962-1769 or 541/593-1000; www.sunriver-resort.com)—Crosswater (only open to resort guests), Meadows, and Woodlands—are the most highly regarded. Expect to pay anywhere from $60 to $155 depending on which course you play and when.

Right in Bend, you'll find more reasonable prices at the Riverhouse resort's **River's Edge Golf Course,** 400 NW Pro Shop Dr. (© 541/389-2828; www. riverhouse.com), where 18 holes will cost you about $25 to $48 in the summer. **Widgi Creek Golf Club,** 18707 Century Dr. (© 541/382-4449; www. widgi.com), is another of the area's highly regarded semiprivate clubs. Greens fees range from $50 to $70.

HIKING   Hiking is one of the most popular summer activities here, but keep in mind that high-country trails may be closed by snow until late June or early July.

Just to limber up or for a quick breath of fresh air, head up to the north end of Northwest First Street, where you'll find a 3-mile-long trail along the Deschutes River. However, our favorite trail is the **Deschutes River Trail** ✪✪, which parallels the Deschutes for nearly 9 miles. To reach the trail, drive the Cascades Lakes Highway 6 miles west from Bend, turn left at a sign for the Meadow Picnic Area, and continue 1.3 miles to the trail head at the picnic area.

The **Three Sisters Wilderness,** which begins just over 20 miles from Bend or Sisters, offers secluded hiking among rugged volcanic peaks. Permits are required for overnight trips in the wilderness area and are currently available at trail heads. Currently, you'll also need a Northwest Forest Pass (available at the Bend and Sisters ranger stations) to park at area trail heads. Contact the **Bend/Fort Rock Ranger Station,** 1230 NE Third St., Bend (© 541/ 383-4000), or the **Sisters Ranger Station** (© 541/549-7700) in Sisters for trail maps and other information.

HORSEBACK RIDING   Down in Sunriver, you can get saddled up and ride the meadows and ponderosa pine forests at **Saddleback Stables** (© 541/ 593-6995), which offers a variety of rides with an hour's ride costing about $25.

MOUNTAIN BIKING ✪✪   Mountain biking is one of the most popular activities in central Oregon, partly because when the snow melts, the cross-country ski trails become mountain-bike trails. Contact the **Bend/Fort Rock Ranger Station,** 1230 NE Third St. (© 541/383-4000), to find out about trails open to mountain bikes. The most scenic trail open to mountain bikes is the Deschutes River Trail mentioned above.

High Cascade Descent (© 800/296-0562 or 541/389-0562; www. paulinaplunge.com) offers guided mountain-bike rides in Newberry National Volcanic Monument. The Paulina Plunge is an easy downhill ride that includes stops at waterfalls and a natural water slide and costs $40 to $45.

WHITE-WATER RAFTING   The Deschutes River, which passes through Bend, is the most popular river in Oregon for white-water rafting, although the best sections of river are 100 miles north of here (see the "North Central Oregon & the Lower Deschutes River" section, above, for details). However, numerous local companies offer trips both on the lower section of the Deschutes and on the stretch of the upper Deschutes between Sunriver and Bend. This latter stretch of the river is known as the Big Eddy run, and though it is short and really has only one major rapid, it offers a quick introduction to rafting. **Sun Country Tours** (© 800/770-2161 or 541/382-6277; www.suncountrytours. com) does both the Big Eddy run ($40) and the lower Deschutes ($95). **Rapid River Rafters** (© 800/962-3327 or 541/382-1514; www.rapidriverrafters. com) also offers full-day trips on the lower Deschutes ($90).

A SCENIC DRIVE ALONG THE CASCADE LAKES HIGHWAY ✶✶

During the summer, the **Cascade Lakes Highway** is the most popular excursion out of Bend. This National Scenic Byway is an 87-mile loop that packs in some of the finest scenery in the Oregon Cascades. Along the way are a dozen lakes and frequent views of the jagged Three Sisters peaks and the rounded Mount Bachelor. The lakes provide ample opportunities for boating, fishing, swimming, and picnicking. At the **Bend Visitor & Convention Bureau,** 63085 N. Hwy. 97, Bend (© 800/949-6086 or 541/382-8048), you can pick up a guide to the Cascade Lakes National Scenic Byway. Keep in mind that from mid-November to late May, this road is closed west of Mount Bachelor because of snow.

The first area of interest along the highway is **Dutchman Flat,** just west of Mount Bachelor. A thick layer of pumice that can support only a few species of plants created this minidesert. A little farther and you come to **Todd Lake,** a pretty little lake that is off the highway a bit and can is reached by a short trail. Swimming, picnicking, and camping are all popular here.

Sparks Lake, the next lake along this route, is a shallow, marshy lake that has lava fields at its southern end. A trail with frequent glimpses of the lake meanders through these forested lava fields. The lake is a popular canoeing spot, though you'll need to bring your own boat. At the north end of the lake, you'll find the trail head for a popular mountain-biking trail that heads south to Lava Lake. Across the highway from the marshes at the north end of the lake is the **trail head for Green Lakes,** a series of small lakes that are in the Three Sisters Wilderness at the foot of Broken Top Mountain. This is one of the most popular backpacking routes in the region and offers spectacular scenery. The hike to Green Lakes can also be done as a day hike. West of the Green Lakes trail head is an area known as **Devils Garden,** where several springs surface on the edge of a lava flow. On a boulder here you can still see a few **Native American pictographs.**

With its wide-open waters and reliable winds, **Elk Lake** is popular for sailing and windsurfing. There are cabins, a lodge, and campsites around the lake. **Hosmer and Lava Lakes** are both known as good fishing lakes, while spring-fed **Little Lava Lake** is the source of the Deschutes River. **Cultus Lake,** with its sandy beaches, is a popular swimming lake. At the **Crane Prairie Reservoir** you can observe osprey between May and October. The **Twin Lakes** are examples of volcanic maars (craters) that have been filled by springs. These lakes have no inlets or outlets.

WHERE TO STAY
EXPENSIVE
Pine Ridge Inn ✶✶   This small luxury inn on the outskirts of town provides an alternative accommodation for anyone who wants first-class surroundings but doesn't need all the facilities (and crowds) of the area's family-oriented

resorts. This is an ideal choice for romantic vacations and honeymoons, but it is also a favorite of business travelers who need to be close to town. The inn is set on a bluff high above the Deschutes River, and though this particular stretch of river is not all that attractive, you still get a river view (and pay extra for it, too). Whether you get a regular room or a suite, you'll have tons of space that includes features such as sunken living rooms and fireplaces. Lots of antiques and artworks by regional artists add a distinctive style. Although the inn doesn't have a restaurant, there is a complimentary afternoon wine-and-cheese tasting.

1200 SW Century Dr., Bend, OR 97702. © 800/600-4095 or 541/389-6137. Fax 541/385-5669. www. pineridgeinn.com. 20 units. $130–$185 double; $190–$325 suite. Rates include full breakfast. AE, DC, DISC, MC, V. **Amenities:** Access to nearby health club; concierge; massage; babysitting; dry cleaning. *In room:* A/C, TV/VCR, dataport, fridge, coffeemaker, hair dryer, iron.

MODERATE

Best Western/Entrada Lodge ⭐ *(Value)*　A few miles west of Bend on the road to the Mount Bachelor ski area, this motel is in a tranquil setting shaded by tall pine trees. Stay here and you'll be just a little bit closer to Mount Bachelor in winter and the region's many lakes and hiking and mountain-biking trails in summer. Although you'll have to drive back into town or to a nearby resort for meals, it's worth that small inconvenience to get such a pleasant setting at economical rates. The Deschutes National Forest borders the property, and the popular Deschutes River Trail is only a mile away.

19221 Century Dr., Bend, OR 97702. © 800/WESTERN or 541/382-4080. Fax 541/382-4080. www. bestwestern.com/entradalodge. 79 units. $69–$99 double. Rates include continental breakfast. AE, DC, DISC, MC, V. Pets accepted ($10 per day). **Amenities:** Outdoor pool; access to nearby health club; Jacuzzi; coin-op laundry. *In room:* A/C, TV, dataport, coffeemaker, hair dryer, iron.

Inn of the Seventh Mountain ⭐⭐ *(Kids)*　As the closest accommodation to Mount Bachelor, this sprawling resort is especially popular with skiers. However, summer is still the high season here, and during the warm months, families descend on the property to take advantage of the seemingly endless array of recreational activities. The guest rooms are done in a country decor and come in a wide range of sizes. Many have balconies and/or kitchens. Our favorites are the rooms perched on the edge of the wooded Deschutes River canyon. Note that there's no golf course on the premises, but there are several close by. In addition to amenities listed below, the resort also has a roller-skating/ice-skating rink, hiking/jogging trails, a miniature golf course, playgrounds and playing fields, and volleyball and basketball courts, and offers rafting and canoe trips and horseback riding.

18575 SW Century Dr., Bend, OR 97702. © 800/452-6810 or 541/382-8711. Fax 541/382-3517. www. 7thmtn.com. 419 units. $63–$135 double; $163–$310 condo. AE, DC, DISC, MC, V. **Amenities:** 2 restaurants (American), lounge; indoor and outdoor pools; tennis courts; access to nearby health club; Jacuzzis; sauna; bike rentals; children's programs; concierge; massage; babysitting; coin-op laundry. *In room:* A/C, TV, coffeemaker, hair dryer, iron.

Mount Bachelor Village Resort ⭐　Set along the top of a narrow ridge overlooking the Deschutes River, this neatly manicured resort on the road to Mount Bachelor is a somewhat more relaxed version of the family ski-and-summer resorts so common in central Oregon. The resort is close enough to town to make going out for dinner convenient but deep enough in the pine forests to feel away from it all. This is a condominium resort; most of the accommodations have separate bedrooms, and many have fireplaces and kitchens. For the best views, request a River Ridge condo, right on the edge of the bluff. These rooms are newer and are quite simply some of the nicest places to stay in the area, with private outdoor hot tubs on the view decks and whirlpool tubs in the bathrooms.

19717 Mt. Bachelor Dr., Bend, OR 97702. ℂ **800/452-9846** or 541/389-5900. Fax 541/388-7401. www. mtbachelorvillage.com. 120 units. $85–$130 double; $130–$340 suite. 2-night minimum stay. AE, DISC, MC, V. **Amenities:** 2 restaurants (Northwest, American), lounge; outdoor pool; 6 tennis courts; health club; 2 Jacuzzis; bike rentals; coin-op laundry. *In room:* A/C, TV, dataport, coffeemaker.

INEXPENSIVE

The Riverhouse ⭐⭐ *Value*   At the north end of town on the banks of a narrow stretch of the Deschutes River, the Riverhouse is one of the best hotel deals we know of in the state; and with its golf course and other resort facilities, it's an economical choice for anyone who wants resort amenities without the high prices. Try to get a ground-floor room; these allow you to step off your patio and almost jump right into the river. However, the rooms on the upper floor have a better view of this rocky stretch of water. All in all, this is the best deal in Bend. Book early. The hotel's main dining room has a view of the river. There is also a poolside cafe and a lounge that features a variety of live entertainment.

3075 N. U.S. 97, Bend, OR 97701. ℂ **800/547-3928** or 541/389-3111. www.riverhouse.com. 220 units. $75–$126 double; $95–$245 suite. Rates include continental breakfast. AE, DC, DISC, MC, V. Pets accepted. **Amenities:** 3 restaurants (steak, American, Chinese), lounge; 2 pools (1 indoor, 1 outdoor); 18-hole golf course; tennis courts; exercise room; Jacuzzi; saunas; room service; coin-op laundry. *In room:* A/C, TV/VCR, dataport, coffeemaker, hair dryer, iron, free local calls.

IN SUNRIVER

The resort community of Sunriver is Oregon's most popular summer destination resort and has hundreds of condos, cabins, and vacation homes at a wide range of prices. **Sunset Realty** (ℂ **800/541-1756** or 541/593-5018; www.sr-sunset. com) is one of the area's bigger rental companies.

Sunriver Lodge & Resort ⭐⭐⭐ *Kids*   This sprawling resort is less a hotel than a town unto itself, and with a wealth of activities available for active vacationers, it is the first choice of many families vacationing in central Oregon. Most of the accommodations overlook both the golf course and the mountains. Our favorite rooms are the loft suites, which have stone fireplaces, high ceilings, and rustic log furniture; although the newest rooms are very luxurious. Lots of pine trees shade the grounds, and 30 miles of paved bicycle paths connect the resort with the surrounding community. However, no matter how impressive the other facilities are, it is the three golf courses that attract the most business. **Meadows at the Lodge** (ℂ **541/593-3740**), the resort's main dining room, features creative Northwest cuisine (entrees are in the $17–$26 range) and has superb views of the mountains. An adjacent lounge offers a cozy fireplace.

P.O. Box 3609, Sunriver, OR 97707. ℂ **800/547-3922** or 541/593-1000. www.sunriver-resort.com. 450 units. $129–$279 double. 2- to 5-bedroom condos and homes also available. Lower rates off-season. AE, DC, DISC, MC, V. **Amenities:** 6 restaurants (Northwest, American), 2 lounges; 2 outdoor pools; 3 18-hole golf courses; 28 tennis courts; Jacuzzi; sauna; watersports; bike rentals; children's programs; concierge; room service; massage; guest laundry. *In room:* A/C, TV, dataport, coffeemaker, hair dryer, iron.

CAMPGROUNDS

The closest campground to Bend is **Tumalo State Park,** 5 miles northwest of Bend off U.S. 20. The biggest campground in the area is **La Pine State Park,** which is accessible from U.S. 97 between Sunriver and La Pine.

Of the many campgrounds along the Cascade Lakes Highway, the walk-in **Todd Lake Campground,** 25 miles west of Bend, is our favorite because it is enough of a walk from the parking lot to keep things pretty quiet. **Devil's Lake Campground,** also a walk-in campground, is another favorite of ours. Farther south, there are lots of campgrounds on the many lakes along this road. Two of our favorites are the **Mallard Marsh** and **South** campgrounds, both of which are on beautiful Hosmer Lake. The campgrounds at **Lava Lake** and **Little Lava Lake** are also fairly quiet, and the view from Lava Lake is the finest at any campground on this stretch of road.

WHERE TO DINE
IN BEND

Coffee addicts will want to drop by **Desert High Espresso,** 2205 NE Division St. (© **541/330-5987**), located in an unusual stone building that is something of a folk-art construction. For good handcrafted ales and pub food, the **Bend Brewing Co.,** 1019 Brooks St. (© **541/383-1599**), is a great alternative to the Deschutes Brewery and Public House (see below). If it happens to be summer and you're craving a meal with an unforgettable view, head to **Mount Bachelor** (© **541/382-2442**) and take the chair lift up to the Pine Marten Lodge, where you can eat at Mile High BBQ or Scapolo's, an Italian restaurant. On summer weekends, there are sunset dinners at Scapolo's.

Broken Top Club Restaurant and Lounge ★★ NORTHWEST Golf courses are among the top attractions of the Bend area, so it should come as no surprise that the city abounds in good golf-course restaurants. This is among the finest of them, offering a posh, rustic ambience, good food, and a superb view of Broken Top Mountain. (There's a golf-course view as well.) For the best experience, make sure your reservation coincides with sunset. The menu here emphasizes regional flavors, and includes dishes such as seared salmon with morels and asparagus on popcorn risotto with vermouth cream; marinated buffalo flank steak; and grilled veal tenderloin with cherry-port glaze. There are also lighter entrees on the menu. The wine list is long and includes quite a few reasonably priced bottles.

62000 Broken Top Dr. © 541/383-8210. www.brokentop.com. Reservations recommended. Main courses lunch $7–$9.50, dinner $16.50–$24. AE, MC, V. Tues–Fri 11:30am–2pm and 6–10pm; Sat 6–10pm.

Deschutes Brewery and Public House ★ (Value REGIONAL AMERICAN For good handcrafted ales (we're partial to the Mirror Pond Pale Ale and the Obsidian Stout) and a range of pub food more creative and tastier than you'd expect, bustling Deschutes Brewery is the place. The buffalo wings are the best we've ever had. Not only do the cooks do an exemplary job on the normal pub menu, but they also prepare more complex daily specials, such as seared blue marlin crusted with pistachios, served with raspberry sauce and wild rice. Mustard, pastrami, root beer, and ginger ale are all made in-house. Bring the family—even the ones who don't drink beer.

1044 NW Bond St. © 541/382-9242. www.deschutesbrewery.com. Main courses $6–$17. MC, V. Mon–Thurs 11am–11pm; Fri–Sat 11am–midnight; Sun 11am–10pm.

Hans ★★ ITALIAN With its white linens and warmly painted walls, this pleasantly stylish little restaurant conjures up a European bistro. We like the Greek chicken pizza with kalamata olives and chevre cheese as well as the salmon piccata pasta. Meat eaters will appreciate blue cheese–stuffed pork tenderloin and the New York steak marinated in balsamic vinaigrette. For dessert, allow yourself to be tempted by the decadent selection of cakes and tortes. There's also a bakery selling good pastries and cookies.

915 NW Wall St. ℭ **541/389-9700**. Reservations recommended for dinner. Main courses $8–$16. MC, V. Tues 11am–4pm; Wed–Sat 11am–9pm.

Pine Tavern Restaurant ⭐ AMERICAN/NORTHWEST   Opened in 1936, the Pine Tavern Restaurant has been a local favorite for generations, and neither the decor nor the view has changed much over the years. Knotty pine and cozy booths give the restaurant an old-fashioned feel, while a 250-year-old ponderosa pine growing up through the center of one dining room provides a bit of grandeur. Most people ask for a table in the back room, which overlooks Mirror Pond. The menu is designed to appeal to a wide range of tastes and includes such comfort foods as meat loaf and filet mignon, but also more creative dishes such as cherry pork Madeira. The restaurant is popular with families.

967 NW Brooks St. ℭ **541/382-5581**. www.pinetavern.com. Reservations recommended. Main courses $13–$22. AE, DISC, MC, V. Mon–Sat 11:30am–9:30pm; Sun 5:30–9:30pm.

IN SUNRIVER

For the best views and food in Sunriver, make a reservation at the **Meadows at the Lodge** restaurant at Sunriver Lodge (see p. 315 for details).

Trout House Restaurant ⭐ 𝘝𝘢𝘭𝘶𝘦 NORTHWEST/AMERICAN   One of the best things about this little restaurant is that it's right on the Deschutes River and is a great place for a waterfront breakfast, lunch, or dinner. It's a popular spot with visitors, so be sure to make reservations during the summer. Seafood predominates, with trout available at all three meals. Razor clams (in season), pan-fried oysters, and blackened salmon with a tequila, lime, and sour-cream sauce can assuage a hunger earned by canoeing on the river or playing an exhausting round of golf.

Next to the Marina in Sunriver. ℭ **541/593-8880**. Reservations recommended. Main courses lunch $5.50–$11, dinner $11–$23. DISC, MC, V. Daily 8am–9pm.

11

Eastern Oregon

So different is eastern Oregon from the wet west side of the Cascades that it is often difficult to remember that it is still the same state. Indeed, the dry eastern ranch lands, deserts, canyons, and mountain ranges of this region have more in common with the landscapes of neighboring Idaho and Nevada. Yet, Oregon it is, and though it is remote, the fascinating geography makes it an interesting region to explore when you've had enough of the verdant landscapes west of the Cascades.

With huge cattle ranches sprawling across the countryside (cattle greatly outnumber people in these parts) and the **Pendleton Round-Up** attracting cowboys and cowgirls from around the country, this region is Oregon's Wild West. This part of the state is also steeped in the history of the Oregon Trail, and although it was to the Willamette Valley that most wagon trains were heading, it is here that signs of their passing 150 years ago still abound. All across this region, **wagon ruts** left by those stalwart overlanders can still be seen, and the history of the Oregon Trail immigrants is chronicled at several regional museums. Although the first pioneers never thought to stop and put down roots in this region, when gold was discovered in the Blue Mountains in the 1860s,

fortune seekers flocked to the area. Boom towns flourished and as quickly disappeared, leaving the land to the cattle ranchers and wheat farmers who still call this area home.

Today, however, the region also attracts a handful of outdoors enthusiasts. They come to hike and horseback ride in the Eagle Cap Wilderness of the Wallowa Mountains, to birdwatch in the Malheur National Wildlife Refuge, to ski in the Blue Mountains, to explore the deepest canyon in the United States, and to raft and fish the Snake, Owyhee, and Grande Ronde rivers. On the north side of the Wallowa Mountains, the small town of Joseph has become a center for Western art, with several bronze foundries casting sculptures sold all over the country.

Because this region is so far from the state's population centers, it is little visited by west-siders, who rarely venture farther east than the resorts of central Oregon. Eastern Oregon is also so vast, and the road distances so great, that it does not lend itself to quick weekend trips. At the very least, it takes a 3-day weekend to get out to Joseph and the Wallowa Mountains or the Malheur National Wildlife Refuge. Should you travel to this part of the state, leave yourself plenty of time for getting from point A to point B.

1 Pendleton

125 miles E of The Dalles, 52 miles NW of La Grande, 40 miles S of Walla Walla, Washington

If not for its famous woolen mills, few people outside the region would be familiar with the Pendleton name. But because the blankets and clothing long manufactured by the **Pendleton Woolen Mills** (here and at other mills around

Eastern Oregon

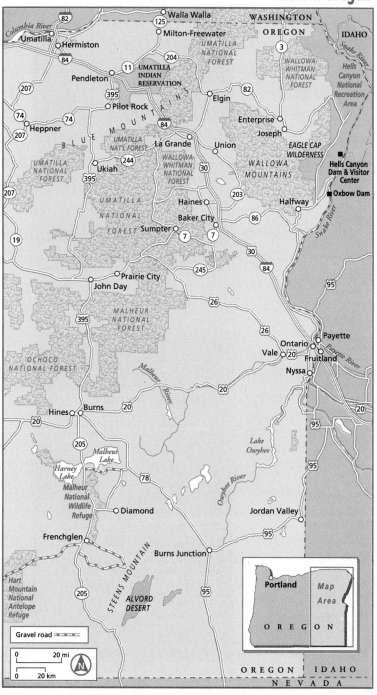

the region) have gained such a reputation, the name has become as much a part of the West as Winchester, Colt, and Wells Fargo. Today, Pendleton blankets and clothing are as popular as ever, and the town's mill is one of its biggest attractions.

But what brings even more visitors to town than the mill is a single annual event—the **Pendleton Round-Up.** Located at the western foot of the Blue Mountains in northeastern Oregon, Pendleton prides itself on being a real Western town; and as the site of one of the largest and oldest rodeos in the West, it has a legitimate claim. Each year in mid-September, the Round-Up fills the town with cowboys and cowgirls, both real and urban. For the rest of the year, Pendleton sinks back into its quiet small-town character and begins preparing for the next one.

Once the homeland of the Cayuse, Umatilla, Walla Walla, and Nez Perce Indians, the Pendleton area began attracting settlers in the 1840s, as pioneers who had traveled the Oregon Trail started farming along the Umatilla River. In the 1850s, gold strikes created boomtowns in the nearby mountains, and Pendleton gained greater regional significance. Sheep ranching and wheat farming later became the mainstays of the local economy, and by the turn of the century, Pendleton was a rowdy town boasting dozens of saloons and legal bordellos. Today Pendleton is a much quieter place, one that few people notice as they rush by on the interstate. But those who do pull off find a quiet town whose downtown historic district is filled with attractive brick buildings and some stately old Victorian homes.

ESSENTIALS

GETTING THERE I-84 runs east to west through Pendleton. From the south take U.S. 395; from the north, Ore. 11, which leads to Walla Walla, Washington. **Horizon Airlines** (✆ **800/547-9308**) has service to the **Eastern Oregon Regional Airport,** which is located about 4 miles west of downtown Pendleton.

VISITOR INFORMATION Contact the **Pendleton Chamber of Commerce,** 501 S. Main St., Pendleton, OR 97801 (✆ **800/547-8911** or 541/276-7411; www.pendleton-oregon.org).

GETTING AROUND **Hertz** rental cars are available at the Eastern Oregon Regional Airport.

THE PENDLETON ROUND-UP

The Pendleton Round-Up and Happy Canyon Pageant, held the second week of September each year, is one of the biggest rodeos in the country and has been held since 1910. In addition to daily rodeo events, there's a nightly pageant that presents a history of Native American and pioneer relations in the area. After the pageant, there's live country-and-western music in the **Happy Canyon Dance Hall.** A country-music concert and a parade round out the events. **The Hall of Fame,** 1205 SW Court Ave. (under the south grandstand), holds a collection of cowboy and Indian memorabilia. The city is packed to overflowing during Round-Up week, so if you plan to attend, reserve early. Tickets sell for $10 to $16, and some types of tickets sell out a year in advance. For more information, contact the **Round-Up Association,** P.O. Box 609, Pendleton, OR 97801 (✆ **800/45-RODEO** or 541/276-2553; www.pendletonroundup.com).

EXPLORING PENDLETON

If you happen to be in town any other week of the year, there are still a few things worth doing. This is the hometown of **Pendleton Woolen Mills,** 1307 SE Court Place. (© **800/568-3156** or 541/276-6911), the famed manufacturer of Native American–inspired blankets and classic wool sportswear. At the mill here in Pendleton, the raw wool is turned into yarn and then woven into fabric before being shipped off to other factories to be made into clothing. Tours are offered Monday through Friday at 9 and 11am, and 1:30 and 3pm. Also at the mill is a salesroom that's open Monday through Saturday from 8am to 5pm.

At one time there were supposedly 10 miles of underground passages and rooms under the streets of Pendleton, where gamblers, drinkers, and Chinese laborers rubbed shoulders. Over the years, these spaces were home to speakeasies and saloons, opium dens, and the living quarters of Chinese laborers who were forbidden to be aboveground after dark. On walking tours operated by **Pendleton Underground Tours,** 37 SW Emigrant Ave. (© **800/226-6398** or 541/276-0730; www.pendletonundergroundtours.com), you can learn all about old Pendleton's shady underside. After exploring the underground, you'll visit a former bordello, whose rooms have been decorated much the way they once might have looked. Tours are offered Monday through Saturday from 9am to 4:30pm; tickets are $10 for adults and $5 for children 12 and under. Reservations are strongly recommended.

At the **Umatilla County Historical Museum,** 108 SW Frazer Ave. (© **541/ 276-0012**), you can learn about the region's more respectable history. The museum is housed in the city's 1909 vintage railway depot and contains exhibits on the Oregon Trail and Pendleton Woolen Mills, as well as a display of beautiful Native American beadwork. The museum is open Tuesday through Saturday from 10am to 4pm; admission is $2 for adults and $1 for seniors and children 12 to 18.

At the **Pendleton Center for the Arts,** 214 N. Main St. (© **541/278-9201;** www.pendletonarts.org), in a renovated Carnegie Library, there are regularly scheduled art exhibits.

If you're looking for glimpses of the **Oregon Trail,** head 20 miles west of Pendleton to the town of Echo, where you can see wagon ruts left by early pioneers. There's an interpretive exhibit in town at Fort Henrietta Park on Main Street; then 2.7 miles west of town on Ore. 320 you can see wagon ruts in Echo Meadows. A mile of ruts can also be seen about 5.5 miles west of town north of Ore. 320. On Ore. 207 north of Ore. 320, there is another Oregon Trail marker.

EAST OF TOWN: NATIVE AMERICAN HISTORY AND A CASINO

East of Pendleton, at exit 216 off I-84, you'll find a complex of attractions that has been developed over the past few years by the Confederated Tribes of the Umatilla Indian Reservation. Included here is the **Wildhorse Casino Resort,** 72777 Ore. 31 (© **800/654-WILD;** www.wildhorseresort.com), which offers 24-hour gambling, including slot machines, poker, blackjack, and keno. There is also a golf course, a motel, an RV park, and the following museum.

Tamástslikt Cultural Institute ☾☾   This modern museum is one of Oregon's four Oregon Trail interpretive centers and differs from others by focusing on the impact the trail had on the Native Americans of this region. The exhibits incorporate artifacts, life-size dioramas, and audio and video presentations to document the effect pioneer settlement had on the indigenous Cayuse, Walla Walla, and

Umatilla Indians who were living in the region when the first settlers arrived. A tour of the museum begins with an exhibit on how the three tribes lived in the days before the arrival of the outsiders. Another exhibit documents the arrival of horses in the region and the way these animals changed the lives of the region's tribes. Other exhibits focus on the coming of missionaries, the advent of Indian schools, treaty negotiations, and the future of the three tribes.

72789 Ore. 331. © **541/966-9748.** Admission $6 adults; $4 seniors, students, and children; free for children under 5. Daily 9am–5pm. Closed Thanksgiving, Christmas, and New Year's Day.

WHERE TO STAY

The Parker House Bed and Breakfast 🏵🏵

Looking very out of place in this Northwest cow town, this Italianate villa seems lifted from the southern California coast. Built in 1917, the home is only 2 blocks from downtown Pendleton and is surrounded by colorful perennial gardens. As befits the villa-like surroundings, a formal atmosphere reigns. The Gwendolyn Room, with its fireplace and semiprivate balcony, is the best room in the house; and in the Mandarin Room, you'll find the original Chinese wallpaper and Asian styling. In all the guest rooms you'll find plenty of antiques. Guest rooms share a bathroom, but what a bathroom it is, with the original multiple-head shower and lots of big old porcelain fixtures. Breakfasts are elaborate and filling, with fresh-baked breads and unusual entrees. If you aren't staying here, you can still tour the home for $5.

311 N. Main St., Pendleton, OR 97801. © **800/700-8581** or 541/276-8581. www.parkerhousebnb.com. 5 units (all with shared bathroom). $75–$135 double. Rates include full breakfast. AE, MC, V. *In room:* A/C, no phone.

Wildhorse Casino Resort 🏵

Whether or not you're interested in gambling, the Wildhorse Casino Resort is a good place to stay in the area. Not only are the rooms modern and comfortable, but there are also plenty of recreational amenities, including the casino with its casual restaurant. The Tamástslikt Cultural Institute (see p. 321) is also nearby. The hotel is 4 miles east of Pendleton and has nice views of the nearby foothills of the Blue Mountains.

72777 Ore. 331, Pendleton, OR 97801. © **800/654-WILD.** Fax 541/276-0297. www.wildhorseresort.com. 100 units. $65–$95 double. Rates include continental breakfast. AE, DC, DISC, MC, V. Pets accepted ($10 fee). **Amenities:** Restaurant (American), lounge; indoor pool; 18-hole golf course; Jacuzzi; sauna; coin-op laundry. *In room:* A/C, TV, coffeemaker, hair dryer.

Working Girls Hotel 🏵 *Finds*

Pendleton likes to play up its Wild West heritage, and there was a time when brothels were legal here. The historic building that now holds the Working Girls Hotel was just such an establishment, and although female companionship doesn't come with the rooms anymore, you will get comfortable accommodations. Although the rooms all have private bathrooms, only one of these is actually in the room; all others have their bathrooms directly across the hall. The hotel is operated in conjunction with Pendleton Underground Tours, and hotel guests get a discount on the tour.

17 SW Emigrant Ave., Pendleton, OR 97801. © **800/226-6398** or 541/276-0730. 5 units. $50–$70 double. MC, V. *In room:* A/C, no phone.

WHERE TO DINE

If you're looking for someplace to get a sandwich or bowl of soup, drop by **The Great Pacific Wine and Coffee Company,** 403 S. Main St. (© **541/276-1350**). Cookies, muffins, truffles, and other sweets round out the menu.

Raphael's Restaurant ★★ NORTHWEST   This restaurant has long been
Pendleton's top fine-dining establishment, and despite being out of commission
for a year or more due to a fire, it is still the best place in town for a first-class
dinner. Housed in a 1904 Queen Anne–style home, the restaurant is known
for its India-style salmon (made with huckleberry purée), hickory-roasted prime
rib, and fettuccine. During October and November you'll also find some interesting wild game dishes, including venison marsala and smoked quail, on the
menu.

233 SE Fourth St. ℂ 541/276-8500. Reservations recommended. Main dishes $12–$27. AE, DISC, MC, V.
June–Aug Tues–Sat 5–9pm; Sept–May Tues–Thurs 5–8pm, Fri–Sat 5–9pm.

2 La Grande, Baker City & the Blue Mountains

La Grande: 260 miles E of Portland, 52 miles SE of Pendleton; Baker City: 41 miles SE of La Grande, 75 miles
NW of Ontario

Though pioneers traveling the Oregon Trail in the 1840s found good resting
places in the Powder River and Grande Ronde Valleys, where Baker City and La
Grande now stand, few stayed to put down roots in this remote region. It would
not be until the 1860s that pioneers actually looked on these valleys as a place
to live and make a living. However, even those first pioneers who just passed
through left signs of their passage that persist to this day. **Wagon ruts** of the
Oregon Trail can still be seen in this region, and outside of Baker City stands the
most interesting and evocative of the state's museums dedicated to the Oregon
Trail experience.

By 1861, however, the Blue Mountains, which had been a major impediment
to wagon trains, were crawling with people—gold prospectors. A gold strike in
these mountains started a small gold rush that year, and soon prospectors were
flocking to the area. The gold didn't last long, and when mining was no longer
financially feasible, the miners left the region. In their wake, they left several
ghost towns, but the prosperity of those boom times also left the region's larger
towns with an enduring legacy of stately homes and opulent commercial buildings, many built of stone that was quarried in the region. Today, the historic
commercial buildings of Baker City, the ornate Victorian homes of Union, and
the Elgin Opera House are reminders of past prosperity. Although the gold has
played out, signs of those raucous days, from gold nuggets to ghost towns, are
now among the region's chief attractions.

One of the most arduous and dangerous sections of the Oregon Trail—the
crossing of the Blue Mountains—lies just west of present-day La Grande. These
mountains are no longer the formidable obstacles they once were, but they are
still among the least visited in Oregon. The Blues, as they are known locally,
offer a wide variety of recreational activities, including skiing, soaking in hot
springs, hiking, mountain biking, fishing, and camping. With their numerous
hotels and restaurants, both La Grande and Baker City make good bases for
exploring this relatively undiscovered region.

ESSENTIALS

GETTING THERE   Both La Grande and Baker City are on I-84. La Grande
is at the junction of Ore. 82, which heads northeast to Joseph and Wallowa
Lake. Baker City is at the junction of Ore. 7, which runs southwest to John Day,
and Ore. 86, which runs east to the Hells Canyon National Recreation Area.

VISITOR INFORMATION   Contact the **Baker County Visitors and Convention Bureau,** 490 Campbell St., Baker City, OR 97814 (ℂ **800/523-1235** or

541/523-3356; www.neoregon.com/visitBaker.html), or the **La Grande/Union County Visitor & Conventions Bureau,** 1912 Fourth St., Suite 200, La Grande, OR 97850 (© **800/848-9969** or 541/963-8588; www.visitlagrande.com).

OREGON TRAIL SITES

Oregon Trail history is on view west of La Grande, in downtown Baker City, and just north of Baker City. At the **Oregon Trail Interpretive Park at Blue Mountain Crossing** (© **800/848-9969**), at exit 248 off I-84, you'll find a half-mile trail that leads past wagon ruts in the forest. Informational panels explain the difficulties pioneers encountered crossing these rugged mountains. On most weekends between Memorial Day and Labor Day, there are living history programs as well.

National Historic Oregon Trail Interpretive Center 🐦🐦   Atop sagebrush-covered Flagstaff Hill, just north of Baker City, stands a monument to what became the largest overland migration in North American history. Between 1842 and 1860, an estimated 300,000 people loaded all their worldly belongings onto wagons and set out to cross the continent to the promised land of western Oregon. Their route took them through some of the most rugged landscapes on this continent, and many perished along the way. This museum commemorates the journeys of these hardy souls, who endured drought, dysentery, and starvation in the hopes of a better life at the end of the Oregon Trail. Through the use of diary quotes, a life-size wagon-train scene, artifacts, and interactive exhibits that challenge your own ability to make the trip, the center takes visitors through every aspect of life on the trail. Outside, a trail through the sagebrush leads to ruts left by the wagons on their journey west.

Ore. 86, Baker City. © **800/523-1235** or 541/523-1843. www.or.blm.gov/nhotic. $5 adults, $3.50 seniors and youths, free for children under 6, or $10 per vehicle, whichever is less. Apr–Oct daily 9am–6pm; Nov–Mar daily 9am–4pm. Closed Christmas, New Year's Day.

Oregon Trail Regional Museum 🐦   In a large building that once housed Baker City's public swimming pool, this museum is filled with pioneer memorabilia, including a large collection of stagecoaches and an extensive mineral collection.

2480 Grove St., Baker City. © **541/523-9308.** Admission $3.50 adults, 75¢ children 6–12. Late Mar–late Oct daily 9am–5pm.

EXPLORING BAKER CITY

At the Baker City Visitors & Convention Bureau, you can pick up a brochure that outlines a **walking tour** of the town's most important historic buildings, including the restored **Geiser Grand Hotel,** which, when it first opened, was one of the finest hotels in the west. (See "Where to Stay" below for details.)

If you'd like to take a look inside one of Baker City's restored old homes, drop by the **Adler House Museum,** 2305 Main St. (© **541/523-9308**), a stately Victorian structure. Everything on the second floor, from the wallpaper to the furniture, is original, dating to the 1890s. The first floor has been refurbished and decorated to look the way it might have more than 100 years ago. The museum is open from May 1 to October 1, Thursday through Sunday from 9am to noon. Admission is $4 per person (free for children 6 and under).

Baker City's fortunes were made by gold mines in the Blue Mountains, and if you'd like to see some samples from those golden years, stop in at the **U.S. Bank** on Main Street in Baker City. The gold collection here includes a nugget that weighs in at 80.4 ounces.

> **Tips** **An Almost Grand Old Opera House**
>
> In the town of **Elgin,** 18 miles north of La Grande on Ore. 82, you can take in a film, play, or concert at the restored **Elgin Opera House,** 104 N. Eighth St. (© **541/437-3456**), which was built in 1912. The opera house is in the same building that once housed Elgin City Hall.

OUTDOOR ACTIVITIES
SPRING THROUGH FALL

If you're interested in **bird-watching,** head out to the **Ladd Marsh Wildlife Area** (© **541/963-4954** or 541/963-2138), 6 miles south of La Grande off I-84 at the Foothill Road exit. In summer, this wetland is home to sandhill cranes, geese, ducks, avocets, black-necked stilts, and numerous raptors. Also keep an eye out for elk. The best way to visit this area is by walking the 1¼-mile nature trail east of I-84 near exit 268. From February 15 to July 31, you can also arrange to use photo/observation blinds.

The **hot springs** of this region have been attracting people since long before the first white settlers arrived, and you can still soak your sore muscles in thermal waters at **Lehman Hot Springs,** in Ukiah, 38 miles west of La Grande on Ore. 244 (© **541/427-3015;** www.lehmanhotsprings.com), which is in a remote forest setting. Here you'll find a large hot swimming pool perfect for an afternoon of lounging around. There are also two smaller and hotter soaking pools (the first of these is too hot to actually get into), as well as an unheated swimming pool (which sees very little use). Also on the premises are campsites and some rustic accommodations, and nearby there are hiking, mountain-biking, cross-country-ski, and snowmobiling trails. The springs are open Wednesday through Sunday in summer from about 10am to 8 or 9pm. (Call for hours the rest of the year.) Admission is $6.

In summer, there are plenty of nearby trails to hike or mountain bike on. Contact the **Wallowa-Whitman National Forest,** La Grande Ranger District, 3502 Ore. 30, La Grande, OR 97850 (© **541/963-7186**), or **Baker Ranger District,** 3165 Tenth St., Baker City, OR 97814 (© **541/523-4476**), for details.

WINTER SPORTS AND ACTIVITIES

With the highest base elevation and the most powder-like snow in the state, **Anthony Lakes Mountain Resort** (© **541/856-3277;** www.anthonylakes. com), 40 minutes west of Baker City, is a good little ski area—small, but with a nice variety of terrain. Daily lift tickets are $28. You'll also find good groomed cross-country-ski trails here, and the area is very popular with snowmobilers.

Winter is also the best time of year to see some of the region's Rocky Mountain elk. Each year December through February, the Oregon Department of Fish & Wildlife feeds a large herd of elk at the **Elkhorn Viewing Area** in North Powder, about halfway between La Grande and Baker City. You can usually see between 150 and 200 elk. During the Christmas holidays, **T and T Tours** (© **541/856-3356;** www.tnthorsemanship.com) takes visitors out to the feeding area by horse-drawn wagon. Tours last about a half hour and cost $4 per person. To reach Elkhorn, take exit 285 off I-84 and follow the Wildlife Viewing signs. For more information, contact the **Oregon Department of Fish & Wildlife** (© **541/898-2826**).

THE ELKHORN MOUNTAIN SCENIC LOOP

Rising up on the outskirts of Baker City is the Elkhorn Range of the Blue Mountains. A paved loop road winds up and around the south side of these mountains, features scenic vistas, access to the outdoors throughout the year, and even a couple of sparsely inhabited ghost towns. Start this loop by heading south out of Baker City on Ore. 245 and then take Ore. 7 west to **Sumpter,** 30 miles from Baker City.

As you approach Sumpter, you'll notice that the valley floor is covered with large piles of rocks. These are the tailings (the refuse left after the mining operations have worked over the land), from the Sumpter Dredge, preserved as the **Sumpter Dredge State Heritage Area** (© 541/894-2486), which has been undergoing restoration. Between 1935 and 1954, the ominous-looking dredge laid waste to the valley floor as it sat in its own little pond sifting through old streambed gravel for gold. Although you can stop and view the dredge any time of year, between May and October it is possible to board the strange machine (open daily 9am–4pm), which now has a few interpretive exhibits on board. Admission is by donation.

In its wake, the dredge left 6 miles of tailings that formed hummocks of rock and gouged-out areas that have now become small ponds. Although such a mining-scarred landscape isn't usually scenic, the Sumpter Valley is surprisingly alive with birds attracted to the ponds.

A favorite way of visiting the Sumpter Dredge is aboard the **Sumpter Valley Railroad** (© 541/894-2268 or 541/523-3453), which operates a classic steam train on a 5-mile run from west of Phillips Reservoir to the Dredge. This railway first began operation in 1890 and was known as the stump dodger. Excursions are operated on Saturdays, Sundays, and holidays from Memorial Day weekend to late September; round-trip fares are $9 for adults and $6.50 for children 6 to 16.

Gold kept Sumpter alive for many decades, and a bit of gold-mining history is still on display in this rustic mountain town, which, though it has a few too many people to be called a ghost town, is hardly the town it once was. In the boom days of the late 19th and early 20th century, Sumpter boasted several brick buildings, hotels, saloons, and a main street crowded with large buildings. However, when a fire destroyed the town in 1917, it was never rebuilt. Today, only one brick building and a few original wooden structures remain. At **The Gold Post** (© 541/894-2362), you can see old photos of Sumpter as well as various artifacts from the town's gold-mining heyday.

Continuing west on a winding county road for another 14 miles will bring you to **Granite** ⭐, another ghost town with a few flesh-and-blood residents. The weather-beaten old buildings on a grassy hillside are the epitome of a Western ghost town, and most buildings are marked. You'll see the old school, general store, saloon, bordello, and other important town buildings.

Beyond Granite, the road winds down to the North Fork of the John Day River and then heads back across the mountains by way of the Anthony Lakes area. Although Anthony Lakes is best known for its small ski area, in summer there are hiking trails and fishing in the area's small lakes. The vistas in this area are the best on this entire loop drive, with rugged, rocky peaks rising above the forest. Also in this same area, you'll catch glimpses of the irrigated pastures of the Powder River Valley far below.

Coming down onto the valley floor, you reach the tiny farming community of Haines, which is the site of the **Eastern Oregon Museum,** Third Street

---

Fun Fact   **Big Fungus Among Us**

The largest living organism on earth is not a whale or a redwood tree, it is a lowly fungus by the name of *Armillaria ostoyae*. These fungi grow underground, and one particular *Armillaria* here in the forests of eastern Oregon is more than 2,400 years old and covers 2,200 acres.

(© **541/856-3564**), a small museum cluttered with all manner of artifacts of regional historic significance. It's open April through October daily from 9am to 5pm; admission is by donation. Here in Haines you'll also find the Haines Steakhouse (see below), a favorite of area residents.

WHERE TO STAY
IN LA GRANDE
Stang Manor Bed & Breakfast ♠   This Georgian colonial mansion, built in the 1920s, looks a bit like the White House and is the best place to stay in La Grande. It's filled with beautiful woodwork and comfortable guest rooms, a couple of which have the original bathroom fixtures, including a footed bathtub. The best deal here is the three-room suite, which has a fireplace and a sun porch that has been converted into a sleeping room. Breakfasts are elegant affairs served in the formal dining room.

1612 Walnut St., La Grande, OR 97850. © **888/286-9463** or 541/963-2400. www.stangmanor.com. 4 units. $85 double; $98 suite. Rates include full breakfast. MC, V. Children 10 and older only. *In room:* TV, dataport, hair dryer, iron.

IN UNION
The Union Hotel ♠ *Value*   Although Union today is a sleepy town, it was once the county seat and a booming little place. This grand little hotel first opened its doors in 1921, but in more recent years it was a decrepit apartment house. An ongoing renovation has turned it into one of eastern Oregon's more interesting historic hotels. Surrounded by lawns and shade trees, the three-story brick hotel now goes a long way toward conjuring up Union's lively past. The lobby, with its white tile floor, could be straight out of a movie set, while the upstairs guest rooms are decorated in various themes. To make the most of a visit here, try to stay in the room with the whirlpool tub. Although Union is 14 miles from La Grande, the location is still fairly convenient for exploring this region.

326 N. Main St. (P.O. Box 569), Union, OR 97883. © **541/562-6135**. www.theunionhotel.com. 13 units. $45–$89 double. DISC, MC, V. **Amenities:** Restaurant (American). *In room:* No phone.

IN BAKER CITY
Geiser Grand Hotel ♠♠ *Finds*   Built in 1889 at the height of the region's gold rush, the Geiser Grand is by far the grandest hotel in eastern Oregon. With its corner turret and clock tower, the hotel is a classic 19th-century Western luxury hotel. In the center of the hotel is the Geiser Grill dining room, above which is suspended the largest stained-glass ceiling in the Northwest. Throughout the hotel, including in all the guest rooms, ornate crystal chandeliers add a crowning touch. Guest rooms also feature 10-foot windows, most of which look out to the Blue Mountains. The two cupola suites are the most luxurious and evocative of the past. These two suites also have whirlpool tubs. Meals are served both in the formal Geiser Grill and in the much more relaxed 1889 Saloon. Way back

in 1968, almost 30 years before the hotel was fully restored, the cast of the movie *Paint Your Wagon* stayed here. Today, no trip to eastern Oregon is complete without a stay at this grande dame of the old West.

1996 Main St., Baker City, OR 97814. ℭ **888/GEISERG** or 541/523-1889. Fax 541/523-1800. www.geisergrand. com. 30 units. $89–$109 double; $129–$259 suite. AE, DC, DISC, MC, V. Pets accepted ($10 per night). **Amenities:** 2 restaurants (American), lounge; indoor pool; access to nearby health club; room service; dry cleaning. *In room:* A/C, TV, dataport, hair dryer, iron.

CAMPGROUNDS

You'll find several national-forest campgrounds along the Elkhorn National Scenic Byway, including **Union Creek Campground,** which is on the shore of Phillips Reservoir southeast of Baker City. Others can be found near Anthony Lakes.

WHERE TO DINE
IN LA GRANDE

For good pastries and fresh-baked bread, stop in at **Kneads,** 109 Depot St. (ℭ **541/963-5413**).

Foley Station ✩✩ *Finds* AMERICAN/NORTHWEST   Although the focus at this surprisingly upscale little restaurant is on breakfasts and lunches, it is also open for dinner 3 nights a week. The menu here is far more contemporary and creative than at any other restaurant in town. A recent menu included Jamaican-jerked crab-stuffed prawns, tournedos of beef with Madeira sauce, and coriander-cured beef tenderloin tamales. At lunch, you can design your own burger (or how about an emu burger?), or opt for dishes such as Chinese barbecue chicken, oyster stew, or Cajun linguine. Definitely *the* place to eat in La Grande.

1011 Adams Ave. ℭ **541/963-7473.** www.restaurant.com/foleystation. Reservations recommended for dinner. Main dishes $6–$15 lunch, $6–$21 dinner. MC, V. Wed and Sun 7am–3pm; Thurs–Sat 7am–9pm.

Mamacita's MEXICAN   With its colorful downtown setting, this small, low-key Mexican place is more college hangout than local Mexican joint. The menu is short but varied, and it includes numerous healthy and vegetarian offerings. Fire-eaters should try the hot salsa verde. Be sure to save room for dessert; the Kahlua pie and chocolate raspberry cake have loyal followers around town.

110 Depot St. ℭ **541/963-6223.** Main courses $3.50–$11.75. No credit cards. Tues–Fri 11am–2:30pm and 5–9pm; Sat–Sun 5–9pm.

Ten Depot Street ✩ *Value* STEAK/SEAFOOD   Housed in a historic brick commercial building, this restaurant has a classic 19th-century feel, complete with a saloon on one side. Although the steaks and prime rib are what most people order, the salads are large and flavorful, and there are even some vegetarian dishes. The $6.95 blue-plate specials on weeknights are a particularly good value, and there are also other inexpensive nightly specials. Also keep an eye out for dishes prepared with emu.

10 Depot St. ℭ **541/963-8766.** Reservations recommended. Main courses $7–$30. AE, MC, V. Mon–Sat 5–10pm.

IN THE BAKER CITY AREA

For pub food and microbrews, there's **Barley Brown's Brew Pub,** 2190 Main St. (ℭ **541/523-4266**).

Baker City Cafe/Pizza à Fetta ✩ PIZZA   When you've just got to have a pizza—and you want more than pepperoni or sausage—this is the place. You can dress your pie with blue cheese, feta, Montrachet, sun-dried tomatoes,

Chinese History in Eastern Oregon

In the town of John Day, the fascinating little **Kam Wah Chung & Co. Museum** ✦✦ (✆ **541/575-0028**), on Northwest Canton Street adjacent to City Park, is well worth a visit. It preserves the home and shop of a Chinese doctor who, for much of the first half of the 20th century, administered to his fellow countrymen who were laboring here. The building looks much as it might have at the time of the doctor's death and contains an office, a pharmacy, a general store, and living quarters. It's open May through October only, Monday through Saturday from 9am to noon and 1 to 5pm, and on Sunday from 1 to 5pm. Admission is $3 for adults, $2.50 for seniors, $1.50 for children 6 to 16, and free for children under 6.

You'll find more Chinese history in Baker City, where an old Chinese cemetery can be seen on Allen Street, just east of exit 304 off of I-84. The Pendleton Underground tour in Pendleton (see p. 321) also focuses on the region's Chinese history.

kalamata olives, or pancetta. Pasta and sandwiches are also available. You can find this place just off Main Street.

1915 Washington Ave. ✆ **541/523-6099.** Pizzas $13–$22. DISC, MC, V. Mon–Fri 9am–8pm.

The Grill ✦ AMERICAN   Located in the central court of the historic Geiser Grand Hotel, this restaurant, with its stained-glass ceiling, conjures a gold rush–era elegance. Mesquite-smoked prime rib and the wide variety of steaks are your best bets here in ranch country. However, there are also plenty of pasta dishes, as well as a few seafood offerings. Before or after dinner, you'll need to spend a little time in the 1889 Saloon just to complete your historical evening. At breakfast there are lots of different omelets and at lunch, you can order a buffalo burger.

Geiser Grand Hotel, 1996 Main St. ✆ **541/523-1889.** Reservations recommended. Main courses $6–$28. AE, DC, DISC, MC, V. Daily 7am–9pm.

Haines Steakhouse ✦ STEAK   Thick, juicy steaks are the specialty of the house here, but it's the decor as much as the food that attracts people. Log walls and booths, a chuck-wagon salad bar, mounted buffalo and elk heads, a totem pole, and an old buggy keep diners amused as they eat. This is a longtime favorite in the area.

910 Front St., Haines. ✆ **541/856-3639.** Reservations recommended. Main courses $6–$20. AE, DC, DISC, MC, V. Mon and Wed–Fri 5–10pm; Sat 4–10pm; Sun 1–9pm.

3 Joseph, Enterprise & the Wallowa Mountains

Joseph: 355 miles E of Portland, 80 miles E of La Grande, 125 miles N of Baker City

The Wallowa Mountains, which stand just south of the town of Joseph, are a glacier-carved range of rugged beauty that has been called both the Alps of Oregon and the Little Switzerland of America. Though the range is small enough in area to drive around in a day, it is big on scenery and contains the largest designated wilderness area in the state: the **Eagle Cap Wilderness.**

In the northeast corner of the mountains lies Wallowa Lake, which was formed when glacial moraines blocked a valley that had been carved by the glaciers. With blue waters reflecting the rocky peaks, the lake has long attracted visitors. In the fall, the lake also attracts bald eagles that come to feed on spawning kokanee salmon, which turn a bright red in the spawning season.

In recent years, the town of Joseph, just north of Wallowa Lake, has become a center for the casting of Western-themed **bronze sculptures,** and there are now several art galleries and foundries in the area. With its natural beauty, recreational opportunities, and artistic bent, this corner of the state today has more to offer than any other area in eastern Oregon.

ESSENTIALS

GETTING THERE   Ore. 82 connects Joseph to La Grande in the west, and Ore. 3 heads north from nearby Enterprise to Lewiston, Idaho, by way of Wash. 129.

VISITOR INFORMATION   For more information, contact the **Wallowa County Chamber of Commerce,** 107 SW First St. (P.O. Box 427), Enterprise, OR 97828 (© **800/585-4121** or 541/426-4622; www.wallowacounty chamber.com).

FESTIVALS   The rowdy **Chief Joseph Days Rodeo,** over the last full weekend in July, and the **Alpenfest,** on the third weekend after Labor Day, are the biggest annual events in the area.

BRONZE FOUNDRIES AND ART GALLERIES

Though the lake and mountains are the main attractions of this area, the presence of several bronze foundries in Joseph and Enterprise has turned the area into something of a Western art community. Along Main Street in Joseph, you'll find several art galleries that specialize in bronze statues and Western art. You'll find more than half a dozen life-size bronze wildlife and Western art sculptures in sidewalk gardens along Main Street.

A good place to start is at the impressive **Manuel Museum,** 400 N. Main St. (© **541/432-7235**), at the west end of town. In addition to housing bronzes by artist David Manuel, the combination gallery/museum includes an outstanding collection of Native American artifacts and a large collection of old wagons. Guided foundry tours are also available. Admission is $6 for adults, $5 for seniors, and $3 for children 10 and under.

Between May and late fall, foundry tours ($5 per person) are offered by **Valley Bronze of Oregon,** 18 W. Main St. (© **541/432-7445**), which is the second-largest bronze foundry in the country and has its foundry at 307 W. Adler St. (© **541/432-7551;** www.valleybronze.com). **Parks Bronze,** 331 Golf Course Rd., Enterprise (© **541/426-4595**), offers foundry tours Monday through Friday ($5 per person). A 24-hour notice is requested. Other bronze galleries in town include the **Bronze Gallery of Joseph,** 603 N. Main St. (© **541/ 432-3106**).

LOCAL HISTORY

At the **Wallowa County Museum,** 110 S. Main St. (© **541/432-4834**), you can see pioneer artifacts, displays on the Nez Perce Indians, and other items donated to the museum by local families. This old-fashioned community museum is housed in a former bank building and is open daily from 10am to 5pm from the last weekend in May to the third weekend in September.

OUTDOOR ACTIVITIES

Down at the south end of Wallowa Lake, you'll find **Wallowa Lake State Park** (© 541/432-4185), where there is a swimming beach, picnic area, and campground. Adjacent to the park is the **Wallowa Lake Marina** (© 541/432-9115), where you can rent canoes, rowboats, paddleboats, and motorboats (open May–Sept). This end of the lake has an old-fashioned mountain resort feel, with pony and kiddy rides, go-cart tracks, miniature golf courses, and the like. However, it is also the trail head for several trails into the Eagle Cap Wilderness. The park is also home to numerous large deer, which have become accustomed to begging for handouts from campers. Although the deer are entertaining, they are still wild animals and can be dangerous.

For a different perspective on the lake, ride the **Wallowa Lake Tramway** (© 877/994-TRAM or 541/432-5331; www.wallowalaketramway.com) to the top of 8,200-foot Mount Howard. This is the steepest tramway in America and provides great views both from the gondolas and from the summit of Mount Howard. The views take in Wallowa Lake and the surrounding jagged peaks. The tramway operates June through September (call for winter hours), daily from 10am to 4pm (in July and Aug until 5pm); the fare is $17 for adults and $10 for children 3 to 12. Food is available at the **Summit Grill & Alpine Patio.**

Because most hikes on the north side of the Cascades start out in valleys and can take up to a dozen miles or so to reach the alpine meadows of the higher elevations, there aren't a lot of great day hikes here. The **backpacking,** however, is excellent. If you're looking for **day hikes,** try taking the tramway to the top of Mount Howard, where there are about 2 miles of easy walking trails with great views. If you'd like to head into the **Eagle Cap Wilderness** to the popular **Lake Basin** or anywhere else in the Wallowas, you'll find the trail head less than a mile past the south end of the lake. For more information on hiking in the Wallowas, contact the **Wallowa Valley Ranger District,** 88401 Ore. 82, Enterprise, OR 97828 (© 541/426-4978; www.fs.fed.us/r6/w-w).

Horse packing into the Wallowas is a popular activity, and rides of a day or longer can be arranged through **Eagle Cap Wilderness Pack Station,** 59761 Wallowa Lake Hwy., Joseph, OR 97846 (© 800/681-6222 or 541/432-4145; www.neoregon.net/wildernesspackstation), which offers trips into the Eagle Cap Wilderness during the summer and into Hells Canyon during the spring. Expect to pay around $175 per person per day for a guided trip. **Millar Pack Station,** 69498 Sherrod Rd., Wallowa, OR 97885 (© 541/886-4035; www.eoni.com/~millar), offers similar pack trips at similar prices.

If you'd like to try **llama trekking** and let these South American beasts of burden carry your pack, contact **Hurricane Creek Llama Treks,** 63366 Pine Tree Rd., Enterprise, OR 97828 (© 800/528-9609 or 541/432-4455; www.hcltrek.com). Most trips last 5 to 6 days and cost between $700 and $875.

This region also offers some of the best **trout fishing** in Oregon, and if you're looking for a guide to take you to the best holes, contact **Eagle Cap Fishing Guides,** P.O. Box 865, Joseph, OR 97846 (© 800/940-3688 or 541/432-9055; www.wallowa.com/eaglecap), or the **Joseph Fly Shoppe,** 203 N. Main St., Joseph, OR 97846 (© 541/432-4343; www.josephflyshop.com). This latter company also offers scenic white-water trips in the area. Expect to pay anywhere from $140 to $200 for a day of fishing.

For **mountain biking** in the area, contact **Crosstown Traffic Bicycles,** 102 W. McCully St., Joseph (© 541/432-2453), charging about $75 for a daylong ride.

"I Will Fight No More Forever"

The Wallowa Mountains and Hells Canyon areas were once the home-land of the **Nez Perce people.** Sometime in the early 1700s, the Nez Perce acquired horses that were descended from Spanish stock and that had been traded northward from the American Southwest. The Nez Perce land, which encompassed rolling hills covered with lush grasses, proved to be ideal for raising horses, and the tribe began selectively breeding horses, emphasizing traits of speed and endurance. Their horses eventually became far superior to those used by other tribes and came to be known as **Appaloosas.** Eventually, the hills in southeast Washington where these horses were first bred came to be known as the **Palouse Hills.**

The Nez Perce had befriended explorers Lewis and Clark in 1805 and remained friendly to white settlers when other Indian tribes were waging wars. This neutrality was "rewarded," however, with treaties that twice cut the size of their reservation in half. When one band refused to sign a new treaty and relinquish its land, the stage was set for one of the great tragedies of Northwest history.

En route to a reservation in Idaho, several Nez Perce men ignored orders from the tribal elders and attacked and killed four white settlers to exact revenge for the earlier murder by whites of the father of one of these Nez Perce men. This attack brought on the ire of settlers, and the cavalry was called in to hunt down the Nez Perce. Tribal elders decided to flee to Canada, and led by Chief Joseph (also known as Young Joseph), 700 Nez Perce, including 400 women and children, began a 2,000-mile march across Idaho and Montana on a retreat that lasted 4 months.

Along the way, several skirmishes were fought, and the cavalry finally succeeded in defeating the Nez Perce only 40 miles from Canada. At their surrender, Chief Joseph spoke the words for which he has long been remembered: "Hear me my Chiefs, I am tired; my heart is sick and sad. From where the sun now stands, I will fight no more, forever."

The town of Joseph is named after Chief Joseph, and on the out-skirts of town, you'll find the grave of his father, Old Joseph. Young Joseph is buried on the Colville Indian Reservation in central Washing-ton. Not far from Joseph, near Lewiston, Idaho, you can learn more about the Nez Perce at **Nez Perce National Historical Park.**

In winter, the Wallowas are popular with cross-country and backcountry skiers. Check at the ranger station in Enterprise for directions to trails. You'll also find a small downhill ski area and groomed cross-country trails at **Ferguson Ridge,** which is 9 miles southeast of Joseph on Tucker Down Road.

Wing Ridge Ski Tours, P.O. Box 714, Joseph, OR 97846 (© **800/646-9050** or 541/426-4322; www.wingski.com), leads experienced skiers on hut-to-hut ski tours for $395 to $495 for a 6-day/5-night trip. The huts can also be rented for $30 per person, per night.

WHERE TO STAY

Chandlers' Bed, Bread, and Trail Inn ⭐   Located right in Joseph, Chandler's is a contemporary home with cedar-shingle walls and a boardwalk that leads through a rock garden to the front door. Inside you'll find a high-ceilinged living room with open-beam construction, folk art, quilts, and a rather eclectic decor. Three of the rooms have mountain views, and there are also three sitting areas for guest use. In warm weather, breakfast is served in a gazebo in the garden.

700 S. Main St. (P.O. Box 639), Joseph, OR 97846. ✆ **800/452-3781** or 541/432-9765. www.eoni. com/~chanbbti. 5 units (3 with private bathroom). $60 double with shared bathroom, $80 double with private bathroom. Lower rates fall through spring. Rates include full breakfast. MC, V. *In room:* No phone.

Eagle Cap Chalets ⭐ *Kids*   Set under tall pines just a short walk from hiking trails and the lake, Eagle Cap Chalets has a wide variety of rooms, as well as an indoor pool and Jacuzzi, and a miniature golf course. Consequently, this place is very popular with families and groups. The rooms here vary from motel style to rustic-though-renovated cabins, and most have phones. Siding on all the buildings makes them appear to be built of logs. Cabins and condos have kitchens. In the early fall, there always seem to be deer hanging out on the lawns here.

59879 Wallowa Lake Hwy., Joseph, OR 97846. ✆ **541/432-4704.** Fax 541/432-3010. www.eaglecapchalets. com. 37 units. $45–$105 double; $75–$125 2- and 3-bedroom. AE, DISC, MC, V. Pets accepted ($6 per night) except during summer. **Amenities:** Indoor pool; Jacuzzi. *In room:* TV.

Ramshead Cottage at Wallowa Lake ⭐ *Finds*   Located in the shady pine forest at the south end of Wallowa Lake, this modern cedar-shingled cottage is operated by Lynn and Doris Steiger, who for years ran a B&B in the wine country outside Portland. The interior decor is rustic yet very comfortable, and the cottage shows the thoughtful touches you expect from a B&B—antique furnishings, an excellent library, quality linens. Light fir floors and pine paneling are found throughout (as opposed to the dark paneling typical of older mountain cabins), and an abundance of windows keeps the rooms bright. The upstairs suite has a living room with a small kitchen, while the downstairs room has a Murphy bed and a private deck. From the cottage, it's just a short walk to either the lake or the start of the trails that lead into the Eagle Cap Wilderness.

84591 Pine Ridge Rd. (P.O. Box 874), Joseph, OR 97846. ✆ **541/432-2002.** Fax 541/432-2002. www.oregontrail. net/~ldsteiger/. 1 2-bedroom cottage. $115 double, $150 4 people. No credit cards. *In room:* TV, kitchen, fridge, coffeemaker.

Wallowa Lake Lodge ⭐   This rustic two-story lodge at the south end of Wallowa Lake was built in 1923 and is surrounded by big pines and a wide expanse of lawn that attracts deer in late summer and early fall. Big comfortable chairs fill the lobby, where folks often sit by the stone fireplace in the evening. The guest rooms are divided between those with carpeting and modern bathrooms and those with hardwood floors, original bathroom fixtures, and antique furnishings (our favorites). All but two of the latter have two bedrooms each, and two rooms have balconies overlooking the lake. The cabins are rustic but comfortable and have full kitchens. The dining room serves a limited menu of well-prepared dishes in the $12.50 to $23.50 range. Hazelnut pancakes with marionberry butter are a breakfast specialty.

60060 Wallowa Lake Hwy., Joseph, OR 97846. ✆ **541/432-9821.** Fax 541/432-4885. www.wallowalake. com. 30 units (including 8 cabins). May to mid-Oct $87–$142 double; $90–$187 cabin. Mid-Oct to Apr $65–$110 double; $75–$122 cabin. 2-night minimum in cabins during summer. DISC, MC, V. **Amenities:** Restaurant (American), lounge. *In room:* No phone.

A GUEST RANCH IN THE WILDERNESS

Minam Lodge ⟨★⟩   Located on the Minam River and surrounded by the Eagle
Cap Wilderness, Minam Lodge is 8½ miles from the nearest road and is accessible only on foot, on horseback, or by small plane, which makes this rustic and
very remote getaway one of the most unusual lodges in the state. Horseback
riding, hiking, fishing, and hunting are guests' primary pursuits. The rustic log
cabins are set atop a low hill and have wood stoves for warmth; good-size windows let in the sunshine and the views. Horseback rides to and from the lodge
are $70 each way, and horse rentals are available ($25 for 2 hr.; $75 for a full
day). Guided overnight pack trips and packages are also available.

High Country Outfitters, P.O. Box 3384, La Grande, OR 97850. ⓒ **888/454-4415** or 541/562-8008. www.
minamlodgeoutfitters.com. 9 units. $120 per person per night (children under 12 half price). Rates include all
meals. DISC, MC, V. Pets accepted ($25 deposit). **Amenities:** Dining room; sauna. *In room:* No phone.

A CAMPGROUND

At the south end of Wallowa Lake, you'll find a campground under the trees at
Wallowa Lake State Park (ⓒ 541/432-4185). In addition to campsites, the
park has two yurts for rent. For campsite reservations, call **Reservations Northwest** (ⓒ **800/452-5687**).

WHERE TO DINE

In addition to the restaurants listed below, you'll find good meat-and-potatoes
meals at the **Wallowa Lake Lodge** (see "Where to Stay" above for details). If you're
just looking for some baked goodies or a light lunch, check out the **Wildflour
Bakery,** 600 N. Main St., Joseph (ⓒ **541/432-7225**), which is set behind an
attractive perennial garden and has a deck out front and wooden booths inside.

Old Town Cafe ⟨★⟩ INTERNATIONAL   This tiny cafe sits right in the middle of Joseph and serves up satisfying portions of excellent food. The menu is
limited, which seems to give the owners plenty of opportunity to perfect their
offerings. For breakfast, don't miss the breakfast burrito, especially if you are
heading out for a day of hiking. These burritos are huge! At lunch, the bottomless bowl of soup is a big hit. Chocoholics should be sure to save room for the
Old Town pie, which has a pecan meringue crust, a chocolate brownie torte
filling, and is covered with cream, chocolate, and nuts—sort of a sundae pie.
Once a month, the restaurant serves an international dinner; call for details.

8 S. Main St., Joseph. ⓒ **541/432-9898.** Main dishes $4.50–$6.50. No credit cards. Daily 7am–2pm.

Terminal Gravity Brewery & Pub ⟨★⟩ INTERNATIONAL   Although it's
small, this brewery on the east side of Enterprise has been getting raves across
the state for its excellent beers. However, you can also get good food in the tiny
brewpub dining room. There are only a couple of tables and a few barstools
(with a few more tables upstairs), but the food is some of the best in this corner
of the state. Each night there is a single dinner special; otherwise, there are only
a handful of basic dishes on the menu.

803 School St., Enterprise. ⓒ **541/426-0158.** Main courses $8–$11. No credit cards. Wed–Sat 3:30–11pm.

Vali's Alpine Restaurant and Delicatessen ⟨★⟩ EASTERN EUROPEAN
Just past the Wallowa Lake Lodge you'll find this little restaurant, which specializes in the hearty fare of Eastern Europe. Only one dish is served each
evening, so if you like to have options, you won't want to eat here. Stuffed
cabbage or Hungarian goulash (Wed), chicken paprikash (Thurs), beef kabobs
(Fri), steak (Sat), and schnitzel (Sun) should help you stay warm on cold

mountain evenings. Luckily, the apple strudel is served every night. Hungarian gypsy music plays on the stereo, and at breakfast there are fresh homemade doughnuts.

59811 Wallowa Lake Hwy. © 541/432-5691. Reservations required. Main courses $8.50–$12. No credit cards. Memorial Day–Labor Day Wed–Sun 9–11am and 5–8pm; Labor Day–Oct and Feb–Memorial Day Sat–Sun 9–11am and 5–8pm. Closed Nov–Jan.

4 Hells Canyon & the Southern Wallowas

South access: 70 miles NE of Baker City; North access: 20 to 30 miles E of Joseph

Sure, the Grand Canyon is an impressive sight, but few people realize that it isn't the deepest canyon in the United States. That distinction goes to **Hells Canyon,** which forms part of the border between Oregon and Idaho. Carved by the Snake River and bounded on the east by the Seven Devils Mountains and on the west by the Wallowa Mountains, Hells Canyon is as much as 8,000 feet deep. Although it's not quite as spectacular a sight as the Grand Canyon, neither is it as crowded. Because there is so little road access to Hells Canyon, it is one of the least visited national recreation areas in the West.

The Hells Canyon area boasts a range of outdoor activities, but because of blazing hot temperatures in summer, when this rugged gorge lives up to its name, spring and fall are the best times to visit. Despite the heat, though, boating, swimming, and fishing are all popular in the summer.

ESSENTIALS

GETTING THERE   The south access to Hells Canyon National Recreation Area is reached off of Ore. 86 between 9 and 48 miles northeast of the town of Halfway, depending on which route you follow. Northern sections of the national recreation area, including the Hat Point Overlook, are reached from Joseph on Ore. 82, which begins in La Grande.

VISITOR INFORMATION   For more information, contact the **Hells Canyon National Recreation Area,** 88401 Ore. 82, Enterprise, OR 97828 (© **541/426-4978;** www.fs.fed.us/r6/w-w/).

EXPLORING THE REGION

Much of **Hells Canyon** ✿ is wilderness and is accessible only by boat, on horseback, or on foot. Few roads lead into the canyon, and most of these are recommended only for four-wheel-drive vehicles. If you are driving a car without high clearance, you'll have to limit your exploration of this region to the road to Hells Canyon Dam and the scenic byway that skirts the eastern flanks of the Wallowa Mountains. If you don't mind driving miles on gravel, you can also head out to the **Hat Point Overlook** east of Joseph.

Southern river-level access begins in the community of Oxbow, but the portion of the Snake River that has been designated a National Wild and Scenic River starts 27 miles farther north, below Hells Canyon Dam. Below the dam, the Snake River is turbulent with white water and provides thrills for jet boaters and rafters. To get this bottom-up view of the canyon, take Ore. 86 to Oxbow, cross the river into Idaho, and continue 22 miles downriver to **Hells Canyon Creek Visitor Center** (© **541/785-3395**), which is located 1 mile past the Hells Canyon Dam. This center has informative displays on the natural history of Hells Canyon and is open daily from May to mid-September.

> ⏜ **Fun Fact**   **Half.com**
>
> In January 2000, the town of Halfway changed its name to Half.com for 1 year. The change was part of a publicity stunt by an Internet company.

To get a top-down overview of the canyon, drive to the **Hells Canyon Overlook,** 30 miles northeast of Halfway on Forest Road 39. From here you can gaze down into the canyon, but you won't be able to see the river.

You'll find many miles of **hiking trails** within the national recreation area, but summer heat, rattlesnakes, and poison oak keep all but the most dedicated hikers at bay. For information on trails here, contact the information center for the recreation area (see above).

The best way to see Hells Canyon is by **white-water raft** or in a **jet boat.** Both sorts of trips can be arranged through **Hells Canyon Adventures,** 4200 Hells Canyon Dam Rd. (P.O. Box 159), Oxbow, OR 97840 (℃ **800/422-3568** or 541/785-3352; www.hellscanyonadventures.com). Jet-boat tours range from $30 for a 2-hour tour to $105 for a 6-hour tour. A day of white-water rafting runs $150.

Horseback trips into the southern Wallowas are offered by **Cornucopia Wilderness Pack Station,** 44256 Eagle Creek Rd., Richland, OR 97870 (℃ **541/893-6400,** or in summer 541/742-5400), with rates around $200 per person per day for fully catered and guided trips. Horses can also be rented here on an hourly or daily basis.

You can also opt to explore the southern Wallowas with a llama carrying your gear. Contact **Wallowa Llamas,** 36678 Allstead Lane, Halfway, OR 97834 (℃ **541/742-2961;** wallama@pinetel.com), for more information. Trips range in price from $395 to $1155.

While in this area, you can learn about bison at **Clear Creek Buffalo Ranch** (℃ **800/742-4992** or 541/742-2238). This ranch outside the town of Halfway offers tours during which you get to see their bison up close, learn more about bison and their cultural significance to the Plains Native peoples, and then have a buffalo dinner. Tour and dinner runs $25. Tours alone are $6 to $12.

WHERE TO STAY

Clear Creek Farm Bed and Breakfast Inn 𝕩𝕩   Located in the hills on the outskirts of Halfway, this comfortable and contemporary farmhouse B&B is part of a buffalo ranch, which makes it one of the most unusual B&B locations in the state. A veranda wraps around three sides of the inn, and there are beautiful flower gardens. Most rooms have mountain or meadow views, and the Garden Room has a claw-foot tub. In addition to the rooms in the main house, there are three rustic cabins that have private bathrooms (which are, however, in a separate bathhouse building). With no insulation and in some cases only screens on the windows, these cabins are just a step above camping and are open only during the warmer months. Meals, which, of course, can include buffalo, can be arranged for an additional charge, and ranch privileges such as the use of bicycles, catch-and-release fishing, birding walks, and various tours, are also available at an additional charge.

48212 Clear Creek Rd., Halfway, OR 97834. ℃ **800/742-4992** or 541/742-2238. Fax 541/742-5175. www. neoregon.com/ccgg. 9 units. $99–$144 double in lodge; $65 double in cabin. Rates include full breakfast. MC, V. **Amenities:** Restaurant (International); Jacuzzi; bike rentals; laundry service. *In room:* No phone.

Pine Valley Lodge ★★ *Finds* This amazing little lodge and restaurant, composed of four old buildings in downtown Halfway, is a Wild West fantasy created by two very creative artists. With handmade furniture and Western collectibles scattered about, the main lodge is a fascinating place just to wander around. Two small guest rooms that combine rustic furnishings with the artistic endeavors of the owners are on the second floor of the main house. Next door is the Blue Dog, with more rustic Western furnishings and four rooms (which can also be combined to form two suites). Outdoorsy types will like the Love Shack bunkhouse, which truly is a shack, albeit a charming one. All in all, this place is unique. The lodge's Halfway Supper Club is across the street in an old church that was built in 1891 (see below for details). On nights when the Halfway Supper Club is not open, lodge guests can, with enough prior notice, arrange dinner.

N. Main St. (P.O. Box 712), Halfway, OR 97834. ✆ 541/742-2027. www.neoregon.net/pinevalleylodge. 6 units (2 with private bathroom), 1 cabin (sleeps 6–10 people). $75–$85 double with shared bathroom, $105–$110 double with private bathroom. Rates include deluxe continental breakfast. No credit cards. Pets accepted ($10). **Amenities:** Restaurant (Continental/Fusion), lounge. *In room:* No phone.

WHERE TO DINE

The Halfway Supper Club ★★ *Finds* MARKET COUNTRY CUISINE Located in an old church that was built in 1891, this restaurant is part of the wonderfully eclectic and rustic Pine Valley Lodge (see above), and it serves the most creative cuisine in this corner of the state. The menu changes weekly based on the chef's whim and what's available in the market. The meals, which might include lamb chops with rosemary and lemon or coq au vin (here known as hunter's chicken), are served amid handmade furniture and pillows and wall coverings painted by the owners. This place is well worth a drive if you're staying anywhere in the vicinity.

N. Main St., Halfway. ✆ 541/742-2027. Reservations recommended. Main courses $18–$28. No credit cards. Fri–Sun 6–8pm.

5 Ontario & the Owyhee River Region

Ontario: 72 miles SE of Baker City, 63 miles NW of Boise, 130 miles NE of Burns

Ontario, the easternmost town in Oregon, lies in the Four Rivers region, at the confluence of the Owyhee, Snake, Malheur, and Payette rivers. Irrigated by waters from the massive Owyhee Reservoir, these wide, flat valleys are prime agricultural lands that produce onions, sugar beets, and, as in Idaho, plenty of potatoes. This region is also where much of the world's zinnia seeds are grown. During the summer, zinnia fields color the landscape in bold swaths. If you're curious to see the flower fields, head south out of Ontario on Ore. 201.

The biggest attraction in the region is the **Four Rivers Cultural Center,** which focuses on the various cultures that have made the region what it is today. However, there is also some Oregon Trail history to be seen nearby, and south of Ontario lies one of Oregon's most rugged and remote regions. This corner of the state is a vast untracked high desert, and along the banks of the Owyhee River and Succor Creek, you can see canyons and cliffs that seem far more suited to a Southwestern landscape.

ESSENTIALS
GETTING THERE Ontario is on the Idaho line at the junction of I-84 and U.S. 20/26, all of which link the town to western Oregon.

VISITOR INFORMATION   For more information on the Ontario area, contact the **Ontario Visitors & Convention Bureau,** 676 SW Fifth Ave., Ontario, OR 97914 (© **888/889-8012** or 541/889-8012; www.ontariochamber.com).

Note: Ontario is on Rocky Mountain time, not Pacific time.

A CULTURAL MUSEUM

Four Rivers Cultural Center & Museum ⚐   Although this remote corner of Oregon may seem an unlikely place for a multicultural museum, that is exactly what you'll find at the Four Rivers Cultural Center & Museum. The museum focuses on four very distinct cultures that have called, and still call, this region home. The Paiutes were the original inhabitants of the area, and an exploration of their hunting-and-gathering culture is the first exhibit. In the mid–19th century, the first pioneers began arriving in the area and quickly displaced the Paiutes. By the late 19th century, many Mexican cowboys, known as vaqueros or buckaroos, had come north to the region to work the large cattle ranches. At the same time, Basque shepherds settled in the area and tended large herds of sheep in the more remote corners of the region. The fourth culture is that of the Japanese, who were forced to live in internment camps in the area during World War II. After the war, many of them stayed in the area.

676 SW Fifth Ave. © 888/211-1222 or 541/889-8191. www.4rcc.com. Admission $4 adults, $3 seniors and children 3–12. Mon–Sat 10am–5pm. Closed all national holidays.

MORE TO SEE & DO: EXPLORING THE REGION

For more Oregon Trail history, head 18 miles west of Ontario to the small farming community of **Vale.** Here you'll find the **Rinehart Stone House Museum,** 283 S. Main St. (© **541/473-2070**), which was built in 1872 and was a stage stop and an important wayside along the route of the Oregon Trail. Today, it houses a small historical museum that is open from April 15 to November 1 Tuesday through Saturday from noon to 4pm; admission is free.

Large historic murals cover numerous walls around Vale, and a good way to see them is by horse-drawn buggy operated by **Wilcox Horse & Buggy** (© **541/473-9251**). The 1-hour tours cost $10 per person. Six miles south of Vale, at Keeney Pass, you can see **wagon ruts** left by pioneers traveling the Oregon Trail.

South of Ontario 15 miles, you'll find **Nyssa,** the "Thunderegg Capital of Oregon." **Rockhounding** is the area's most popular pastime, and thundereggs (also known as geodes) are the prime find. These round rocks look quite plain until they are cut open to reveal the agate or crystals within. You'll find plenty of cut-and-polished thundereggs in the rock shops around town. If you'd like to do a bit of rockhounding yourself, you can head south to **Succor Creek State Park** ⚐, a rugged canyon where you'll find a campground, picnic tables, and thundereggs waiting to be unearthed.

If you have a four-wheel-drive or high-clearance vehicle, you can continue another 30 minutes to **Leslie Gulch** ⚐⚐, an even more spectacular canyon with walls of naturally sculpted sandstone. If you're lucky, you might even see bighorn sheep here. Few places in Oregon have more of the feel of the desert than these two canyons, and just as in the desert Southwest, here, too, rivers have been dammed to provide irrigation waters and aquatic playgrounds. **Lake Owyhee,** 45 miles south of Ontario off Ore. 201, is the longest lake in Oregon and offers boating, fishing, and camping. The Owyhee River above the lake is a designated State Scenic Waterway and is popular for **white-water rafting** ⚐⚐. If you're interested in running this remote stretch of river, contact **Destination**

Wilderness (© **800/423-8868** or 541/549-1336; www.wildernesstrips.com), or **Oregon Whitewater Adventures** (© **800/820-RAFT** or 541/746-5422; www.oregonwhitewater.com), both of which occasionally run this river. Expect to pay $750 to $900 for a 5-day trip. Below the Owyhee Dam, 12 miles southwest of the town of Adrian, you'll find a signposted **"Watchable Wildlife" area** that offers excellent bird-watching. You may also spot beavers, porcupines, mule deer, and coyotes.

WHERE TO STAY

For the most part, Ontario is a way station for people traveling along I-84, and as such, the city's accommodations are strictly off-ramp budget motels. Motel options include a **Best Western Inn,** 251 Goodfellow St., Ontario, OR 97914 (© **800/828-0364** or 541/889-2600), charging $78 to $160 double; a **Super 8 Motel,** 266 Goodfellow St., Ontario, OR 97914 (© **800/800-8000** or 541/889-8282), charging $55 to $62 double; and a **Motel 6,** 275 NE 12th St., Ontario, OR 97914 (© **800/466-8356** or 541/889-6617), charging $42 double.

At nearby **Farewell Bend State Recreation Area** (© **541/869-2365**), 25 miles northwest of Ontario on I-84, you'll find not only campsites but also covered wagons that can be rented for overnight stays ($27 per night). Don't look for horses to hitch up, though; these wagons stay put. There are also teepees for rent. For campsite, covered-wagon, and teepee reservations, contact **Reservations Northwest/Reserve America** (© **800/452-5687**; www.reserveamerica.com).

WHERE TO DINE

In downtown Ontario, you'll find a couple of basic Mexican restaurants and some places specializing in steaks, but that's about it.

6 Southeastern Oregon: Land of Marshes, Mountains & Desert

Burns: 130 miles SE of Bend, 130 miles SE of Ontario, 70 miles S of John Day

Southeastern Oregon, the most remote and least populated corner of the state, is a region of extremes. Vast marshlands, the most inhospitable desert in the state, and a mountain topped with aspen groves and glacial valleys are among the most prominent features of this landscape. Although cattle outnumber human inhabitants and the deer and the antelope play, it's birdlife that's the region's number one attraction. At **Malheur National Wildlife Refuge,** birds abound almost any month of the year, attracting flocks of bird-watchers, binoculars and bird books in hand.

Because this is such an isolated region (Burns and Lakeview are the only towns of consequence), it is not an area to be visited by the unprepared. Always keep your gas tank topped off and carry water for both you and your car. Two of the region's main attractions, **Steens Mountain** and the **Hart Mountain National Antelope Refuge,** are accessible only by way of gravel roads more than 50 miles long. A visit to the Alvord Desert will also require spending 60 or more miles on a gravel road.

ESSENTIALS

GETTING THERE   The town of Burns is midway between Bend and Ontario on U.S. 20. Malheur National Wildlife Refuge, Steens Mountain, and Hart Mountain National Antelope Refuge are all located south of Burns off Ore. 205.

VISITOR INFORMATION For more information on this area, contact the **Harney County Chamber of Commerce,** 76 E. Washington St., Burns, OR 97720 (© **541/573-2636;** www.harneycounty.com).

EXPLORING THE REGION

Because water is scarce here in the high desert, it becomes a magnet for wildlife wherever it appears. Three marshy lakes—Malheur, Harney, and Mud—south of Burns cover such a vast area and provide such an ideal habitat for birdlife that they have been designated the **Malheur National Wildlife Refuge** ⊛. The shallow lakes, surrounded by thousands of acres of marshlands, form an oasis that annually attracts more than 300 species of birds, including waterfowl, shorebirds, songbirds, and raptors. Some of the more noteworthy birds that are either resident or migratory at Malheur are trumpeter swans, sandhill cranes, white pelicans, great blue herons, and great horned owls. Of the more than 58 mammals that live in the refuge, the most visible are mule deer, pronghorn antelope, and coyotes.

The refuge headquarters is 32 miles south of Burns on Ore. 205, but the refuge stretches for another 30 miles south to the crossroads of Frenchglen. The refuge is open daily from dawn to dusk. The **visitor center,** where you can find out about recent sightings and current birding hot spots, is open weekdays and most weekends during the spring and summer, while a **museum** housing a collection of nearly 200 stuffed-and-mounted birds is open daily. Camping is available at two campgrounds near Frenchglen. For more information on the refuge, contact Refuge Manager, **Malheur National Wildlife Refuge,** HC-72, Box 245, Princeton, OR 97721 (© **541/493-2612;** http:pacific.fws. gov/malheur).

Steens Mountain, a different sort of desert oasis, is 30 miles southeast of Frenchglen on a gravel road that's usually open only between July and October. Even then the road is not recommended for cars with low clearance, but if you have the appropriate vehicle, the mountain is well worth a visit. Rising to 9,733 feet high, this fault-block mountain was formed when the land on the west side of a geological fault line rose in relationship to the land on the east side of the fault. This geologic upheaval caused the east slope of Steens Mountain to form a precipitous escarpment that falls away to the Alvord Desert a mile below. The panorama out across southeastern Oregon is spectacular. The mountain rises so high that it creates its own weather, and on the upper slopes the sagebrush of the high desert gives way to juniper and aspen forests. From Frenchglen, there's a 66-mile loop road that leads to the summit and back down by a different route.

More wildlife-viewing opportunities are available at the **Hart Mountain National Antelope Refuge** ⊛, which is a refuge for both pronghorns, the fastest land mammal in North America, and California bighorn sheep. The most accessible location for viewing pronghorns, which despite the common name, are not true antelopes, is the refuge headquarters, 49 miles southwest of Frenchglen on gravel roads. Bighorn sheep are harder to spot and tend to keep to the steep cliffs west of the refuge headquarters. Primitive camping is available near the headquarters at **Hot Springs Campground.** For more information, contact the **Hart Mountain National Antelope Refuge,** P.O. Box 111, Lakeview, OR 97630 (© **541/947-3315**).

WHERE TO STAY & DINE

Frenchglen Hotel *Finds*   Frenchglen is in the middle of nowhere, so for decades the Frenchglen Hotel (now owned by Oregon State Parks) has been an important way station for travelers passing through this remote region. The historic two-story hotel is 60 miles south of Burns on the edge of Malheur National Wildlife Refuge. Though the historic setting will appeal to anyone with an appreciation for pioneer days, the hotel is most popular with bird-watchers. The guest rooms are on the second floor and are small and simply furnished. This hotel is often booked up months in advance. Three meals a day will cost $20.50 to $30 per person, and the hearty dinners are quite good.

Frenchglen, OR 97736. © **541/493-2825.** Fax 541/493-2828. fghotel@ptinet.net. 8 units (all with shared bathroom). $60–$63 double. DISC, MC, V. Closed Nov 16–Mar 14. **Amenities:** Restaurant (American). *In room:* No phone.

Hotel Diamond *☆*   Located 54 miles south of Burns off Ore. 205, the Hotel Diamond, built in 1898, is on the opposite side of the Malheur National Wildlife Refuge from Frenchglen. The historic hotel was completely restored in the late 1980s and now has rooms with hand-stitched quilts on the beds and artwork by one of the owners. There's a big screened porch across the front and a green lawn that attracts deer. Family-style dinners are available for $15.50 to $18.50 (make reservations at least 24 hr. in advance). There's also a three-bedroom house available nearby.

HC-72, Box 10, Diamond, OR 97722. © **541/493-1898.** www.central-oregon.com/hoteldiamond. 8 units (3 with private bathroom). $65 double with shared bathroom, $90 double with private bathroom. MC, V. **Amenities:** Restaurant (American). *In room:* A/C, no phone.

Appendix:
Oregon in Depth

At 97,073 square miles (roughly 1½ times the size of New England), Oregon is the 10th-largest state in the Union, and it encompasses within its vast area an amazing diversity of natural environments—not only lush forests, but also deserts, glacier-covered peaks, grasslands, alpine meadows, and sagebrush-covered hills. Together, these diverse environments support a surprisingly wide variety of natural life.

The **Oregon coast** stretches for nearly 300 miles from the redwood country of Northern California to the mouth of the Columbia River, and for most of this length is only sparsely populated. Consequently, this coastline provides habitat not only for large populations of seabirds, such as cormorants, tufted puffins, and pigeon guillemots, but also for several species of marine mammals, including Pacific gray whales, Steller's sea lions, California sea lions, and harbor seals.

Each year between December and April, more than 20,000 **Pacific gray whales** pass by the Oregon coast as they make their annual migration south to their breeding grounds off Baja California. These whales can often be seen from shore at various points along the coast, and numerous whale-watching tour boats operate out of different ports. In recent years, more and more gray whales have been choosing to spend the summer in Oregon's offshore waters, and it is now possible to spot these leviathans any month of the year. More frequently spotted, however, are **harbor seals** and Steller's and California **sea lions,** which are frequently seen lounging on rocks. Sea Lion Caves and Cape Arago State Park, both on the central Oregon coast, are two of the best places to spot sea lions.

The **Coast Range,** which in places rises directly from the waves, gives the coastline its rugged look. However, even more than the mountains, it is **rain** that gives this coastline its definitive character. As moist winds from the Pacific Ocean rise up and over the Coast Range, they drop their moisture as rain and snow. The tremendous amounts of rain that fall on these mountains have produced dense forests that are home to some of the largest trees on earth. Although the south coast is the northern limit for the coast redwood, the **Douglas firs,** which are far more common and grow throughout the region, are almost as impressive in size, sometimes reaching 300 feet tall. Other common trees of these coastal forests include Sitka spruce, Western hemlocks, Port Orford cedars, Western red cedars, and, along the southern Oregon coast, evergreen myrtle trees. The wood of these latter trees is used extensively for carving, and myrtle wood shops are common along the south coast.

More than a century of intensive **logging** has, however, left the state's forests of centuries-old trees shrunken to remnant groves scattered in largely remote and rugged areas. How much exactly is still left is a matter of hot debate between the timber industry and environmentalists, and the battle to save the remaining old-growth forests continues, with both sides claiming victories and losses with each passing year.

Among this region's most celebrated and controversial wild residents is the **Northern spotted owl,** which, because of its requirements for large tracts of undisturbed old-growth forest and its listing as a federally endangered species, brought logging of old-growth forests to a virtual halt in the 1990s. Concern next focused on the **marbled murrelet,** a small bird that feeds on the open ocean but nests exclusively in old-growth forests. Destruction of forests is also being partially blamed for the demise of trout, salmon, and steelhead populations throughout the region.

Roosevelt elk, the largest commonly encountered land mammal in the Northwest, can be found throughout the Coast Range, and there are even designated elk-viewing areas along the coast (one off U.S. 26 near Jewell and one off Ore. 38 near Reedsport).

To the east of the northern section of the Coast Range lies the **Willamette Valley,** which because of its mild climate and fertile soils, was the first region of the state to be settled by pioneers. Today, the Willamette Valley remains the state's most densely populated region and is home to Oregon's largest cities. However, it also still contains the most productive farmland in the state.

To the east of the Willamette Valley rise the mountains of the 700-mile-long **Cascade Range,** which stretches from Northern California to southern British Columbia. The most prominent features of the Cascades are its **volcanic peaks:** Hood, Jefferson, Three Fingered Jack, Washington, the Three Sisters, Broken Top, Thielsen, and McLoughlin. The eruption of Washington's Mount St. Helens on May 18, 1980, reminded Northwesterners that this is still a volcanically active region. However, here in Oregon, it is the remains of ancient Mount Mazama, which erupted with great violence 7,700 years ago, that provide the most dramatic reminder of the potential power of Cascade volcanoes. Today, the waters of **Crater Lake,** Oregon's only national park, fill the shell of this long-gone peak. Near the town of Bend, geologically recent volcanic activity is also visible in the form of cinder cones, lava flows, lava caves, and craters. Much of this volcanic landscape near Bend is now preserved as **Newberry National Volcanic Monument.**

The same moisture-laden clouds that produce the near rain-forest conditions in the Coast Range frequently leave the Cascades with heavy snows and, on the highest peaks (Mount Hood, Mount Jefferson, the Three Sisters), numerous glaciers. The most readily accessible glaciers are on **Mount Hood,** where ski lifts keep running right through the summer, carrying skiers and snowboarders to slopes atop the Palmer Glacier, high above the historic Timberline Lodge.

East of the Cascades, less than 200 miles from the damp Coast Range forests, the landscape becomes a desert. The **Great Basin,** which reaches its northern limit in central and eastern Oregon, comprises a vast, high-desert region that stretches east to the Rockies. Through this desolate landscape flows the **Columbia River,** which, together with its tributary the Snake River, forms the second-largest river drainage in the United States. During the last Ice Age, roughly 13,000 years ago, glaciers repeatedly blocked the flow of the Columbia, forming huge lakes behind dams of ice. These vast prehistoric lakes repeatedly burst the ice dams, sending massive and devastating walls of water flooding down the Columbia. These floodwaters were sometimes 1,000 feet high and carried with them ice and rocks, which scoured out the **Columbia Gorge.** Today, the gorge's many waterfalls are the most evident signs of these prehistoric floods.

Today, it is numerous large, modern **dams,** not ice, that dam the Columbia, and they have become the focus of one of the region's hottest environmental battles. The large dams, mostly built during the middle part of the 20th century, present a variety of barriers both to returning adult salmon and to young salmon headed downstream to the Pacific. Though many of the dams have fish ladders to allow **salmon** to return upriver to spawn, salmon must still negotiate an obstacle course of degraded spawning grounds in often clear-cut forests, slower river flows in the reservoirs behind the dams, turbines that kill fish by the thousands, and irrigation canals that often confuse salmon into swimming out of the river and into farm fields. Overfishing for salmon canneries in the late 19th century struck the first major blow to salmon populations, and for more than a century, these fish have continued to struggle against manmade and natural obstacles. Compounding the problems faced by wild salmon has been the use of fish hatcheries to supplement the wild fish populations (hatchery fish tend to be less vigorous than wild salmon). A salmon recovery plan was adopted in the 1990s to attempt to save threatened runs of native salmon, but farmers, electricity producers, shipping companies, and major users of hydroelectric power have continued to fight the requirements of the recovery plan, which include lowering water levels in reservoirs to speed the downstream migration of young salmon. In the late 1990s, the focus turned to the removal of some of the dams on the Snake River, which proved to be a very controversial idea. In 2001, high electricity rates (and the consequent demand for more water to send through hydroelectric dams) and a court ruling against the listing of certain salmon on the endangered species list struck a double blow to salmon recovery efforts.

South-central and southeastern Oregon are the most remote and unpopulated regions of the state. However, this vast desert area does support an abundance of wildlife. The **Hart Mountain National Antelope Refuge** shelters herds of pronghorn antelope, which is the fastest land mammal in North America. This refuge also protects a small population of California bighorn sheep. At **Malheur National Wildlife Refuge,** more than 300 bird species frequent large shallow lakes and wetlands, and at the **Lower Klamath National Wildlife Refuge,** large numbers of bald eagles gather each winter. Several other of the region's large lakes, including Summer Lake and Lake Abert, also attract large populations of birds.

2 Oregon Today

Oregon is a state dominated by a **love of the outdoors** and this isn't surprising when you realize just how much nature dominates beyond the city limits. From almost anywhere in Oregon, it's possible to look up and see green forests and snow-capped mountains, and a drive of less than 2 hours from any Willamette Valley city will get you to the mountains or the Pacific Ocean's beaches.

Oregonians don't let the weather stand between them and the outdoors. The temptation is too great to head for the mountains, the river, or the beach, no matter what the forecast. Consequently, life in Oregon's cities tends to revolve less around cultural venues and such other urban pastimes as shopping than around parks, gardens, waterfronts, rivers, mountains, and beaches. Portland has its Forest Park, Rose Garden, Japanese Garden, and Waterfront Park. Eugene has its miles of riverside parks, bike paths, and even a park just for rock climbing. In Hood River, the entire Columbia River has become a playground for wind-surfers, and when the wind doesn't blow, there are always the nearby mountain-bike trails and rivers for kayaking. In Bend, mountain biking and downhill skiing are a way of life. These outdoor areas are where people find tranquillity, where summer festivals are held, where locals take their visiting friends and relatives, and where they tend to live their lives when they aren't being interrupted by such inconveniences as work and sleep.

This is not to say, however, that the region is a cultural wasteland. Both Portland and Eugene have large, modern, and active **performing-arts centers.** During the summer months, numerous **festivals** take music, theater, and dance outdoors. Most impressive of these are the Oregon Shakespeare Festival and the Britt Festivals, both of which are staged in southern Oregon. Many other festivals feature everything from chamber music to alternative rock.

Word of the state's natural beauty and the Oregon good life has been spreading far and wide in recent years, and the state has been experiencing unprecedented growth. As the population in urban areas of the Willamette Valley has expanded, **politics** have developed a very pronounced urban-rural split here in Oregon. Citizens from the eastern part of the state argue that Salem and Portland are dictating to rural regions that have little in common with the cities, while urban dwellers, who far outnumber those living outside the Willamette Valley, argue that majority rule is majority rule. This split has pitted conservative voters (often from rural regions) and liberal voters (usually urban) on a wide variety of issues, and the reality of Oregon politics is now quite a bit different from the often-held perception of a state dominated by liberal, forward-thinking environmentalists and former hippies. Medical use of marijuana and assisted suicide, both of which were legalized in Oregon in the late 1990s, have both continued to generate controversy and court cases.

For more than a decade, until the **economy** began slowing in 2001, Oregon had been one of the fastest-growing states in the nation. The state's economy boomed as high-tech industries built manufacturing facilities here and Californians, fed up with that state's pollution, crime, congestion, and high cost of living, moved north in search of a better quality of life. However, the state's reliance in recent years on high-tech manufacturing means that this state has been particularly hard hit by the slowing economy. As the price of tech stocks has plummeted, so too has the Oregon economy. By the middle of 2001, the state had one of the highest unemployment rates in the country. However, despite the rapid growth of recent times and the more recent high-tech slowdown, Oregonians continue to work hard to preserve the state's unique character and to keep Portland and the state's other major cities as livable as they have always been.

3 Oregon History 101

EARLY HISTORY The oldest known inhabitants of what is now the state of Oregon lived along the shores of huge lakes in the Klamath Lakes Basin some 10,000 years ago. Here they fished and hunted ducks and left records of their passing in several caves. These peoples would have witnessed the massive eruption of Mount Mazama, which left a hollowed-out core of a mountain that eventually filled with water and was named

Dateline

- **13,000 B.C.** Massive floods, as much as 1,000 feet deep, rage down Columbia River and carve the Columbia Gorge.
- **10,000 B.C.** Earliest known human inhabitation of Oregon.
- **5,000 B.C.** Mount Mazama erupts violently, creating a caldera that will later fill with water and be known as Crater Lake.

continues

Crater Lake. Along the coast, numerous small tribes subsisted on salmon and shellfish. In the northeast corner of the state, the Nez Perce Indians became experts at horse breeding even before Lewis and Clark passed through the region at the start of the 19th century. In fact, the appaloosa horse derives its name from the nearby Palouse Hills of Washington.

However, it was the **Columbia River tribes** that became the richest of the Oregon tribes through their control of Celilo Falls, which was historically the richest salmon-fishing area in the Northwest. These massive falls on the Columbia River east of present-day The Dalles witnessed the annual passage of millions of salmon, which were speared and dip netted by Native Americans, who then smoked the fish to preserve it for the winter. Today, Native Americans still fish for salmon as they once did, perched on precarious wooden platforms with dip nets in hand. However, Celilo Falls are gone, inundated by the pooling water behind The Dalles Dam, which was completed in 1957. Today little remains of what was once the Northwest's most important Native American gathering ground, a place where tribes from hundreds of miles away congregated each year to fish and trade.

Even before this amazing fishing ground was lost, a far greater tragedy had been visited upon Northwest tribes. Between the 1780s, when white explorers and traders began frequenting the Northwest coast, and the 1830s, when the first settlers began arriving, the Native American population of the Northwest was reduced to perhaps a tenth of its historic numbers. It was not war that wiped out these people, but European diseases—smallpox, measles, malaria, and influenza. The Native Americans had no resistance to these diseases, and entire tribes were soon wiped out by fast-spreading epidemics.

- **A.D. 1542** Spanish exploratory ship reaches what is now the southern Oregon coast.
- **1579** Englishman Sir Francis Drake reaches the mouth of the Rogue River.
- **1602** Spain's Martín de Aguilar explores the coast of Oregon, probably as far as Coos Bay.
- **1792** Robert Gray becomes the first explorer to sail a ship into a great river he names the Columbia, in honor of his ship the *Columbia Rediviva*.
- **1805–06** Expedition led by Meriwether Lewis and William Clark crosses the continent and spends the winter at the mouth of the Columbia River.
- **1810** Americans attempt first settlement at the Columbia River's mouth.
- **1819** Spain cedes all lands above 42° north latitude.
- **1824–25** Russia gives up claims to land south of Alaska; Fort Vancouver founded by Hudson's Bay Company on Columbia River near present-day Portland.
- **1834** Methodist missionary Jason Lee founds Salem, which later becomes the state capital.
- **1840** First settlers move to what is now Oregon.
- **1842** Jason Lee founds first school of higher learning west of the Mississippi.
- **1843** First wagons cross the continent on the Oregon Trail; Asa Lovejoy and William Overton stake claim on land that will soon become Portland.
- **1844** Oregon City becomes the first incorporated town west of the Mississippi.
- **1846** The 49th parallel is established as the boundary between American and British territories in the Northwest.
- **1848** Oregon becomes first U.S. territory west of the Rockies.
- **1851** Portland is incorporated; gold is discovered in southern Oregon.
- **1915** Columbia Gorge scenic highway is constructed.
- **1935** Angus Bowmer stages *As You Like It* in Ashland and plants the seed of the Oregon Shakespeare Festival.
- **1940s** Kaiser shipyards in the Portland area become the world's foremost shipbuilders.

continues

THE AGE OF EXPLORATION

Though a Spanish ship reached what is now southern Oregon in 1542, the Spanish had no interest in the gray and rainy coast. Nor did famed British buccaneer Sir Francis Drake, who in 1579 sailed his ship the *Golden Hind* as far north as the mouth of the Rogue River. Drake called off his explorations in the face of what he described as "thicke and stinking fogges."

However, when the Spanish found out that Russian fur traders were establishing themselves in Alaska and along the North Pacific coast, Spain took a new interest in the Northwest. Several **Spanish expeditions** sailed north from Mexico to reassert the Spanish claim to the region. In 1775, Spanish explorers Bruno de Heceta and Francisco de la Bodega y Quadra charted much of the Northwest coast, and though they found the mouth of

- 1945 Oregon becomes the only state with civilian war casualties when a Japanese balloon bomb kills six children.
- 1957 The Dalles Dam is completed; backwaters inundate Celilo Falls, the region's most productive Native American salmon-fishing grounds.
- 1974 In a bold step toward making Portland a more livable city, a freeway along the city's downtown waterfront is removed.
- 1995 Sen. Bob Packwood resigns after the Senate Ethics Committee recommends his expulsion for sexual misconduct.
- 1999 Eight species of salmon and steelhead in the Willamette River are listed as federally threatened species.
- 1999 The freighter *New Carissa* runs aground off Coos Bay.
- 2001 The state experiences its driest year in a century, causing conflicts over water rights in the Klamath Basin.

the Columbia River, they did not enter it. To this day four of the coast's most scenic headlands—Cape Perpetua, Heceta Head, Cape Arago, and Cape Blanco—bear names from these early Spanish explorations.

It was not until 1792 that an explorer, American trader Robert Gray, risked a passage through treacherous sandbars that guarded the mouth of the long speculated upon Great River of the West. Gray named this newfound river Columbia's River, in honor of his ship, the *Columbia Rediviva*. This discovery established the first American claim to the region. When news of the Columbia's discovery reached the United States and England, both countries began speculating on a northern water route across North America. Such a route, if it existed, would facilitate trade with the Northwest.

In 1793, Scotsman Alexander MacKenzie made the first overland trip across North America north of New Spain. Crossing British Canada on foot, MacKenzie arrived somewhere north of Vancouver Island. After reading MacKenzie's account of his journey, Thomas Jefferson decided that the United States needed to find a better route overland to the Northwest. To this end, he commissioned Meriwether Lewis and William Clark to lead an expedition up the Missouri River in hopes of finding a single easy portage that would lead to the Columbia River.

Beginning in 1804, the members of the **Lewis and Clark expedition** paddled up the Missouri, crossed the Rocky Mountains on foot, and then paddled down the Columbia River to its mouth. A French Canadian trapper and his Native American wife, Sacagawea, were enlisted as interpreters, and it was the presence of Sacagawea that helped the expedition gain acceptance among Western tribes. After spending the wet and dismal winter of 1805–06 at the mouth of the Columbia at a spot they named **Fort Clatsop,** the expedition headed back east. Discoveries made by the expedition added greatly to the scientific and geographical knowledge of the continent. A replica of Fort Clatsop is now a

Did You Know?

- Oregon was home to America's first policewoman, Lola Greene Baldwin, who joined the Portland force in 1908.
- Matt Groening, creator of *The Simpsons*, got his start in Portland.
- Portland is home to the world's smallest dedicated park—Mill Ends Park—measuring only 24 inches in diameter.
- Oregon is one of the few states with no sales tax.
- Astoria, in the very northwest corner of the state, is the oldest American community west of the Mississippi.
- Oregon's Crater Lake is the deepest lake in the U.S.
- Hells Canyon is the deepest gorge in North America.
- Oregon is home to the world's shortest river, the 120-foot-long D River.
- Port Orford, Oregon, is the westernmost incorporated town in the contiguous 48 states.

national memorial and one of the most interesting historical sites in the state. Outside of The Dalles, a campsite used by Lewis and Clark has also been preserved.

In 1819, the Spanish relinquished all claims north of the present California-Oregon state line, and the Russians gave up their claims to all lands south of Alaska. This left only the British and Americans dickering for control of the Northwest.

SETTLEMENT   Fur Traders, Missionaries & the Oregon Trail   Only 6 years after Lewis and Clark spent the winter at the mouth of the Columbia, employees of John Jacob Astor's Pacific Fur Company managed to establish themselves at a nearby spot they called **Fort Astoria.** This was the first permanent settlement in the Northwest, but with the War of 1812 being fought on the far side of the continent, the fur traders at Fort Astoria, with little protection against the British military presence in the region, chose to relinquish control of their fort. However, in the wake of the war, the fort returned to American control, though the United States and Britain produced no firm decision about possession of the Northwest. The British still dominated the region, but American trade was tolerated.

With the decline of the sea-otter population, British fur traders turned to beaver and headed inland up the Columbia River. For the next 30 years or so, fur-trading companies would be the sole authority in the region. Fur-trading posts were established throughout the Northwest, though most were on the eastern edge of the territory in the foothills of the Rocky Mountains. The powerful Hudson's Bay Company (HBC) eventually became the single fur-trading company in the Northwest.

In 1824, the HBC established its Northwest headquarters at **Fort Vancouver,** 100 miles up the Columbia near the mouth of the Willamette River; and in 1829, the HBC founded **Oregon City** at the falls of the Willamette River. Between 1824 and 1846, when the 49th parallel was established as the boundary between British and American northwestern lands, Fort Vancouver was the most important settlement in the region. A replica of the fort now stands outside the city of Vancouver, Washington, across the Columbia River from Portland.

In Oregon City, several homes from this period are still standing, including that of John McLoughlin, who was chief factor at Fort Vancouver and aided many of the early pioneers who arrived in the area after traveling the Oregon Trail.

By the 1830s, the future of the Northwest had arrived in the form of **American missionaries.** The first was Jason Lee, who established his mission in the Willamette Valley near present-day Salem. (Today, the site is Willamette Mission State Park.) Two years later, in 1836, Marcus and Narcissa Whitman, along with Henry and Eliza Spaulding, made the overland trek to Fort Vancouver, then backtracked into what is now eastern Washington and Idaho, to establish two missions. This journey soon inspired other settlers to make the difficult overland crossing.

In 1840, a slow trickle of American settlers began crossing the continent, a 2,000-mile journey. Their destination was the Oregon country, which had been promoted as a veritable Eden where land was waiting to be claimed. In 1843, Marcus Whitman, after traveling east to plead with his superiors not to shut down his mission, headed back west, leading 900 settlers on the **Oregon Trail.** Before these settlers ever arrived, the small population of retired trappers, missionaries, and HBC employees who were living at Fort Vancouver and in nearby Oregon City had formed a provisional government in anticipation of the land-claim problems that would arise with the influx of settlers to the region. Today, the best places to learn about the experiences of the Oregon Trail emigrants are at the Oregon Trail Interpretive Center outside Baker City and the End of the Oregon Trail Interpretive Center in Oregon City. In many places in the eastern part of the state, **Oregon Trail wagon ruts** can still be seen.

In 1844, Oregon City became the first incorporated town west of the Rocky Mountains. This outpost in the wilderness, a gateway to the fertile lands of the Willamette Valley, was the destination of the wagon trains that began traveling the Oregon Trail, each year bringing more and more settlers to the region. As the land in the Willamette Valley was claimed, settlers began fanning out to different regions of the Northwest so that during the late 1840s and early 1850s many new towns, including Portland, were founded.

Though the line between American and British land in the Northwest had been established in 1846 at the 49th parallel (the current U.S.–Canada border), Oregon was not given U.S. territorial status until 1848. It was the massacre of the missionaries at the Whitman mission in Walla Walla (now in Washington state) and the subsequent demand for territorial status and U.S. military protection that brought about the establishment of the first U.S. territory west of the Rockies.

The discovery of **gold** in eastern Oregon in 1860 set the stage for one of the saddest chapters in Northwest history. With miners pouring into eastern Oregon and Washington, conflicts with Native Americans over land were inevitable. Since 1805, when Lewis and Clark had first passed this way, the **Nez Perce tribes** (the name means "pierced nose" in French) had been friendly to the white settlers. However, in 1877 a disputed treaty caused friction. Led by Chief Joseph, 700 Nez Perce, including 400 women and children, began a march from their homeland to their new reservation. Along the way, several angry young men, in revenge for the murder of an older member of the tribe, attacked a white settlement and killed several people. The U.S. Army took up pursuit of the Nez Perce, who fled across Idaho and Montana, only to be caught 40 miles from the Canadian border and sanctuary.

INDUSTRIALIZATION & THE 20TH CENTURY   From the very beginning of white settlement in the Northwest, the region based its growth on an extractive economy. **Lumber** and **salmon** were exploited ruthlessly. The history of the timber and salmon-fishing industries have run parallel for more than a century and led to similar results in the 1990s.

The trees in Oregon grew to gigantic proportions. Nurtured on steady rains, trees such as Douglas fir, Sitka spruce, Western red cedar, Port Orford cedar, and hemlock grew tall and straight, sometimes as tall as 300 feet. The first sawmill in the Northwest began operation near present-day Vancouver, Washington, in 1828, and between the 1850s and the 1870s, Northwest sawmills supplied the growing California market as well as a limited foreign market. When the transcontinental railroads arrived in the 1880s, a whole new market opened up, and mills began shipping to the eastern states.

Lumber companies developed a cut-and-run policy that leveled the forests. By the turn of the century, the government had gained more control over public forests in an attempt to slow the decimation of forestlands, and sawmill owners were buying up huge tracts of land. At the outbreak of World War I, more than 20% of the forestland in the Northwest was owned by three companies—Weyerhaeuser, the Northern Pacific Railroad, and the Southern Pacific Railroad—and more than 50% of the workforce labored in the timber industry.

The timber industry has always been extremely susceptible to fluctuations in the economy and experienced a roller-coaster ride of boom and bust throughout the 20th century. Boom times in the 1970s brought on record-breaking production that came to a screeching halt in the 1980s, first with a nationwide recession and then with the listing of the **Northern spotted owl** as a threatened species. When the timber industry was born in the Northwest, there was a belief that the forests of the region were endless. However, by the latter half of this century, big lumber companies had realized that the forests were dwindling. Tree farms were planted with increasing frequency, but the large old trees continued to be cut faster than younger trees could replenish them. By the 1970s, environmentalists, shocked by the vast clear-cuts, began trying to save the last **old-growth trees.** The battle between the timber industry and environmentalists is today still one of the state's most heated debates and tree-sitters continue to attract media attention as they attempt to stop the cutting of old-growth forests.

Salmon was the mainstay of the Native Americans' diet for thousands of years before the first whites arrived in the Oregon country, but within 10 years of the opening of the first salmon cannery in the Northwest, the fish population was decimated. In 1877, the first fish hatchery was developed to replenish dwindling runs of salmon, and by 1895, salmon canning had reached its peak on the Columbia River. Later, in the 20th century, salmon runs would be further decimated by the construction of numerous dams on the Columbia and Snake rivers. Though fish ladders help adult salmon make their journeys upstream, the young salmon heading downstream have no such help, and the turbines of hydroelectric dams kill a large percentage of fish. One solution to this problem has been barging and trucking young salmon downriver. Today the **salmon populations** of the Northwest have been so diminished that entire runs of salmon have been listed as threatened or endangered under the Endangered Species Act. Talk is now focusing on the removal of certain dams that pose insurmountable barriers to salmon. However, there is great resistance to this, and long, drawn-out legal battles continue to wend their way through the courts.

Surprisingly, during the dry summer of 2001, the Columbia River saw its largest runs of salmon in more than a decade.

The dams that have proved such a detriment to salmon populations have, however, provided irrigation water and cheap electricity that have fueled both industry and farming. Using irrigation water, potato and wheat farms flourished in northeastern Oregon after the middle of the 20th century. The huge reservoirs behind the Columbia and Snake River dams have also turned these rivers into waterways that can be navigated by huge barges, which often carry wheat downriver from ports in Idaho. Today, the **regional salmon recovery plan** is attempting to strike a balance between saving salmon runs and meeting all the other needs that have been created since the construction of these dams.

Manufacturing began gaining importance during and after World War II. In the Portland area, the Kaiser Shipyards employed tens of thousands of people in the construction of warships, but the postwar years saw the demise of the Kaiser facilities. Recent years have seen a diversification into **high-tech industries,** with such major manufacturers as Intel, Epson, and Hewlett-Packard operating manufacturing facilities in the Willamette Valley.

However, it is in the area of **sportswear manufacturing** that Oregon businesses have gained the greatest visibility. With outdoor recreation a way of life in this state, it comes as no surprise that a few regional companies have grown into international giants. Chief among these is Nike, which is headquartered in the Portland suburb of Beaverton. Other familiar names include Jantzen, one of the nation's oldest swimwear manufacturers; Pendleton Woolen Mills, maker of classic plaid wool shirts, Indian-design blankets, and other classic wool fashions; and Columbia Sportswear, which in recent years has become one of the country's biggest sports-related outerwear manufacturers. If you like to play outside, chances are you own some article of clothing that originated in Oregon.

4 Eat, Drink & Be Merry

Although there is no specifically Oregon cuisine, there is a regional cooking style that, although somewhat diluted by various international influences in recent years, still can be distinguished by its pairings of meats and seafood with local fruits and nuts. This cuisine features regional produce such as salmon, oysters, halibut, raspberries, blackberries, apples, pears, and hazelnuts. A classic Northwest dish might be raspberry chicken or halibut with a hazelnut crust.

Salmon is king of Oregon fish and has been for thousands of years, so it isn't surprising that in one shape or another, it shows up on plenty of menus throughout the state. It's prepared in seemingly endless ways, but the most traditional method is what's known as **alder-planked salmon.** Traditionally, this Native American cooking style entailed preparing a salmon as a single filet, splaying it on readily available alder wood, and slow-cooking it over hot coals. The result is a cross between grilling and smoking. Today, however, it's hard to find salmon prepared this traditional way. Much more readily available, especially along the Oregon coast, is traditional **smoked salmon.** Smoked oysters are usually also available.

With plenty of clean cold waters in many of its bays and estuaries, Oregon raises large numbers of **oysters,** especially in Tillamook and Coos bays. Then there are the mussels and clams. Of particular note are **razor clams,** which can be tough and chewy if not prepared properly, but which are eagerly sought after along north-coast beaches when the clamming season is open. After salmon, though, **Dungeness crab** is the region's other top seafood offering. Though not as large as an Alaskan king crab, the Dungeness is usually big enough to make a meal for one or two people. Crab cakes are also ubiquitous on Oregon restaurant menus.

The Northwest's combination of climate and abundant irrigation waters has also helped make this one of the nation's major fruit-growing regions. Hood River Valley and the Medford area are two of the nation's top **pear-growing regions,** and just a few miles east of Hood River, around The Dalles, cherries reign supreme, with the blushing **Rainier cherry** a regional treat rarely seen outside the Northwest. The Willamette Valley, south of Portland, has become the nation's center for the production of **berries,** including strawberries, raspberries, and numerous varieties of blackberries. All these fruits show up in the summer months at farm stands, making a drive through the Willamette Valley at that time of year a real treat. Pick-your-own farms are also fairly common throughout the Northwest. So famed are Oregon's fruits that the Harry and David's company has become a mainstay of the mail-order gift industry, shipping regional produce all over the country.

When hunger strikes on the road, Oregon offers what seems to be a regional potato preparation that just might be the only truly Northwestern cuisine. **Jo-jos** are potato wedges dipped in batter and fried. Traditionally served with a side of ranch dressing for dipping, these belly bombs are usually purchased as an accompaniment to fried or baked chicken.

One last Northwest food we should mention is the **wild mushroom.** As you'd expect in such a rainy climate, mushrooms abound here. The most common wild mushrooms are morels, which are harvested in spring, and chanterelles, which are harvested in autumn. You'll find wild mushrooms on menus of better restaurants throughout the state, so by all means try to have some while you're here.

Oregon's thriving wine industry has for quite a few years now been producing **award-winning varietal wines.** Oregon is on the same latitude as the French wine regions of Burgundy and Bordeaux and produces similar wines. Oregon Pinot Noirs are ranking up there with those from France, and Pinot Gris, Rieslings, and other varietals are getting good press as well. Wineries throughout the state are open to the public for tastings, with the greatest concentrations to be found southwest of Portland in Yamhill County, just west of Salem, and northwest of Roseburg.

Oregon is at the center of the national obsession with **craft beers,** and new brewpubs continue to open across the state. Oregon breweries such as Bridgeport, Full Sail, and Widmer, which have long been at the forefront of the state's craft brewing industry, have grown so large that the term "microbrewery" no longer applies to them. Although Portland is still the state's (and the nation's) microbrewery mecca, brewpubs can now be found throughout the state.

Although local wines may be the state's preferred accompaniment to dinner and microbrews the favorite social drink, it is **coffee** that keeps Oregonians going through long gray winters—and even through hot sunny summers, for that matter. Although Seattle gets all the press for its espresso obsession, this dark and flavorful style of coffee is just as popular in Oregon. There may still be a few small towns in the state where you can't get an espresso, but you certainly don't have to worry about falling asleep at the wheel for want of a decent cup of java. In parking lots throughout the state, tiny espresso stands dispense all manner of coffee concoctions to the state's caffeine addicts.

Index

FROMMER'S® COMPLETE TRAVEL GUIDES

Alaska
Alaska Cruises & Ports of Call
Amsterdam
Argentina & Chile
Arizona
Atlanta
Australia
Austria
Bahamas
Barcelona, Madrid & Seville
Beijing
Belgium, Holland & Luxembourg
Bermuda
Boston
British Columbia & the Canadian
  Rockies
Budapest & the Best of Hungary
California
Canada
Cancún, Cozumel & the Yucatán
Cape Cod, Nantucket &
  Martha's Vineyard
Caribbean
Caribbean Cruises & Ports of Call
Caribbean Ports of Call
Carolinas & Georgia
Chicago
China
Colorado
Costa Rica
Denmark
Denver, Boulder & Colorado Springs
England
Europe
European Cruises & Ports of Call
Florida
France

Germany
Great Britain
Greece
Greek Islands
Hawaii
Hong Kong
Honolulu, Waikiki & Oahu
Ireland
Israel
Italy
Jamaica
Japan
Las Vegas
London
Los Angeles
Maryland & Delaware
Maui
Mexico
Montana & Wyoming
Montréal & Québec City
Munich & the Bavarian Alps
Nashville & Memphis
Nepal
New England
New Mexico
New Orleans
New York City
New Zealand
Nova Scotia, New Brunswick &
  Prince Edward Island
Oregon
Paris
Philadelphia & the Amish Country
Portugal
Prague & the Best of the Czech
  Republic
Provence & the Riviera

Puerto Rico
Rome
San Antonio & Austin
San Diego
San Francisco
Santa Fe, Taos & Albuquerque
Scandinavia
Scotland
Seattle & Portland
Shanghai
Singapore & Malaysia
South Africa
South America
Southeast Asia
South Florida
South Pacific
Spain
Sweden
Switzerland
Texas
Thailand
Tokyo
Toronto
Tuscany & Umbria
USA
Utah
Vancouver & Victoria
Vermont, New Hampshire
  & Maine
Vienna & the Danube Valley
Virgin Islands
Virginia
Walt Disney World & Orlando
Washington, D.C.
Washington State

FROMMER'S® DOLLAR-A-DAY GUIDES

Australia from $50 a Day
California from $70 a Day
Caribbean from $70 a Day
England from $75 a Day
Europe from $70 a Day

Florida from $70 a Day
Hawaii from $80 a Day
Ireland from $60 a Day
Italy from $70 a Day
London from $85 a Day

New York from $90 a Day
Paris from $80 a Day
San Francisco from $70 a Day
Washington, D.C., from $80
  a Day

FROMMER'S® PORTABLE GUIDES

Acapulco, Ixtapa & Zihuatanejo
Amsterdam
Aruba
Australia's Great Barrier Reef
Bahamas
Baja & Los Cabos
Berlin
Big Island of Hawaii
Boston
California Wine Country
Cancún
Charleston & Savannah
Chicago
Disneyland

Dublin
Florence
Frankfurt
Hong Kong
Houston
Las Vegas
London
Los Angeles
Maine Coast
Maui
Miami
New Orleans
New York City
Paris

Phoenix & Scottsdale
Portland
Puerto Rico
Puerto Vallarta, Manzanillo &
  Guadalajara
San Diego
San Francisco
Seattle
Sydney
Tampa & St. Petersburg
Vancouver
Venice
Virgin Islands
Washington, D.C.

FROMMER'S® NATIONAL PARK GUIDES

Family Vacations in the National
  Parks
Grand Canyon

National Parks of the American
  West
Rocky Mountain
Yellowstone & Grand Teton

Yosemite & Sequoia/
  Kings Canyon
Zion & Bryce Canyon

FROMMER'S® MEMORABLE WALKS

Chicago	New York	San Francisco
London	Paris	

FROMMER'S® GREAT OUTDOOR GUIDES

Arizona & New Mexico	Northern California	Vermont & New Hampshire
New England	Southern New England	

SUZY GERSHMAN'S BORN TO SHOP GUIDES

Born to Shop: France	Born to Shop: Italy	Born to Shop: New York
Born to Shop: Hong Kong, Shanghai & Beijing	Born to Shop: London	Born to Shop: Paris

FROMMER'S® IRREVERENT GUIDES

Amsterdam	Los Angeles	San Francisco
Boston	Manhattan	Seattle & Portland
Chicago	New Orleans	Vancouver
Las Vegas	Paris	Walt Disney World
London	Rome	Washington, D.C.

FROMMER'S® BEST-LOVED DRIVING TOURS

Britain	Germany	New England
California	Ireland	Scotland
Florida	Italy	Spain
France		

HANGING OUT™ GUIDES

Hanging Out in England	Hanging Out in France	Hanging Out in Italy
Hanging Out in Europe	Hanging Out in Ireland	Hanging Out in Spain

THE UNOFFICIAL GUIDES®

Bed & Breakfasts and Country Inns in:	Florida with Kids	New Orleans
California	Golf Vacations in the Eastern U.S.	New York City
New England	The Great Smoky & Blue Ridge Mountains	Paris
Northwest	Hawaii	San Francisco
Rockies	Inside Disney	Skiing in the West
Southeast	Las Vegas	Southeast with Kids
Beyond Disney	London	Walt Disney World
Branson, Missouri	Mid-Atlantic with Kids	Walt Disney World for Grown-ups
California with Kids	Mini Las Vegas	Walt Disney World for Kids
Chicago	Mini-Mickey	Washington, D.C.
Cruises	New England & New York with Kids	World's Best Diving Vacations
Disneyland		

SPECIAL-INTEREST TITLES

Frommer's Adventure Guide to Australia & New Zealand
Frommer's Adventure Guide to Central America
Frommer's Adventure Guide to India & Pakistan
Frommer's Adventure Guide to South America
Frommer's Adventure Guide to Southeast Asia
Frommer's Adventure Guide to Southern Africa
Frommer's Britain's Best Bed & Breakfasts and Country Inns
Frommer's France's Best Bed & Breakfasts and Country Inns
Frommer's Italy's Best Bed & Breakfasts and Country Inns
Frommer's Caribbean Hideaways

Frommer's Exploring America by RV
Frommer's Gay & Lesbian Europe
Frommer's The Moon
Frommer's New York City with Kids
Frommer's Road Atlas Britain
Frommer's Road Atlas Europe
Frommer's Washington, D.C., with Kids
Frommer's What the Airlines Never Tell You
Israel Past & Present
The New York Times' Guide to Unforgettable Weekends
Places Rated Almanac
Retirement Places Rated

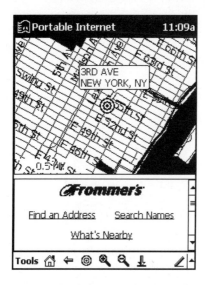